Robert Lane proposes a provocative new approach for assessing the strengths and weaknesses of the market economy. Rather than judge the market solely by its ability to provide economic well-being, we must, Lane argues, also consider the contribution the market makes to people's overall life satisfaction and to human development. Economic welfare must be recognized as only one factor in overall life satisfaction, and the market must be evaluated as it contributes to and inhibits a range of other factors, such as the development of self-esteem and a sense of control over one's environment. In addition, Lane argues, we must recognize our involvement with the market, both through work and through other economic activities, as a major influence in adult development and so must evaluate the market's developmental effects.

Lane draws on economic philosophy, psychological theory and research, economic anthropology, and the sociology of work in analyzing the broad range of market experiences in terms of their contributions or detriments to people's life satisfaction and individual development. Particular themes explored include the limitations and costs of rational calculation, the importance of work experience and distribution of workplace learning, the effects of the market emphasis on material rewards versus intrinsic rewards, and the limitations of the concept of utility versus that of life satisfaction.

The market experience

The market experience

ROBERT E. LANE

Yale University

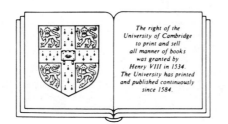

The right of the
University of Cambridge
to print and sell
all manner of books
was granted by
Henry VIII in 1534.
The University has printed
and published continuously
since 1584.

CAMBRIDGE UNIVERSITY PRESS

Cambridge

New York   Port Chester

Melbourne   Sydney

Published by the Press Syndicate of the University of Cambridge
The Pitt Building, Trumpington Street, Cambridge CB2 1RP
40 West 20th Street, New York, NY 10011, USA
10 Stamford Road, Oakleigh, Melbourne 3166, Australia

© Cambridge University Press 1991

First published 1991

Printed in the United States of America

Library of Congress Cataloging-in-Publication Data
Lane, Robert Edwards.
The market experience/by Robert E. Lane.
p. cm.
ISBN 0-521-40391-X. – ISBN 0-521-40737-0 (paperback)
1. Economics – Psychological aspects. 2. Markets. I. Title.
HB74.P8L26 1991
330.1–dc20   91-9109
                                                        CIP

British Library Cataloguing in Publication Data
Lane, Robert E.
The market experience.
1. Capitalism
I. Title
330.122

ISBN 0-521-40391-X hardback
ISBN 0-521-40737-0 paperback

Symbolism and Economic Rationality,'' in Richard M. Couglin, ed., *Socio-Economic Perspectives 1990* (Armonk, NY: M. E. Sharpe, 1990); ''Market Choice and Human Choice,'' NOMOS 31 (1989); ''Procedural Goods in a Democracy: How One Is Treated vs. What One Gets,'' *Social Justice Research* 2 (1988): 177–92; ''Market Justice, Political Justice,'' *American Political Science Review* 80 (June 1986): 383–402; ''Individualism and the Market Society,'' NOMOS 25 (1983); ''Political Observers and Market Participants: The Effects on Cognition,'' *Political Psychology* 4 (1983); ''Market Thinking and Political Thinking,'' in Adrian Ellis and Krishan Kumar, eds., *Dilemmas of Liberal Democracies: Studies in Fred Hirsch's ''Social Limits to Growth''* (London: Tavistock Publications, 1983); ''Government and Self-Esteem,'' *Political Theory* 10 (February 1982): 5–31; ''Motives for Liberty, Equality, Fraternity: Effects of Market and State'' (Presidential Address, 1979), *Political Psychology* 1 (1979): 3–20; ''Markets and the Satisfaction of Human Wants,'' *Journal of Economic Issues* 12 (1978); ''The Regulation of Experience: Leisure in a Market Society,'' *Social Science Information* 17 (1978); ''Autonomy, Felicity, Futility: The Effects of the Market Economy on Political Personality,'' *Journal of Politics* 40 (1978): 2–24.

I have greatly benefited from comments received following presentations at the meetings of the International Society of Political Psychology (especially the comments of James Davies), Yale's faculty Political Theory Seminar, and the Institute of Social and Policy Studies' Complex Organizations Workshop; in connection with the last of these, I found Charles Perrow's subsequent severe comments especially helpful in giving focus to a diffuse presentation. Emily Loose, my editor at the Cambridge University Press, has done much to improve the coherence of the text; and my copy editor, Marilyn Prudente, has saved me from many errors. C. E. Lindblom's weekly luncheon critiques have kept me within the bounds of reasonable coherence. Lindblom, indeed, is the godfather of this project.

New Haven and Oxford, September 1990

Contents

Acknowledgments

My degree is in political economy and government, my research work and teaching have been at the intersection of psychology and politics; I have followed the diagonal path to political economy and psychology.

Without knowing it, I started this book in 1972–3 while on a Fulbright Fellowship at Churchill College, Cambridge. I had been blindsided in the 1960s by the counterculture; as a rejoinder I would write a sober book on "progress." Fortunately, when I returned to New Haven, my colleague and then Director of Yale's Institution for Social and Policy Studies, Charles E. Lindblom, organized a seminar on the Market-Oriented Society and Personality. The seminar, whose members, in addition to Lindblom, included psychologist Leonard Doob, philosopher Karsten Harries, economist Michael Montias, anthropologist Leopold Pospisil, sometimes political theorists Thomas Pangle and David Johnston, and sometimes lawyer Leon Lipson. The seminar survived for a remarkable four years. Almost nothing substantive in this book stems directly from the seminar, and almost all of my feeling that the project was exciting and worth doing is the product of the seminar. Such are the strange ways of intellectual stimulation.

While working on this project I have benefited from fellowships and hospitality from a number of institutions. In addition to Churchill College, these were: National Endowment for the Humanities Fellowship (resident in New Haven), 1977–8; Resident Scholar, London School of Economics, 1978–9; Fellow, Netherlands Institute for Advanced Study, 1982–3; Fellow, National Humanities Center, 1984; Visiting Fellow, Research School of Social Sciences, Australian National University, 1985; Visiting Scholar, Nuffield College, Oxford University, 1986. These grants and institutional homes have done much to improve my work, undermine sectarian and parochial tendencies, and make life enjoyable. For enduring logistical support, I am grateful to Yale's Institution for Social and Policy Studies and to Nuffield College whose Fellows have generously admitted me to their fellowship every summer since 1986.

Intellectual stimulation and support have no geographical home. In this field of psychosocial economics, without the work of the following authors, among others, this book could not have been wirtten: Herbert Simon, Albert Hirschman, Tibor Scitovsky, Shlomo Maitel, Burkhard Strumpel, George Katona, Kenneth Boulding, Amitai Etzioni, David Sears, Amos Tversky, Daniel Kahneman, the pioneering group of British psychologists, Stephen E. G. Lea, Roger Tarpy, and Paul Webley, the sociologists Alex Inkeles, Melvin Kohn, and Carmi Schooler, the political scientist, Ronald Inglehart, and two teams from the University of Michigan studies of the quality of life, Frank Andrews and Stephen Withey, and Angus Campbell, Philip Converse, and Willard Rogers.

In modified form, I include portions of several articles and book chapters: "Money

PART I

Introduction

Introduction

About this book

The premise of this book is that the market should be judged by the satisfactions people receive as a consequence of their market experiences and by what they learn from them. I would substitute these criteria for the current criterion: efficiency in producing and distributing goods and services. That is, goods and services – and the income that purchases them – are only intermediate goods, whereas satisfaction or happiness and human development are final goods. I believe that the argument and evidence in the book are a challenge not only to market institutions but also to market economics and to the humanist and socialist critiques of markets.

The challenge is a fundamental one, for if the analysis is accurate it changes the very axis of debate that has dominated most of the twentieth century. That debate has dealt substantially with the relative merits of capitalist and socialist economies, the relative merits of markets and states in governing economies, and the best ways to achieve *economic* welfare. Although it may be that the capitalist–socialist argument is now moot, the arguments over the relative merits of markets and states and over the best ways to achieve economic welfare continue unabated. In this debate human development has hardly been seriously considered as a market purpose (in spite of brief acknowledgments by Marshall, Pigou, and others – to be discussed) and and has not been seriously investigated at all.

In contrast, I propose a wholly different debate, one that has a dual focus. First, if one accepts the substantial evidence in Part VII showing that individual economic welfare (above a decent minimum) has only a minimal relationship to a sense of well-being, the proposed debate would then turn directly to the real sources of overall well-being in which the market plays an important role. The debate turns on the question, What is the market's contribution to happiness or satisfaction with life-as-a-whole? In answering the question the market will be judged by what it produces and distributes and by the *processes* of production and distribution. The second item for the proposed debate is the market's role in human development. In this respect it will be judged by a whole new set of criteria. By shifting the debate from an argument that falsely identifies life satisfaction with wealth to one that does not make that identification, this book seeks to rotate the axis of debate from the one that dominated the twentieth century to a different axis in the twenty-first century, one embracing values closer to those given priority by most philosophers.

The story line in the book is not linear as inevitably must be so when one seeks to explain the multiple *outcomes* of some single source, in this case the market. Explanations of outcomes contrast with explanations of the multiple *causes* of some phenomenon where the arguments all lead to a single focus on the phenomenon to be explained. Linearity is also inhibited when interpreting a *social system* where

3

each act influences other acts and there must, therefore, be a reflexive quality to the argument. It is for these reasons that the reader will find many cross references in the book.

Some of the topics deal with the interpretation of the market experience by economists who assume responsibility for interpreting and guiding the market, as in the cases of my treatment of rationality, emotionality, and symbolism in market behavior (Chapters 3 and 4). In these comments I treat only microeconomics, not macroeconomics, which seems to have little to do with its microeconomic cousin. Other topics deal with the inherent features of the market, for example, my discussion of the possibilities of giving priority to worker welfare in a competitive market economy (Chapter 16). Still other topics clarify the goals of market behavior, thus, it is hoped, illuminating both economists' interpretations of utility and the grounds of well-being for market participants (Part VII). Many of the topics include criticism of the market critics, especially humanist philosophers and democratic socialists. Neither economists nor their critics seem to comprehend that economic behavior is simply another form of behavior for which behavioral theories developed by psychologists and other behavioral scientists are the guiding disciplines. In this book I attempt to repair these deficiencies.

In spite of the variety of markets over time and across cultures, I believe that it is possible to conceive of a *market experience* that is typical, frequent, and paradigmatic for those who do market work for pay, use money and buy – rather than make, inherit, or receive from government – the commodities with which they adorn their lives. The book is not phenomenological, not a view from inside the experience. Rather, I have sought to discover how psychological and social principles govern the thinking, feeling, and behavior of participants in a market economy.

Attribution of causal influence is always difficult; attribution to the market is unusually so. In comparing the experience in market economies to similar experiences in command economies one is not so much comparing institutional influences as comparing Americans (or British or French) with Russians (or Poles or Cubans) – a different set of topics. Comparing household economies in agricultural societies to market economies in inevitably more advanced societies is little better. The chosen topic permits no evasion: We must infer from psychological theory and experiments, from survey evidence, and from analogy the complex patterns of influence that shape the market experience. The findings and the inferences and the evaluations will be as tentative as the weakness of the evidence demands and the frailty of the arguments may suggest.

The selection is severe; I say very little about socialization for the market, consumer behavior, the effects of advertising, saving and investment. Nor do I give a proper attention to ethical issues. Although I present a model of human development, I do not treat ethical development in any detail and treat matters of fairness and justice only in the context of other issues. The work also fails to treat the uses of leisure as a supplement to or substitute for the work-oriented society advocated as the main source of happiness and personal development. Thus the programs of those who find leisure, rather than work, to be the main new opportunities for human development are not given the space they may deserve.

We shall be discussing in some detail market effects in two major life domains, human relations and work (and the rewards from work). There are, of course, other life domains influenced by the market, such as family life and leisure activities, but, a little like Freud who said that love and work were the principal features of life, we think of relations with others and work as comprising two major sources of well-being – and of work as the major source of adult development. These two aspects of life also represent those features that, aside from ethical issues, have been thought to be most influenced by the market and have been most criticized by humanist and socialist commentators.

This book is evaluative. The criteria are those implied by any effort to increase the satisfaction that people receive from their lives and their own personal development. Looking as fairly as possible at what evidence we can find and inferring from it what seems most probably true, we then (and I hope only then) judge some outcomes better than others. Explicit credos in prefaces have never helped readers to sort out facts from judgments, so I do not offer one here. None of the criteria are arcane or, I think, idiosyncratic: It is better for people to be happy, more cognitively complex, to think of themselves as worthy, and to take responsibility for their own lives where they can influence events than the other way around.

The theories and evidence that inform this analysis derive mostly from experimental social and cognitive psychology, with some help from economic anthropology, the sociology of work, and what Joan Robinson calls "philosophical economics." Psychology is the science of behavior, cognition, motivation, value formation, and human development; it is the natural source of theories of economic behavior as well. In order to give credibility to the arguments made here, I will present enough of the experimental or observational bases for psychological inferences to make them plausible and to give the reader a fair chance to evaluate the applicability of the evidence and the relevance of the theories.

This Introduction deals with three things: The next section sets forth some preliminary challenges to market economics and to the humanist and the socialist (noneconomic) critiques of the market. I then define our maximands – happiness and our concept of human development – and, finally, define the features of the market that concern us.

A challenge to microeconomics and to market critics

What follows here is a synopsis of some of the main criticisms of microeconomics and humanist and socialist criticisms made in this book.

A challenge to microeconomics

The analysis of economic behavior as a specialized application of theories of human behavior inevitably challenges certain microeconomic concepts.

Utility and satisfaction. It is well known that economics has no independent measure of its dependent variable, utility (Chapter 23). Whereas market economics holds that because of the commodities that money buys, money income is the primary source of utility (satisfaction or happiness), the evidence shows that income does not contribute so much to life satisfaction as, for example, people's beliefs that they have met life's challenges (economic or otherwise) and their experience of work enjoyment (Chapter 22). It is most often in the sphere of work, not consumption, that the greatest subjective well-being lies (Chapter 13). It follows that one fundamental proposition of market economics is wrong: Work is not a disutility or sacrifice for which income is the compensation. And pay, therefore, serves a very different set of purposes in the economy than is assigned to it by market economics (Part VI).

Many of the most important sources of human satisfaction do not go through the market, not only intrinsic work enjoyment but also satisfactions from interaction with friends and family, solitary reflection and thought, honors and achievements of all kinds (including economic achievements that have no price), religious reassurance, and many more. None of these are adequately accounted for by the market value of leisure. The market may or may not be a superior device for "the satisfaction of human wants" (Chapter 23), but for many wants it is not even the theatre of greatest importance.

Rationality and cognition. Rational calculation is thought by market economics to be the way individuals maximize their utilities (Chapter 3). Along with a growing number of others I challenge this assumption, showing the complexity of cognitive processes in making market and other choices. The fact is that the market is a cockpit of emotions whose influences must be analyzed before it is possible to assess the actual cognitive processes engaged in the market experience (Chapter 4). Like psychoanalysis, however, microeconomics has no theory of cognition.

Developing wants. Economists treat as exogenous the origins of wants, but they cannot at the same time claim as the object of their discipline the study of how to "satisfy wants in human society" and ignore the nature of satisfaction and of wants and wanting (Chapter 23). Even if it were possible to employ purely rational decision processes in the market, these would not contribute much to human happiness if people did not know the sources of their own happiness or the ways to achieve it. I will show (Chapter 27) a degree of popular ignorance in this respect that challenges the market's premise that happiness is best achieved by relying on individually self-selected goals. (The argument challenges many other cherished theories as well.)

Human motivation. The assumption that a sufficient accounting of market behavior may rest on a simple motivation for more money has been widely, if ineffectively, challenged. Economists have acknowledged the accuracy but not the force of this criticism, arguing that people may not want more money per se, but that money serves as a means for acquiring the goods they do want and that the net force of their desires is, then, appropriately measured by money. My analysis challenges this assumption, showing that the emotional arousal of the market is much richer and more complex than this simple theory of motivation implies (Chapters 4 and 24).

The neutrality of money. Whereas market economics holds that money is a neutral medium of exchange whose influence is exhausted by its power over goods and services, my findings suggest that money is itself an emotionally charged symbol that, in its own right, influences the character of market transactions (Chapters 6 and 7). This contributes to the thesis that market *processes* are often as influential in their effect on satisfaction and learning as are market outcomes in productivity and consumption.

A theory of behavior. As mentioned, economic behavior is not different in its basic elements from behavior in other spheres of life. It relies, for example, on the same principles of perception, memory, cognition, motivation, attitude and value formation, social reference, reliance on social norms, ambivalences and other internal conflicts, and affective responses as does behavior in schools, homes, civics, and churches. In spite of theories of the situational specificity of behavior, these general principles apply. None of the studies of behavior in these other areas are successfully examined by reference to the axioms of greed and rationality (Chapter 3).

The social system. Economic behavior is caused by and has consequences in other features of the social system. We live in systems where any change in one element influences other elements; the moral, psychological, social, and economic aspects of the market experience are so intertwined that specialized prescriptions seem blind to the costs the prescriptions would incur (Chapter 2). *Coeteris paribus* is the analyst's crutch that protects us from harm, keeps us going – and prevents us from learning to walk straight.

Underlying these differences in causal theories of economic behavior is an evaluative difference, namely, that the value of persons is as great as the value of commodities.

The challenge to humanist and socialist critiques

The humanist critique. The argument and evidence in this book is no less challenging to the humanist and ethical critique of the market than to conventional market economics. Without adequate guiding theories of social behavior these critiques cannot be persuasive. As a consequence of this deficiency, the causal attributions of market influence on character assumed by the humanist critique are generally mistaken: An exchange economy has no discernible tendency to convert *people* into exchangeable commodities; there is no evidence that people are more materialistic in market economies than they were in peasant economies or in the recently deceased command economies (Part IV); it is not true that in market societies people work primarily for pay – rather they work for a variety of goals including the exercise of skill and discretion (Chapter 17); whereas the market is not a reliable teacher of ethics, the evidence suggests that ethical reasoning and, to a lesser extent, practice is as high in the most marketized as it is in the least marketized economies.

Moreover, there is much evidence that the members of affluent societies have the qualities desired by the humanists in greater measure than the members of poorer societies. And the market is the engine of affluence. Rawls is right to emphasize a form of justice that protects productivity – though it is not clear that economic differentials have the effect he believes they have. The strong emphasis on ethics in the humanist critique risks creating a stick figure, "ethical man," no more human and no more realistic than economic man. We need a critique based on what is known about human development and its various elements. (The humanist criticisms of the market's influence on personal relations are discussed in Part IV.)

Standards. Most market criticisms are ambiguous regarding the standards employed, that is, they do not specify whether "the market" (undifferentiated) fails to meet some ideal standard or whether it fails to do as well in the specified respects as traditional economies or command economies, or as well as some known or imagined mixed economies. Nor is it clear whether the observed market fails to do as well as another, superior kind of market (such as market socialism) might do, or whether, instead, the defects are inherent in any market economy.[1]

But if we are to deal with the body of criticism as it presents itself, we must accept this ambiguity and take it to mean that compared to some other economic system, ideal or historical, certain qualities of materialism, individualistic selfishness, competitiveness, exchange orientation, and so forth are learned both from market experience and market culture; they are rewarded by status and power and wealth, and taught to children as conditions of success. What is learned, then, both governs the domain of life covered by the market *and* generalizes to the larger nonmarket life domains where it influences behavior and becomes internalized as socially functional features of personality.

What is striking to me is how wide of the mark these humanist and socialist criticisms are, not because the market is better than assumed, but because the indictments are quite different from the ones I find cogent.

The socialist critique. Without entering into the economics of socialism, certainly never tested by experience in the successor to the tsar's former empire and its satellites, this book challenges socialism on other fronts. Marx was right in emphasizing the work experience rather than the distribution of income (a matter he thought relevant only to bourgeois justice), but on most other counts he was wrong, especially in his materialistic emphasis. The more interesting case is democratic socialism, where two caveats from the themes of this book are especially relevant.

[1] When the standards are idealized, some name-calling is evident: "We can say that a society is sick when its basic institutions and relations, its structure, are such that they do not permit the use of available material and intellectual resources for the optimal development and satisfaction of individual needs." Herbert Marcuse, *One Dimensional Man* (Boston: Beacon, 1964), 251. Even the most enthusiastic market supporter must agree that market fails by this test of optimal development. The sick society, says Marcuse, then invites "surplus repression," more repression than is necessary to maintain order.

First, the loosening of the relation between income and happiness (Chapter 26) tells us that the redistribution of income in an egalitarian direction will not have the payoff in equality of well-being that its proponents claim for it. The socialists' emphasis on economic equality, therefore, is not so much wrong as it is misplaced. What should be redistributed is discretionary, challenging work – as many democratic socialists already know.

Second, the dominant current variant of democratic socialism is *market social-ism,* and yet it is the market itself that prevents an emphasis on producer well-being.[2] Although socialists of this persuasion hope to gain the economic and psychological benefits of markets, their policies threaten to repeat the ills that we have identified with the very institution on which they pin their hopes (Chapter 16).

In these and other respects this book is a challenge to the market's critics as well as its dominant interpreters, market economists.

From products to processes. Both microeconomists and ethical market critics have tended to focus on the market's products – microeconomists on the *production* of goods and services, ethical critics on the *distribution* of these products. There is a fundamental shift from these foci in my analysis, a focus that is orthoganal, if not directly antithetical, to market analysis: the importance of economic transactions as a *process* rather than as a means to superior *outputs*. It is from the processes that people gain their greatest satisfactions and learn the features of human development we will identify. The priority given to producer satisfactions, which are more closely related to overall satisfaction with life than are goods and services, challenges the inherent, and I believe inevitable, market priority given to consumer satisfactions.

Two maximands: happiness and human development

Happiness

Subjective well-being has two overlapping measures, happiness and satisfaction with life-as-a-whole. More than a temporary mood, happiness is defined as a more or less enduring and comprehensive emotional state, whereas life satisfaction is more of a judgment, a cognitive appraisal of one's life. Neither can be achieved by summing local utilities, although each is the sum of feelings and thoughts about particular aspects of one's life. If utilities refer to local and often transient satisfactions, summing them does not imply life satisfaction nor, more emphatically, happiness (Chapter 28). Adding utilities in conformity with market economic doctrine is, in this respect, most misleading.

Nonutilitarian philosophers are not content with happiness as a final good and even utilitarians in the full exposition of their theories are not satisfied with any particular individual's happiness. John Stuart Mill makes the point by his preference for an unsatisfied Socrates over a satisfied fool. Whereas some nonutilitarian phi-

[2] Frank Roosevelt, "Market Socialism: A Humane Economy?" *Journal of Economic Issues* 3 (1964): 3–20.

losophers (e.g., Ross) may add justice and knowledge to their concepts of the good,
I have added human development.

Human development

Human development is our second maximand. Although most humanist and socialist critics of the market make human development an implicit or explicit goal, few
economists do so. Most economists and some socialists hold explicitly that the
payoff for an economy is the *maximization of utility*, or "the satisfaction of human
wants" whatever the character of these wants may be. But the character of the
wants is not a matter of indifference not only because of ethical considerations but
also because they do not serve the criterion of human development.

We shall limit our attention to three aspects of human development: the development of cognitive complexity, self-attribution (the belief that a person is effective
in influencing his or her fate), and self-esteem.

Cognitive complexity. Complex thinking has the following properties: (1)
It is conceptual in the sense that from a sufficient store of concepts or schemata, it
employs these concepts systematically and appropriately to identify and classify
objects; (2) it holds these concepts with sufficient flexibility to permit change when
evidence or experience conflicts with their tenets; (3) complex cognition operates at
an abstract rather than a concrete or largely perceptual level, thus facilitating thinking about those things that are distant in time or space; (4) it differentiates the parts
of a stimulus complex, recombines them, and integrates them in new forms; (5) it
characterizes the properties of an object more on the basis of relevant object or
situational characteristics than on the basis of preferences, that is, it "detaches [the]
ego from the outerworld and from inner experiences."

Cognitive complexity enables an individual to do certain things: "to assume a
mental set willfully and consciously, . . . to account for one's acts to oneself or to
others and to verbalize the act, . . . to shift reflectively from one aspect of the
situation to another, . . . to [hold in mind] simultaneously various aspects [of a
situation], . . . to grasp the essentials of a given whole, breaking it into parts,
isolating them, and synthesizing them," . . . to abstract common properties and
form hierarchic concepts, and to plan ahead and assume the attitude of the mere
possible; to think counterfactually.[3] Compare this ideal with the ideal of rationality
(Chapter 3).

[3] I have borrowed heavily from O. J. Harvey, David Hunt, and Harold M. Schroder, *Conceptual Systems
and Personality Organization* (New York: Wiley, 1961), 10–34; I have also added some Piagetian
concepts. The recent emphasis on *social* cognition adds concepts of cognitive balance, attribution, and
schemata. For an analysis of these forms of cognition, see Susan T. Fiske and Shelley E. Taylor, *Social
Cognition* (New York: Random House, 1984). For a somewhat different approach and analysis of our
tendencies to fall short of accurate cognition, see Richard Nisbett and Lee Ross, *Human Inference:
Strategies and Shortcomings of Social Judgment* (Englewood Cliffs, NJ: Prentice-Hall, 1980). Inevitably, specific measures abstract from these general cognitive abilities, focusing variously on abilities to
see both liked and disliked features of an object (Bieri), ability to discern a figure in a complex background (an ability sometimes called "field independence" and sometimes "differentiation" by Witkin,
and by Berry), discernment of commonalities in diverse objects – called "concept attainment" (Bruner
et al.), imaginative solutions to puzzles (Wertheimer), and so forth. See Herman A. Witkin, R. B. Dyk,
H. F. Faterson, D. R. Goodenough, and S. A. Karp, *Psychological Differentiation* (New York: Wiley
& Sons, 1962).

Self-attribution. In addition to cognitive complexity, human development includes a sense of personal effectiveness that, in the end, is based on a person's belief that he or she is a *cause* influencing the events that shape a person's daily life (Chapter 9). This belief can be misleading, and it is not good epistemology, but it has been shown to be a necessary ingredient in both effectiveness and happiness. In this respect, the market performs well. Self-attribution is learned from experiences of acting and seeing the world respond, contingent responses. A transaction, I will argue, requires mutually contingent responses; therefore an economy based on transactions teaches self-attribution. In addition, the market's indifference to the fate of persons requires people to develop what is likely to be called *self-reliance,* which, in turn, is also based on self-attribution.

Self-esteem. The third quality of human development is self-esteem. Self-esteem is not pride nor complete satisfaction with the self, but rather a belief that one is a person, like others, deserving of respect and decent treatment. Unlike Rawls, I do not hold that self-esteem is a good in itself, for its goodness depends on the grounds for a person's esteem of the self, as we shall see in Chapter 10. Its relation to the market is complex. Contrary to the implications of market theory, after a certain minimum income is achieved, self-esteem is not closely related to level of income but it *is* closely related to discretion and challenge at work. Whereas the market would enlist self-esteem as a stimulus to striving for income, the evidence suggests that the payoff in self-esteem is greater from work that enlists internal standards of excellence and gives a person greater discretion in what he or she does at the workplace. But the basic challenge to market doctrine is in making self-esteem a direct criterion for market performance and not an indirect criterion mediated by income. To repeat, this change is justified by the fact that the market doctrine's implicit belief in income as the main source of self-esteem is usually wrong.

Markets: definition and selected properties

Definition

"The market mechanism is a form of economic organization in which individual consumers and business interact through markets to determine the central problems of economic organization." According to Samuelson and Nordhaus, these central problems are: "(1) What goods shall be produced? (2) How shall these goods be produced? and (3) For whom shall the goods be produced?" For these purposes, "The market is a process by which the buyers and sellers of a good interact to determine its price and quantity."[4] Since my purpose in examining the market experience is somewhat different from the purposes of most economists, who put exchange at the center of the stage, I must fill in this definition with some other particulars.

As mentioned, there are many kinds of markets, and over the years the character

[4] Paul A. Samuelson and William D. Nordhaus, *Economics,* 12th ed. (New York: McGraw-Hill, 1985), 24, 41, 43.

of these markets has changed drastically, but we may search for central defining features. As an instrument for deciding what is to be produced, in what manner, and for whom, the market is serviceable to sections of command economies and to household economies as well as to what we call a market economy. Household and command economies are not market economies because (1) prices are set by custom or executive order, and/or (2) prices do not serve to decide for society in general what will be produced, in what way, and for whom.

Insofar as the market *experience* is concerned (as contrasted to the role of markets and hierarchies in governing the economy), there has been and continues to be a substantial increase in both labor and consumer market experiences. This increase occurs partly through the entry into the labor market of housewives and partly because more goods are bought and fewer made at home. The labor market and the consumer market are now populated by more people than has ever been the case before.

"Marketization" of a society is a continuum: An economy is more or less marketized. It is more marketized to the extent that (1) transactions (exchange of goods and services for money) are widespread and frequent. The market is a *network of transaction;* each transaction in theory affects every other one – because there is a more or less continuous chain of substitution at the margin of the economical use of each good. Whether a definition should be burdened with the concept of transaction costs is uncertain, but since *some* information about prices is necessary, it is reasonable to say, (2) the market implies an information network where each person is helped to calculate his or her next move according to the price information recently received. (3) Social control and coordination are achieved within the economy through transactions; (4) the principle of substitutability is maximized, that is, values (tastes, people, goods, services) are easily and frequently substituted for each other, for example, capital for labor, one kind of good for another; (5) coordination is achieved through price mechanisms; (6) the criterion for success within the economic system for individuals is income and wealth (past income), and for firms is profits; (7) wealth commands resources within the market system. (8) Because values are linked to costs and fungible in money terms (see item 4) certain forms of thinking, often called "rational calculation" ("formal rationality," as Weber would say), are facilitated and often required; (9) competition, in the sense of alternatives (not necessarily of people) competing against each other for scarce resources, is present; (10) there is no regnant center of control; and (11) political and economic authorities are separate. In this system, coordination is achieved through multiple decision centers operating on the principle of unit gain informed by a price-rich information network and regulated by feedback (consumer demand) in a cyberneticlike process. In this sense, as Weber observed, the market is *autocephalic.* It is a *system* with characteristic subsystems, sometimes partially autonomous.

This leaves open the ownership of the means of production. "The foundation of the process is the *private ownership* of productive resources – a synonym for freedom," said Knight.[5] With apologies to Mises[6] as well as to Knight, private own-

---

[5] Frank H. Knight, *Risk, Uncertainty and Profits* (1921; reprint Chicago: University of Chicago Press, 1971), 56. Knight emphasizes "ownership" to which I have added emphasis on "private."
[6] "When one reaches the conclusion, strictly by the canons of scientific procedure, that private ownership

ership of the means of production is neither logically implied by the concept of a market nor empirically without disconfirming cases.[7] What is implied is that each unit sets its own price for its goods.

An economic coordinating system is in some sense like a constitution; it orders power relationships, locates who shall make what decisions, distributes values. And to the extent that market doctrine is not itself an ideology, the market is further defended by a system of ideas elaborated in the discipline of economics, *The American Business Creed*,[8] and the ideology of capitalism.

Selected influential market properties

Certain properties of the market bear a close, fundamental relationship to the character of the market experience, as the following topics point out.

Consumer driven. As mentioned, the wants to be satisfied by market economies are consumer, not worker, wants; the criterion for firm decisions is whether some act will yield a profit in meeting demand, not whether it provides work or enriches jobs (Chapters 15 and 16). Consumer sovereignty refers to more than supply responsive to demand; it means that the consumer, not the worker, has, as Grotius would say, that power over which there is no superior power – except where consumer sovereignty gives way to those who decide what the consumer wants[9] (Chapter 23).

The efficiency norm. Giving managers and owners a stake in reducing costs in order to widen profit margins is a central advantage for market economies. This familiar feature of the market creates an efficiency norm that has other, sometimes less widely appreciated effects (Chapter 16). When the efficiency norm overrides other considerations in a consumer-driven economy, it sacrifices designing work to meet the needs and desires of workers; it lends credibility to government reluctance to redistribute income; it limits the force of ethical considerations; it uproots community life; it undermines ecological reparations. Sometimes called "the profit motive," the efficiency norm is wider and deeper than that suggests; it is a system of value priorities and causal explanations. And it greatly modifies the market experience.

Exchange. "At the center of the economist's stage is the market . . . exchange. That act of exchange is the source and proof of all economic gain, which

of the means of production is the only practicable form of social organization, this is neither an apology for capitalism nor an improper attempt to lend the authority of science to the support of liberalism." Ludwig von Mises, "Epistemological Problems of Economics," in *Socialism: An Economic and Sociological Analysis*, trans. J. Kahane (1936; reprint Indianapolis: Liberty Fund, 1981), 39.

[7] In many societies that meet the given definitions of the market, gas, electric, and water utilities, automobile firms, oil wells, demonstration farms, railroads and bus lines, naval ports and airports, and so forth are owned by the state, by municipalities, or by public corporations. Depending on how prices were set, the Webb's municipal socialism might have met these market requirements. Market socialism is a live issue, not in spite of but because of the ferment in the 1990s of what have been command economies.

[8] Francis X. Sutton, Seymour Harris, Carl Kaysen, and James Tobin, *The American Business Creed* (Cambridge: Harvard University Press, 1956).

[9] John Kenneth Galbraith, "Economics in the Industrial State: Science and Sedative – Economics as a System of Beliefs," *American Economic Review* 60 (1970): 469–78. The rejoinders to Galbraith following this presidential address are partially persuasive.

explains the economist's preoccupation with it."[10] Among the many things that cannot be exchanged, however, are intrinsic enjoyments of work, friendship, aesthetic enjoyments, and, indeed, a large variety of *activities* that totally escape the market (Chapters 13 and 18). Yet it is through exchange that people learn that they are, or are not, causes of the events that govern their lives (Chapter 9).

Contingency. The market's reliance on exchange creates a set of contingencies such that no market goods are available without some effort or sacrifice. This situation approaches the ideal requirement for learning theory and for its allied sense of personal control, that is, the experience of acting and having the environment respond. The matrix – defined by action/no action and response/no response – makes the two cells – act and response, no action and no response – a perfect confirmation that one is effective.[11] Buying and selling in the consumer market answers to that description (Chapter 9).

Apportioning rewards and tasks in the same act. Referring to the problems of assigning tasks to people and rewarding them appropriately for their work performances, Frank Knight said, "The first essential of the existing system is that it solves its two fundamental problems together as one. . . . It apportions tasks through the apportionment of rewards."[12] If this is, indeed, "essential," money rewards necessarily control work behavior, for they must be used to assign tasks as well as to inform (by rewarding) people about their performances. Alternative rewards, such as intrinsic work enjoyment, praise, and honor do not have the same capacity to direct, without coercion, labor to where it is "needed," that is, to where enterprises are called upon to meet the demand for their products. As we shall see (Chapter 20), it is precisely this conjunction of rewarding and allocating labor by the same act that stands in the way of creating what I shall call a "producer's economy," where the things that contribute most to life satisfaction can be given priority.

One feature of the market is its alleged self-regulating quality, but this begs the fact that the market is itself a collective good that, by all definitions of the market, is excluded from this self-regulating quality. Thus the market experience takes place in the context of an institution that cannot, of its own accord, govern its boundaries or transcend its own rules.

The market economy as a collective good. Collective or public goods are the kinds of goods where "those who do not purchase or pay for any of the public or collective good cannot be excluded from sharing in the consumption of the good, as they can where noncollective goods are concerned."[13] This certainly applies to

[10] Tibor Scitovsky, *The Joyless Economy* (New York: Oxford University Press, 1977), 133. Scitovsky further points out that many sources of satisfaction are not reciprocated and are, therefore, not exchanges.
[11] Martin E. P. Seligman, *Helplessness: On Depression, Development, and Death* (San Francisco: Freeman, 1973).
[12] Knight, *Risk, Uncertainty, and Profits,* 56.
[13] Mancur Olson, *The Logic of Collective Action: Public Goods and the Theory of Groups,* rev. ed. (Cambridge: Harvard University Press, 1971), 15.

living in a market economy. If I paid no income taxes I would not be excluded from the market, as alien visitors and those beneath the lowest tax bracket are not. In this sense, the market is like the courts; it is protected by rights, in this case the right to buy and sell without paying a fee for this right. In some respects, we are all free riders on the market economy, and in most respects contributions to the system are extremely uneven. Furthermore, just as the egalitarianism of an economic distribution is a public good that must be decided upon collectively and that market principles of choice cannot decide,[14] so it is impossible to decide by market principles whether or not to have a market economy.

The significance of locating the market economy in the realm of public goods is to liberate us from the idea that market is responsible only to itself, and that market principles should apply to the selection of an economy itself. The self-regulating economy must be selected and appraised by extra-system, exogenous criteria. Like the democratic experience, the market experience is in some sense collectively chosen and derives some of its legitimacy from this imputed act of choice.

Summary

This book is an effort to shift the axis of debate from an economistic one that does not deal directly with how economic life contributes to either happiness or human development to a debate that does. These two elements of life, happiness and development, then become the criteria by which the market may be judged. In this shift of axes, economic behavior is treated as a special application of general theories of behavior and we therefore look to these theories for guidance in explicating the *market experience*, that is, the typical experiences of those who enter the labor and consumer markets. Within this framework two activities are selected for special attention, relating to others and working, with the latter developed into a theory of major market deficiencies.

The challenge to microeconomics focuses on concepts of utility, rationality, concepts of wants and wanting, and the desire for more money (mistakenly thought to be a neutral medium) as the single or at least dominant motivation. As a theory of behavior, economics has much to learn from the disciplines that study behavior in all its applications. Since it is not possible to insulate economic life from other aspects of life, we suggest that economic behavior may fruitfully be located in a more general theory of social *systems*.

Although humanist and socialist criticisms of the market implicitly employ theories of behavior, like microeconomics they are usually innocent of the theories of behavior that the behavioral disciplines have laboriously developed. Moreover, also like microeconomics, they are economistic in the assumptions about what makes people happy. Under these circumstances, these critics have a relatively poor record in framing their theories about the influence of markets, especially with respect to the market's influence on human relations. The economism of the socialists leads them to place far too much emphasis on income distributions and not enough on

[14] J. E. Meade, *The Just Economy*, vol. 4 of *The Principles of Political Economy* (London: Allen & Unwin, 1976), 17–18.

what happens at work. And their reliance on markets in their currently preferred plan of market socialism threatens to reintroduce many of the deficiencies of market capitalism. Both economists and their critics place far too much emphasis on the *outcomes* of the productive process and not enough on the *processes* themselves.

Happiness and satisfaction with life-as-a-whole are not achieved by summing local satisfactions of utilities. In this respect the market's notion of summing utilities is misleading. In any event, happiness by itself is an insufficient social maximand for it must be supplemented by human development. This second maximand is defined in this book as growth in cognitive complexity, the sense that one is an effective person, and self-esteem, the last of these only when the grounds of esteem are properly qualified.

Although there are many kinds of markets, a market *economy* is characterized by a network of transactions where relative prices determine what shall be produced and who shall receive the products. Market economies do not require private ownership of the means of production, but they inevitably place consumer welfare over worker welfare, derive their emphasis on efficiency from the interest in profits of managers and owners, emphasize exchange that undermines the value of goods that cannot be exchanged, provide goods only contingent on sacrifice, and allocate resources by the same acts that reward the owners of these resources. But the market itself is a collective good governed by the same principles that govern all collective goods.

Chapter 1 begins the substantive treatment of the market experience with an appraisal of theories of human capital serving as economists' version of human development, continuing with an analysis of market consciousness and implicit theory, and concluding with an evaluation of the influence of market-inspired prosperity, the *affluence effect*.

Chapter 2 deals with the importance of recognizing that we live in systems each part of which affects others. The main message is that it is impossible for economists to understand productivity, for ethicists to understand the grounds of moral behavior, and for psychologists to understand personality development in the market without, in each case, also considering features of the system outside their specialties. To protect the special values that concern these specialists, they must cope with the causal forces and values that concern other specialists.

1 Persons and markets

This chapter first presents an analysis and criticism of an economic theory of human development. Next, aspects of market consciousness and the highly theoretical character of the underlying assumptions of market participants are treated. In the last section I analyze criticisms of growth and show the extent of benefits that seem to have been concealed from the critics (the *affluence effect*).

The value of persons

It normally takes little persuasion to convince people that it is the persons served by institutions, not the institutions themselves, that have the greater value. The point is made in varying terms; sometimes the value is expressed as "human flourishing,"[1] sometimes as "developed existence,"[2] sometimes as "mind." As the philosopher David Ross comments, "Contemplate any imaginary universe from which you suppose mind entirely absent, and you will fail to find anything in it that you can call good in itself. . . . The value of material things appears to be purely instrumental, not intrinsic."[3] And, of course, there is the authority of Kant for the claim that, inasmuch as all other things are exchangeable for something else, only the human person has that supreme value that Kant calls dignity. Inevitably the market shapes how humans flourish, the development of their existences, their minds, and their dignity. As a group of British psychologists have pointed out, "Those who frame economic policy are indirectly framing human psychology. . . . There will always be human consequences, and usually human costs, to be considered."[4]

Criteria for judging market effects on personality

One standard, among many, for evaluating personality development is mental health. Two definitions of mental health by psychiatrists suggest both the common and variant themes that enter these definitions:

Let us define mental health as the adjustment of human beings to the world and to each other with a maximum effectiveness and happiness. . . . It is the ability to maintain an even temper, an alert intelligence, socially considerate behavior, and a happy disposition.[5]

In very simple terms, a mature and mentally healthy person is one who (1) respects and has confidence in himself and, because he knows his true worth, wastes no time in proving it to himself and others; (2) accepts, works with, and to a large extent enjoys other people; (3)

[1] Margaret J. Radin, "Justice and the Market Domain," in John W. Chapman and J. Roland Pennock, eds., *Markets and Justice*, NOMOS 31 (New York: New York University Press, 1989).
[2] William A. Galston, *Justice and the Human Good* (Chicago: University of Chicago Press, 1980).
[3] W. D. Ross, *The Right and the Good* (Oxford, UK: Clarendon Press, 1930), 140.
[4] Stephen E. G. Lea, Roger M. Tarpy, and Paul Webley, *The Individual in the Economy* (Cambridge, UK: Cambridge University Press, 1987), 523.
[5] Karl Menninger, quoted in W. A. Scott, "Conceptions of Normality," in E. F. Borgatta and W. W. Lambert, eds., *Handbook of Personality Theory and Research* (Chicago: Rand McNally, 1968), 974

17

carries on his work, play, and family and social life with confidence and enthusiasm and with a minimum of conflict, fear, and hostility.[6]

These may be compared with two other models: Economic Man, characterized as possessing greed and rationality, and Ethical Man, characterized by benevolence, virtue, and the will to see justice done but not much more. The idea of a mature and mentally healthy person must be made from other materials.

Partly because of the work of social psychologists in analyzing and measuring certain elements of mental health, we have focused on these elements: happiness ("cheerful disposition"), self-esteem ("respects and has confidence in himself"), a sense of effectiveness or control over one's own life ("maximum effectiveness," "carries on . . . with confidence"), and another element characteristically omitted by psychiatrists, cognitive complexity. The ideas of "adjustment . . . to each other" and "enjoying other people," on the one hand, and of "carrying on [one's] work . . . with confidence and enthusiasm," on the other, are treated respectively in Parts IV and V, not as definitions of human development but as ways of enjoying life and learning developmental skills.

Rival claims. In spite of the general indifference to human development by market analysts, some economists, like Marshall, refer in passing to their beliefs that the market favors certain forms of development. However, without a theory of development those claims that are made tend to be uninformed and grandiose. Thus, Wilhelm Röpke claims that the market serves "to adapt economic policy to man, not man to economic policy." This adaptation is benign because

the market economy . . . [fosters] individual effort and responsibility, absolute norms and values, independence based on ownership, prudence and daring, calculating and saving, responsibility for planning one's life . . . proper tension between the individual and the community, firm moral discipline, respect for the value of money, the courage to grapple on one's own with life and its uncertainty, a sense of the natural order of things, and a firm scale of values.[7]

On the other hand, for socialism, Friedrich Engels claims that the socialization of the means of production "guarantees to [all people] the completely unrestricted development and exercise of their physical and mental faculties," and he reassures his public: "This possibility now exists for the first time, but it does exist."[8] The validity of these competing claims will be examined further in this book; their validity is a matter for investigation, not assertion.

We now turn to the major defense of the market's concern for human beings, a defense based on the concept of *human capital,* sharply differentiated from physical capital represented by factories and tools, offices and inventories used in production.

[6]T. A. C. Rennie and L. E. Woodward, *Mental Health in Modern Society* (New York: The Commonwealth Fund, 1948), 334. Of the dozen definitions listed by Scott, only one or two list the ethicists' central criterion, benevolence, and none mentions the alleged central property of economic choice, rationality. William A. Scott, "Conceptions of Normality."
[7]Wilhelm Röpke, *A Humane Economy: The Social Framework of the Free Market,* trans. E. Henderson (1958; reprint Chicago: Regnery/Gateway, 1971), 6, 98.
[8]Friederich Engels, *Socialism: Utopian and Scientific,* reprinted in V. Adoratsky, ed., *Karl Marx: Selected Works* (Moscow: International Publishers, n.d.), 185.

The human capital approach

As the evidence accumulated that growth in economic productivity was *not* a function of the growth of physical capital,[9] Theodore Schultz (and a few others) "invented" the idea of human capital to explain this phenomenon.[10] Schultz offers a powerful argument for believing that the market enhances the value of the human person and that as a consequence of market influences there has been a "secular rise in the economic value of man."[11] "Investment in human capital," he says, "rests on the proposition that there are certain expenditures (sacrifices) that are made deliberately to create productive stocks, embodied in human beings, that provide services over future periods. These services consist of producer services revealed in future earnings and of consumer services that accrue to the individual as satisfactions over his lifetime."[12] The producer services are increased occupational skills, nonspecific forms of judgmental abilities, competence and willingness to find suitable jobs and to move to locations where jobs are more plentiful, advanced forms of literacy, and so forth. Economic development increases the need for complex cognitive skills, thereby also increasing the need for and value of education. Above all, it is human knowledge that contributes to economic growth. Schultz emphasizes that, with the increased earning power of women, their time becomes more valuable and therefore their investment of that time in children becomes more precious. As a consequence women and society invest in quality rather than quantity of children. In short, "the investment in population quality and in knowledge in large part determines the future prospects of mankind."[13]

Under these circumstances, are there any grounds for claiming that the market ignores the welfare and dignity of individuals? The prior question of the grounds given for appreciating the value of human beings creates an initial objection. The idea that humans derive their value from their ability to produce goods is quite antithetical to the philosopher's notion that the human mind is good in itself or that the dignity of humankind cannot be sustained by a consequential argument; people are not, in the first instance, valued for any other reason than that they are human. This is not an argument that could be supported by market usefulness or by consumer enjoyment. But if the matter is rephrased so that we do not argue that human beings are worthy *because* they are productive, but rather ask whether the market cherishes and protects their intrinsic worthiness, promoting their happiness and development, the question about market effects on the value of persons becomes both acceptable and important. This book is a kind of answer to that question. The an-

[9] Moses Abramovitz, "Resource and Output in the United States Since 1870," *American Economic Review* 46 (1956); see also Robert Solow, "The Insignificance of Capital Accumulation," in *Economic Organization and Social Systems* (Indianapolis: Bobbs-Merrill, 1967), chap. 7.

[10] Theodore W. Schultz, *Investment in Human Capital: The Role of Education and Research* (New York: Free Press, 1971). Given Weber's earlier treatment of the intellectual property of professionals, the verb *rediscovered* might be a better term than *invented*.

[11] Ibid., 247.

[12] Theodore W. Schultz, "Fertility and Economic Values," in Schultz, ed., *Economics of the Family* (Chicago: University of Chicago Press, 1974), 6.

[13] Theodore W. Schultz, *Investing in People: The Economics of Population Quality* (Berkeley: University of California Press, 1981), xi.

swer must be made in the light of the human capital argument pointing to "the rising values of human beings."

The rising value of the human being. Contemporary evidence shows that the return on human capital is as great as or greater than the returns on physical capital,[14] a powerful incentive for both individuals and society to invest further in human capital. Because the returns to society are likely to be larger than the returns to individuals, the need for public investment is also supported.[15] In this respect Schultz's argument is endorsed: Economic growth is primarily a consequence of the improved quality of human resources and increased knowledge.[16] The idea that the market's restless search for novelty and efficiency is *necessarily* linked to increasing reliance on knowledge and that "knowledge is our most powerful engine of production"[17] promises a continued high value assigned to the human mind.

The consequences are enormous. As we shall see, two major feedback cycles are set in motion: Economic growth is a major source of cognitive development, which, in turn, is a source of economic growth (Chapter 7); and economic growth has (contrary to recent argument by Easterlin[18] and others) a major impact on subjective well-being or happiness, which also has effects on various facets of behavior that increases productivity and which, in turn, increases the sense of well-being (Chapters 26 and 28).

Caveats and modifications

A reversible trend. Recall that in the industrial revolution of the late eighteenth and early to mid-nineteenth centuries the British and American markets showed just the opposite tendencies. Furthermore, if the "deskilling hypothesis," which says that it is profitable for owners to reduce the need for skills in production so as also to reduce wages to the level of the unskilled,[19] were valid, we would be faced with a genuinely market inspired, and not just a technologically promoted, continuation of those unhappy earlier tendencies. Apparently the hypothesis has been true for certain periods of American history and, until recently, has been more true for

[14] Jeffrey G. Williamson and Peter H. Lindert, *American Inequality: A Macroeconomic History* (New York: Academic Press, 1980), 202.

[15] Martin Neil Baily and Alok K. Chakrabarti, *Innovation and the Productivity Crisis* (Washington, DC: Brookings Institution, 1988).

[16] Schultz, *Investing in Human Capital*, 33 and passim. A more definitive account of the contribution of education and knowledge to economic growth is available in Edward F. Denison, *Trends in American Economic Growth, 1929–1982* (Washington, DC: Brookings Institution, 1985). The attribution to increased knowledge, however, refers to a residual category that has been called the measure of our ignorance of the causes of growth. Education and knowledge are treated separately.

[17] Schultz, "Fertility and Economic Values," 18.

[18] Richard A. Easterlin, "Does Economic Growth Improve the Human Lot?" in Paul A. David and Melvin W. Reder, eds., *Nations and Households in Economic Growth: Essays in Honor of Moses Abramovitz* (Stanford: University of Stanford Press, 1974); Idem, "Does Money Buy Happiness? *The Public Interest,* no. 30 (Winter 1973): 3–10.

[19] Compare Harry Braverman, *Labor and Monopoly Capital* (New York: Monthly Review Press, 1974) and Kenneth I. Spenner, "Prometheus Deciphered: Temporal Change in the Skill Level of Work," *American Sociological Review* 48 (1983): 824–37.

women than for men. But currently the deskilling hypothesis is not an accurate description of trends in the labor market (Chapter 14). Consider, then, how fragile this reliance on a pattern that currently prevails may be. "When returns exceed cost, population quality will be enhanced. This means that an increase in any quality component is a response to a demand for it."[20] But when returns are less than costs, population quality will be depreciated. In the end, constant market principles with reversible effects will prevail. This is a strange way to treat a summum bonum.

Children: from producer goods to consumption goods. Schultz's argument is based almost exclusively on the increased productive value of human persons, but, in a discussion not fully integrated with the main thrust of his argument, he points out that children are no longer regarded as productive assets to a family but rather as "consumer goods."[21] The alarm in the 1980s and 1990s over what seemed to be increasing child neglect[22] (and sometimes abuse), suggests that as consumer goods, children may be less valued and less well cared for than when they were productive assets.

Consider environmental psychology's way of thinking of the relationship between the economy and the value of children as reflected in theories of child development. "The basic problem of the socialization theorist is to trace the economy → economic activity → social coordination → child rearing paths invented and transmitted by various cultures."[23] It is quite possible that this second way of thinking about economic outputs has much more to do with the satisfaction of wants in human society than has conventional analysis. In this formulation the character of the children shaped by the economy is the explanandum, the dependent variable. Perhaps they are trained to be future producers, rather than current consumer goods, but at least the focus is on the human beings produced by the economy. It will be at least a generation before we know how microeconomics fits into environmental psychology, from which this model was borrowed.

The rising value of human capital makes those without such capital worse off. The burden placed on those without such capital represents a further caveat to the human capital approach. The evident academic satisfaction (not to say, gratification) in the message that "knowledge is our most powerful engine of production" must be tempered by some sense of the increased depreciation of those without the appropriate human capital or with meager stores of capital of any kind. The split between the man of knowledge and the productive worker that Marx decried has simply shifted its devisive force downward a few notches and enlarged the sense by the disadvantaged of being left out.

[20] Schultz, *Investing in People*, 12
[21] Schultz, "Fertility and Economic Values," 7–8.
[22] For an early manifestation of this alarm, before the child abuse stories became dominant in the news, see National Research Council (National Academy of Sciences), Committee on Child Development, *Toward a National Policy for Children* (Washington, DC: National Academy of Sciences, 1976).
[23] Laboratory of Comparative Cognition, "What is Cultural about Cross-Cultural Cognitive Psychology?" *Annual Review of Psychology* 30 (1978): 145–72 at 155.

Valuing persons without understanding them. A further caveat asks whether it is possible to value something without seeking to understand it. The religious person seeks, partly through his or her church, to understand God; the materialist seeks devoutly to understand the inner working of a system that promises money. Can it be that the market and its agents value the human being without seeking to understand that being? Marshall reports that economists *are* concerned with the "desires, aspirations and other affections of human nature. . . . But the economist studies mental states rather through their manifestations than in themselves, and if he finds they afford evenly balanced incentives to action, he treats them *prima facie* as for his purpose equal."[24] Thus, "desires, aspirations and other affections of human nature" are dropped from sight and represent only a set of influences in a field of larger forces. Along similar lines, John R. Hicks reports that "the econometric theory of demand does study human beings, but only as *entities* having certain patterns of market behaviour; it makes no claim, no pretence, to be able to see inside their heads."[25] How much value can be assigned to individuals who are studied only for their economic behavior or the net effects of their behavior?

Businesspeople's antiintellectualism. With some unfairness to the market, I add here a set of attitudes toward "the life of the mind" attributed to the market's custodians and agents, businesspeople. "The common strain that binds together the attitudes and ideas which I call anti-intellectualism," said Hofstadter, "is a resentment and suspicion of the life of the mind and of those who are considered to represent it; and a disposition constantly to minimize the value of that life. . . . I put business in the vanguard of anti-intellectualism in our culture," he says, not because it is more philistine but because it is more powerful. "This is true both in the sense that the claims of practicality have been an overweening force in American life and in that sense that, since the mid-nineteenth century, businessmen have brought anti-intellectual movements more strength than any other force in society."[26]

Since Hofstadter wrote, industry and commerce have become more supportive of science and technology, but the smaller businesspeople, Rotary Clubs, and trade journals still tend to respect "practicality" over the abstract and to view intellectuals with suspicion. For example, Charles Wick, a businessman appointed by President Reagan to direct the International Communications Agency, explained his views on intellectuals as follows:

I don't want to knock intellectuals. There's a tremendous need for those kinds of people . . . [But] I wouldn't trust them to fix my car. Reagan would identify the problem swiftly, get someone to fix it who didn't necessarily go to Harvard. . . . [America is] just a giant busi-

[24] Alfred Marshall, *Principles of Economics,* 8th ed. (London: Macmillan, 1938), 15, 16.
[25] John R. Hicks, *A Revision of Demand Theory* (Oxford, UK: Oxford University Press, 1956), 6, cited in Amartya Sen, "Behaviour and the Concept of Preference," *Economica* 41 (1973): 242–54 at 242, my emphasis.
[26] Richard Hofstadter, *Anti-Intellectualism in American Life* (New York: Knopf/Vintage, 1963), 7, 239. Hofstadter's other main source of antiintellectualism in the United States is democratic egalitarianism.

ness. Other people who have run the country – social scientists – have never met a payroll. That's what brought us to this calamitous point.[27]

The value of individuals and of individuality in an ecological system

It is possible to value the human species without valuing its individual members, or, put differently, to sacrifice individuals for the preservation of the species. The ecological metaphor helps us to understand market evaluations of individuals. The market is an ecology with properties very like a Darwinian system, that is, it is indifferent to individuals and to specific firms but is designed, if that is the word, to protect the species of firms. In nature, the system may be profligate with individuals, arranged, for example, so that the sacrifice of a third of the individual birds in winter will still preserve the gene pools of those best fitted to that environment. Similarly, the market is arranged so that many individuals or firms may be ''lost'' but the fittest will survive. Indeed, it is only through the sacrifice of individuals in a labor market and in bankruptcy proceedings that the market can achieve its purposes. This is neither cruel nor compassionate toward individuals; it is merely indifferent. Like nature, the market is a winnowing process.

The institution of the market is not alone in its indifference to individuals. Bureaucracies are devised to produce a standard product without relying on specific persons; the judicial system is no respecter of persons (a phrase Weber used to describe the market); and the military, in addition to sharing this person-indifference with bureaucracy and the judicial system, is devised explicitly so that individuals and whole units may be sacrificed to consummate some purpose. But none of these achieve their purposes by deliberately winnowing the weak.[28] This market method modifies the claim that the market is an engine for increasing the value of the human individual.

Substitutability, ecology, and individuality. The argument over the homogenization of ''market man'' in his gray flannel suit has, finally, given ground to the recognition of modern individuality.[29] Approval of individuality, however, is different from valuing the individual. To value an individual is to value John Doe in a particularistic manner; to value individuality is to value variations in persons irrespective of any particular exemplars. It is possible for the market to substitute one person for another without concern for the particular individual sacrificed, and

[27] Sidney Blumenthal, ''Whose Side is Business on, Anyway?'' *New York Times Magazine,* 25 October 1981, p. 93.

[28] In contrast to all of them, the Christian religion is said to hold every soul precious in the eyes of God. The problem for humanists, and Christians, too, is to reconcile the ethical worth (or dignity) of each individual to the indifference of the market.

[29] The grounds for the homogenization argument were the market's substitutability of one person for another. Without much evidence, this substitutability has been said to lead to the neutralization of personality, to ''moral neutralization,'' and generally to the alienation that stifles learning. I know of no evidence showing more amorality in market than in household or command economies, and some evidence going the other way, but there is abundant, if casual, evidence that individual members of the labor force are treated as ''hands'' rather than persons – at least until they become in some way uniquely valuable to the production process. See Paul Diesing, *Reason in Society* (Urbana: University of Illinois Press, 1962), 23–4.

at the same time to increase variation among the individuals thus treated so casually. As a changing ecology with ever finer niches for specialists, the market necessarily produces ever more differentiated people to fit these specialized niches.[30] Thus, even an ecological analysis produces grounds for believing that individuality, but not individuals, might be favored by a market economy.[31]

The market that we are familiar with may be said to be based on an *econocentric* model, but it is possible to think of a market based on what I shall call (Chapter 25) a *psychocentric* model. The econocentric market is certainly not the enemy of human development. In many ways it is an ally, but it fails to foster happiness and human development in crucial respects. This book proposes to explore this mixed support.

But the market experience has two different aspects, for living and working in a market economy is different from living and working in a society that the market has made prosperous. We turn to this difference now.

Market consciousness and subliminal theories

Exchange effects and affluence effects. The difference is explained by reference to two sets of market effects, the first being the *affluence effect,* the experience of social affluence in a society that, judging from contemporary history, must have employed the market to achieve that affluence. The second is the *exchange effect,* which, for want of a better name, we use to describe the market processes employed in a market economy – a kind of residual, basic experience in any market society. Although there are criticisms of the affluence effect in various treatments of economic growth (see below) most humanist and socialist criticisms of the market focus on the exchange effects, as we shall see in our treatment of friendship in Part Four.

Engagement in the market and market consciousness

The ordinary person is deeply engaged in only two markets – the labor market and the consumer market – almost never in interfirm markets and only glancingly, when he or she saves, in the capital market. Success in the labor market establishes one's place in the economy and to a large extent one's status in the community; it gives one the means for entry into the consumer market. Although on the average one person enters the labor market only about twelve times during a lifetime, the fact that one *sells* one's labor, talents, and devotion can be expected to influence one's thought and perhaps one's personality throughout life. A person's economic anxieties, sense of independence or dependency, alienation (in all of the Marxian senses), self-respect, and self-reliance will depend more on the labor market than on the consumer market (Part V).

The consumer market is another matter. In 1965 for the American population the

---

[30] Here I side with Durkheim against Marx in finding that specialization and the division of labor can enrich individuals as well as society. See Emile Durkheim, *The Division of Labor in Society*, trans. G. Simpson (1893, 1911; reprint New York: Free Press, 1964).
[31] Marginal analysis shows how workers are not paid according to their individual productivity but according to the productivity of the least efficient member of a set of workers.

average time spent marketing and shopping was thirty-one minutes a day, an increase of 40 percent over the preceding thirty years. Women spend more time shopping than men, the French and West Germans spend more time shopping than Americans.[32] The figures do not include such market experiences as eating in restaurants and exposure to advertising, the latter greatly increasing children's exposure to market norms. The critics' argument is that a person's exchange orientation, the "commodification" of friendship (Part IV), as the phrase goes, pricing of the intrinsic, and so forth is learned from and reinforced by these experiences in the consumer market.

The labor market experience is different from the consumer market experience, but both share a *market culture* that is said to permeate all institutions and practices in market societies: literature, religion, politics, family. Given what is thought to be the primacy of economic institutions, this assumption of the penetration of market culture has some initial plausibility, but it must be examined in the light of the many theories of the autonomy of art, the family, religion, and even politics.[33] We shall find that market penetration into other domains of life encounters many internal and external obstacles. It is impermissible, therefore, to claim that market attitudes, values, and skills generalize to nonmarket domains without examining the situational specificity of these values.

The importance of the market in shaping our consciousnesses has a direct and an indirect aspect. Only a modest element of our daily consciousness is focused directly on market-related things. A much larger portion is occupied by work (which is quite different from the labor market), family, friendship, uncommercialized leisure, education, worship, musing/reflecting/wool gathering – whatever people do when they are unoccupied and alone – eating and drinking, sleeping, health care and health worry, growing up, gardening, walking down the street. Allowing seven hours for sleeping (which is about the United States average), what people think about in the sixteen hours and twenty-nine minutes wakeful time when they are not shopping and in the fifty-eight years of their allotted seventy in which they are, on the average, not looking for a job, has little to do with money and markets. Those who doubt this perspective might reflect upon how much of their conscious life is devoted to thinking about market-related things. Nor is the unconscious much more occupied with such things. For example, in one analysis of the dreams of 1,000 men and women, only 43 dreams had to do with money, compared to 149 dealing with automobiles (adventure and symbol more than price), 125 with "rooms" (of which more were living rooms than bedrooms!), 118 with "home," 62 with water, 49 with hands, and 46 with faces.[34]

[32] Alexander Szalai, *The Use of Time* (The Hague: Mouton, 1972), 578.

[33] The autonomy of politics has long been disputed by Marxists, but recently even this autonomy has been acknowledged: See Peter B. Evans, Dietrich Rueschmeyer, and Theda Skocpol, eds., *Bring the State Back In* (New York: Cambridge University Press, 1985). In a more conventional analysis, Eric A. Nordlinger writes on *The Autonomy of the Democratic State* (Cambridge: Harvard University Press, 1981). The autonomy of art is proclaimed in a strange place: Jurgen Habermas, "Science and Technology as Ideology" in his *Toward A Rational Society,* trans. J. J. Shapiro (Boston: Beacon, 1970).

[34] Calvin S. Hall and Robert L. van de Castle, *The Content Analysis of Dreams* (New York: Appleton-Century-Crofts, 1966), 243–72. Studies of the content of daydreams reveal more economic content, but

But the indirect effect of the market on the way we think is substantial. We assume without thought that goods are exchanged for precise money amounts and not given in the manner of gift exchange economies. We think of goods as individually and not collectively owned and that their usufruct pertains to their individual owners. We accept that we must earn our living in the labor market, that it is shameful to be dependent on kin, that the money in our pockets is exchangeable for commodities, and so forth. If we do not think *about* market-related things, what we do think about often (but certainly not always) reflects what we have *learned from* the market. To a large extent the assumptions that we learn are, in fact, *causal theories* about ourselves and the institutions that affect our lives.

The basic economic sequence (BES)

We will organize these theories in terms of a basic economic sequence (BES). For any household or individual engaged in economic work to earn a living the following basic sequence applies: (1) To satisfy a want (motive), a person must (2) exert effort or make a sacrifice, for (3) a reward, which is then (4) consumed, traded, or saved (5) for the benefit of self or others, (6) within a time framework, e.g., now or later, (7) yielding gratification (or not), and (8) somehow justified.

What we would like to stress about the sequence is that it comprises a bundle of theories. A common formula for a theory of motivation is set forth as follows:

The tendency to strive for a given goal is a function of the strength of the enduring motive (Mg) times the value of the goal target or incentive (Ig) times the probability that by striving one will achieve the goal (Pg) minus any aversions toward the goal or the means to the goal.[35]

Underlying this theory is a set of nested others. The term Pg is a theory of causation implying and drawing on more general theories of effective action, such as the rational expectations theory involving a payoff matrix. This rational expectations theory itself involves further theories of what causes increases in a person's income in this society, and if, as Adam Smith claimed, money is sought to win the favorable "sentiments of mankind," there is the added theory of the effect of money on favorable sentiments. Since the agent is the self, the most important causal attribution is to the self – or, alternatively, to others, fate, or society generally.

Interpreting the strength of the underlying motive (Mg) has been assumed in economic discourse to be unproblematic, but the more this interpretation of the sources of one's own behavior is examined, the more it appears to be a complex and often misleading process (Chapter 27). The complexity is illustrated by theories and research on arousal showing that the interpretation of a motive is often a process of seeking a label for and then an explanation of one's aroused state (Chapter 28). The explanation is often found, not from privileged insight, but from available, conventional theories of why any person in the given circumstances would feel as that person does.[36] To this set of problems is added the definition of the self and the

in that area it is work and not pay, buying, selling, money, or exchange that people turn to in their musings.

[35] This formula is an amalgam taken from two related sources: John W. Atkinson, "Motivation for Achievement," in Thomas Blass, ed., *Personality Variables in Social Behavior* (New York: Halsted/ Wiley, 1977), and David Winter, *The Power Motive* (New York: Free Press, 1973).

[36] Daryl J. Bem, "Self-Perception Theory," in Leonard Berkowitz, ed., *Advances in Experimental Social Psychology*, vol. 6 (New York: Academic Press, 1972).

self's longer term interests. In simpler societies (we think) people had ascribed identities, but in modern society, with its multiple models and conflicting demands, people are likely to have to forge for themselves achieved identities.[37]

Finally, for many of the same reasons, the interpretation of whether the target will, in fact, gratify the puzzled person (Ig) is more complicated than it seems. One source of complication is that gratification, like other emotions, is dependent on specific situations: The purchase of clothing that is rewarding among peers is not rewarding when worn in the presence of parents; the car that conveys the right image in the company parking lot may not be the one a person would choose for its powers of acceleration. One of the most poignant problems of situationally defined rewards is in interpreting the meaning of wages or commissions and bonuses. Interpreted as a reward for excellence, they are welcome, but interpreted as an effort to control one's discretion at work, they are sometimes resented.[38]

People do more than "satisfice;" they simplify, routinize their decisions, purchase by habit, adapt to familiar situations, all to economize on their scarce cognitive resources.[39] But it is possible that the market makes demands upon its participants that exceed their modest powers (Chapter 8).

What we now see is that the material self-interest that lies behind and is said to drive the BES is both compelling and so complex as to be often deceiving. It is compelling in part because the market makes it so (yet it has great attractiveness to premarket traditional societies); it is complex because it involves the interpretations and theories mentioned, taxing the cognitive powers of many people. The underlying materialist interpretation of the world and the self will be both popular and misleading. As we shall see, it is not quite a case of "fool's gold," for material rewards are moderately associated with greater life satisfaction, but the link between money and subjective well-being is far more slender and fragile than most people think (Chapter 26). Between 1957 and 1976 the association between money and happiness declined for the better off and better educated.[40] We may be seeing a slow process of social learning in which the deceptively attractive idea that money buys happiness is gradually perceived more accurately as very likely to be a disappointing purchase.

Affluence effects

The market generates the wealth of nations. Could it be that the affluence created by the market has a desirable effect on experience and personal qualities but that

[37] Eric Erikson, "The Problem of Ego Identity," *Journal of the American Psychoanalytic Association* 4 (1956): 58–121; Edmund Bourne, "The State of Research on Ego Identity: A Review and Appraisal, Part I, *Journal of Youth and Adolescence* 7 (1978): 223–51.

[38] Mark R. Lepper and David Greene, eds., *The Hidden Costs of Rewards: New Perspectives on the Psychology of Human Motivation* (Hillsdale, NJ: Erlbaum, 1978).

[39] George Katona, *Psychological Economics* (New York: Elsevier, 1975). The concept of the "cognitive miser" expresses this tendency toward parsimonious thought. See Susan T. Fiske and Patricia Linville, "What Does the Schema Concept Buy Us?" *Personality and Social Psychology Bulletin* 6 (1980): 543–57.

[40] Angus Campbell, Philip E. Converse, and Willard L. Rodgers, *The Quality of American Life* (New York: Russell Sage, 1976), 28; Angus Campbell, *The Sense of Well-Being in America* (New York: McGraw-Hill, 1981), 233–4.

the *process* of generating that wealth has a set of undesirable effects? Is living in a market society the disutility for which the compensating utility is living in an affluent society? Keynes put the problem in a moral perspective:

When the accumulation of wealth is no longer of high social importance, there will be great changes in the code of morals. We shall be able to rid ourselves of many of the pseudo-moral principles which have hag-ridden us for two hundred years, by which we have exalted some of the most distasteful of human qualities into the position of the highest virtues. We shall be able to afford to dare to assess the money-motive at its true value."[41]

By this line of reasoning, we must be modestly immoral to become an affluent society but can shed this immorality at that beautiful moment when we have become affluent enough. Is the same delayed gratification necessary for developing ourselves to our full capacities and for becoming genuinely happy?

The controversies over growth/no growth and the effects of growth or affluence on character, the environment, "status goods," uses of leisure, have been well rehearsed; I summarize them here. But note that the affluence effect is controversial only after incomes achieve a certain level; none criticize the developing nations for their increments of national income, and all mourn the post-1970 regression into even more abject poverty of the African nations. In what follows we consider *social* affluence for the developed nations, roughly measured by per capita GNP (or GDP), not individual wealth (see Chapter 26).

The critics of social affluence

Keynes was writing in the 1930s and anticipated that his grandchildren might experience the "permanent problem of mankind," namely, learning to live well. In the 1990s, Keynes's grandchildren are now middle-aged. Since his time, per capita GNP in the economically advanced countries has at least doubled, but only a relative few are ready to "rid themselves" of the profit motive.

The analysis of affluence does not cover the historic difficulties of getting there, the pains of economic development. Before turning to affluence, we must acknowledge that point: Whereas the process of first making people more miserable in the period 1760–1830 before making them better off at a later time may never have been what Marx and others claimed,[42] the misery was acute and prolonged. Oddly, the developing nations seem not to suffer from this perverse process of immiseration.[43] Yet major social changes are disruptive, not least because in the case of the developing nations much of the change is prompted from outside.[44] There is a psychic agony in the first stages of economic growth, whether or not it is market inspired,[45] an agony that wanes but in the traumas of all major life changes[46] does not ever fully expire. Affluence itself has other defects:

[41] John Maynard Keynes, "Economic Possibilities for our Grandchildren," in his *Essays in Persuasion* (London: Macmillan, 1931), 63. Keynes seems to suggest that only people living in economically developed societies can afford genuine morality, a thesis that ethicists would find repulsive.

[42] T. S. Ashton, *The Industrial Revolution: 1760–1830* (London: Oxford University Press, 1948).

[43] Alex Inkeles and David H. Smith, *Becoming Modern* (Cambridge: Harvard University Press, 1974).

[44] Margaret Mead, ed., *Cultural Patterns and Technical Change* (New York: Mentor, 1955).

[45] Leonard W. Doob, *Becoming More Civilized: A Psychological Exploration* (New Haven: Yale University Press, 1960).

[46] Thomas H. Holmes and Minoru Masuda, "Life Change and Susceptibility to Illness," in Barbara

1. Schumacher and his allies point to the double damage done by rich societies: They impoverish their (and everyone's) children by consuming the capital endowment of our common natural resources as though it were income and at the same time poison the air and water used by the current generation.[47] We now see, however, that it is the richest nations that can alleviate pollution where the struggling middle-level nations cannot and the command economies did not.

2. Hirsch argues that so many of the advantages we enjoy are enjoyable only if others do not have them, for "the satisfaction that individuals derive from goods and services depends in increasing measure not only on their own consumption but on consumption by others, as well." Hirsch calls these depreciated items "status goods" and, unfortunately for his case, cites education as an example.[48]

3. Mishan's indictment of the effects of growth are more substantial: There is no necessary connection between economic growth and the relief of poverty and inequality; growth multiplies useless and wasteful choices; wealth creates disamenities in the environment, particularly in cities; it reduces privacy, makes rare artistic monuments or places of natural beauty crowded and ugly, and does nothing to improve the enjoyment of work. To remedy these defects by market means, Mishan proposes three conditions, none of which can be met: (a) *All* goods must be assigned an accurate cost and all marginal costs must be equal; (b) the "the relative income hypothesis" must be false (people's well-being must not be a function of their neighbors' well-being); and (c) welfare or well-being from nonmarket goods must represent only a small portion of the total.[49]

4. In his *People of Plenty,* David Potter argues that the anxiety and insecurity of the prosperous American people is traceable to their perpetual striving after an illusory success.[50]

5. Durkheim's description of the anomie of affluence is a familiar indictment of market influence; it is a state where "reality seems valueless by comparison with the dreams of fevered imagination; reality is therefore abandoned when it in turn becomes reality."[51] Like the exchange effect, whose critics will be given a louder

Snell Dohrenwend and Bruce P. Dohrenwend, eds., *Stressful Life Events* (New York: Wiley, 1974). It should be noted that the most stressful life events are not economic in their nature.

[47] E. F. Schumacher, *Small Is Beautiful: Economics as if People Mattered* (New York: Harper/Colophon, 1973). In a horrifying, but fortunately inaccurate, account of this process, the Meadows and their collaborators, writing on behalf of the Club of Rome in 1972, prophesied that within a generation we should have choked ourselves to death with industrial waste. See Donella H. Meadows, Dennis L. Meadows, Jørgen Randers, and William W. Behrens, III, *The Limits to Growth* (New York: Potomac/Earth Island, 1972).

[48] Fred Hirsch, *Social Limits to Growth* (Cambridge: Harvard University Press, 1976), 2. The example is unfortunate, for although it may be true that as the educational level of the population increases, any particular level is less and less of a credential for its possessor for status and jobs, it is also true that the externalities of living in an educated society for an educated person are benign and far more important.

[49] E. J. Mishan, *The Costs of Economic Growth* (Harmondsworth, UK: Penguin, 1969).

[50] David M. Potter, *People of Plenty: Economic Abundance and the American Character* (Chicago: University of Chicago Press, 1954).

[51] Emile Durkheim, *Suicide,* trans. J. A. Spaulding and G. Simpson (Glencoe, IL: Free Press, 1951), 256. Elsewhere Durkheim asks, "Even from a purely utilitarian point of view, what is the point of increasing abundance, if it does not succeed in claiming the desires of the greatest number, but, on the

voice in a later chapter, the affluence effect has its cogent critics, but note that the socialists are missing; they have no case against affluence. Yet against the indictment, the benefits of affluence seem more substantial.

The defense of social affluence.

The affluent society has two auxiliary strengths: higher levels of cognitive development and higher levels of life satisfaction. By themselves, these seem to make the positive case, but they have further consequences that will be briefly mentioned after the general effects of affluence.

Direct affluence effects. Better health and longevity are the least controversial effects of affluence, with higher levels of education a close second. As the product of knowledge, affluence is necessarily associated with increased knowledge and employment in a "knowledge industry";[52] affluence is also associated more generally with a selective upgrading of a variety of (but by no means all) occupations. One of the most important gains from increased per capita income is the opportunity it offers for housewives to leave the drudgery of housework for market jobs that do not simply duplicate that drudgery (Chapter 14). With a greater, and especially a growing, surplus, governments are more redistributive. They can redistribute new income in Pareto optimal manner: No one gets absolutely less and the poor, sick, and disadvantaged can get more. It should be noted that the equality does not flow automatically from greater wealth in a market society, but rather from the policies of governments in richer societies.[53] Those socialized in periods of affluence and security are less "materialistic" and have more of the "post-materialist" values identified by Inglehart, such as appreciating beauty and wanting to live "in a society where ideas count."[54] There is a positive correlation between per capita income and the institutions of democracy, judicial independence, and freedom of expression, a correlation that is as strong at the top of the scale, in the region we are examining, as it is at the bottom.[55]

Altering the perspective slightly we include the benefits of growth and the rising phase of the business cycle among the benefits of affluence. With economic growth there are gains in the quality of other social institutions. The rise of totalitarian regimes is more likely to occur during recessions or depressions.[56] In contrast to recessions, during prosperous periods people tend to convert to more liberal and humanistic religions.[57] The media seem to be more "authoritarian" in their report-

contrary, only serves to arouse their impatience?'' See Emile Durkheim, *Professional Ethics and Civic Morals,* trans. C. Brookfield (London: Routledge & Kegan Paul, 1957), 16.

[52] Fritz Machlup, *The Production and Distribution of Knowledge in the United States* (Princeton: Princeton University Press, 1962).

[53] Robert W. Jackman, *Politics and Social Equality: A Comparative Analysis* (New York: Wiley, 1975), especially p. 198; see also Giorgio Gagliani, "Income Inequality and Economic Development," *Annual Review of Sociology* (1987): 313–86.

[54] Ronald Inglehart, *The Silent Revolution* (Princeton: Princeton University Press, 1972).

[55] For an early example of research supporting these hypotheses, see Arthur S. Banks and Robert B. Textor, *A Cross-Polity Survey* (Cambridge: M.I.T. Press, 1963); many of the same relationships are reported in Kenneth Kanda, *Political Parties: A Cross National Survey* (New York: Free Press, 1980).

[56] Lea et al., *The Individual in the Economy,* 432, citing work by T. Geiger.

[57] S. M. Sales, "Economic Threat as a Determinant of Conversion in Authoritarian and Non-Authoritarian Churches," *Journal of Personality and Social Psychology* 23 (1972): 420–8.

ing of news during economic crises and to turn to superstition and astrology in recessions.[58] In short, many democratic and social institutions operate better under circumstances of economic growth than in its absence – at least once the taste for growth has been acquired.

Indirect affluence effects: cognitive contributions. Affluence is associated with greater cognitive complexity throughout society, from which a number of other benefits follow. In line with Keynes's moral argument, the greater cognitive complexity in advanced countries is associated with higher levels of moral reasoning;[59] greater cognitive complexity also implies increased capacities for divergent or imaginative thinking;[60] because of their higher levels of cognition and moral reasoning, people in affluent societies have lower levels of authoritarianism and are therefore less vulnerable to "malignant obedience," that is, unthinking obedience to authority without consulting their own consciences;[61] the cognitively complex are less ethnically prejudiced, more accepting of complexity; people in affluent societies are somewhat more likely to believe that they are responsible for their own fates[62] and considerably more likely to value and have the capacity for self-direction at work.[63] Finally, to complete the circle, the cognitively complex also contribute more to production and thus to affluence itself, especially in the post-industrial age where knowledge is the main source of productivity.

A market economy is a great engine for greater affluence. If the processes of achieving wealth by market means are sometimes infelicitous and damaging to human development, the product in greater affluence is clearly a substantial gain. A condition where people are more cognitively and morally sophisticated, more democratic, more autonomous, healthier, more productive, less materialistic, and happier is better than a condition where people have fewer of these qualities.

Summary

In this chapter we have begun the substantive analysis of the market experience by focusing on three things: market economists' concepts of the developed person as human capital, concepts that may be useful but are totally inadequate as concepts of personality with intrinsic values; the experience of living in a market where exchange is the central organizing concept for economists and the central coordinating

---

[58] D. O. Jorgenson, "Economic Threat and Authoritarianism in Television Programs: 1950–1974," *Psychological Reports* 37 (1975): 1153–4; V. R. Padgett and D. O. Jorgenson, "Superstition and Economic Threat: Germany 1918–1940," *Personality and Social Psychology Bulletin* 8 (1982): 736–41. Both are reported in Lea et al., *The Individual in the Economy*, 429.

[59] Lawrence Kohlberg and R. Kramer, "Continuities and Discontinuities in Childhood and Adult Moral Development," *Human Development* 12 (1969): 92–120.

[60] Frank Baron, *Creativity and Personal Freedom*, 2d ed. (New York: Van Nostrand, 1968).

[61] Stanley Milgram, *Obedience to Authority: An Experimental View* (New York: Harper & Row, 1974); Herbert C. Kelman and V. Lee Hamilton, *Crimes of Obedience: Toward a Social Psychology of Authority and Responsibility* (New Haven: Yale University Press, 1989), 189, 227.

[62] Gerald Gurin and Patricia Gurin, "Personal Efficacy and the Ideology of Individual Responsibility," in Burkhard Strumpel, ed., *Economic Means for Human Needs* (Ann Arbor, MI: Institute for Social Research, 1976).

[63] Melvin Kohn and Carmi Schooler, *Work and Personality: An Inquiry into the Impact of Social Stratification* (Norwood, NJ: Ablex, 1983), 32, 48–9, 77, 92.

element for market institutions; and the beneficent experience of living in an affluent economy born in pain from the womb of the exchange economy.

Unfortunately, the human capital approach to human development rests on properties of the market that have not always valued human capital and may not do so at another time. Nor does the approach seem to protect children now that they are thought to be expensive consumer goods rather than productive assets. From another point of view, the more valuable and necessary is human capital, the more tragic are the cases of those without it. Human capital is defined so as to require no understanding of persons, but to value people without bothering to understand them is a superficial approach to human dignity. Finally, using an ecological metaphor we saw that it is quite possible to value individuality without valuing individuals.

If the market's exchange effect influences human behavior, it does so by imprinting unconscious assumptions about the world rather than by influencing consciousness. But probably without human intention, the market is so devised as to make consumer welfare dominant over worker welfare. And in the pursuit of welfare in a market economy, the basic sequence of thoughts and acts rests on a most complicated and rarely comprehended set of causal theories, so complicated that only the "epigrams" of the theories are captured and used.

Economic growth producing relative social affluence may have the infelicitous consequences alleged by critics of growth, but the tendencies for economic growth to increase health and education, to improve both cognition and moral reasoning, and to create more democratic and tolerant societies readily overcome these defects.

2   Choices in social systems

We live in systems

Nature and society are systemic but our disciplines partition these systems to suit our convenience rather than to fit the phenomena we seek to analyze. In this chapter I seek to show the importance of a systemic, multidisciplinary approach to the market experience, illustrating it by showing the interlocking nature of several of the main criticisms of the market.

There are five major targets of criticism of the market: influence on politics, efficiency, distributive justice, personality, and quality of life. Market influences on any one of these also influence the other four; hence criticism of market influences on any one implies something about the others. As the ecologists say, "You can't do just one thing." In this discussion I shall combine the last two targets of criticism, personality and the quality of life, under the heading of *the market experience,* and in the interest of brevity I will omit political influences. Efficiency (productivity), justice, and personality are intimately interrelated (in a tripartite system each element has two relationships, one with each of the other elements; the numbering system reflects this set of relationships, e.g., 1.a, 1.b; 2.a, 2.b, etc.):

1.a. Levels of efficiency and productivity affect justice. Most obviously, a just distribution depends upon production, and the relief of poverty requires resources. Many justice theorists have recognized this. Vlastos once pointed out that any just custodian of goods must, as a condition of his fiduciary responsibilities, maximize the resources available to his wards;[1] as Rawls reminds us, even egalitarians must make provision for resource development unless they prize equality over well-being.[2] In quite a different sense, economic growth permits Pareto optimal increments to the poor. Finally, and less certainly, there seems to be a curvilinear relationship between economic growth and egalitarian distribution such that at a late stage of industrial development some intrinsic properties of market systems favor a (modestly) more egalitarian distribution of the product.[3] If efficiency and equality represent "the big tradeoff,"[4] a person can choose to emphasize one over the other, but responsible moral theorists cannot choose to ignore the effects of the one upon the other.

1.b. Economic efficiency affects personality. Everywhere poverty is the enemy of personality development and a decent quality of life (Chapter 7). Scrambling for

[1] Gregory Vlastos, "Justice and Equality," in Richard B. Brandt, ed., *Social Justice* (Englewood Cliffs, NJ: Prentice-Hall, 1962).

[2] John Rawls, *A Theory of Justice* (Cambridge: Harvard University Press, 1971).

[3] Simon Kuznets, "Economic Growth and Income Inequality," *American Economic Review* 45 (1955): 1–28.

[4] Arthur M. Okun, *Equality and Efficiency: The Big Tradeoff* (Washington, DC: Brookings Institution, 1975).

a living is preoccupying and, even without the "culture of poverty" (which is said to be a feature only of capitalist societies),[5] the poor cannot reflect upon themselves to achieve self-knowledge; they cannot devote their meager resources to cultural enrichment or self-development. Across societies members of the more developed economies have higher levels of moral reasoning, or at least develop them earlier in adolescence; within the modern American society, the college educated are overwhelmingly more likely than those without such education to develop standards of principled moral reasoning.[6] College education costs money. Cognitive development, which is the foundation of moral reasoning and has many other desirable personality effects, is a function of resources given to education. Higher per capita GNP is certainly not a sufficient condition for personality development in a broad spectrum of the public, but up to a point (perhaps one we have now reached) it is a necessary one.

2.a. Distributive justice affects efficiency, partly because it affects incentives to produce – hence Rawls's difference principle. Carelessly applied, the distribution of money (but not of work) based on principles of need seems to undermine initiative and enterprise. Although in both the British and American economies most people believe that they get about what they deserve,[7] some strikes, labor turnover, and withdrawal of initiative stem from a sense of injustice and do have efficiency costs.

2.b. Justice affects personality and some aspects of life quality, although it affects these things less than does efficiency. This is because poverty has a much greater effect on personality than does inequality (Chapter 7). For example, above the level of decent subsistence, that primary good, self-esteem, is only minimally related to level of income[8] (Chapter 10). On these narrow grounds, and taking due care not to create feelings of dependency, the justice of need seems better devised to protect personality than does the justice of equality (where these two kinds of justice may be distinguished).

3.a. Personality affects efficiency in all the obvious senses. Work ethic, entrepreneurial spirit, sense of responsibility, ability to delay gratification, and self-reliance are all related to economic development. About one-sixth of the American productivity increases in the 1929–69 period were attributable to the development of human capital.[9]

3.b. Personality affects justice in a variety of ways. Variations in belief in a "just world" create variations in tendencies to justify injustices;[10] most people show a strong tendency to desire that any person's (often the self's) ratio of input (cost

[5] Oscar Lewis, *La Vida: A Puerto Rican Family in The Culture of Poverty – San Juan and New York* (New York: Random House/Vintage, 1966).
[6] Lawrence Kohlberg and R. Kramer, "Continuities and Discontinuities in Childhood and Adult Moral Development," *Human Development* 12 (1969): 93–120.
[7] Wesley H. Perkins and Wendell Bell, "Alienation and Social Justice in England and the United States: The Polity and the Economy," in R. F. Tomasson, ed., *Comparative Social Research,* vol. 3 (Greenwich, CT: JAI Press, 1980).
[8] Angus Campbell, *The Sense of Well-Being in America* (New York: McGraw-Hill, 1981), 216–17.
[9] Edward F. Denison, *Accounting for United States Economic Growth 1929–1969* (Washington, D.C: Brookings, 1974).
[10] Melvin J. Lerner, *The Belief in a Just World: A Fundamental Delusion* (New York: Plenum, 1980).

or effort or sacrifice) to outcome (pay or status or power) is the same as any other's similar ratio, but people differ in their responses to unbalanced ratios;[11] the level of moral reasoning mentioned, especially the capacity to rise above conventional reasoning based on consensus or law and order to levels of principled reasoning, is a personality trait; so is the sense of responsibility for the fate of others that must precede prosocial or altruistic acts.[12] All these qualities, although often situationally influenced, are differentially distributed in the population, that is, they reflect dispositions or personality.

We live in social systems where the systemic effects are reflexive. For example, the market's efficiency effects on personality in turn affect the market's efficiency. For this reason those market critics who desire to alter one relationship must think of the second-order effects of that alteration on the relationship criticized and on the values that the criticism is designed to advance. The unintended consequences of any one policy, whether it is the current policy or a proposed reform, are substantial and often self-defeating.[13]

The fact that society is a system where alterations in one element affect others is obvious enough, but its realization is inhibited by a general feature of our analytical world and by a special feature of some ethical thought. The general feature is the division of labor among analysts: economists devote their attention to efficiency, ethicists to justice, psychologists and psychiatrists to personality, and everyone, it seems, to observations on, if not the study of, the quality of life. In order to promote rigor, each discipline believes it must treat the others as *coeteris paribus*. It is a rigor bought at a high price in understanding system qualities and in the consequences of policies based on that understanding.

One implication is that the economic system cannot be studied in isolation of the social system. This has long been evident in lessons learned from attempted application of the principles that govern advanced market systems to the systems of the Less Developed Economies,[14] but even between advanced economies cultural differences modify the effects of economic changes in the different societies. I will illustrate this in Chapter 14 with a report on research by Duncan Gallie showing the very different responses of French and British labor to the introduction of automation. Holding constant the degree of marketization and levels of technology, Gallie found that worker response patterns to the same major technological changes varied greatly between the two cultures.[15] Whatever may be said about invariant economic "laws," it is clear that market constraints tend to channel worker responses to technology less than do variations in culture, ideology, and worker expectations. It

---

[11] Elaine Walster, Ellen Berscheid, and G. William Walster, "New Directions in Equity Research," *Journal of Personality and Social Psychology* 25 (1973): 141–76.

[12] Shalom H. Schwartz, "Moral Decision Making and Behavior," in J. Macaulay and L. Berkowitz, eds., *Altruism and Helping Behavior* (New York: Academic, 1970).

[13] The social system, of course, is much larger than the economic system, with families, communities, religious institutions, and so forth all sharing in the system effects, but there is enough to do in the preceding analysis without complexifying it further.

[14] An early report on the changed assumptions needed for the analysis of economic growth in the LDC is available in Walt W. Rostow, *The Process of Economic Growth* (New York: Norton, 1952).

[15] Duncan Gallie, *In Search of the New Working Class* (Cambridge, UK: Cambridge University Press, 1978), 16–21.

is a salutary lesson in the subordination of market systems to social systems, the embeddedness of the market in society. Consequently, "the" market experience is, in fact, a series of different market experiences depending on where it takes place.

The special impediments to systematic thought are of two kinds. One is the narrow deontological claims to the priority of duty over other considerations, such as efficiency and mental health. The other is the proposition that rights are absolute. It is the virtue of some rights theorists, like Dworkin,[16] that they recognize the limits to absolute claims. Emphasis on good will, rigorous performance of duty, and absolute rights in a world of poverty is heroic but empirically unlikely to influence events.

Walls and systems

Whereas the recognition of the interrelatedness of things is sometimes impeded by the parochialism of the social sciences, it is sometimes wisely reflected in society by efforts to protect or wall off one cherished value from contamination by the other elements of the system. Since it is impossible to perform an efficiency act without consequences to justice or personality, or to be virtuous without affecting both justice and efficiency, this solution by spheres and walls and boundaries and tiers offers problems that we shall have to examine.

How can it be that in a system where each element affects others, we could ever hope to erect a wall between the market and certain protected kinds of practices? Walls may do two things. They may insulate the subsystem from "pollution" by other subsystems, and/or they may insulate the subsystem from "pollution" by the purposes of the overall system. (To avoid such infelicities of expression I hereafter refer to *subsystems* as *institutions* or *practices,* and *the overall social system* as *society.*)

Partitioning institutions and practices from each other
The first of these purposes (protecting one set of practices from infection by another) is more familiar, as illustrated by Walzer's *Spheres of Justice.* The spheres are protected by "blocked exchanges" protecting such institutions as criminal justice and such practices as merit awards from contamination by the institutions and practices of the market. For Walzer, the main purpose of these blocked exchanges is to keep separate the power of money from other kinds of power and the criteria of wealth from other kinds of criteria.[17]

This kind of insulation has many guises in both theory and social practice. In theory construction, Rawls's "lexical ordering" of freedom is a form of boundary creation. In such social practices as those represented by law, to serve the interest

[16] Ronald Dworkin, *Taking Rights Seriously* (Cambridge: Harvard University Press, 1977).
[17] Robert E. Goodin proposes to insulate ethical decisions from materialistic ones on the grounds that "material incentives destroy rather than supplement moral incentives" (p. 113). This formulation ignores the system properties of societies, as outlined in the text, and also runs into the difficulty that few ethical decisions are free of material consequences, and few material decisions can be divorced from ethical considerations. See his *Political Theory and Public Policy* (Chicago: University of Chicago Press, 1982), chap. 6.

of personality development the law prohibits child labor, thus insulating children from demands for direct and immediate contributions to productivity, and we establish an elaborate system of rights to protect certain acts from trespass by the government. In business, to promote productivity both capitalist and socialist firms protect factories from ethical demands based on the justices of need and equality.

Internal, mental walls. The wall metaphor has generally been applied to external constructions, for example, whereby parents are forbidden by law to sell their children and people are denied opportunities to buy commissions in the armed services. *Professional codes,* enforced by professional ethics commissions, are also walls. Walls are internal as well as external: The professional codes derive more of their power from their acceptance by members of the profession than from professional policemen. Sociologists find in *roles* the device that instructs role occupants in appropriate behavior. Harry Truman explained his switch from the segregationist policies, once "appropriate" for a senator from Missouri, to his presidential support for desegregation in the armed services on the grounds that as president something different was appropriate. Like professional codes, roles become internalized and are internally policed. Psychologists find that *situational* explanations account for as much of the variance in behavior as do explanations based on personal dispositions.[18] Between situations there are invisible boundaries that account for behavioral transformations; the individual defines situations as similar or different, largely on the grounds of what is required of him or her in each situation.[19] Finally, the quality-of-life studies find that people can mentally divide their lives into *domains,* a rather mixed concept of locus and activity: religion, health, marriage, leisure, work. The ease with which respondents assess their separate satisfactions in each domain, suggests that their habits of mental compartmentalization may also divide behavioral codes in the same way. Walls, then, are much more than blocked exchanges; they are mental sets as well. The pollution of nonmarket spheres by the market is inhibited, but certainly not prevented, by these walls.

Dangers in isolating a domain. The fear of pollution risks a damaging isolation. For example, the family has been called the agent of society; thus, if one insulates family ethics from commercial ethics, one deprives commercial ethics of its ethical nourishment from family ethics, and once again, one has frustrated one's own purposes. Institutional arrangements can fruitfully insulate one sphere from another for the very purpose of protecting the system, as is illustrated by the injunction (in spite of Posner)[20] to the courts to ignore efficiency considerations in rendering justice. But systems thrive on communication and information exchange among their elements. In this respect, the wall metaphor is dangerous.

Insulating an institution from its parent society
The second function of walls, the insulation of the institution or practice from the overall norms, codes, and purposes of the larger society is more complicated and

[18] See Walter Mischel, *Personality Assessment* (New York: Wiley, 1968).
[19] David Magnusson, ed., *Towards a Psychology of Situations* (Hillsdale, NJ: Erlbaum, 1981).
[20] See Richard A. Posner, *The Economics of Justice* (Cambridge: Harvard University Press, 1983).

hazardous. If a wall (blocked exchanges, reduced communication, mental compart-mentalization) insulates an institution from the regulatory features of a society, its government and general codes of behavior, the institution becomes *self-regulating* and achieves a degree of autonomy that may frustrate the larger purposes of the society. This is a particularly acute problem if we accept Churchman's idea that in any system the system goal determines the goals of all its subsystems.[21] Would it not be the case that agents of the market subsystem behind a wall of this kind, designed, in Walzer's phrase, to reduce the power of money and "to make money harmless"[22] might come to believe that their agencies are, by some magical, per-haps invisible, hand, serving a valuable social purpose in every act? The insulation that prevents the market from contaminating government becomes a barrier pre-venting government, as the agent of society, from guiding the market toward larger goals. Barriers rigidify, become reified, and lend to institutions pretensions of au-tonomy.

> *The idea of overarching social purpose reexamined.* There have been many attempts to define a single or small group of ultimate goods: W. D. Ross proposes four such ultimate goods: (1) "virtuous disposition and action," (2) merited hap-piness, (3) justice, and, more ambiguously, (4) knowledge.[23] Of this group, the market gives priority to the satisfaction of wants or what, in utilitarian terms, might be described as happiness, merited or not, as the ultimate good. Others, like Radin, suggest that "human flourishing" should be that ultimate good. She is critical of efforts to wall off the market wherein it may promote its version of the good, because such a wall would protect only some aspects of her summum bonum, leav-ing practices outside the wall free to trespass on human flourishing.[24] Her concept of the overriding societal goal is more attractive than the market's concept, and more congenial to our point of view, but unless it can be reconciled with other concepts of the good, it represents only one more vague formulation of a supreme good. We cannot follow Churchman's precept requiring that each institution in society serve the overall purpose of society because we cannot now specify that purpose.

Without an overall ruling purpose, systematicity demands something else. We may ask of every criticism and every defense of the market not only whether it would serve the short-run purposes for which it is established or proposed, but also how it does or would affect other social purposes, specifically, democratic govern-ment, economic efficiency, justice, personality development, and the quality of life.

For example, we cannot defend rent control because it protects the rights of tenants to circumstances favorable to their quality of life without also asking how it affects the production of housing and therefore the interests of the homeless. Nor can we propose that all jobs be devised to develop human potentials without also asking how this affects labor costs and therefore unemployment – bearing in mind

---

[21] C. West Churchman, *Challenge to Reason* (New York: McGraw-Hill, 1968).

[22] Michael Walzer, *Spheres of Justice* (Oxford, UK: Robertson, 1983), 107.

[23] W. D. Ross, *The Right and the Good* (Oxford, UK: Clarendon Press, 1930), 134–40.

[24] Margaret J. Radin, "Justice and the Market Domain," in John W. Chapman and J. Roland Pennock, eds., *Markets and Justice*, NOMOS 31 (New York: New York University Press, 1989).

that our Taiwanese competitors whose jobs might be protected by an expensive job enrichment program in the United States are also people with moral claims.

Ethically informed proposals to promote justice and virtue must, like economic proposals to promote efficiency and like psychological proposals to promote mental health (or human flourishing), ask these kinds of questions about system effects and weigh the answers with care. If they do not, in each case they not only risk jeopardizing the other values they have ignored, but also, because of systematic interconnections, risk defeating their own purposes.

There is one other aspect of systematicity: Just as each institution or practice influences institutions and practices, so it shares with other institutions the burdens of educating and shaping its subjects. Whereas a fruitful study of the market experience cannot avoid dealing with the systematicity of the forces shaping that experience, it cannot avoid also considering the division of labor in the system. To complain that the market does not do everything sounds like that form of "high IQ whimpering" that was characteristic of the brief life of the existentialists, so recently deceased.

Summary

I have put the assessment of the market experience in the context of a system where efficiency, justice, personality, and quality of life are so interrelated that any change in one of these factors influences the others. The focus has been on the critics of the market, but the main thrust can now be seen: Any *defense* of the market in purely efficiency terms is inadequate; any discipline that seeks to deal with only one of these facets of the market experience is, because of reflexive influences, failing to cope with its own materials. This is true of ethical justifications, economic analysis, and psychological appraisals. The system is unresponsive to logical implications derived from the principles of any one discipline because its premises are multidisciplinary.

The concept of walls as barriers between institutions includes mental components (code, role, situational, domain) as well as externally enforced ones. Whereas walls protect institutions, they also insulate them from overarching social purposes. Since these are plural, it is not possible to derive institutional purposes from a single social good.

PART II

Cognition and emotion

Part II begins the analysis of market effects on human development, with only incidental references to our other desideratum, happiness. As mentioned, I have isolated three facets of development: cognitive complexity, a sense of personal control over the features of one's life, and self-esteem. Part II focuses on the first of these, cognitive complexity. It contributes to the overall themes of this book by illuminating both thinking and emotion in the market experience. The devotion of six chapters to this subject is justified by both the prominence of misleading concepts of rationality and the paucity of ideas of emotion in economic analyses. I seek to correct these deficiencies by substituting concepts of cognitive complexity and cognitive functioning for rationality and by showing the ways emotion and cognition interact in the analysis of transactions. Two chapters are devoted to the role of money in market behavior because of the centrality of money in market analyses and in economic behavior.

Before entering upon the analysis of actual thinking processes in the market, Chapter 3 explores the relation of the market to two kinds of idealized modes of cognition, rationality and cognitive complexity. We will discover that rationality, as it is usually employed in market analysis, is misleading even as an ideal, and damaging to analyst and "practionaer" alike when it is used descriptively as a way of understanding behavior. This chapter, then, is devoted more to what economists have said than to the way the market actually works. In Chapter 4 I turn to market functioning, introducing research reports to show how emotions influence cognition and vice versa. One of the major conclusions of the chapter is that rationality, as contrasted to cognitive complexity, is incompatible with happiness. The analysis of emotion and cognition may also be fruitfully contrasted to the earlier concepts of "the passions and the interests" reported by Hirschman.[1]

In Chapter 5 I first distinguish between cognitive development and cognitive facilitation, the latter treating money as the market's principal tool for coping with the complexity of transactions. As price, money is the central concept in the market's self-regulating system; I show the way money facilitates a variety of cognitive functions and hinders others. In Chapter 6 the analysis of money continues, returning to the influence of emotions on market transactions and analyzing the way money symbolism greatly alters "rational" calculation in the market.

Chapter 7 offers an account of the reciprocal influences of cognitive development and economic development, showing, among other things, the effect of the several stages of economic technology (hunting and gathering, agricultural cultivation, and industry) on cognitive development. We also explore the equally important influ-

[1] Albert O. Hirschman, *The Passions and the Interest: Political Arguments for Capitalism Before Its Triumph* (Princeton: Princeton University Press, 1977).

41

ence of poverty on cognitive failure. Continuing this theme of cognitive development, Chapter 8 shows the contribution to cognitive functioning of the kind of stimulus-rich environment offered by the market – and the way the market erodes the gains thus achieved by its uncertainty and stress.

3 The costs of rationality

This chapter first distinguishes between two concepts with overlapping meanings, rationality and cognitive complexity. Rationality is the concept employed by economists to analyze market behavior. As I will show, however, it is in fact a misleading ideal, even for their purposes, and not descriptive of actual market or any other behavior. Cognitive complexity is also an ideal, the ideal included as a prime element and goal in human development. Psychologists reveal in great detail how people fall short of this ideal. They do not employ it to describe behavior; rather they investigate actual behavior to discover the underlying principles that govern various kinds of behavior in various circumstances.

Following this analysis of meanings, I turn to some of its uses and a defense of the rational model, a specification of its inadequacy in general and in its application to the logic of collective action; I compare it to other forms of analysis with equal claim to rationality, point to the kinds of crucial decisions where it is unhelpful, discuss its failure to understand market learning, show some of the unhappy consequences for those who adopt it as a guide, and in detail show how the axioms of consumer behavior based on this rational model systematically undermine our understanding of market behavior.

Rationality and cognitive complexity

As mentioned in Chapter 1, cognitive complexity includes capacities to see the relations among several aspects of a problem, to see both the good and the bad features of an object, to go beyond *perception* to the *abstraction,* to *analyze* and then *synthesize* in a new combination the elements of a complex stimulus, to see a figure in a complex ground, to derive commonalities or rules from concrete cases, and much more. Clearly cognitive complexity of this kind is an ideal, an ideal properly compared to the ideal of rationality.

The concept of rationality employed by economists refers to decision making, not scientific investigation or textual analysis. As such, it has four parts: (1) the consistent, coherent (transitive) scheduling of preferences such that one has one's priorities right, (2) the development of a matrix of alternative means whereby to achieve each preferred goal, (3) assigning risks and probable payoffs in satisfaction for the ordered preferences, and (4) choosing accordingly. The second of these parts is a version of the familiar concept of ends–means rationality. Although they need not be, the ends are assumed, because the overwhelming body of work on economic rationality suggests a single maximand, money,[1] making economic rationality more

---

[1] "The individual who attempts to obtain these respective maxima [utility and money] is also said to act 'rationally'." John von Neuman and Oskar Morgenstern, *Theory of Games and Economic Behavior,* 3d ed. (Princeton: Princeton University Press, 1953), 9.

like Weber's *wirtrationality*, where the end is given and the calculations are restricted to means. Weber distinguishes this from *zweckrationality*, where ends are to be weighed and compared, and from "substantive rationality," which deals with the selection of ends that truly reflect an individual's or society's genuine priorities after consideration. Weber's illustrations of *wirtrationality* focus on the goal of salvation, the economists' on economic gain; the parallel is instructive.

Because economists do not examine how "tastes" or preferences or, as others might say, "ends" are selected, or how people actually arrive at their choices of means, or their actual decisional procedures in selecting the appropriate means for any given ends, or what enters into their selection of risks (except the formal elements of probability theory), their version of economic rationality hardly comprehends the elements of cognitive complexity that are, in fact, implied. In my opinion, to be a helpful standard for decision making, rationality would have to include a set of standards for the component processes implied: It would have to offer criteria for analyzing the relations among the parts of a problem, for accurate appraisal of the good and bad features of an object, for going beyond perception to abstraction, and for embracing the other elements of cognitive complexity. Without analysis at this level of cognitive processing of information, defaults from the standard are difficult to correct. As a standard, cognitive complexity is more useful for most purposes because it specifies more of the dimensions of cognition than the economic rationality economists employ. The economists' policy of looking only at the outcome of decisional processes and their consequences for the economy is understandable, but self-limiting and unhelpful for remediation.

Both rationality and cognitive complexity, then, are ideals or standards; neither describes behavior. One might say that rationality is a thin version of cognitive complexity, wherein the crucial *intellectual processes* are unspecified. As reported below, Simon refers to the economists' version as "objective rationality" to distinguish it from the "subjective rationality" describing the processes of decision making, but it is also informative to make a different contrast with a different kind of "objective rationality," one referring to procedures of investigation as well as decision. This form of objective procedural rationality implies a variety of processes that are to some extent summarized in treatments of the scientific method: clarifying concepts, inquiring into facts ascertained by suitably controlled observations and measures, testing theories with these observations, exploring alternatives, sound inference and valid logic, and so forth. Economic rationality ignores these supplementary standards.

As a description of the way people do make their decisions, all theories of objective rationality are grossly optimistic and almost invariably misleading, as we shall see. A discipline based on these theories of human information processing will also be misleading. More than that, to the extent that people adopt procedural rationality as a description of their own behavior, they will misinterpret that behavior. It is even possible, as I will show, that if in their concern to be "rational," people seek to eliminate emotional elements from their responses, they will choose less wisely and even suffer social rejection. In this and the following chapters I will show that, compared to theories of cognition, all theories of rationality are inadequate descriptions of behavior, and compared to cognitive complexity, objective rationality is a most incomplete ideal or standard of behavior.

The consequences of hyperrationalism

"The rational attitude," Schumpeter said, "presumably forced itself on the human mind from economic necessity; it is to everyday economic tasks to which we as a race owe our elementary training in rational thought and behavior – and I have no hesitation in saying that all logic derived from the pattern of the economic decision." So much is merely economic, not necessarily market inspired. But "capitalism develops rationality and adds a new edge to it in two interconnected ways. . . . [First] it exalts the monetary unit . . . into a unit of account," and then "the cost–profit calculus in turn reacts upon that rationality . . . [and] powerfully propels the logic of enterprise."[2]

Later, economists propelled the *theory* of rational calculation into other fields. For example, Gary Becker, one of the leaders of this expanded enterprise, claims that "the combined assumption of maximizing behavior, market equilibrium, and stable preferences, used relentlessly and unflinchingly, form the heart of the economic approach" and can be applied to human behavior in all fields.[3] There is controversy over whether these efforts have been successful and whether their successes and failures have anything to do with rationality, depending, instead, on the assumptions employed[4] (see subsequent text).

The reliance in market theory on rationality has been well-described elsewhere;[5]

[2] Joseph A. Schumpeter, *Capitalism, Socialism, and Democracy*, 3d ed. (London: Allen & Unwin, 1950), 122–3.

[3] Gary S. Becker, *The Economic Approach to Human Behavior* (Chicago: University of Chicago Press, 1976), 5. For examples of the application of the method, see Becker's *Human Capital: A Theoretical and Empirical Analysis, with Special Reference to Education*, 2d ed. (New York: National Bureau of Economic Research with the Columbia University Press, 1975), and *A Treatise on the Family* (Cambridge: Harvard University Press, 1981).

[4] See, for example, the critique of Becker by Joan Huber and Glenna Spitze, *Sex Stratification: Children, Housework, and Jobs* (New York: Academic, 1983), 77. These authors point out that Becker's theory does not specify which comes first, assignment to housework and *therefore* lower wages, or lower wages and therefore assignment to housework. Economists assume that women's socialization makes them more productive in the home, but the failure to consider the historical order of the assignment to housework makes misleading Becker's theory that differential economic productivity causes the prevailing household division of labor and lower wages for women.

[5] Max Weber, *The Theory of Social and Economic Organization*, trans. and ed. Talcott Parsons (New York: Oxford University Press, 1947), especially 115–18; Talcott Parsons, *The Structure of Social Action* (New York: McGraw Hill, 1937); Karl Mannheim, *Man and Society in an Age of Reconstruction*, trans. E. Shils (New York: Harcourt Brace, 1948), 51–75; Schumpeter, *Capitalism, Socialism, and Democracy*, 121–30. Of the vast contemporary literature perhaps the most relevant for our purpose are: Tibor Scitovsky, "Are Men Rational or Economists Wrong?" in *Human Desire and Economic Satisfaction: Essays on the Frontiers of Economics* (New York: New York University Press, 1986), chap. 6; M. Hasheim Pesaran, *The Limits to Rational Expectation* (Oxford, UK: Blackwell, 1987); Brian Barry and Russell Hardin, eds., *Rational Man and Irrational Society?* (Beverly Hills, CA: Sage, 1982); Jon Elster, *Sour Grapes: Studies in the Subversion of Rationality* (Cambridge, UK: Cambridge University Press, 1983); Robin M. Hogarth and Melvin W. Reder, eds., *Rational Choice: The Contrast Between Economics and Psychology* (Chicago: University of Chicago Press, 1987). On the more general question of rationality, see: C. J. Friedrich, ed., *Rational Decisions*, NOMOS 7 (New York: Atherton, 1964); Byron R. Wilson, ed., *Rationality* (Oxford, UK: Blackwell, 1970); Nicholas Rescher, *Rationality: A Philosophic Inquiry Into the Nature and Rationale of Reason* (Oxford, UK: Oxford University Press, 1988).

here I wish to add to the account only a few observations on the way this emphasis on rationality may have influenced certain features of the market experience. Although our main interest, of course, is not with economic science,[6] we must first concern ourselves with the usefulness of the rational approach in describing the market experience. Then, second, we will consider some experimental consequences should people adopt the rational approach as a guide to their own behavior.

One reason for examining the premises of a discipline when we are actually interested in the behavior that the discipline purports to describe is the possibility that in the social sciences, science becomes the lore of a relevant public and guides the thinking and behavior of those quite ignorant of the original science. Features of the science of economics thus become the unconscious assumptions of producers and consumers. The same fear has been expressed with reference to law: If the law teaches "rational, cost-accounting images of man . . . essentially self-seeking, balancing in some cognitive ledger the personal costs and gains of a given behavior," there is a danger that people will then behave that way.[7] In looking at the rationality premise of economics we are also looking at a source of economic behavior.

Analytical costs of hyperrationalism in the market experience
A rich literature shows that people do not behave according to the rational decision-making model,[8] a literature supported by observations to follow. It is equally true that there are analytical gains in a model permitting, as the rational model does, deductive analysis based on theories of maximisation. As Friedman points out, the test of a theory is not the truth of its assumptions, but the fruitfulness of the analysis that follows from the use of that theory.[9] And it is true that there are analytical advantages in formulating a standard, as in ethics, permitting a comparison of behavior with the standard. But there are costs in the form of an imprecise or misleading theory based on erroneous assumptions.

The misleading character of the rational decision-making model. Simon suggests that the rationality assumptions do not help us to infer anything about behavior, for "human subjects do not possess consistent utility functions or probability assignments." As a consequence, it is not assumptions of rationality that advance our understanding. Rather, "the key premises in any theory that purports

---

[6] There is some pathos in a current distress over economic assumptions. Following the failure of the U.S. economy to develop in the 1970s, "some U.S. economists have felt a serious professional guilt – they need to explain why macroeconomic performance should have deteriorated *while the tools of their trade have advanced in sophistication.*" Robert J. Gordon, "U.S. Stabilization Policy: Lessons from the Past Decade," in Arnold C. Harberger, ed., *World Economic Growth* (San Francisco: Institute for Contemporary Studies, 1984), 125, emphasis added.

[7] Dean E. Peachey and Melvin J. Lerner, "Law as a Social Trap," in Melvin J. Lerner and Sally C. Lerner, eds., *The Justice Motive in Social Behavior: Adapting to Times of Scarcity and Change* (New York: Plenum Press, 1981), 452.

[8] Robert P. Abelson, "Social Psychology's Rational Man," in S. I. Benn and G. W. Mortimore, eds., *Rationality and the Social Sciences* (London: Routledge & Kegan Paul, 1976); Richard Nisbett and Lee Ross, *Human Inference: Strategies and Shortcomings of Social Judgment* (Englewood Cliffs, NJ: Prentice-Hall, 1980).

[9] Milton Friedman, *Essays in Positive Economics* (Chicago: University of Chicago Press, 1953), 14ff.

to explain the real phenomena . . . are the assumptions about goals and, even more important, about the ways in which people characterize the choice situation.''[10]

Simon further showed that the assumptions that economic rationality made about human capacities, knowledge, and information-processing procedures were quite unreasonable. The consequence was his model of "bounded rationality" that did not sacrifice the concept of rationality, but rather substituted subjective rationality for objective rationality and argued (what was later proved) that individuals limit the alternatives considered, value their information-processing costs more highly than assumed, and settle for a process of "satisficing," that is, they assure themselves that the consequences of their decisions will be "good enough" for their purposes and proceed accordingly.[11]

The cognitive psychologist Robert Abelson proposed an alternative model where "the application of predictable processes which happen not to correspond to the rules of formal logic . . . [are applied] by the individual to a specifiable but not necessarily accurate picture of the world." The idealized rational model cannot predict behavior; consequently,

rationality as an ideal is very liable to be superseded by strong psychological mini-principles limited in scope and high in subjectivity. . . . We have pictured the individual as overloaded with information which he does not quite know how to process even if he were motivated to invest considerable mental energy. . . . Individual mental processes are subject to illusion and oversimplification because of biased or misleading experience, motivated self-enhancement, and insufficient awareness of social pressure, even though the individual may honestly try to follow common sense.

The economist's assumption of rationality, he said, provides for a "succession of steps grossly implausible as a model of standard human functioning," and is, therefore, too *prescriptive* and *presumptive;* and, because it focuses attention on "default from a standard," too *preemptive.*[12]

Lea and his colleagues conclude, "We have been able to find [cases and data compatible with the principle] of rationality but it has also consis*ently failed to make interesting predictions."[13] Subsequent colloquia where economists and cognitive psychologists have argued these issues seem to me to have conclusively established the misleading character of the rational decision-making paradigm.[14]

The case of the misleading logic of collective action

The logic of collective action is a leading exemplar of the proposition that people decide on a course of action in a rational fashion in order to maximize individual returns to themselves. It holds that any person or subgroup who can gain advantages by not paying the costs of some collective benefit accruing to a larger group will do

[10] Herbert Simon, "Human Nature in Politics: The Dialogue of Psychology with Political Science," *American Political Science Review* 79 (1985): 293–304 at 296, 301.

[11] Herbert Simon, "A Behavioral Model of Rational Choice," in Simon, *Models of Thought* (New Haven: Yale University Press, 1979), 7–19.

[12] Robert Abelson, "Social Psychology's Rational Man," 61, 62, 83.

[13] Stephen E. G. Lea, Roger M. Tarpy, and Paul Webley, *The Individual in the Economy* (Cambridge, UK: Cambridge University Press, 1987), 480.

[14] Hogarth and Reder, eds., *Rational Choice;* Princeton Conference on Behavioral Economics, report on the conference in "Behavior Studies Alter Economic Theory," *APA Monitor*, October 1984.

so. The main message of this logic is that, as in the case of public goods, if benefits and sacrifices are separated or disproportionate to each other, people will avoid the sacrifices.[15] Public goods are defined informally as those kinds of goods where "those who do not purchase or pay for any of the public or collective good cannot be excluded from sharing in the consumption of the good, as they can where non-collective goods are concerned."[16] If they cannot be excluded, people will become "free riders," benefiting from collective goods but not paying for the benefits.

Social psychologists have explored the same kinds of situations predicting free riding with initially similar results. In their experiments, Latané, Williams, and Harkin call free riding *social loafing*.[17] This behavior occurs when people are asked to cooperate in a task with no division of labor in order to produce a joint, additive result. At first, individual contributions cannot be identified, though later this last condition is relaxed. Their experiments showed that when people pull on a rope, or are requested to make the loudest noise they can, or are asked to grade applications either individually or as a team, efforts by isolated individuals are always greater than efforts by the same individuals in groups. That is, people tend to be free riders.

Szymanski and Harkins noticed that the anonymity condition in these experiments was such that when the experimenter could not assess the individual efforts of the subjects, neither could the subjects assess their own individual efforts. Perhaps, the experimenters argued, it was the participants' ignorance of the contributions others were making that produced social loafing. They tested the idea that "the opportunity for the participants to evaluate themselves would be sufficient to eliminate the loafing effect."[18] First, however, they measured the effects when only the experimenter knew the participants' efforts and found, as others had, that this condition was sufficient to eliminate social loafing. The next experiment involved a situation where only the participants themselves, and not the experimenter, knew the comparative efforts put forth by each: "When the experimenter could not evaluate the participants' outputs [but the participants could evaluate their own outputs], the potential for self-evaluation reliably improved participant performance."[19]

A study by Weldon and Gargano tested twenty-five male and twenty-five female undergraduate business administration students on the care they took in assessing the various merits of job candidates for student summer employment. The task was devised so that numeric scores could be given to amount of information used and to various shortcuts (e.g., sampling) in the task performance. Like the other social-loafing studies, the task was such that no division of labor took place; each person did the same work as others with an additive value of pooled judgments. The familiar *individual versus shared* responsibility dimension was manipulated by telling

[15] Mancur Olson, *The Logic of Collective Action: Public Goods and the Theory of Groups*, rev. ed. (Cambridge: Harvard University Press, 1971).
[16] Ibid., 15.
[17] Bibb Latané, Kipling Williams, and Stephen G. Harkins, "Many Hands Make Light Work: The Causes and Consequences of Social Loafing," *Journal of Personality and Social Psychology* 37 (1979): 822–32.
[18] Kate Szymanski and Stephen G. Harkins, "Social Loafing and Self-Evaluation with a Social Standard," *Journal of Personality and Social Psychology* 53 (1987): 891–7 at p. 891.
[19] Ibid.

some subjects that they were alone in making the assessment while others were told that they were members of a committee of sixteen persons reading the same files. But to this was now added an *accountability* dimension, manipulated by getting the names and telephone numbers of some students and telling them: "We may want to contact you later to ask you to explain your evaluations." Accountability of this kind "is assumed to raise concerns about social evaluation, so that an individual's interest in appearing thoughtful, logical, and industrious overcomes motivation to loaf."[20]

The results confirmed the authors' hypotheses: Judges who shared responsibility and were not accountable for their judgments "used less effortful judgment strategies." Those judges who believed that decisions hinged on their judgments alone and who were accountable worked hardest. In between, the shared-responsibility-but-accountable judges and the individually-responsible-but-unaccountable judges were each less diligent, but along somewhat different dimensions. Accountability does not fully make up for individual responsibility in reducing social loafing. The authors comment that "these data demonstrate the debilitating effect of shared responsibility, suggesting once again that two heads are not always better than one." The study also shows that "accountability discourages cognitive loafing in co-acting groups." By and large, these authors believe, "decision makers prefer 'least effort' solutions to information processing demands, so that information processors exert only enough effort to satisfy those to whom they must account."[21] To this, Szymanski and Harkins would add that the self may be the person "to whom they must account."

If all it takes to eliminate free riding or social loafing is (1) that some authority knows the degree of effort put forward, or (2) that individuals know their performance compared to that of others, or (3) that individuals are made in some way accountable for their performances, the force of the logic of collective action is greatly diminished. Notice the applicability of Simon's point: Rationality assumptions are irrelevant; what are relevant are the factual assumptions regarding what goal is to be pursued. It seemed that the goals are as likely to be social approval and self-approval as they are to be conservation of sacrifice whether that be money or effort. Can you have free riders when the goal is, as it usually is, the approval of others?

Economic rationality as a standard for decision making
The risk that any one model of decision making should be regarded as *the* standard is probably not very great, but if it were, the costs would be considerable. Consider five examples of rationality quite different from that embraced by the market's rational decision-making model.

[20] Elizabeth Weldon and Gina Gargano, "Cognitive Loafing: The Effects of Accountability and Shared Responsibility on Cognitive Effort," Personality and Social Psychology Bulletin 14 (1988): 159–71 at 160. Philip E. Tetlock found accountability also improved the cognitive performance of politicians: "Accountability and Complexity of Thought," *Journal of Personality and Social Psychology* 43 (1983): 74–83.
[21] Weldon and Gargano, "Cognitive Loafing," 169.

Scientific decision making. The processes of validation in science are now well understood (e.g., Popper, Nagel, Hempel), but the process of deciding which hypothesis to explore, a special form of decision making, is not explained by the philosophy of science. Rather it is described as a process of intuition, imagination, analogy, metaphor, divergent thinking, and associative thinking.[22] But these qualities do not appear in the formula for rational economic decision making. Physical science, moreover, might challenge Schumpeter's allegation that rationality came from economic life. Butterfield points out that it was the scientific "modes of thought . . . which were beginning to change the face of the West in the latter half of the Seventeenth Century" that were exported to the rest of the world.[23]

Legal decision making. Legal scholarship deals explicitly with decisions. Again the processes of analyzing decisions and of making them may be confounded, but in making decisions the judge must draw on the same skills employed by the analyst. These include refined methods of taxonomic or classificatory analysis (this case is governed by this rule), and exegesis (an accurate reading of this rule finds it to mean so and so). Again these are not to be found in the arsenal of the economic rational model.

Utopian decision making. The most "rational" of all political thought is, according to Popper, utopian thought: First decide on the goals of society and the character of the social good, then find the means to implement them. However, says Popper, the efforts to reconcile a fractious population to these self-defined goals can lead to tyranny as the disastrous consequence. Better, he says, to identify the ills of society and then, with their remedy as the stipulated ends of one's effort, find the appropriate means to effectuate the remedy. These approaches differ in their reasonableness, but not in their rationality. The point is that the selection of the ends is the most important decision; the selection is not, again according to Popper, a process lending itself to rational thought,[24] certainly not to a rationality where "tastes" are taken as given.

Market decision making. Within the smaller scope of economic and decision-making rationality, the standard "calculated rationality" of the economic decisional model is only a small part. March gives a fertile analysis of possible alternatives within that concept: *limited rationality,* which is rational because it recognizes the limited capabilities of the human mind; *contextual rationality,* which understands the fact that decisions reflect the contexts within which they are made; *game rationality,* which notes the problem of individual preferences in a field where others also seek to advance their preferences and offers game theoretical solutions; *process rationality,* often employed by philosophers, which focuses on the processing of

[22] See, e.g., Norwood Russell Hanson, *Patterns of Discovery* (Cambridge, UK: Cambridge University Press, 1958).
[23] Herbert Butterfield, *The Origins of Modern Science, 1300–1800,* 2d ed. (New York: Macmillan, 1957), 191.
[24] Karl Popper, "Utopia and Violence," *Conjectures and Refutations: The Growth of Scientific Knowledge* (London: Routledge & Kegan Paul, 1963), 337–63.

information. To this list March adds other alternatives based on experiential learning: the rationality of survival in a competitive ecology, the rationality that seeks to anticipate how to maximize, after the event, the sense that one has chosen wisely, and those rationalities that take into account how the very decisions to be made will endogenously change the preference of the decision maker. March's main point is that the ambiguities and uncertainties that are called error by advocates of calculated economic rationality are, in fact, the unconscious wisdom of people with changing, ambiguous preferences, often ordered in different schedules that are wisely kept apart, operating in a world where their rational estimates of probable payoffs are extremely fallible.[25]

Ego-syntonic decision making. Finally, and most important, there is that form of rationality which correctly selects one's basic, enduring preferences when they are opposed by more emphemeral, less "ego-syntonic" preferences, those failing to express one's deepest values and wants. We will take up this form of rationality again in Chapter 27.

Unhelpfulness in the market experience
Not only do the assumptions of rationality mislead both analysts and ordinary people about the nature of economic decision making, they also fail to offer help on crucial social decisions – a grave defect in a heuristic designed to be helpful.

Societal priority or individual priority. In a collection by Barry and Hardin, *Rational Man and Irrational Society?*, modern game theorists point with puzzlement to the apparently injurious consequences to the social order of individual rational behavior, a "paradox" anticipated by Garrett Hardin's "The Tragedy of the Commons" fourteen years earlier.[26] Rapaport seeks to solve the dilemma by suggesting two different forms of rationality, a social form and an individual form,[27] but this does not help a person to decide *which* rationality to employ. Gauthier finds ways to reconcile maximizing self-interest with concern for society: In order to preserve opportunities for future maximization of self-interest, it is more rational to support societal interests now.[28] This flies in the face of the logic of collective action, which shows that among rational people, even if one wanted to advance the interests of a collectivity, it is not possible to do so when others might take advantage of any lapse in the pursuit of short-term self-interest by any member of that collectivity.[29]

A rationality that cannot justify itself. "The spirit of capitalism," said Weber, "is best understood as part of the development of rationalism as a whole."

[25] James G. March, "Bounded Rationality, Ambiguity, and the Engineering of Choice," *The Bell Journal of Economics* 9 (1978): 578–608.
[26] Garrett Hardin, "The Tragedy of the Commons," *Science* 162 (1968): 1,243–8.
[27] Anatol Rapaport, "Prisoner's Dilemma – Recollections and Observations," in Barry and Hardin, eds., *Rational Man and Irrational Society?*
[28] David Gauthier, "Reason and Maximization," *Canadian Journal of Philosophy* 4 (1975): 418–33.
[29] Olson, *The Logic of Collective Action.*

But it is a *rationalism that cannot justify itself*.[30] In a finer grained analysis of rationalism, Weber points out that "formal rationality" of economic calculation is different from "substantive rationality" that provides "the bases from which to judge the *outcome* of economic action,"[31] thus restoring meaning to otherwise meaningless calculations. In Weber's view the *formal* rationality of the market is thus unable to judge the worth of its own activities.

Rationalism and market learning

One of the main concerns of this text is what people learn in their experiences with the market. They will learn less if they adopt the rationalistic perspective because they will misunderstand the learning process. This reduction in learning is important for market analysis, since the theory of "long-run" tendencies that validate market theories of more or less perfect competition relies on learning. In the rationalistic version, learning, which is, in fact, often slow and misguided, is treated by economic rationalists as though it were prompt and responsive to the information in market feedback. People are, however, impeded in their learning by a variety of processes: (1) they have tendencies to verify (rather than to falsify) whatever initial hypothesis comes to mind; (2) their blunt and inaccurate perceptions of correlations among events distorts their causal attributions; (3) they are biased by their desires to protect and favor themselves or their preferred outcomes,[32] (4) people's attributions of causes focus on the dispositions of others (a focus called "the fundamental attribution error"); (5) attending closely to their own cases and aware of the constraints on their own action, people focus on exculpating circumstances; (6) they reinterpret evidence dissonant with their more important beliefs to make the evidence more harmonious with these beliefs; (7) their schemata are often mere stereotypes, yet the default values (inferences therefrom) of these sketchy schemata guide their actions; (8) their explanations of their own actions are often not the product of insight but rather their inferences of why persons (any person) in that culture would do what they did.[33] Risk calculations are not rational, partly because people are risk averse in cases of possible gain but risk accepting in cases of preventing loss.[34] Learning under stress is different from learning in tranquility;[35] learning through experience is different from learning by imitation or from tuition; learning to work for pay is very different from learning to work for quality or high standards. As the psychologists show in their commentary on economists' faith in the power of successive approximations to achieve rational outcomes, human learning is not so reliable as rationalists imagine.[36] As a consequence, the long run is not likely to approximate the perfect model.

[30] Max Weber, *The Protestant Ethic and the Spirit of Capitalism*, trans. T. Parsons (1904; reprint New York: Scribner's Sons, 1958), 79, 181, 182.
[31] Weber, *The Theory of Social and Economic Organization*, 184, 186.
[32] Jonathan Baron and John C. Hershey, "Outcome Bias in Decision Evaluation," *Journal of Personality and Social Psychology* 54 (1988): 569–79.
[33] See Abelson, "Social Psychology's Rational Man;" Nisbett and Ross, *Human Inference*.
[34] Amos Tversky and Daniel Kahneman, "The Framing of Decisions and the Psychology of Choice," *Science* 211 (30 January 1981): 435–58.
[35] Irving Janis and L. Mann, *Decision Making: A Psychological Analysis of Conflict, Choice, and Commitment* (New York: Free Press, 1977).
[36] Hogarth and Reder, eds., *Rational Choice*.

The rationalists' experiences

To the extent that the rational approach is accepted and executed, the costs again are substantial, illustratively, in interpersonal relations, in confidence in one's judgment, and in appraisals of justice. *Interpersonal relations* are likely to be injured because people who make a point of their rationality, especially as it appears to subordinate their emotions, are regarded as *cold,* and the warm/cold dimension seems to dominate all others in people's assessment of each other; people dislike coldness in their associates and think of cold people as selfish.[37] *Confidence in one's own judgments* is greater when those opinions are based more on emotional or intuitional processes than when they are based on purely cognitive processes.[38] No doubt this is why advertisers find that "reasons-why" advertisements are far less effective than appeals to the emotion.[39] As for *assessments of justice,* the rationalists' focus on payoffs and outcomes misleads people, for litigants and defendants are more influenced by how they are treated, the procedures of justice, than they are by the outcomes, and among the features of the procedures that impress them is the apparent sympathy of the judges. Rational justice is not more appreciated by litigants and defendants than sympathetic justice.[40]

Repressing or diverting the emotions. Assuming that there are elements of the market experience that would profit from emotional neutrality (or "affective neutrality," in Parson's characterization of modernity),[41] we will examine four theories of the effect on decision making of repressing emotions.

First, Shlomo Maitel takes a favorable view of constrained emotionality, suggesting that the requirement for scheduling preferences or desires actually enhances pleasures; they become less chaotic, less demanding, and budgets tend to constrain excess. Even the provision of credit permits the scheduling of pleasures by some criterion other than immediately available cash[42] – and, on the other hand, invites indulgence at the same time, something Maitel acknowledges only later when he ascribes inflation to the advent of credit cards.

Two of the other theories of emotionality under cognitive control rely on what remains of psychoanalytic theory. Even if hydraulic theories of emotionality are rarely persuasive, we must see that cognitive control of the emotions may well not be the end of the matter. Thus, a second interpretation of the effect of controlling emotions in a rationalistic system relies on a theory of redirecting the emotion to

[37] Seymour E. Asch, "Forming Impressions of Personality," *Journal of Abnormal and Social Psychology* 41 (1946): 258–90.

[38] Robert B. Zajonc, "Feeling and Thinking: Preferences Need No Inferences," *American Psychologist* 35 (1980): 151–75.

[39] Paul Thomas Young, *Emotion in Man and Animal: Its Nature and Dynamic Basis,* 2d rev. ed. (Huntington, NY: Krieger, 1973), 4.

[40] E. Allan Lind and Tom R. Tyler, *The Social Psychology of Procedural Justice* (New York: Plenum, 1988); Robert E. Lane, "Procedural Goods in a Democracy: How One Is Treated Versus What One Gets," *Social Justice Research* 2 (1983): 177–92.

[41] Talcott Parsons and Edward Shils, "Values, Motives, and Systems of Action," in Parsons and Shils, eds., *Towards a General Theory of Action* (1951; reprint New York: Harper Torchbook, 1962), 83.

[42] Shlomo Maitel, "Novelty, Comfort, and Pleasure: Inside the Utility-Function Black Box," in Paul J. Albanese, ed., *Psychological Foundations of Economic Behavior* (New York: Praeger, 1988).

another, more available target, that is, *sublimation.* If this process should prevail, cognitive control is not threatened and the emotion is not stifled but, rather, redirected.

The third theory posits that if the impulse or emotion is *repressed,* then we may expect the "return of the repressed," often in an ugly form – as scapegoating, or self-punishment, or perversion – each making rational choice more difficult. Whatever affective neutrality might then prevail is temporary and hazardous. In a tentative, if blunt, way, one might suggest that the market, with its presentation of alternatives and training in choice, is a better instrument for sublimation than for repression.

Finally, the theory that frustration tends to be followed by aggression and that aggression tends to be preceded by frustration suggests a further, and unattractive, manner of channeling (but not harnessing) the emotions associated with frustration.[43]

In short, the consequences of an emotionally neutral, wholly "rational" approach to decision making in the market are hard to predict, but it is clear that an assumption that better decisions are made when emotions other than antiseptic "preferences" are withheld is likely to be false.

Some substantive assumptions of market rationality

There are grounds for believing that the rationality hypothesis rests on and follows from certain misleading "laws" or axioms about strictly economic behavior. These are explicated in Hausman's "eight lawlike statements" extracted from microeconomic equilibrium theory[44] and in the axioms of demand theory set forth by P. J. Simmons in *Choice and Demand.*[45] If the rationality premise is wrong, these "lawlike statements" and axioms derived from that premise are also likely to be wrong. To see if this is the case, we will examine four of Simmons's five axioms describing consumer behavior: the axiom of completeness, the axiom of transitivity, the axiom of greed, and the axiom of continuity.

The axiom of completeness

The axiom of completeness is like the normal logical axiom proscribing an undistributed middle. For any two bundles A and B, consumers prefer A to B, or B to A, or they are indifferent between them. (1) This axiom makes no room for *ambivalence,* which cannot be described as indifference; rather it is a condition of conflicted desires. Ambivalence is not an exotic state: March finds it to be a major characteristic of preferences,[46] Jahoda said that it was the main finding of research

[43] John Dollard, Leonard Doob, et al., *Frustration and Aggression* (New Haven: Yale University Press, 1939).
[44] Daniel M. Hausman, "Are General Equilibrium Theories Explanatory?" in Hausman, ed., *The Philosophy of Economics: An Anthology* (Cambridge, UK: Cambridge University Press, 1984), 344–59.
[45] P. J. Simmons, *Choice and Demand* (London: Macmillan, 1974). To the four axioms presented here, Simmons adds a fifth: the "axiom of convexity," which says that if B is a mixture made by taking $x\%$ of A with $y\%$ of C, where $x + y = 100\%$, then neither A nor C will be preferred to B (but B may well be preferred to A or C or both).
[46] March, "Bounded Rationality."

on attitudes toward work,[47] and it seems to have a biological source. In a discussion of the conflicting tugs of biologically programmed dispositions Wilson points out that "ambivalences stem from counteracting pressures on the units of natural selection."[48] We are programmed for ambivalences falling in the space between $A > B$ and $B > A$. (2) The axiom of completeness is a statement of how people categorize schemata, but in actual practice, taxonomies are created by very different principles having more to do with levels of concreteness than of completeness.[49]

The axiom of transitivity

Empirical support for the second axiom, the axiom of transitivity, is equally fragile. The axiom says if A is preferred to B and B is preferred to C, then A must be preferred to C. Lea reports experimental work with students offered a choice among marital partners possessing such bundles of attributes as: beauty, average charm, and being well off, versus: plain, very charming, and very rich. About a quarter of the choices were intransitive.[50] A better study, by Tversky and Kahneman, taking into account the stochastic nature of choices, involved entertainment tickets and gambling choices where the evidence suggests that within a single decision frame "a great majority of people choose transitively." But Tversky and Kahneman's evidence suggests again that transitivity can be violated when *different decision frames* are presented. Consider the fact that most people (88 percent) say that if they arrived at a theater to buy a ticket for a play and then discovered that they had lost ten dollars on the way, they would buy a ticket anyway. But if they had paid for the ticket in advance and discovered when they arrived in the theater that they had lost it, most (54 percent) say they would *not* buy another ticket. In the one case the ticket is preferred to ten dollars; in the second case ten dollars is preferred to the ticket.[51] The compartmentalization of our internal budgeting interferes with transitivity. Whereas most choices seem to be transitive, if transitivity is an "axiom" of rationality, then a very large number of cases violate that axiom and cannot, therefore, be called rational.

The axiom of greed

Simmons provides a motive in his list of axioms: the axiom of greed, which says that if A contains more of one good than B, and as much as B of other goods, consumers prefer A to B – a kind of one-man Pareto optimality. *Satisficing* will violate this axiom if the value at stake is not one of the criterial priority dimensions of choice, in which case the presence of B is ignored because the decision rule has been satisfied. Also, there are goods of which both too little and too much is undesirable, leisure being a case in point. Thus at a certain moment, everything else remaining the same, more leisure is not preferred and the axiom of greed is violated.

---

[47] Marie Jahoda, *Employment and Unemployment: A Psychological Analysis* (Cambridge, UK: Cambridge University Press, 1982).

[48] Edward Wilson, *Sociobiology: The New Synthesis* (Cambridge: Harvard University Press, 1975), 3, 4.

[49] Eleanor Rosch, "Principles of Categorization," in Rosch and Barbara B. Lloyd, eds., *Cognition and Categorization* (Hillsdale, NJ: Erlbaum, 1978).

[50] Lea et al., *The Individual in the Economy*, 113–14. For what it is worth, Lea reports that in animal studies "preference is nearly always intransitive when the schedules of rewards differ in kind" (p. 114).

[51] Amos Tversky and Daniel Kahneman, "The Framing of Decisions," 457.

Then, finally, there is the semantic problem: Does one call a person "greedy" if the good in question is altruism? or the performance of duty? It is a possible usage, but it is the rare philosopher who calls the benevolent person greedy.

There is another approach to this problem of greed that shows that whatever is a reward in one case may be a cost in another. Based on his studies with animals, Premack shows that mammals will learn to "work" on an exercise wheel to earn water, or learn to drink water to earn the right to exercise.[52] In the axiom X is the good of which A has more than B. Y and Z are the goods of which A has the same quantity as B. A is preferred to B solely because it has more X. If X is a positive utility, the axiom makes sense, but if X is the cost or disutility of acquiring Y or Z, the axiom of greed is misstated. In summarizing research relevant to greed, Lea et al. conclude, "Organisms have 'ideal' distributions of their time between different activities. If they are deprived of one activity, they will work to get its rate back to the ideal ('baseline') level." Token economics have shown similar behavior among humans. Thus, from such research as is available, one may conclude with Lea et al. that "the evidence is that the axiom of greed must be rejected, because real people, unlike *Homo Economicus,* are not insatiable."[53]

The axiom of continuity

Finally, Simmons proposes an axiom of continuity, which says that similar bundles are close to each other in preference ordering. If the axiom is not tautological (similarity being defined as closeness in preference ordering), this axiom also runs into difficulties. The axiom rules out lexical ordering or Guttman scaling where one choice is necessarily *prior* to another. It seems (although there is some room for doubt) that choices among different *kinds* of goods are also ruled out. From the example of the theater tickets and the lost money, we already know that money and goods can be thought of as different *kinds* of goods, thus emptying the axiom of much of its market relevance.

In another sense, however, Simmons is right. As we shall see in Chapter 25, people like exchanges within categories: things like money exchanged for goods or services, things like love exchanged for status and intimate services.[54] But it is doubtful if this exchange helps to support the axiom of continuity.

There are other criticisms of the rationality assumption and its uses in economic analysis, of which the most important question the following propositions, each of which is treated later in this book: (1) People know what makes them happy and can choose rationally appropriate means to achieve happiness (Chapter 27); (2) the feedback from market experience is veridically perceived and systematically used to inform further market purchases (Chapter 6); (3) the enjoyment of intrinsic pleasures of work and buying are rationally accounted for by their money benefits and

---

[52] D. Premack, "Catching up with Common Sense or Two Sides of a Generalization: Reinforcement and Punishment," in R. Glaser, ed., *The Nature of Reinforcement* (New York: Academic, 1971), reported in Lea et al., *The Individual in the Economy*, 110–11.

[53] Lea et al., *The Individual in the Economy*, 111.

[54] Uriel Foa, "Interpersonal and Economic Resources," *Science* 171 (29 January 1971): 345–51.

costs (Chapter 18); (4) money's contribution to rationality is made possible by the neutral "colorlessness" of money, as contrasted to the view that where money is concerned, as elsewhere, "the medium is the message."

Summary

"The rational attitude" may have emerged from "economic necessity," as Schumpeter states, but the paradigm of rational decision making emerged from economics. The model has its cost: It adds nothing to analysis of behavior that is not present in the factual assumptions embraced; it severely misrepresents the behavior of individuals engaged in the market experience; embedded in the logic of collective action, it has created misunderstanding about the inevitability of free riding, a misunderstanding corrected by psychological experiments on *social loafing* showing that feedback on performance and provision for simple accountability almost eliminate free riding.

Competing theories of rational decision making show that scientists, lawyers, and even consumers employ quite different models; applied to politics, the rationalism of utopians is likely to prove disastrous.

The rational decision-making model is unhelpful in solving two problems: (1) assigning priority to social or individual benefits, and (2) justifying what is to be rationally decided upon.

The rational model seems to support market paradigms by assuming a learning process that provides for correction over the long run, but the learning process assumed does not conform to what is known about how people learn.

The experience of people who might adopt the rational model would lead them to great unpopularity, reliance on a cognitive process that excludes the affective processes that give individuals a greater sense of confidence in their judgments, and, through overemphasizing outcomes and payoffs, would lead to a misinterpretation of justice processes where procedures that have been found to be more related to participant satisfaction than outcomes would be slighted. Furthermore, repressing or diverting emotions, although sometimes hedonically beneficial, risks the return of the repressed or aggression following frustration.

The substantive axioms of rational consumer behavior dealing with "completeness," transitivity, greed, and "continuity" are incomplete and misleading.

4   Affect, cognition, and well-being in a market economy

The concept of market rationality discussed in the previous chapter assumes a kind of emotional neutrality (except for the anemic schedule of preferences) that is totally unrealistic. In the following discussion we turn first to the central role of emotions in the market economy and then to certain ways in which affect (emotions) and cognition influence each other, as when cognitive processes are called upon to define arousal or when, in reverse, a positivity bias changes perception. Research on emotions greatly alters our understanding of market satisfactions or utility. We then turn to the effects on emotions of market success and failure, followed by a discussion of the effects of good mood on market work and thought. The chapter concludes with a discussion of the relation between happiness and cognition, including speculation on whether rationality is really compatible with happiness, which is the ultimate maximization of utility.

Markets as theaters of emotion

If it be agreed that the theory of market rationality as an approximation to economic behavior is a mischievous fiction, what is to take its place? Some combination of emotion and cognition, no doubt, but the relation between these two is complex. We turn here to a few of the market relevant aspects of this relationship.[1]

Affect and *arousal* are the most encompassing of the terms dealing with this general area; *emotions* refer to something more specific, like fear, or pity; *mood* refers to an affect without specific target. The market stimulates arousal and is saturated with emotion: pride and shame and guilt (the three emotions that are identity-related); anger and aggression; self-love, the foundation emotion, as Adam Smith pointed out. Further, the approval motive, which Smith thought was the principal manifestation of self-love, is enlisted in all aspects of market life but egregiously so in the appeals of consumer advertising.

Investigating emotional responses to financial success and failure, Eliot Smith and James Kleugel found the following feelings representative: happiness, worry, guilt, confidence, disappointment, thankfulness, frustration, and satisfaction.[2] Economists, too, have occasionally recognized this emotionality in economic affairs. If Keynes is right, management investment decisions reflect "animal spirits,"[3] and if Knight is right, in economics as elsewhere "human activity is largely impulsive, a relatively unthinking and undetermined [sic] response to stimulus and

---

[1] In the following discussion I am guided by Susan T. Fiske and Shelley E. Taylor, *Social Cognition* (New York: Random House, 1984), especially Chapter 11.
[2] Eliot R. Smith and James R. Kluegel, "Cognitive and Social Bases of Emotional Experience: Outcome, Attribution, and Affect," *Journal of Personality and Social Psychology* 43 (1982): 1,129–41.
[3] John Maynard Keynes, *A General Theory of Employment, Interest and Money* (London: Macmillan, 1936), 161.

suggestion.''[4] Moreover, in the very concept of a preference schedule, so much more important in the rationality formulae than the payoff matrix, is embedded the possibility of very strong feelings. Income and money, with their implications for rank, deference, prestige, and all the trappings of wealth and power, imply two of the most affect-laden elements of life. The negative emotions may be even stronger: fear of failure, of unemployment, of bankruptcy, of humiliation. Anxiety, as we shall see in Chapter 24, radically undermines the positive hedonic gains of the market experience.

This emotionality is to be contrasted to the simplistic greed plus rationality schema that is said to characterize economic behavior.

The consumer market encourages emotionality. The consumer market is licentious, inviting self-indulgence, tempting people to go beyond the bounds of prudence. As the priest invites fervor, and the spouse lust, so the consumer market invites greed. The consumer market shouts *carpe diem* – not *caveat emptor*.

The consumer market constrains the passions. But there are, of course, constraints. The household budget is the ego to restrain the consumer's pleasure principle; the scheduling of preferences is not reinforced so much by rationality as by necessity. Very often, however, the combination of rationality and budgets is insufficient to prevent short-term preferences from overwhelming those wants that have their payoff in the longer term.[5] My analysis of money will show the differences between those who can stop wanting what they cannot have, and those who have no such capacity.

The labor market restrains emotionality. The labor market and, more particularly, firms' internal labor markets constrain desire by making consumption contingent on work and holding a job contingent on performance. The efficiency norm (Chapter 16) serves as well as the Protestant ethic ever did in constraining emotionality. The market experience must refer constantly to the exchange of effort for pay, payment for goods, very little for nothing. Contingency is a teacher of discipline.

The labor market arouses emotion. Whatever is the source of people's evaluations of themselves arouses the most intense emotions; success at work in a market society is just such a basis for self-evaluation. Internal standards, and therefore internal rewards and punishments, are enlisted; comparisons with others engendering rivalry, envy, and smugness are fairly common (though not so important as they are thought to be); and above all the negative emotions of fear, anxiety, and sense of insecurity (Chapter 24) are aroused at work and in the labor market.

[4]Frank Knight, *The Ethics of Competition and Other Essays* (New York: Augustus Kelly, 1935), 50. I discovered Robert H. Frank, *Passions Within Reason: The Strategic Role of the Emotions* (New York: Norton, 1988) too late for appropriate inclusion in the discussion.
[5]The most serious case of excessive arousal and unconstrained desire is addiction. It is not easy to indict the market for its encouragement of addiction because most market societies do not suffer this to the same extent as the command economy of the Soviet Union, where alcoholism is said to be an overwhelmingly serious problem.

Thus in each of the markets that engage the ordinary market participant, there is conflict between emotional responses and cognitive constraints of these emotions.

Market choices: affective and cognitive interaction

Emotions interfere with cognition

Hirschman has given an account of the way relabeling avarice as an "interest" pacified some of its critics and led to the triumph of capitalism.[6] Emotionality has often been thought to interfere with rationality, as in Weber's analysis: "For the purposes of a typological scientific analysis it is convenient to treat all irrational, affectually determined elements of behavior as factors of deviation from a conceptually pure type of rational action" – as in a panic on the stock exchange.[7] Some psychologists seem to lend support to this view. A standard text describes emotion as "a perturbation, a departure from a normal level of non-emotional activity. . . . When emotion arises there is a disorganization of smooth, adaptive behavior."[8] Emotionality in infancy may also inhibit learning cognitive skills later.[9] The theory of "interrupts" is an example of the "perturbations" mentioned.

Market arousal and the stimulation of thought

"Physiological arousal is produced by 'interrupts' or unexpected events that alert the organism to cope with an environmental contingency." These interrupts arise either when there is some perceptual anomaly that requires interpretation or when some plan is unexpectedly frustrated.[10] Thus, the market's tendency to disturb life by its pattern of constant changes is a frequent source of arousal, with the consequence that the market first stimulates and invites emotion and then requires cognitive interpretation of the arousal and the labeling or the emotion. That is, the market's stimulation of cognition (but not necessarily rationality) is in part a by-product of its stimulation of emotionality.

Almost all analysts now agree that emotions and cognition are best viewed not as disruptive forces, but rather as different dimensions that are possibly rooted in different systems,[11] a fact that permits each dimension to vary in a manner independent of the other, and yet, as we shall see, to rely on the other for crucial support. One

[6] Albert O. Hirschman, *The Passions and the Interests: Political Arguments for Capitalism Before Its Triumph* (Princeton: Princeton University Press, 1977).

[7] Max Weber, "The Fundamental Concepts of Sociology," in *The Theory of Social and Economic Organization,* ed. and trans. T. Parsons (New York: Oxford University Press, 1947), 92.

[8] Paul Thomas Young, *Emotion in Man and Animals: Its Nature and Dynamic Basis,* 2d rev. ed. (Huntington, NY: Krieger, 1973), 21, 22.

[9] There is evidence that mammals with cognitively enriching experiences in infancy are less emotional and less aggressive. Their cognitive gains are thought to be promoted in part by the reduction of "emotionality" in their infancy. Patricia Wallace, "Complex Environments: Effects on Brain Development," *Science* 185 (10 September 1974): 1,035–7.

[10] Ibid., 317–18, citing work by Mandler.

[11] McGuire says that cognition and affect "are not at different ends of a single continuum but tend rather to be separate . . . dimensions." William McGuire, "The Nature of Attitudes and Attitude Change," in Gardner Lindzey and Elliot Aronson, eds., *Handbook of Social Psychology,* vol. 3 (Reading, MA: Addison-Wesley, 1969), 202. The two-systems view is given in Robert B. Zajonc, "Feeling and Thinking: Preferences Need No Inferences," *American Psychologist* 35 (1980): 151–75.

way in which their incompatibility has been overemphasized is revealed in research on people's *range* of emotions that found "à strong positive relationship between emotional range [as contrasted to intensity] and both role taking and cognitive complexity in the description of other persons."[12] And another path to compatibility lies in the suspension of self-reference when solving problems, mentioned in the definition of cognitive complexity above. There are many others.

Arousal. Some analysts of emotional life find that two major dimensions organize most of the main emotions: a positive–negative dimension, and an arousal (high–low) dimension. On a two-dimensional diagram, the concept "angry" was placed high on arousal and moderately negative, whereas "miserable" was very negative but represented only moderate arousal.[13] At a glance we see the market invokes emotions at both ends of the positive–negative dimension: "pleased," "glad," "delighted," "excited" (but not "serene") at the positive end, and "frustrated," "distressed," "miserable," "depressed" (but not "gloomy") at the negative end. On the arousal dimension, the market elicits more of the high-arousal emotions than the low-arousal ones, that is, "angry," "alarmed," "astonished," "excited" at the aroused end, but not "sleepy," "calm," "relaxed," "droopy" at the low arousal end. This condition is important, for the more aroused a person is the more intensely he or she feels the need to express the emotion. These inferences, and those from the discussion of money, in Chapters 5 and 6, contradict Scitovsky's stimulating analysis of the *Joyless Economy* in which he chides the American consumer for lack of arousal – and therefore lack of pleasure.[14]

Labeling arousal and market feedback

As mentioned, the market is an instrument for emotional arousal of many kinds. William James believed that emotional arousal preceded our identification of an aroused state that we then label as "fear," or "anger," or some other specific emotion according to context. The physiology of arousal needs a name before it can be interpreted – and naming is a cognitive operation. The search by aroused individuals for the source of their feelings has many expressions. Actions may be prompted by unconscious motives or they may be responses to some autonomic muscular condition, but those actions also need to be classified to give them meaning. Muscular configurations can precede the emotions they are supposed to be responses to. By mechanically forcing the face into a smile or a frown and then observing the effects on subjectively reported feelings, research has shown that people actually feel more cheerful when forced to smile and more dispirited when forced to frown.[15]

The market relevance of the *arousal-labeling* theory lies in the problem it raises for interpreting market satisfaction. If people do not know why they are feeling good and attribute the good feeling to their purchases, the whole apparatus of market feedback has lost its informative quality (Chapter 27). Nonmarket arousals spill

---

[12] Shula Sommers, "Emotionality Reconsidered: The Role of Cognition in Emotional Responses," *Journal of Personality and Social Psychology* 41 (1981): 553–61.

[13] J. A. A. Russell, "A Circumplex Model of Affect," *Journal of Personality and Social Psychology* 39 (1980):1,161–78.

[14] Tibor Scitovsky, *The Joyless Economy* (New York: Oxford University Press, 1977).

[15] Fiske and Clark, *Social Cognition,* 313.

over into market evaluations, and market arousals, in turn, influence evaluations at home and in leisure activities.

Emotions are contagious: the collectivization of satisfaction

Emotions may be "learned" from others, indeed, they are often modeled on what is inferred from others' behavior – as in flight or panic. "Modeled affect generates vicarious arousal through an intervening self-arousal process in which the observed consequences are imagined mainly as occurring to oneself in similar situations."[16] The most obvious cases involve what is called empathy, but there are others that more closely resemble "infection," such as the influence on individuals' job satisfaction exerted by the satisfaction of coworkers.[17] Clearly, under these circumstances, the idea that the individual utility function is unaffected by the utilities of others is untenable. But beyond this correction of microeconomic theory, the matter is important because it collectivizes satisfaction or dissatisfaction (one rotten apple in a barrel spoils the lot), changes the focus from the individual to the group, and offers a countermechanism to envy and invidiousness.

Cognition defines emotion – and cognitions are borrowed from the group

The theory of stereotypes is familiar. A schema with a high affective loading is applied to a stimulus person and the person is assigned both the affective and the cognitive defined attributes of the schema. In the previous cases affect preceded cognition, but in this case cognition precedes affect; yet this ordering does nothing to ensure that the emotions are "appropriate" or well-considered.

Stereotypes offer what is called *default value,* that is, in default of other information the stereotypical schema fills in the empty space with its set of attributes. This schema economizes cognition at the cost of reducing complexity. But stereotypes are, almost by definition, socially constructed; they are, therefore, representative of the culture in which an individual lives and, so to speak, they deindividuate thought at the same time that they deprive emotions of any relation to the thinking process (except for rough-and-ready categorization) of the individual. Attitudes toward jobs and commodities do not, then, summarize an individual's experience, but summarize the lore of collective experience – a lore that, because it is often untested, persists in the face of each individual's private knowledge. It is in this fashion that stereotypes of bureaucracy survive disconfirming experience of the individuals who have had favorable bureaucratic encounters.[18]

Thought moderates – and polarizes – feeling

The more complex a person's thinking about a subject, the less his or her views are likely to be. This is illustrated again by reference to stereotypes: "People tend to

[16] Albert Bandura, *Social Learning Theory* (Englewood Cliffs, NJ: Prentice-Hall, 1977), 66.

[17] See Christopher Jencks, Lauri Perman, and Lee Rainwater, "What is a Good Job? A New Measure of Labor-Market Success," *American Journal of Sociology* 93 (1988): 1,322–57.

[18] Daniel Katz, Barbara A. Gutek, Robert L. Kahn, and Eugenia Barton, *Bureaucratic Encounters: A Pilot Study in the Evaluation of Government Services* (Ann Arbor, MI: Institute for Social Research, 1975).

evaluate out-group members (low complexity) more extremely than in-group members,'' in part because they simply know them less well. ''Thus, the greater the complexity of a knowledge structure, the more moderate the affect it elicits.''[19]

There is a counterprinciple: The more one thinks about a matter, the more likely one is to line up supporting opinions and information in a consolidated and polarized fashion. ''Because [complex thought] leads to a tighter organization of the attributes of a given stimulus, for those who possess a schema for thinking about it, . . . affect becomes polarized over time as a result of complexity.''[20] The tendencies to confirm, rather than disconfirm, and to reduce dissonance facilitate polarized, ideological thinking with its freight of emotional commitments.

What we see here is a paradigmatic conflict between science and ideology, between *Consumer Reports* and the struggle for brand loyalty. The reader of *Consumer Reports* finds that some brands and models do one thing better whereas others do something else better. The chosen brand is considered marginally superior because, say, safety is preferred to convenience. Advertising prefers the choice of a brand on emotional (self-image) grounds, knowing that once a customer has bought the item, knowledge of its qualities will be organized so as to confirm the wisdom of the purchase.

Emotions and calculability

People need predictability, partly for economic reasons, partly because being able to predict events is a major contribution to the sense that one is in control of one's own life. And that, in itself, is an important contribution to happiness and life satisfaction.[21] It is true that emotional responses are more difficult to predict than cognitive responses, partly because it is the emotional responses that are more vulnerable to external stimuli,[22] at least in contrast to such internal stimuli as may be represented by a schedule of preferences. Emotions also have an order of their own, for people seem to organize their ideas by similarity of feeling as well as by similarity of meaning. Market stimuli that arouse feelings of a similar tone will therefore evoke behavior of a similar kind, with the emotions governing the classificatory procedures. Thus, rather curiously, emotionality in the market implies somewhat more responsiveness to market signals than does the conventional calculated rationality and, if not exactly rational, these responses are ordered in an understandable fashion once the key to this ordering is comprehended.

Cognition, emotion and memory

To the extent that memory is organized by emotional tone rather than cognitive significance, the market, whose operation has been compared to the stimulus-response theories of Watson, will search for the emotional trigger to those feelings. Since people tend to recall memories ''affectively congruent with their current emotional

[19] Fiske and Taylor, *Social Cognition,* 321, citing research by Linville.

[20] Ibid., 321–2, citing research by Tesser.

[21] Robert I. Sutton and Robert L. Kahn, ''Prediction, Understanding, and Control as Antidotes to Organizational Stress,'' in Frank M. Andrews, ed. *Research on the Quality of Life* (Ann Arbor, MI: Institute for Social Research, 1986).

[22] Fiske and Taylor, *Social Cognition,* 336.

state''[23] and their memories will be guided by their current mood, the affective associations connected to a person or event will be retained when other learning is forgotten. And, because such learning has lost its verbal handle, "affective conditioning can be extremely resistant to extinction."[24]

Market choices that reflect a history of feeling tones about previous experiences regarded as somehow similar represent a great economy of effort, but a great impediment to learning and innovation. Most repeated purchases, says Katona, are neither rational nor irrational, but merely habitual;[25] now it seems that habit is not just the condensation of what has been learned from previous experiences, but rather a thing that changes with current mood. In a different context, Edmund Burke is challenged along with the rationalists whom he decried, because "traditions," whose interpretation is now seen to change with mood, are not the intergenerational constants he thought they were.

The effect of market success and failure on the emotions

Although level of income makes only a very modest difference to subjective well-being, sense of achievement contributes powerfully to it.[26] Belief that one has been more or less successful in life combines these two mental qualities. Smith and Kleugel studied feelings aroused by self-defined success and failure in terms more complex than satisfaction or happiness. In their study respondents to a national survey first reported their interpretation of the degree of success they had achieved, then they explained this success or lack of it, and finally stated the particular emotions they felt about the matter. The attributed causes of their success (or failure), internal or external, turned out to be important mediating factors.[27] Several of their findings, significant for our purposes, may be summarized as follows:

1. The emotions were most influenced by the actual degree of success respondents believed they had achieved; if successful they felt "satisfied" (but not "happy"), "confident," "thankful," and "proud;" if they believed they were unsuccessful, they felt "disappointed" and "frustrated," but not necessarily more worried or guilty.

2. After controlling for beliefs in their success or failure, external attribution (the belief that their fates were due to circumstances beyond their control, e. g., luck, deprived childhood, parental discouragement, etc.) consistently lowered positive feelings and increased negative feelings.[28] This supports the claim that personal control contributes to feelings of well-being under both favorable and unfavorable circumstances.

The study has implications for stratification and the relations between the classes or, more precisely, between the rich and poor.

3. Income, occupation, and education do not directly influence the expression of

[23] G. H. Bower, "Mood and Memory," *American Psychologist* 36 (1981): 129–48, cited in ibid., 566.
[24] Ed Diener, "Subjective Well-Being," *Psychological Bulletin* 95 (1984): 542–75, at 566.
[25] George Katona, *Psychological Economics* (New York: Elsevier, 1975): 220.
[26] Ibid., passim. See the extended discussion in Part VII.
[27] Eliot R. Smith and James R. Kleugel, "Cognitive and Social Bases of Emotional Experience: Outcome, Attribution, and Affect," *Journal of Personality and Social Psychology* 43 (1982): 1,129–41.
[28] Ibid., 1135.

the emotions, a finding consonant with other evidence, to be presented later, of the surprisingly weak contribution of income to happiness. But these factors do indirectly influence well-being by influencing belief in a sense of personal control: higher status is associated with a higher sense of personal control.

4. If lower status people *do* have a sense of personal control, their emotional patterns in success and failure are like those of upper status people. The sense of personal control wipes out social class difference in patterns of responses to success or failure. Self-attribution is an equalizer: Whatever contributes to self-attribution contributes to psychological equality. And the market contributes to self-attribution! (Chapter 9).

5. Those who make external attributions, crediting and blaming anything but themselves for their particular levels of success or failure, felt *more guilty* than those who considered themselves responsible for their own fates. On logical and psychological grounds, it has long been assumed that feelings of guilt were the products of *self*-blame, not the blaming of others – but the Protestant ethic theory could be resuscitated, as the authors point out, by attributing the guilt to the very process of external attribution. Guilt in the Protestant ethic economy would not then be due to a sense of having failed, but rather to a sense of not having taken responsibility for one's own fate. This interpretation is modestly supported by the fact that "thankfulness," which had been expected to be related only to external attribution (otherwise one seems to be thankful to oneself), was equally related to internal attribution – people were thankful for the gifts that enabled them to be successful.

Success in the labor market, then, does more than contribute to that nondescript concept of "utility;" it increases "confidence," "thankfulness," and "pride." It creates those feelings mainly among those who attribute their success to their own acts, however, not to those who attribute their success to luck, or to their family upbringing or something outside themselves. This proves true quite irrespective of income level or social class. It is for this reason that the self-attribution we have included in our analysis of human development is so important in analyzing the market experience. And, parenthetically, it seems that feelings of guilt are attributable more to failure to take responsibility for one's own acts, for deficient self-reliance, than to self-perceived failure in the labor market.

Positivity and cognition

There are enduring moods representing personality dispositions that may characterize a person for a very long time (traits), and there are shorter term dispositions that are situationally determined (states). I examine one of these moods, happiness, at length in Part VII of this book; here I wish to point mainly to the relationship of good and bad moods to certain cognitive responses in order to give further content to the concept of utility and to show how good moods greatly alter market behavior.

Positivity bias. People prefer happy endings to stories, and given an opportunity to do so, they will reconstruct a story to give it a happy ending[29] (Chapter

[29] Robert P. Abelson, "Social Psychology's Rational Man," in S. I. Benn and G. W. Mortimore, eds., *Rationality and the Social Sciences* (London: Routlege & Kegan Paul, 1976), 66–7.

24). They tend to recall pleasant events more than unpleasant events, to process pleasant words more quickly than unpleasant words, to look for the good or for the silver lining in every disappointment, to anticipate progress, and so forth. This complex of events has been appropriately called the positivity bias or, more graphically, the "Pollyanna Principle,"[30] and is revealed in surveys (where people tend to choose positively over negatively phrased items),[31] in person perception, [32] and in many other spheres of expression and interpretation. The "happy consciousness" that Marcuse thought was a market product reflecting the abundance of goods made available in a market society, has a much wider, though not universal, provenance.[33]

There are some physiological factors partially accounting for some of the happy consciousness. Jean Piaget reports on children's positivity as follows:

Everything is aimed at the primacy of the positive during the elementary stages, and the positive corresponds to what, on the level of experience, represents the "immediate data," whereas negation depends either on derived verifications or on more or less labored constructions as determined by the complexity of the systems.[34]

Negation not only implies absence, or a counterfactual, it also requires the brain to work harder, for it involves an extra step in encoding: "Any series interpreted in terms of 'good' will be easier to deal with than any series interpreted in terms of 'bad.' "[35] The positivity bias has a wonderful effect on the satisfaction of human wants – in the market or elsewhere.

Good moods are self-amplifying. The positivity bias is lodged in memory as well as in the topical "happy consciousness." Thus, the tapping of networks of mood-congruent associations in memory, mentioned before, reinforces the cognitive biases favoring the good over the bad. Moods influence thought and behavior in many ways. "People in good moods are more helpful, more open to conversation with strangers, like others more, and are more satisfied with their cars and other possessions compared to people in neutral moods."[36] Bad moods, or negative affect, have similar, if reversed, effects. These effects are weaker than those for good moods, for it seems to be the case that people can to some extent voluntarily change their moods. Furthermore, the brain cooperates, for a negative current mood seems to be more weakly associated with negative memories than a good mood is with

[30] Margaret Matlin and David J. Stang, *The Pollyana Principle: Selectivity in Language, Memory, and Thought* (Cambridge, MA: Schenkman, 1978).

[31] Angus Campbell, Philip E. Converse, and Willard L. Rodgers, *The Quality of American Life* (New York: Russell Sage, 1976), 99.

[32] David O. Sears, "The Person-Positivity Bias," *Journal of Personality and Social Psychology* 44 (1983): 233–58.

[33] Herbert Marcuse, *One Dimensional Man* (Boston: Beacon, 1964), 78. For cross-national variations, see Ronald Inglehart and Jacques-Rene Rabier, "Aspirations Adapt to Situations – But Why Are the Belgians so Much Happier than the French? A Cross-Cultural Analysis of the Subjective Quality of Life," in Frank M. Andrews, *Research on the Quality of Life.*

[34] Jean Piaget, *The Origins of Intelligence in the Child,* trans. M. Cook (New York: Norton, 1977), 17.

[35] Michael I. Posner, *Cognition: An Introduction* (Glenview, IL: Scott Foresman, 1973), 160.

[36] Fiske and Taylor, *Social Cognition,* 326, 328, citing research by Clark and Isen.

positive memories, and bad moods, in turn, are generally (with notable exceptions) less salient and less retrievable (Chapter 19). Finally, positive affects are more likely to lead to behavior than are negative affects.[37] The consequence is that people like each other, their jobs, and their daily lives more than social critics believe that objective circumstances warrant.

Dissatisfaction with market products is also inhibited by these positivity forces, including highly transient sources of good moods. For example, when people in a shopping mall received a gift from one source and were approached later for an apparently unrelated marketing survey, those whose moods were elevated by the gift reported that their cars and television sets performed better and had better service records than those who had not received the gift.[38] Satisfaction with current purchases, that is, their *utility*, varies with antecedent events, implying that "aspects of life are not evaluated in terms of a single utility scale and standard."[39]

The effect of good mood on cognition and behavior

If the market economy is justified as a means of satisfying human wants and in this capacity serves as a source of subjective well-being, we can turn this justification around and ask whether subjective well-being then influences market behavior? Although some have doubted such effects,[40] we have just seen examples of relevant impacts of mood on both consumer and productive behavior. More than that, if moods generalize beyond the specific occasion that caused them, utility is not attributable to a specific purchase but to other elements in a person's life. And if moods affect cognition, those mental processes the economists call "rational choice" are not only the causes of utility maximization, but the products as well.

Good mood as a more or less enduring trait usually, but not always, predicts behavior similar to good mood as a temporary state;[41] in this discussion I combine

---

[37] Ibid., 326–8.

[38] Margaret S. Clark and Alice M. Isen, "Toward Understanding the Relationship Between Feeling States and Social Behavior," in Albert H. Hastorf and Alice M. Isen, eds., *Cognitive Social Psychology* (New York: Elsevier North-Holland, 1982), 78.

[39] Marshall Dermer, Sidney J. Cohen, Elaine Jackson, and Erling A. Anderson, "Evaluative Judgments of Aspects of Life as a Function of Vicarious Exposure to Hedonic Extremes," *Journal of Personality and Social Psychology* 37 (1979): 247–60.

[40] "It would be naive to think that a person's behavior at any one time could be closely predicted from his feelings without taking into account social and physical constraints that impinge on that person." Frank M. Andrews and Stephen B. Withey, *Social Indicators of Well-Being: Americans' Perceptions of Life Quality* (New York: Plenum Press, 1976), 215.

[41] For example, short-term positive feelings induced by a loaded questionnaire produced a sense of general well-being. Although this effect did not survive an eight-week interval, negative moods similarly induced did survive the delay! Darlene E. Goodhart, "Some Psychological Effects Associated with Positive and Negative Thinking about Stressful Outcomes: Was Pollyana Right?" *Journal of Personality and Social Psychology* 48 (1985), 216–32. In Campbell et al.'s study of *The Quality of American Life* simple measures of satisfaction with life-as-a-whole correlated at .5 with simple questions on happiness; more complex measures of well-being had higher correlations (p. 8). There are exceptions, however. Circumstantial positivity, such as that produced by good grades, does not relate in the same way to attribution as does a longer term disposition to feel cheerful, happy, or satisfied with one's life. See Gerald I. Metalsky, Lisa J. Halberstadt, and Lyn Y. Abramson, "Vulnerability to Depressive Mood Reactions: Toward a More Powerful Test of the Diathesis-Stress and Causal Mediation Components of

them, because measures of affects indicate that moods are often surprisingly durable and stable.[42]

Mood generalization. Among the properties of this complex of positive feelings, several help us to relate them to the economy. First, good mood in one area tends to generate good moods and satisfaction in other areas of life. For example, a good mood produced quite simply by asking subjects to think positive thoughts, had the effect of increasing estimates of past and future successes and of improving self-evaluations. Moreover, after failure, those in a bad mood lowered their expectations about the future and lowered their estimates of themselves, but those in a good mood seemed invulnerable to these failure effects.[43] A good mood also seems to protect a person against stress at a later time, although the delay must be only moderate.[44]

For our purposes, this generalization effect is important as an indication of the power of market pleasures – or displeasures – to affect general moods, to increase expectations of better things to come, to improve a person's self-esteem. That is, what is called "utility" in some treatments is not in itself a general state of satisfaction, but it can help to generate such satisfactions by the generalization effect. Of course, the generalizations work both ways: Some satisfaction at home, some happy moments with one's children, can increase market utility quite without reference to prices and demand schedules. And all of this is thoroughly unconscious to the choosing person; generalization of this kind is an affective process without cognition.

Cognition and mood. Good moods raise expectations, often to an unattainable level[45] – a factor to be taken into account in any consideration of "rational expectations." In contrast, depressed people are much more accurate than happy people in their predictions of what will happen to them over the next few months and in estimating their own degrees of control over uncertainly controllable events. The depressed are also better at estimating how they are judged by others.[46] Nondepressed people have a self-enhancing bias that leads them to overestimate the probabilities of success and underestimate the probability of failure. Depressed people do not share that bias; hence they are more accurate in their views of their own

the Reformulated Theory of Depression," *Journal of Personality and Social Psychology* 52 (1987): 386–93. Further, some studies suggest that it is not so much the presence of a good mood that has the indicated effects as the absence of negative feelings. See Goodhart, "Some Psychological Effects," 216. In order not to burden the discussion with detailed exceptions, we shall, except where attributions are significant, follow the Clark and Isen findings on the effects of even temporary good moods.

[42] Norma D. Feshbach and Seymour Feshbach, "Affective Processes and Academic Achievement," *Child Development* 58 (1987): 1,335–47. Special issue on schools and development.

[43] Jack Wright and Walter Mischel, "Influence of Affect on Cognitive Social Learning Person Variables," *Journal of Personality and Social Psychology* 43 (1982): 901–14.

[44] Goodhart, "Some Psychological Effects."

[45] Wright and Mischel, "Influence of Affect on Cognitive Social Learning," 901.

[46] Clive Wood, "Sadder but Wiser," *Psychology Today* 22 (January 1988), 8, reporting research by Timothy Osberg, Lauren B. Alloy, and Lynn Y. Abramson. Alloy et al. show that this invulnerability to the illusion of control is more of a characteristic of temporary circumstantially induced moods than natural depressed states. See Lauren B. Alloy, Lyn Y. Abramson, and Donald Viscusi, "Induced Mood and the Illusion of Control," *Journal of Personality and Social Psychology* 41 (1981): 1,129–40.

future.[47] If rational expectations were a necessary guide to negotiating the byways of the market economy, the depressed would have a considerable advantage over happy people. But there are other cognitive effects of good moods that counterbalance this market advantage of the unhappy!

Alice Isen, who has studied the effects of moods for about twenty years, has discovered many of these qualities (Chapter 27). Among her findings, the following are relevant: (1) Happiness increases imagination: in word association tests, those who feel happy "give more unusual and diverse association to neutral stimulus words."[48] (2) Compared to people in neutral moods, good moods improve problem solving in some ways, but not in others. "Positive emotions . . . encourage people to look beyond the normal problem-solving method to try different options;" they are more flexible and innovative. These qualities are rarely found in depressed or sad individuals. (3) On the other hand, happy people "tend to simplify complex decisions by relying on intuition." For example, subjects put in a good mood by receiving a small gift [it really seems to be that simple] tend to guess at solutions for which more complex analysis is more appropriate and more often used by those in neutral moods – "and their answers tend to be wrong." But the lack of weighty analysis had its compensations, for (4) happy people "performed tasks more efficiently than controls . . . [e.g., in buying a car]. They took less time in reaching a decision by eliminating unimportant information and spending less time rechecking information already considered." But, again (5) there is a cost in loss of precision: on a word-classification task, happy people "were more likely to rate 'fringe' examples as members of a group," for example, classifying "purse" and "ring" in the category "clothing."

(6) Happy people are more risk averse – in a special way. Compared to persons whose mood was neither elevated nor depressed, happy people tended to bet more real money on a low-risk bet but less on a high-risk bet. When there was no real money at stake, however, happy people were more likely to take a high-payoff long shot. The evidence suggests a desire to maintain the happy mood by avoiding risks of real losses, but where little real loss was at stake, they were stimulated by more adventurous opportunities.[49] Other evidence on children's tendencies toward self-indulgence is interpreted in the same way: A good mood is too valuable to lose by taking risks or incurring disapproval,[50] or, put differently, losses are more keenly felt by people who are happy. As Isen said to a reporter in explaining this phenomenon, "When you're feeling happy, you want to keep it that way."

Good mood, work, and savings. Finally, happiness leads to hard work and (sometimes) to greater achievement. Feshbach related the affect levels of 8–9 and

[47] Lauren B. Alloy and Anthony H. Ahrens, "Depression and Pessimism for the Future: Biased Use of Statistically Relevant Information in Predictions for Self and Others," *Journal of Personality and Social Psychology* 52 (1987): 366–78.

[48] Report in *The APA Monitor* 19 (1988): 6–7, summarizing Isen's work; the quotations are from the report unless otherwise specified.

[49] Alice M. Isen and Robert Patrick, "The Effect of Positive Feeling on Risk Taking: When the Chips Are Down," *Organizational Behavior and Human Performance* 32 (1983): 194–202.

[50] Louise C. Perry, David G. Perry, and David English, "Happiness: When Does It Lead to Self-Indulgence and When Does It Lead to Self-Denial?" *Journal of Experimental Child Psychology* 39 (1985): 203–11.

10–11-year-old children to their academic achievements. In both age groups the happier children were better achievers, although the relationship was weakened for the older boys whose interest in athletics may have accounted for the falling off in their grades.[51] Among adults feelings of well-being tend to lead to harder work and longer hours, though this is mediated by various other psychological and demographic characteristics.[52] In general, too, a good mood facilitates saving,[53] but, conversely, there is some survey evidence that prudent savers tend to be unhappier than those who take their futures more casually and save less,[54] this latter finding suggesting that constraints of prudence and rational calculation are hedonically costly (to be discussed below).

The market effects of good moods. If the market is the source of good moods (which it often is not), by this benign act it raises expectations that it must often frustrate. The revolution of rising expectations (which may be a myth)[55] has been said to have left a trail of unhappy people in its wake. The cycle of good mood, higher expectations, and bad mood following frustration is not a felicitous one. On the other hand (as mentioned), to the extent that rationality is identified with "rational expectations," only the depressed can be expected to be truly rational – and therefore to maximize the satisfaction of their wants in the market. There is more than the pleasure of a paradox in this observation, for it reveals how dependent the market is on "the animal spirits" that Keynes said guided investment,[56] or the desire for a "private kingdom" and the "will to conquest – as in sport," rather than the will to make money per se, that Schumpeter said characterized entrepreneurs.[57] In fact, since good moods are more likely to be acted on than bad moods, the reliance on the "rational expectations" of the depressed would provide us with a society of excellent, but poverty-stricken, prophets.

Happiness *or* cognition

There are several strands of thought that weave in and out of the relation between happiness or good mood, on the one hand, and cognition or rationality, on the other. Since rationality is only a thin and biased version of full cognitive complexity (Chapter 3), where it is used in this analysis it must serve as only a rough indicator of the richer, fuller concept. Similarly, we will here group together a set of comparable terms for hedonic well-being: *satisfaction with life-as-a-whole*, which involves a

[51] Feshbach and Feshbach, "Affective Processes and Academic Achievement."

[52] Jeffrey H. Greenhaus, Arthur G. Bedeian, and Kevin W. Mossholder, "Work Experiences, Job Performances, and Feelings of Personal and Family Well-Being," *Journal of Vocational Behavior* 31 (1987): 200–15.

[53] Clark and Isen, "Toward Understanding," 88.

[54] Carin Rubenstein, "Money and Self-Esteem, Relationships, Secrecy, Envy, Satisfaction," *Psychology Today* 15 (1981): 29–44.

[55] See Marylee C. Taylor, "Improved Conditions, Rising Expectations, and Dissatisfaction: A Test of the Past/Present Relative Deprivation Hypothesis," *Social Psychology Quarterly* 45 (1982): 24–33.

[56] Keynes, *A General Theory*, 161.

[57] Joseph A. Schumpeter, *The Theory of Economic Development: An Inquiry into Profits, Capital, Credits, Interest, and the Business Cycle*, trans. R. Opie, 2d ed. (Cambridge: Harvard University Press, 1936).

more critical and therefore cognitive appraisal; *happiness,* which is a state of being primarily governed by affect without any necessary cognition; and *good mood,* which can represent general satisfaction or happiness and implies a current, perhaps temporary, hedonic feeling.

At one level, the issue is whether two of the main themes of market analysis are compatible: market rationality and that supreme utility, happiness. I treat these themes as hypotheses to be examined in the light of the modestly probative empirical evidence available.

In *religious* thought the tension is seen in the consequences of curiosity for Prometheus and Adam and Eve, the latter sacrificing paradise for their inadvertently acquired knowledge of good and evil. The Faustian myth is a second warning. More recently Protestant theologian Rienhold Niebuhr warned against the "hybris" of believing that man can know himself through unaided reason; Niebuhr finds this kind of cognitive pride to be a cause of much current unhappiness.[58] Excessive emphasis on cognition risks unhappiness.

Philosophy takes the opposite view. Rather than being in conflict, happiness and knowledge are generally harmonious. Since thinking is their trade, philosophers have almost always believed that happiness and complex thinking were related; indeed, thinking *is* happiness. For Plato, wisdom, the contemplation of the good, was the only certain route to happiness. In a minimalist position, John Stuart Mill believed that it was hedonically better to be a dissatisfied Socrates than a satisfied fool. Recent philosophical arguments over the elements of well-being claim that one cannot be truly happy and deluded about the causes of one's happiness at the same time.[59] If they had to choose between happiness and knowledge, some would choose a properly qualified happiness (merited happiness), but others would choose knowledge as part of the concept of the fully developed human personality.[60] American lay philosophers (the general public) seem to believe that the two are somewhat in opposition to each other in the sense that if a person chooses one of the values, he or she is unlikely to choose the other ($r = -.17$).[61]

The third strand of thought is *psychological.* A continuing argument about the dominant pattern of causal priority between affects (such as happiness) and cognition (such as rationality) remains unresolved and variable.[62] We have seen evidence that sometimes emotional arousal comes first and takes on meaning only when cognitively labeled as a pleasant or unpleasant emotion and other evidence showing

[58] Reinhold Niebuhr, *Faith in History* (New York: Scribner's, 1951), 12, 89.

[59] James Griffin, *Well-Being: Its Meaning, Measurement, and Moral Importance* (Oxford, UK: Clarendon Press, 1986), 9.

[60] For example, Ross puts knowledge last among the ultimate goods, after merited happiness and justice. See W. David Ross, *The Right and the Good* (Oxford, UK: Clarendon Press, 1930). In his discussion of the good, contemporary political philosopher William Galston makes "developed existence," that is, the developed and mature personality, one of his three primary goods. William A. Galston, *Justice and the Human Good* (Chicago: University of Chicago Press, 1980).

[61] Milton Rokeach, *The Nature of Human Values* (New York: Free Press, 1973), 44.

[62] For the priority of affect, see Robert B. Zajonc, "Feeling and Thinking," 151–75. For a critical view of that priority, see Howard Leventhal, "The Integration of Emotion and Cognition: A View from the Perceptual-Motor Theory of Emotion," in Margaret S. Clark and Susan T. Fiske, eds., *Affect and Cognition* (Hillsdale, NJ: Erlbaum, 1982).

that people can think their way into happiness or unhappiness. Complex thinking is not identified as a source of happiness and, although good feelings improve some aspects of cognition, depression improves accuracy in predicting and assessing matters close at hand.

The fourth, *economic,* strand emerges from the belief that hedonic maximization follows a strict rational ordering of preferences and from rational interpretation of means to achieve that maximum within preferred risk tolerance. Whereas the philosophers hold that knowledge (or wisdom) is itself a source of happiness, the economists believe that whatever intrinsic value it may have, the main function of knowledge is to guide people in selecting and scheduling their preferences so as to maximize their satisfactions. There is no interest in the reverse relationship. The relationship between the two, but not their relative priorities, is an empirical question.

Education, intelligence, and happiness

One way of seeking to disentangle this puzzle is to examine the relationship between subjective well-being among those with more and those with less developed cognitive capacities. We take education and intelligence measures as rough indicators of cognitive development. In a study embracing data on eleven advanced countries, Inglehart and Rabier report, "The more educated are happier and more satisfied with their lives than the less educated. But the differences between the most educated and the least educated amount to only six or seven percentage points." The impact of education is greater than that of sex or age, but less than that of, for example, going to church.[63] Compared to a *change* in income, the effects of education are much slighter; compared to *level* of income at any one time, the income effect dominates the education effect, though neither is very powerful.[64] As for intelligence, Michalos reports on two studies, one showing that intelligence has no independent influence on feelings of either satisfaction or of happiness, and another study finding that happiness with life-as-a-whole was in no way associated with verbal intelligence.[65]

Neither the philosopher's nor the economist's view that happiness is associated with complex thinking is supported. Similarly, this rough evidence of little or no relationship is incompatible with the beliefs of the religionists. It is, of course, compatible with the evidence of the psychologists.

Why education and intelligence do not lead to greater happiness

Why are education and intelligence so unrelated to subjective well-being when they should offer the very tools that lead people to lives with higher hedonic payoffs?

---

[63] Inglehart and Rabier, "Aspirations Adapt to Situations," 20. In a very different kind of sample, Jonathan Freedman comes to the same conclusion of perceptible but small effects of education on happiness. See his *Happy People* (New York: Harcourt Brace, 1980).

[64] Andrews and Withey, *Social Indicators of Well-Being,* 322; Norman M. Bradburn and David Caplovitz come to the same conclusion. See their *Reports on Happiness* (Chicago: Aldine, 1965), 10.

[65] Alex C. Michalos, "Job Satisfaction, Marital Satisfaction, and the Quality of Life: A Review and a Preview," in Andrews, ed., *Research on the Quality of Life,* 62. Michalos is reporting work by Sigelman (1981) and by Kamman (1978).

The answer to this question is useful in preparing the way to the next one: Can economic rationality lead to happiness?

Inglehart and Rabier turn to an adaptation-level explanation. We become accustomed to our circumstances very easily and only *changes* in circumstances affect our moods; level of education is established early and rarely changes.[66] Although this might explain why education per se does not make people happy, it does nothing to explain why education and intelligence do not serve as tools for maximizing hedonic values, as the economists would predict.

A different line of explanation suggests that the promised advantages of education are increasingly frustrated by the very increase in numbers of people educated. In Hirsch's term, education is a "positional good," one whose comparative advantage depends upon whether or not others also have a given level of education; each generation, then, achieves what would have been commanding heights in its parental generation, only to find that the achieved level is so crowded that their hopes are frustrated.[67] This interpretation seems unlikely since only 10 percent of a national American sample (1973) were generally dissatisfied with "the usefulness for you, personally, of your education," and it was those with the least education that were most dissatisfied[68] – as had been true for a century or more. In any event, there are as good reasons to be pleased that others are educated, especially those with whom one associates, as for being unhappy about the rivalry over status and jobs that others present.

A better explanation, it seems to me, is that education trains people both in criticality and in thinking of situations contrary to fact – what might be or might have been as well as what is and was. Fiske and Taylor report on research showing that schemata of "what might be" or "what might have been" induce some feelings of anticipation and relief, but more often feelings of disappointment and regret, contrasting what is with something else.[69] That kind of cognitive complexity that includes imagination of situations contrary to fact could depress subjective well-being even in a life that is rather better planned than average.

A fourth line of explanation follows the finding (already mentioned) that the more one thinks about something and the more one knows about it, the more moderate the emotions attached to it become. Complex cognitions apprehend complex situations so that simple good and bad responses seem inappropriate.[70] In that sense, cognition depresses affectivity and, since evaluations of one's satisfaction with life-as-a-whole tend to be positive, the depression of affectivity would represent a regression to some more affectively neutral point.

Bryant and Veroff follow a fifth line of reasoning. They find that although the better educated are more self-confident, they are also more likely to feel uncertain about the future. "Thus education may . . . lead to more worrying, anxiety, and dissatisfaction about life." The longer term payoff is more "foresightful coping"

[66] Inglehart and Rabier, "Aspirations Adapt to Situations," 5–6.
[67] Fred Hirsch, *Social Limits to Growth* (Cambridge: Harvard University Press, 1976).
[68] Andrews and Withey, *Social Indicators of Well-Being*, 258, 146.
[69] Fiske and Taylor, *Social Cognition*, 324–5. The citation for research on "what might be" is to Robert Abelson; that for research on "what might have been" is to work by Tversky and Kahneman.
[70] Ibid., 321.

and increased capacity to handle the anticipated stress when it comes,[71] but apparently the long-term advantages are bought at the cost of short-term anxiety.

Sixth, to the extent that it takes intellectual effort to counter the normal positivity bias (Chapter 24), the educated may be better prepared to undertake that effort than those without such education. This would imply that for any given level of objective advantage, the more educated would apply a discount factor reducing the satisfaction/pleasure score by the amount the positivity bias had added to it. A group critical of modern emphases on material welfare, called "post-materialists,"[72] are drawing upon their superior cognitive ability, reinforced by their higher education, in overcoming acquiescence and positivity. Thus the link between intellectuals and criticality or disaffection relies upon "intellect" to overcome positivity and their moral expression in "just world"[73] tendencies.

Finally, a somewhat different kind of explanation relies on the superior intraceptivity (willingness to probe one's unconscious and semiconscious) of the better educated. On good psychoanalytic principles, we would infer that being in touch with one's emotions is a necessary ingredient for happiness – but there are other considerations. In a study of how Americans view their own mental health, Gurin et al. find "a heightened self-probing – both for strengths and weaknesses – that can and evidently does result from increased education. . . . The social and cultural conditions that lead to introspection may also lead not only to a realistic self-criticism but to a generally negative self-percept."[74] In a similar manner, such consciousness of self as may be induced, for example, by seeing oneself in a mirror or hearing one's voice on a tape recorder, is painful. Because it reminds people of their deficiencies, it does not make them happy.[75] Education, and to some degree social status generally, is associated with a greater consciousness of self, a greater concern for one's character, and a lesser concern for one's objective circumstances, especially health and money.

Speculation on the opposition between rationality and happiness

Emotions and life satisfaction. In a review of many studies of subjective well-being, Diener reports that cognitive evaluation of the elements of one's life tends to have a weaker relationship to assessments of overall life quality than do affective measures.[76] In the language we have borrowed from Albert Hirschman, the passions contribute more to subjective well-being than do the interests.

But specifically in the market domain, cognitive responses explain more of the feelings of subjective well-being. Andrews and Withey found that whereas the family domain makes its contribution to subjective well-being directly through the af-

---

[71] Fred B. Bryant and Joseph Veroff, "Dimensions of Subjective Mental Health in American Men and Women," in Andrews, ed., *Research on the Quality of Life,* 139.

[72] Ronald Inglehart, *The Silent Revolution* (Princeton: Princeton University Press, 1972).

[73] Melvin Lerner, *The Belief in a Just World: A Fundamental Delusion* (New York: Plenum Press, 1980).

[74] Gerald Gurin, Joseph Veroff, and Sheila Feld, *Americans View Their Mental Health* (New York: Basic Books, 1960), 81, 83.

[75] Robert A. Wicklund, "Objective Self-Awareness," in Leonard Berkowitz, ed., *Advances in Experimental Social Psychology,* vol. 8 (New York: Academic Press, 1975).

[76] Ed Diener, "Subjective Well-Being," 550.

fective feelings or "passions" it evokes, market satisfactions make their lesser contributions to well-being through more cognitive processes. Andrews and Withey's two market related sets of questions, one set dealing with money and another with goods and services, are much more likely to produce higher feelings of satisfaction than of happiness.[77] What the market evokes, then, are the more cognitive, evaluative feelings of satisfaction, rather than the more affective feelings of happiness. This tells us only that thought processes contribute more to satisfaction with life-as-a-whole than to happiness, but nothing about whether more rigorous thought processes contribute to (or detract from) either.

Does rationality impede the happiness it is supposed to foster? If depression is associated with more veridical and sober estimates of the way others view the self and more accurate assessments of the probable frequency of negative events and of the possibility that plans will be frustrated, perhaps it is because these cognitions make a person unhappy, rather than because the bad mood improves cognition. Like Jeremiah, these people might be unhappy *because* they see the future clearly. This assumption can be ruled out by the experimental methods used, however. Subjects are first made unhappy by their own ideation, or by a contrived or natural event, like receiving poor grades on an examination, and only *then* do they reveal their superior "rational expectations." But it seems that dispositional, enduring forms of depression have somewhat different effects from the circumstantial, "recent-failure-of-exam" variety that are employed in experiments.[78] Thus, there remains a question that, to my knowledge, has not been investigated: Does the concern to get the right answer, to think something through to the end, to avoid wishful thinking, to reduce possible losses due to carelessness, to avoid missing some fact or inference, in short, to apply the canons of rationality to every problem – does this kind of scrupulous rationality make people unhappy?

One route might be through anxiety, for anxiety, of course, reduces happiness.[79] But the process may be more subtle and extensive. If emotionality, including, it may be supposed, feelings of joy and sorrow, hinders cognitive development, as Wallace's studies with animals suggest (see next chapter), might it not be true that cognitive development hinders feelings of joy, or that our prized rationality is bought at the price of happiness? Freud suggested this when he considered the possibility that "our so-called civilization itself is to blame for a great part of our misery, and we should be much happier if we were to give up and go back to primitive conditions."[80] Is the theory of rationality developed by von Neuman and Morgenstern a theory of behavior that carries with it an underlying, if discreet, melancholy?

Again we must sort out the hedonic effects of cognitive complexity from those of rationality. From the evidence on the lack of relationship between education or intelligence, on the one hand, and measures of happiness or satisfaction with life-as-a-whole, on the other, it seems that *cognitive complexity* is not a consistent source

[77] Andrews and Withey, *Social Indicators of Well-Being*, 169.
[78] Metalsky et al., "Depressive Mood Reactions."
[79] Antonia Abbey and Frank M. Andrews, "Modeling the Psychological Determinants of Life Quality," in Andrews, *Research on the Quality of Life*.
[80] Sigmund Freud, *Civilization and its Discontents*, trans. J. Riviere (London: Hogarth Press, 1951), 44.

of either happiness or unhappiness. Cognitive complexity and happiness are compatible under certain circumstances and not others. But such blunt relationships often mask conflicting tendencies and other evidence suggests that education, again as a surrogate for complex cognition, reduces hedonic levels by increasing introspection and thus alerting people to their own deficiencies, by making them aware of life's alternatives not chosen, and by increasing their consciousness of the risks and uncertainties that they face. At the same time, more complex thinkers are more self-confident about their capacities to cope with these uncertainties (because they believe they are more in control of their own fates – see Chapter 9) and, in fact, do cope with vicissitudes more successfully. Finally, the market's justification of things as they are, on the grounds that everyone in the market gets his or her deserts, might satisfy the less well educated but is perceived to be untrue by the better educated, or at least by the college educated.[81] The lack of relationship is due to the interaction of these conflicting tendencies.

We do not have similar surrogate measures of *rationality* but find in the concept certain properties that suggest that, compared to others, people who follow its precepts are indeed *less* likely to be happy, although we would be less certain of their satisfaction with life-as-a-whole. The reason for the difference between the effects of happiness and life satisfaction is that happiness is explicitly an emotional mood, whereas satisfaction is a more cognitive appraisal of one's life. This negative relationship, or incompatibility, between rationality and happiness would occur because of the implied suppression of emotionality by the rational, the inference regarding its cold calculation of ends and means and therefore its tendency to offend people who search for warmth in their relationships (see Chapter 11), and its unnecessary but economically implied concentration on maximizing self-interest. Cognitive complexity carries no similar implication.

The difference between the relationship between cognitive complexity and happiness, on the one hand, and rationality and happiness, on the other, is further suggested by Isen's research. She finds that people who have been inducted into a good (happy) mood, compared to those who have not, make more rapid decisions that turn out to be satisfying, with more self-confidence, less rechecking of facts already ascertained, and more intuitiveness. But these happy people lack those qualities that are characteristic of *rational* decision makers: methodological scrupulousness, care in rechecking facts, and freedom from error.[82] It is not necessarily true, of course, that because happy people are, in this limited sense, likely to be less rational, that rational people are likely to be less happy. With the limited evidence at hand, however, we can at least point to the increased probability that happiness and rationality are negatively correlated.

---

[81] Gurin and Gurin sort out "personal efficacy" from what they call "economic control ideology," the latter measuring the belief that people in general, not just the self, get what they deserve. All except college graduates tend to accept this ideological view; college graduates tend to reject it. See Gerald Gurin and Patricia Gurin, "Personal Efficacy and the Ideology of Individual Responsibility," in Burkhard Strumpel, ed., *Economic Means for Human Needs,* (Ann Arbor, MI: Institute for Social Research, 1976), 139.

[82] Alice M. Isen, "Positive Affect, Cognitive Processes, and Social Behavior," in L. Berkowitz, ed., *Advances in Experimental Social Psychology,* vol. 20 (New York: Academic Press, 1987).

The weight of speculation and evidence falls upon the side of modest incompatibility between rationality and happiness. To the extent that the market favors rationality, the market is more of a cause of rational sobriety than of happiness. The
paradox mentioned earlier – only the depressed can be truly rational in their pursuit
of happiness – has its obverse: The market's rational utility maximizers can never
be truly happy! Yet the market rationale rests on its capacity to satisfy human wants,
of which happiness is preeminent.

Summary

Market behavior is saturated with emotions. The consumer market arouses affects
and constrains them through budgetary processes; the labor market constrains affects through performance criteria and arouses them through the desire for achievement and self-rewarding or self-punishing demands for excellence.

Sometimes emotions do interrupt ongoing cognitive processes (often for good
reason) and sometimes the two go their separate ways. But their main relation is
mutual support, cognition interpreting arousal and emotion stimulating further cognition.

Emotional responses are more vulnerable to external stimuli than cognitive responses, and are organized by principles different from those of cognitive responses. Thus, market stimuli appeal to emotional assessments disturbing the original schedule of preferences, and their organizational principles lead to kinds of
behavior different from those prompted by cognitive organizational patterns.

The fact that emotional arousal may acquire a label from some irrelevant source
means that market feedback conveys distorted information. The market's capacity
to arouse people requires them to explain their arousal to themselves and so stimulates thinking. But inasmuch as the thinking is not directly linked to people's insights into their own behaviors, they borrow interpretations from the general public,
reinforcing the tendency to "collectivize" and standardize explanations for feelings
generated both in the market and elsewhere. Thinking about a matter moderates
emotions, thus opening the door to greater market rationality, but at the same time
the thinking leads people to *discover* after the fact various reasons why one choice
is better than another, a form of partisanship. Tendencies for memories to be affected by current moods reduces the validity of market experience as a guide to
choice.

A positivity bias makes market goods liked without the goods having "earned"
it. Good moods increase the positivity bias so that, again, the satisfaction in any
particular purchase is not just a function of that purchase but also of the mood at
the time of purchase and the history of all purchases lodged in memory. Given these
effects on temporary moods and biases, it would be well to think of utility curves
varying with time and circumstance; a person has many utility curves.

People who attribute their failure to some external cause are *more* likely both to
be more depressed and to feel more guilty than those who attribute it to something
in their own behavior. I speculated that it was the very evasion of responsibility that
prompted this guilt. Internal attribution by all social ranks seems to lead people,

first, to be more alike, and, second, to accept arguments that do not emphasize social structure.

Good moods or happiness seem to favor productivity by increasing self-confidence, imagination, and increasing prudence and saving. On the other hand, the depressed are more accurate in their forecasts and view of how others see them. On balance, good moods favor productivity, especially through buoyant entrepreneurs.

Whether or not two of the main themes of the market experience, rationality and the maximization of utilities, are compatible seems uncertain. But from the evidence that (1) efforts to be meticulously rational are associated with less happiness; (2) cognitive development takes place where organisms are less emotional; (3) intellectual sophistication increases both knowledge of how things might be otherwise (alternative payoffs – a feature of rationality) and anxious planning for the future; and, finally, (4) rationality limits other, and possibly more congenial, forms of cognition, we find some incompatibility. Isen's findings seem to be contrary but the thought patterns of the happy, relying on intuition and worrying less about error, seem to apply to forms of cognitive complexity that do not fit the rationality pattern. We tentatively concluded that there were reasons to believe in a paradox: Rational utility maximizers are likely to achieve lower utility yields than others.

5   Money and cognitive complexity

*And Mony (of what manner soever syned by the Sovereign of a Common-wealth)
is a sufficient measure of the valuye of all things else [beyond gold and silver],
between the Subjects of that Common-wealth. . . . In so far as this Concoction is,
as it were, the Sanguinifcation of the Common-wealth; for naturall Bloud is in
like manner made of the fruits of the earth; and circulating, nourisheth, by the
way, every Member of the Bod of Man.*

Thomas Hobbes, Leviathan

In this chapter and the next I will focus on money. There are sound economic and
psychological reasons for this focus. The economic reason for this attention to money,
which Schumpeter said was "exalted" by the capitalist system, is that money is the
medium for executing the market's central function: coordinating economic activity. The very concept of a *self*-regulating market requires monetary feedback, and
the market's network of transactions depends upon the information that money prices
provide. The coordinating function of the market would not work without it. But it
is the cognitive function that is of concern here.

Whereas the concept of *cognitive development* employed in the previous chapters
means the growing capacities of the mind to cope with increasingly complex events,
cognitive facilitation means the removal of concepts or circumstances that inhibit
such development and the use of conceptual technology that permits people to think
more clearly about their problems. Money may contribute to cognitive development; I think it does, but it is primarily an instrument of cognitive facilitation, a
tool for thinking, and, as we shall see, money may also be a fetter that constrains
clear thinking.

We will first examine the way money schemata, attributions, and abstractions
help individuals to cope with their environments, then turn to the relation of money
to thinking about space and time and social barriers. These, we will say, are aids to
thought. At the same time, however, the very advantages of money can limit thought
to channels that are not satisfying nor illuminating nor ethically justified. But to
some extent the market's very success loosens these fetters.

Cognitive facilitation

The mind has limited processing capacities: its short-term memory is truncated, its
rationality is severely "bounded," psychologists speak of people as "cognitive
misers," hoarding their small capacities for important uses.[1] The use of money
schemata both strains these limitations by substituting abstract money terms for
perceptually visible commodities like milk and meat, and relaxes these limitations
by reducing complexity and releasing mental space for more urgent uses. We use

---

[1] See, for example, Susan T. Fiske and Patricia Linville, "What Does the Schema Concept Buy Us?"
Personality and Social Psychology Bulletin 6 (1980): 543–57; Herbert Simon, *Models of Bounded Rationality,* 2 vols. (Cambridge: M.I.T. Press, 1982).

the terms *cognitive facilitation* to mean such aids to thinking and *cognitive fetters* to mean the associated handicaps. Given any individual's capacities for cognitive complexity, or for "formal operations" (Piaget), or for abstract thinking, the use of money schemata enhances these capacities in certain ways – and may distort thought in other ways.[2] First, we turn to specifications of the means whereby money clarifies and extends thinking processes.

The assistance of signs and symbols to thinking processes is widely appreciated. For example, Bandura says

The capability for intentional action is rooted in symbolic activity. Images of desirable futures foster courses of action designed to lead toward more distant goals. Through the medium of symbols people can solve problems without having to enact all the various alternative solutions. . . . Without symbolizing powers, humans would be incapable of reflective thought. A theory of human behavior therefore cannot afford to neglect symbolic activities.[3]

It is this power of money signs and symbols, sometimes called *schemata* by psychologists, that we will be exploring.

1. MONEY SCHEMATA AS TOOLS FOR THOUGHT. Among its many effects on the complex procedures of schema selection and use,[4] money permits the *reduction in the number of schemata* necessary to grapple with a problem. For example, instead of thinking of deprivation as lack of sufficient food and clothing and shelter and other things, a person using money schemata may conceive of deprivation as the lack of funds to buy these things. Most people prefer to employ only one schemata at a time, anyway;[5] money provides a convenient schema to fit this preference. Second, a money schema often permits a *more inclusive* criterion capturing more, though by no means all, desiderata. Third, given the tendency to let one schema stand for others, it is better that it should be a *representative* one, one that more adequately represents the class of things one is concerned about. Fourth, a money schema also permits *comparison* among specifically unlike things, as Weber and others have observed and as I shall further elaborate. For purposes of justice, Aristotle found in this standardizing capacity an excuse for money. Finally, money schemata awaken the sense of *potentiality,* for money "signs," that is, money's denotative meanings (but not money "symbols" representing its connotative meanings – see next chapter) are valued mostly for what money will fetch in exchange. Thus, whereas attention to money schemata may be conservative in one sense, their cognitive effect is to encourage, within a small ambit, thought about how things might be otherwise. As we shall see, however, money schemata may be constraining and limiting, as well.

2. CAUSAL ATTRIBUTION. In dealing with physical things, causal attribution increases with the physical and temporal proximity of a perceived "forcing" object and a perceived "receiving" object. When one physical object, A, "strikes" an-

[2] See Robert E. Lane, "Political Observers and Market Participants: The Effects on Cognition," *Political Psychology* 4 (1983): 455–82.
[3] Albert Bandura, *Social Learning Theory* (Englewood Cliffs, NJ: Prentice-Hall, 1977), 13.
[4] See Robert Axelrod, "Schema Theory: An Information Processing Model of Perception and Cognition," *American Political Science Review* 67 (1973): 1,248–66.
[5] Robert P. Abelson, "Social Psychology's Rational Man," in S. I. Benn and G. W. Mortimore, eds., *Rationality and the Social Sciences* (London: Routledge & Kegan Paul, 1976), 77.

other, B, if the two are adjacent and if B moves without delay, A is said to be the cause of that motion; if there is a distance between the two and a delay of a certain period, A is not said to have caused that movement.[6] With many variations this is the paradigm case of causal attribution among things. But money causes its effects in many different ways, often across great distances and over long and delayed time periods, imperceptibly, silently, even secretly. Whereas these silent, distant, delayed effects lead to creative fantasies of all kinds, they also liberate causal attributions from the here and now, from physical force and contiguity.

3. SENSE DATA AND MENTAL TRANSFORMATIONS. William James suggested that the "tender-minded" alternative to "tough-minded" reliance on a "sensationalistic" orientation, was an "intellectualistic" one, that is, a reliance more on the mind than the senses.[7] The mind does not merely receive and record sense data; it transforms them. In growing up, "the child . . . is translating redundancy [of sensory impressions] into a manipulable model of the environment that is governed by rules of implication." The child can then deal with "the nonpresent, with things that are remote in space, qualitative similarity, and time from the present situation."[8] These are the capacities that are stimulated by money schemata and their expanded causal attributions.

4. ENLARGING PRACTICALITY. The practicality and tough-minded orientation of the thing-minded materialist may well be retained by the users of money schemata, but that orientation is enlarged and liberated from physical property. Practicality in gemeinschaft dealt directly with land and things; in gesselschaft (i.e., a market economy) it deals with land and things as forms of capital convertible to money.[9] In *Middlemarch* George Eliot has her early nineteenth-century landed squires view the local banker with scorn as a mere "speculator." Forms of practicality change; for the businessperson the practicality of the market economy requires a more sophisticated knowledge of investment, multiple markets, distant opportunities, changing currencies, the prospects of a variety of industries, and much more; for the rest of us it requires a knowledge of wage schedules, pension schemes, mortgage rates, tax deductibles, as well as of houses and consumer durables. We must be alert; money values change more rapidly than do physical things, and require monitoring.

5. ABSTRACT THINKING. As mentioned, money is more abstract than physical things in the sense that as a representational symbol it has few intrinsic properties, and is generally represented in such invisible forms as credit or debit or as a set of records. Thus money lends itself to abstract thinking, a form of thought generally capable of handling problems intractable to concrete thinking.[10]

---

[6] A. Michotte, *The Perception of Causality* (New York: Basic Books, 1963).

[7] William James, *Pragmatism: A New Name for Some Old Ways of Thinking* (London: Longmans, Green, 1908), 12.

[8] Jerome S. Bruner, "The Course of Cognitive Growth," *American Psychologist* 19, no. 1 (1964); reprinted as Warner Module no. 400 (1973): 13.

[9] Tönnies observed the increase in cognitive demands by this transformation: "It marks great progress in thinking . . . when the individual and society begin to handle land as a special kind of property and capital." Ferdinand Tönnies, *Community and Society*, trans. and ed. C. P. Loomis (1887; reprint New York: Harper Torchbook, 1963), 86.

[10] Most of the many formulations of this view stem ultimately from Jean Piaget. See his *Psychology of Intelligence*, trans. M. Piercy and D. E. Berlyne (1947; reprint Totowa, NJ: Littlefield, Adams, 1960).

Two illustrations will reveal different facets of the way abstract thinking frees the individual from restraints. One has to do with the involvement of the self in a problem. The vivid, immediate, and personally compelling things or events before the eyes (the *availability heuristic*) are likely to be heavily ego-involved; indeed, that is what makes their images compelling. But raising them to a more abstract level inevitably implies other people; rules and principles governing others as well as the self come into view and Piagetian "egocentricity" (only "my" thoughts are real) is overcome. Generalization of this kind is, for example, the method of ethics.

The second illustration has to do with a different form of abstraction involving calculating abilities. Before children can calculate ratios, they divide shares equally regardless of contribution; when they have learned to do ratios they often choose the justice of proportionality.[11] Do children who are more experienced in dealing with money learn proportionality quicker and better? H. G. Furth has argued that children who use money in their own active construction of reality have a head start in certain respects.[12] We do not know the answers, but we do know that early experience with verbal language greatly favors child development. Perhaps it is also true of money languages as well.

Given people's preferences for concrete thinking, for what has been called "sweeping concretization," and their general tendency to ignore "pallid" background material in favor of the vivid and the personal, any aid to abstract thinking must be regarded as a welcome assistance to a difficult process.

6. EMOTIONAL DISENGAGEMENT. Simmel's view that money payments liberate the individual from entanglements with persons and things suggests the kind of separation of self from involvement in a process of thought forming part of our definition of cognitive complexity. Simmel says, "Full liberation becomes possible only after the money economy has succeeded the natural [traditional] economy and the money payment the factual obligation. The personality is then divorced from the product and at full liberty to obtain that money in whatever way it may choose."[13] Elsewhere Simmel speaks of intellectuality as a protection against overinvolvement. Given people's emotional involvement with money, the point has merit only in comparison to such physical things as heirlooms, family homesteads, sentimental gifts, or possibly the "known and fondled objects" in the family circle of *The World We Have Lost*.[14]

7. QUANTIFICATION. To return to a point made in Chapter 3: "The money economy," says Simmel, ". . . has filled the days of . . . many people with weighing, calculating, with numerical determinations, with a reduction of qualitative values to quantitative ones."[15] "[T]he results of incessant quantification have become too gross and life threatening to be ignored," said Lewis Mumford.[16] Thought has

[11] J. Hook and Thomas Cook, "Equity Theory and the Cognitive Ability of Children," *Psychological Bulletin* 86 (1979): 429–45.
[12] H. G. Furth, *The World of Grown-ups: Children's Conceptions of Society* (New York: Elsevier, 1980).
[13] Georg Simmel, *The Philosophy of Money*, trans. T. Bottomore and D. Frisby (1887; reprint London: Routledge & Kegan Paul, 1963), 219–20.
[14] Peter Laslett, *The World We Have Lost*, 2d ed. (New York: Scribner's, 1971), 22.
[15] Georg Simmel, "The Metropolis and Mental Life," in Kurt H. Wolff, ed. and trans. *The Social Theory of Georg Simmel* (Glencoe, IL: Free Press, 1950), 154.
[16] Lewis Mumford, "The Integration of Science and Life," in Robert Caravillano, L. Skehan, and W.

become "logistics," said Horkheimer and Adorno.[17] The revolt against the "clio-metricians" (Barzun) by historians[18] reflects this same theme. But, in fact, the nomothetic use of cases by lawyers, social workers, and clinicians as well as the flourishing narrative history of historians blunts the criticism. How would one tell if the quantification that money encourages displaces appreciation of the unique or exploration of qualitative differences? If a quantitative measure of skills is not disqualified by the very terms of the argument, one might search the record of aptitude scores for a decline in verbal and a rise in quantitative skills, but in fact they are *positively* correlated and rise and decline together, although there are many individual divergences.

8. ANALYTICAL THINKING: WHOLES AND PARTS. Anticipating the discussion in Chapter 7 of *differentiation,* which is one kind of cognitive development, we ask if the return of differentiating skills after their relative deemphasis in agricultural societies can be traceable to the development of a money economy. Differentiation requires people to break some observation, event, or problem into its component parts, a capacity called "field independence" and is contrasted to "field dependence" where things are viewed only holistically.[19] Two features of monetary thinking suggest reasons why experience with money may promote field independence. First, it seems that by their very nature, money sums are made of differentiable parts; they are aggregated and disaggregated many times a day. Second, as we shall see in the same later discussion, in less developed societies it is those who work for money wages, as contrasted to those who remain in the household economies, who are more field independent, that is, more able to see the parts and reassemble them in different combinations.[20] Also, in primitive societies people seem to be less able than Westerners to imagine alternatives, to "shuffle things around in their heads."[21] Whereas this inability has been attributed to the lack of the kind of training presented by Western education, it is plausible to believe that, in smaller part, it also may be due to lack of experience in disaggregating wholes and in thinking about the kinds of alternatives made available by discretionary money expenditures.

9. PREFERENCE FOR DISJUNCTIVE EXPLANATIONS. People prefer *disjunctive* explanations (either this *or* that) to conjunctive ones (this *plus* that), for example, as in the (conjunctive) analysis of variance.[22] One of the advantages of money is its

Janes, eds., *Science and the Future of Man* (Cambridge: M.I.T. Press, 1970), 107.

[17] Max Horkheimer and Theodor W. Adorno, *Dialectic of Enlightenment,* trans. J. Cumming (1944; reprint New York: Herder & Herder, 1972), 37.

[18] Jacques Barzun, *Clio and the Doctors: Psycho-History, Quanto-History, and History* (Chicago: University of Chicago Press, 1974). In this chorus of voices raised against quantification, the critics of the business schools may seem out of place. Yet the recent decline in American productivity has been attributed to "management by the numbers" instead of by intimate substantive knowledge of technology and the productive process. See Robert H. Hayes and William Abernathy, "Managing our Way to Economic Decline," *Harvard Business Review* 58 (1980): 67–77.

[19] Herman A. Witkin, R. B. Dyk, H. F. Faterson, D. R. Goodenough, and S. A. Karp, *Psychological Differentiation* (New York: Wiley/Erlbaum, 1974). For a criticism of the measures used, see E. A. Zigler, "A Measure in Search of a Theory?" *Contemporary Psychology* 8 (1963): 133–5.

[20] Thomas J. Gamble and Pauline Ginsberg, "Differentiation, Cognition, and Social Evolution," *Journal of Cross-Cultural Psychology* 12 (1981): 445–59.

[21] Barbara Lloyd, *Perception and Cognition* (Harmondsworth, UK: Penguin, 1972), 132.

[22] Abelson, "Social Psychology's Rational Man," 77. Incidentally, this preference for disjunctive ex-

divisibility, and thinking about money focuses on the contributions of component parts to make a sum large enough for the purpose at hand. Things are more or less expensive. Tentatively one might infer that thinking about money encourages concepts of degree so essential to conjunctive explanations.

One might also expect money to help prepare people for another form of disliked explanation, probabilistic explanation, if only because money facilitates wagers. But given people's poor records in estimating probabilities and their tendencies not to use the full range of information on probabilities that may be given to them, this hypothesis must await investigation.

10. PSYCHOLOGICAL MOBILITY. Psychological mobility means the capacity to think of oneself or others in situations contrary to fact or, more generally, to imagine how situations might be other than what they are. It is inhibited by thing-mindedness, concrete thinking, and stimulus boundedness. In Daniel Lerner's analysis of Middle Eastern societies, psychological immobility (he used the term first) was said to be the most important cause of the failure of these societies to modernize their (then) poverty-stricken economies. Lerner's respondents were unable to imagine themselves or others in positions different from the ones they occupied.[23] To the degree that thinking about the *potential* and *alternative* uses of money generalizes to other situations, the lack of a developed money economy may have inhibited psychological mobility as it inhibited economic development. Lerner believed that psychological mobility was a product of literacy and urbanism, but again it is plausible to believe that the market also contributes to this skill by encouraging the search for alternatives; for example, Lerner's prototypical case of a person with emerging psychological mobility was a grocer. And the skill may, indeed, generalize across situations: Inkeles and Smith report that experience in a third world factory expands horizons to include preferences among public policies totally alien to the village world from which the factory workers came.[24] Exposure to factory and urban conditions lifted these factory workers out of their parochial village mentalities and made the larger world relevant, but by receiving pay for their work, in some measure they had also experienced the expanded experience of choosing among alternatives made possible by their pay.

Space, time, and cosmopolitanism

Poverty, wealth, and cognitive facilitation. Poorer people and poorer countries might be expected to respond to the "cognitive facilitation" of money in ways different from richer people and countries. In advanced societies, the very poor understand all too well the value of money; indeed, they "tend to be obsessed

planation has the great disadvantage that once some easily available monetary explanation has been settled on, further dispositional or situational explanations are discouraged. Perhaps it is for this reason that once the critics of the market have explained some social defect as due to materialism, they do not look further, and, even worse, once market defenders have discovered a material advantage in one course of action, they believe they have exhausted the process of explanation.
[23] Daniel Lerner, *The Passing of Traditional Society* (New York: Free Press, 1958).
[24] Alex Inkeles and David Smith, *Becoming Modern* (Cambridge: Harvard University Press, 1974).

by money."[25] Above the poverty level, however, income is not closely related to attitudes toward money.[26] One reason is that experience with money does not teach (children) prudential uses of their money unless the parents set a good example,[27] a finding that suggests a limitation on the experiential theory we have been interpreting. That limitation would be to the effect that experience is a better teacher if it is assisted by following a model.

Among the developing countries, the way money facilitates thought is likely to be different in some respects from the way money facilitates thought in a developed economy. People in countries or regions moving from household economies to cash economies are inevitably confused, apparently tending to understand the equivalence of money for purchasable things, but not the uses of money as a "store of value" or the more sophisticated uses of the money language.[28] The conversion from a currency with intrinsic values, like cattle, to a money currency is widely disruptive.[29] For some developing societies, whatever analytical skills may stem from using money must be learned at first under circumstances of substantial stress.

The lifting of spatial horizons

Like ownership of physical property, ownership of money implies "a right of control over things . . . [that] must be exclusive as against others,"[30] but in itself does not exclude others from space. On the other hand, it makes relevant to the imagination spaces other than that which one occupies. With enough of it, no country is beyond reach. Furthermore, because of the vast world network of money, what happens in distant countries is immediately and practically relevant to most of us: the wages and skills of the electronic workers in Taiwan and the miners in Chilean copper mines, the fiscal policies of Japan, and the oil policies of Saudi Arabia all affect our standard of living or our job security. Like its sponsoring market, money is geographically mobile and expansive, creating stakes (and therefore interests) in distant places. But the cognitive facilitation that collapses distances does not also collapse loyalties and animosities, for the world network of monetary, usually mutually beneficial, relations reduces parochialism, patriotism, or other primordial loyalties only very slowly, if at all.[31]

The extension of temporal horizons

As a store of value and a standard of deferred payment money facilitates saving, debt, and interest. A money economy facilitates a comparison of present and future

[25] Adrian Furnham and Alan Lewis, *The Economic Mind: The Social Psychology of Economic Behaviour* (Brighton, UK: Wheatsheaf/Harvester, 1986), 56.

[26] Kent Yamauchi and Donald Templer, "The Development of a Money Attitude Scale," *Journal of Personality Assessment* 46 (1982): 522–8.

[27] H. Marshall and L. Magruder, "Relations Between Parent Money Education Practices and Children's Knowledge and Use of Money," *Child Development* 31 (1960): 253–84. Furth, on the other hand, finds that children who have had more experience with money understand monetary concepts better. See Furth, *The World of Grown-ups.*

[28] Leonard Doob, *Becoming More Civilized* (New Haven: Yale University Press, 1960), 91–2, 223.

[29] Margaret Mead, *Cultural Patterns and Technical Change* (New York: Mentor, 1955), 240.

[30] L. T. Hobhouse, *Sociology and Philosophy* (London: G. Bell & Sons, 1966), 82.

[31] See Henry Bretton, *The Power of Money* (Albany: State University of New York Press, 1980), 219.

needs, borrowing from the future to serve the present and providing for the future by deferring present gratification. At the same time that it makes provision for the future more easily possible, it also makes it more necessary, necessary at least if we compare the wage earner to the land-owning farmer. The first sense of cognitive facilitation through temporal comparisons and control lies in the way money makes time more calculable, controllable, and valuable. "The price system," said Daniel Bell, "is a mechanism for the efficient rationing of time."[32]

1. MONEY SCHEMATA DO NOT OVERCOME THE DESIRE FOR GRATIFICATION NOW. In their "rational life plans" Americans save as best they can for: emergencies, that is, for a rainy day, unemployment, illness" (45% of all savings); for retirement (31%); for their childrens' education and other predictable family needs (22%); and for purchasing a house (8%), durable goods (7%), and so forth.[33] But the facilitation is more cognitive than conative, for people have trouble acting on their cognitions. Just as the internationalization of money only marginally affects "locals" whose attention remains close to home, so the possibility of rationing time through money only marginally affects many people who find the present unbearably urgent. The desire for goods and the physical "materialism of present-day society [are] having an adverse effect on saving, . . . [for] the desire to save is frequently pushed into the background and saving becomes residual."[34] Money schemata apparently do not make the desires of the future as "real" as the desires of the present, especially in American society where saving rates are lower and installment buying is more extensive than in other modern economies.

2. THE STIMULUS VALUE OF MONEY IS REDUCED BY ITS ABSTRACTNESS AND IN-CREASED BY ITS POTENTIALS. Compared to the claims of *things,* the claims of money are temporally liberating in a sense that partially conflicts with what I have just said. Attractive things within one's field of vision are likely to be more seductive than something as abstract as money, which represents only potential indulgences. Children confronted with a choice between more attractive but deferred snack foods and less attractive but immediately available snack foods tend to choose the *less* attractive but immediately available items when both are visible during a voluntary waiting period. However, after a brief introduction to the goods, when neither is visible during the waiting period, children are willing to defer gratification to get the more attractive items. *Informational,* as contrasted to vivid *consummatory* cues (the "crunchy, salty taste of pretzels"), helped children to delay consumption.[35] Is it not possible that because of its "colorness and indifference" (Simmel), a money

[32] Daniel Bell, *The Coming of Post-Industrial Society* (New York: Basic Books, 1973), 452.
[33] George Katona, *Psychological Economics* (New York: Elsevier, 1975), 235. Data are for 1966.
[34] Ibid., 237.
[35] Walter Mischel, "Processes in the Delay of Gratification," in Leonard Berkowitz, ed., *Advances in Experimental Social Psychology,* vol. 7 (New York: Academic Press, 1974). In a similar experiment Ross found that the visibility of a promised reward reduced the intrinsic interest in an enjoyable task. See M. Ross, "Salience of Reward and Intrinsic Motivation," *Journal of Personality and Social Psychology* 32 (1975): 245–54.

schema offers more informational cues than consummatory ones, permitting deferral more easily than a commodity schema with its consummatory cues would do.

The contrary influence emphasized the wider potentials of money and the provision of credit in a money economy. The stimulus value of money's many potentialities and the greater ease of borrowing might mean that money stimulates what has been called our desire for "instant gratification," making the problem of saving more difficult.[36] The forces at work are in conflict; their resolution in a money economy is uncertain: The Japanese save about 15 percent of their income and the Americans less than 5 percent. One reason for this complexity is that the decision to provide for the future through saving is not a simple process of "waiting" (Marshall) or a characterological trait of "patience" (Fisher) or a function of government pensions (Friedman), but rather is a complex process involving a variety of dispositional traits, of which the most important is the sense of personal control (Chapter 9).

3. MONEY FACILITATES A LONGER TERM TELEOLOGICAL PERSPECTIVE – IN SOME CASES. Fleshing out the concept of "potentialities" employed here, Simmel mentions another way that a money economy encourages futurity: *longer term purposiveness*, a teleological orientation that necessarily points to the future. In a characteristic turn of the century (1907) statement, Simmel suggested that "the impulsiveness and emotional character of primitive people is undoubtedly due in part to the shortness of their teleological series. . . . Extension of the teleological series is in the first place due to the introduction of money."[37] Although laboratory work finds no relationship between impulse control and future time orientation,[38] Simmel's interpretation of the time orientation of less developed societies is supported by a major work on the psychology of time: "Embedded as they are in a network of [current] mutual obligations and with fewer choices available, traditional peoples are likely to pay relatively little attention to the future."[39]

Comparative studies are instructive. In Kluckhohn and Strodtbeck's study comparing the time orientations of Navaho, Zuni, Mexican-Americans, Mormons, and Texas Anglo-Presbyterians, they do find that the more commercialized Texan Presbyterians and Mormons are more future oriented.[40] In seeming confirmation of Simmel's view, Trinidadian blacks generally spend their money as soon as it is received. But,

the same people saved money, planned elaborately, and were willing to give up competing immediate gratifications in order to plan ahead for future outcomes (such as annual feasts, religious events, and carnival celebrations) whose preparation and realization was under their

---

[36] See Shlomo Maitel, *Minds, Markets, and Money: Psychological Foundations of Economic Behavior* (New York: Basic Books, 1982). Maitel, like many others, believes that advertising and easy credit are the causes of the decline in saving in the United States.

[37] Simmel, *Philosophy of Money*, 232–3.

[38] Leonard Doob, *Patterning of Time* (New Haven: Yale University Press, 1971), 264.

[39] Ibid., 53.

[40] Florence Kluckhohn and Fred L. Strodtbeck, *Variations in Value Orientations* (Evanston, Ill.: Row, Peterson, 1961).

own control . . . making it evident that any generalization about their cross-situational "impulsivity" are quite unwarranted.[41]

Clearly, social norms (including the norm of deferral) make a difference; the Western "time gestalt" is not characteristic of other societies.[42] The attractiveness of whatever it is that is being saved for also makes a difference, especially whether the object of saving is in some sense one's own and under one's own control.[43] These are all modifying elements of any money schema employed.

4. TRUST IS A CONDITION FOR DEFERRED GRATIFICATION, WITH OR WITHOUT MONEY. The sense of *trust,* meaning both trust in the future and trust of others, makes a difference in the way money is employed to calculate and provide for future needs. Contrary to the critics' (e.g., Erich Fromm's) view that money economies breed suspicion of others, measures of trust/distrust in people show higher rates of trust in countries that developed money (market) economies earlier and have had them longer.[44] There is also other evidence that the low level of mutual trust in some developing societies makes market transactions difficult to consummate.[45] In her studies comparing the deferral of gratification among poorer Eastern and better-off Western Jews in Israel, Sharone Maitel found that the two groups held similar values on the advantage of saving and deferred gratification, but that in actual practice the Eastern Jews were not able to live up to their verbally expressed values because of their lack of trust in the promises of those who said that subjects would get more if they waited.[46]

Money and the price system is, indeed, "a mechanism for the efficient rationing of time" and may help to distance tempting goods, but the mechanism does not run by itself, for its operators must be endowed not just with the economists' "patience," but with a sense of control, purposiveness fitted to some goal for which the money is useful, and a sense of trust. Nor will the influence of money on temporal ordering work without barriers across life's domains. Reviewing family history studies, Tamara Haraven says that it has been "particularly important" to realize "that family behavior was paced differently in different domains, that peo-

---

[41] Mischel, "Processes in the Delay of Gratification," 254–5.

[42] Irvin L. Child, "Personality in Culture," in Edgar F. Borgatta and William W. Lambert, eds., *Handbook of Personality Theory and Research* (Chicago: Rand McNally, 1968), 82–145 at 86.

[43] See T. D. Graves, *Time Perspective and Deferred Gratification Patterns in a Tri-ethnic Community* (Boulder: University of Colorado Press, 1961).

[44] Ronald Inglehart and Jacques-Rene Rabier, "Aspirations Adapt to Situations – But Why are the Belgians so Much Happier than the French? A Cross-Cultural Analysis of the Subjective Quality of Life," in Frank M. Andrews, ed., *Research on the Quality of Life* (Ann Arbor, MI: Institute for Social Research, 1986), 52. Alex Inkeles and Larry Diamond, "Personal Development and National Development: A Cross-Cultural Perspective," in Alexander Szalai and Frank M. Andrews, eds., *Quality of Life: Comparative Studies* (Beverly Hills, CA: Sage, 1980), 73–109, at 97. See also Gabriel A. Almond and Sidney Verba, *The Civic Culture: Political Attitudes and Democracy in Five Nations* (Princeton: Princeton University Press, 1963), 267.

[45] In the Philippines, "among those people fully involved in the commercial sector of the economy, one of the most powerful and obvious impediments to corporate economic activities is a pervasive mistrust of others, fortified by innumerable accounts of double dealing in the town." D. L. Szanton, *Estancia in Transition,* quoted in George M. Guthrie, "A Social Psychological Analysis of Modernization in the Philippines," *Journal of Cross-Cultural Psychology* 8 (June 1977): 186.

[46] Sharone Maitel, "An Analysis of Delay of Gratification as a Two-Part Process" (Master's thesis, Tel Aviv University, 1976), reported in Maitel, *Minds, Markets, and Money,* 63–4.

ple could be 'modern' at work and 'traditional' at home, and that the family exercised the power of initiative and choice in accepting new ways of life.''[47] The
family can choose and vary its own time scheduling, employing or not employing
the facilitating and hindering temporal influences of money.

Cosmopolitanism

Horizons are broadened by including other people in one's world of discourse and
recognition. Unlike nationality or most forms of community, the network of persons
connected by money is boundless; one enters it without permission or passport
(other than money itself, of course) and, if one is suitably concealed behind a business identity, without the hazards of racial or religious prejudice. Where money has
supplanted kinship as an organizing principle for society, "strangers" with money
may be admitted to trade and custom and personhood (no mean thing) although they
may not be admitted to honor or, precisely, to kinship. Money, as a lingua franca,
talks. Through their command of money, marginal peoples (the Scots in Britain;
the Jews, Lebanese, and Armenians in Europe and the United States; the Ibo in
Nigeria) can often change castelike restrictions to class advantages – and national
economic advantages as well. If people are to be judged by externals, it is better
that they be judged by their money than by their races or ethnicities.

A market economy has been said to erode "primordial loyalties" of these kinds;
it has also been said to exploit them,[48] thus exacerbating them. The record is more
favorable to the erosion of invidious religious distinctions than racial ones, but
where a racial minority has had market experience, even racial discrimination has
been said to be undermined.[49] Is it possible that the British Bill of Rights of 1689
was favored by the rise of commerce and the consequent redefinition of statuses in
income rather then religious terms, and that the Civil Rights Act of 1964 in the
United States found support from the perception of blacks as a group characterized
by remedial *poverty* rather than by irremediable race? Praying to money, as Marx
said we did, might be better than praying to a jealous god though there are better
objects of prayer.

Cognitive fetters: the single standard

Choosing the standard for evaluation. If comparisons of dissimilar things
are made on only one dimension – in the case of the market the dimension is money
– is it not likely that this dimension will be overemployed not only as a matter of
convenience but as a way of economizing scarce cognitive resources? The cognitive
facilitation we have examined makes choices easier and to some extent enlarges

[47]Tamara K. Haraven, "Family Time and Historical Time," in Alice S. Rossi, Jerome Kagan, and
Haraven, eds., *The Family* (New York: Norton, 1978).
[48]Stanley B. Greenberg, *Race in Capitalist Development: Studies in South Africa, Alabama, Northern
Ireland, and Israel* (New Haven: Yale University Press, 1980).
[49]Thomas Sowell, "Three Black Histories," *The Wilson Quarterly* 3 (Winter 1979): 96–106. For further
treatment see Sowell's *Markets and Minorities* (New York: Basic Books, 1981). The proposition that
Caribbean blacks do better in the United States has been challenged by evidence that their higher status
is due to their concentration in New York, where black mobility is higher than elsewhere.

them; it makes space, time, and variety of persons (cosmopolitanism) easier to manage. Yet genuine cognitive facilitation does not take any single standard of evaluation, such as money, for granted, but rather, from a higher perspective, chooses among standards.

If any single standard is given by the society, or subtly rewarded to the exclusion of other more appropriate standards, that standard is as much a fetter as a source of facilitation. Does the erosion of social norms, widely attributed to the market, achieve only the institution of a single, coercive market norm in their place? We will examine one aspect of this question, the influence of exchange on personal relations, in Chapter 11; here we deal with the closely related question of the effect of a money standard on personal relations and go on to examine nonpecuniary values of things, the self, the regulation of human behavior, ethics, and other processes dealing with intrinsic values. Where the single monetary criterion obstructs others, it may fairly be said to constrain thought. We turn briefly to these in the following text.

Persons: monetizing human relations. In a capitalist society, said Erich Fromm, "People are . . . experienced as the embodiment of a quantitative exchange value."[50] In Marx's famous phrase about assuming "man as man" he protested the misapplication of the money schema in bourgeois society, because then money can buy love.[51] Marx was dealing with multiple conflicting tendencies, some of which are quite independent of what might be called the "monetization of reality." does money *buy* love, or is it that people with money are somehow endowed with other favorable characteristics, an endowment following cognitive balance theory, which organizes perceptions such that all good things cluster together separately from all bad things, which also cluster together?[52]

Although the cold–warm dimension dominates person perceptions,[53] the rich–poor dimension has similar, if weaker, powers. As we will see in Chapter 11, experiments show that people do use "rich" and "poor" as default values for assessing the desirable personality qualities a person has. In this study by Luft, "the hypothetical rich man was seen as relatively healthy, happy, and well adjusted, while the hypothetical poor man was seen as maladjusted and unhappy." In fact, the measured qualities of real poor men in the sample had no more nor less of the unwholesome qualities attributed to them than others in the vicinity.[54]

[50] Erich Fromm, *The Sane Society* (New York: Rinehart, 1955), 116.
[51] Karl Marx, "The Meaning of Human Requirements," in Dirk Struik, ed., M. Milligan, trans., *Philosophical Manuscripts of 1844,* (New York: International Publishers, 1964), 169.
[52] In the process of socialization, "by the mid-teens young people tend to evaluate general inequalities, riches and rich people positively, and poverty, unemployment and poor people negatively." Barrie G. Stacey, "Economic Socialization," in Samuel S. Long, ed., *Political Behavior Annual,* vol. 1 (Boulder, CO: Westview Press, 1984), ms. copy p. 40.
[53] Seymour E. Asch, "Forming Impressions of Personality," *Journal of Abnormal and Social Psychology* 41 (1946): 258–90.
[54] Joseph Luft, "Monetary Value and the Perception of Persons," *Journal of Social Psychology* 46 (1957): 245–51. The richer students were more prone to this judgment than the poorer students, illustrating another principle: People prefer others like themselves. Compare Lord Bryce: "The feeling of the American public towards the very rich is, so far as a stranger can judge, one of curiosity and wonder rather than of respect. . . . They are admired as a famous runner or jockey is admired. . . . But they do

1. Thus, the money schema is a fetter because it uses money as a misleading default value in evaluating others.

The appropriateness of the money standard for evaluating people, however, is largely denied. Most Americans (about 60%) disagree with the proposition that people *should* be judged by their wealth.[55] Given the evidence from Luft's study, these denials cannot be taken as generally operative; rather they serve as an indicator of a social norm that discourages a money standard in evaluating persons.

2. It seems that the American culture offers resistance, preferring a standard of character and personality integral to persons.

Does money increase invidious social comparisons? A second facet of this problem of monetary standards in interpersonal comparisons deals with the possibility that the facilitation of comparisons by the ready availability of a single standard *encourages invidiousness,* or, to use a more neutral term, *social comparisons.* This would be undesirable on at least three grounds: It encourages rivalry as well as competition, discourages cooperation, and, it has been found, is associated with a lower sense of well-being than that associated with self-comparisons – employing one's own best efforts as a standard.[56]

Although it seems to be the case that people are more likely to make social comparisons of their levels of pay than of their housing,[57] a careful study in the 1970s of *Income Equity among U.S. Workers* found that in fact wage comparisons, when they were made, did not prompt self-damaging feelings of envy or loss of well-being. Thus: "wage comparisons had no direct effect on satisfaction with living standards" and only a "limited and indirect effect" on more basic economic satisfaction.[58] Other "relative deprivation" studies tend to confirm this finding.[59] In the United States, at least, there is a surprising lack of envy in comparisons of money income or possessions across broad income strata, partly because there is a general consensus on what people in various occupations and life strata should

not necessarily receive either flattery or social deference." *The American Commonwealth* (New York: Macmillan, 1910), 814. For British attitudes, see Adrian Furnham, "Attributions for Affluence," *Personality and Individual Differences* 4 (1983): 31–40.

[55] But the 19 percent of the national sample who believed that "money is one of the most important things" in life were very modestly more likely to judge others by their wealth. Morris Rosenberg and Leonard I. Pearlin, "Social Class and Self-Esteem Among Children and Adults," *American Journal of Sociology* 84 (1978): 53–77.

[56] Jonathan Freedman, *Happy People* (New York: Harcourt, Brace, 1980), 75. See also Chapter 12 in this volume on "downward comparisons."

[57] On wages, see Ephraim Yuchtman (Yaar), "Effects of Psychological Factors on Subjective Well-Being," in Burkhard Strumpel, ed., *Economic Means for Human Needs: Social Indicators of Well-Being and Discontent* (Ann Arbor, MI: Institute for Social Research, 1976); on housing, see Angus Campbell, Philip E. Converse, and Willard L. Rodgers, *The Quality of American Life* (New York: Russell Sage, 1976), chap. 6.

[58] Richard T. Curtin, *Income Equity among U.S. Workers: The Bases and Consequences of Deprivation* (New York: Praeger, 1977), 55.

[59] Faye J. Crosby, *Relative Deprivation and Working Women* (New York: Oxford University Press, 1982); W. G. Runciman, *Relative Deprivation and Social Justice* (Berkeley: University of California Press, 1966). In fact, both of these studies show that the sense of relative deprivation is minimal. It is uncertain whether the facilitation of comparisons made possible by money schemata increases invidious comparisons where reference to the uniqueness of things or material possessions (thing-mindedness) would not.

receive[60] and partly because people believe incomes of those in more elevated occupations are generally "earned" (with luck considered to be an appropriate basis for income).[61] In any event, praise or privileges granted to another but withheld from the self are likely to be regarded with even more invidiousness than pay. Indeed, there is some evidence that comparisons employing public and objective data arouse *less* envy than those employing private data, because, without information, the imagination always suspects that others are better treated than they actually are.[62] In this sense, the employment of money schemata does not encourage invidiousness across the social spectrum. This is a stabilizing, indeed pacifying, force in society.

3. We do not find that money, especially wages, increases invidiousness and in that sense it is not a fetter to such cognitions as person perception or such emotions as benign feelings toward others.

The gains to cognitive power that come from the widespread use of money cost something, though less than has been feared. They increase the use of money as a false criterion for judging people; money criteria do seem to dominate the belief that people should be judged by what they are, rather than what they earn, but we find little evidence that they provide grounds for invidiousness or hostile person perceptions.

Things as commodities

Another familiar criticism of the money schema is the conversion of things to commodities, that is, items for sale whose value does not derive from use but from actual or potential exchange. Cognitively, this is thought to have the effect of blunting perception. Tönnies puts it this way: "Goods become commodities. A commodity is for its owner nothing but a means to acquire other commodities. This essential quality makes all commodities as such equal and reduces their differences to a quantitative level. Money is the expression of this equality."[63] Stripped of hyperbole, the argument has merit; by definition the use of price to facilitate exchange implies a common denominator that may govern evaluation where other properties of the thing in question, such as its beauty or its serviceability would do better. Not only does exchange value "hollow out," aesthetics (Simmel), it also reduces the variety of the world; it makes a mockery of uniqueness. When a businessman looks at the Black Forest in terms of lumber, he has narrowed his cognitive span. Wilde defines such a person as a *cynic* ("a man who knows the price of everything and the value of nothing"). I know of no evidence that indicates an increase in this form of materialism and there is some evidence of its decline,[64] but

[60] Sidney Verba and Gary R. Orren, *Equality in America: The View from the Top* (Cambridge: Harvard University Press, 1985).
[61] Robert E. Lane, *Political Ideology: Why the American Common Man Believes What He Does* (New York: Free Press, 1962); Lee Rainwater, *What Money Buys: Inequality and the Social Meanings of Income* (New York: Basic Books, 1974).
[62] Edward E. Lawler, III, "Pay and Organizational Effectiveness," in Richard M. Steers and Lyman W. Porter, eds., *Motivation and Work Behavior* (New York: McGraw-Hill, 1975).
[63] Tönnies, *Community and Society,* 181. Marx and Lukacs's expression, "the fetishism of commodities" is misleading, for fetishes are unique and not exchangeable for each other.
[64] See Chapter 17 in this volume, "Maximizing Pay: Costs and Consequences;" also Ronald Inglehart, *The Silent Revolution* (Princeton: Princeton University Press, 1972).

it is plausible to believe that the salience of price information will dominate other information in a monetary economy and thus become a fetter.

In this sense (4) money reduces, rather than expands, the number of schemata employed.

Judging the self on the single dimension of money

Since people tend to judge themselves along the same dimensions conventionally used for judging others, all the arguments against assessing persons by their incomes apply to self-assessment. But there is one other argument dealing with self-assessment by a single standard that must be counted against the dominance of the money dimension. That critical good, self-esteem (Chapter 10), is greatly aided if people can *choose* the dimension on which they are to be judged – employing the principle of *psychological centrality,* that is, selecting favorable grounds for assessing the self. We know that in high school children are relatively free to choose their own grounds among three principal criteria – athletics, social popularity, and academic achievement – with great variation among schools and social classes.[65] The substitution in adulthood of the single money standard would narrow the choice further and deprive many young adults of their previous grounds for self-esteem.

Certainly (5) the imposition of an exclusive money standard for judging the self would be a most unfortunate fetter, but in a society where there is scope to choose the grounds on which a person will be judged, that single standard will be resisted.

Money rewards as a substitute for understanding

The use of short-term money rewards to regulate behavior may represent a substitution of stimulus–response mechanisms for understanding. Token economies and a form of behavioral therapy are based on this principle.[66] In these ways money payments serve as an instrument of control that shortcuts education and eliminates cognition, following the Skinnerian doctrine that each person is the history of his or her reinforcements and not a reflective or even curious individual.

(6) Money payments that reinforce behavior as a substitute for explanation, persuasion, and understanding also substitute a money schema for a much more complex set of schemata that would truly represent cognitive facilitation; this usage represents genuine cognitive fetters.

Consumer markets avoid this characterization because of their persistent efforts at persuasion. Internal labor markets, however, like the token economies they sometimes resemble, are vulnerable (Chapter 17).

Ethics and the monetary dimension

Money is not necessarily a dimension of evil and corruption: Not only is there philanthropy, but also thrift, ambition, prudence, and financial independence to be enlisted on the moral side. Is it not the case, however, that the contemplation of every value as an alternative to money threatens all intrinsic values? Walzer's "blocked

---

[65] Morris Rosenberg, *Society and the Adolescent Self-Image* (Princeton: Princeton University Press, 1965).
[66] See Teodor Ayllon and Nathan Azrin, *The Token Economy: A Motivational System for Therapy and Rehabilitation* (New York: Appleton-Century-Crofts, 1968); J. Wolpe, *Psychotherapy by Reciprocal Inhibition* (Stanford: Stanford University Press, 1958).

exchanges''[67] do not also block the use of money as a ''standard of value'' (Chapter 2). There is nothing in the market or in the concept of money that would inhibit the widespread use of this money standard, and even government is powerless to influence such private thought.

There is a residual consideration. Morality involves intention; the measuring rod of money has no means of measuring that – nor responsibility, nor good will, nor benevolence and beneficence. Critics of utilitarianism have amply demonstrated the inadequacy of consequentialist arguments to give an ethical accounting of an act.[68] Like the market itself, money accounts are indifferent to *why* a person acted as he or she did. We tread familiar ground; these are no more than reminders.

Loosening the fetters: limits to the single standard

The multiple values of a market society (as contrasted to gemeinschaft) – the variety of personalities in a society where individualism licenses (but does not always encourage) individuality, the many social functions requiring specialized knowledge where command of that knowledge rather than money brings honor and self-esteem, the cultural variety facilitated by international trade, and the cosmopolitanism that is protected by the substitution of a money schema for ethnic and religious schemata – all offer resistances to the single standard. With increase in per capita national income, the value of money to individuals seems to decline. For example, in Japan, the nation that has experienced the most radical cultural change in the postwar years, the declining proportions of people of successive age cohorts agreeing that ''money is the most important thing'' to teach a child reveals in Table 5.1 in exaggerated form similar cultural changes in other countries. The data clearly show that it is not so much that individuals change their minds about the value of money as that they are gradually replaced by those who find other values more important. Later data in the West have revealed that this kind of rapid change does not survive recessions and the slowing down of economic growth, but the cohorts growing up in affluence and peace retain their relative depreciation of the importance of money, compared to other values, through their mature years.[69]

The process is familiar to economists: Scarcity makes a wanted good precious; relieve the scarcity and the relative importance of the good declines.

Summary

The denotative, descriptive meanings of money facilitate thought as they are supposed to do. By gathering together in one schema the disparate qualities of many

[67] Michael Walzer, *Spheres of Justice* (Oxford, UK: Robertson, 1983). Walzer makes the point that when things have only ''use value and individualized symbolic values, their unequal distribution doesn't matter.'' (p. 108) But inasmuch as symbolic values are a prime source of feelings of well-being and it is the equality of well-being that, in the end, is crucial for egalitarians, this view must be discarded.
[68] See, for example, Amartya Sen and Bernard Williams, ''Introduction,'' in Sen and Williams, *Utilitarianism and Beyond* (Cambridge, UK: Cambridge University Press, 1982).
[69] Ronald Inglehart, ''Post-Materialism in an Environment of Insecurity,'' *American Political Science Review* 75 (1981): 880–900.

Table 5.1 *Percentage of Japanese adults agreeing that "money is the most important thing" to teach a child, 1953–1978*

Year	1953 cohort aged 20–24 followed through successive years	Members of successive 20–24 aged cohorts questioned in each designated year
	Percentage	Percentage
1953	60	60
1963	58	43
1968	59	34
1973	46	22
1978	56	18
Differences 1953–78	4	42

Source: Ronald Inglehart, "Changing Values in Japan and the West," *Comparative Political Studies* 14 (1982): 445–79; adapted from Table 5, p. 465.

otherwise unlike things, money schemata conserve cognitive capacities, facilitate comparisons, put a handle on the rationing of time and of possibilities for the future. They extend the range of causal attributions and liberate people from dependence on perception and the here and now. Causal thinking is also enlarged by the new possibilities for conjunctive thinking, the layman's analysis of variance. To be practical in a money culture is not to be merely thing-minded, but rather practicality is extended to the abstract, where conceptualization must always take place. Rather than substituting quantity for quality, the quantified thinking encouraged by money enriches both quantities and qualities. Emotionally less arousing than the consumer goods it buys, money may help to defer gratification – but its rich potentialities and the ease of borrowing it makes possible may interfere with such deferrals.

As money is extensive in time and space, so does it help to extend spatial and temporal horizons, encouraging a kind of psychological mobility that facilitates counterfactual ideas, the imaginary, the idea of the self doing something else somewhere else. It may not help to overcome the bias toward present time, but if the will is there, it helps to plan for the future. Additionally, as it erases temporal and spatial boundaries, it also erodes ethnic and religious boundaries and substitutes for them the more porous barriers of social class.

Money hampers and fetters as it facilitates, for the very qualities that facilitate the thinking process invite overuse, indiscriminate assessments, inappropriate classification. Money as a measure of other people, of the total sum of the qualities of nature, or ethics, and of the self leaves the mind wounded, with a broken wing. That great advantage of the market, the facilitation of choice, is not reflexive, it does not facilitate choosing among the facilitators.

But in true dialectical fashion, the market may undermine the conceptual importance of money as it makes money more abundant.

6 Money symbolism and economic rationality

Criteria for individual rationality

In Chapter 3 we saw the inadequacies of the economist's version of rationality and in Chapter 4 we developed a more sophisticated concept of cognitive complexity, one that seems to give a superior account of economic behavior. That later chapter also introduced us to some ways of thinking about emotional responses to economic stimuli and showed the interdependence of cognition and emotion in economic life. Now, following the analysis of the way money facilitates, and hinders, cognition in the market I seek to continue this treatment of money and to integrate several of these themes.

Economic rationality is a thin and unsophisticated version of cognitive complexity; it clearly enlists complicated cognitions but it is ignorant of the grounds for preferences, their relation to the deepest trends in a person's psyche, the way they change, and the way people match means to ends. Yet we need a realistic standard for decision making in the market, one that is judged not only by psychological standards but also on grounds of its efficiency in guiding a person to get what he or she wants. Here, for the limited purposes of this chapter, I take the liberty of devising such a standard and, so as not to sacrifice a useful word, will name it *insightful rationality*.

This invention permits us to get on with the substantive purpose of the chapter: to analyze how attitudes toward money affect the (insightfully) rational decisions that people make in their economic transactions. In Chapter 5 we saw how money, taken in its denotative sense as a *sign,* altered and usually improved people's cognitions about the market. But money is a *symbol* as well as a sign, that is, it is charged with emotional and connotative meanings that also alter patterns of economic thought, sometimes in ways quite different from what the plain economic value of money would suggest. By looking at money as a symbol in this way, we reintroduce the influence of emotions in economic thinking, making our analysis of the market experience more realistic.

After explicating the concept of *insightful rationality* I devote the large middle section of the chapter to analysis of empirical studies of people's connotative, emotional responses to money symbols. The third section interprets these findings in the light of the standards of rationality thus developed.

Insightful rationality

I will specify two criteria, each of which has several conditions. The first criterion for insightfully rational preference formation requires that four conditions be met. (1) In accordance with accepted doctrine, preferences must be framed so that they are consistent and transitive,[1] but also flexible enough to accommodate learning. In

---

[1] "At a minimum, rationality comprises two ideas: consistency and the choice of appropriate means to one's ends." Brian Barry and Russell Hardin, "Epilogue," in their edited, *Rational Man and Irrational*

most other definitions stability, rather than flexibility, is emphasized and adaptive learning is assumed but not specified. (2) Preferences must be made in the light of alternatives, that is, utility maximization implies rejecting some preferences as well as choosing some others. This condition is important because it implies that even the most relaxed standards of subjective rationality must be informed; it is not satisfied by habit (unless that is itself a conscious decision) and takes into account decision making and information costs. These two conditions are more or less standard criteria for any kind of rationality, including Simon's "satisficing," and Abelson's "predictable mental processes which happen not to correspond to the rules of formal logic . . . [applied] to a specifiable but not necessarily accurate picture of the world."[2]

The next condition to be met (3) is insight. The preferences or values pursued must be "ego-syntonic," that is, they must be such that if they are achieved or consummated they yield genuine satisfaction. Elster has pointed out one way in which stated preferences are misleading: If those preferences are conditioned on the belief that certain otherwise desirable objects are unattainable ("sour grapes"), or, alternatively, that only the unattained and unattainable is preferable ("the pastures are greener on the other side of the fence"), they are not an adequate guide to satisfaction.[3] The grapes would and the pastures would not yield satisfaction. Similarly, it would be absurd to accept as rational a schedule of preferences whose purpose was to maximize the economic equivalent of what the psychiatrist calls "neurotic gain" at the cost of some greater satisfactions that, with more insight, an individual would welcome. I will elaborate on this crucial condition in Chapter 27.

(4) A fourth condition for accepting a schedule of preferences as rational reflects an important requirement for maximizing satisfaction: A person's aspirations must be within the bounds of potential achievements. Again, the important characteristic here is that a person has some insight into what he or she can do or get or be. Studies of people's satisfaction with their housing, for example, reveal that satisfaction depends heavily on the relationship among aspirations, expectations, and achievement. The objective character of the housing is much less important than the relation of achievement to aspirations.[4] One reason why the more mature members of the population are more satisfied with their lives than the younger members is that they have brought their aspirations into closer line with their achievements – but everyone has, and generally uses, a subjective upgrading of "achievements" to help this process of reconciling the desired with the achieved.[5] This condition also rules out the insatiability of appetites that Durkheim said led to *anomie*. Thus, we cannot be content with the simple criterion of stable and transitive preferences, and

Society? (Beverly Hills, CA: Sage, 1982), 371. See also Lionel Robbins, *An Essay on the Nature and Significance of Economic Science* (London: Macmillan, 1935), 78.

[2] Robert Abelson, "Social Psychology's Rational Man," in S. I. Benn and G. W. Mortimore, eds., *Rationality and the Social Sciences* (London: Routledge & Kegan Paul, 1976), 61, 62.

[3] Jon Elster, *Sour Grapes: Studies in the Subversion of Rationality* (Cambridge, UK: Cambridge University Press, 1983).

[4] Angus Campbell, Philip E. Converse, and Willard L. Rodgers, *The Quality of American Life* (New York: Russell Sage, 1976), chap. 6.

[5] Ibid., 171–98.

of course neither can we be satisfied with the tautology implied by the doctrine of "revealed preferences," that is, the pattern of purchases is ipso facto evidence of utility maximization within a given budget.[6]

The second criterion for insightful rationality is ends–means rationality, a criterion that has two conditions. (1) Within the information reasonably available (available within the time-and-effort budget dictated by some satisficing criteria) the selected means must be chosen efficiently to bring about the preferred ends. In more formal terms, the selection of means within a payoff matrix must match the preferences in the matrix of utilities. But this is insufficient, especially in a market economy where consumer pleasures tend to dominate considerations of what Juster calls "process benefits,"[7] for it seems to ignore the intrinsic satisfaction of the means. As Charles Fried reminds us, all means have some intrinsic satisfactions or dissatisfactions that are, therefore, proximate ends in themselves.[8] Thus, insightful rationality must not only account for the effectiveness of the means, but also (2) their intrinsic hedonic qualities, a matter for which insight into what a person enjoys *doing* as well as getting and having is essential. My intention is to be sure to include work satisfaction in the rational calculus, but, with a little extension, this consideration might also include the satisfaction of conscience in the process of acquisition.

When discussing economic rationality of any kind one must consider whether rationality implies exclusive attention to *self-interest*. I reject this idea, partly on the grounds that it is often tautological and sometimes ambiguous: For example, David Gauthier distinguishes between "self-interest" and "self-directed aims,"[9] and extended self-interest may incorporate not only family and friends but also the nation, thus blending with altruism. But, more importantly, I reject it on the grounds that from the individual point of view it is as rational to follow the Kantian imperative or to follow the line of reasoning in Rawls's *A Theory of Justice* as it is to be solely selfish. No one would say that altruism is irrational unless he or she accepted a self-interest premise, thus begging the question. It is better to leave unspecified the beneficiaries of the utilities a person seeks to maximize.[10] The rationality of the

[6] With certain exceptions, economists are usually satisfied to take preferences as given. See Gary Becker and George Stigler, "De Gustibus Non Est Disputandum," *American Economic Review* 67 (1977): 76–90. One can imagine an economist responding to the suggestion that economic formulae include the elements of symbolic thinking by observing that these may be absorbed by simple notations. The symbolist might respond with gratification – but only if the notations referred to empirical findings and not merely hypothetical difficulties, and if the theories of economic behavior that the notation represented were accordingly modified. Economists might argue further that commodity bundles are as "multivalent" as are money symbols and do not pose difficulties for traditional economic analysis; but, the symbolist would point out, that is because the multivalence of the bundles are, in fact, reduced to the single dimension of money value. I am indebted to James Bennett for suggesting this imaginary discourse.

[7] F. Thomas Juster, "Preferences for Work and Leisure," in Juster and Frank P. Stafford, eds., *Time, Goods, and Well-Being* (Ann Arbor, MI: Institute for Social Research, 1985).

[8] Charles Fried, *The Anatomy of Values: Problems of Personal and Social Choice* (Cambridge: Harvard University Press, 1970).

[9] David Gauthier, "Reason and Maximization," in Barry and Hardin, eds., *Rational Man and Irrational Society?*, 93.

[10] From the point of view of the social system, altruism is not irrational, but from the point of view of the economy, the matter is less certain, an uncertainty we do not need to enter upon here. Most econo-

market accommodates all altruism mediated by purchases (for it does not matter whether a person buys flowers for his or her own enjoyment or for a gift), but it is disturbed by altruism expressed in the satisfaction a person receives from other people's income and welfare (e.g., interdependent utilities) when they are achieved without any economic act of the altruistic individual.[11]

The neutrality of money

What we wish to explore is the way attitudes toward money, the symbolization of money, affect these various criteria for economic rationality, in this case an enlarged and insightful rationality. Most economists, and even their critics, hold that the meaning of money is exhausted by its command over goods and services. After rehearsing the various materials used in primitive society as money and the period when money was "backed" by precious metals, the economist Walter C. Neale says, "Today . . . the paper and the tokens 'stand for' nothing except what they can do for their owners: make payments to payees who will accept the paper and tokens in payment."[12] Georg Simmel, too, claims that the value of money is relative to its command over goods and services; therefore "money is nothing but the symbol of this relativity. . . . It expresses the relativity of objects of demand through which they have economic value." As time passes, "money becomes more and more a mere symbol [sic], neutral as regards its intrinsic value."[13] Finally, Karl Polanyi suggests the neutrality of money symbolism by analogizing it to the symbols of weights and measures.[14] Of course, economists recognize that the money *system* affects and sometimes distorts the production and distribution of commodities,[15] but this does not affect the phenomenology of money, which is treated almost without exception as directly dependent on what money can buy.

As we have seen, however, money is symbolized in such a way as to be phenomenologically anything but neutral; it is invested with a variety of fears, obsessions,

mists assume self interest, but it has been said that "to run an organization *entirely* on incentives of personal gain is pretty much a hopeless task." Amartya K. Sen, "Rational Fools: A Critique of the Behavioral Foundations of Economic Theory," *Philosophy and Public Affairs* 6 (1977): 335. Further, some arguments claim that self-interested rationality leads to societal irrationality. (Cf. Barry and Hardin, eds., *Rational Man and Irrational Society?*) Moreover there are sufficient treatments of how the market may accommodate altruism to accept the view that the kind of individual rationality required of the market is not necessarily dependent on self-interest. See: Howard Margolis, *Selfishness, Altruism, & Rationality* (Cambridge, UK: Cambridge University Press, 1982); David Collard, *Altruism and Economy: A Study of Non-Selfish Economics* (New York: Oxford University Press, 1978); Robert H. Frank, "If *Homo Economicus* Could Choose His Utility Function, Would He Want One with a Conscience?" in his *Passions Within Reason: The Strategic Role of the Emotions* (New York: Norton, 1988).
[11] See Tjalling C. Koopmans, *Three Essays on the State of Economic Science* (New York: McGraw-Hill, 1957), 41.
[12] Walter C. Neale, *Monies in Societies* (San Francisco: Chandler & Sharp, 1976), 16–17. Neale goes on further to desymbolize money meanings: "What matters is that there is a record which can be used to enforce rights and duties of members of the society. [Demand deposits] are analogous to the records of land deeds in a county court house."
[13] Georg Simmel, *The Philosophy of Money*, trans. and ed. T. Bottomore and D. Frisby (1907; reprint London: Routledge & Kegan Paul, 1978), 123, 127, 130, 152.
[14] Karl Polanyi, "The Semantics of Money Uses," in his *Primitive, Archaic, and Modern Economies* (Boston: Beacon Press, 1971).
[15] See, for example, Arthur C. Pigou, *The Veil of Money* (London: Macmillan, 1949).

and inhibitions that distort its serviceability for market calculations. This elaboration of meanings is further complicated by the fact that the symbolization of money is often matched by a symbolization of particular commodities ("the fetishism of commodities"), and, it seems, from dream content, especially of automobiles.[16] Tversky and Kahneman's study of the framing of decisions mentioned in Chapter 3 shows that there is often a mental framework for particular commodities and a separate framework for money in general, with the result that "this paradoxical variation in the value of money is incompatible with the standard analysis of consumer behavior."[17]

One measure of the difference in the hedonic value of money symbols and the commodities they purchase is suggested by their different contributions to measures of subjective well-being. Thus, one such account, a score on a "money index" contributes about 15 percent of the variance on an overall measure of life satisfaction, whereas a score on a "consumer index" contributes about 7 percent. If one were to follow economic practice and identify the sign value of the money to what money buys (the consumer index), the remaining symbolic value of the money would contribute about 8 percentage points of the total 15 percent that the "money index" contributes to a sense of well-being. By this calculation, the symbolic value of money contributes more to well-being than does the sign, descriptive value.[18] Of course, these calculations are merely suggestive, but whatever measure of well-being is used (satisfaction, happiness, etc.), the overall result is the same.

A broad and tolerant concept of economic rationality can accommodate many of these symbolizations; the criterion for this accommodation is whether or not money symbols permit a person to maximize his or her utilities in the market. Following the above set of criteria, such symbolization interferes with individual "rationality" most generally when emotions dominate thought, and more specifically when the symbolization inhibits the formation of (1) consistent but flexible, (2) comparatively assessed, (3) ego-syntonic, (4) feasible preferences. It does this by distorting thinking about (5) how to achieve the goals implied by these preferences, and (6) by ignoring or exaggerating the intrinsic value of the means employed. That is, those money symbols that bias perceptions, bend preferences, inhibit transactions for desired goods or invite transactions for undesired goods, or, like anxiety and obsessions, distort market calculations – these symbolic uses of money may be said to damage market rationality as I have defined it.

[16] Calvin S. Hall and Robert L. van de Castle, *The Content Analysis of Dreams* (New York: Appleton-Century-Crofts, 1966), app. A.

[17] Amos Tversky and Daniel Kahneman, "Judgment under Uncertainty: Heuristics and Biases," in D. Kahneman, P. Slovic, and A. Tversky, eds., *Judgment under Uncertainty: Heuristics and Biases* (New York: Cambridge University Press, 1982), 457.

[18] Frank M. Andrews and Stephen B. Withey, *Social Indicators of Well-Being: Americans' Perceptions of Life Quality* (New York: Plenum Press, 1976), 124. The money index was composed of the following questions: "How do you feel about . . . how secure you are financially? the income you (and your family) have? how comfortable and well-off you are?" The consumer index was composed of answers to the following questions: "How do you feel about . . . the way you can get around to work, schools, shopping, etc.? the doctors, clinics, and hospitals you would use in this area? the goods and services you can get when you buy in this area – things like food, appliances, clothes?" Admittedly, they diverge from ideal questions for the point at hand.

We may conceive of some of these money symbolisms as *transaction costs,* that is, the impediments to utility maximization imposed by money symbols increases the "price" of the commodities purchased. But it would be more accurate to think of them as *price distortions,* changing the value of the commodities in the market. In a clinical analogy they may be said to represent *neurotic gain,* short-term advantages purchased at the cost of long-term satisfaction. In the language of metaphor, inviting a person with some of the money symbolism we shall examine to enter the market is like inviting a person with agoraphobia to enjoy the view of a Kansas prairie. Sometimes, too, under the influence of symbolization, market calculations become like the decision to fly to an appointment in Paris made by a person who fears (or craves) flying. There is a lot more going on than calculating the relative satisfactions to be derived simply from the objects purchased.

Money symbolism

Condensation symbols, with their dense configurations of meaning "allowing for the ready release of emotional tension in conscious or unconscious form,"[19] may be tapped in discursive accounts and word-association tests. A simpler, though quite compatible, approach to money meanings is through conventional attitude research. In the following discussions I combine these approaches and attempt to synthesize the findings of four studies.

1. In 1981 Carin Rubenstein reported four main clusters of attitudes (scales) derived from a nonrepresentative mail return sample of 20,000 respondents self-selected from the readers of *Psychology Today.* The sample was younger, more affluent, and included more professionals and business people than would a representative national sample.[20]
2. In 1982, seeking to systematize psychoanalytic and other theories of money attitudes, Yamauchi and Templer found four main independent factors in a study employing sixty-two questions given to a heterogeneous American sample of 300. These factors accounted for 33 percent of the variance.[21]
3. In 1984 Adrian Furnham, employing sixty-four questions (many of them borrowed from Rubenstein's and Yamauchi and Templer's items) in a study of a heterogeneous British sample of 226, found seven independent factors accounting for 17 percent of the variance.[22]
4. Earlier, in 1972, Wernimont and Fitzpatrick employed a different method, the "semantic differential"; that is, they asked their 533 heterogeneous subjects to respond to forty statements of the following kind: "To me money is something that is. . . . 'good/bad,' 'embarrassing/not embarrassing,' 'successful/unsuccessful,' " etc. In many ways this method is better designed to discover the more subtle meanings of money. Again, the authors analyzed the results by factor analysis, finding six independent factors accounting for 55 percent of the variance.[23]

[19] Edward Sapir, "Symbolism," *Encyclopedia of the Social Sciences,* vol. 14 (New York: 1934), 493.
[20] Carin Rubenstein, "Money and Self-Esteem, Relationships, Secrecy, Envy, Satisfaction," *Psychology Today* 15 (May 1981): 29–44.
[21] Kent T. Yamauchi and Donald I. Templer, "The Development of a Money Attitude Scale," *Journal of Personality Assessment* 46 (1982): 522–8.
[22] Adrian Furnham, "Many Sides of the Coin: The Psychology of Money Usage," *Personality and Individual Differences* 5 (1984): 95–103.
[23] Paul F. Wernimont and Susan Fitzpatrick, "The Meaning of Money," *Journal of Applied Psychology* 50 (1972): 218–26.

I also employ the reports of a psychoanalyst, Edmund Bergler, on two of the many cases he treated that revolved around money problems.[24] In the following reports, the sources are indicated by the name of the authors in brackets.

Obsession with money and money consciousness

Agreeing with such propositions as the following obviously indicates an unusual concern about money: "I put money ahead of pleasure;" "I feel that money is the only thing that I can really count on" [Furnham]; "Next to health, money is the most important thing in the world."[25] In a more discursive vein, those who believe they think "much more" about money than others, or who say they fantasize about money "all or much of the time," may be said to be "money conscious" [Rubenstein]. As might be expected, the poor more than the rich, the less well educated more than the better educated, fall into this classification.

Microeconomics is silent about such obsessions. It may be that these are stable and transitive preferences fulfilling the usual criteria of market rationality. And they may even permit pursuit of feasible goals pursued efficiently. But obsessions are not flexible; they block learning. Almost by definition, an obsession is not ego-syntonic in the sense that it does not correspond to those desires that, with more self-knowledge, a person would continue to desire; given help, people are happy to be free of obsessions. Evidence that such obsessive concern about money fails, for such reasons as these, to permit utility maximization comes from the studies themselves, for there is a reported tendency for people with such money obsessions to be dissatisfied with their work, their love lives, and their social relations. They are unhappy.[26] Of course, we do not know whether their money obsessions contribute to their unhappiness or merely reflect a more general malaise, but it seems unlikely that such obsessions permit choices leading to happiness.

The word-association study [Wernimont & Fitzpatrick] found one factor (out of six), called a "pooh-pooh attitude," revealing a tendency to depreciate the importance of money. Some of the adjectives associated with money in this factor were "weak," "unprofessional," "dissatisfying," "unimportant." It seems on the face of it to represent the opposite of obsession with money.

Again, there is no reason to believe that such an attitude interferes with consistent, flexible, ego-syntonic, feasible preferences, although it may rule out one source of pleasure: For many people part of the fun of life lies in meeting economic challenges by making money. This form of utility maximization is apparently barred by the pooh-pooh attitude. On the other hand, this depreciation of the value of money

---

[24] Edmund Bergler, *Money and Emotional Conflicts* (Garden City, NY: Doubleday, 1951), 230–4. Regarding these five sources, we must enter certain caveats on the general applicability of the data: Surveys and clinics are not markets – people behave differently in these differing situations; attitudes often do not predict behavior [see Icek Ajzen and Martin Fishbein, *Understanding Attitudes and Predicting Social Behavior* (Englewood Cliffs, N.J.: Prentice-Hall, 1980)]; the representativeness of the samples used is uncertain. My claim is only that some of the people, some of the time, are guided by such symbolism as is reported in these works.

[25] This item has been added to an "Anomia" scale originally devised by Leo Srole. See John P. Robinson and Philip R. Shaver, *Measures of Social Psychological Attitudes: Appendix B* (Ann Arbor, MI: Institute for Social Research, 1969), 175.

[26] Rubenstein, "Money and Self-Esteem," 42.

may facilitate choices contributing to overall life satisfaction. For most people, satisfaction with leisure and with family life makes more of a contribution to life satisfaction than does satisfaction with standard of living. And, most strangely, satisfaction with the standard of living may itself be enhanced by considering money unimportant.[27] Unlike obsessions with money, there is nothing qualifying the pooh-pooh attitude as a violation of the criteria for economic rationality. Indeed, by limiting the scope of a person's aspirations, the pooh-pooh attitude may facilitate a more congenial ratio of aspirations to achievements. The irony flowing from the greater economic rationality of those who place a *lower* value on money will not be lost on a public taught to be believe that economic rationality depends on maximizing income.

Anxiety

In two studies "anxiety" emerged as a major factor differentiating responses to money; it is indicated by such sentiments as: "I show signs of nervousness when I don't have enough money;" "I spend money to make myself feel better" [Furnham; Yamauchi & Templer]. For these people, it seems, money symbolism either stands for previous disturbing experiences or otherwise prompts chronic states of anxiety. These attitudes were independent of people's incomes, but they were closely associated with a general measure of mental disturbances.

Perhaps the attitude is compatible with consistent, comparative, and feasible preferences, but few clinicians would say that people choose ego-syntonically during anxiety. From social psychological studies we know that mild anxiety improves performance but more severe anxiety reduces the quality of performance because the individual is thinking more of himself or herself than the task at hand. Anxiety foreshortens perspectives and reduces realistic assessment.[28]

Control over one's money

Folk expressions and popular verse often reflect the sense that money is out of control: "That's the way the money goes,/Pop goes the weasel;" "Money burns a hole in my pocket." The sentiment is reflected in a group labeled "the money troubled," characterized by their sense that they were poorer than their friends (even though they were not), aspirations beyond their means, inability to save, and the tendency to charge things they could not currently afford – and hence encumbrance by debt [Rubenstein; see also Furnham]. In contrast, another group, called "the money contented," have a sense of control over their finances and say that if they cannot afford something they either save for it or forget it; they keep their aspirations within their means and (borrowing from a similar constellation in another study) such people report that "I always know how much I have in my savings account" [Furnham]. Again, these attitudes toward money are not related to level of income.

There is nothing in the concept of consistent preferences that prevents overspend-

[27] Campbell et al., *The Quality of American Life*, 76.
[28] Charles D. Spielberger, ed., *Anxiety: Current Trends in Theory and Research*, vol. 1 ((New York: Academic Press, 1972), 39–42.

ing, or that implies a sense of control over one's finances, yet these attitudes and behaviors interfere with rational allocation of budgets over time. Specifically, this use of money violates the criterion for individual rationality represented by aspirations within one's means and rational ends–means calculations. Further, we know that a sense of control over one's fate is a central and indispensable ingredient of life satisfaction[29] (i.e., utility maximization). For those who have lost control over their money, money cannot represent a set of neutral symbols, like the weights and measures that Polanyi says are comparable to money symbols; rather money is fraught with trouble, entailing a sense of inadequacy in dealing with it.

Money retention and saving

A tendency to value saving over spending is not just the opposite of the lost sense of control (the corrective factor that would set things right), but rather a factor in its own right, and not a happy one. In two studies it is characterized by a tendency to agree with the following statements: "I often say 'I can't afford it' whether I can or not;" and "Even when I have sufficient money I often feel guilty about spending money on necessities like clothes, etc." [Furnham; Yamauchi & Templer]. There are no income differences that mark off this group. In another study, the author developed a "Midas scale"; those who scored high on this scale reported themselves to be "penny pinchers" and stated that they do not "really enjoy spending money" [Rubenstein].

For these groups the consistent preference is to deny oneself the commodities for which it is necessary to spend money, that is, there is a high transaction cost for every transaction. Since transaction costs (like information costs) represent charges against utility maximization, those who dislike spending money gain less from their purchases than others because the "price" has been increased. In assessing how this syndrome fits into the concept of economic rationality one could think of Midas himself as maximizing his utilities by hoarding, but, unlike Midas, the persons ranking high on the Midas scale derive little happiness from their savings. For example, the attitudinal cluster includes agreement with the statement, "I often feel inferior to others who have more than myself, even when I know that they have done nothing of worth to get it." Rather, it seems, the retentiveness syndrome is (again) equivalent to a neurosis where the "neurotic gain" interferes with long-term, ego-syntonic satisfaction. For example, the "Midases" in this study had low self-esteem, were unhappy about their jobs, friends, and sex lives, and had frequent headaches,[30] evidence witnessing the implausibility of utility maximization along this route. But then, the Protestants who devised the Protestant ethic of thrift (and work) never placed a high value on happiness.

Impression management

As mentioned, there is no reason to consider "conspicuous consumption," or impression management, irrational in market terms; after all, as noted in Chapter 5, Adam Smith held that the main reason people sought money was "to be observed,

---

[29] Angus Campbell, *The Sense of Well-Being in America* (New York: McGraw-Hill, 1981), 217–18.
[30] Rubenstein, "Money and Self-Esteem," 43.

to be attended to, to be taken notice of with sympathy, complacency, and appreciation."[31] Thus, finding a cluster of attitudes toward money that indicates that the meaning of money for some people is the power they think it gives them over other people's attitudes toward themselves is not surprising or in itself economically irrational. Fashion is built on just such a set of attitudes. We see this cluster in the favorable responses to such statements as: "I sometimes buy things I don't need or want to impress people because they are the right things to have at the time;" "I sometimes 'buy' friendship by being very generous with those I want to like me;" and "I often give large tips to waiters/waitresses that I like" [Furnham].

The preference expressed, so far as we can tell, is consistent with other preferences, but it may lead to a kind of intransitivity in actual purchases. Seeking to buy friendship or approval from Group A today, the individual ranks commodity X over Y, but seeking to buy the friendship of Group B tomorrow, he ranks commodity Y over X. His preference for approval retains its priority, but, as others have observed, a person's intransitive commodity preferences risk his or her becoming a "money pump," trading a discounted Y for X today and then a discounted X for Y tomorrow. Going beyond the logic of the transactions, we might observe the risk of failure in the underlying "approval motive;" when it is severe it is self-defeating, for people do not want to be courted insistently and they therefore spurn the suitor.[32] And recalling Marx's comment on the use of money to buy love,[33] one might conclude that what is rational in market terms becomes irrational in terms of a larger life plan that reserves friendship for a separate domain.

Distrust and suspicion

"When I make a purchase, I have a suspicion that I have been taken advantage of"; "I argue or complain about the cost of things I buy" [Yamauchi & Templer]. Through such questions a cluster of attitudes marked off a group of distrustful purchasers, a group measurably (on a separate measure) more paranoid than most.

Like the group purchasing approval, this group risks having an intermediate purpose, in this case avoiding being taken advantage of, distort consumer preferences. There is nothing irrational about emphasizing reputations for integrity, choosing commodities according to the warranties offered, or going only to places where one is known, but the priority given to risk-aversive tactics at the cost of other properties of transactions and of things to be purchased seems likely to be costly in other ways. In any event, true paranoia cannot be reassured, for there are always grounds for suspicion. Therefore, the preference fails the feasibility criterion. It is comparable to Durkheim's insatiable appetites, and *any* insatiability violates one of the canons of rational preferences: aspirations within reach of achievements. It also violates ends–means rationality, for no means can achieve these ends.

---

[31] The social psychologist Albert Bandura makes the same point: Reinforcements, such as money, influence behavior more because they promise sympathetic attention than because they promise other forms of benefits. See his *Social Learning Theory* (Englewood Cliffs, NJ: Prentice-Hall, 1977), 97–8.

[32] Douglas P. Crowne and David Marlowe, *The Approval Motive* (New York: Wiley, 1964).

[33] Karl Marx, "The Power of Money in Bourgeois Society," in *Economic and Philosophical Manuscripts of 1844*, trans. M. Milligan and ed. D. Struik (New York: International Publishers, 1964).

Shameful failure

In the semantic differential study, a factor called "shameful failure" was the most discriminating of the factors found. As mentioned, the factor emerged as people responded to the question, "To me money is something that is . . . ," with the adjectives "unsuccessful," "retreating," "embarrassing," "discouraging," "degrading." Those most likely to score high on this factor were hospital sisters, a group of unemployed in training, and freshmen and sophomores in college; the low scorers were managers and salesmen. That is, those for whom money was not important in their daily occupations (at least at the time of the questioning) viewed money as "embarrassing" or "discouraging," whereas those successfully engaged in making money did not. The same division occurs on another dimension, money as "socially acceptable or unacceptable" [Wernimont & Fitzpatrick].

Two forces affecting the stability of preferences seem to be at work in these responses: (1) The study was conducted in 1970 or 1971 when the counterculture was still active. For the students, at least, there was available a ready-made, negative response to money symbols that would disappear as the more conventional attitudes of the later 1970s reassumed their original force. Preferences cannot be expected to remain stable when the zeitgeists blow them hither and yon. (2) What is rational in one role is not rational in another. When the freshmen and sophomores become managers and salesmen or when the unemployed in training have jobs, money symbolism will almost certainly not carry this freight of possible failure, embarrassment, and degradation. For only the mature hospital sisters is this likely to be a stable and transitive "preference," but for the others, something like Mannheim's "self-transformation"[34] (with the aid of the changing zeitgeist and new responsibilities) seems at work – a different form of life rationality. In the meantime, to the extent that these attitudes imply behavior consonant with the attitudes reported (which is not always true), there remains an aversion to earning money that will frustrate certain forms of economic rationality.

Money masochism

A taciturn and bitter criminal lawyer came into the office of psychiatrist Edmund Bergler, answered questions in resistant monosyllables, and when told that he must give more information, he broke down and wept. He than told a story of how he defended, by brilliant maneuvers, a group of chiseling clients in the plastics business. These "chiselers," however, persuaded the lawyer to accept, in lieu of payment, a partnership scheme in their business. In order to rescue his investment the lawyer spent more and more time trying to save himself from losses, and as a consequence, neglected his legal work and lost more money.

A public accountant told Bergler a similar story. Deciding that he could not get rich by his accountant's practice, he was lured by his clients into investing in the cinder block business. It turned out that the business was in shambles and that in order to save his investment he poured more money into the scheme with few pros-

---

[34] Karl Mannheim, *Man and Society in an Age of Reconstruction,* trans. E. Shils (New York: Harcourt Brace, 1948).

pects for success. Bergler asked him, " 'How could you, a specialist at figures and account sheets, fall for these crooks you allowed to become your partners?' 'You know the human weakness for getting rich,' he answered."[35]

But, of course, the answer concealed the special forces at work in his own case. In both cases, given the special competences of lawyers and accountants, Bergler interpreted their failures as reflecting desires to punish themselves, a form of "money masochism," based on unconscious wishes to prove their own incompetence, or to assuage their guilt, or for some other reason.

Economic rationality makes no room for either the fear of success, now said to characterize some women in the professions and business,[36] or masochistic tendencies. It would do no good to find that their preferences were consistent and feasible, and it would violate the canons of mental health to label masochism as ego-syntonic. The obvious problem for economic rationality, however, is how to interpret utility maximization through self-punishment, pleasure through pain.

Moral evil

In the word-association test, one group associated money with the adjectives "dishonest," "dishonorable," "unfair." The syndrome was called "moral evil" and, strangely, was almost as frequently found among salesmen and managers as among students and hospital nurses [Wernimont & Fitzpatrick]. For the salesmen some inconsistency among "preferences" is apparent in the fact that they also found money "socially acceptable," and associated it with the adjectives "relaxed," "happy," and "dependable." One source of inconsistency is the ambivalence characteristic of symbols, that is, both positive and negative feelings about the same object, a frequent enough set of attitudes and yet qualifying as irrational by the economist's standards, especially since ambivalence might easily lead to intransitivity. For utility maximization, two unhappy outcomes might stem from ambivalence: (1) Making and spending money might not lead to pleasure because the dark side of the ambivalence would detract from that pleasure; and (2) prior to consummation of an ambivalent desire, the individual might hold back as the negative side of his or her feelings made itself felt. Furthermore, with respect to money as "moral evil," the stage is set for a classic moral dilemma: achieving a desired good through means thought disreputable. It is hard to achieve utility maximization when each component pleasure is balanced by an associated, sometimes greater, sometimes lesser, pain.

Money-contented, secure, acceptable

Some of the attitudes toward money and money symbolization reflect a sense of control over one's funds, a sense that money is desirable primarily as a source of security, and that it is a socially acceptable medium of exchange. In contrast to the "money troubled" the "money contented" say that if they can't afford something they save for it or forget it [Rubenstein]. Those who find money a source of security report that "I always know how much I have in my savings account" [Furnham].

---

[35] Bergler, *Money and Emotional Conflicts*, 234.
[36] David W. Tresemer, *Fear of Success* (New York: Plenum Press, 1977).

The social acceptability of money is reflected in the word-association study by such adjectives as "trusting," "loyal," "healthy," "friendly," "controllable" [Wernimont & Fitzpatrick]. The studies indicate that these groups are reasonably populous but do not form a majority of the respondents studied. We do not know whether these attitudes are associated with rational economic behavior, but they seem quite compatible with the criteria and conditions we have employed.

Market ideology

A somewhat different kind of attitude set, and a powerful one, is represented by acceptance or rejection of the market ideology itself. Labeled respectively "American Dream" and "American Nightmare," these two attitude sets both reflected and caused various aspects of money symbolism. The American Dream syndrome holds that (1) hard work always pays off; (2) wealth is a measure of intelligence, mental health, and happiness; (3) the Dreamers' own futures are considered bright. The Dreamers also tend to be (4) more religious than others and (5) more money conscious.

In contrast, the American Nightmare cluster holds that (1) success is a matter of luck or connections (or greed), and (2) people have little control over their financial prospects. In addition the Nightmare people are (3) less happy and less optimistic than others, and (4) they tend to be agnostic and skeptical about life [Rubenstein].

This rich pair of syndromes tells us little about consistent, flexible, ego-syntonic, feasible preferences, but it tells us something about utility maximization. To increase one's happiness in a market economy one's preferences should include support for market methods; one should believe in market fairness and one's own efficacy in the market. As it turns out, for some people these beliefs and preferences are indeed so stable that they survive every kind of misfortune in the market (including structural unemployment), that is, market system symbols are so strong that they foreclose some relevant learning from market misfortune. Even those who lose their jobs because of business failure or recession often continue to believe in that portion of the market ideology holding that one is responsible for one's own fate, a belief that only increases their misery.[37] In this sense, ends–means rationality is certainly not a feature of market ideology.

Symbolic thinking and rationality

If money were only a sign, or a neutral quantity like measures of weights, it would be merely a tool for the normal processes of rational inference. We have seen this is not the case, however. The symbolization of money has implications for rational inference going beyond our confined definition of economic rationality, implications to which we now turn.

Interpreting meanings and market choices

At the beginning of this discussion I said that rationality in general implies emotions under cognitive control. As reported in Chapter 4, the relationship between cogni-

---

[37] Kay L. Schlozman and Sidney Verba, *Injury to Insult: Unemployment, Class, and Political Response* (Cambridge: Harvard University Press, 1979).

tion and affectivity is not that of a single dimension, with rationality at one end and emotion at the other; rather these two aspects of human responses are said either to lie along two different dimensions,[38] or to be governed by two different systems. It is worth repeating the point made by psychologist R. B. Zajonc:

Affective responses to stimuli are often the very first reactions of the organism. . . . Affective reactions can occur without extensive perceptual and cognitive encoding, are made with greater confidence than cognitive judgments, and can be made sooner. . . . [A]ffect and cognition are under the control of separate and partially independent systems that can influence each other in a variety of ways, and . . . both constitute independent sources of effects in information processing.[39]

As mentioned in Chapter 5, responses to symbols tend to give priority to affect, the "like–dislike" dimension, and only secondarily to lead to a search for cognitive content or appropriate disposition. One of the purposes in the use of symbols is to arouse or pacify the emotions, playing on this primacy of affective responses. Certain things follow from this:

1. It is hard to hold the affect-laden attitudes we have been examining in suspension while considering various alternative choices. Of course, people do this in making their purchases or choosing jobs, but the symbolization of money makes this more difficult and is an impediment to the economist's idea of "value-weighing" rationality.
2. The relatively weak cognitive content of symbols means that the dispositions they arouse may be inconsistent and incoherent. "Affective reactions," says Zajonc "need not depend on cognition," and "may be separated from content."[40]
3. The multivalence of the symbolic meaning of money implies multiple possible referents from which the individual must choose.[41] For example, when money means "distrust and suspicion" or "shameful failure," the rich association behind such interpretations are likely to suggest a multitude of responses that may be quite inconsistent and incoherent. In the cases of the lawyer and accountant described by Bergler, the inconsistency of manifest and latent goals led to the self-defeating behavior that Bergler said was intended but that might also be interpreted as the result of cognitive confusion due to multivalent stimuli.

Inference and truth values

The vague and underspecified cognitive content of the symbols makes logical inference difficult, for logic requires clear conceptual boundaries for its processes of inclusion and exclusion. If money were a neutral sign pointing to desired commodities or desired savings instead of a symbol of anxiety, suspicion, pride, and ideology, logical inference would be more nearly possible.

The truth or validity of a symbol cannot be verified or falsified, depriving rationality of one of the means of disposing of the untrue or invalid. Langer suggests that a symbol is an affectively and imaginatively endowed *concept*;[42] as Hempel

[38] William McGuire, "The Nature of Attitudes and Attitude Change," *Handbook of Social Psychology,* 2d ed., vol. 3 (Reading, MA: Addison-Wesley, 1969), 202.

[39] Robert B. Zajonc, "Feeling and Thinking: Preferences Need No Inferences," *American Psychologist* 35 (1980): 151.

[40] Ibid., 158, 159.

[41] See, for example, Mircea Eliade, *Images and Symbols: Studies in Religious Symbolism,* trans. P. Mariet (1952; reprint New York: Sheed & Ward, 1969).

[42] Susanne K. Langer, *Philosophy in a New Key* (1942; reprint New York: Mentor, 1948), 58.

said many years ago, concepts are neither true nor false, they are simply fruitful or unfruitful.[43] But the test of fruitfulness in the case of money symbols is only partly that of utility maximization in the market; perhaps a larger part is subjective satisfaction from the symbolic process itself.[44] Using money symbols has its process benefits – and costs.

The noncausal nature of symbolic thinking limits rational assessment of the consequences of one's own acts or purchases in the market. And yet such questions as the following cannot be answered without careful attention to causes: What effects will buying a house have on my budget? How will an education affect my chances of getting a job? Does saving now for a vacation make sense in an inflationary economy?

One of the processes of inference is to infer from a little information some larger construct of meaning: What does a price/earnings ratio tell a person about a stock? What does price tell a person about the quality of a product? Money symbols tend to be overloaded with meaning. In this respect symbols are like stereotypes; they seem to offer more information (default values) than it is possible for them to convey. Thus, a money symbol is likely to be invested with inferences about a person who is poor that are quite unwarranted by the facts.[45] Or an apparent desire to make money may give to the phrase "promising investment" more meanings than the mere phrase can convey – as in the cases of the lawyer and accountant in Bergler's reports.

The vivid, emotionally cathected, often personally relevant loadings of a symbol tend to dominate the background, sometimes statistical, situationally relevant information about the phenomena the symbol refers to. In this sense, symbols invite what is called *the availability heuristic,* that is, the tendency to focus on what is readily available to the senses and memory rather than what is determinative for more scientific information processing.[46] Thus, money symbols (standing for status, power, moral evil, as well as price) may dominate information on the quality or usefulness of a commodity, again frustrating utility maximization.

Symbols are said to "represent" something, but they may not be representative of the events or people they stand for. Because they are so much "things-in-themselves," they do not lend themselves to concepts of sampling; they invite that common defect of thinking called *the representativeness heuristic* that says people

[43] Carl G. Hempel, *Fundamentals of Concept Formation in Empirical Science,* in *Foundations of the Unity of Science,* vol. 2, no. 7 of *International Encyclopedia of Unified Science* (Chicago: University of Chicago Press, 1952).

[44] "The symbol itself is enjoyed. . . . Here aesthetic factors in a wide sense become relevant." Harold D. Lasswell and Abraham Kaplan, *Power and Society: A Framework for Political Inquiry* (New Haven: Yale University Press, 1950), 113.

[45] Joseph Luft, "Monetary Value and the Perception of Persons," *Journal of Social Psychology* 46 (1957): 245–51.

[46] Tversky and Kahneman, "Judgment under Uncertainty." One should not, however, exaggerate the power of price information to determine consumer decisions. See G. J. Stigler, "The Economics of Information," *Journal of Political Economy* 69 (1961): 213–25. Examining research evidence on consumer behavior, Lea et al. comment: "It seems that the economy of information is not a major influence on real consumer behavior." Stephen E. G. Lea, Roger M. Tarpy, and Paul Webley, *The Individual in the Economy* (Cambridge, UK: Cambridge University Press, 1987), 530.

tend to pick as representative of a set the exemplar that has the most immediately salient characteristics of the set being typified.[47] Asked to describe the characteristics of mammals, people describe the characteristics of dogs and cats – but forget about whales.

Thinking about condensation symbols is often metaphorical, employing analogy to yield significance or meaning. As mentioned, metaphors are fruitful sources of creativity and invention, but they may not be serviceable in providing consistent and coherent preferences or in leading to the ends–means rationality required to maximize utilities in the market. Like all analogies, metaphors select the similarities in some comparison but ignore the dissimilarities. Thus, government debt is analogized to household debt, with bankruptcy as its perilous outcome. In the hidden interstices of language, economic metaphors convey subtle meanings. It has been pointed out that the phrase "labor is a resource" analogizes human labor to that of raw materials, thereby concealing the dignity of labor.[48] Psychoanalytic interpretations of money rely heavily on metaphor. The power of money triggers analogies to sexual potency, but thinking of money as sexual potency is not a preferred route to maximization of utilities in the market.

The interpretation of condensation symbols sometimes relies on *insight,* which may be defined as perception of a hidden pattern in some complex ground. The search for patterns is ubiquitous. From a few instances (and some indoctrination), one "finds" that "hard work pays off," "people can't be trusted," "people get what they deserve." Like analogies, these discerned patterns may lead to discoveries, but they are only ambiguously related to consistent, flexible, ego-syntonic, feasible preferences and appropriate ends–means rationality. Once the pattern has been discerned, it may trigger a response appropriate to that pattern. As in the case of the distrustful person who "finds" himself always being cheated, however, these discerned patterns may be inappropriate to the real-life situation. That is, given our bounded rationality, people employ few (rational) reality checks on their "insights."

Symbols help to *define situations* and thus to guide responses considered appropriate to that situation. British anthropologist Geoffrey Gorer said that Americans were exceptionally generous until the situation was defined as a business situation, at which point they became shrewd and calculating.[49] But defining situations by using money symbols, such as those suggested by the labels "money retentiveness," "uncontrollability," or "distrust and suspicion," is likely to lead to responses frustrating utility maximization in any long-term, ego-syntonic sense.

Finally, when a proposition is symbolized the task of interpreting its meaning is complicated by the fact that a respondent must disentangle the meaning of the symbol from that of the context or situation. Borrowing from the symbolic politics

[47] Tversky and Kahneman, "Judgment under Uncertainty."
[48] George Lakoff and Mark Johnson, *Metaphors We Live By* (Chicago: University of Chicago Press, 1980), 236.
[49] Geoffrey Gorer, *The American People* (New York: Norton, 1948). Defining situations is like employing the "frameworks" that Amos Tversky and Daniel Kahneman discuss in "The Framing of Decisions and the Psychology of Choice," *Science* 211 (30 January 1981), 453–8.

literature, we turn to a study by Lance Bennett that offered similar population samples two statements, one straightforward and the other symbolized: "This country should take some of the money it spends on defense and the space program and use it to solve problems here at home" and "Above all, the flag should fly with pride above America. We should take some of the money we spend on defense . . ." The consequence of adding the symbolic rhetoric was, first, to stabilize opinion and, second, to cause ideas on the use of defense money to cluster these now stabilized opinions in ways reflecting the symbol rather than the proposition to which it was attached. For the less sophisticated the symbol simplified their thought on the matter because the symbol dominated policy considerations, but for the more sophisticated it complicated things because they recognized that they had to sort out the separate meanings of symbol and statement, rather than confound them.[50] In some such fashion the symbolization of money complicates the meaning of a purchase, for there are two messages to be sorted out: the money message and the commodity message.

Ranking preferences

Ranking implies that a good, A, is ranked higher than another good, B, because A has more of the desiderata for that class of goods than B.[51] But if it is money, rather than the goods themselves, that holds the desiderata of a person, it may be because that person is interested in warding off being cheated, or avoiding moral evil, or fearful of failure. If that is the case, then these fears and desires are what is ranked and the utility maximization lies in successfully coping with these symbolic concerns. This form of utility maximization is just as "real" and just as rational as the ranking of pleasures to be derived from each item in an array of candidates for purchase. It is certainly a different market, however, from the one envisaged by market economists. This picture represents an "economy of love and fear," although in quite a different sense from that employed by Boulding.[52]

There are several properties inherent to symbolism that help to explain the problem of ranking goods or values in symbolic thinking:

1. Symbolic thinking is nonlogical, nonlinear, and, as we said, employs loosely bounded concepts whose wide and vague boundaries defy ranking.
2. Whereas money as a sign creates a *unidimensional* scale along which to rank and compare the value of goods, money as a symbol treats such references as "moral evil," "impression management," "ideology of the market," and "shameful failure" as different and often incomparable dimensions. Thus, with the symbolization of money we have deprived it of one of its main functions: serving as a standard of value permitting all goods to be ranked on a single dimension.
3. Two of the properties of symbols already mentioned also impose barriers to sensible ranking: the ambivalence arising from the simultaneous positive and negative feelings that symbols arouse in the same person at the same time, and the situational specificity of those feelings.

[50] Lance Bennett, *The Political Mind and the Political Environment* (Lexington, MA: Heath/Lexington Books, 1975), 98–101.
[51] Kurt Baier, "What is Value? An Analysis of the Concept," in Baier and Nicholas Rescher, eds., *Values and the Future* (New York: Free Press, 1969).
[52] Kenneth E. Boulding, *The Economy of Love and Fear* (Belmont, CA: Wadsworth, 1973).

Ego-syntonic preferences

Just as "affective judgments implicate the self" in a way uncharacteristic of more cognitive judgments,[53] so symbols are incorporated in the personality in a way not characteristic of signs. There is some irony in this, for, according to Simmel, one of the values of a money economy is the way money frees its owners from entanglements of personality and permits a certain detachment or blasé attitude toward life.[54] The incorporation into the self of money symbols and the definition of the self in terms of money shatters this detachment and with it some portion of a person's capacity to assess each situation without believing that his or her self-concept is at stake. Rubinstein's study shows that those who are "money troubled" and those who are niggardly and savings conscious tend to have lower self-esteem than others.

Information costs

Both the market and individuals perform better when information costs are minimal, but it is characteristic of condensation symbols to conceal as well as to distort information for the purpose of arousing or influencing an audience. This goes beyond the selective use of metaphor mentioned earlier, and the more obvious case of advertising, for it points to such problems as those revealed in the discussion of obsession with money. As mentioned, obsessions shut out other information, hence a person with a money obsession answering "I put money ahead of pleasure" (i.e., utilities) is shielded from information about other kinds of pleasures – and forfeits utility maximization. In this respect, obsession with money is like any other obsession, except that in economic matters its scope is probably wider than that of other obsessions. Quite frequently the symbolization of money impedes information searches and shuts out relevant available information, thus violating the comparison condition in the formation of preferences.

As Marx observed, money conceals and remedies such personal deficiencies as unlovability and lack of taste. Research shows that this concealment works: Without meaning to, we attribute to the wealthy favorable attributes denied to the poor.[55]

Risk assessment

We already know that people are poor judges of probability. The heuristics they use often "lead to large and persistent biases with serious implications for decision making in areas as diverse as financial analysis and the management of natural hazards."[56] Behind these general attitudes lie certain individual differences associated, in the case of money, with such attitudes as distrust, as was mentioned earlier. More generally, the goodness and badness of money symbols seem sufficient in themselves to accept or reject the symbol distorting calculations of risk even beyond

[53] Zajonc, "Feeling and Thinking," 157.
[54] Georg Simmel, "The Metropolis and Mental Life," in *The Sociology of Georg Simmel*, trans. and ed. Kurt H. Wolff (Glencoe, IL: Free Press, 1950).
[55] Luft, "Monetary Value and the Perception of Persons."
[56] Paul Slovic, Baruch Fischhoff, and Sarah Lichtenstein, "Facts versus Fears: Understanding Perceived Risk" in Daniel Kahneman, Paul Slovic, and Amos Tversky, eds., *Judgment under Uncertainty: Heuristics and Biases* (New York: Cambridge University Press, 1982), 464–5.

the "large and persistent biases" that frequently prevail. This subordination of calculation to emotion is the function of patriotic symbols in war and, to lesser degree,
is evident in money calculations, as well. But without some consideration of risk of
failure, enterprises will be more vulnerable to bankruptcy, and without some grasp
on probability, investment in education, career choices, and the purchase of consumer durables will certainly not maximize satisfaction.

Borrowed meanings

Finally, money symbols borrow meanings from other life domains, meanings used
by the market but not generated by it. For example, the meanings of money influence and are influenced by family life. People who grew up in families where
money was a central feature of conversation are more likely to be "money troubled" [Rubenstein]. As cause or symptom, family quarrels often center on the handling of money.[57] Thus, in assessing market rationality we must allow for the fact
that in using their money, people are fighting old quarrels (which they never win)
or reflecting childish illusions of omnipotence that Bergler finds carried over into
adulthood. This is a rather different and less satisfying way of "maximizing satisfaction" than that described by market rationality.

Summary

A more realistic approach to market behavior includes the treatment of money as a
symbol as well as a sign pointing to price or exchange value. Money symbols stand
for, suggest, and imply such things as personal inadequacy, the fruits of effort or
luck, shameful failure, moral evil, social unacceptability, suspicious behavior,
comfortable security, and much more. Money symbols distort economic rationality,
the formation of consistent, flexible, comparative, ego-syntonic, feasible preferences in many ways. They inhibit rational ends–means calculations and they reveal
and often exaggerate the intrinsic value of money. Symbolization of money increases transaction costs, distorts "prices," and impairs judgments for many people; for others it makes the transaction itself the primary object of attention. As a
consequence money symbols undermine utility maximization in the market.

And yet, if the political literature is any guide, the rational pursuit of monetary
self-interest is more or less inert.[58] Without symbolizing money, few (beyond the
subsistence level) would exert themselves to earn much more of it, few would value
it once they had it, seldom would people rouse themselves for great enterprises, and
we would "silently unbend the springs of action" that make the system go.

---

[57] Edith Neisser, "Emotional and Social Values Attached to Money," *Marriage and Family Living* 22
(1960): 132–8.
[58] Donald R. Kinder and D. Roderick Kiewiet, "Economic Discontents and Political Behavior: The Role
of Personal Grievances and Collective Economic Judgments in Congressional Voting," *American Journal of Political Science* 23 (1979): 495–527; David O. Sears, Richard R. Lau, Tom R. Tyler, and Harris
M. Allen, Jr., "Self-Interest vs. Symbolic Politics in Policy Attitudes and Presidential Voting," *American Political Science Review* 74 (1980): 670–84.

7 Economic and cognitive development in a market society

The nuclear cataclysm is over. The earth is covered with gray dust. In the vast silence no life exists, save in a little colony of algae deep in a leaden cleft long inured to radiation. The algae perceive their isolation; they reflect upon the strivings of all life, so recently ended, and on the strenuous task of evolution to be begun anew. Out of their reflection could emerge a firm conclusion: "Next time, no brains."

Ian McHarg, "Man and Environment"

In Chapter 4 we noted the lack of empirical relation between intelligence and education, on the one hand, and measures of happiness, on the other. Stimulated by this finding, and by other considerations, we questioned the actual compatibility of one pattern of cognition, the economists' version of rationality, and happiness. If happiness were our sole maximand, any incompatibility between happiness and cognition should cause us to lose interest in cognition. Such is not the case because our criteria for judging the market is two-fold; it embraces both hedonic well-being *and* a version of human development embracing complex cognition. In pursuing this interest in market effects on cognition here, we will now examine a very long period embracing what have been called "stages of civilization." For this purpose we will go beyond what we have called the *exchange effect*, the effect of market operations on those who participate in those operations, to the *affluence effect*, the effect of market-induced prosperity on those who benefit from it. We treat the market-cognition relationship reciprocally: How does economic development promote complex cognition? and How does complex cognition influence firm and national prosperity? If we find a pattern of mutual support, we will know that there is firm foundation for the belief that markets favor complex cognition.

After reviewing the definition of cognitive complexity in the first section, we turn in the second section to the record across stages of civilization: from hunting, gathering, and fishing economies to agricultural economies to industrial economies. In this section the main lesson is that it is the way people earn a living that determines the way they think. In a sense this represents a confirmation and correction of Schumpeter's idea that "it is to everyday economic tasks that we as a race owe our elementary training in rational thought." A second theme deals with the value for cognition of an economic surplus. We will see in this discussion evidence that an economic surplus may actually reduce the stimulus to live by one's wits – and so to reduce reliance on wits.

In the next section of the chapter, the contribution of a surplus to cognition is restored, *provided* that the surplus is used to reduce poverty, for in industrial societies poverty is the main impediment to cognitive development. Thus, the two main economic sources of cognitive development are challenging work and absence of poverty.

115

In order to understand the incentives of firms to encourage cognitive complexity among their workers, the last section puts forward the reversal of the causal inference: How does cognitive development contribute to economic development in a market economy? We find a paradox. Aggregate data suggest a major contribution, chiefly through education, but disaggregated data on specific causal pathways are much more ambiguous.

Cognitive complexity

Cognitive complexity and IQ. Recall from Chapter 1 that cognitive complexity has the following properties: It is the systematic and comparative use of concepts held with sufficient flexibility to permit appropriate change, operating at an abstract rather than a concrete or largely perceptual level, differentiating the parts of a stimulus complex and recombining them in new forms. It characterizes the properties of an object more on the basis of relevant object or situational characteristics than on the basis of preferences, thus enabling individuals

to assume a mental set willfully and consciously, . . . to account for one's acts to oneself or to others and to verbalize the act, . . . to shift reflectively from one aspect of the situation to another, . . . to [hold in mind] simultaneously various aspects [of a situation], . . . to grasp the essentials of a given whole, breaking it into useful parts, and to plan ahead and assume the attitude of the mere possible; to think counterfactually.[1]

Just as these dimensions are not well captured by the concept of "rational calculation," so they are also inadequately comprehended by IQ type tests. Yet we are constrained to use the results of these tests for most comparative purposes because there are no others. This use may be justified on three grounds: (1) the general importance in many tasks of the abstract problem-solving abilities that IQ is thought to measure, (2) most authorities acknowledge that intelligence tests contain some sort of general or "g" factor that accounts for the intercorrelation of the various measures of mental abilities, even across cultures,[2] and (3) the emphasis on linguistic skills in IQ tests. The importance of *language* is stressed by almost all authori-

[1] I have borrowed heavily from O. J. Harvey, David Hunt, and Harold M. Schroder, *Conceptual Systems and Personality Organization* (New York: Wiley, 1961), 10–34; I have also added some Piagetian concepts. The recent emphasis on *social* cognition adds concepts of cognitive balance, attribution, and schemata. For an analysis of these forms of cognition, see Susan T. Fiske and Shelley E. Taylor, *Social Cognition* (New York: Random House, 1984). For a somewhat different approach and analysis of our tendencies to fall short of accurate cognition, see Richard Nisbett and Lee Ross, *Human Inference: Strategies and Shortcomings of Social Judgment* (Englewood Cliffs, NJ: Prentice-Hall, 1980). Inevitably, specific measures abstract from these general cognitive abilities, focusing variously on abilities to see both liked and disliked features of an object (Bieri); ability to discern a figure in a complex background (an ability sometimes called "field independence" and sometimes "differentiation" by Witkin, and by Berry); discernment of commonalities in diverse objects – called "concept attainment" (Bruner et al.); imaginative solutions to puzzles (Wertheimer), and so forth. See Herman A. Witkin, R. B. Dyk, H. F. Faterson, D. R. Goodenough, and S. A. Karp, *Psychological Differentiation,* (New York: Wiley & Sons, 1962).
[2] "Despite arguments against the usefulness of a concept of g [for general factor], there is considerable evidence for its utility." John L. Horn and Gary Donaldson, "Cognitive Development in Adulthood," in Orville G. Brim, Jr., and Jerome Kagan, eds., *Constancy and Change in Human Development* (Cambridge: Harvard University Press, 1980), 445–529 at 465. Nevertheless, the cultural emphases differ greatly. For example, in Muslim cultures (Malaysia and Uganda) more emphasis is placed on social skills, the concept of intelligence being associated with such terms as "friendly," "honorable," "happy," and "public." (pp. 460–1)

ties. Vernon, for example, points out that the acquisition of intellectual abilities is dependent on language skills; among his conditions for high IQ scores is the cultivation of language and conversation in the home and among peers.[3]

Cultural bias. Authorities no longer speak of "culture-free" tests of intelligence, but rather of "culturally reduced" tests, such as the Ravens Progressive Matrices test. This test, however, is said to measure only one aspect of intelligence, "abstract problem-solving ability."[4] Again, the presence of the g factor found in the standard intelligence tests (Stanford-Binet, Wechsler) is some slight insurance of cultural fairness.

Inherited or learned. There is an important distinction between *fluid* intelligence (e.g., "series reasoning with abstract elements, identifying optional classifications, completing visual patterns") and *crystallized* intelligence (e.g., "verbal comprehension, the ability to use social conventions . . . in making reasonable decisions for which information is relevant.") Fluid intelligence is thought to depend less on education and experience, that is, to be more nearly innate, whereas crystallized intelligence is more a product of experience and education, though education makes some contribution to fluid intelligence as well.[5] In fact, the best estimate of the inheritance from parental genotype to child genotype seems to be "between 0.30 and 0.40"[6] If market experiences contribute to intelligence at all, they will contribute only to crystallized intelligence.

Kinds of intelligence. In reconceptualizing intelligence Sternberg has produced a three-part breakdown of the concept: (1) *componential:* high test scores and superior verbal skills; (2) *experiential:* ability to combine disparate experiences and to synthesize them in creative or at least useful ways; (3) *contextual:* "street smarts," ability to perceive ways to manipulate the environment and to develop strategies to achieve goals.[7] Standard IQ measures tap the first component, which successfully predicts academic performance, but not teacher performance or medical performance. It seems that the second and third parts of the concept are more relevant to success in the market. The antiintellectualism of businesspersons reported in Chapter 1 might well be based on their resentment toward "intellectuals" who command the heights of componential intelligence and then patronize those who have "mere" contextual intelligence. None of the intelligence tests measure motivation or purposiveness.

[3] Philip E. Vernon, *Intelligence and Cultural Environment* (London: Methuen, 1969), 47–9, 230.
[4] James R. Flynn, "Massive IQ Gains in 14 Nations: What IQ Tests Really Measure," *Psychological Bulletin* 101 (1987): 171–91.
[5] Horn and Donaldson, "Cognitive Development in Adulthood," 460–1.
[6] Christopher Jencks, *Inequality: A Reassessment of the Effect of Family and Schooling in America* (New York: Harper/Colophon, 1972), 271.
[7] Robert J. Sternberg, *Beyond IQ: A Triarchic Theory of Human Intelligence* (New York: Cambridge University Press, 1984). Sternberg (Yale) and Howard Gardner (Harvard) report that there are over a dozen types of intelligence, of which standard IQ tests measure only one or two. These authors have developed an instrument that measures insight, tacit knowledge (practical savvy useful in business and daily life), "social perception," and other aspects of intelligence not captured by the various versions of the Stanford-Binet, Wechsler, or other IQ tests.

What seems missing in all these accounts of cognitive complexity and intelligence is any reference to the ingredients of economic rationality, preference scheduling and the development of payoff matrices. Does this neglect, again, suggest the inadequacy of the rationality concept? In his introduction to his book *Productive Thinking,* Wertheimer points out that although "training in traditional logic . . . contributes to critical-mindedness; . . . it does not, in itself, seem to give rise to productive thinking. In short, there is the danger of being empty and senseless, though exact; and there is always the difficulty with regard to real productiveness."[8]

The influence of economic development on cognitive development

We turn here to an examination of the relation of economic development, mostly at early stages, and cognitive development. What I will show is that there is no *necessary* relation between economic surpluses and cognitive development, although in industrial societies where the surplus improves the standard of living of the poorest group, the contribution is massive. The main influence over the large sweep of human history seems to be in the way people earn their livings. In this sense, the discussion is an anticipation of the discussion in Chapter 13 on the effects of various work tasks on cognition. What follows is a specification of the broader themes of environmental psychology focusing in this case on economic influences over cognitive style.[9]

From hunting and gathering to agriculture to industry
The most extensive work linking cognition to economic patterns has been done by John W. Berry, employing measures with "culture reduced" content whose core concepts are "disembedding" a figure or thought from its holistic background. The tests are designed to measure *discrimination,* "making relatively fine visual discrimination from a fairly uniform background; . . . *analysis,* . . . the visual extraction of a small figure from an organized context; . . . *restructuring,* . . . the reorganization of materials following analysis; and *spatial and inferential behavior,* . . . more complex operations subsequent to these earlier ones."[10] In his extensive cross-cultural studies of differentiation (the central concepts in the tests) involving twenty hunting-and-gathering, pastoral, and agricultural societies from ten different cultures, Berry found that the capacity to differentiate objects and to separate parts

[8] Max Wertheimer, *Productive Thinking,* rev. ed. (New York: Harper, 1959), 10.
[9] In spite of the great advances in cross-cultural psychology in the past decade, we are handicapped by the fact that some of the most extensive research focuses either on cognitive differences *or* on the effect of economic forces on personality but not on cognition. Thus Dasen's cross-cultural work on Piagetian psychology is not linked to economic variables, and the extensive research by the Whitings on the relations among "maintenance systems," socialization, and child and adult behavior does not treat cognitive styles. See, for example, Pierre R. Dasen, ed., *Piagetian Psychology: Cross-Cultural Contributions* (New York: Gardner/Wiley/Halsted, 1977); Beatrice B. Whiting and John W. M. Whiting, *Children of Six Cultures* (Cambridge: Harvard University Press, 1975).
[10] John W. Berry, *Human Ecology and Cognitive Style* (Beverly Hills, CA: Sage/Halsted, 1976), 61–2, 136. The underlying concept is *differentiation,* originally called "field independence" by the author of some of these tests and the originator of the conceptual analysis, Herman Witkin, and contrasted to "field dependence," a tendency to accept wholes as indivisible gestalts. See Witkin et al., *Psychological Differentiation.*

from wholes was, compared to agricultural economies, relatively high in hunting-and-gathering societies. The members of agricultural economies seemed less able to analyze parts and wholes, and in some tests, to separate themselves from the object examined. As measured by these kinds of tests, differentiation is associated with independence and desire for autonomy, as contrasted to an obedience and more passive, group acceptance facilitating accommodation to more hierarchical social structures.[11] Berry tested his hypothesis with a different (Asch-type) measure of conformity and again found that nomadic peoples, and those with a loosely knit pastoral or hunting organization of their economies were more independent and less conformist than people in the more stable agricultural economies.[12]

Berry also studied the effects on these "less developed" societies of contacts with Western culture, focusing on education, wage labor, and urbanization. He found that both the societies and the individuals with differentiated thinking patterns adjusted better to Western culture, with less stress and trauma, than societies without these patterns. Although he does not treat the influence of "wage labor" in detail, as part of his index of the degree and persistence of the culture contact with the West, wage labor was a relatively inoffensive feature of market economics wherever societies already had the kind of differentiated cognition that Western societies possess.[13] Observe that because of their cognitive readiness for market conditions, it is the "more primitive" hunting-and-gathering societies, rather than the "more advanced," agricultural societies that accommodate to Western culture with less strain.

Although not specifically focusing on thinking processes, an earlier study by Barry, Child, and Bacon followed a somewhat similar course of reasoning and came to a similar conclusion. Arguing that "economic role tends to be generalized to the rest of behavior," these authors focused on the relation between degree of food accumulation and certain personality characteristics implying different degrees of innovation and individualistic patterns of thinking. "In societies with low accumulation of food and resources, adults should tend to be individualistic, assertive and venturesome [whereas adults in] societies with high accumulation should be . . . conventional, compliant and conservative."[14] Food accumulation, they held, had the effect of encouraging routine patterns of behavior and risk aversion. Animal husbandry involved the greatest degree of food accumulation, agriculture (cereals and roots) the next, and fishing and hunting the least. Socialization stressed responsibility and obedience in animal husbandry economies, and to a lesser degree in stable agricultural economies, and least in hunting and fishing economies. In contrast, socialization for achievement and independence (and, for girls, self-reliance) was most stressed in hunting and fishing economies, less so in agriculture, and least in animal husbandry economies. Combining these measures into an index of "pressure toward compliance," these authors found that this pressure was greatest among

[11] Berry, *Human Ecology and Cognitive Style,* chaps 7 and 8.
[12] J. W. Berry, "A Cultural Ecology of Social Behavior," in L. Berkowitz, ed., *Advances in Experimental Social Psychology,* vol. 12 (New York: Academic Press, 1979), 190–200.
[13] Berry, *Human Ecology and Cognitive Style,* chap. 8.
[14] Herbert A. Barry, Irvin L. Child, and Margaret K. Bacon, "Relation of Child Training to Subsistence Economy," *American Anthropologist* 61 (1959): 51–63 at 52–3.

those engaged in animal husbandry, less in agricultural economies, and least among the fishing and hunting groups.[15]

The economic history of the West has consistently taught that economic surpluses were the very source and foundation of civilization. They provided the basis for urban living, for supporting education, art, and invention, and for the general growth of knowledge. It is stimulating to discover that certain prized elements of modern civilization – achievement orientation, intellectual independence, and a kind of cognitive complexity – were more related to what people did for a living than how well they lived.

From these two studies we learn of the powerful effects of broad ecological/economic pressures on cognitive style (Berry) and on personality dimensions closely related to cognitive styles. The explanation of these effects is a functional one: People learn to think in ways that help them earn a living. Rejecting genetic selection as a cause of the differences in degrees of differentiation between agricultural and hunting-and-gathering (and fishing) societies, Berry stresses cultural adaptation and socialization as the main explanations, especially adult adaptation since his measures of socialization show only modest relations to his measure of differentiation. People and societies are selectively rewarded by higher standards of living for adopting a pattern of cognition that is adaptive to their economic and social tasks. And, to introduce a different line of argument, the obedience and compliance of peasants in agricultural societies reward the elite rather better than the peasants.

Concepts of progress in economic and cognitive development

What is interesting about this pattern is the incompatibility of what we might think of as economic progress and cognitive progress over human history. Economic progress might be defined in efficiency terms (higher per capita GNP) or, more neutrally, in terms of serving better whatever pattern of living has been "chosen." Thus Berry, understandably reluctant to call agriculture a "higher" stage than hunting and gathering, says that "wherever it is possible [because of temperature and rainfall], societies produce or grow their own food rather than gathering or chasing it."[16] In the same manner, it is possible to speak of economic "development" without ethnocentrism by grounding "development" in the tendency for developing countries to *choose* industrialization and some other aspects of modernity – the material rather than the political and cultural aspects.[17] (Few scholars would applaud this selection of the values of a material over an intellectual civilization, revealing once again the ambiguous advantages of marketlike reliance on individual choices.)

Concepts of cognitive development, shunned by most modern anthropologists, might be based on the same kind of reasoning. Since the value of a cognitive style is tied to the purposes of a society, one might speak of cognitive development as that form of cognition that best suits the purposes of any given society. Thus, says

[15] Ibid., 57.
[16] Berry, *Human Ecology and Cognitive Style*, 48.
[17] See Leonard W. Doob, *Becoming More Civilized: A Psychological Exploration* (New Haven: Yale University Press, 1960).

Berry, "high differentiation would be 'better' in a hunting and gathering society and low differentiation would be 'better' in agricultural societies. . . . No universal value is likely to be applicable, given the nature of extant cultural differences; it is ethnocentric to argue otherwise."[18] We must reject this definition because it would lead to support for the idea that when work is routine and unchallenging, cognitive dullness appropriate to that work represents cognitive development. The definition of cognitive complexity employed here is not depreciated because work does not employ such complexity. Rather, it is the work that is at fault.

The evidence presented here to the effect that *"less* advanced" stages of economic development (in the sense indicated) are associated with *"more* advanced" stages of cognition suggests that economic progress in various segments of its journey may not depend on cognitive development, contrary to Schultz's human capital theory. If the two have no necessary relation to each other in the step from hunting and gathering to agriculture, we have no reason to think that the transitions from agriculture to industry will be associated with increased cognitive powers, nor later, the transition from the age of coal and iron to the age of electronics and computerization. Berry's evidence that there is a curvilinearity in the relation between economic modes of production and differentiated thinking such that the thinking pattern favorable to hunting-and-gathering economies is also favorable to modern market economies[19] is hopeful, but does not permit reliance on economic changes to accelerate cognitive complexity.

It is better to think of each technological advance (water wheel, horse collar, moldboard plow, computerized production, etc.) as each having its own cognitive effect and therefore each subject to separate evaluation on those grounds. Concepts of "progress" tend to assume what has to be proven.

Cognitive development in socialist economies

If the economic forces that propel cognitive development are some combination of (1) the reduction or elimination of poverty, (2) occupational tasks that require more cognitive complexity, and (3) increased average levels of education, there seems little that is specifically related to market processes that is necessary for cognitive development. Any prosperous, industrialized economy might do the same, whether state socialist or worker-owned and -managed cooperatives. A brief examination of the work of Soviet psychologist A. R. Luria on cognitive growth in the Soviet Union, and certain studies of the kibbutz society will help us to discover what is special about the market in this respect.

Reports on cognitive development in the Soviet Union. Luria examined the development of cognition in an economic system that deemphasized individual gain, self-reliance, and individual material wealth, emphasizing instead collective gains, social rather than material rewards, and team productivity. In that milieu, Luria

---

[18] Berry, *Human Ecology and Cognitive Style*, 219.
[19] "In any systematic study of relationships between sociocultural variables and ecological or behavioral ones, this nonlinearity must now be taken into account." Berry, *Human Ecology and Cognitive Style*, 23; see also p. 61.

developed a theory of cognitive progression from external instruction to overt self-instruction to implicit self-instruction involving symbolic rehearsals of various alternatives. Instead of following Pavlov, who dominated Soviet psychology during the first fifteen years of the Soviet regime, Luria sought to explain cognitive development (1931–2) among the peasants in Uzbekistan and Kighizia by a theory similar to Berry's.[20] Employing tests of color classification, classification of objects, logical reasoning, and tests of imagination, Luria compared the cognitive levels of traditional village men and women with those participating in collective farms and given literacy training. He was able to show the higher cognitive levels of those who had entered the Soviet version of the modern economy.[21]

These Soviet developmental gains are similar to, though less marked than, those of Puerto Rican children entering a market economy. Moreover, to the extent that Luria relies on occupational roles, there is little reason to believe that they would be different within occupational categories in any market economy – although slower movements from farms to cities would retard developmental processes in the Soviet Union.[22] We cannot, therefore, use this comparison to reveal the effects of the exchange and contingency paradigm, internality, self-reliance, frequency of choice, or the other elements of market economies that concern us. Moreover, the autonomy of economics from culture and politics is inappropriate, as our emphasis on systemic interrelations in Chapter 2 implies. Witkin, Berry, and others have reported that cognitive development (as indexed by differentiation) is slower in more authoritarian societies,[23] a matter that Luria did not discuss.

Cognitive development in the kibbutz. Reports on children of the kibbutz vary in the measures they employ and the cognitive developments that concern them. Rorschach tests suggest that, compared to other Israeli children, the "kibbutz group reacts more immediately with less anxiety and inhibition," have "higher intellectual development," but show no differences in achievement tests; they also seem generally less motivated and less ambitious.[24] Other studies show slower initial intellectual development, but, in the end, development to a level equal to that of children reared outside the kibbutz.[25] A study of moral judgment shows kibbutz children to be more rigid and "absolutistic" than Israeli city children who are more

---

[20] A. R. Luria, *Cognitive Development: It's Cultural and Social Foundations.* (Cambridge: Harvard University Press, 1976).

[21] Ibid., 29. Luria's "materialist psychology" borrows nothing from Marx and, like many Western theories, relies on the effects of occupational demands and educational practices within cultural milieux that have been historically shaped. But whatever the theory, the results have been sufficient to impress even Western psychologists. See Vernon, *Intelligence and Cultural Environment,* 230.

[22] Subsequent reports of Luria's studies, available only in Russian, might reveal ways in which cognitive development in a command economy relied on processes different from those of any other developing nation, including market economies, but there is nothing in Luria's work in English that suggests a difference.

[23] Witkin et al., *Psychological Differentiation,* 145–6.

[24] Albert J. Rabin, "Kibbutz Adolescents," in Dorothy Rogers, ed., *Issues in Adolescent Psychology* (New York: Appleton-Century-Crofts, 1969), 592–606. Many psychologists believe that Rorschach tests have as many interpretations as there are interpreters and doubt their validity.

[25] Irvin L. Child, "Personality in Culture," in Edgar F. Borgatta and William W. Lambert, eds., *Handbook of Personality Theory and Research* (Chicago: Rand McNally, 1968), 82–145 at 116.

flexible and more likely to take into account the special circumstances of each case. The conflicting influences on the city children were thought to make them more cognitively flexible.[26]

The comparison of the effects of economic development on cognition in a market economy with the effects in a command economy and in socialist kibbutzim suggests that the effects of collectively or nationally owned property on cognition is minimal. Given the lack of comparability between these studies and studies in market economies, we can say with more confidence that cognitive development is facilitated by modern occupational roles and educational processes, as Inkeles and Smith have established for six developing nations regardless of the presence or absence of market institutions.[27] And given the preceding reports on the kibbutzim and recent reports on the USSR, it also seems probable that the lack of motivational pressures for personal advancement retards some forms of "street smarts," although the reduction of anxiety (to be discussed in the next chapter) liberates other unspecified cognitive qualities. People do learn cognitive complexity without career rewards, but they probably learn more and better with them.[28] The motivation offered by the sense that one's success relies on personal skills must inevitably be a consideration. I examine some of these market features in Chapter 9.

Industrialism, poverty and cognitive development

Poverty

In all societies poverty is the principal enemy of cognitive development. Poverty implies "poor nutrition and health, overcrowded homes, lack of intellectual stimulation, inferior language background, lack of parental interest in education, poor schooling, and insecure economic future."[29] These effects are cumulative as is made clear by an early (1923) study of English canal boat children whose IQs declined from age four to six years (mean IQ = 90) to adolescence (mean IQ = 60). In this study of poverty-stricken children the correlation between IQ and age was −.75. The cumulative effect of circumstances that fail to foster intellectual development starts early: "It is commonly observed in a progressive drop in the IQs for children of the poor between the ages of fifteen or eighteen months and five or six years."[30] Although recent research may reveal earlier differences,[31] the current

---

[26] Avner Ziv, David Green, and Joseph Guttman, "Moral Judgment Differences Between City, Kibbutz, and Israeli Arab Preadolescents on the Realistic-Relativistic Dimension," *Journal of Cross-Cultural Psychology* 9 (1978): 215–25.

[27] Alex Inkeles and David H. Smith, *Becoming Modern* (Cambridge: Harvard University Press, 1974).

[28] "People differ in the value they place on approval, money, material possessions, social status, exemption from restrictions, and the like. Values determine behavior in that prized incentives can motivate activities required to secure them, disvalued incentives do not. The higher the incentive value, the higher the level of performance." Albert Bandura, *Social Learning Theory* (Englewood Cliffs, NJ: Prentice-Hall, (1977), 139.

[29] Vernon, *Intelligence and Cultural Environment,* 33.

[30] J. McV. Hunt and Girvin E. Kirk, "Social Aspects of Intelligence: Evidence and Issues," in Robert Cancro, ed., *Intelligence: Genetic and Environmental Influences* (New York: Grune & Stratton, 1971), 296.

[31] Whereas previous tests of infant intelligence using motor skills have had "zero predictability" for later cognitive abilities, research in the late 1980s using visual memory has had considerable success in

evidence that the children of all social classes seem to have similar measured "intelligences" until about the age of two, when the effects of wealth and poverty begin to make them diverge, is a startling comment on the power of economics to influence intelligence.

Some of the effects of poverty are purely physiological: the human brain is particularly vulnerable to diet deficiencies from three months prior to six months after birth – and the effects are irreversible. Compared to children from poor families without dietary supplements, children whose mothers were given such supplements during pregnancy gained five IQ points.[32] Of the twenty-three million babies born in India each year, nineteen million will survive, and of these 84 percent will suffer more or less serious malnutrition, undermining the development of their natural cognitive and other abilities.[33]

Many of the effects of poverty, however, are due to poor socialization and lack of early stimulation. An experiment in Milwaukee took twenty preschool children of poor black mothers in day-care facilities with one caretaker for every twenty infants and transferred them to a day-care facility with one professional caretaker for every three children. The children's average IQs increased from 75 to 124. When they were returned to their homes and ordinary schooling their IQs regressed to 109, a loss but "nevertheless the . . . effect of the educational day care during preschool years continued to be manifest in their superiority over [children without such an enriched experience]. . . . Plasticity can cut both ways, but early gains tend to be maintained."[34]

Compared to middle-class children, the children of working- and lower-class parents fail to learn future planning, are less likely to be made responsible for their own behavior, receive more commands and fewer instructions, become more present- and less future-oriented, and do not learn that the environment is more or less lawful and can be mastered. "Life for the lower class family is less purposive since future economic circumstances, housing, and so forth are largely outside their control." These children also have poor linguistic models and learn a form of speech that is parochial both in its handling of referents and in its grammatical and lexical forms. As a consequence of these linguistic patterns, schools, inevitably middle-class in speech and reference, are uncongenial and do not elicit effort.[35] Fortunately, not only do enriched day-care facilities improve cognitive performance, but also "teaching mothers of poverty to be better teachers of their own infants and preschool children"[36] has similar, if less dramatic, effects.

Industrialization and modernization. Industrialization, which under early market conditions led to the brutalization of children, now seems often to have the

predicting both subnormal and superior intellectual performances later in childhood. Gina Kolata, reporting work by Joseph Fagan and by Marc H. Bornstein and Susan Rose in the *New York Times,* 4 April 1989, p. C1.

[32] Vernon, *Intelligence and Cultural Environment,* 35–7.

[33] *The Economist* 286 (18 March 1983).

[34] Hunt and Kirk, "Social Aspects of Intelligence," 275.

[35] Vernon, *Intelligence and Cultural Environment,* 50–5. Vernon refers to Bernstein's work on the typical speech patterns of working class and middle class children. See Basil Bernstein, *Class, Codes, and Control* (St. Albans, UK: Paladin, 1973).

[36] Hunt and Kirk, "Social Aspects of Intelligence," 296.

opposite effect. A 1966 study of Puerto Rico, then experiencing accelerated industrialization,

found children aged 7 and 8, who enjoyed the advantages of prosperity associated with the coming of industrialization, with mental ages as high as or higher than those of their parents who were reared in the rural poverty characteristic of the inland portion of the island before industrialization. In this study children and parents were tested at the same time. The parents, despite their low IQs, were functioning adequately in their traditional roles, [but were less well prepared than their children for the roles of the newly industrialized community].[37]

The concept of early capitalism, frozen in the Marxist ideology for a hundred years, assimilates such evidence only with difficulty.

To the extent that cognitive development is a product of education and better health, economic development throughout the world has similar effects. For the quarter century from 1950 to 1975 in low-income countries (excluding India and China) primary school attendance increased from 50 percent to 83 percent for males and from 24 percent to 55 percent for females, and high school attendance increased from 6 percent to 19 percent. Health improvements were equally impressive, with life expectancy increasing in the low-income countries from forty-one years in 1960 to fifty-eight years in 1981, and with middle-income countries increasing a decade, from fifty to sixty in the same period. These educational and health gains were associated with substantial gains in per capita GNP during much of this period: 2.9 percent per year among the poor countries and 3.7 percent per year in the middle-income countries, the latter exceeding the growth rates (3.5 percent) of the advanced countries.[38] Unhappily, this trend of advancing prosperity and educational and cognitive development was reversed in the later 1970s and 1980s with the consequence that at least in sub-Saharan Africa "four fifths of the 39 countries experienced declines [in GNP]. For the first time since World War II . . . a whole region has suffered retrogression over a generation."[39] The economic basis of cognitive development could not be portrayed more graphically.

Recessions and cognitive development. Scholars have been made familiar with the effect of economic recessions on mental illness by the work of Harvey Brenner;[40] it now seems clear that there is a similar effect on intelligence or cognitive complexity of many kinds. The effect works chiefly through thrusting a cohort of infants and children into poverty, depriving them of their cognitive abilities and accelerating the losses of intelligence associated with poverty. Socialization suffers

[37] Ibid., 275.
[38] Arnold C. Harberger, "Economic Policy and Economic Growth," in Harberger, ed., *World Economic Growth* (San Francisco: Institute for Contemporary Studies, 1984), 365–6.
[39] World Bank, *Financing Adjustment with Growth* (April 1986), reported in Glenys Kinnock, "Preface," in Joan Lestor and David Ward, *Beyond Band Aid: Charity is Not Enough* (London: Fabian Society, 1987), 2–3.
[40] M. Harvey Brenner, *Mental Illness and the Economy* (Cambridge: Harvard University Press, 1973). Brenner's work, relying substantially on differential rates of admission to mental hospitals, has been criticized on the grounds that increased admissions during recessions do not necessarily mean increased incidence or prevalence of mental illness, but rather that families that had been able to take care of their mentally disturbed members found themselves unable to do so during a recession and turned to mental hospitals to care for their ill members. See papers presented at the National Institute of Mental Health Conference on Mental Health and the Economy, Center for Metropolitan Studies, Hunt Valley, Maryland, June 1–3, 1978. Some of these papers are summarized in the *New York Times,* 6 April 1982, p. C1.

when the father is unemployed, though girls seem to suffer more than boys from this effect.[41] Some of these losses may be recaptured later with the return of prosperity, but some are, as Vernon reports, irretrievably lost. These, then, are lifetime losses whose consequences will be felt throughout the lives of the deprived – and possibly by their children. Beveridge spoke of ignorance as one of the Giant Evils to be banished by the welfare state; how much more urgent is the need to banish the decrements of thinking power associated with poverty and regularly inflicted on a portion of the population by the down phases of the business cycle!

The market contributes mightily to cognitive development by its success in creating the conditions for economic growth. It detracts from this contribution whenever it reduces growth and more especially whenever GNP per capita declines. The market's tendencies toward inequality are, by themselves, quite irrelevant to this contribution, but wherever that inequality implies poverty, market economies lose some of their credits. Relying on the market's immanent unfolding processes is no solution; the market must be helped.

Cognitive development as a source of economic development

If economic development has a large potential, but variable, effect on cognitive devlopment, is the reverse causal effect similarly potent? Does cognitive development contribute to economic development? The matter is important because if the two are mutually and reciprocally supportive, improvement of one will tend to contribute to the other. In a market economy, however, it is possible for a general improvement of cognition to benefit firms without any single firm having sufficient incentive to further that improvement. As in the case of industrial skills, firms investing in training an employee risk losing the trained individual to other firms who have not so invested. Thus, in a market economy, to find that cognitive complexity promotes economic development in general does not guarantee that those measures necessary for that development will be adopted.

From the estimates of the contribution of education and human capital to economic growth and increased productivity, one would infer that cognitive complexity has an immediate and strong effect on that productivity. That may well be true, but the path is unclear and the relationships, which we draw from a variety of sources, are complex. To help clarify these relationships, and yet to avoid a detailed and intricate analysis of the causes of economic growth (which is, in any event, beyond our powers and unnecesary to our purpose), consider the matrix in Figure 7.1. Human capital is conceived as some combination of cognitive skills and personality that is in unknown degree derivative from education.

Three of the independent variables, education, growth in knowledge, and the summary variable, human capital (duplicating education and adding health), behave as predicted.

Education contributes to increased economic productivity. As mentioned in Chapter 1, macro measures show that increases in level of education in a popu-

[41]Glen H. Elder, Tri Van Nguyen, and Avshalom Caspi, "Linking Family Hardship to Children's Lives," *Family Development: Child Development* 85 (1985): 361–75.

Independent variables	Mediating variables	Dependent variable

1. Years of education
2. Cognitive skills (IQ)
 	
3. Personality,
  e.g., industriousness
 	
Human capital
	5. Individual occupational
	  and income attainment
	
	6. Job performance
		7. Increase in per capita GNP

4. Knowledge: State of arts

Figure 7.1. *Cognitive skills and increases in per capita GNP*

lation are strongly related to increases in GNP. During the 1929–69 period, increased education contributed about a quarter of the total gain in economic growth of that period,[42] with later estimates showing an acceleration of that contribution during the period of the 1970s when the influence of other factors actually declined.[43] Denison gives an explanation for this relationship.

The continuous upward shift in educational background has upgraded the skills and versatility of labor and contributed to the rise of national income. It has enhanced the skills of individuals within what are conventionally termed occupations, often with considerable changes in the work actually performed; it has also permitted a shift in occupational composition from occupations in which workers typically have little education and low earnings toward those in which education and earnings are higher. Education also heightens a person's awareness of job opportunities and thereby the chances that he is employed where his marginal product is greatest. A more educated work force also is better able to learn about and use the most efficient production practices.[44]

The analytical problem that confronts us is to reconcile this view with the more detailed evidence on two major sets of relationships: first, the weak relation between measures of cognitive complexity and (1) job performance, (2) income, and (3) occupational attainment; and second, the uncertain relation between individual occupation achievements and the increases in economic productivity measured by GNP. In short, the microstudies show only a minimal relationship between IQ and performance or income, and the macromeasures show the greatest gains in IQ in

---

[42] Edward F. Denison, *Accounting for United States Economic Growth 1929–1969* (Washington, DC: Brookings Institution, 1985), 113.

[43] Martin N. Baily and Alok K. Chakrabarti, *Innovation and the Productivity Crisis* (Washington, DC: Brookings Institution, 1988), 15.

[44] Denison, *Trends in American Economic Growth, 1929–1982* (Washington, DC: Brookings Institution, 1985), 15. Baily and Chakrabarti, *Innovation and the Productivity Crisis,* 15–16, take issue with the allegation that the decline in the *quality* of education accounts for the productivity slowdown. The decline in Scholastic Aptitude Test scores from the cohort born in 1945 to the cohort born in 1962 is substantial, but half of that decline is attributable to the fact that "as more and more students finished high school, the bottom tail of the distribution lengthened." Thus the value of having more people receive the benefits of education must be weighed against the fact that the average effect of education is weakened. Moreover, the increased proportion of young people in the work force was not large enough to account for much of the slowdown in productivity – and that increase was reversed in the 1980s.

those post-war years when growth of GNP was actually declining.[45] We will examine the relationships more closely.

Human capital contributes to increased economic productivity. Although human capital has been defined rather narrowly by economists (i.e., skills and knowledge related to finding, holding, and performing well in market jobs), it includes some of those cognitive powers and cognitions that are embraced by the larger concept of cognitive complexity already outlined. As mentioned in Chapter 1, the return on human capital has recently been higher than the return on physical capital with the consequence that "human capital has become the more dominant form of accumulation, and both private and public expenditures on education and medical care have grown at rapid rates in the past half century."[46]

Knowledge (managerial and technological) contributes to economic productivity. Separate from the growth of education and human capital is the somewhat ill-defined and residual factor of "advances of knowledge;" it is a very important one. For the 1929–69 period these "advances in knowledge" contributed an additional amount equal to twice the contribution of education, representing the largest single allocated contribution to economic growth.[47] Advances in knowledge must surely be the product of complex cognition, but it could be by a very small group, in which case general levels of IQ would not be related to increases in productivity.

Education increases cognitive skills. Among the independent variables, amount of education [1] (numbers in brackets refer to variables in Figure 7.1) makes a clear contribution to [2] cognitive skills (as measured by IQ), though the size of this contribution is somewhat controversial. Jencks tells us that each year of schooling increases IQ by only about one point[48] – not overwhelming, but cumulatively important. Vernon, on the other hand, finds schooling more important: "In Western countries the level of adult intelligence depends on the kind and amount of the adolescent's secondary schooling and occupation."[49] Schooling and cognitive skills may be measured independently, but they are fairly closely correlated. Dasen's cross-cultural Piagetian research finds that "school attendance is a necessary but not sufficient condition for the attainment of formal operations."[50]

Education increases individual occupational attainment. Evidence from Blau and Duncan also tells us that the strongest path to occupational attainment is from [1] education to [5a] first job to [5b] later occupational attainment, with a

---

[45] Flynn, "Massive IQ Gains in 14 Nations."
[46] Jeffrey G. Williamson and Peter H. Lindert, *American Inequality: A Macroeconomic History* (New York: Academic Press, 1980), 202. Unhappily, the emphasis on human capital has the effect of increasing economic inequality and "has a strong anti-poor bias." Ibid.
[47] Denison, *Accounting for United States Economic Growth*, 113.
[48] Jencks et al., *Inequality*, 88.
[49] Vernon, *Intelligence and Cultural Environment*, 222.
[50] Pierre R. Dasen, "Introduction," in Dasen, ed., *Piagetian Psychology*, 7.

strong support for a more direct route from [1] education to final [5] occupational attainment.[51]

Personality factors contribute to individual occupational attainment. The relationship between [2] personality and [5] individual attainment is also fairly well established. Thus Jencks found that teacher ratings of student qualities were directly related to achievement and, by inference, may have contributed to actual job performance, although this was unmeasured. "While no single, well-defined trait emerged [from teacher ratings] as a decisive determinant of economic success," says Jencks, "the combined effects of many different measures were typically as strong as the combined effects that we used to measure cognitive skills." Of the nine teacher ratings, "industriousness" was the most important in predicting occupational success, a personality quality highly correlated with "cooperativeness," "dependability," and "emotional control." Although these qualities had a great deal to do with staying in school (and thus might be confounded with educational achievement), they also had sturdy independent effects of their own. As for income, teacher ratings of "executive ability" were more predictive than "industriousness."[52] In sum:

Noncognitive measures explained at least as much of the variance in men's status and earnings as test scores did. While we could not isolate any single personality characteristic that was critical to success, we can say that the relevant traits are largely independent of both cognitive skills and parental status. . . . Men's traits at the time they enter the labor force could well explain 55 to 60 percent of the observed variance in their later occupational status [and throughout their working lives].

Something like half of the observed variance in these men's annual earnings is attributable to stable personal characteristics that they carry with them from one job to the next.[53]

But [2] cognitive skills are apparently not related to [3] the kinds of personality qualities that contribute to occupational achievement.[54]

Education may or may not contribute to relevant personality factors. At this point, the crucial question is the contribution of [1] education to [3] these predictive personality variables. On the one hand, education has been said to do more than provide credentials and improve cognitive complexity; it also changes attitudes and trains people in disciplined work habits.[55] On the other hand, these findings are somewhat (but not wholly) dissonant with the findings of a longitudinal study of a group of inner-city working-class youth first interviewed at about age fourteen. The research showed that *work experience,* including, but by no means

[51] Peter M. Blau and Otis D. Duncan, *American Occupational Structure* (1967; reprint New York: Free Press, 1978), 170.
[52] Christopher Jencks, Susan Bartlett, et al., *Who Gets Ahead? The Determinants of Economic Success in America* (New York: Basic Books, 1979), 222–3. In studies of both national economic productivity and individual economic success there are very large residual terms; for productivity studies these unexplained residuals are assigned to "advances in knowledge;" for individual achievement studies they are assigned by Jencks to "luck." (pp. 307–8)
[53] Ibid., 230, 301, 305.
[54] Ibid., 230.
[55] Howard R. Bowen, *Investment in Learning: The Individual and Social Value of American Higher Education* (San Francisco: Jossey-Bass, 1978); Herbert H. Hyman, Charles R. Wright, and John S. Reed, *The Enduring Effects of Education* (Chicago: University of Chicago Press, 1975).

limited to, hard work at school (as measured by achievements above the predicted level) predicted, after thirty years, occupational success and other criteria of superior social adjustments. The evidence on early perseverance in and dedication to one's work was a better predictor than knowledge of parental background or other demographic statuses. Intelligence "was not a critical mediating factor."[56] Early induction into disciplined, purposive work – the "industriousness" that Jencks's teacher ratings revealed – serves at least as well as the cognitive abilities measured by IQ tests or grades to prepare people for work in a market – or probably any – economy.

So far, (1) cognitive complexity seems not to be related to personality factors that explain as much of the variance in personal achievement as do IQ measures, and (2) education is by no means a necessary condition for the relevant personality factors.

The relationships among the mediating variables is less clear.

Cognitive skills (IQ) are not closely related to income or occupational attainment. Lester Thurow reports that "standard economic variables (skills, I.Q., hours of work, etc.) could [in the relevant research] explain only 20 to 30 percent of the variance in individual earnings. Either economics is missing some key factor or . . . the world is much less deterministic and much more stochastic . . . than had been suspected."[57] And Jencks says, "The relationship between test scores and economic success is even more attenuated than [other relationships]. To begin with, occupational success depends on a wide variety of factors besides on-the-job performance. In addition, on-the-job performance depends on noncognitive as well as cognitive skills, and on attitudes and motivation. The net effect . . . is to reduce the association between test scores and economic success to a rather modest level."[58]

Among managers and professionals there is considerable evidence that performance has little to do with pay and promotion. Two large studies show that although education is related to initial job placement and grade level, measured performance is either unrelated to or negatively related to pay level or pay increases.[59] There is even greater doubt about the relationship of the pay of chief executive officers and their performances.[60]

[56] George E. Vaillant and Caroline O. Vaillant, "Natural History of Male Psychological Health: Work as a Predictor of Positive Mental Heath," *American Journal of Psychiatry* 138 (1981): 1,322–440.

[57] Lester Thurow, "Economics 1977," *Daedalus* 106 (Fall 1977), 81.

[58] Jencks et al., *Inequality*, 57. This, however, is not a necessary market relationship – or lack thereof – since, as Jencks points out, the Swedish relationship between IQ and earnings is more substantial. Very possibly the lack of influence of IQ on job performance is exaggerated in the American market. Environmentalists will be pleased to find that the genes that influence IQ scores appear to have relatively little influence on income." (p. 255)

[59] Gene Dalton and Paul H. Thomson, "Accelerating Obsolescence of Older Engineers," *Harvard Business Review* 49 (1971): 57–67; unpublished research at Harvard by James L. Medoff and Katherine G. Abraham, both reported in Shlomo Maitel, *Minds, Markets and Money: Psychological Foundations of Economic Behavior* (New York: Basic Books, 1982), 96–7.

[60] See Robert H. Hayes and William J. Abernathy, "Managing Our Way to Economic Decline," *Harvard Business Review* 58 (1980): 68; Lester Thurow, "Toward a Definition of Economic Justice," *Public Interest*, no. 31 (Spring 1973): 56–80; Steven Prokesch, "America's Imperial Chief Executive," *New York Times*, 12 October 1986, sec. 3, pp. 1, 25. But, in fact, among 300 of the largest firms, 5

Cognitive skills are very modestly related to job performances. Jencks reports: "Test scores have only a modest effect on actual competence at work. Supervisor ratings have an average correlation of about 0.30 with workers' IQ scores in most occupations." For example, for teachers this correlation is a little less and for medical interns it is about average.[61] Jencks regards correlations of .30 as too small to explain much, but given the noise in the system, the large measurement errors, and the cumulative effect of a .30 correlation, I would consider them important enough to bear some explanatory weight in accounting for occupational performance – and perhaps for increases in national economic productivity. In this reduced form the possibility remains that increases in IQ, mostly in the area of fluid intelligence, especially abstract problem-solving ability, help to account for increases in individual productivity.

But our concern is with the final variable, economic productivity, more than with what makes people individually successful or even productive, and here we run into difficulties worth more extended discussion, borrowing in this case from a literature concerned about low productivity gains in the 1970s and 1980s.

The cognitive skills and personality traits of the work force have minimal relationship to economic productivity. One of the explanations of the decline in productivity during this period was a decline in quality of work force, largely because of the increase in young and inexperienced workers and women with, it was thought, both less experience and less commitment. Whereas not explicitly focused on cognitive skills, these were included in the reference to "quality of workers." In his analysis of the contributing factors to the productivity slowdown in the 1973–82 period, Edward Denison could find no evidence of the decline of work effort in the work force and dismissed the evidence on decline in quality.[62] Baily and Chakrabarti agree on the basis of similar evidence.[63] Both sets of scholars conclude that with respect to the decline of work force quality and work effort: "To date the evidence for either is thin and inconclusive."[64] The clear inference is that individual qualities (including cognitive skills) and changes in national economic productivity are at least somewhat independent, although, of course, other factors may mask a genuine relationship.

The main reason for minimal productivity effects of variation of worker's cog-

percent of the CEOs were dismissed, mainly for reasons of poor firm profitability. Whether this is a "large" or a "small" proportion depends on criteria not at our command. See David R. James and Michael Soref, "Profit Constraints on Managerial Autonomy: Managerial Theory and the Unmaking of the Corporation President," *American Sociological Review* 46 (1981): 1–18.

[61] Jencks et al., *Inequality*, 187.

[62] Although he has no independent evidence, Denison doubts the accuracy of impressionistic studies revealing national productivity decreases due to lack of work commitment, and he faults statistical studies on methodological grounds. Both in 1978 and again in 1985 he pointed to the difficulty of using the "people don't want to work anymore" argument to explain a sharp decline in 1973 and cites evidence from cohort studies to support these further grounds for skepticism. Denison, *Trends in American Economic Growth*, 47.

[63] Baily and Chakrabarti, *Innovation and the Productivity Crisis*, 17, citing Frank Stafford and Greg J. Duncan, "The Use of Time and Technology by Households in the United States," in Ronald A. Ehrenberg, ed., *Research in Labor Economics*, vol. 3 (Greenwich, CT: JAI Press, 1980), 335–75.

[64] Baily and Chakrabarti, *Innovation and the Productivity Crisis*, 18.

nitive skills (within nations) has to do with their opportunities for influence: *Workers have little influence over decisions affecting the major causes of productivity gains and losses.* Even if their skills influenced worker productivity, variation in worker productivity attributable to increased general cognitive skills is a small part of the complex forces shaping productivity. We must, then, turn from these general skills to structural *opportunities* for influencing such things as shortages of resources, the management of the business cycle, and at least three of the major measured contributions to productivity: decisions on the allocation of resources (a management function), changes in the economies of scale, and states of technical knowledge. The last is particularly important: Workers seem at first to have no influence on the largest single factor in economic growth, the development or application of science and technology. We examine this point briefly.

Both industrial psychologists and economists agree that, by and large, changes in the state of the arts [(4) knowledge – Figure 7.1] are the most important influences on changes in productivity,[65] but neither blue collar nor white collar employees can make much of a positive contribution to this dominant factor. In this respect Marx's comments on the division of labor into thinking and working were partly right.[66] Indeed, since the time that Marx pointed to the appropriation of science by capital as a way of reducing the autonomy and creativity of labor so as "to render [the worker's] muscular power entirely mechanical and obedient,"[67] the division between contribution of new knowledge and the contribution of worker's skills has grown. This is due, in part, to the increasing dependence of technology on theoretically based science; apprenticeship is not so relevant a training as it once was. As a consequence, fundamental technical improvements are not likely to come from production workers.

There is a codicil to this inference of worker irrelevance to major gains in productivity: Employees make a contribution in the adoption of technology by positively *accepting* the new technology, an acceptance that usually requires learning new skills and disrupting old routines, both of which are painful and facilitated by education. It is not just the invention of technology by engineers and adoption of technology by businesspersons that are at stake, for, so to speak, technology is a state of mind; its acceptance is a matter of cultural congeniality and popular welcome.[68] The relevant state of mind is more a matter of socialization than a rational decision, except, perhaps, as a person becomes conscious of the tradeoffs and sac-

[65] Denison, *Trends in American Economic Growth;* Baily and Chakrabarti, *Innovation and the Productivity Crisis.*

[66] Karl Marx, *Capital* (New York: Everyman, 1910), 382. Marx seems to have borrowed some of these themes from Dugald Stewart and, in turn, contributed greatly to Mannheim's formulation.

[67] Marx, ibid., quoting W. Thompson, *An Inquiry into the Principles of the Distribution of Wealth* (London, 1824).

[68] See Lawrence E. Harrison *Underdevelopment Is a State of Mind: The Latin Case* (Lanham, MD: University Press of America, 1985). The American productivity slowdown has been said to have similar cultural causes. Jordan Lewis suggests that it is the Japanese "sense of purpose" in contrast to the American "drift," the Japanese emphasis on consensualism in contrast to the American emphasis on individualism and conflict, that give the Japanese an advantage in adopting technological changes – an advantage incurred without greater expenditures on research and development than in the United States. See Jordan D. Lewis, "Technology, Enterprise, and American Economic Growth," *Science* 215 (5 March 1982): 1,204–11.

rifices involved. Alain Touraine offers some principles for locating those more likely to accept technical change: The economically secure, better educated, and urban members of the work force will accept changes more easily.[69] Acceptance of technology is only in small degree a product of cognitive complexity.

The value of cognitive complexity and "wisdom" in a market economy

The culture within which a market is embedded has a partially independent role in fostering or hindering cognitive complexity. The American culture does not seem particularly favorable. In that culture, perhaps because of the special influence of businesspeople's "antiintellectualism,"[70] people do not value highly cognitive complexity, at least as it may be described by the following terms: "intellectual – intelligent, reflective"; or "logical – consistent, rational"; or "imaginative – daring, creative." In a ranking of eighteen instrumental values, these ranked, respectively, fifteenth, seventeenth, eighteenth. Qualities of character were more highly valued, with "honest," "responsible," and "ambitious" ranking first, second, and third. In a list of terminal values, "wisdom – a mature understanding of life" does somewhat better, ranking seventh, but far below the first three values of "peace," "family security," and "freedom."[71] Perhaps cognitive complexity is not valued because it does not lead to happiness or life satisfaction, as previously reported. Now we find another set of reasons: Although the market does reward many cognitive skills, it rewards aspects of personality just as much. For example, it may reward "honest," "responsible," and "ambitious" people better than "intellectual," "logical," and "imaginative" people, suggesting once again the influence of market rewards on popular culture.

If those kinds of cognitive complexity measured by IQ make only a minimal contribution to better job performance, and therefore at the national level to economic productivity, nevertheless, in seeming contradiction, aggregate measures show education as a potent contribution to national prosperity. Some of these larger contributions rest on the schools' development of relevant personality characteristics, some on the actual work experience in school, and some on an unmeasured contribution to technique and knowledge, which are potent influences on national productivity. The disvalued qualities of logic, reflection, and imagination must then find exogenous support in selective universities in order to survive.

There is an alternative interpretation more favorable to the market. In that growing number of cases where an economy demands these logical, reflective, and imaginative qualities for certain occupations, the market is working against the cultural

[69] Alain Touraine, with Claude Duranc, Daniel Pecaut, and Alfred Willener, *Workers' Attitudes to Technical Change* (Paris: OECD, 1965). Contrary to such critics of market-sponsored technology as Mumford and Ellul, this strain is not just a market-induced burden for there has been a record of Soviet Ludditism that could not be kept from surfacing from time to time. Mark Frankland, "The Soviet 'Luddites,' " London *Observer*, 5 June 1983. For most workers, the strain is minimal because they enjoy working with and welcome technology. Eva Mueller, *Technological Advance in an Expanding Economy* (Ann Arbor, MI: Institute for Social Research, 1969).

[70] Richard Hofstadter, *Anti-Intellectualism in American Life* (New York: Knopf, 1963), chap. 2.

[71] Milton Rokeach, "Change and Stability in American Value Systems, 1968–1971," *Public Opinion Quarterly* 38 (1974): 222–38.

grain and such support for these qualities is then largely attributable to the market – as Schumpeter alleges. Or the increasing professionalization of the work force, partly antithetical to the market's exchange orientation, may foster greater logic, reflection, and imagination.

Cognitive skills and economic performance

If individual firms cannot individually support measures that improve cognitive flexibility, they may collectively support public education. Do markets or business firms in a market economy support or reward cognitive complexity? I can think of six reasons for believing that they do not. First, although general popular support for education in the United States has been strong, business support has often been weak. For example, in the United States, the proportion of state income going to public education in more rural states was just as generous as the proportion in the more marketized industrial states. Nor is the case much stronger in Europe, or at least in Germany. When the two Germanies represented different economic systems, West Germany's educational effort was no greater than East Germany's.[72] Recently, however, businesses have begun to recognize the high cost of low educational effort and it seems that new support has been forthcoming.

Second, market rewards are thought to produce the incentives that call forth those abilities valued by the market. If so, cognitive complexity, as measured by IQ, will not be called forth by the market, for income and occupation are not closely related to IQ.

Third, it seems that personality factors are quite as important in both occupational attainment and in job performance as are cognitive skills, to the limited extent that IQ reflects these skills. Like individuals, as Rokeach's value study shows, the market seems not greatly to value cognitive complexity except in the scientific and some managerial elite. The market is no friend of high levels of complex cognition, but rather values specific job-related skills and industriousness.

Fourth, job performance, at least among professionals and managers, especially top managers, is not closely related to pay. This is a market defect in the market's own efficiency terms.

Fifth, inasmuch as inventors and entrepreneurs rarely reap the full rewards of their innovation,[73] the market does not fully reward these contributions to productivity, but rather rewards managers who are sufficiently acute to employ, or borrow from, the works of these innovators. These are the skills, cognitive or not, that are most generously rewarded.

More generally, sixth, those things that contribute to individual occupational and income attainment are only tenuously related to increases in economic productivity. Since the market incentives and rewards are all related to individual attainments,

---

[72] Robert E. Lane, "Political Education in a Market Society," *Micropolitics* 3 (1983): 39–65.

[73] Baily and Chakrabarti point out that "part of the knowledge R&D generates provides benefits not to the company performing the R&D, but to other companies and consumers"; only part becomes a *private* return. This condition applies to innovative entrepreneurs as well and for the same reason: Knowledge is public and is appropriated by those who did not spend anything to discover it. Baily and Chakrabarti, *Innovation and the Productivity Crisis,* 38.

the focus of rewards on individual promotions and economic gain erodes much market leverage on productivity increases.

These findings and their interpretations tend to reduce (although not to eliminate) the instrumental value of cognitive complexity in average market work, but, again as Jencks points out, this reduction does not hold for those kinds of jobs that resemble the academic work for which IQ tests are good predictors.

For the majority of workers, it is not abstract cognitive complexity but local occupational skills and *character*, especially perseverance and industriousness, that earn market rewards and, it seems, that also contribute most to economic productivity. The contribution of education may be greatest in teaching perseverance and industriousness for the mass, and cognitive complexity for the scientists and technicians whose work contributes to technology, enlarging the pool from which emerge the innovators and inventors – who are largely rewarded by considerations outside the market.

For most people, however, if complex thinking abilities are to be assigned value, it is primarily their intrinsic worth that must recommend them.

Summary

Georg Simmel proposed that the money (or market) economy was the source of a new high value placed upon intellect: "The idea that life is essentially based on intellect, and that intellect is accepted in practical life as the most valuable of our mental energies, goes hand in hand with the growth of a money economy."[74] We have reason to believe that this is only partly true and, in any event, selectively misleading.

Although IQ captures only a fraction of the elements of cognitive complexity, the abstract analytical skills it represents are important and IQ may be employed as an indicator of the abstract skills in the large concept of cognitive complexity.

Looking at the long haul from hunting and gathering to agricultural to industrial societies, research shows that hunting-and-gathering societies have higher cognitive levels than agricultural ones and, because of these higher abilities, the transition from hunting and gathering to modern wage labor societies seems easier than from agricultural to industrial societies. These findings, taken together with those showing that societies with *less* accumulated surplus have higher achievement motives than those with more surplus, suggest that it is not affluence but what people do for a living that determines their cognitive development. Where national wealth may be cumulative, changes in modes of production to promote learning at work has no necessary directionality; "progress" is uncertain.

The Soviet Union has experienced some of the same kinds of cognitive gains from modernization that have been described in the West, but the authoritarian culture and the lack of individual motivation in the USSR may have retarded development. Development of children in the kibbutzim seems roughly comparable to

[74] Georg Simmel, *The Philosophy of Money*, trans. T. Bottomore and D. Frisby (1907; reprint London: Routledge & Kegan Paul, 1978), 152.

that of Israeli city children, but lacks the cognitive flexibility gained from conflict-ing points of view outside the kibbutz and may also suffer from somewhat lower motivation – though this latter point is less certain.

In industrial societies, the contribution of the economy to cognitive development also rests on what people do for a living (Chapter 13), but the reduction of poverty is more important; even the intermittent losses during recessions of these welfare gains are costly in cognitive development. Much of the market influence derives from the acceleration of industrialization and modernization that it brings about – a very different situation prevailing now from that of early nineteenth-century Britain.

In the modern American market society, indicators of cognitive complexity such as education and IQ do not contribute to either happiness or satisfaction with one's life-as-a-whole; and cognitive complexity (as measured by IQ) seems to have only modest effects on job performance, income, and occupational attainment. Since education and other components of human capital do relate strongly to growth in GNP, there is a strong suggestion that it is the perseverance and industriousness that those who finish higher levels of education must have had, which is the cause of these macro relationships. The cognitive complexity that education contributes to is economically valuable chiefly for the elites, especially the scientists and tech-nicians whose contribution registers so strongly in the knowledge components of sources of increased productivity. Workers make a major contribution only in not resisting technological advances. Markets fail to reward scientists, inventors, and entrepreneurs to the full extent of their economic value but rather reward those who select and use their ideas.

We now turn to another facet of cognition and economic development, the prob-lem of decision overload.

8 Environmental complexity and cognitive complexity

In the previous chapter we found that markets contribute to cognitive complexity largely through their influence on the kinds of work people do and their relief of poverty. On the other hand, firms often did not systematically reward complex cognition (often they could not afford to train for it) and they have not, until recently, banded together to give political support for a level of public education appropriate to its influence on the economy. In this chapter I continue the examination of market effects on cognitive complexity by turning to the influence of environmental stimulation and stress on cognition.

The market, as a source of both challenge and stress, by its very nature demands difficult cognitive responses. As a self-regulating system the market is not equipped to regulate or inhibit overstimulation. It has no terminal facilities for stimuli. There is no systemic brake or inhibition (except for individual choice) that might tailor demands to the variety of capacities among market participants. The thesis of this chapter is that market effects on cognition follow a curvilinear pattern whereby they first increase cognitive complexity by their challenges, innovations, and propensities for rapid change, and then often overload the capacities of their participants by their demands for complex cognitions. I first present evidence of curvilinearity in laboratory, field, and historical studies, then turn to evidence of market complexities leading to overload. After exploring some social consequences of this pattern, we will examine models where environmental complexities occur either simultaneously or in sequence, concluding with an examination of adaptive responses in these different circumstances.

Cognitive development and environmental complexity

A model of environmental complexity and cognitive complexity
A simple, general theory of the relation between environmental stimulus/complexity and cognitive complexity is presented in Figure 8.1. The curve in this figure describes individual responses and, perforce, group responses. We will concentrate here on group responses, partly because the relevant research has been done with groups, but also because many of the crucial decisions by firms are made by committees and other groups. In this vein, this figure presents average cognition for some collectivity, summarizing a family of individual curves representing different abilities and different trauma points. In group problem solving, groups cannot rise much higher than their weakest members: "In groups, as in persons, structural evolvement [to higher forms of cognition] begins at the simpler level and progresses to higher levels only if the conceptual level of individual members permits."[1] Thus,

[1] Harold M. Schroder, Michael J. Driver, and Siegfried Streufert, *Human Information Processing* (New York: Holt, Rinehart & Winston, 1967), 12.

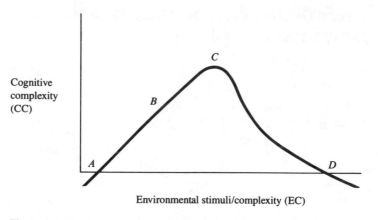

Figure 8.1. *Environmental complexity and cognitive complexity*

it will not be the case that the best minds can solve the problems for the others; group solutions [in this example] are necessary.

The curvilinearity of this figure arises from the fact that the human mind is stimulated to higher performance by increasing environmental stimuli, novelty, and challenge up to a point of overload, when performance declines and people adopt simpler forms of cognition. Stimulus deprivation, represented in the figure below the *x*-axis at the beginning of that axis, injures the mind, as does severe trauma, at the other end of the *x*-axis, where again performance declines below normal. It is assumed that learning to cope with environmental challenges continues after the ratio of success to failure becomes discouraging and the intrinsic pleasure in the challenge ceases. On the graph *B* is the point where the intrinsic pleasure of an experience ceases; thus we may assume motivated performance during the *AB* portion of the curve. The *BC* portion of the curve may also represent motivated responses, but for this portion only instrumental motivation, for example, work for pay, is operative. At point *C* stress and overload take place and performance declines to a simpler level of cognition, perhaps going beyond some normal average level to cognitive decrements. I present some evidence first on the cognitive gains from increasing environmental complexity and then on the general curvilinear relation.

Environmental complexity increases cognitive complexity. Studies of rats show that "if animals are reared in an environment that is more complex than the standard laboratory cage, interesting changes occur in key brain areas."[2] For the enriched environment to have these effects it must include both rearing in groups and "playthings that are changed daily;" neither alone has the physiological effects. These effects are associated with better long-term memory, higher metabolic rates, increased size of the synaptic junctions, facilitating information transmission,

[2]Patricia Wallace, "Complex Environments: Effects on Brain Development," *Science* 185 (20 September 1974): 1,035–7 at 1,035.

and more branching of the nerve cells, implying more connections. The enriched rats are less emotional and less aggressive, states that facilitate learning. Fewer, but highly suggestive, studies with monkeys show similar effects. Nor is the effect dependent upon "critical years," or early conditioning. Most investigators "firmly deny that it is a critical-period effect which is strictly limited to early life and cite evidence that brain structure and chemistry can be modified by enrichment even in 'elderly' rats." When animals are "transferred to an impoverished environment, many of the brain changes produced by the enrichment gradually diminish." There may, however, be differences between the physiological mechanisms of early and later enrichment, the early enrichment achieving its effects partly by reducing the emotionality of the young rats while "the cortex may benefit from enrichment throughout the animal's life."[3] It will be recalled that Vernon and others have also pointed to the increases in IQ produced by verbal, graphic, and kinesthetic stimulation.[4]

Too much environmental complexity produces cognitive regressions: the curvilinear theory. Among both human children and adults, there is a curvilinear relationship between environmental complexity and cognitive complexity. Among children, "degree of arousal appears to have a curvilinear relation to developmental level. Children manifest their highest level at an intermediate degree of arousal and lower levels as arousal increases or decreases from that point."[5] In the relevant laboratory studies of adults, environmental complexity means the number of alternative dimensions or ideas presented, the number of rules required by a test, the speed of change, and the discrimination necessary to solve a problem.[6] In the field studies and inferences therefrom, environmental complexity means urbanization, mass media exposure, physical mobility, and educational stimuli.[7] The laboratory and the field studies agree that cognitive complexity embraces the number of "dimensions" (schemata, scripts, rules, etc.) with which people work, their capacities to discriminate among the presenting situations (as in the Berry study), empathy in the special sense of being able to imagine the self in the position of another, openmindedness or intellectual flexibility.[8]

The curvilinear theory connects these two kinds of complexity, cognitive complexity matches environmental complexity to higher and higher points, and then, when the environment becomes too complex, "stress" or "trauma" reduces cognition to simpler levels – perhaps even below the starting points. There are substantial individual differences in the way minds react to complexity with the greatest

[3] Ibid. Hunt confirms this view of age specificity: "Rodents that have experienced the enriched condition have regularly done better than rodents reared in isolation. For some tests, early postweaning experience seems most beneficial while for others no sensitive period is evident." J. McVicker Hunt, "Psychological Development," *Annual Review of Psychology* 30 (1979): 103–43 at 132.

[4] Philip E. Vernon, *Intelligence and Cultural Environment* (London: Metheun, 1969), 222.

[5] Kurt W. Fischer and Louise Silvern, "Stages and Individual Differences in Cognitive Development," *Annual Review of Psychology* 36 (1985): 613–48 at 639.

[6] Schroder et al., *Human Information Processing,* chap. 3.

[7] Frederick Frey, "Communication and Development," in Ithiel de Sola Pool and Wilbur Schramm, eds., *Handbook of Communication* (Chicago: Rand McNally, 1973).

[8] Schroder et al., *Human Information Processing,* 10.

differences at the peaks of individual's respective performances[9] (point C on the graph). Although not topic bound, cognitive complexity for each individual varies with his or her familiarity with the subject at hand.

As mentioned, the portion of the curve below the y-axis on the left represents the effects of sensory deprivation. Deprived of all external stimuli, the mind starts circling on itself, hallucinating and rendering the deprived individual exceptionally vulnerable to suggestion. Prolonged sensory deprivation risks irreversible damage.[10] In the more limited range of everyday life, extreme boredom may represent a very modest degree of sensory deprivation and is "extremely unpleasant."[11] A feeling that one has "time on one's hands" is even more damaging to life satisfaction than a sense that one is always under the pressure of time – which is damaging enough. Thus, a curve representing the relations between the sense of time pressure and life satisfaction closely resembles the curve relating environmental complexity to cognitive complexity.[12]

Curvilinear relationships of stress and arousal. The curvilinearity of the relationship between environmental complexity and cognitive complexity is grounded in several established theories, one of which is the relation between stress and distress. As Selye points out, there is no life without stress of some kinds and, indeed, it would not be healthy: "all agents to which we are exposed . . . produce a non-specific increase in the need to perform adaptive functions and thereby to establish normalcy. . . . Stress is not something to be avoided. . . . Complete freedom from stress is death."[13] But there can be too much, of course, as well as too little: "Deprivation of stimuli and excessive stimuli are both accompanied by an increase in stress, sometimes to the point of distress."[14] These responses are based on the homeostatic physiology of the body, which, says Selye, may not always know best; it is sometimes necessary to intervene with consciously created adaptive mechanisms.[15]

Berlyne suggests a different, epistemic reason for a curvilinear relation between environmental complexity and level of cognition. Beginning with the concept of "arousal" or the physiological "orientation response" produced by a stimulus, Berlyne explains the ensuing cognitive activity as in part a desire to continue or discontinue that state, depending on whether it is considered pleasant or not. When too great, "high arousal may act as an aversive state whose alleviation can be rewarding."[16] On the other hand, "when a stimulation is monotonous or scanty, the resulting state of stimulation, which is, of course, what we call 'boredom,' is relieved by receipt of stimulation from any source provided that it brings the colla-

[9] Ibid., 40, 157.
[10] See T. Schaefer and N. Bernik, "Sensory Deprivation and its Effect on Perception," in P. H. Hoch and J. Zubin, eds., *Psychopathology of Perception* (New York: Grune & Stratton, 1965); Michael I. Posner, *Cognition: An Introduction* (Glenview, IL: Scott, Foresman, 1973), 144–6.
[11] Leonard Doob, *Patterning of Time* (New Haven: Yale University Press, 1971), 111, 167–70.
[12] Angus Campbell, Philip E. Converse, and Willard L. Rodgers, *The Quality of American Life* (New York: Russell Sage, 1976), 357.
[13] Hans Selye, *Stress Without Distress* (New York: New American Library, 1975), 15–20.
[14] Ibid., 26.
[15] See Alvin Toffler, *Future Shock* (New York: Random House, 1970).
[16] Daniel E. Berlyne, *Structure and Direction in Thinking* (New York: Wiley, 1965), 252.

tive [intellectually integrative] properties of the environment up toward an optimal level."[17] Berlyne also provides a causal sequence with more conscious intellectual content. Curiosity is stimulated by perceptual or conceptual conflict, in the sense of the unexpected, or by the conflict between two concepts. People are thus led to attempt to resolve the conflict by seeking more information or by thinking more about the anomaly. But there are costs to the inquiry or cogitation – uncertainty, fear of failure, fatigue – with the result that at a certain point in the attempt to cope with the stimuli, inquiry and thought cease, returning to the level of origin.[18] Scitovsky places the participants in the American economy on the low end of the optimal arousal continuum; given symptoms of stress and anxiety in the American population, I disagree. In Andrews and Withey's study of the areas of satisfaction and dissatisfaction in the American public, the kind of relief from excessive arousal indicated by "family security" ranks very low, 10 percent feel "unhappy" or "terrible" and another 11 percent are "mostly dissatisfied" with their security.[19] Their experience with unpleasant novelty may have dulled their appetites for new experiences that might be more pleasant.[20]

There are also theories of overload relying on the sheer limits of the mind to assimilate further information, the bottlenecks in the sensory systems, limits of the channel capacities, and the strain on the nervous system. "Briefly, cognitive overload theories build upon the general conceptualization of the human being as a resource-limited information processor who, on occasion, is confronted with a greater number, variety, complexity, or intensity of stimulus inputs than he or she can efficiently manage."[21] Overload increases with the complexity of the problems. As Simon says, "The capacity of the human mind for formulating and solving complex problems is very small compared to the size of the problems whose solution is required for objectively rational behavior in the real world." There are, he points out, both linguistic and neurological causes for these limits.[22] Although these theories do not explain the ascending relation between environmental complexity and cognitive complexity (AC), they describe the limits of that ascent and the reasons for the descent, often a sharply accentuated one.[23]

Market stimulation and overstimulation

Market stimuli are generally familiar:

Proliferation of choices among commodities. The virtue of the market, multiple voluntary choices, is both a challenge and a source of strain. Choices

[17] Ibid., 254–5.
[18] Ibid., 261–7.
[19] Frank M. Andrews and Stephen B. Withey, *Social Indicators of Well-Being: Americans' Perceptions of Life Quality* (New York: Plenum Press, 1976), 254.
[20] Tibor Scitovsky, *The Joyless Economy* (New York: Oxford University Press, 1977).
[21] John M. Darley and Daniel T. Gilbert, "Social Psychological Aspects of Environmental Psychology," in Gardner Lindzey and Elliott Aronson, eds., *Handbook of Social Psychology*, 3d ed., vol. 2 (New York: Random House, 1985), 949–91 at 976.
[22] Herbert Simon, *Models of Man* (New York: Wiley, 1957), 198.
[23] Posner, *Cognition*, 127, 135–9. Whereas the curvilinear theory has many advocates and is supported by considerable research, note the incompatibility of the idea of a trauma point and decline with Piagetian

among commodities, jobs (where possible), and between present and future enjoy-ment, have the effect of encouraging individual capacities for choice. "Decision-ism" in the market cannot rely on the rule-consciousness of the law.

The processing skills that seem so simple to the habituated consumer, embrace some fairly difficult information-processing procedures that may be illustrated by what children must learn when confronted with television advertising. These in-clude "(1) selection of performance attributes in considering a television purchase, (2) comparing brands on the basis of functional characteristics, (3) awareness of a variety of sources of information about new products, (4) awareness of brands, and (5) level of understanding of the function of television advertising."[24] A blue-collar worker whom I interviewed in Eastport in 1957 complained of his fatigue and ex-asperation over "the many tiny messages" assaulting him daily.[25]

Constant change and demands for counterfactual anticipation. More than command or household economies, markets encourage change; the environmental complexity, then, is a dynamic complexity, never quite the same in each period. In the face of change, adaptive flexibility is rewarded, indeed, creating and anticipat-ing change may be even better rewarded. Those kinds of cognition that imagine things not yet perceptible to the senses and that adapt to changing stimuli, therefore, will be encouraged – up to the breaking point.

Pressures for efficiency, for cost-benefit analysis. The efficiency norm (Chapter 16) enforces adaptation under pain of loss of job, loss of approval, reduced self-esteem, bankruptcy, or economic loss more generally. Competition is the ex-ternal sanction; internal standards and even conscience are the internal sanctions. Compared to nonmarket economies, in the market economy "efficiency considera-tions usually predominate over welfare considerations."[26] These are pressures that strain cognition in directions not present in other kinds of economies.

Money. Money simplifies thinking in a variety of familiar ways but there are several complexities in this process of "simplification:" (1) The usefulness of money is so great that it invites complex analyses beyond the powers of most peo-ple; (2) money is abstract whereas goods are concrete, and abstractions are more difficult to conceptualize than concrete things one can see and handle; and (3) the very thing that makes money useful also deprives people of one of their principal ways of grabbing hold of phenomena: familiar categories. That is, the iconic cate-gories "cornflakes," "soup," and "bread" are lost in a budget item for food des-ignated by a number. There is a class dimension to this increase in conceptual difficulty. Whereas middle-class children classify things and their symbols in the

natural stages theory, a theory of immanent unfolding of powers that are not so greatly affected by environmental complexity.

[24] Scott Ward, Daniel B. Wackman, and Ellen Wartella, *How Children Learn to Buy* (Beverly Hills, CA: Sage, 1977), 77.

[25] Robert E. Lane, *Political Ideology: Why the American Common Man Believes What He Does* (New York: Free Press, 1962).

[26] Theodore Geiger, *New International Realities* 2 (October 1976), 19.

same way, "children of poverty succeed in classifying only concrete objects in a fashion resembling the classification of children of middle-class backgrounds. The classifications which children of the poor tend to make of the pictures of those objects and of the names of those objects differ from the classifications which they make of the concrete objects."[27] Although these references refer to verbal symbols, the same "distancing hypothesis" that applies to words and pictures applies even more strongly to numbers.

Time preference. The market increasingly requires a set of decisions regarding the uses (or investment) of time: (1) especially for women, whether to work part-time or full time (if the labor market offers a choice); (2) for both sexes, whether to work while going to school and whether to start full-time work immediately after high school; (3) when to retire (if given a choice); (4) whether to moonlight; (5) whether to invest time in household production and maintenance.[28]

Place of work and with whom to work. Without exaggerating the array of choices available to most people, increased geographical mobility by members of the working class as well as the middle class creates a set of difficult choices, at least in American, if not British and some other labor markets.[29] Some work satisfaction studies also show a concern for workmates that suggests the choice of with whom one works may affect selection of jobs – again, where such selection is possible.[30]

Social incoherence and heterogeneity. The market, partly because of its erosion of gemeinschaft, is more directly responsible for the mixing of persons with different backgrounds, the presentation of an array of life-styles, and for the cafeteria of entertainments and leisure agendas that lead to what might be called "cosmopolitanism" (Chapter 5). These disparate elements come to a focus in the metropolis. Simmel gives the consequence of these various influences a cognitive twist: "The metropolitan type of man – which, of course, exists in a thousand variants – develops an organ protecting him against the threatening currents and discrepancies of his external environment which would uproot him. He reacts with his head instead of his heart. . . . Metropolitan life, thus, underlies a heightened awareness and a predominance of intelligence in metropolitan man. . . . Intellectuality is thus seen to preserve subjective life against the overwhelming power of metropolitan life."[31] The interesting point here is that instead of responding with cognitive sim-

[27] J. McV. Hunt and Girvin E. Kirk, "Social Aspects of Intelligence: Evidence and Issues," in Robert Cancro, ed., *Intelligence: Genetic and Environmental Influences* (New York: Grune & Stratton, 1971), 297–8.

[28] F. Thomas Juster, "Investments of Time by Men and Women," in Juster and Frank P. Stafford, eds., *Time, Goods, and Well-Being* (Ann Arbor, MI: Institute for Social Research, 1985).

[29] See, for example, R. M. Blackburn and Michael Mann, *The Working Class in the Labor Market* (Atlantic Highlands, NJ: Humanities Press, 1979).

[30] See Harold L. Sheppard and Neal Q. Herrick, *Where Have All the Robots Gone? Worker Dissatisfaction in the '70s* (New York: Free Press, 1972).

[31] Georg Simmel, "The Metropolis and Mental Life," *The Sociology of Georg Simmel,* trans. and ed. Kurt H. Wolff (Glencoe, IL: Free Press, 1950), 153.

plicity, as the theory of overload suggests, Simmel's metropolitan man responds by buffering the effects of overload with a sophisticated, blasé cognitive style. As a defense against overstimulation, however, this intellectuality represents more of a pose than a coming to grips with the stimuli. Simmel's theory has a different emphasis from, but is not incompatible with, the posture Milgram suggests: withdrawal from obligations and from unsolicited social contacts.[32] Both represent devices for protecting the overloaded individual from the stress of too many diverse stimuli.

Some insight into the way the market generates stress, both the stress leading to higher cognition and stress leading to simpler cognition, may be gathered from looking at a cross-culturally validated list of "stressful life events" (Chapter 24). The consequence of such stressful events is a greatly increased incidence of physical as well as mental illness over the ensuing two years. The list of stressful life events includes forty-three items scaled according to level of stressfulness, from "death of spouse," (scored 100) to "minor violation of the law" (scored 11).[33] Of the forty-three items, about fourteen or roughly one-third can be related to market sources, including "fired at work" (scored 47), "business readjustment" (scored 39), and "wife begins or stops work," (scored 26). The most stressful seven events are familial and personal, almost totally irrelevant to economic or market changes. Nor is a fully developed market economy a condition for the occurrence of the fourteen job- and money-related items. In less developed countries, for example, those who "are changing" compared to those who are not changing or those who "have already changed" are more disturbed and anxious.[34] Rather, the market relevance lies in the tendency of market economies to generate these kinds of events more frequently than traditional or (probably) central decision economies, and to offer less protection against their distressing consequences.

Mild stress, as in test anxiety, often improves performance but further stress leads to decrements of various kinds:[35] Loss of curiosity is a consequence of both stress and anxiety;[36] a focus on procedures rather than purpose provides for the anxious a defense against criticism; under circumstances of stress, stereotypical thinking flourishes; Rokeach finds that closed-mindedness and dogmatism are increased by anxiety.[37] Schroder et al., whom we discussed as a source of the curvilinear theory, point out that whereas mild criticism increases cognitive performance, intense criticism reduces it. Under these circumstances of greater stress, thought becomes more

[32] Stanley Milgram, "The Experience of Living in Cities: A Psychological Analysis," in Frances Korten, Stuart W. Cook, and John I. Lacey, eds., *Psychology and the Problems of Society* (Washington, DC: American Psychological Association, 1970), 152–73.

[33] Thomas H. Holmes and Minoru Masuda, "Life Change and Illness Susceptibility," in Barbara S. Dohrenwend and Bruce P. Dohrenwend, eds., *Stressful Life Events* (New York: Wiley, 1974).

[34] Leonard W. Doob, *Becoming More Civilized: A Psychological Exploration* (New Haven: Yale University Press, 1960).

[35] Eric Gaudry and Charles D. Spiegelberger, *Anxiety and Educational Achievement* (Sydney: Wiley Australasia, 1971).

[36] Abraham H. Maslow, *Toward a Psychology of Being*, rev. ed. (Princeton, NJ: Van Nostrand, 1968), 62–5.

[37] Milton Rokeach, "A Factorial Study of Dogmatism and Related Concepts," *Journal of Abnormal and Social Psychology* 53 (1956): 356–60.

concrete and less abstract, as though there were more security in perception than in abstract cognition.[38] And Janis and Mann elaborate how decision making becomes less efficient and information is assigned less veridical implications when the decision are made under stress.[39] Some of this curvilinearity is a product of increased motivation to succeed against the odds: "Increasing the intensity of motivation will enhance performance up to a point; after that, further motivation will result in poorer performance."[40]

The curvilinear theory of cognitive and environmental complexity has political implications beyond those mentioned here. In the cross-cultural field studies of differentiation, it has been found that authoritarianism is associated with low differentiation. This condition may be because agricultural communities, with their hierarchies and low levels of differentiation, lend themselves to authoritarian political institutions, but it may also be because authoritarianism is itself a form of cognitive simplicity, as is suggested by authoritarians' "intolerance of ambiguity," leading to gross, undifferentiated stereotyping. Whenever in a single culture measures of authoritarianism have been correlated with differentiation (field independence), "in most of these a significant relationship in the expected direction was found,"[41] that is, the more authoritarian a group, the less its members employed differentiated cognition. And in studies measuring other kinds of attitudes toward authority, "men who showed a tendency to accept authority were significantly more field dependent (undifferentiated) than men who did not." Witkin holds that "this relationship reveals that people with an undifferentiated cognitive style require greater support for guidance than people with an analytical approach."[42]

Manifestations of curvilinearity

The curvilinear theory has the advantage of helping to organize a variety of social phenomena.

Acculturation. The curvilinear theory helps to explain the differences in acculturation that Berry found were related to the strength and persistence of contact with the West. Holding constant many of the ecological factors that concerned him, Berry found that a modest, initially gradual exposure to Western institutions could lead to adaptive acculturation, whereas a sudden, intense exposure could be traumatic and cognitively disruptive. The difference between the cultural adaptation to

---

[38] Schroder et al., *Human Information Processing*, 90–1. These authors also cite (at p. 92) Osgood, Succi, and Tannenhaus to the effect that "under stress, complexity in the dimensions of political cognition disappeared."

[39] Irving Janis and L. Mann. *Decision Making: A Psychological Analysis of Conflict, Choice, and Commitment* (New York: Free Press, 1977).

[40] John C. McCullers, "Issues in Learning and Motivation," in Mark R. Lepper and David Greene, eds., *The Hidden Costs of Rewards: New Perspectives on the Psychology of Human Motivation* (Hillsdale, NJ: Erlbaum, 1978).

[41] Herman A. Witkin, R. B. Dyle, H. F. Faterson, D. R. Goodenough, and S. A. Karp, *Psychological Differentiation* (New York: Wiley/Erlbaum, 1974), 140. For a criticism of Witkin's measures, see E. A. Zigler, "A Measure in Search of a Theory?" *Contemporary Psychology* 8 (1963): 133–5.

[42] Witkin et al., *Psychological Differentiation*, 140.

Western influences of the relatively remote Canadian Eskimos and the traumatic disintegration of the cultures of many American Indian tribes reveals the difference in even greater detail.[43] Whereas Western law and the practices of democracy may be introduced to third world countries by stages (as was often the case in the various phases of British expansion), left to its own devices the market has no means of staging its imperialism to accommodate to native habits and mores.

Crowding, density, and social stimulation. The attraction of the stimulating life in the Western metropolises, inviting rural people to share in the excitement, often leads to disenchantment and to a numbing of the companionable impulses of the ordinary human being. Milgram's explanation of the tendency of metropolitans to avoid helping others on the grounds of just such a sensory overload[44] has been used to explain the negative effects of crowding in dormitories or other housing.[45] Thus, the curvilinear theory of cognitive complexity would be matched by a similar pattern of social stimulation – too little and one is lonely, too much (and too little privacy) and one is overloaded and unable to cope. The damaging effects of "overload" of this kind can be relieved without actually reducing the stimuli by giving threatened individuals a sense that they *can* control the stimuli if they want to.[46] In this case, as in Berry's analysis of cognitive differentiation and in other instances, there are individual skills and attitudes that can retard the onset of trauma and the decline of cognitive performances. But what indigenous market force inhibits the crowding in cities, subways, and highways?

The burden of rationality. A third example of how the curvilinear theory helps to organize social phenomena is represented by situations where individual capacities are exceeded by collective complexities on a very large scale. Mannheim suggests that this mismatch leads to a simplifying search for charismatic leaders.[47] Erich Fromm's treatment of the German *Escape From Freedom* can be interpreted to mean that when the burdens of escape from gemeinschaft into a world of individualistic choices become too great, people choose to deindividuate themselves, thrusting the burden of choice onto a mass movement or its leader.[48] Other theorists suggest that the need to place *some* construction upon events, when these events are otherwise inexplicable, leads people into religious or political cults offering simple ex-

[43] Nelson H. H. Graburn, "Traditional Economic Institutions and the Acculturation of Canadian Eskimos," in George Dalton, ed., *Studies in Economic Anthropology* (Washington, DC: American Anthropological Association, 1971).

[44] Milgram, "The Experience of Living in Cities: A Psychological Analysis." It should be added that a Dutch study of the relationship between urban stressors (noise, traffic) and helpfulness (agreeing to be interviewed, returning a dropped key, helping a lost stranger) did not reveal the predicted relationship between stress and helpfulness. See Charles Korte, Ido Ypma, and Anneke Toppen, "Helpfulness in Dutch Society as a Function of Urbanization and Environmental Input Level," *Journal of Personality and Social Psychology* 32 (1975): 996–1,003.

[45] Janet E. Stockdale, "Crowding: Determinants and Effects," in L. Berkowitz, ed., *Advances in Experimental Psychology*, vol. 11 (New York: Academic Press, 1978).

[46] Darley and Gilbert, "Social Psychological Aspects of Environmental Psychology," 977.

[47] Karl Mannheim, *Man and Society in an Age of Reconstruction* (New York: Harcourt, Brace, 1948), 71–5.

[48] Erich Fromm, *Escape From Freedom* (New York: Rinehart, 1941).

planations – essentially the interpretation that Dodds offers of the retreat from rationality into Eastern mysticism of the Alexandrine Greeks.[49] The episodic retreats
from modernizing and rationalizing tendencies among third world nations (e.g.,
Iran) may reflect the same set of processes. It would be ironic, indeed, if market
overstimulation and stress drove people away from market institutions to religion
and to (ersatz) gemeinshaft.

The relevance of this curvilinear theory to our analysis of markets and cognitive
complexity lies in the tendency of the market to offer both stimulation and stress in
unmeasured, uncontrolled degrees. The sequence is not always as the curve suggests, for enjoyable challenge and distressing complexity occur at the same time (a
source of the ambivalence so often found toward market institutions), but when the
challenge outweighs the distress, cognitive powers are engaged; when distress outweighs the challenge, cognitive powers are overwhelmed.

More speculatively, the conflict between market economics and its various socialist alternatives (the kibbutzim as well as the various command economies) has
often been said to have its sources in the conflict between "freedom" and "security," or in the terms employed here, between uncontrolled, often traumatic challenges and protection against the traumas of cognitive and sensory overload. Furthermore, it might be said in blunt exaggeration that the welfare system is devised
to provide not only for those whose economic bases have collapsed, perhaps through
no faults of their own, but also for those who have been traumatized by the insecure,
unpredictable demands of a system that offers more stimuli and information than is
within their capacities to assimilate? One might then say that the function of government is to prevent the environmental complexity generated by the market from
overwhelming the individual, from leading to the stress that causes a perverse cognitive simplicity and so threatens the very order and security that both government
and market rely upon for their separate functions.

Change and responses to change

We have been examining market-induced environmental complexity, illustrated by
cognitive overload and stress, in static situations. Social change may be differentiated from other kinds of environmental complexity by its movement from one
complex situation to another, perhaps superimposing a new complexity on an old
one, perhaps simply moving from one complex situation to another. The superimposition adds to the cognitive demands at any given time; the sequential process
adds transition costs to the original complexity.

Figure 8.2 represents the superimposition of a new complexity on an old one; the
original figure (*ABCD*) relating environmental complexity (EC) to cognitive complexity (CC) at Time 1 is the same as in Figure 8.1 to which an additional curve
(*WXYZ*) representing an increase in environmental complexity at Time 2 has been
added. Recall that these figures represent averages with some people learning complexity more rapidly than others and some reaching their individual trauma points
sooner than others. In Figure 8.2 the superimposition of new complexity has been

[49] E. R. Dodds, *The Greeks and the Irrational* (Boston: Beacon, 1957).

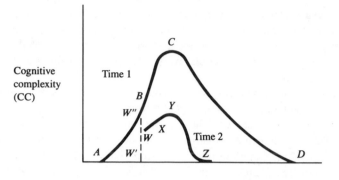

Figure 8.2. *Superimposed complexity*

so rapid that the cognitive development that the original EC would have encouraged has not had time to take place. The shift in an initial EC from *A* to *W'* means that for all persons the learning represented by the portion of the original curve from *A* to *W* has been lost. Some of the weakest members have already reached their trauma points and dropped down to a lower level of cognition, depressing the average. This explains why the curve for Time 2 starts at *W* rather than *W'*. The CC curve for Time 2 therefore starts lower and rises only to *Y*, rather than to *C* as in the curve for Time 1.

Recall, too, that the cognitive powers of groups are limited by the powers of their weakest members and the strongest in the group cannot carry the burden for the others. As a consequence of the new complexity at Time 2, fewer people rise to the level of the previous situation and more people find the complexity traumatic and adopt simple solutions. One further consequence is that measured by its capacity to solve its own problems, the society has become *less "intelligent."* The increased environmental complexity has forced a kind of simplicity of cognition on those who, in the simpler circumstances of Time 1, were actually operating at a higher level of cognition. Displaced persons, American Indian tribes, Palestinians in the Gaza camps, all reflect some such compounding of adjustment problems.

Figure 8.3 represents the sequential ordering of environmental complexity; the new EC arrives after the cognitive learning at Time 1 has taken place and people can make use of that learning for adapting to the new complexity. Thus, the curve *EFGH* in Figure 8.3 takes off from the position already gained on the old curve, and rises higher to *G*, rather than to *C*, because the previous learning facilitates learning for all, except those who have already reached their trauma points in Time 1, and the delay of traumas extends the curve to *H*, rather than *D*, along the EC dimension.

Figure 8.4 represents a situation where education has increased the cognitive complexity of the members of the community and where previous experience with societal complexity has also given the members new powers of cognition. *ABCD*

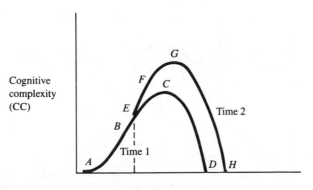

Environmental complexity (EC)

Figure 8.3. *Sequentially ordered complexity*

again shows the relation between environmental complexity at Time 1, but by Time 2 there has been an independent increase in cognitive complexity due to education as well as learning from the EC at Time 1. Starting with the new degree of complexity at J' on the EC dimension, the initial level of cognitive complexity is J'', rather that A, and new, tougher problems give intrinsic pleasure (K versus B). Fewer people reach an early trauma point, more people can cope with the new degree of complexity, both elements raising the average peak from C to L. The increased average level of cognition permits the resolution of old problems more easily; there are fewer cases of trauma at each level of EC, and the society is better off.

Adaptation and regression

The overload theory just explained is challenged by a competing theory, namely that of adaptation-level responses. The two theories must be reconciled.

Adaptation level versus trauma and stress. Adaptation-level theory says that after a period of adjustment to change, people derive the same pleasure or pain from improved or deteriorated situations as they did from the original situations. Based on physiological theory explaining eye responses adjusting to brightness, muscle responses adjusting to heaviness, and so forth, the central concept is that all evaluations are relative to some previous circumstances or referents that themselves change over time.[50] If this adaptation-level theory were to apply to stress or to responses to stress, the downturn of the curvilinear theory relating environmental complexity to cognitive complexity would not occur or, after an initial trauma, cognitive complexity would quickly return to its previous normal level. Overload theory and adaptation-level theory seem to be in conflict.

The causes of the difference, of course, lie in the inherently different natures of

[50] See Philip Brickman and Donald T. Campbell, "Hedonic Relativism and Planning the Good Society," in M. H. Appley, ed., *Adaptation-Level Theory: A Symposium* (New York: Academic Press, 1971).

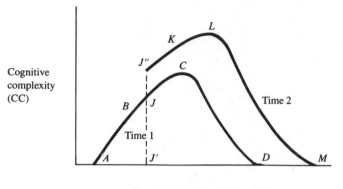

Environmental complexity (EC)

Figure 8.4. *Sequential ordering plus education*

affective and cognitive systems. Emotions satiate and pleasures cloy. Because affects employ largely internal standards and referents for evaluations, people's adaptations tend to adjust to situations so as to minimize demands upon their easily exhausted resources. Cognition, on the other hand, is capable of linear development in such a way that each new capacity opens doors to other new capacities; in that sense cognition is progressive. It is one of the ironies of utility theory that the doctrine of declining marginal utility applying more or less well to commodities applies not at all to "process-benefits," to skills. Thus, although emotional capacities, like cognitive capacities, may be overloaded, the result is not a "regression" to simpler emotions – for there is no such emotional capacity scale. In contrast, because cognition is a genuinely objective skill, there is a cognitive capacity scale down which traumatized individuals may descend.

Cognitive regression may occur without any sense of hurt or shame on the part of the regressing individual, for individuals may be equally pleased with a low level of cognitive response and a high level. Theories that assume an inner drive for ever better performance are likely to be disappointed.[51] It is here that extrinsic market rewards make a difference. Unless a person has internalized a set of standards that always call for doing better,[52] extrinsic rewards of an objective judge, such as a personnel officer or a bankruptcy court, may be necessary to create dissatisfaction with mediocre performance. Social learning theory stresses the value of *internal* standards and consequent inadequacy of extrinsic control, but it acknowledges the need for external, objective criteria and agents. "Adults who were treated indulgently later self-rewarded their own performances more generously than those who had been stringently trained, even though the actual achievements of both groups

---

[51] "Most successes do not bring lasting satisfaction; having accomplished a given level of performance, individuals ordinarily are no longer satisfied with it and make further positive self-evaluation contingent upon higher attainments." Albert Bandura, *Social Learning Theory* (Englewood Cliffs, NJ: Prentice-Hall, 1977), 161.
[52] Ibid., 133–65.

were comparable."[53] As in adaptation-level theory, without external reinforcement of higher standards one can all too easily adapt to poor cognitive performance. It is for these reasons that cognitive regression occurs without protest when environmental complexity exceeds cognitive complexity.

Choosing one's own level of complexity. In certain domains, such as politics, the levels of complexity offered are unchosen, but in other areas, such as the arts, people can choose just the level of complexity that they can manage. In the market people can choose their own levels of complexity to some extent. For example, within rather tight constraints, they can choose jobs within their cognitive powers (in any event, they will be chosen for jobs at a manageable level of difficulty), they can purchase goods by engaging in discriminating taste and extensive comparative shopping or by habit and by modeling others, and they can use their leisure to expose themselves to complex or simple fare. By selecting their own niches in the economy (aided by promotion and placement by employers) and by adjusting strategies of regret minimization, people can sometimes move up the learning curve of complexity to their own optimum performances and avoid the traumas that will cause them to regress to simpler cognitive styles. But there is no way in which the market can, or cares to, adjust environmental complexity to the abilities of those who suffer trauma – so long as the positions it creates are appropriately manned. The social reward of this indifference is constant stimulation to higher levels of complexity for some, and the social cost is the loss of the traumatized.

Regression in the service of affiliation. Not all cognitive regression stems from cognitive overload; much of it comes from social pressure – peer groups as adolescents, work groups and relatives as adults. There is an apparent hedonic tradeoff between thinking for oneself and groupthink, a tradeoff visible both in studies of the quality of life and in public policy making.[54] Inasmuch as neither intelligence nor higher levels of education contribute much, if anything, to happiness, we can expect people not to resist the decline of cognitive complexity when they feel threatened by cognitive overload and to turn to affiliation (friendship, a sense of solidarity with others) with its clear and immediate hedonic rewards.

Cross-generational transmission. Leonard Doob suggests a "spiraled explanation:" The innovative individuals of one generation succeed and are imitated in their own generation, and they and their imitators then teach their children an innovative frame of mind. The main effect, as with scientific paradigms, is thought

[53] Ibid., 134. But, social learning theory research shows that the market's results are more usually achieved by modeling others who have high standards for themselves.

[54] Irving L. Janis, *Victims of Groupthink* (Boston: Houghton Mifflin, 1972). Some quality of life studies show that a low level of social support can nevertheless lead to a high sense of well-being if the individual has a strong sense of personal control – and vice versa. The two together do not make a person happier than a strong presence of one or the other. See Antonia Abbey and Frank M. Andrews, "Modeling the Psychological Determinants of Life Quality," in Frank M. Andrews, ed., *Research on the Quality of Life* (Ann Arbor, MI: Institute for Social Research, 1986), 110.

to be the training of new cohorts for whom the old ways have no emotional signif-icance.[55] The consequence is that the cognitive regression of a majority of an older generation leaves the field open for the new generation to imitate the successful innovators.

Where entrepreneurship is a feature of the economy, one might expect that so-cialization to novelty and preparation for adaptation to make each new generation more flexible will take place. In contrast, one would expect bureaucratic socializa-tion to be rigid and rule bound. Two psychologists, Miller and Swanson, compared the socialization processes of entrepreneurs and bureaucrats. The entrepreneurs comprised the self-employed and others whose income was at least half derived from profits and fees or who worked in a small, unbureaucratized firm (less than two levels of hierarchy); the bureaucrats were those of matched status who worked for and received a salary from someone else in an organization marked by several levels of bureaucratic hierarchy. The entrepreneurs, often born on a farm, were differentiated from the bureaucrats by their greater sense of self-reliance, their greater concern for thrift and delayed gratification, opposition to sensuality, and support for self-denial. The bureaucrats were more open to a variety of enjoyments, to a relaxed view of self-indulgence, and to a reasoning, rather than a moralizing, ap-proach to the world. Socialization procedures did not follow the predicted occupa-tional themes of the two groups. Rather, entrepreneurial parents were more influ-enced by their own socialization milieux, for it was the rural/moral/controlled themes of their backgrounds that influenced them; for the bureaucrats it was the urban/permissive/reasoning elements of their background. The consequence was that in bringing up their children the entrepreneurs required more *unthinking obedience,* more internal control, less expressiveness, and less exploration.[56] As we saw in Chapter 7, it is not so much cognition that shapes a person's behavior and destiny as it is personality and character – to the extent that it is not circumstance that controls destinies.

A perspective on environmental complexity

Before turning to self-attribution in the next chapter, let us integrate the findings and argument of this chapter into the overall argument on cognitive complexity. I have shown the economist's concept of rationality to be at best a thin, selective, and uninformed version of the larger concept of cognitive complexity, a version that fails to account for economic behavior and that misleads both analysts and market participants about what they are actually doing and where their true interests

[55] Irvin, L. Child, "Personality in Culture," in Edgar F. Borgatta and William W. Lambert, eds., *Hand-book of Personality Theory and Research* (Chicago: Rand McNally, 1968), 82–145 at 118, citing Leon-ard Doob, *Becoming More Civilized.* See also Everett E. Hagan, *On the Theory of Social Change: How Economic Growth Begins* (Homewood, IL: Dorsey, 1962).

[56] Daniel R. Miller and Guy E. Swanson, *The Changing American Parent* (New York: Wiley, 1958), 68–113 and passim. The distinctions between entrepreneurs and bureaucrats that Miller and Swanson report are very similar to those found between owners and managers in Francis K. Sutton, Seymour Harris, Carl Kaysen, and James Tobin, *The American Business Creed* (Cambridge: Harvard University Press, 1956). Note that, like Vernon, Miller and Swanson find that authoritarian socialization reduces cognitive development – but for Miller and Swanson it is the entrepreneurs who are more authoritarian.

lie. In this chapter we see another reason why rationality fails to explain economic behavior: The market both stimulates cognition and often overloads it; the consequent stress inhibits rationality along with other forms of cognitive complexity.

Chapter 4 dealt with the way emotions influence cognition. Again we find that the material in this chapter sheds light on this influence. The market arousal mentioned in Chapter 4 may be followed by the emotions associated with stress and overload: fear, anxiety, uncertainty, and eroded motivation. And these are emotions that depress cognitive complexity.

Chapter 7 showed how, over the long haul, it was how people earned a living that shaped their cognitive development. But the effect of occupational challenge may be sharply modified by the environment of insecurity that they experience, an insecurity that may be directly attributable to market-induced social changes. Even the most challenging task is less likely to stimulate cognition under circumstances of stress. We also found a curiously weak relationship between IQ and performance at work and a more robust relation between certain qualities of character and performance. Could it be the case that among the unmeasured qualities of personality is a capacity to tolerate stress? Evidence is presented in the next chapter that one of these personality qualities is the sense of personal efficacy stemming from a belief that any individual is the cause of what happens in the course of his or her life.

Summary

Increased stimulation increases the cognitive powers of animals at any point in the life cycle; children, too, experience cognitive growth when appropriately stimulated. Laboratory experiments show that beyond a certain point of complexity, a point different for each individual, people regress to simpler styles of cognition. Studies of psychological mobility among developing nations have parallel curvilinear patterns of growth and trauma. Curvilinear responses to stress and to arousal seem partially to explain these patterns of cognitive growth up to a point and then decline to more simplified modes of thought.

Many features of the market stimulate and perhaps overstimulate market participants: the variety of choices, market-accelerated changes, pressures toward efficiency, the symbolization of concrete things by the abstract medium, money, strain to provide for the future, conflict over jobs and places of work, and the stimulation of the variety of things represented by heterogeneity and cosmopolitanism. All these factors represent stimulation that might first challenge and then traumatize cognition. Although the most disturbing "life events" are not strictly market events, the pressures of the market on various aspects of life may make their effects more serious.

Examples of the curvilinear challenge and trauma theory may be found in the way less advanced people adjust to modernity, in the way a belief in personal control first reassures and then loads the individual with more responsibility than can be easily borne. The theory is also borne out by the pattern of response of such societies as Weimar Germany and Alexandrine Greece when they were faced with demands beyond their capacities.

If the assaults on the system occur sequentially in a manner that permits adjustment and learning after the first assault and before the second, we anticipate a progressive set of adaptations. If, however, the second assault arrives before the effects of the first one are assimilated, cumulative decrements will take place. The best pattern is a timing such that adjustment plus increases in education take place before the second assault, in which case the second assault may carry the society to even higher levels of complexity.

Adaptation theory predicts outcomes different from those shown because adaptation rests on satiable emotions of satisfaction, whereas we are dealing here with progressive capacities for cognitive complexity. But where satisfaction has a built-in drive for more, cognition has no such immanent force and people adjust easily enough to their own mediocre performances. The market has an advantage over some other institutions in that it permits people to choose their own levels of complexity – but the advantage is limited because the market has no effective means of tailoring complexity to individual capacities. Cognitive overload is by no means the only source of cognitive regression; the desire for social approval also often serves to inhibit cognitive growth. The transmission of complexity is likely to be across generations, but there is a risk, as in the case of the entrepreneurial parents and their children reported here, that parents will indoctrinate the children and moralize the belief system that was a successful adaptive device for the parents.

Reflections on Part II

Markets are excellent devices for the efficient production of goods and services; they are not designed for and have no special mechanism to promote human development. They neither necessarily reward agents (firms) that do promote that kind of development, nor individuals who develop themselves along the lines I have identified: cognitive complexity, self-attribution, and the added quality not yet discussed, self-esteem. Neither is it necessarily true that these qualities would be supported by market agencies if it could be shown that the qualities contribute to productivity, for firms cannot afford to invest in these or any other forms of human capital when the beneficiary of their investments can move next door to serve their competitors. Human beings are like the grassy commons in "the tragedy of the commons:" It pays all firms to exploit their potentials but it does not pay the firms to invest in improving that potential.

It is not true, however, that there is nothing immanent in the idea or practice of markets that favors human development: Economic development and affluence are both immanent and contributory to cognitive complexity; exchange is immanent and contributory to self-attribution. And on these bases, much else may be built.

In this part we have been concerned mainly with the market's effect on the development of cognitive complexity. We turn in the next part to analyses of the two other elements of human development that have been identified: self-attribution and its associated sense of personal control (Chapter 9) and self-esteem (Chapter 10).

Self-attribution and self-esteem

The criteria for a successful market are its contributions to happiness (or utility) and to human development. Human development, in turn, is composed of the cognitive complexity we examined in Part II and of two other elements: a sense of personal control (which is based on self-attribution) and an appropriately high sense of one's own worth, self-esteem. Here in Part III I deal with these two additional elements of the developed personality, treating them more briefly than was thought necessary for cognitive complexity.

Chapter 9 relates the development of a sense of personal control to exchange, claiming that market exchange is the kind of contingent response situation that teaches people that when they act the environment responds. From such experiences of effective action people learn self-attribution, that is, that they are the (partial) causes of the events in their own lives. The correlates of a sense of personal control give it a high status among the elements of a developed personality, but the implied belief that each person controls his or her own fate risks both a false view of causal forces in the environment and an unattractive ethical perspective in which victims deserve their victimization. By itself, therefore, a sense of personal control, enlisting self-attribution as it does, is not a final good.

In Chapter 10 I take up the self-esteem that Rawls has called the most important of the primary goods. After refining the concept and emphasizing its purely instrumental character, I analyze the market's influence on self-esteem: how the market's tendency to base esteem on achievement rather than ascription is a contribution to both social productiveness and individual learning; the uses and perils of the market's emphasis on free choice in favoring the way the individual can choose the dimensions of life on which to base his or her self-esteem; the effects of the division of labor on multiplying these dimensions, and the relative power of participation in politics and in the regulation of work life to enhance self-esteem. Borrowing from the discussion in Part VII, I further point out how the loose relation between income and self-esteem influences our understanding of the justices of equality and proportionality.

As the discussion of self-attribution and self-esteem proceeds, we will find that the three elements of human development form a syndrome in the sense that each element contributes to the others. Cognitive complexity contributes to the development of a sense of personal control, and personal control facilitates the exploratory learning that enhances cognitive complexity. The self-confidence derived from a sense of personal control is one of the principal dimensions on which people evaluate themselves to arrive at their estimates of their own worth. And in reverse, a high self-evaluation gives people the confidence that they can influence their immediate environments, that is, a high sense of internality and personal control. By contributing to any one of these, the market contributes to the others, although the way these contributions are made will differ in each case.

There are common themes in the treatment of the two qualities discussed in Part III. The first is the demotion of a sense of personal control and of self-esteem from the status of final or primary goods to instrumental goods. The merits of these two qualities as features of human development, then, depend on refining their meanings to eliminate the malign features. For the sense of personal control, this means restoring an understanding of circumstantial (external) attribution in the explanation of events and eliminating from the concept any implication that people always get what they deserve. In the case of self-esteem, the refinement means purging the concept of invidious elements and basing self-evaluations on values that are themselves meritorious. When this is accomplished, we can say that the value of self-attribution and self-esteem is truly dependent on their contributions to happiness and to human development – but only after this latter concept has been corrected by the refining of its three components.

A second common theme is the emphasis on contingency, that is, on earned rewards. In Chapter 9 contingency is shown to be an important source of a sense of personal control. This theme is repeated in Chapter 10 where we will discover that self-esteem based on achievement is both more socially effective and more personally productive than self-esteem based on ascription. The analysis of exchange as a form of contingency links these two beneficial results to the central feature of markets – and points to the way markets also fail to protect these developmental goods from erosion.

9   Self-attribution: market influences

In this chapter we leave the problems of the market's influence on cognitive complexity and turn to the second of our criteria for human development, self-attribution. Because this concept refers to the sources of "control" of events, it is often called "personal control," or "internal locus of control," the latter abbreviated as *internality*. Internal locus of control is the belief by an individual that when he or she acts the environment responds; it is a powerful feature of personality, contributing to feelings of effectiveness, autonomy, subjective well-being, and to cognitive complexity. Self-attribution, like all attributions, is a form of cognition, the topic presented in Part II.

The thesis of this chapter is that there is a powerful causal connection between the emphasis on *exchange* in a market economy and the belief among market participants that they are endowed with an internal locus of control. The connection is both direct and indirect, the indirect route running from exchange through *contingency,* that is, a situation where benefits (or punishments) are contingent on the prior acts of the benefited (punished) person – to internality. There is also a partially independent route from ideas about the market (doctrine and ideology) to internality that is not wholly congruent with practices of exchange and contingency. The internality induced by exchange, contingency, and market ideology, in turn, offers strong support for cognitive complexity.

I first explain the character of internality, and follow with three kinds of market influences on this internality: exchange, contingency, and doctrine. Discussion of the effects of markets on socialization for internality (personal control, self-attribution) in childhood and adulthood follows. Cross-national comparisons are used to buttress the thesis. Finally, internal attribution is linked to cognition and thus to the discussion in the previous two chapters. I conclude with an analysis of some of the social and individual costs of internality.

Internal attribution: personal control

The psychologists Richard Nisbett and Lee Ross claim that belief in the causal source of what happens to the self (and to others) is the most "profound" and "far-reaching" psychological theory a person can adopt.[1] The principal alternatives in the process of attribution are beliefs in the causal force of *dispositions,* that is, something internal to the person or persons, and beliefs in *circumstances*. And, if one relies on dispositions, then one must decide whether one's own fate is the product of one's own skill, effort, and will, or of those of others. Emphasis on dispositions or situations each has its advocates. Most humanists, philosophers,

[1] Richard Nisbett and Lee Ross, *Human Inference: Strategies and Shortcomings of Social Judgment* (Englewood Cliffs, NJ: Prentice-Hall, 1980), 30.

157

clinical psychologists, and many historians believe that individual decisions and skills pretty much determine the course of individual lives, and perhaps, though less certainly, of history itself. As contrasted to a belief in fate or historical determinism, "a rather general *'dispositional theory'* is shared by almost everyone socialized in our [Western] culture. Certainly, it is a part of the world view of the so-called Protestant ethic that one's virtues and failings reflect one's worthiness and, conversely, that one's vices and failings reflect one's unworthiness." There may be good and bad luck to modify the outcomes, "but one's fate will eventually mirror one's character, and one's personal traits and abilities will ultimately prevail over circumstances."[2] This is what we teach our children almost without knowing that there is any alternative. As mentioned, some psychologists call it "the fundamental attribution error."[3] The alternative, *situationist* view is held by most contemporary psychologists, sociologists, on a grand scale by Marxists, and increasingly by many humanists when they seek to explain poverty and crime.[4]

The psychological evidence against the dispositionist view has two parts: (1) the consistent failure of research to find anything like a cross-situational consistency in behavior that could be attributed to personality traits, and (2) "many studies . . . demonstrate that seemingly insubstantial manipulations of situational factors can control behavior dramatically and can greatly restrict individual differences."[5] The solution, of course, is what is called an *interactionist* position that considers the interesting phenomena as the joint product of environment and person.[6]

The concept of internal locus of control or personal control

The idea that one of the prime motives of humans and other species is to control their own environments was initiated by a seminal article by Robert White, examining clinical material, children's maturation, and cross-species behavior.[7] Reluctantly, he coined the word "effectance:" "Effectance motivation . . . aims for the feeling of efficacy"; feeling effective and in control of one's circumstances is pleasurable in itself and is not just instrumental for other goals. "Effectance motivation may lead to continuing exploratory interests or active adventures when in fact there

---

[2] Ibid., 31, emphasis added.

[3] Lee Ross, "The Intuitive Psychologist and His Shortcomings," in L. Berkowitz, ed., *Advances in Experimental Psychology*, vol. 10 (New York: Academic Press, 1977).

[4] Moral and moralist critics, on the other hand, claim that by exculpating the dependent person for his dependency and the criminal for his crime, thus relieving them of the responsibilities for their own acts, this "humane" view has encouraged the very dependency and criminality it deplores.

[5] Nisbett and Ross, *Human Inference*, 32. A very sharp controversy has raged in psychology over the disposition/situation interpretation of behavior. Although chronic, the recent discussion has been stimulated by Walter Mischel, *Personality Assessment* (New York: Wiley, 1968).

[6] "The recent debate over the existence of such [cross-situational] consistencies appears now to have evolved into a consensus that it is the interaction between the person and the situation that supplies most of the psychologically interesting variance in behavior." Daryl J. Bem and David C. Fundor, "Predicting More of the People More of the Time: Assessing the Personality of the Situation," *Psychological Review* 85 (1978): 485–501 at 485–6. The interactionist position, however, leaves open the weights to be assigned to each of these two determinants of behavior.

[7] Robert W. White, "Motivation Reconsidered: The Concept of Competence," *Psychological Review* 66 (1959): 297–333.

is no longer any gain in actual competence or any need for it in terms of survival. . . . The motive is capable of yielding surplus satisfaction well beyond what is necessary to get the biological work done."[8] Thus the motive for being effective in dealing with the environment is independent of other motives – but they are not independent of it, for they may have to rely on it for execution.

A second stream of thought comes from attribution theory, a complex strand initiated by Heider and made more sophisticated by Harold Kelley.[9] Kelley's contributions included the idea that in their causal analyses people behave like scientists (following John Stuart Mill's paradigm of the scientific method in his *Logic*). Examining "co-variance," they base their attributions to actor or circumstance in a given case on (1) whether the actor always or uniquely (in this case) behaved in the given way: *distinctiveness;* (2) whether the objective of his or her acts was always or uniquely of the given character: *consistency;* and (3) whether others usually behaved as the actor did in this case: *consensus.* The idea of attribution joins the idea of effectance in reflecting the concept of control: "The purpose of causal analysis – the function it serves for the species and the individual – is effective control . . . [The attributor's] latent goal in gaining knowledge is that of effective management of himself and his environment."[10] The locus of control in a person's attributional pattern could be either persons or circumstances, but more importantly, either self or circumstances. If to the self, the individual has an internal locus of control (internality), compared to those who attribute causal force to their environments (externality). Internality is conceived in two ways: as a more or less enduring feature of a personality *trait* with cross-situational applications, and as a more temporary *state,* induced by a particular stimulus or situation.

A third important stream of thought emerged from the increasingly sophisticated theory and research originated by B. F. Skinner, operant conditioning. Seligman developed this into a theory of "learned helplessness," or belief that whatever one does, nothing happens. Table 9.1, a simple fourfold table, presents the four possible relationships between action and response. People learn that they are effective if cell (1) is more or less consistently *Yes* and cell (4) is more or less consistently *No* and the cross-diagonal cells (2) and (3) are consistently neither *Yes* nor *No.* Alternatively, they would be effective if cell (1) were consistently *No* and cell (4) *Yes* and the cross-diagonals as before. The environment is then seen to respond when people perform the act and the environment fails to respond when they do not, or vice versa. They then experience the rare moments when a person's act is a necessary and sufficient condition for an environmental response. Under these circumstances people learn that they are effective and believe that "control" is vested in themselves. If, on the other hand, when people act and there is no relation between their acts and environmental responses, they learn that they are ineffective, they

[8] Ibid., 323.

[9] Fritz Heider, *Psychology of Interpersonal Relations* (New York: Wiley, 1958); Harold H. Kelley, "Attribution Theory in Social Psychology," in *Nebraska Symposium on Motivation* (Lincoln: University of Nebraska Press, 1967), 192–238.

[10] Harold H. Kelley, "Attribution in Social Interaction," in E. E. Jones, D. E. Kanouse, H. H. Kelley, R. E. Nisbett, S. Valins, and B. Weiner, eds., *Attribution: Perceiving the Causes of Behavior* (Morristown, NJ: General Learning Press, 1972), 22.

Table 9.1. *Individual acts and environmental responses*

	Environmental response: present/absent	
	(1)	(2)
Given act	yes/no	yes/no
Individual act		
	(3)	(4)
No such act	yes/no	yes/no

develop "learned helplessness." Seligman's research and that of others show that this is a condition not only for helplessness but for depression.[11]

Yet the idea that one learns effectiveness through simple contingent response mechanisms must be qualified. As we shall see in the discussion of token economies and payment by results (Chapter 17), unless the responding individual has some discretion in the kinds of responses he or she will make and some understanding of the goal for which the response is made, he or she learns little of transferable quality and almost nothing about the self.

With a fruitful theory in place, the next step was to work out a measure of internal or external locus of control, something which J. B. Rotter did with initial success.[12] Among the items of his widely used test were paired choices: (1) "When I make plans, I am almost certain that I can make them work," or, "It is not always wise to plan too far ahead because many things turn out to be a matter of good or bad luck;" (2) "People who are born poor have less of a chance to get ahead than other people," or, "People who have the ability and work hard have the same chance as anyone else, even if their parents were poor." Later research revealed that the test measured two different kinds of things: a genuine test of a person's feelings about his or her own efficacy, reflected in the first question, and a test of "control ideology" reflected in the second question that was focused not on the self but on others in general.[13] The better educated tend to discriminate between the two concepts, scoring high on personal control and lower on control ideology, that is, they tended not to believe that others, whatever their circumstances, were responsible for their own fates. But the less well educated accepted the package: Everyone got what he or she merited.

[11] Martin E. P. Seligman, *Helplessness: On Depression, Development, and Death* (San Francisco: Freeman, 1975), 13–20. Environmental responses are not likely to be so invariably contingent as this; they are probabilistic and people are not very good at estimating probabilities or perceiving covariances. "Extinction," the decline of a learned response, occurs more slowly when the environment sometimes responds and sometimes does not in a fashion the individual cannot fathom.

[12] J. B. Rotter, "Generalized Expectancies for Internal versus External Control of Reinforcement," *Psychological Monographs* 80 (1966): 609.

[13] Gerald Gurin and Patricia Gurin, "Personal Efficacy and the Ideology of Individual Responsibility," in Burkhard Strumpel, ed., *Economic Means for Human Needs* (Ann Arbor, MI: Institute for Social Research, 1976).

We want to know whether and by what means a market economy might encourage internality. I will argue that the process of exchange is a major contribution to self-attribution and feelings of personal control, distinguishing market transactions from purely social interactions or social exchanges.

Market effects: exchange

It is easy to exaggerate the salience of exchange in a consumer transaction. A man enters a department store to buy a pair of gloves; he encounters a saleswoman who attracts his admiration; he discusses the materials – suede, pigskin, and some anonymous leather; he is concerned with the roughness of his hands as he tries on the gloves; he offers some pleasantry on "cold hands mean a warm heart" with the saleswoman and she smiles at him; he looks at his watch to see if his lunchtime has been exceeded; does he want the gloves wrapped or will he wear them? He pays by credit card and leaves.[14] It is by no means clear that among the various impressions he records, the fact that this is an exchange for a commodity is likely to be the salient one for this glove buyer. In a way, that is the point: As in language, the *marked* features are the unusual ones, the ones to which people pay attention. The unmarked features nevertheless communicate their meanings, but largely in the preconscious. An assumption that things are acquired through exchange is the basic, if unconscious, premise of living in a market economy.

The causal connection between market exchange and the experience of control can be illustrated by contrast with other forms of exchange, including the implicit exchanges in any kind of choice, rule application, and acts governed by obedience to conscience.

1. Two kinds of *social* exchange offer one set of contrasts.[15] (a) DYADIC SOCIAL EXCHANGE is probably that kind of exchange that is most likely to reinforce – but also to undermine – feelings of personal control. Social exchange comprises such acts as deference exchanged for patronage, favors exchanged for flattery.[16] Such uneven social exchanges raise questions about *whose* personal control is being reinforced. Moreover, the uncertain reciprocation and the vagueness of the terms of the anticipated return weakens the sense of personal control. By way of contrast, market exchanges are contracts that are precise and enforceable. (b) THE EXTENDED (OR CHAIN) EXCHANGES of gemeinschaft societies, where A gives to B who gives to C, each with the understanding that he or she will be similarly favored,[17] offers even less control.

2. CHOICES AND THEIR OPPORTUNITY COSTS. Every good that is chosen has an

---

[14] What is required to capture the subtleties of such situations is the kind of analyses portrayed in Roger Barker's *The Stream of Behavior* or Erving Goffman's *The Presentation of Self in Everyday Life*. Roger G. Barker, ed., *The Stream of Behavior* (New York: Appleton-Century-Croft, 1963); Erving Goffman, *The Presentation of Self in Everyday Life* (New York: Doubleday, 1959).

[15] Compare, for example, George Homans, *Social Behavior: Its Elementary Forms* (New York: Harcourt, Brace & World, Inc., 1961) with Albert Bandura, *Social Learning Theory* (Englewood Cliffs, NJ: Prentice-Hall, 1977), 39–50, 129–58.

[16] Peter M. Blau, *Exchange and Power in Social Life* (New York: Wiley, 1964).

[17] See Peter P. Ekeh, *Social Exchange Theory: The Two Traditions* (London: Heinemann, 1979).

opportunity cost measured by the values of the goods not chosen (Chapter 11). When a father chooses to read the newspaper instead of playing with his daughter he "prices" the value of the newspaper higher and the cost lower than playing with his daughter. To choose something is to "exchange" it for something you might have had if you had chosen something else. Giving up a less preferred good for a more preferred good is an exercise of personal control in only a limited sense: It reflects the ability to choose, which *reactance theory* says is, indeed, an important act of control.[18] But it is only in the act of choosing, which could be done wholly in the mind, that one exercises control. The world responds when the choice is consummated in some act that involves nature or society. It is that overt act and the worlds's response that instructs the individual that he or she is an effective person; the choice by itself will not offer this proof of effectiveness.

3. RULE APPLICATION. The manipulation or interpretation of rules to extract some benefit or avoid a penalty yields evidence that a person can influence his or her environment and thus confirms a sense of effectiveness or control. But one's behavior is governed within the context of a rule – a context that steals from personal control that autonomy that gives personal control much of its savor. Normally it is a defensive act: If one gets the interpretation right, some benefit may flow, but the overriding power is in the rule maker. It is not a reciprocal relationship like a contract.

4. EXCHANGES AND PUNISHMENTS. Rule-based systems rely on punishments from external sources for enforcement; exchange-based systems rely on rewards and, of course, denial of rewards. It is arguable that a deprivation of a good is a punishment ("No dessert for you tonight, young man!"), but, as Skinner points out, there are two crucial differences: (1)Punishments for infraction of rules or commands teach the punished to avoid the punishing agent and similar situations in the future; the punished leave the field. Rewards, and even their deprivation, provide incentives to remain within the field and to keep in touch with the agent of rewards. (2) Rewards teach a person what he or she did right and therefore what can be done in the future to gain other rewards; punishments teach only what a person did wrong; he or she may be quite ignorant of how to correct errors made.[19] Rewards teach personal control in a way not true of punishments. Adam Smith was the first to point out that voluntary exchanges in their very nature are rewarding to *both* participants – otherwise they would not consummate the exchange.

Unfavorable exchanges exact their own punishments without external agencies; they teach a person not only what he or she did wrong (in a sequence of mixed exchanges) but also what he or she did right. They are participatory in a way such that the individual is both subject and object of his or her own choices, not the object of a decision by another. In many ways, this absence of an external authority and punishing agent is the secret of market success and of the failures of command economies.

---

[18] Reactance theory and research show that if a person prefers A to B and is told that he or she cannot have B, that person changes his or her preferences so as to prefer B to A as a way of preserving autonomy. See Jack W. Brehm, *Responses to the Loss of Freedom: A Theory of Psychological Reactance* (Morristown, NJ: General Learning Press, 1972).

[19] B. F. Skinner, *Science and Human Behavior* (New York: Macmillan, 1953).

5. EXCHANGE: LEARNING RECIPROCITY AND SOCIOCENTRICITY. Piaget claims that it is in the give-and-take of peer group, rather than parental, relations that children learn reciprocity – and therefore, he says, learn both logic and sociocentricity, the latter meaning an understanding that others, as well as the self, have legitimate claims and valid ideas.[20] Market exchange is more like peer group relations, and rule application is more like parental relations. Inherent in exchange is the idea of understanding the claims of the exchange partner so as to maximize gain; that is, the selfishness of the market erodes Piagetian "egocentrism," by which he means the belief that what is in an individual's own mind is the only reality. In the process of cognitive maturation, egocentrism of this kind is a handicap that must be overcome.

6. EXCHANGE: RELAXING THE GRIP OF CONVENTION. It is in the give-and-take (exchange) relations with a peer group that children learn that rules are not given in the nature of things but may be modified to suit the convenience of the players. Whereas the givenness of things is the enemy of cognitive development, a system in which exchange is free to transgress on any given arrangement is likely constantly to erode the rules of the status quo. A situation where what is bought and sold in a constant flow of transactions determines social wealth teaches something different from the teachings of a hereditary landowning system.

7. CONSCIENCE. Finally, obeying the rules of conscience tells the moral individual that he or she is good – or even powerful, but only against temptation. It is a wholly internal power, satisfying in many ways, but it is not evidence that a person's control extends to an external environment. Ethical philosophers who find in benevolence a final good, do not appreciate the further advantages of beneficence whereby a person's sense of effectiveness may be tested and learned.

Work roles: the market's Achilles' heel. We will examine the relationship of work to self-attribution in Chapter 13, but regarding this matter of internality and work it is necessary to note the undermining character of the wage contract. A person is expected to be internal and self-directive in foraging for jobs, choosing them as befits that person's aspirations and talents, but once possessing a job he or she is often deprived of discretion, of the opportunity to act and see the effects of that act, of acquiring a favorable history of contingent reinforcement. What the worker sells is his or her labor power, that is, an availability for management direction – not, on the surface, a circumstance favoring a sense of control over one's environment. This is the great exception to the theory of exchange and internality set forth here.

Market effects: contingency

As mentioned in the introduction to this chapter, exchanges are a form of contingent acts, which, in turn, are the principal sources of internal attribution. The main focus here is on the market's demand that one must give something – money, labor,

[20] Jean Piaget, *The Moral Judgment of the Child,* trans. M. Gabin (1932; reprint New York: Free Press, 1965).

sacrifice – in order to get something. Contingent relations of this kind are again best understood by contrast with three related concepts. (1) The concept of *the intrinsic* is foreign to contingency, for "intrinsic" refers to something that is of value in and by itself. (2) The idea of *altruism* is alien to contingency. In a contingency-dominated culture the marketized recipient of a generous act asks, "I wonder what he wanted?" Altruism is thus converted into a game of reciprocity, as social exchange theorists would specify. Thus, market contingency implies instrumentalism and, if among persons, self-interest. (3) Contingency is also opposed to the concept of *unconditional rights,* the rights of citizens or simply of persons, as the term "unconditional" implies. In short, contingency flies in the face of much moral theory, of good will as a good in itself, of virtue, and of rights.

But contingency is a great teacher. Termed "reinforcement," contingency is at the heart of the original Watson-Skinner theory of learning and is respected by the more sophisticated social learning theorists:

Reinforcement does play a role [for example] in observational learning, but mainly as an antecedent rather than a consequent influence. Anticipation of reinforcement is one of several factors that can influence what is observed and what goes unnoticed. . . . Moreover, anticipated benefits can strengthen retention of what is learned observationally by motivating people to code and rehearse modeled behavior that they value highly. . . . In social learning theory, reinforcement is considered a facilitative rather than a necessary condition because factors other than response consequences can influence what people attend to.[21]

School teachers deprecate the grades-for-work concept of schooling, but students do develop cognitively in an atmosphere loaded with contingency relations.

There are good reasons for preferring intrinsic learning to contingent learning: What is learned is not only more but different when curiosity is the stimulus. On the other hand, reliance on contingent relations in economic life has, when compared to other kinds of motivation in other economies, proved superior to reliance on conscience, for example, when work is "volunteered" because of its social value, or on feelings of social solidarity, as when someone joins a work team that needs the person, or, indeed, on intrinsic work motivation based wholly on internal rewards[22] (Chapter 18). In Utopia we will rely wholly on internal rewards; in the meantime we may accept with gratitude the learned sense of personal control that comes from the external rewards of contingent reinforcement.

Overreliance on contingent rewards

Perhaps we should modify our gratitude for external rewards, because reliance on them, untempered by an acknowledgement of people's capacity for self-rewards, implies a substantial loss of autonomy – as well as realism. Psychologists and sociologists have amused themselves at the expense of the assumption that people are governed by contingent extrinsic rewards: "If actions were determined solely

---

[21] Bandura, *Social Learning Theory,* 37. "A vast amount of evidence lends validity to the view that reinforcement serves principally as an informative and motivational operation rather than as a mechanical response strengthener." (p. 21)

[22] See Mark R. Lepper and David Greene, eds., *The Hidden Costs of Rewards: New Perspectives on the Psychology of Human Motivation* (Hillsdale, NJ: Erlbaum, 1978). Chapters 18 and 19 in this text are devoted to the analysis of the intrinsic.

by external rewards and punishments people would behave like weathervanes, constantly shifting directions to conform to the momentary influences impinging upon them.''[23] And the economist's "conception of man is that of a lightening calculator of pleasures and pains, who oscillates like a homogeneous globule of desire of happiness under the impulse of stimuli that shift him about the area."[24] The implied version of humanity is of mindless creatures, with no more self-determination than moths flying toward light or cockroaches shunning it. In fact, of course, humans are to a large extent "self-regulators," selecting goals and behaviors that satisfy their internal standards and purposes, sometimes moved by the contingent relations offered, and sometimes not. "Behavior is . . . regulated by the interplay of self-generated and external sources of influence," which means that to some extent, all behavior is at least partially "under self-reinforcement control."[25]

Market doctrine and latitude for personal control

We will distinguish between (1) *market doctrine*, the letter and spirit of market economics, and (2) *market imperatives*, what market institutions actually require of people for them to benefit from market institutions. We turn first to market doctrine. The central issue is whether market "laws" are so confining that individuals cannot exercise the kinds of choices that contribute to their individual sense of effectiveness. Economists do not have to take a stand on whether internal locus of control is encouraged by the market; rather their position is that if a society wants efficiency in material production, its members must choose to follow market laws. Within those laws, freedom of choice is a central tenet of the doctrine. And within those constraints, all people are free to employ their skills to gain whatever success those skills entitle them to. Markets are assumed to be responsive to effort. Each person is assumed to act alone, guided solely by concepts of individual household well-being. By forbidding consideration of intersubjective utility and requiring that "the satisfaction of each consumer is affected only by his own consumption and work, and not in addition by other people's consumption,"[26] the market doctrine assumes internal reference and control.

Price and budget constraints. Like psychologists, economists are inevitably interactionist, but unlike psychologists they stipulate that one pair of circumstances and one internal constraint will together decide the outcome of all market choice processes. The circumstances are budgets and prices and the internal constraint is taste; given budgets and taste, price is a sufficient determinant of consumer behavior, or given taste and prices, budgets are sufficient. It is this assumption that leads to the observations about people as "weathervanes" turning in the direction that the wind (price) decides for them, or as "homogeneous globules of desire for happiness" whirling in response to prices. If taste is autonomously determined,

[23] Bandura, *Social Learning Theory,* 128.

[24] Thorstein Veblen, "Why is Economics Not an Evolutionary Science?" in *The Portable Veblen* (New York: Viking, 1949), 232. Original essay published 1919.

[25] Bandura, *Social Learning Theory,* 129.

[26] Tjalling C. Koopmans, *Three Essays on the State of Economic Science* (New York: McGraw-Hill, 1957), 41.

however, individual behavior is still self-determined and not similar to that of a weathervane or globule.

Given ends. Market doctrine assumes that people are income and leisure maximizers, whereas those with a genuine sense of internal control do not wish to have their ends assumed for them. They may sacrifice *both* income and leisure to work at something with intrinsic appeal. The consequence is that they are in fact income and leisure satisficers, where alternative ends in friendship and family life, both of which may imply some sacrifice of income and leisure, are weighed in the balance. People are not self-determining when their ends are given to them. But it is doctrine, not practice, that "gives" those ends.

Iron laws. In addition, economics has not entirely passed beyond the kind of iron laws that Malthus and Ricardo thought constrained economic behavior. Commenting on countries who have seen their GNPs decline, Harberger says that "a crude sort of 'justice' prevails in the economic policy realm. Countries that have run their economies following the policy tenets of the professionals [i.e., market economists] have on the whole reaped good fruit from their effort; likewise, those who have flown in the face of these tenets have had to pay the price."[27] There is only one route to economic efficiency.

In fact, there are many routes and many different voices among the "policy professionals" and Harberger's own prescriptions are very loosely framed.[28] Some of the successful economies have high taxes and some have low ones; some have deficits and others balanced budgets; some depend upon foreign trade and others on domestic trade; some have large public sectors and some small ones; welfare policies very; trade union policies vary; monetary policies vary. It may be fairly argued that it is the relations of these policies to each other that matter, which is true, of course, but does not alter the range of variation.

The system of the policy professionals is not so confining as it seems, for it leaves out of account many of the most important variables: the *culture* of enterprise, thrift, work ethic, trust (Chapter 16), the family patterns, educational level, and level of development of the society. It is more nearly right to say with Harrison that "underdevelopment is a state of mind"[29] and that state of mind will determine the success of any one of the policies proposed by the policy professionals. States of mind seem much more amenable to personal control than economic laws. The iron laws that might constrain self-determination and limit personal control may be as Engels said they were:

The forces of production in society work exactly like the forces operating in nature. . . . But when once we have recognized them and understand how they work, their direction and their

[27] Arnold C. Harberger, "Economic Policy and Economic Growth," in Harberger, ed., *World Economic Growth* (San Francisco: Institute for Contemporary Studies, 1984), 462.
[28] Ibid., 428–35.
[29] Lawrence E. Harrison, *Underdevelopment Is a State of Mind: The Latin Case* (Lanham, MD: University Press of American, 1985).

effects, the gradual subjection of them to our will and the use of them for the attainment of our aims depends entirely upon ourselves.[30]

Within the context of economic laws, the individual in a market society is not only free to choose his or her own destiny but free to choose within economic laws that are less restrictive than those who look strictly at economic policy will allow.

How markets teach a sense of personal control

Childhood socialization

Economic socialization is a topic unto itself; here I note only a few of the patterns that influence internality and cognitive development. The childhood socialization we examine first is usually conceived as forming *traits* that are likely to endure into adulthood.

Much of parental policy seems independent of economic system. Lefcourt reports that internality is fostered by initial affection and warmth followed by and associated with selective reinforcement of control behavior; indiscriminate reinforcement and total failure to reinforce children's exploratory efforts both fail to encourage independence and internal locus of control. One report mentions a mother's "coolness and criticality" and parents who "push their children toward independence" as conditions for learning that the self is, indeed, a cause. Learning internal locus of control is also a condition for learning the skills that make up "intelligence"[31] (discussed in Chapter 7). This is congruent with Vernon's specification of the conditions that favor higher intelligence: a "demanding" but "democratic" family emphasizing internal controls and early training for independence.[32] Family effects on cognitive complexity discussed in Chapters 7 and 8 apply to self-attribution, as well.

Parents teach self-reliance – when they have learned its benefits in the market. It is generally assumed that parents teach their children those traits that the parents think will be functional for their children in adulthood.[33] At least in the American culture, self-reliance (internal locus of control) is thought to be just such a functional trait,[34] but within this overall pattern there are differences based on

[30] Friedrich Engels, *Socialism: Utopian and Scientific,* in V. Adoratsky, ed., *Karl Marx: Selected Works* (Moscow: International Publishers, n.d., c. 1933), 180–1.

[31] Herbert M. Lefcourt, *Locus of Control: Current Trends in Theory and Research* (Hillsdale, NJ: Erlbaum/Wiley, 1976), 97–104.

[32] Philip E. Vernon, *Intelligence and Cultural Environment* (London: Methuen, 1969), 218, 230.

[33] This is the general assumption of the literature on personality and culture. See, for example, John M. Whiting, "Socialization Process and Personality," in Francis L. K. Hsu, ed., *Psychological Anthropology: Approaches to Culture and Personality* (Homewood, IL: Dorsey, 1961), 355–80. But the doctrine is modified by the fact that parents tend to socialize children in the manner in which they themselves were socialized. See Abram Kardiner with the collaboration of Ralph Linton, Cora DuBois, and James West, *The Psychological Frontiers of Society* (New York: Columbia University Press, 1945).

[34] Margaret Mead claims that this is the typical goal of the American family; see her *And Keep Your Powder Dry* (New York: Morrow, 1942).

parental occupation. Training for independence is generally taught in homes where the parents have had jobs where initiative, rather than obedience, has been functional. What seems at first to be a class-determined pattern, turns out to be a product of parental occupational learning. Regardless of class, if the parents learned initiative in their jobs, they value this for their children; if their jobs required obedience, they teach *that* to their children.[35] Influenced by the way the market economy (and, more importantly, technology) structures and distributes occupations, parents will teach their children either that they can influence their environments through their own initiative, or that they should adapt to their environments as these are given to them.

Competition between markets and children for mothers' time. The market influences socialization in another way. The Whitings found that among their six communities of study (including a New England village), if the division of labor was such that the mother was so heavily engaged in earning the family living that the children had to take care of each other, as contrasted to situations where the mother was dependent on her husband for economic support and had more time for her children, the children grew up more nurturant and more community minded. More motherly attention, on the other hand, was associated with greater independence and self-interestedness in children[36] – a syndrome, I judge, closer to that of internal locus of control. As the market absorbs more and more mothers into employment, motherly attention becomes scarce, although there is little evidence that the children of working mothers suffer in other ways.[37] How market forces allocate mothers' time powerfully influences the way children learn a sense of personal control.

Adult socialization: exchange as contingency
The most important congruence between market doctrine and practice, on the one hand, and internal locus of control, on the other, is in the acceptance of the concept of contingency. As Weber said, the market "is no respecter of persons." It does not offer goods based on membership in a community, ascriptive status, or personhood. It does not recognize need. To live well in a market is to have a history of contingent reinforcement – the very thing that Seligman and others have said is the condition of internality. People wanting to live well must learn to accept contingent reinforcement; people living in an environment of contingent reinforcement are more likely to learn internality. Internal locus of control implies that when a person acts, the environment responds; the market says in order for the environment to respond, a person must act. Whereas it is certainly not universally true that "when a person

[35] Leonard J. Pearlin and Melvin L. Kohn, "Social Class, Occupation, and Parental Values: A Cross-Cultural Study," *American Sociological Review* 31 (1966): 466–79.
[36] Beatrice B. Whiting and John W. M. Whiting, *Children of Six Cultures* (Cambridge: Harvard University Press, 1975).
[37] Lois Wladis Hoffman and F. Ivan Nye, *Working Mothers* (San Francisco: Jossey-Bass, 1974). But later studies suggest that if the combined burden of home and market work is heavy and not shared with the husband, the mother and children often suffer.

acts, the environment responds" (e.g., structural unemployment), internality is learned on those occasions when it is true.

From this we infer three things: people who live well in a market economy are likely to have learned internality – an inference supported by the fact that level of income (not education) is the single best demographic predictor of internality.[38] Conversely, internals are more likely than externals to do well in a market economy. This fact is confirmed by several studies, one of which found that those business school students who were high on internal locus of control earned more in later business life than others who were lower in this respect – and, in turn, increased their sense of internal control, probably as a consequence of their success.[39] Another study found that among those who had been out of the labor market, those who were more internal before reentry advanced more rapidly over a two-year period than those who were less internal, and in addition, those who reentered compared to those who did not, developed greater internality.[40] Finally, if the market, rather than wealth and education, is the source of internality, those who are closer to market operations and for whom these operations are more important should have greater faith in internal locus of control than those with similar demographic backgrounds but less of an investment in the market. One study seems to confirm this inference: Compared to professionals and all other groups, business "managers scored highest of all subgroups on generalized fate-control,"[41] a measure of internality.

Noncontingent income. In the 1970s the federal government sponsored a massive income maintenance program to test whether security of income for the poor might not lead to more vigorous job searches, greater job satisfaction, less dependence on welfare, and greater family integrity. It did not turn out that way.

In an exhaustive review of the labor supply effects of the income maintenance program, Robins found "an unambiguous negative impact of the experiment on annual hours of work." Compared to a control group, the guaranteed noncontingent income reduced the labor supply of husbands by 5 percent, wives by 22 percent, and single female heads of families by 11 percent, with few differences by race or site or duration in the program.[42] Moreover, "in addition to causing a reduction in annual hours of work for persons employed, the experiment also reduces the probability of working. . . . Husbands in the experimental group tend to remain out of work for longer periods of time and to work for shorter hours of time than husbands

[38] Gurin and Gurin, "Personal Efficacy," 137. The correlation is such ($r = .24$) that many other factors are also relevant.
[39] Ibid., 140.
[40] P. J. Andrisani and G. Nestel, "Internal–External Control as Contributor and Outcome of Work Experience," *Journal of Applied Psychology* 61 (1976): 156–65. The measure of internal to external was an eleven-item Rotter scale.
[41] Burkhard Strumpel with the assistance of Richard T. Curtin and M. Susan Schwartz, "Economic Life-Styles, Values, and Subjective Welfare," in Strumpel, ed., *Economic Means for Human Needs*, 54.
[42] Philip K. Robins, "Labor Supply Response of Family Heads and Implications for a National Program," in Philip K. Robins, Robert G. Spiegelman, Samuel Weiner, and Joseph G. Bell, eds., *A Guaranteed Annual Income: Evidence from a Social Experiment* (New York: Academic Press, 1980), 63.

in the control group. . . . Wives and female heads exhibit a somewhat larger reduction in the probability of employment than husbands.''[43] To crown the disappointment of the advocates of the income maintenance program, it was found that families in the experiment were more likely to dissolve than were families in the control group, a finding not predictable from models of economic man and attributed in this case to the ''stress'' of even this benign change in circumstances.[44] Finally, although one might expect the sense of security given by income maintenance to improve job satisfaction, apparently this did not happen. A supplementary noncontingent source of income had no effect at all on husbands' job satisfaction, very modestly increased job satisfaction of wives, and actually *reduced* job satisfaction of single female heads of families.[45]

The evidence is strong that noncontingent money, ''welfare money'' as it was called, fails to convey the message that a person is effective, does not teach self-attribution or personal control, and therefore does not improve morale.

Unemployment. In theory and by the evidence, people who fail in the labor market learn that their acts do not elicit favorable responses from the (market) environment. They learn externality, passivity, helplessness, the importance of luck, chance, and fate.[46] Or, if the market ideology persists in the face of the frequent evidence that the individuals' unemployment is not their fault, many will learn self-blame, demoralization, and depression.[47] The contingency imperative of the market is a device for encouraging internality, rewarding those who have it, and punishing those who either do not have it to begin with or who learn externality in the market forum.

Social loafing. To round out this picture, recall the discussion in Chapter 3 showing that social loafing occurred when individuals' contribution to group effort was anonymous and the individual was not accountable to anyone. But also recall how both the identification of comparative individual effort, if only privately to each participant, and accountability to others reduced social loafing. Contingent rewards can be self-awarded, but this works better when others are observing the rewarding procedure.

There is one codicil: People at the bottom of most strata learn to control their own fates within small ambits by manipulating their ''masters,'' as James Scott

[43] Ibid.

[44] See Peggy Thoits and Michael T. Hannan, ''Income and Psychological Distress,'' in Robins et al., *A Guaranteed Annual Income*. An alternative explanation might be Goode's hypothesis that divorce is a function of available income to support the wife in case of marital dissolution.

[45] Robins, ''Job Satisfaction,'' in Robins et al., *A Guaranteed Annual Income*, 129.

[46] Marie Jahoda, *Employment and Unemployment: A Psychosocial Analysis* (Cambridge, UK: Cambridge University Press, 1982).

[47] N. Feather, ''Unemployment and its Psychological Correlates: A Study of Depression Symptoms, of Self-Esteem, Protestant Ethic Values, and Attributional Style and Apathy,'' *Australian Journal of Psychology* 34 (1982): 309–23; see also Kay L. Schlozman and Sidney Verba, *Injury to Insult: Unemployment, Class, and Political Response* (Cambridge: Harvard University Press, 1979).

has vividly portrayed in his *Weapons of the Weak*,[48] by exaggerated deference, faking incompetence, petty theft and secret "borrowing," and much more.

Individual or collective rewards

[Situations where] one's outcomes are personally determined encourage self-reliance and self-interest. Collective contingency systems subordinate self-interest to group welfare. This is achieved by rewarding and punishing the entire group so that members are affected by each other's behavior. . . . Group-oriented contingencies are most prevalent in societies espousing a collectivist ethic. . . . Individually oriented reinforcement . . . is well suited for creating independent, self-seeking people.[49]

There is evidence that compared to the Taiwanese and Americans, the Japanese have an internality of a slightly different, but no less authentic, character. Thus the following report raises a number of questions: "Whereas the American ideal might be individualistic achievement as a goal, the Japanese concept of achievement is integrally associated with a person's group role and status, especially with respect to one's family." Japanese goals are, therefore, likely to be group oriented – in industry as well as in the household.[50] Because of such evidence, we should modify the belief that individualistic attitudes are necessary for the development of a sense of internal control. Inasmuch as the Japanese *pay* their employees individually, however, I retain the belief that pay loosely contingent on performance is probably a more effective way to teach people that their outcomes are dependent on their prior acts.

Benign and malign cycles

The cited evidence shows that internals were more successful in the labor market and at work and that this success, in turn, reinforced their internality. Similarly, externals were less successful in finding work and if they did, their experience on the job was unlikely to provide them with the discretion that confirms internality. If they did not find work, they were (or might be) reinforced in their lack of faith in their own efforts.

Some of the psychological machinery for these cycles has been explored with children. Under conditions of failure, the internals (called "mastery oriented children") focused on remedies, whereas externals ("helpless oriented children") focused on causes; internals "made surprisingly few attributions but instead engaged in self-monitoring and self-instructions." When pressed, internals explained their failures as due to lack of sufficient effort and other surmountable factors, whereas externals attributed their failures to lack of abilities beyond their capacities to master – even when the abilities of the two groups are identical. Internals, believing that the fault was remediable, also believed that they would do better next time; exter-

[48] James C. Scott, *Weapons of the Weak: The Everyday Forms of Peasant Resistance* (New Haven: Yale University Press, 1985).

[49] Bandura, *Social Learning Theory,* 116, 117.

[50] Richard W. Brislin, "Cross-Cultural Research in Psychology," *Annual Review of Psychology* 34 (1983): 363–400 at 375.

nals believed that they would never do any better. Their perceptions of their own successes and failures also differed: Internals were a little more likely to overestimate their successes and underestimate their failures, whereas the externals consistently underestimated their successes and overestimated their failures. "Thus, for helpless (external) children, successes are less salient, less predictive [of future successes], and less enduring – less successful."[51]

Even more than life itself, the market seems constantly to support the Matthew Principle (Matt. 25:29): "For unto every one that hath shall be given, and he shall have abundance; but from him that hath not shall be taken away even that which he hath."

Comparison with less marketized societies

If the forces of exchange and contingency and the ideology of self-reliance stem from market sources, we should expect people in more marketized societies to exhibit more internality. There is, in fact, a cross-cultural ordering of the belief in internal locus of control that might be interpreted as evidence for market support: Among three cultures, American Indians are the least internal, Mexican-Americans more internal, and Anglo-Americans the most.[52] This sequence tends to support the idea that the more marketized the culture, the more likely are its members to have internal locus of control. Rosina Lao reports on a variety of cross-cultural studies showing that "Americans seem to be more internal than individuals from other less industrialized countries."

Lao's explanation, however, relies more on the effect of industrialization on the family and community than on market imperatives. "In a more industrialized culture, there is a higher dependency on the 'self,' and individuals are less under the control of family, tribe, or even chance factors such as drought, hurricane, and so on."[53] Lao's own study finds that Taiwanese and American college students are very little different in their beliefs about personal control. Even in 1977, Taiwan was a highly commercial society; that evidence says nothing, then, about market effects.

Lao, however, gives figures from a comparable study of Japanese students (1974), whose pattern of beliefs represent a level of personal control comparable to that of Americans, but it is based on a lower sense of general internality and a higher feeling of freedom from the control of "powerful others."[54] This alerts us again to the multidimensionality of the concept, but so far we have weak evidence support-

[51] Carol I. Diener and Carol S. Dweck, "An analysis of Learned Helplessness: Continuous Changes in Performance, Strategy, and Achievement Cognitions Following Failures," *Journal of Personality and Social Psychology* 36 (1978): 451–62; idem, "An analysis of Learned Helplessness: II. The Processing of Success," *Journal of Personality and Social Psychology* 39 (1980): 940–52.
[52] T. D. Graves, *Time Perspective and Deferred Gratification in a Tri-ethnic Community* (Boulder: University of Colorado Press, 1961), cited in John Condry and James Chambers, "Intrinsic Motivation and the Process of Learning," in Mark R. Lepper and David Greene, eds., *The Hidden Costs of Rewards: New Perspectives on the Psychology of Motivation* (Hillsdale, NJ: Wiley/Erlbaum, 1978), 78.
[53] Rosina C. Lao, "Levenson's IPC (Internal Control) Scale: A Comparison of Chinese and American Students," *Journal of Cross-Cultural Psychology* 9 (1977): 113–24 at 121.
[54] Ibid., 117.

ing Lao's belief that industrialized (in these cases marketized) societies encourage a higher sense of "self" – a self that is more in control of its own fate.

It is at least tangentially relevant that the "sense of (political) competence," defined as a belief that a person can exert political influence in various ways, was highest in two of the then (1963) most commercially advanced countries, the United States and Britain, and lowest in the sample's two least commercially advanced countries, Italy and Mexico.[55] Among Western countries, the United States regularly scores higher than other countries on indicators both of sense of personal control over one's own fate and of support for the market,[56] revealing at least an ideological affinity between the two. Finally, there seems to be a recent trend in the United States to find increasing satisfaction in independence: A major study of changes in American attitudes from 1957 to 1976 found that "many more people in the 1976 population look at their own independence as a source of their well-being . . . [and are] seeing the self as generally more efficacious."[57] The usual problem of tracing these psychological developments to market influences pertains; at least it seems that market economies in general, and the American economy in particular, offer hospitable soil for nurturing feelings of personal control.

Internality and cognitive complexity

Internality and cognitive style
I have shown that market exchange is a form of contingent reward that promotes internal locus of control. Now we will relate this very internality back to cognitive complexity that occupied much of Part II. What is the relationship between internal locus of control and cognition? The short answer is that, compared to externals, internals are likely to be more cognitively complex, more perceptive, and more independent in their thinking. The evidence is subtle and persuasive. In the first place, internals do better at school, partly because they assume responsibility for their own success or failure: "Boys who assumed responsibility for success and girls who assumed responsibility for failure were the most likely to have obtained higher grades and achievement scores."[58] Internals are more verbally fluent and more skillful at pattern recognition, particularly when this recognition involves invention of labels and names.[59]

One reason that internals have higher achievement is that their concerns are better fitted to the difficulty of the tasks. When tasks are difficult, internals value success

[55] Gabriel A. Almond and Sidney Verba, *The Civic Culture* (Princeton: Princeton University Press, 1963), 184–6. Although it is true that a sense of political efficacy has declined in the United States since 1964, that decline has been in the political part of the measure; the sense of *personal* efficacy has held up rather better.

[56] See, for example, George Katona, Burkhard Strumpel, and Ernest Zahn, *Aspirations and Affluence: Comparative Studies in the United States and Western Europe* (New York: McGraw-Hill, 1971), 21–2.

[57] Joseph Veroff, Elizabeth Douvan, and Richard Kulka, *The Inner Americans: A Self-Portrait from 1857 to 1976* (New York: Basic Books, 1981), 535.

[58] S. R. Messer, "The Relation of Internal–External Control to Academic Performance," *Child Development* 43 (1972): 1,456–62, cited in Lefcourt, *Locus of Control,* 146. The sex differences are supported by other studies.

[59] Lefcourt, *Locus of Control,* 145, citing work by Brecher and Denmark (1969).

more highly than externals; when the tasks are easy, internals fear failure more. Thus their concerns offer a more rational pattern than that of the externals whose fears of failure fail to match the difficulty of the tasks.[60]

Internals are more intellectually flexible; they are quicker at perceiving change. In a study ostensibly on verbal facility, the list of words increasingly employed sexual double entendres ("rubber," "bust," etc.). The internals were quicker than the externals to see the double meanings, laughed sooner, and enjoyed the joke more.[61] Internals are also more perceptive in seeing and remembering matters incidental to a task; asked to proofread a story for typographical errors, internals did at least as well as externals in spotting the "typos" and, in addition, could remember the names, dates, and incidents in the story rather better. Similarly, asked to memorize the dates in a story, they did better in remembering the names as well.[62]

More than externals, internals seek information relevant to the problem or task confronting them. In an infirmary for tubercular patients, internals sought more information about tuberculosis, even though the information might be painful; in a boys' reformatory, internals knew more about parole than externals; asked to persuade others about Vietnam, internals sought out more relevant information than externals.[63]

Compared to externals, internals are more interested in skill-related information than chance-related information. In a task requiring the matching of various names and symbols, internals spent more time and worked harder when the task was labeled a task of skill than when it was labeled a task of chance, whereas these labels made no difference to externals – except for a slightly greater interest in the chance task. In general, the authors of this study report that internals vary their attention, concern, and interest in a more purposive way.[64]

Internality: its resistance to obstacles to cognitive complexity

Conformity and resistance to authority. Conformity is an enemy of complex cognition and internals tend to resist conformity more than externals. In a study where individuals were asked to assess the relative lengths of two lines in circumstances in which a group of confederates all assessed the longer line as the shorter one, internals were only very slightly more independent than externals – but they were much less certain of their (group-influenced) assessments than were externals. In a story writing study where an experimenter sought, through smiles and nods of the head, to encourage longer stories, internals (more than externals) wrote shorter stories. Asked about the persuasiveness of a message, internals and externals did not differ, but where externals were influenced by the prestige of the alleged author, internals were uninfluenced by these attributions. Reporting on his own studies, Lefcourt said, "Internals were unresponsive to the experimenter's instructions, sug-

[60] Ibid., 147, citing work by Karabenick (1972).
[61] Ibid., 60–2, citing work by Lefcourt, Gronnerud, and McDonald (1973).
[62] Ibid., 64, citing work by Wolk and Ducette (1974).
[63] Ibid., 52–3, citing work by Seeman and Evans (1962), Seeman (1963), Davis and Phares (1967).
[64] Ibid., 57–8, reporting work by Rotter and Mulry (1965).

gestions, and manipulations, whereas externals readily capitulated, behaving, almost to a man, in accord with task directions."[65]

Like conformity, submission to authority undermines independent cognition. The resistance to experimenters in the studies reported is partial evidence that internals are more likely than externals to be independent in their thinking. In summarizing these and other research reports, Lefcourt said, "The internal resists being placed in positions where he is the pawn who is 'put down,' so to speak, by the assumed knowledge of others."[66] Lefcourt believes that what Eichman in Germany and Lt. Calley (who claimed that he was carrying out orders when he, himself, ordered the murder of women and children in Vietnam) lacked was exactly this kind of internal locus of control. A study of American reactions to the arrest of Lt. Calley reports on the mechanism: "Those who resist in these situations have somehow managed to maintain the framework of *personal causation* that applies in 'normal' situations."[67]

Stress. Like conformity and obedience to authority, stress reduces cognitive complexity – as we saw in some detail in the analysis of environmental complexity (Chapter 8). "Laboratory research on learned helplessness suggests that independence between outcomes and responses may directly reduce motivation [and] interfere with cognitive processes."[68] Just as control over the incidence of stressful events, even when they cannot be avoided, improves cognition, so does the sense of control, even when it is not exercised.[69]

In an indirect fashion internality contributes to the relief of stress (and to improved cognition of a special kind) by contributing to happiness or the sense of subjective well-being. In one study, internal control, together with a sense of social support and of achievement "accounted for 75 percent of the variance in evaluations of life as a whole."[70]

The costs of internal locus of control

Stratification and power
Within a society, the experience of control over one's own circumstances, acting and having someone respond, is directly related to power positions in that society. Thus, whites are more internal than blacks and other minorities who have been discriminated against; the rich are more likely to be internal than the poor; men are

[65] Ibid., 41–6, citing, in the order reported, studies by Crowne and Leverant (1963), Gore (1962), Ritchie and Phares (1969). Quotations from ibid., 46.
[66] Ibid., 42.
[67] Herbert C. Kelman and Lee Hamilton Lawrence, "Assignment of Responsibility in the Case of Lt. Calley: Preliminary Report on a National Survey," *Journal of Social Issues* 28 (1972): 177–212 at 181.
[68] Robert I. Sutton and Robert L. Kahn, "Prediction, Understanding, and Control as Antidotes to Organizational Stress," in Frank M. Andrews, ed., *Research on the Quality of Life* (Ann Arbor, MI: Institute for Social Research, 1986), 345.
[69] David C. Glass and Jerome E. Singer, *Urban Stress: Experiments on Noise and Social Situations* (New York: Academic Press, 1972).
[70] Antonia Abbey and Frank M. Andrews, "Modeling the Psychological Determinants of Life Quality," in Andrews, *Research on the Quality of Life*, 105.

more internal than women; and internality tends to increase with age to the middle years (where it remains on a plateau for most of the rest of one's life).[71] In the benign cycle, internals tend to succeed in the market and their successes increase their beliefs in their own causal effectiveness.

Given the control by the richer, older, white, male members of society over the definition of social values, we cannot be surprised that the self-reliance and internality they share, rather than piety, courage, scholarly ability, or altruism, is given such value priority. Nor, given the worth assigned to self-reliance by such diverse figures as Emerson, Mill, and Kant, does this seem unduly partisan. The social cost of the high value placed on internal locus of control lies in what the Gurins have called "control ideology":[72] the related belief that most people (and not only the self) do control their own destinies and that, therefore, they get what they deserve. That belief justifies privilege and pacifies and immobilizes the disadvantaged. It obliterates the fact that people do not start with equal advantages, that internality and externality are unevenly distributed by the circumstances of birth. The stratification of attributional beliefs reveals how self-serving it is for the better off. Two British studies found that the richer a person is, the more likely he or she is to attribute poverty and unemployment to the defects of the poor and the unemployed, whereas the poor and unemployed were somewhat more likely to explain their conditions as products of bad luck or a faulty economy.[73] Internal attribution reinforces inequality by justifying it.

Internality as a useful social fiction

If most of the variance in individual behavior *is* accounted for by situational stimuli, what standing can the belief in internal locus of control have? One possibility is that the value of the belief is not in its truth value but in its value to the society; it is a "noble lie." Societies are richer, as well as more cultivated and egalitarian, if people *believe* that they control their own destinies, whether they do or not. In a Darwinian fashion, the species benefits by a trait that is often individually dysfunctional, as with the instinctual emission of danger signals by birds who give notice to their peers at the cost of attracting attention to themselves.

Another justification is that probabilistically the individual will personally be better off if he or she believes in personal control over his or her own destiny. If the individual pursues his or her aims, chances for success may be low, but they are zero if the individual does not try.

Third, as Robert White pointed out, it is intrinsically satisfying to believe that one controls one's own fate, and people deceive themselves in this respect both because of this intrinsic gratification and because of its gratifying implications about their qualities of strength, determination, and character. Like the power of social influence, it seems that it might be hard to demonstrate that the market is responsi-

---

[71] James E. Birren, Walter R. Cunningham, and Koichi Yamamoto, "Psychology of Adult Development and Aging," *Annual Review of Psychology* 34 (1983): 543–75 at 562.
[72] Gurin and Gurin, "Personal Efficacy."
[73] Adrian Furnham, "Explanations of Unemployment in Britain," *European Journal of Social Psychology* 12 (1982): 335–52; Alan Lewis, "Lay Explanations for the Causes of Unemployment in Britain: Economic, Individualistic, Societal, or Fatalistic," *Political Psychology* 8 (1987): 427–39.

ble for a belief that offers so many other satisfactions and so many social advantages. But, as noted, the belief varies a great deal across cultures.

Internality as veridical distortion

As mentioned, the belief that causal explanation for personal and social outcomes is exclusively attributable to individuals has been called "the fundamental attribution error." Social action is *always* due to interaction between persons and circumstances, with the weight usually assigned to persons when their behavior deviates from a norm and to circumstances when their behavior is conventional or normal. What a belief in internal locus of control does is systematically to misread this interaction, thus systematically to simplify and distort cognition. In doing this, it exaggerates the natural desire of persons to believe in their own effectiveness, their usual tendencies to convert chance situations to skill situations, their "illusion of control."[74] Whereas it would be desirable to establish norms that counter natural tendencies to distort inferences, the ideology of self-reliance reinforces these tendencies. The consequence may be distortion of remedial policy.

Flexible individual attributional policies permit assignment of causes now to circumstance, now to persons, sometimes to self, and sometimes to others or society. It is not that internal attribution is always wrong; rather it is not always right. The definition of cognitive complexity given in Chapter 1 includes the proposition that concepts are held with sufficient flexibility to permit change when evidence or experience conflicts with their tenets; the undiluted doctrine of internality violates that proposition. Moreover, such fixity of conception interferes with learning and adaptation. Madsen found that, compared to kibbutz and Mexican children, children reared in urban market economies could not change their individualistic, personal controlling, competitive pattern to fit changed rules of a game for which this pattern was a sure loser.[75] As a doctrine, internality is self-contradictory: One cannot, in fact, control one's own fate unless one can also understand that at appropriate times other persons or groups control that fate.

Loss of ethical perspectives

Internals behave in more ethical ways than externals. In completing stories about heroes subjected to immoral temptations, internal boys, more than externals, have the hero resist the temptations; internal girls do not cheat in situations where external girls do.[76] Internal subjects were more likely to help another person on a task of sorting small objects when they were subjected to mild electric shocks for this helping behavior. In reporting on this experiment, Lefcourt says: "This study indicates that internals are more tolerant of discomfort in doing what they consider to be correct than are externals."[77]

---

[74] Ellen J. Langer, *The Psychology of Control* (Beverly Hills, CA: Sage, 1983).

[75] Millard C. Madsen, "Cooperative and Competitive Motivation of Children in Three Mexican Subcultures," *Psychological Reports* 20 (1967): 1,307–20.

[76] Lefcourt, *Locus of Control*, 48–9, reporting research by Johnson, Frank, and Fionda (1968) and by Johnson and Gormly (1972).

[77] E. Midlarski, "Aiding Under Stress: The Effects of Competence, Dependence, Visibility, and Fatalism," *Journal of Personality* 39 (1971): 132–249, reported in Lefcourt, *Locus of Control*, 49.

It seems uncharitable, therefore, to fault internality for lack of moral sensitivity. Moreover, ethics itself is dispositional: Virtue is an individual property, as are goodwill and good intentions. But there are three counts against internality (and its extension to others as "control ideology") as it is in fact, though not in logic, expressed in ethical thinking.

1. INTERNALITY IMPLIES THE JUSTICE OF DESERTS. Internal attributions at least suggest and perhaps imply (but certainly do not require) the justice of deserts, proportionality, or, as psychologists say, equity. If I am responsible for everything that happens to me, it is only fair that I should receive rewards proportionate to my contributions. It takes an extra cognitive step to explain why this should not be so, and because they are "cognitive misers," people avoid extra cognitive steps whenever possible. Whatever the logic may be, people who extend their own internality to include others (control ideology) are very likely to believe in the justice of deserts, the deserving being those who have done well.[78] This is a limiting cognition, depriving people of a fair consideration of the justices of need and equality.

2. OTHERS ARE RESPONSIBLE FOR THEIR FATES, BUT I AM NOT. Internality is a conservative cognition as well, for the idea that people are responsible for their own outcomes implies the *Just World* syndrome: Whatever happens to people is just; the victims always bring upon themselves their own fates.[79] Such a perception stifles the impulse for reform. An even less attractive use of the extended belief that people in general have that power of control (control ideology) may be seen when it is combined with evasion of a sense of responsibility for one's own outcomes. "Individuals seem to be able to believe in the Protestant ethic enough to use it to explain unemployment and poverty without necessarily feeling that they are individually responsible for their own personal economic situation."[80]

3. SELF-FAVORING SELECTIVE INTERNALITY. In practice, though not necessarily in theory, internals tend to believe that they are responsible for their own successes but that circumstances are responsible for their failures. This is in contrast to the usual belief that others are responsible for whatever they do, good or bad.[81] Thus, this self-serving bias is a violation of the ethical command to treat the self in the same way one treats others.

But there is a reverse twist to this line of ethical assessment:

Egalitarian rewards may teach learned helplessness in a market society. People learn that they are effective by the experience of acting on their environments and seeing the environment respond; they control rewards and punishments. If, as the market assumes, money is the principal reward and if people get the same money reward regardless of their acts, the acting persons might well conclude that the world is unresponsive to their acts. This is the condition of (1) income equality and (2) learned helplessness. It is at this point that egalitarian ethicists will

[78] Gurin and Gurin, "Personal Efficacy."
[79] Melvin Lerner, *The Belief in a Just World: A Fundamental Delusion* (New York: Plenum Press, 1980).
[80] Gurin and Gurin, "Personal Efficacy," 148.
[81] Edward E. Jones and Richard E. Nisbett, "The Actor and the Observer: Divergent Perceptions of the Causes of Behavior," in Jones et al., *Attribution: Perceiving the Causes of Behavior*.

turn to theories of self-rewards in social learning theory. But just as the rationalists' assumptions represent a cognitive overload, the egalitarian ethicists overload the internal standards and conscience of unaided self-regulation. Perhaps a strong dispositional internality is a necessary condition for continued belief that the self *is* effective even though economic rewards are not responsive to individual effort.

Summary

Self-attribution (internality, a sense of personal control) may not be an adequate basis for explaining events, but it helps people to feel autonomous, resist pressures toward conformity, and lead happier lives, and is associated with more complex cognition. Market contractual exchange, compared to various kinds of social exchange, internal exchanges reflected in assessing opportunity costs, conformity to conscience, and rule application, contributes to self-attribution because it provides experiences where the world responds to a person's acts. The major exceptions are labor exchanges where the individual employee loses a sense of reciprocal control.

Underlying the exchange paradigm is the idea of contingency: Pleasures and pains are contingent on prior performances. Contingent relations of this kind omit the intrinsic, altruism, and unconditional rights, thus violating many ethical principles while providing a superior form of teaching internality. But overreliance on contingent rewards slights the force of self-regulation and seems to make of people weathervanes blowing in the wind.

On the one hand, market doctrine emphasizes self-attribution and self reliance, but on the other hand, its stipulated ends of material advancement and its "iron laws" of policy seem to constrain the role of the individuals in controlling their own destinies. In fact, economic "laws" are rather relaxed and fail to include many of the crucial elements that influence economic outcomes.

Markets encourage parents to teach children self-attribution, but this is undercut by the socialization of their parents to obedience at work. Moreover, the amount of mothers' time that is needed to socialize children into autonomous adults endowed with a sense of personal control is often influenced by the appeal of market work. Other facets of socialization favoring self-attribution, such as a democratic but demanding family, have no market relevance.

Adults learn self-attribution through the contingency training they receive in a market economy, partly because of the many choices they must make and partly because rewards are individual, rather than collective. They are more successful if they have this sense of personal control, and, in turn, they learn the underlying self-attribution by market experience. Failure is both a cause and an effect of lack of self-attribution. Thus benign and malign cycles of success and failure are encouraged by the market.

Modest support for these views comes from cross-cultural research showing that people in more marketized (and industrialized) societies have stronger feelings of personal control. The research also shows that it is possible to have a collective orientation (e.g., the Japanese) and also to attribute outcomes to the self.

Internality is closely associated with a variety of kinds of cognitive complexity,

partly because self-attribution is a protection against conformity, unthinking obedience, and stress.

The social costs of internality are the encouragement it gives to hierarchical views
of society, the misleading explanations of events that it fosters, and a limited ethical
perspective favoring only the justice of deserts and leading to a concept of the world
as just. Another cost is the painful inferences of self-blame by people who fail in
the competitive system.

10 Markets and self-esteem

The quality of persons analyzed in this chapter, self-esteem, was said by Rawls to be "perhaps the most important primary good."[1] In this he is in harmony with the contemporary concern for *self-respect* as a superordinate value, an end in itself.[2] I shall take issue with this evaluation, suggesting that, instead, self-esteem is an instrumental good whose value depends upon its contributions to the two final or primary goods that we have identified as criteria for judging the market: happiness and human development.

As one might expect, self-esteem is closely correlated with self-attribution and internal locus of control discussed in the previous chapter. The similarities are obvious: Both imply favorable beliefs about the self, both are treasured features of an identity, and both are subject to perceptions distorted to favor a more flattering self-image. Just as self-attribution is said to be the most "profound" and "far-reaching" cognition a person can adopt, so opinions about the self are said to be "the most treasured" of all our opinions.[3] In dealing with these two aspects of the self, we touch the foundations of personality. The two aspects are also related to each other by their reciprocal support: The belief that when the self acts, the environment responds is certain to support self-esteem, and the belief that one is worthy supports the idea that one is an effective cause. Both are also closely related to the sense of well-being or happiness,[4] but self-esteem has the closer relationship; indeed, measures of self-esteem may be substituted for measures of subjective well-being.[5] These close relationships mean that as the market encourages and undermines self-attribution, it also encourages and undermines self-esteem.

But even though the two concepts are similar to each other in a variety of ways, they are different in several important respects. Self-esteem is primarily an evaluation, whereas self-attribution is a cognition; a cognition may be judged right or wrong by outsiders, but an evaluation includes preferences that outsiders cannot easily assess as right or wrong. This difference means that it is difficult to "correct" self-evaluations by offering "proof" of error (although cognitive therapy makes the effort). A second difference lies in the fact that, unlike self-attribution, self-esteem is not necessarily learned through action, for self-esteem may be acquired

This chapter borrows substantially from an earlier article, "Government and Self-Esteem," *Political Theory* 10 (1982): 5–31. The substance of that article, in turn, had been presented to the Institute of USA and Canada, Academy of Sciences of the USSR, June 1981; also at the Annual Meeting of the International Society of Political Psychology, Mannheim, Germany, June 1981.
[1] John Rawls, *A Theory of Justice* (Cambridge: Harvard University Press, 1971), 440.
[2] Harold D. Lasswell and Abraham Kaplan, *Power and Society* (New Haven: Yale University Press, 1950), xxiv, 56.
[3] Morris Rosenberg, *Conceiving the Self* (New York: Basic Books, 1979), chap. 2.
[4] Angus Campbell, *Sense of Well-Being in America* (New York: McGraw-Hill, 1981), chap. 13.
[5] Frank M. Andrews and Stephen B. Withey, *Social Indicators of Well-Being: Americans' Perceptions of Life Quality* (New York: Plenum Press, 1976), 323.

from admiring others without any acts on the part of the self. In contrast, self-attribution (as the enduring belief in one's effectiveness) usually requires a history of active reinforcing experiences. Third, the fruit of self-attribution, a sense of effectiveness, is only one of the many dimensions employed in self-evaluation. It must compete, for example, with opinions about the self's attractiveness, moral probity, popularity, and so forth. For these reasons it is possible for the market to have an effect on self-esteem that is independent of its influence on self-attribution, for example, by influencing the weight given to effectiveness, by raising or lowering the standards of effectiveness required, or by readmitting some lost ascriptive standards to the list of criteria that includes effectiveness. Thus self-attribution and self-esteem are fundamental features of personality that are sufficiently different from each other to suffer different fates at the hands of the market.

In this chapter I will first define the concept of self-esteem and some of its correlates, then take up the question already mentioned, Is self-esteem a good in itself? The answer to this question depends on the processes and values employed in developing self-esteem, for its goodness rests on how it is achieved and the values on which it is based. When these have been explored, we enter an analysis of the relationship of market processes to self-esteem and the ways the market encourages and hinders its development. Among these are market effects on social comparison with the invidiousness it implies; the encouragement of achievement-based esteem rather than ascriptive esteem, and the effect of the market on aspirations – the "feverish imagination" that alarmed Durkheim. We deal then with two aspects of choice in a market economy: the freedom of choice of dimensions on which one is to be judged and the number of dimensions the society offers. Finally, there is the influence of the distribution of income on the distribution of self-esteem, and here we find that in this crucial matter the market's inegalitarianism is less of a handicap in fostering self-esteem among the less advantaged than most critics have supposed.

The concept of self-esteem

The "global" concept of self-esteem (in contrast to some narrower definitions) comprises "evaluations of such things as worth, goodness, health, appearance, skills, and social competence." Because it is multidimensional, deficits in some areas may be made up by strengths in others;[6] this is why I shall be arguing for the importance of choice in the dimensions on which people evaluate themselves and are evaluated by others. Like self-attribution, self-esteem is considered to be both a trait, that is, an enduring feature of the personality, and a *state,* meaning self-estimates that vary with circumstances. A large discrepancy between ideal self and observed self at the level of personality implies a low-*trait* self-esteem that is a serious problem, but a

---

[6] Philip Robson, MD, "Improving Self-Esteem," *Harvard Medical School Mental Health Letter* 6, no. 12 (June 1990): 3–5 at 3. In greater specification, Robson lists the following as common bases of self-esteem: "competence, resilience, control over events, contentment, a sense of significance, a sense of worth, perceived attractiveness, approval by others, a sense of the value of existence, a capacity for self-evaluation independent of the view of others." (p. 4)

discrepancy between a high standard of performance and actual performance is considered healthy.[7] Without the latter, people are unlikely to learn from experience, but it has been found that the trait, usually learned early in life, is resistant to change, thus enlarging the influence of early socialization and limiting the influence of the market. (Unless otherwise specified, further references to self-esteem in this chapter refer to self-esteem as a trait.) Self-evaluations can refer to a variety of selves: the presenting self, the self to which one is committed, the observed self, and the ideal self.[8] Self-esteem is often measured by the discrepancy between the observed and the ideal selves, making the measure and its concept dependent not so much on the worthiness others might assign to a person as upon the level of the ideals to which the person aspires.

I seek to give a specificity to our discussion by relying on studies that use a standard measure. The concept is best indicated, then, by citing some of the (ten) questions in the measure: "On the whole, I am satisfied with myself." "At times, I feel that I am no good at all." "I am able to do things as well as most other people." "I wish I could have more respect for myself." The author of this measure, Morris Rosenberg, comments:

High self-esteem, as reflected in our scale items, expresses the feeling that one is "good enough." The individual simply feels that he is a person of worth; respects himself for what he is; . . . he does not necessarily consider himself superior to others. . . . Our high self-esteem students do not simply accept themselves for what they are; they also want to grow, to improve, to overcome their deficiencies."[9]

The concept certainly does not mean smugness.

The correlates of this measure suggest the contribution of self-esteem to, or at least the association with, various aspects of human development in addition to the sense of well-being and internal locus of control. Compared to those with low self-esteem, people with high self-esteem participate more in the affairs around them – largely because they are confident of their relations with others; they are more tolerant of deviance, less authoritarian, more exploratory in their thinking, less anxious, more capable of self-discipline, and generally in better physical health.[10] And their marriages are likely to be more successful, for "self-depreciation is a handicap in love-making relations. People who do not like themselves feel both a strong urge for love and understanding but at the same time cannot believe that the other party really likes them."[11] Self-esteem is clearly a desirable attribute, but it is not the primary good that Rawls and others believe it is.

---

[7] "In fact, to some theorists optimum self-esteem or self-satisfaction is manifested by moderately small (rather than large or zero) discrepancies between the subject's descriptions of self and ideal self." Ruth C. Wylie, *The Self-Concept* (Lincoln: University of Nebraska Press, 1974), 127.

[8] Rosenberg, *Conceiving the Self*, 38–51.

[9] Morris Rosenberg, *Society and the Adolescent Self-Image* (Princeton: Princeton University Press, 1965), 31, 440. This chapter owes more to Morris Rosenberg than even the frequent references to his work suggest.

[10] Ibid.

[11] Ruut Veenhoven, "Does Happiness Bind? Marriage Chances on the Unhappy," in Veenhoven, ed., *How Harmful is Happiness? Consequences of Enjoying Life or Not* (Rotterdam: Universitaire Pers Rotterdam, 1989), 57.

The preferred bases of self-esteem

Thinking of oneself as worthy, or estimable, or deserving in respect, cannot be treated philosophically as a final good any more than philosophers can think of happiness as a final good without considering whether or not it is deserved.[12] Therefore, in order to provide a standard whereby to assess the market's contribution, we must refine the concept to indicate what kind of self-esteem is, indeed, valuable. For this purpose it will be useful to weigh the processes by which esteem is achieved and the values on which it may be based. They are not all equally desirable.

Rosenberg suggests four processes used in self-evaluation. One process occurs when people see themselves as they think others see them and judge themselves accordingly (reflected appraisal). A second process involves social comparison: Because one must have some standards to know where one stands on whatever dimensions one may choose for evaluation, one compares one's qualities and achievements with others. Third, one examines one's record, sees what one has done, notes one's achievements in various circumstances, and judges oneself accordingly (self-attribution). And fourth, one selects among one's various qualities and performances those that seem to yield the greatest promise for favorable self-evaluation (psychological centrality) – at least one selects these qualities when free to do so by a society that does not dictate a single criterion for esteem.[13] I will refer to these processes to show, first, the surprisingly light use of social comparison by market agents, and then to show the way the market uses two of the other processes to good advantage: achievements of which an individual is proud (self-attribution), and self-selection of dimensions on which to be judged.

Of the four *value bases* for self-esteem indicated by Coopersmith[14] – power, significance, virtue, and competence – *power* is the least promising, for insofar as it implies power over others, it means that someone's gain in self-esteem is someone else's loss. Except as money implies power over others (which it often does, but it is through "bribes" not commands), the market is less likely than any hierarchy to use power as a basis for self-esteem and more likely to use money.

Significance, implying the need for attention, honor, "narcissistic supplies," or even respect, is important as a baseline condition, but beyond that it is ethically and socially marginal. The market makes significance dependent on wealth – or contribution to wealth, but in the concept of "contribution to wealth" is buried a large set of desirable criteria included under *competence*, such as skill, responsibility, and, by all accounts, cooperation and teamwork.

If *virtue* refers to benevolence, it is a valuable element of self-esteem; if it refers to a satisfied conscience, the assessment depends on the contents of the conscience; if it is comparative ("I am holier than thou"), it is dangerous. In the market, virtue is only tangentially a basis for self-esteem, and then mainly on only two dimensions

---

[12] Nicholas Rescher, *Distributive Justice: A Constructive Critique of the Utilitarian Theory of Distribution* (Indianapolis: Bobbs-Merrill, 1966); W. David Ross, *The Right and the Good* (Oxford, UK: Clarendon Press, 1930).

[13] Rosenberg, *Conceiving The Self*.

[14] Stanley Coopersmith, *The Antecedents of Self-Esteem* (San Francisco: W. H. Freeman. 1967).

of virtue: appropriate effort or sacrifice in exchange for the income offered and assuming responsibility for the self and family.

Competence, assuming that the competence is exercised in a valuable activity, is equally essential for an acceptable evaluation of the self, for it serves as the source of individual and social achievements. Competence is the market's avowed basis for self-esteem. If virtue and competence are the preferred grounds for self-esteem, the market may be seen as defective in one and strong in the other.

Based on Rosenberg's processes and Coopersmith's values, the rules governing the assessment of self-esteem, now treated as an instrumental good, might be set forth as follows:

1. Discourage power-based self-esteem, encourage noninvidious virtue-based and competence-based self-esteem; give to each the talisman of significance needed to make significance-based esteem of diminished importance.
2. Discourage invidiousness; reduce the importance of social comparison while increasing the importance of self-comparison; so far as possible, make all market encounters grounds for enhanced reflected appraisal, that is, let the salesclerks, Smith's "butcher, brewer, or baker," provide dignity along with the goods, and let the employer exchange for the work he receives a modicum of dignity along with pay.
3. Let people set their own standards for their ideal selves within an environment that encourages personal growth.
4. Encourage appreciation of others' needs for their self-esteem as criteria for estimating performances that merit self-esteem for any given individual; relate virtue, significance, and competence to these criteria.
5. Convey, and encourage others to convey, to each person the sense of dignity, of being an unconditional "end in oneself;" *and* award praise, if nothing else, conditional on performance.
6. Except for the ascribed baseline condition of personhood, encourage self-esteem based on achievement rather than on ascription.
7. Diversify the dimensions along which people are graded and grade themselves; let each person choose a basis for individual self-appraisal consistent with high self-appraisal for others (maximize Mill's "individuality").

These are high standards for the market to meet; simply encouraging people to "feel good about themselves" will not do. To what extent does, or can, the market meet these high standards?

Social comparisons

Self-esteem based on invidious comparisons is socially damaging, as Nozik suggests.[15] Such comparisons invite envy (the most despicable of emotions, according to J. S. Mill) and rivalry, the invidious world of Thorstein Veblen. One cannot do away with social comparisons because all evaluations use external standards to some extent, but the preferred standard is the self, either the ideal self or the actual self on another occasion.[16]

[15] Robert Nozick, *Anarchy, State, and Utopia* (New York: Basic Books, 1974), 239–46.
[16] Rousseau's distinction between *amour de soi* and *amour-propre,* the latter often masquerading as benevolence, captures some of the meaning intended here. For a discussion of this distinction, see Marshall Berman, *The Politics of Authenticity* (New York: Atheneum, 1972), 147.

Although it seems to be the case that people are more likely to make social comparisons of their levels of pay than of their housing,[17] a careful study in the 1970s, *Income Equity among U.S. Workers,* found that, in fact, when wages were compared the comparisons did not prompt self-damaging feelings of envy or loss of well-being. Thus, "wage comparisons had no direct effect on satisfaction with living standards" and only a "limited and indirect effect" on more basic economic satisfaction.[18] Other "relative deprivation" studies tend to confirm this finding.[19] In the United States, at least, there is a surprising lack of envy in comparisons of money income or possessions across broad income strata, partly because there is a general consensus on what people in various occupations and life strata should receive.[20]

Although humanist and socialist critics of the market have long believed that it encourages invidious comparisons, I cannot find much evidence for that view. Indeed, based on the same kinds of anecdotal and impressionistic evidence employed to support these criticisms, the household economies of gemeinschaft societies or their modern pale imitations in rural villages seem to encourage more social comparisons of almost every kind (Chapter 12).

Contingency: doing versus being or having

My thesis is that the market contributes to many people's self-esteem by offering them opportunities for achievement – and, of course, erodes the esteem of those who fail these opportunities. But ascriptive-based self-esteem, even when based on personhood, has more serious disadvantages, including a common form of erosion for those claiming from some authority their basic ascriptive rights.

There is a gradient of hedonic payoffs from self-esteem that orders earned esteem achieved by *doing* something ahead of ascriptive-based self-esteem merited by *being* something – a person, a white, Protestant, or whatever. Self-esteem based on an earned reward seems to give the most happiness. Of all the specialized satisfactions included in a massive study of subjective well-being, the satisfactions that were most related to overall life satisfaction were measured by these items: "How do

---

[17]On wages, see Ephraim Yuchtman (Yaar), "Effects of Psychological Factors on Subjective Well-Being," in Burkhard Strumpel, ed., *Economic Means for Human Needs: Social Indicators of Well-Being and Discontent* (Ann Arbor, MI: Institute for Social Research, 1976); on housing, see Angus Campbell, Philip E. Converse, and Willard L. Rodgers, *The Quality of American Life* (New York: Russell Sage, 1976), chap. 6.

[18]Richard T. Curtin, *Income Equity among U.S. Workers: The Bases and Consequences of Deprivation* (New York: Praeger, 1977), 55.

[19]Faye J. Crosby, *Relative Deprivation and Working Women* (New York: Oxford University Press, 1982); W. G. Runciman, *Relative Deprivation and Social Justice* (Berkeley: University of California Press, 1966). In fact, both of these studies show that the sense of relative deprivation is minimal. It is uncertain whether the facilitation of comparisons made possible by money schemata increases invidious comparisons where reference to the uniqueness of things of material possessions (thing-mindedness) would not.

[20]Sidney Verba and Gary R. Orren, *Equality in America: The View from the Top* (Cambridge: Harvard University Press, 1985), 154–66.

you feel about: . . . "the way you handle the problems that come up in your life?" "what you are accomplishing in your life?" and "yourself?"[21]

Compared to ascription, achievement not only yields more happiness but also more self-esteem; achievement is more esteem-efficient in modern society.[22] And it is both more socially efficient and efficient for human development: Achievement-based self-esteem serves as a source of energy for society and it is a source of important learning and growth. Whereas ascription, by definition, is given by race, or sex, or family, or, indeed, personhood (a philosophical favorite), achievement stimulates individual growth where ascription does not.

These considerations lead to examination of an alternative to market-derived self-esteem, that is, to esteem based on *rights,* a basis favored by Rawls (see following). A reward that is a right to which individuals may make unconditional claims, when their circumstances permit such claims, offers them a dignity in their status as claimant that at least does not damage their self-esteem. But many such rewards are available only upon petition at the discretion of another, perhaps an official. This is demeaning to dignity because it establishes an inferior–superior relationship. Often there is an implicit exchange, namely gratitude or deference in exchange for the reward, that is, lowering the esteem of the petitioner to enhance the esteem of another. Market exchanges are usually less demeaning because each party has something the other wants.

Negative rewards or punishments are demeaning, as they are intended to be, inasmuch as part of the punishment is the "indignity" attached to it. The market "punishes" by withdrawal of rewards for failure to perform, a kind of indignity that seems to me to be generally less demeaning than a direct punishment for infraction of a rule. This is true partly because the market's failure to reward is impersonal and partly because it is not described publicly as a penalty for antisocial behavior.

Contrary to much liberal theory, this gradient suggests that one feels better, enhances one's self-esteem more, when one argues that one's claim for a right, say due process, rests not so much upon one's personhood as upon one's earned rights as taxpayer or veteran, converting the basis of one's claim from "the rights of man" to the rights of taxpayers or veterans who have earned these rights. That is, people seem to want contingent rewards in preference to rewards of other kinds. There are good reasons for minimizing this line of thought, but the self-esteem advantages of the conditional earned right over the unconditional personhood right deserve some recognition. At the very least, it helps to explain why people ground their claims in something other than the personhood with which ethicists cloak them. Personhood does not feel like sufficient dress.

But the main inferences from the gradient must apply to Rawls's argument that awarding, even in an economically unequal society, equal rights and liberties will provide all with equal bases for self-esteem:

[21] Frank M. Andrews and Stephen B. Withey, "Developing Measures of Perceived Life Quality: Results from Several National Surveys," *Journal of Social Indicators Research* 1 (1974): 1–26.
[22] Morris Rosenberg, "Group Rejection and Self-Rejection," in Roberta G. Simmons, ed., *Research in Community and Mental Health,* vol. 1 (Greenwich, CT: JAI Press, 1979).

In a well-ordered society the need for status is met by the public recognition of just institutions, together with the full and diverse internal life of the many free communities of interests that equal liberty allows. The basis for self-esteem in a just society is not then one's income share but the publicly affirmed distribution of fundamental rights and liberties. And this distribution being equal, everyone has a similar and secure status of being equal, everyone has a similar and secure status when they meet to conduct the common affairs of the wider society.[23]

If when people reflect upon their merits, achieved credits dominate ascribed credits, the Rawlsian system will not work. As Rosenberg has pointed out, it will not be possible under these circumstances to strip "one's income share" of esteem implications, especially since differential earned income is allowed precisely in order to motivate and reward superior economic performance.[24] Rawls's proposition is serviceable for improving the distribution of self-esteem in traditional or slave societies, the basis for revolutions of the past, since more dignity is derived from claiming rights than from petitioning grace, or mercy, or charity. And such petitions, in turn, are more compatible with dignity than punishments or avoiding punishments. Rawls, then, is talking about the bases of justice in a pre- or nonmarket society.

The important right suggested by the mentioned esteem gradient is the right to work, the right to earn self-esteem. This takes precedence over the right to subsistence income that personhood implies, for *earned* income is a source of self-esteem whereas welfare income is not. An equally important feature of the right to work is the right to consider oneself a functioning member of society, for functionless people, "useless" people, must regard themselves with a degree of contempt. The right to work is the first right, more important to self-esteem than the political rights Rawls mentions, more important to most people than the right to express their opinions. But the market fails to recognize the right to work and by its very nature cannot do so. Of all the blemishes in the market's record of support for self-esteem, the failure to assure its participants of the opportunity to earn that esteem through work is the most disfiguring.

Converting achieved esteem to ascribed esteem

With all its blemishes, the market is nevertheless a more or less vigilant guard against a kind of recidivism toward ascriptive security by two kinds of people, elites seeking to make secure their achieved status and those who claim elite status on the grounds of ethnic or other ascriptions. In this sense, it is a protector of the achievers against the claims of others. With respect to the first group, elites will seek to convert their achieved statuses to ascribed statuses as a method of perpetuating their privileges and of investing their persons as well as their work with esteem-conferring attributes. An identity choice is implied: "I am a Brahmin," rather than, "I am a lawyer." Yet examine this illustration once again. The ordinary son of a famous father may choose his lineal identity; the famous son of a famous father will want to be known for his own achievements. The ordinary lawyer may choose the

[23] Rawls, *A Theory of Justice*, 544.
[24] Morris Rosenberg, "Rawls' 'Unwelcome Complication': Social Status and Self-Esteem." (Paper presented at the Annual Meeting of the International Society of Political Psychology, Boston, June 1980), 12.

family identity; but the lawyer who has won a difficult case will want to be known for that achievement. Although in such cases achievement is preferred to ascription, in market societies as elsewhere ascriptive esteem is more secure. Any attempt to convert achieved esteem to ascribed esteem is likely to be prudential, an insurance against failure. The ascribed status can be passed on to one's children – without effort. More generally, in an achieving market society, ascriptive self-esteem may be thought of as a protection against the fear of low achievement; it is the bulwark against free riders.

For the second group, for example, the ethnocentrics and the Daughters of the American Revolution whose self-esteem flows from pride of race or lineage, the market's emphasis on performance is a constant challenge. It is a difficult group to cope with since, on closer examination, the ethnic lineal claims are often based on low self-esteem.[25] For them, the pride in ascription is compensatory. The fact that low self-esteem is generally associated with prejudice, intolerance of minorities (as well as of heterodox views), and lack of support for democratic values[26] raises the stakes for a wide distribution of self-esteem. In a market society the protector of these high stakes is a successful market. And something more: The value of personhood so recently dismissed as an inadequate basis for self-esteem is also a protector.

Personhood: not a sword but a shield. Consider the seeming paradox: Ascriptive personhood is an insufficient and ineffective basis for self-esteem and at the same time it is a valuable innoculant against ethnic, class, and religious claims for special status and deference. That is, the most general ascription of all, personhood, serves as a protection against lesser ascriptions. More than that, a strong cultural doctrine holding that the weak and indigent have value in themselves protects them against abuse by governments, firms, and persons alike (but not by the impersonal market). What does not suffice as a basis for self-esteem, personhood, is nevertheless a necessary protection against the abuse or denigration of others. It is the confusion between these two functions of personhood that leads Rawls and others to believe that the rights of personhood are themselves the sources of self-esteem. A high ascriptive value given to personhood is not a sword by which self-esteem can be won, but a shield against denigration of a person's esteem by others. And if the market offers swords to those who can use them, it fails to offer shields to all the others. This is a second disfiguring blemish.

Property rights

If achievement is a more socially and individually useful basis for self-esteem than ascription, what shall we do with property rights? Using the related concept of "function" in place of achievement, R. H. Tawney provides an answer: Deprive property of the status of "rights which stand by their own virtue" and reward property and its owners according to their usefulness, the functions they perform.[27]

---

[25] T. W. Adorno, Elsa Frenkel-Brunswick, Daniel Levinson, and Nevitt Sanford, *The Authoritarian Personality* (New York: Harper & Row, 1950), 421–9.
[26] Paul M. Sniderman, *Personality and Democratic Politics* (Berkeley: University of California Press, 1957), 194, 198.
[27] R. H. Tawney, *The Acquisitive Society* (New York: Harcourt, Brace, 1920), 24, 26

Although this may strip the owners of the esteem that flows from the ascribed rights of property ownership, rewarding them on the basis of their functions and services is a better way of achieving self-esteem – better for society because, as I said, it enlists energy and directs effort; and better for the individual because it leads to learning, growth, and, if successful, a less defensive, if sometimes less secure, self-esteem. As we saw in the evidence from the quality of life studies, the achiever will be happier than the owner. Doing is better than having.

Conditional versus unconditional self-esteem

Ascriptive self-esteem is unconditional; earned self-esteem is conditional. The income maintenance study reported in the previous chapter showed that unearned, guaranteed incomes led to a kind of demoralization, that is, to low self-esteem. The rewards received were not contingent on any contribution from the recipients. The value of contingency is illustrated again in Morris Rosenberg's research, this time by an example, not of unconditional income, but of unconditional approval. In his large sample of New York State students, Rosenberg found one group that seemed to have unconditional high self-esteem: only sons surrounded by sisters, especially older sisters. For most adolescents doing well in school, in athletics, or in popularity was a condition for high self-esteem. Not so for these only sons; they believed themselves to be of superior worth regardless of their performance. It was, as Rosenberg suggests, a poor preparation for life.[28] They had complete confidence that their personhood was sufficient to merit their high self-esteem. Thus the value of achieved rewards is demonstrated by two counterexamples: The unconditional income that cannot be justified by a person's good luck, by his or her hard work, or by a parent's hard work does not seem to be a suitable basis for the self-esteem that prompts search for employment; unconditional admiration based on gender leads to high self-esteem but not to productive work. These opposites share one thing: unconditional rewards.

The solution is difficult to achieve yet relatively easy to prescribe. It involves the differential use of the two levels of each individual's split-level self-esteem, composed of an enduring personality trait of high self-esteem and variable performance-related *states* of self-esteem vulnerable to the blows of poor performance. Rosenberg's sample of only sons had the first but not the second. It seems that the unresponsive group in the income maintenance experiment had neither. Thus the valuable version of self-esteem is a split-level phenomenon that is both unconditional and conditional in these two respects.

The relation between these two levels is such that over long periods of time each modifies the other. If the trait level of self-esteem stems primarily from family socialization and unspecified biological endowments, the market's influence is initially limited to the more variable-state self-esteem, but one may be sure that repeated defeats over time will reach beyond the current, variable states of self-evaluation to influence the traits established earlier. The market's influence will be through work and money income; but we know that levels of income have relatively

[28] Rosenberg, *Society and the Adolescent Self-Image*, 122–7.

little long-term influence over self-esteem. In Part VII I explain the weakness of this influence in more detail; here notice that one reason for this weakness may be that its initial influence is through shorter term changes in income affecting only the more superficial level of state self-esteem.

Psychological centrality: choice of grounds for self-esteem in the market

To what extent and in what ways does the market facilitate or hinder people's choice of the dimensions on which they may judge themselves and be judged by others? Isaiah Berlin's concept of *negative freedom* represents a useful point of departure, even though he slights the concept of "opportunity" and passes over the problem of "capacity to choose," both integral to a full treatment of the grounds for choosing a rewarding dimension for self-evaluation. The boundaries of negative freedom, says Berlin, are defined by the answer to the question, "What is the area within which the subject – a person or group of persons – is or should be left to do or be what he is able to do or be, without interference by other persons?"[29] Berlin's concept of freedom is especially relevant because his criterion for assessing the value of freedom is the same as the human development criterion we have employed in judging the market: "the development of [a person's] natural faculties."

Since received concepts of negative freedom are silent on the one right we said was crucial to self-esteem, the right to *earn* a living, and since the relation between participation in political or civic affairs and self-esteem is more plausibly reversed (self-esteem is a condition for self-expression, not the reverse), the first impression is that negative freedom is an irrelevant condition for self-esteem. This impression is corrected, however, when we consider the importance for individuals of freedom to choose the grounds on which they judge themselves and wish others to judge them, the device that Rosenberg called "psychological centrality." Following William James ("our self-feeling in this world depends entirely on what we *back* ourselves to be and do"),[30] we see that freedom to choose some attribute of the self, expressed in some activity, is the central gift by freedom to self-esteem.

Whereas it is true that the freedom to choose the grounds on which people may judge themselves fosters self-esteem, as Rosenberg points out, this in itself is not a guarantor of human development. It is a beginning, for self-esteem is a condition for the exploratory learning that promotes human development.[31] But what if the grounds for self-esteem thus chosen do not favor human development? Here the market's facilitation of choice, however much that may favor self-esteem, must be reexamined. Inevitably, some dimensions of esteem, the grounds on which people "back themselves," are trivial, others are coarse, many are comfortably unchallenging, and most are routinely conformist with the conformity unrecognized.

The dilemma is apparent: The market may be credited with the values of achieved

---

[29] Isaiah Berlin, *Four Essays on Liberty* (London: Oxford University Press, 1969), 122.
[30] William James, *Psychology: The Briefer Course* (1882; reprint New York: Harper & Row, 1961), 54.
[31] Rosenberg, *Society and the Adolescent Self-Image;* Coopersmith, *The Antecedents of Self-Esteem;* Sniderman, *Personality and Democratic Politics.*

self-esteem, which is better than ascribed esteem, but it cannot be said that the values favored by the market are selected for their contributions to human development. The market is no friend of sophisticated culture, aesthetic sensibility, reflective self-knowledge, or, as we have seen, most virtues. The market defines human development in terms of human capital, not an unworthy goal but one that does not include these other qualities and is far short of the Enlightenment's high standard.

If we fail to accept people's own selections of the dimensions on which they wish to be judged, we may not only erode the value of individual autonomy but we may also erode self-esteem itself by saying that these people are not what they ought to be. Self-criticism would solve this problem, but it rarely is self-generating; it must be encouraged.[32] When others encourage a person to develop along different lines the message is not merely the critical one, however, for there is embedded a double message: "You are not as estimable as you think you are" *and* "You are worth attention, encouragement." In industry, the "Hawthorne effect" revealed the importance to individuals of authoritative concern for their well-being. Rosenberg found that parental criticism, even punitiveness, did not affect adolescents' self-esteem, but parental lack of interest in their children's work and lives greatly reduced it.[33] Lefcourt reports studies showing that after parental unconditional support has served its purposes, parental criticism helps children to develop that cognate quality, a sense of personal control over their own fates.[34] The point is that it is not criticism but indifference that erodes self-esteem. Families, schools, and universities are agencies for guidance and criticism; the market is indifferent.

Multiple choices, individuality, and uncertainty

Negative freedom implies differentiation, Mill's individuality; its purpose is exactly that. Nozick's multiple dimensions, Rosenberg's specialization, lead to that end. The end is heterogeneity, with its implied uncertainty regarding not only what is to be desired, but also what is desirable. Consider in this context three findings showing how uncertainty undermines self-confidence and self-esteem. Examining *The Antecedents of Self-Esteem,* Coopersmith found that clear parental directives and norms, and firm but loving discipline in the household (in contrast to certain versions of "permissiveness") clearly promoted the development of a child's self-esteem.[35] In examining the kinds of occupations that promoted self-esteem, Kohn and Schooler found that certain kinds of risks and uncertainties were associated with lower self-esteem.[36] In his study of New York State high school students, Rosenberg found that being a member of a minority religion in an otherwise homogeneous

---

[32] In the American society women have slightly lower self-esteem than men, not because of lower achievement, but because they are more self-critical. Women are the pioneers. See Campbell, *Sense of Well-Being in America,* 216–17.

[33] Rosenberg, *Society and the Adolescent Self-Image,* chap. 7.

[34] Herbert M. Lefcourt, *Locus of Control: Current Trends in Theory and Research* (Hillsdale, NJ: Erlbaum, 1976), 103.

[35] Coopersmith, *The Antecedents of Self-Esteem,* chaps. 10, 11.

[36] Melvin L. Kohn and Carmi Schooler, "Occupational Experience and Psychological Functioning: An Assessment of Reciprocal Effects," *American Sociological Review* 38 (1973): 105.

neighborhood (a Protestant in a Catholic neighborhood or a Catholic in a Protestant neighborhood) lowered a person's self-esteem.[37] Later he found that being black in a white school had the same effect.[38] In part, these effects stemmed from uncertainty regarding what was right, what was acceptable, or, by implication, learning that one was "wrong" in certain important respects.

There is another dilemma here: Although high (trait) self-esteem is a protection against the ravages of criticism, even trait self-esteem is vulnerable to uncertainty about what is right. The market's proliferation of choices that we said might lead to overload in Chapter 8 seems also to lead to uncertainty regarding the "rightness" of any given choice or state of being. The dilemma is partially circumvented by another of Rosenberg's findings: Habituation to minority status is a protection against the damages of uncertain standards, for Jews, prepared by history and by family support, suffered less from being different than did others. Being "different" is hazardous to self-esteem, but people can arm themselves against those hazards. And self-esteem is itself an effective armament.

Heterogeneity, uncertain norms, and minority status seem to impede the development of self-esteem. Yet these conditions are precisely the consequence of multiple dimensions for self-assessment. A free society is likely to be a heterogeneous society and so, countering the advantages to self-esteem of free choice on which attributes to choose for self-judgment, freedom also has a contradictory effect through the heterogeneity that it promotes. Fortunately, the market promotes within its domain the precious freedom of choice that licenses a variety of dimensions; unfortunately, the domain is narrow and the market has no way of protecting against the damages to self-esteem that come with uncertainty.

Aspirations and the market

Long ago William James pointed out that our evaluation of ourselves is based on a ratio: achievements/aspirations. With respect to the market this faces us with a problem of value distortion and with a dilemma. The *value problem* is the result of the familiar market pressure toward hypereconomics: how to preserve aspirations for better family life, better civic life, and better selves. Whereas there is some evidence that prosperity itself relieves the priority of economic values,[39] the problem persists and market aspirations remain inflated when measured against the standards of both happiness and of human development.

More relevant here is the *dilemma,* one horn of which is the unlimited aspirations that seem to follow from market pressures and promises.

Unlimited aspirations
It is said that to the extent that freedom relaxes social norms, it also obliterates the criteria for setting levels of achievement to which a person may legitimately and

[37] Rosenberg, *Society and the Adolescent Self-Image,* chap. 4.
[38] Morris Rosenberg and Roberta G. Simmons, *Black and White Self-Esteem: The Urban School Child* (Washington DC: American Sociological Association, 1971).
[39] See Joseph Veroff, Elizabeth Douvan, and Richard A. Kulka, *The Inner Americans: A Self-Portrait from 1957 to 1976* (New York: Basic Books, 1981).

confidently aspire. It erases the benchmarks by which people judge themselves along whatever dimension they may choose. With respect to the commercial dimension, Durkheim said:

From top to bottom of the ladder, greed is aroused without knowing where to find ultimate foothold. Nothing can calm it, since its goal is far beyond all it can contain. Reality seems valueless by comparison with the dreams of fevered imagination; reality is, therefore, abandoned, but so too is possibility when it in turn becomes reality.[40]

Without the hyperbole, other studies suggest something of this hedonic treadmill. Homans reports a study showing that when people are promoted their levels of aspiration rise, rather than being newly satisfied by their recognition and increased salaries. As Homans comments, "If his level of aspiration goes up without a corresponding increase in the rewards he is getting, the amount he still desires will increase and his satisfaction decrease."[41] There are two mechanisms at work: changes in cognitive expectations of future success, and changes in the affective aspects of motivation.[42] Both mechanisms are enlisted to assure that the increments of self-esteem derived from promotion are rapidly eroded by changes in expectations and in level of aspiration. Given that increased demand is an important motor to increase economic activity, market agencies are unlikely to ease the pain of aspirations beyond all possibility of achievement. That pain must find balm in psychological solutions.

Relating aspirations to achievement

The other horn of the dilemma is posed by the consequences of reduced aspirations. If we suggest that self-esteem should be furthered by lower aspiration levels, we risk an economically passive population and a more stagnant economy. But the dilemma is more apparent than real, for reality itself offers a solution. The study of aspirations in housing and neighborhoods mentioned earlier shows that aspirations are anchored to previous experience that has a stabilizing force on fevered imagination. Wherever social comparisons provide the standard for self-evaluation, this stability is missing, for there is always someone better off than the self to set a standard. But expectations, as contrasted to aspirations, operate to reduce the feverish imagination. Expectations are tied to aspirations, but lower, again reducing the source of disappointment, for it is frustrated expectations rather than frustrated aspirations that cause most of the anguish.

Empirical studies show a second consideration: the steady adjustment of both aspirations and expectations to match achievements. The basis for the relatively high level of trait self-esteem among the poor as well as the rich, the less competent as well as the more competent,[43] the less "significant" and even the less virtuous as well as the more "significant" and virtuous is achieved by lowering standards.

[40] Emile Durkheim, *Suicide*, trans. J. A. Spaulding and G. Simpson (Glencoe, IL: Free Press, 1951), 256.
[41] George Homans, *Social Behavior: Its Elementary Forms* (New York: Harcourt, Brace & World, Inc., 1961), 275–6.
[42] John W. Atkinson and Joel O. Raynor, *Personality, Motivation, and Achievement* (New York: Wiley/Halsted/Hemisphere, 1978), 179.
[43] Campbell, *Sense of Well-Being in America*, 216.

If all were to employ the same high standards, self-esteem in these disadvantaged groups would plummet. Those who condemn lowered aspirations also condemn the device that eases the pain of the elderly, those who were extravagantly hopeful in their youth, and those who were misled by the market's promises.

A more fundamental solution of the dilemma lies in the lack of relationship between income and happiness. Because income does not relate closely to happiness, the perpetually higher economic aspiration levels encouraged by the market are based on a mythical source of well-being (Part VII); if they are frustrated, people may be temporarily dissatisfied but not permanently unhappy. Inglehart and Diamond's research shows that enduring characteristics, including *level* of income, have very little effect on happiness, whereas *changes* in current income have substantial effects.[44] If the same pattern prevails for the related quality of self-esteem, dissatisfaction arising from frustrated expectations may modify the more vulnerable *state* self-esteem but leave untouched the basic *trait* self-esteem. Through its influence on state self-esteem the market can stimulate people's striving for economic rewards, but the failure to meet these ever receding goals will not touch the basic trait self-esteem.

Nevertheless, the market-induced frequency of social changes that makes yesterday's experience less relevant for judging the self today and that moves some friends up the ladder and some down does threaten the kind of certainty that seems to favor self-esteem.

The division of labor and self-esteem

Having dealt briefly with the question of freedom of choice, we turn here to the question of the number of dimensions for evaluation offered by the market. The two are related by the fact that individuals with different talents or other assets will press to have their own strengths registered as appropriate dimensions. As Rosenberg points out, the pianist and the violinist are not rivalrous when categorized by their specialties, although when categorized as "musicians" they may, indeed, be rivalrous.[45] From the kind of problem this situation illustrates one sees a solution in the specialization of labor.

To some extent, the same arguments apply to the multiplication of dimensions as applied to individual choice, but here it is the market's influence on the division of labor that is benign, whereas again it is the market's monopolization of standards that is corrosive.

Representative conservatives and liberals disagree on the appropriate basis of self-esteem, liberals finding it in the distribution of equal political and legal rights, conservatives in the sphere of the market. That arch exponent of unregulated market contract, Robert Nozick, argues that in order to minimize the comparisons that foster envy and to distribute self-esteem more broadly, society would "have no

---

[44] Ronald Inglehart and Jacques-Rene Rabier, "Aspirations Adapt to Situations – But Why Are the Belgians So Much Happier than the French? A Cross-Cultural Analysis of the Subjective Quality of Life," in Frank M. Andrews, ed., *Research on the Quality of Life* (Ann Arbor, MI: Institute for Social Research, 1986).

[45] Rosenberg, "Rawls' 'Unwelcome Complication,' " 14.

common weighting of dimensions; instead [society] would have diversity of different lists of dimensions and of weightings."[46] "And one might worry," he adds, that "*if* the number of dimensions is not unlimited and if [government reduces the number of dimensions by promoting equality], that as the number of differentiating dimensions shrinks, envy will become more severe. For with a small number of differentiating dimensions, many people will find that they don't do well on *any* of them."[47] If the government has a role at all, which is doubtful in Nozick's theory, it is to multiply dimensions of evaluation, not to restrict them, as might be the case if government were to restrict income differences and base self-esteem on political rights.

Where Rawls sought to avoid economic criteria and to narrow the dimension for evaluating self-esteem to the single ground of equal rights, Nozick seeks to multiply the grounds by embracing the dimensions offered in the market. Rawls's argument is weakened by the fact that equal political rights are insufficient grounds for self-esteem and by the impossibility of making unequal incomes irrelevant. Nozick's argument is weakened not only by his (false) assumptions about the weight given to social comparison, but also by the assumption that each dimension along which people judge themselves is independent of others. This is false because of the "halo effect" whereby one salient dimension, such as high income in the market or good behavior in school, infects the influence of others.

Within its special ambit, the market makes its contribution to self-esteem in Nozick's direction, by accelerating (but not causing, which is a matter for technology) the division of labor that fosters a variety of dimensions, each creating a different pyramid of positions where, among these pyramids, many more can be superior and where fewer competitors are involved. And then the market undermines this contribution by trespassing on the rightfully independent domains of family, community, leisure activities, and civic life.

Although Nozick's and Rosenberg's[48] suggestions of the advantages of specialization and the division of labor are appealing, they threaten another peril. By reducing the size of the group within which one compares oneself, there is created a group whose members are known to each other, thus converting anonymous *competition* to interpersonal *rivalry*. Competition with unknown others is less invidious than rivalry with known others; because it is impersonal and invites external attributions (to fate or "the system"), competition is less damaging than rivalry to self-esteem. Alternatively, rivalry turns to collusion and the strictly economic benefits of the division of labor are jeopardized.

Positive freedom: self-direction and participation

Self-esteem is said to flow from participation in the governing of one's own affairs. Although this may be true in the small arenas of daily life, and especially at work, the principle has been mainly applied by liberal (but not Marxist) philosophers to

---

[46] Nozick, *Anarchy, State, and Utopia*, 239–46 at 245.
[47] Ibid.
[48] Rosenberg, "Rawls' 'Unwelcome Complication,' " 14–18.

civic and political life. Inasmuch as this route to self-esteem has been presented as the main alternative to market routes, we will examine the proposals in some detail. Rawls says:

The effect of self-government where equal political rights have their fair value is to enhance the self-esteem and the sense of political competence of the average citizen. His awareness of his own worth developed in the smaller associations of his community is confirmed in the constitution of the whole society. . . . These freedoms [to participate] strengthen men's sense of their own worth, enlarge their intellectual and moral sensibilities, and lay the basis for a sense of duty and obligation upon which the stability of just institutions depend.[49]

Unhappily, there is very little evidence to support Rawls's hypothesis and much evidence that the reversed causal relationship is more important. Thus, adolescents and adults with low self-esteem tend to have fewer memberships in voluntary organizations, are less likely to be leaders, and are much less well informed about and participate less frequently in political activities. For the most part their withdrawal, ignorance, and indifference are due to their incompetence in relations with others, causing them to drop out of the social networks that inform and inspire such activity. These people with low self-esteem are also too busy managing their anxieties to concern themselves with distant political matters.[50] As Sniderman points out, anxious people divide attention between self and task, and in so doing, whatever the task, they do less well at it. They learn less from their own experiences and less from observing and listening to others.[51]

These findings[52] pose certain problems for Rawls's hypothesis. The reversed causal force means that only people already endowed with "a sense of their own worth" (and possibly with "enlarged intellectual and moral sensibilities") create and enjoy "self-government where equal political rights have their fair values." These people are not the "least advantaged" with whom Rawls is most concerned; if participation has the benefits alleged, those who need these benefits most are not benefiting from it.

Why do people with low self-esteem not take advantage of this opportunity to enhance their power and status through participation? The answer lies in the *capacity* to choose, a matter omitted by Rawls. People with low self-esteem are ridden with anxieties, fears, self-consciousness, and autisms. They cannot be said to "choose" their isolation from others, their inability to learn, or their deep engagement with their own problems. They cannot help themselves; miseries are rarely self-chosen.

There are grounds for questioning Rawls's premise that participation in government and politics increases self-esteem. Even some modest success does not im-

---

[49] Rawls, *A Theory of Justice*, 234.

[50] Rosenberg, *Society and the Adolescent Self-Image*, chaps. 10, 11.

[51] Sniderman, *Personality and Democratic Politics*, 145–51, 153–61.

[52] These research reports are quite in conflict with Lasswell's hypothesis that persons with doubts about themselves enter politics to relieve those doubts. Both Rosenberg and Sniderman, in the works cited immediately above, refer to the Lasswellian hypothesis in order to refute it. Lasswell's hypothesis may be found scattered through his works, but the most explicit statement is as follows: "Our key hypothesis about the power seeker is that he pursues power as a means of compensation against deprivation. *Power is expected to overcome low estimates of the self.*" Harold D. Lasswell, *Power and Personality* (New York: Norton, 1948), 39, emphasis in the original.

prove the self-esteem of those with a disposition to low self-esteem[53] for they attribute their own successes to chance and their failures to their own deficiencies.[54] Thus, level of self-esteem shapes the interpretation of experience in a way that undermines Rawls's assumption. Under these circumstances, even extensive political participation is not enough to produce the esteem effects that Rawls predicts.

But the main reason why the exercise of participatory rights in political life is unlikely to affect self-esteem is that politics is of marginal interest to most people. For people to derive self-esteem advantages through exercising their political rights, they would have to define their political interests as important in their self-concepts – politics would have to be psychologically central. Comparing themselves to others (all of whom enjoy the same rights), they would need to see themselves as more competent or more virtuous than others in these political participatory respects. They would have to believe that others see in their political persona something worthwhile, but being active in politics is not often endowed with such honorific cachet. (Rather, people ask, "What's in it for them?") And the political activity would have to be such that participating individuals might see themselves as having "done well," or even as having made a difference. These effects are difficult to perceive in the opaque world of politics. In any event, only 26% of the population has "ever worked for a party or candidate during an election" and only 30% has ever "attempted to persuade others to vote as they were."[55]

Rawls has confused *granting* of rights, which might make an esteem difference at the time of the grant because it would represent a *change*, with the *exercise* of these rights once granted, which is an unchanging circumstance that is unlikely to influence self-esteem. But more than that, Rawls has simply overestimated the salience of politics, at least in contemporary society, and underestimated the importance of the domain of work where skill, effort, identity, reputation, and recognition all weigh heavily in a person's estimate of his or her worth. For contributions to the self-esteem of adults, we must look to the spheres of life where they believe themselves to be tested – chiefly, but by no means exclusively, economic life.

Work and self-esteem

There is evidence that exercise of discretion on the job, which is not so much a right as a requirement of complex tasks, has more substantial effect on self-esteem than any exercise of familiar political rights has ever had. Kohn and Schooler's studies of the effects of self-direction on the job, participating in controlling what one does at work, show how important these forms of self-direction are for improving a person's self-concept.[56] A second study, although not directly measuring self-

[53] Dean B. McFarlin and Jim Blacovich, "Effects of Self-Esteem and Performance Feedback on Future Affective Preferences and Cognitive Expectations," *Journal of Personality and Social Psychology* 40 (1981): 521–31.

[54] Gordon Fitch, "Effects of Self-Esteem, Perceived Performance, and Choice on Causal Attributions," *Journal of Personality and Social Psychology* 16 (1970): 311–15. For an interpretation of the relation between self-esteem and feelings of competence, see Barry Fish and Stuart A. Karabenick, "Relationship Between Self-Esteem and Locus of Control," *Psychological Reports* 229 (1971): 784.

[55] Sidney Verba and Norman H. Nie, *Participation in America* (New York: Harper & Row, 1972), 31.

[56] Melvin L. Kohn and Carmi Schooler, "The Reciprocal Effects of the Substantive Complexity of Work

esteem, seems to confirm this report. This study of a privately owned, highly automated paper products plant that devolved to worker groups such decisions as who
would work where, production goals, budget forecasting, and so forth, is illuminating. The "worker self-management" teams, in contrast to others, developed a
sense of efficacy and "personal potency" that was not characteristic of those working under the usual hierarchical management. As mentioned, these feelings of efficacy and potency form one of the dimensions on which people evaluate themselves.
Moreover, in this study, feelings of efficacy generated in the workplace were generalized to political participation – a more effective route to Rawls's participatory
efficacy.[57]

The clear inference is that one should add to the basic right to work mentioned
earlier, the right to participate in the decisions affecting one's work. These are the
prior rights to which Rawls should give lexical precedence. They are economic
rights, but not rights recognized either by the market doctrine or practice.

Income, equality, and self-esteem

Both liberal critics and conservative supporters of the market are likely to agree that
the market contributes to and undermines popular self-esteem through its distribution of economic rewards. They have accepted the economistic premises of the
market to the effect that somehow people will evaluate themselves as they are evaluated by the market. For them, money buys self-esteem just as it buys utility or
happiness. But in neither the case of utility nor the case of self-esteem is this true.
It follows that the market's inegalitarian distribution of income is not a major handicap to a more egalitarian distribution of self-esteem.

In the United States there is no difference among children in self-esteem by parental income, among adolescents there is a very small difference, and among adults
there is a modest difference; for adults the correlation (gamma) is .233.[58] Thus,
income equality would have only a relatively small effect on self-esteem. That
effect would depend in part on the importance and kind of social comparisons enlisted in evaluating oneself under conditions of income equality. For example, the
relationship between income and self-esteem is greater among those who think their
friends, relatives, or neighbors have either more or less income than they do. No
doubt for those who thought these other groups had more, the equalization of income would tend to increase their self-esteem; for those who thought that others
had less, equalization might tend to decrease their self-esteem. But only about a
third of the sample believed their friends, relatives, or neighbors had incomes different from their own.[59] Thus, whereas social comparisons currently contribute

and Intellectual Flexibility: A Longitudinal Assessment," *American Journal of Sociology* 87 (1978):
24–53.
[57] Maxwell J. Elden, "Political Efficacy at Work: The Connection between More Autonomous Forms of
Workplace Organization and a More Participatory Politics," *American Political Science Review* 75
(1981): 43–58.
[58] Morris Rosenberg and Leonard E. Pearlin, "Social Class and Self-Esteem Among Children and Adults,"
American Journal of Sociology 84 (1978): 54–8.
[59] Ibid., 62.

something to the effect of income inequality on self-esteem, the group for whom equalization of income would make these kinds of social comparison irrelevant is relatively small, and the effect of income equality would not work in the same way for even the members of this small group. But, as we have seen, social comparison is only one of the devices employed in establishing one's worthiness.

One of these other ways (psychological centrality) is through defining money as more or less important. The Rosenberg and Pearlin study we discussed asked respondents to agree or disagree with the following statement: "One of the most important things about a person is the amount of money that he has." Among the 60 percent who "strongly disagreed," the relationship between income and self-esteem was much weaker than among those who agreed, suggesting again that one's self-esteem is based on those qualities one thinks important and wishes to measure oneself on. Equalization of income would eliminate the importance of money in evaluating self-esteem, bringing the relationship between money and self-esteem closer to that of those who believe money is unimportant in evaluating people. This brings the correlation down from the reported .233 for the entire sample, to .214 for the group that "strongly disagrees" that evaluation of others should be made on the basis of money,[60] a difference of .019, hardly significant.

Under these circumstances, might it not be the case that the modestly lower self-esteem of the poorer members of the population is due to the cumulative effects of things that are not individually strong correlates of self-esteem: the hassles of poverty, intermittent unemployment (which does substantially decrease self-esteem), low education (which is not closely related to self-esteem), low occupational prestige, and the lack of challenging work already mentioned? It follows that the route to higher and more equal self-esteem is not so much through equalization of income as through policies that improve the condition of the poor, increase education, and especially promote work redesign that makes work more challenging and rewarding.

The untoward effects of equality – and their rebuttal

The arguments minimizing the value of equality for self-esteem find a kind of support from an early source of concern about equality in America:

If the members of a community, as they become more equal, become more ignorant and coarse, it is difficult to foresee to what pitch of stupid excesses their selfishness may lead them and no one can foretell into what disgrace and wretchedness they would plunge themselves lest they should have to sacrifice something of their own well-being to the prosperity of their fellow creatures.[61]

In this interpretation, the increased invidiousness is the consequence of economic similarity, and the increased materialism is the consequence of having been told of the importance of *economic* equality. The inference (if not the language) is clear. The market's resistance to equality is a protection against the selfishness, coarseness, and stupid excesses that equality might bring!

[60] Ibid., 69.
[61] Alexis de Tocqueville, *Democracy in America*, vol. 2, trans. H. Reeve and ed. Phillips Bradley (New York: Knopf, 1945), 124.

One further lesson from Tocqueville: Equality of condition, he says, leads to only small ambitions. Self-esteem, rather than being increased by the social comparisons encouraged by equality, is lowered because one then sees oneself as "the little man," "the common man." According to Tocqueville, such a person "has so contemptible an opinion of himself that he thinks he is born only to indulge in vulgar pleasure. He willingly takes up with low desires without daring to embark on lofty enterprises, of which he scarcely dreams." Some source of self-esteem other than equality is necessary. "I would have endeavors made," says Tocqueville, "to give them [Americans] a more enlarged idea of themselves and of their kind. Humility is unwholesome to them; what they want is, in my opinion, pride. I would willingly exchange several of our small virtues for this one vice."[62] Again, by resisting the doctrine of equality, the market protects us from the sin of humility and opens the way for pride and the lofty enterprises that it then invites.

Tocqueville's hypotheses inspire a thought experiment. The order of posttax income equality (gini) of eleven nations as measured in the mid-1970s is as follows: Netherlands (most equal), Sweden, Norway, United Kingdom, Japan, Canada, Australia, United States, Germany, Spain, and France.[63] Would it be the case that citizens of the Netherlands, Sweden, and Norway, compared to those of Germany, Spain, and France, are more jealous of their own material well-being vis-à-vis others, are more likely to base their own self-esteem on material grounds, are more fearful to "embark on lofty enterprises," and in general, are more lacking in healthy pride? Tocqueville's hypotheses fail this test. Income equality will do less to promote self-esteem than the relief of poverty, but not for the reasons that Tocqueville mentioned.

We conclude, therefore, that the market's inherent inegalitarianism does little to reduce the self-esteem of the less advantaged. Nor is it inegalitarianism that inflicts market damage on the truly poor; it is their poverty. As Rosenberg and Simmons report after finding that blacks in white schools do better academically but have lower self-esteem than blacks in black schools, "The central problem of the black in American society today is not low self-esteem but poverty."[64] Again, self-esteem is not a final good.

Occupational equality

Markets have much less effect on occupational status than on income, as may be seen by the relative independence of the ordering of occupational prestige compared to an ordering by income.[65] But if occupational prestige cannot be easily changed by altering levels of pay, it may defy the egalitarian for other reasons. Whereas rankings do not reveal, say, the level of respect accorded to the bottom (or to the top), the relative invariance of these rankings throughout the world suggests something about their intractability to change:

[62] Ibid., 248.
[63] Malcolm Sawyer, "Income Distribution in OECD Countries," in *OECD Economic Outlook* (Paris: Organization for Economic Cooperation and Development, 1976), 19.
[64] Rosenberg and Simmons, *Black and White Self-Esteem*, 135.
[65] Donald J. Treiman, *Occupational Prestige in Comparative Perspective* (New York: Academic Press, 1977).

In all complex societies, industrialized or not, a characteristic division of labor arises that creates intrinsic differences among occupational roles with respect to power; these in turn promote differences in privilege; and power and privilege create prestige. Since the same process operates in all complex societies, the resulting prestige hierarchies are relatively invariant in all such societies, past or present.[66]

This holds true for (former) communist as well as capitalist societies, except that in communist societies, the "ratio of wages of manual workers to those of white collar workers appears to be substantially higher on the average than in Western Europe," with consequent prestige reversals.[67] For maximizing self-esteem in society, no useful purpose is served by increasing the prestige of blue-collar workers at the cost of downgrading white-collar workers. More generally, although it may be possible to equalize incomes (perhaps at the cost of efficiency),[68] if Treiman is right, it is not possible to equalize occupational prestige.

The proposal to increase the division of labor is a feasible substitute for the seemingly more difficult proposal to flatten the occupational prestige curve, with the added advantage that it promises to increase the total supply of self-esteem rather than merely to redistribute it. And it chimes with current market processes rather than challenging them.

The justices of equality and equity (proportionality)

There are two senses in which the doctrine of equality may injure self-esteem. First, market doctrine, if not market institutions, emphasize an equality of economic *opportunity* that places the responsibility for success on the shoulders of each individual. But inevitably some people must fail; their self-esteem is lower than it would have been if they were to believe that success is available in disproportionate degree to the already advantaged. The economically less successful solve this, as we have seen, by lowering their economic aspirations and by choosing some noneconomic bases for their self-judgment, but a residuum remains. Second, relative equality of *condition* enlists a familiar psychological device: People compare themselves to similar others. But relative equality of condition makes many similar to each other, and the normative doctrine of economic equality (people *should* be equal) makes these comparisons salient, that is, encourages comparisons of material well-being.

This line of argument on equality suggests that the justice of equality is less likely to promote self-esteem than the justice of equity (or proportionality). Equity is, indeed, the justice of the market, provided that the "inputs" meriting rewards are exclusively effort and skill and never ascribed statuses. This emphasis on equity does not rule out equal incomes, as in the kibbutz, for praise and social esteem may serve as an alternative currency, again as in the kibbutz,[69] but this only changes the currency, not the principle on which justice is based. Praise inequalities are as invidious as money inequalities – or more so because of their intensely personal quality, although they will not lead to inequalities of standard of living.

The market has a mixed record in promoting self-esteem, but its inegalitarianism,

[66] Ibid., 128.
[67] Ibid., 145.
[68] Cf. Arthur M. Okun, *Equality and Efficiency: The Big Tradeoff* (Washington DC: Brookings Institution, 1975).
[69] Melford E. Spiro, *Kibbutz: Venture in Utopia* (Cambridge: Harvard University Press, 1965), 26.

which is morally offensive to some, must be indicted on other grounds. Poverty, however, is a different matter.

Summary

We have unseated self-esteem from its throne, asking it to serve the two goods that represent our criteria for the market itself, namely, happiness and human development. In sorting out the kinds of self-esteem that are suitable for that service we specified how one may select from the processes that contribute to self-esteem and the values on which it rests those elements that are humanly beneficial.

For this purpose of refinement, we substituted self-comparison for social comparison, finding to our surprise that the market did not encourage the invidiousness claimed for it.

Because achievement leads to more happiness and better learning than does ascription, achievement offers better grounds for self-esteem. In this the market is a strong ally to self-esteem both in offering opportunities for achievement and in fighting the rearguard action of the ascription-minded recidivists. In any event, that ascriptive esteem based on personhood does not yield much self-esteem, although it is an appropriate protection against the claims of lesser ascriptions. In arguing for conditional self-esteem based on effort or sacrifice, we found that property rights might also be divided along the same lines: their ascriptive (functionless) portion may be stripped of rewards and barren of esteem-yielding value but their achievement portion may be properly fruitful of self-esteem. We found no machinery or will in the market, however, either to give personhood its proper role (or, indeed, any role at all) or to divide the rights of property into useful and useless functions. (Nor do we know that they are, in fact, divisible.)

The enemies of self-esteem are the authorities, customs, and group pressures that prevent individuals from choosing the dimensions on which they wish to judge themselves. Here, again, the market is an ally, for its general encouragement of choice makes the choice of dimensions easier. But the market is a *partisan* ally, inviting people to enter the marketplace for the kinds of self-esteem they might better look for at home or in the public forum. Unhappily, the uncertainty this very freedom of choice encourages then subtly undermines the self-esteem thus achieved.

The market's tendency to invite higher aspirations than it can fulfill is checked by two psychological forces: the common tendency to resist this invitation by reducing aspirations to match achievements, and the equally common tendency to perceive one's achievements as more substantial than objective criteria would indicate. In any event, the blows to self-esteem from falling short of aspirations are blows only to the more flexible, less enduring, circumstantially influenced *state* self-esteem.

By accelerating the division of labor, the market contributes to the creation of specialties whose multiple pyramids accommodate more demands for specialized success than would be available, for example, from a single class hierarchy. This multiplicative process of the market is a more fruitful source of esteem than a single-minded focus on political rights.

If political participation is an inadequate source of self-esteem, partly because only those who already have self-confidence participate, participation in decisions at the workplace, especially self-direction in one's own job, does yield substantial esteem dividends.

Finally, the discovery that, beyond the poverty level, self-esteem is largely independent of income freed us from the belief that the market allocates dignity when it allocates pay. This knowledge divorced the benefits of income equality from the benefits of self-esteem equality and permitted us to examine two risks to self-esteem from the justice of equality. One was the fact that emphasis on equality of opportunity thrusts on individuals the responsibility for their own fates and therefore the burden of their own failures. The second was that wherever equality of income (that is, of outcome) prevails, people's tendency to compare themselves to others like themselves finds more scope for comparison because there are more people within this class of similars. Also, because of the value placed on similarity of income, small differences take on a larger significance in allocating esteem.

PART IV

Human relations

As stated in the introductory chapter, there are two maximands in economic life as there are in other aspects of life: a sense of well-being (happiness and satisfaction with life-as-a-whole) and human development. Whereas Parts II and III dealt with the relation of the market to the three elements of human development we have identified (cognitive development, a sense of autonomy and personal control, and self-esteem), Part IV begins the analysis of market effects on the other desideratum, a sense of well-being, with references to ethical problems and human development along the way.

The substantive features of the market experience that are given attention here are human relations and work, these two features representing the subjects that (in addition to the ethics of distribution) have been most severely criticized by market critics. The criticisms of friendship and work have different validities. In Part IV we find that the criticism of market influences on human relations is largely unjustified, whereas in Part V we will discover that the criticism of work in a market economy is trenchant and well conceived. Partly for that reason we will spend much more time on work than on human relations.

Chapter 11 takes up the specific arguments about how an institution whose central feature is exchange influences our interpersonal relations. I point out that in many ways the choices people make in market transactions are no different from other choices made in the ordinary course of social life, but there is a set of specific differences between market and other choices that helps to account for the alarm over exchange as a way of life. The second section of the chapter continues the examination of exchange by examining how the extrinsic rewards requisite to exchange influence the intrinsic rewards requisite to friendship. Referring to the differences between social exchange and market exchange and to the differences between the two domains of friendship and economic life, I conclude that the market fails to corrupt warm interpersonal relations. In the third section we will examine some empirical evidence on trends in human relations in the American setting, incidentally showing how humanist criticisms of these relations can, with reference to social science materials, be made more or made less plausible.

In contrast to the criticisms of an exchange orientation made here, recall how Chapter 9 showed how exchange can be a valuable teacher of that crucial feature of human development, self-attribution. In Part VI I will show how, as the humanist criticism of exchange implies, the market's emphasis on exchange is inherently incompatible with intrinsically enjoyable work activities. Thus, the effects of the market's emphasis on exchange are both beneficial and malign.

Chapter 12 approaches the effect of the market on human relations from a different perspective. Here we will analyze how the alleged competitiveness and rivalry of market life may infect human relations, making them also competitive and rivalrous. In this treatment I present evidence that the trait of *competitiveness* is not rewarded by the market, that comparisons with one's own experiences at an earlier time are more prevalent than are social comparisons, and that, in any event, comparisons with others is only one of a number of ways of establishing a standard for judging one's own well-being. Although comparisons with those less well-off than the self do improve a person's sense of well-being, these downward comparisons are most frequently made by those already unhappy. Again I conclude that, in spite of the humanistic criticism, the market is not a major source of invidious comparisons.

Finally, in Chapter 12 I ask by what standard a person should choose the psychic rewards of friendship over the psychic rewards of income in situations where these are presented as alternatives. I conclude that there is a standard that is not dependent on "the measuring rod of money," namely, choosing according to whichever option promises to make the greatest *contribution to overall life satisfaction* as this measure is described in the quality of life studies.

11 Friendship and market exchange

> *Money lowers all the gods of mankind and transforms them into a commodity.*
> *Money is the universal self-constituting value of all things. It has, therefore,*
> *robbed the whole world, both the human world and nature, of its own peculiar*
> *value. Money is the essence of man's work and existence, alienated from Man,*
> *and this alien essence dominates him and he prays to it.*
>
> Karl Marx,
> On the Jewish Question

The humanist criticism of the market often focuses on the risk that the market's reliance on exchange will lead us to think of each other as instrumental items of exchange. In Chapter 9 I pointed out the way exchange helped people to achieve a sense of personal control; here we examine whether the price of exchange is "the commodification" of friendships. Exchange has its costs, but they are not the devaluation of friendship. It is not the case that because we exchange *goods,* we think about *people* in the same way as we think about goods, or that people are degraded by taking part in the processes of exchanging goods for money.

The cash nexus among people

Society has long been embarked on a process of moving from status to contract (Maine), from gemeinschaft to gesselschaft (Tönnies), from communal to associative relations (Weber). The transition has provoked a variety of criticism with a long lineage: Montesquieu commented on "the monetization of all human relations"; Carlyle's phrase on the reduction of human relations to "cash payment" is, of course, echoed in Marx and Engel's "cash nexus"; like others, the authors of the *Communist Manifesto* refer to the conversion of human value into "exchange value"; both Simmel and Lukacs speak of the way human relations in a market economy are cold and anonymous. Fromm gives this interpersonal orientation a name: "The character orientation which is rooted in the experience of oneself as a commodity and of one's value as exchange value I call the marketing orientation . . . [which] has been growing rapidly."[1] Many of these critics allege that "warmth" has gone out of human relations in market societies, with the consequence that people become, as Simmel said, "intellectually calculating egoisms . . . [who] need not fear any deflection because of the imponderables of personal relationships."[2]

To deal with this set of criticisms one must first put exchange or transactions in their proper context, and then treat the "infection problem" a little more systematically.

[1] Erich Fromm, *Man for Himself* (New York: Holt, Rinehart & Winston, 1947), 76.
[2] Georg Simmel, "The Metropolis and Mental Life," *The Sociology of Georg Simmel,* trans. and ed. Kurt H. Wolff (Glencoe, IL: Free Press, 1950), 154.

Ordinary exchanges and desperate exchanges

All goods have "shadow prices." The central feature of market economies, transactions, may be compared to opportunity costs to clarify what exchange
for money has in common with all choices. All choices imply "pricing" the objects
chosen in terms of the alternatives not chosen – the costs of the opportunities foregone. The "price" or cost of one's use of time is the next preferred use of that
same time: When I choose to play squash rather than to visit George in the hospital,
the cost is born by George spending a lonely hour wondering where his friends are
– and by me in assuaging my guilty conscience. In some sense, therefore, it is not
just the market that gives everything a "shadow price"; the very need to select
among alternatives implies shadow prices.

There are differences. Transactions are always interpersonal and therefore public;
they lend themselves to pricing in money terms without injury to the transacting
persons or the objects exchanged. Opportunity costs are features of all choices,
including those involved in transactions; they include both intrapersonal and interpersonal private choices. When others are involved, placing a money price on the
opportunity cost may injure a partner, say, a chosen friend; when alone, pricing a
prayer or enjoyment of beauty is offensive. The general rule is that when a choice
involves something with intrinsic value, opportunity costs should not be priced in
money terms (Chapter 18).

*Transactions are not necessarily more materialistic or selfish because they
involve exchange for money.* Market exchanges may or may not be more "materialistic" than other kinds of choices. If we take "materialism" to mean the nature
of the goods chosen or exchanged, contrasting them, for example, with love and
knowledge, I am as "materialistic" when I choose a chisel instead of a screwdriver
as when I sell my chisel (now nicked) for money. If we take "materialism" to
mean valuing wealth over, for example, friendship, I am as materialistic when I can
my fruit to save money, instead of talking to friends, as when I sell my canned fruit
in the farmers' market.

And market exchanges may or may not be more "selfish" or "self-interested"
than other kinds of choices. My squash game is as selfish and self-interested as
when I bargain with the butcher, the brewer, and the baker over the price of my
dinner.

If the objections to transactions are not properly based on these grounds, how do
transactional choices differ from other kinds of choices and exchanges? I suggest
four aspects of market exchange that differentiate it from nonmarket choices.

Overspecification of the terms of exchange. Making conscious and manifest what was unconscious and latent does have consequences. Although it may be
true that all gift giving follows the norm of reciprocity, the act of giving is perceived
differently from the act of selling by both the giver and the receiver. Giving, even
at Christmastime when gifts are exchanged, is more of an expression of sentiments
(often genuine) of respect, affection, and solidarity that is clearly not true of selling

or exchanging exact equivalences. In some ways, the stipulated exactness of the equivalence in a market transaction is what undermines the solidarity, in comparison with the inexactness of reciprocal gifts, for it expresses a conventionalized distrust in the partner. And, in spite of the doctrines of social exchange theory, there are many acts of generosity where the relevant return is not "gratitude" and "deference"[3] but a private (intrinsic) pleasure in the welfare of another. Anonymous philanthropy represents just such a case. The idea of an extended ego, where what happens to another who is linked by some tie to the self, however remote that tie may be (as in the cases of common ethnicity or nationality), makes altruism a selfish pleasure that does not rely upon the returns stipulated by social exchange theory.

Narrowing the criteria for assessment. Normally choices are made on the basis of multiple criteria: the intrinsic pleasures of friendship, curiosity, achievement motivation, revenge. The kinds of evidence by which we judge the success or failure of these choices are also multiple; in addition, they are often subtle, hidden in the small signs we get from others or from ourselves. Market transactions, however, are made under circumstances where there are public indicators that all may read: price, cost, comparative economic value. Even if price and economic value are only rarely the sole or even the principal criteria employed in consumer purchases,[4] nevertheless, following a variety of known cognitive heuristics, people tend to use the most visible, cognitively available information they have – and that is often price. Furthermore, since price is a dimension permitting comparisons of many choices – its great advantage over qualitative criteria running over several dimensions – price is used as a surrogate measure, in the absence of others, of subjective profit. The very advantage of economic choices over the other kinds of choices mentioned, their comparability, tends to twist evaluations, and indeed values, along the price dimension. Even the opportunity costs of leisure, as Linder has pointed,[5] tend to be priced.

The exaggerated default value of the price. Price is also a surrogate for other information. Just as a more expensive good is thought to be "better" than a less expensive one, so a richer person is thought to be "better" than a poorer person. Given information on a person's wealth and nothing more, people tend to infer a host of favorable personality qualities for a hypothetical prosperous man and unfavorable qualities for a hypothetical poor man. This is wholly spurious; that is, poor men taking the same personality test that was used for the hypothetical evaluations by the subjects of the study, had personality profiles much more favorable than those assigned to the hypothetical poor man.[6] In this more limited sense, human relations *are* affected by the money consciousness taught by market econo-

[3] See Peter M. Blau, *Exchange and Power in Social Life* (New York: Wiley, 1964).
[4] See, for example, James F. Engel, Roger Blackwell, and David T. Kollat, *Consumer Behavior* (Hinsdale, IL: Dryden, 1978).
[5] Steffan B. Linder, *The Harried Leisure Class* (New York: Columbia University Press, 1970).
[6] Joseph Luft, "Monetary Value and the Perception of Persons," *Journal of Social Psychology* 46 (1957): 245–51.

mies. (Whether this same stereotypical behavior would be seen if knights and dukes were compared to yeoman and peasants in feudal society, or section chiefs and clerks in a bureaucracy, or party members and nonparty members in the Soviet Union remains to be seen; the "halo effect" is probably universal.)

Desperate exchanges. Forced and coerced choices are always unfortunate; it is the circumstances of the choice and not whether or not money changes hands that should affect our judgment of the choice or exchange. The concepts of forced and coerced choices may be explicated as follows:[7]

1. All choices are constrained by nature, human possibility, and so forth. Choices constrained only by these factors are not coerced; they are choices among *limited alternatives*.
2. Where there are universal social constraints applying to all individuals within a society and we know that customs and institutions could be different, the choices are *forced* but not coerced.
3. Where an individual, John Doe, has choices P and Q, but P involves serious and punitive consequences, then Q is *coerced* if and only if:
   a) we know that there are feasible choices R and W that are not ruled out by nature or universal social practices; and
   b) there are others who are like Doe in relevant respects but unlike him in the respect that robs Doe of choices R and W and
   c) this respect is by some standard wrong; and
   d) Doe knows of these alternatives. (If Doe does NOT know of these alternatives and could choose them if he knew them, the choice is not coerced, but Doe is *deprived*.)

Not market exchange, but forced and coerced choices are the enemy of human choice. As Walzer says, "there is nothing degrading about buying and selling – nothing degrading in wanting to own that shirt (to wear it, to be seen in it). . . . If the sphere of money and commodities is properly bounded" there is no great harm in trying to sell more. What is degrading is a "desperate exchange,"[8] such as one requiring long hours of unremunerative work from a person with no alternatives, or prostitution, perhaps at any time (or perhaps not if one is a popular courtesan), but certainly under duress. Although there are many choices quite outside the market that are degrading (ingratiation toward a tyrannical father, supplication for grace from an intolerant priest), the most common situs for forced exchanges is in that area where a livelihood is to be gained: in a market economy, the market. (As a parenthetical remark, I might note that in my opinion the sale of one's blood and organs is rather like the sale of one's labor, although probably less degrading because less intimately tied to self-esteem, for one's blood and organs are rarely matters of pride or so vulnerable to criticism as one's work. Selling either one's labor or one's blood and organs in a desperate exchange or under threat of starvation are both equally degrading.)

---

[7] The following explication has been greatly assisted by comments by Ian Shapiro and others in a discussion of the Yale Political Science Department Political Theory Seminar, November 1988. See also Ian Shapiro, *The Evolution of Rights in Liberal Theory* (New York: Cambridge University Press, 1986), 180–5 and 290–9.

[8] Michael Walzer, *Spheres of Justice* (Oxford, UK: Robertson, 1983), 109–10, 102.

Friendship: infection by extrinsic motivation

If market exchange relations generalize to or infect social relations, will they not tend to substitute reliance on extrinsic rewards for the rewards intrinsic to friendship? Friendship thrives where friends are valued for themselves and not for favors and complements and services that deprive affectionate relations of their intrinsic value. This *infection problem* surfaces in a variety of contexts such as the discussion of the creation of walls and spheres in social systems (Chapter 2) and in the generalization of learning and emotion from one domain to another (Chapter 25). Here, I focus on the specific problem of the infection of the intrinsic in affectionate relations by the extrinsic orientation of the market.

What is learned in the market does infect other domains. We will see evidence in the Breer and Locke studies to be reported in Chapter 13 that both cooperative and competitive task orientations generalize to ideologies of cooperative or competitive world views. In the Kohn and Schooler studies reported in the same chapter there is evidence that what is learned in challenging, self-directed work "spills over" into those leisure pursuits that are more challenging and intellectually demanding. It is also true that among the things learned at home exchange orientations, as contrasted to rule orientations, lead children at school to offer help only when help may be reciprocated.[9] On the face of it the case is strong that the exchange of work-for-pay orientation would similarly generalize to social relations. To answer questions on the generalization of exchange orientations, we turn to social exchange theory.

Differences between market exchange and social exchange.
Social exchange theories developed by George Homans,[10] Peter Blau,[11] and others, seek to explain human relations as a process whereby each partner in a relationship "exchanges" affection, reassurance, deference, patronage, favors, and other forms of gratification for some similar gratifications of roughly equal subjective value. More formally, social exchange may be defined as "those actions that are contingent on rewarding reactions from another and that cease when these expected reactions are not forthcoming."[12] This sounds like a market relation, but "social exchange is distinguished from strictly economic exchange by the unspecified obligations incurred in it and the trust both required for and promoted by it." There is a third difference: The contingency relations of the market stipulating that nothing is free, that rewards are always contingent on performance (Chapter 9), is subtly converted in social exchange to a moral obligation to repay services – the *norm of reciprocity*.[13] The contractual obligations of the market become moral obligations in social exchange. Finally, the transferability of market wealth but the nontransfera-

[9] Leonard Berkowitz, "A Laboratory Investigation of Social Class and National Differences in Helping Behavior," *International Journal of Psychology* 1 (1966): 231–42.
[10] George Homans, *Social Behavior: Its Elementary Forms* (New York: Harcourt, Brace & World, 1961).
[11] Blau, *Exchange and Power in Social Life*.
[12] Ibid., 6.
[13] Alvin W. Gouldner, "The Norm of Reciprocity," *American Sociological Review* 25 (1960): 161–78.

bility of popularity, respect, and attraction, representing the "wealth" of social exchange, means that the entire concept of *property* changes. Goods that are not transmissible thereby lose much of their exchange value. These differences between market and social exchange will, in their several ways, inhibit infection of market exchange characteristics to social exchange. So far, the intrinsicness of friendship is protected by the different characteristics of the two kinds of exchange,[14] but there are other barriers erected by the differences between money and verbal rewards.

As we shall see in Chapter 18, it is the threat of *control* that makes extrinsic payments impair intrinsic work satisfaction, but compared to money, social approval fades into the background of accepted norms: "It appears that verbal reinforcement is generally less likely to produce detrimental effects than reinforcement procedures involving tangible rewards." One reason is that "social pressures typically do not appear sufficient as explanation for one's actions unless they are made unusually explicit and salient."[15] Self-perception processes, therefore, do not activate the sense of loss of control, the sense that one has been bought by flattery. In the case of friendship or love, one does not, then, explain one's affection on the basis of rewards by the other; therefore affection, being unbought, is interpreted by the self as genuine.

Another reason is that praise and social approval are more likely to be interpreted as information than control, a circumstance that greatly reduces the feeling that one has been bought (Chapter 18). No author, reviewing his own insincere expressions of approval of another's manuscript and comparing it with his own belief in the sincerity of another's similar review of his own manuscript can fail to notice the way flattery is converted to authentic information. Indeed, "information" of that kind often increases intrinsic feelings of warmth.[16]

There is another reason why control among friends is not so important as control in commercial relations. As Aristotle observed, friendship is more congenial among equals, substantially, I might add, because equals are less likely than unequals to seek to control their partners. Their intercourse is based on exchange of information, jokes and laughter, pensive reflections, troubles, exculpations, and perhaps obliquely of affection, but not, usually, of power plays. The bond of friendship is strained or broken by efforts to control the other for these are incompatible with friendship.[17]

---

[14] Blau explicitly allows for intrinsic rewards. He says the basic motive in social exchange is "social attraction;" if the attraction is intrinsic, the reward is an internal sense of being liked or approved of or respected by another; if extrinsic, the individual "expects association with [another] to be in some way rewarding to himself, and his interest in the expected social rewards draws him to the other." Blau, *Exchange and Power in Social Life*, 20. These rewards may be nonmaterial – deference, gratitude, reputation – as well as material or something of material worth, such as favors, introductions, publicity, and so forth, but the overwhelmingly most important reward is social approval. (p. 63)

[15] Mark R. Lepper and David Greene, "Overjustification Research and Beyond," in Lepper and Greene, eds., *The Hidden Cost of Rewards: New Perspectives on the Psychology of Motivation* (Hillsdale, NJ: Erlbaum/Wiley, 1978), 130.

[16] Edward L. Deci, "The Effects of Externally Mediated Rewards on Intrinsic Motivation," *Journal of Personality and Social Psychology* 18 (1971): 105–15; see also Richard Koestner, Miron Zuckerman, and Julia Koestner, "Praise, Involvement, and Intrinsic Motivation," *Journal of Personality and Social Psychology* 52 (1987): 383–90.

[17] "A man who seeks affection does not want kindness. Approval of an individual's specific qualities

A further reason why extrinsic relations in the market do not infect personal relations is that the ease of exit from friendship relations is a powerful deterrent to control and a safeguard against feelings of being controlled. Indeed, all three of Hirschman's control devices, *Exit, Voice, and Loyalty*,[18] are more easily enlisted in personal relations than in firm–employee relations, giving each partner in social relations reciprocal control and reasons for refraining from attempts to dominate.

Foa has demonstrated that people prefer to exchange like goods for like goods, money for money and love for love (see Chapter 25). This tends to separate social exchanges from money exchanges. The separation is further increased by the fact that money is universalistic – a dollar has the same objective value to everyone – but friendship or love is particularistic to each of the partners. Money can be exchanged where friendship and love cannot. Money can be acquired swifly and spent even more swiftly, but friendships must be cultivated and love usually incubates over a long period of time.[19] Therefore, what people learn about the uses of money cannot easily be transferred to friendship or love relationships.

Finally, the market system itself is a protection against the use of friendship as a device for controlling others because control is taken over by market relations. In gemeinschaft, where approval rather than money is the main mechanism of control, approval will be more visible; approval will extend throughout the hierarchy and be less equal; exit will be more difficult, and control by approval will be more coercive. Under those circumstances, it is quite likely that a person will conform to group opinion; he or she will be controlled. In contrast, where price can carry the burden of control, human relations can be devoted to other things, including intrinsic enjoyment of each other. The same line of argument leads anthropologist Paul C. Rosenblatt to argue that romantic (intrinsic) love increases when the economic bases of marriage decline.[20] Instead of "hidden costs" (the term I employ in Chapter 18 to describe the way money payments tend to *reduce* work enjoyment and, therefore, where extrinsic payments tend to replace the intrinsic rewards), this is a case of hidden gains, where the intrinsic replaces the extrinsic.

I conclude that there are protections in the nature of the different reward systems and institutions against the conversion of interpersonal relations to marketlike transactions dependent on extrinsic rewards.

Commodification of human relations

If market exchange lacks some of the distinctive defects alleged, is sufficiently different from social exchange to be inapplicable in social relations, and is inhibited

that becomes diffuse approval of his composite qualities as a person is the source of intrinsic attraction to him." Blau, *Exchange and Power in Social Life*, 69. See also Karen S. Rook, "Reciprocity of Social Exchange and Social Satisfaction Among Older Women," *Journal of Personality and Social Psychology* 52 (1987): 145–54.

[18] Albert O. Hirschman, *Exit, Voice, and Loyalty: Responses to Decline in Firms, Organizations, and States* (Cambridge: Harvard University Press, 1970).

[19] Uriel G. Foa, "Interpersonal and Economic Resources," *Science* 171 (29 January 1971): 345–51.

[20] Paul C. Rosenblatt, "Cross-Cultural Perspective on Attraction," in Ted L. Huston, ed., *Foundations of Interpersonal Attraction* (New York: Academic Press, 1974).

by the nature of the rewards from replacing intrinsic rewards by extrinsic rewards, does this not settle the matter? Not entirely, because these conclusions are derived more from theory than from observation and evidence and it is always wise to examine the data to see if the theories are right. The allegation that friendship is infected by commercial relations sometimes goes by the name of "the commodification of human relations." In pursuing this matter I wish not only to discover facets of the market experience, but also on the way, to suggest to humanist (and Marxist) critics who make this allegation the value of empirical research and the complex theories that such research generates. The point is not to defend the market but to defend scholarship in an area saturated with ideology.

What is to be explained seems clear enough from the introductory passages: People are treated instrumentally, coldly, as objects to be used for one's own advantage. But the evidence for the increase in these unfavorable qualities paralleling the rise of the market economy is not offered; perhaps there is nothing of this sort to be explained, or, miraculously, what must be explained is the *decline* of cold, stiff, formal relationships. The allegations certainly seem dissonant with the alleged dominance of "other-directedness," that exaggerated concern for what others think of the self.[21] Only after some estimate of the truth of the allegations will it be worthwhile trying to assess whether it is the market economy, or urbanization, or the division of labor, or the market's effects on these mediating forces, or something else that accounts for whatever changed human relations has taken place.

Observations on the character of human relations are easily made, hard to prove or disprove. Impressionistic observers of the American character, for example, differ on how to characterize the way we treat each other: Tocqueville says "the temper of the Americans is vindictive," whereas Bryce says the Americans typically take a "charitable view of wrongdoers." Max Lerner, like Laski, speaks of the "friendliness" of the Americans, but Tocqueville noticed a certain "coolness" and anxiety in their mutual relations. Are the observers wrong, or between Tocqueville and Bryce or Lerner and Laski have the Americans become less vindictive, warmer, and more friendly? Those who characterize the temper of the times, or of Western market civilization more generally, also differ from each other: Like Simmel, Lewis Mumford characterizes the human relations of modern man as "cold," whereas Allen Wheelis, a psychiatrist, says, "The key words for our time are 'flexibility,' 'adjustment,' and *'warmth.'* "[22] If observations are ambiguous in one way, statements of "felt need" are ambiguous in another. Psychologist Seymour Sarason speaks of the widespread, deeply felt, contemporary American need for closer personal ties, "the sense that one was part of a readily available, mutually supportive network of relationship upon which one could depend."[23] But is this because of our isolated, atomized lives (more isolated and atomized than a farm household in Nebraska in the 1880s?), or because we have developed a higher standard of human

[21] David Riesman, with Nathan Glazer and D. Ravel, *The Lonely Crowd* (New Haven: Yale University Press, 1950).
[22] Allen Wheelis, *The Quest for Identity* (New York: Norton, 1958), 85.
[23] Seymour Sarason, *The Psychological Sense of Community* (San Francisco: Jossey-Bass, 1974), 1.

relations than we had before? or a lower standard? Psychologist Abraham Maslow says that *needing* others, as contrasted to wanting them, is a sign of incomplete personality development.[24]

Systematic studies with controlled observations and better conceptualization do not tell us of the effect of markets, but do give a clue as to what it is that must be explained. A detailed study of people's beliefs about themselves, their social roles and life concerns, shows a shift between 1957 and 1976 toward a greater attention to and a higher evaluation of personal intimacy and more concern with personal relationships, as contrasted to an emphasis on relatively impersonal status and role relationships earlier.[25] Another American national study using 1957 and 1978 survey material reports that "most [but not all] people in this country are surrounded by a network of relatives and friends whom they see frequently and who provide for them feelings of satisfaction with family and friendships which we know to be important to the individual's sense of well-being."[26] For our purposes, the important point is that those lacking this supporting friendship network are not those most exposed to the market but those marginal people who have failed in the market, a fact suggesting an explanatory theory very different from the ones mentioned. There is, therefore, reason to doubt the range and depth of the phenomena alleged to be characteristic of modern market societies.

Causes and evaluation of commodification

The causal sequence that might bring about the commodification of human relations cannot be elaborated here, but we might take a tentative excursion in that direction by glancing at a few of the alleged causes. The first of these alleged causes follows the critics' argument already discussed: They say we learn human relations in the market (not the home, where gemeinschaft still prevails) and that as a consequence other people become primarily instruments for enhancing our wealth. This argument does not square with the evidence: People's contemporary value systems place friendship and community ahead of wealth. For example, in a national sample of the American people [1971] on an eighteen-item scale, "true friendship" ranks tenth, three places ahead of "a comfortable, prosperous life," which ranks thirteenth.[27] Also, in a different study, number of friends was a much better predictor of life satisfaction in this market society than family income."[28] Finally, in ranking

[24] Abraham H. Maslow, *Toward a Psychology of Being*, 2d ed. (Princeton, NJ: Van Nostrand, 1968), 26, 401–42.

[25] Joseph Veroff, Elizabeth Douvan, and Richard A. Kulka, *The Inner Americans: A Self-Portrait from 1957 to 1976* (New York: Basic Books, 1981), 530–1, 537.

[26] Angus Campbell, *The Sense of Well-Being in America* (New York: McGraw-Hill, 1981), 110. Not all research reports are so favorable to the idea of warm contemporary human relations. Richard Christie and Florence L. Geis report the rise of a manipulative attitude toward people that would seem to support one of the critics' themes. See Christie and Geis, *Studies in Machiavellianism* (New York: Academic Press, 1970).

[27] Milton Rokeach, "Change and Stability in American Value Systems, 1968–1971," *Public Opinion Quarterly* 38 (1974): 222–38. Both of these values, incidentally, rank far below "a world at peace," "freedom," and "equality."

[28] Angus Campbell, Philip E. Converse, and Willard L. Rodgers, *The Quality of American Life* (New York: Russell Sage, 1976), 368.

the qualities desired at work, people value congenial workmates about the same as pay, which in turn generally ranks below interesting work.[29]

The second causal exploration deals with the effect of changing role relations. Assume that Parsons is right and that human relations in modern market societies are characterized by more "role specific" behavior and that, by way of contrast, in gemeinschaft people are known to each other in their several capacities or roles: A person is not just "the postman" but also a neighbor and father of one's children's friends. Because the market (but also the command economy) does seem to facilitate the division of labor where "role specificity" might flourish, an indirect causal relationship would be established and these relatively more anonymous relationships might be interpreted as "cold" and "exchange oriented." If that were true, then we would still have a choice. On the one hand, Godfrey and Monica Wilson suggest a multiplicative effect: The number of interpersonal contacts times the depths of these relationships equals a constant.[30] On the other hand, Lyn Lofland suggests an additive relation: "The cosmopolitan did not lose the capacity for knowing others personally, but he gained the capacity for knowing others only categorically."[31] Studies of friendship networks in cities suggest that the Wilsons' theory may be marginally true for the working class, whereas Lofland's observation is more valid for the middle class.

A third line of exploration follows the idea that the market effect on human relations is not a product of exchange orientation, but rather of the market's encouragement to geographical mobility: going where the jobs are. We did not grow up with our neighbors; we are all transient "strangers" to each other. The plausibility of this hypothesis is partially undermined by the research findings that (1) after five years people usually have as many friends in the place to which they have migrated as they did in the old place,[32] and (2) there seems to be no difference in willingness to share confidences, to lend and borrow, and to experience intimacy with relatively new friends compared to old ones.[33]

As for the *evaluation* of this alleged decline of intimacy, consider some alternative evaluative puzzles: How much prosperity should we sacrifice (if that is necessary) for a marginal gain in the kind of human relations embraced by community solidarity? If, as seems to be the case, looser social networks are associated with decreased sex discrimination and an increase in the activities married couples do together,[34] is the cost greater than the gain? The title to Richard Sennett's book,

[29] Robert P. Quinn and Linda J. Shepard, *The 1972–73 Quality of Employment Survey* (Ann Arbor, MI: Institute for Social Research, 1974), Table 3.28.

[30] Godfrey Wilson and Monica Wilson, *The Analysis of Social Change* (Cambridge, UK: Cambridge University Press, 1945). Jencks and associates studied what people like most about their work and they report, "We believe that the most plausible interpretation of our findings is that nonmonetary job characteristics are far more important to workers than most of us ordinarily assume." Christopher Jencks, Lauri Perman, and Lee Rainwater, "What is a Good Job? A New Measure of Labor-Market Success," *American Journal of Sociology* 93 (1988): 1,322–57 at 1,343.

[31] Lyn H. Lofland, *A World of Strangers* (New York: Basic Books, 1973), 177.

[32] John B. Lansing and Eva Mueller, *The Geographic Mobility of Labor* (Ann Arbor, MI: Institute for Social Research, 1967).

[33] Nicholas Babchuk and Alan P. Bates, "The Primary Relations of Middle Class Couples: A Study of Male Dominance," *American Sociological Review* 28 (1963): 377–84.

[34] Elizabeth Bott, *Family and Social Networks* (New York: Free Press, 1971).

The Tyranny of Intimacy, presents the dilemma posed by the Wilsons. Intimacy, says Sennett, impedes sociability.[35] Is a wider but looser set of relations better or worse than fewer but more intimate relations? Finally, in this abbreviated, illustrative list is the problem of a tradeoff between cognitive development and intimate human relations. If it were the case that the market's stimulative effects and thrust toward self-reliance increased alertness and learning capacities (as new playthings do for monkeys and rats; see Chapter 8), but, on the other hand, the market destroyed the easy bonding of neighbors, by what criteria of happiness and human development should we choose among these goods? Warm, intimate social relations are good, but where they imply costs, their goodness must be weighed against the costs.

Comparative evidence on commodification

If the complex and multifaceted criticisms of market effects on human relations had validity, we would expect market societies to reveal more damaged relations than either command economies or household (peasant) economies. Two studies on human relations in command economies suggest caution in attributing the alleged rise in "coldness" and impersonality to markets a greater degree of responsibility than is attributable to other economies. One, entitled "From Friendship to Comradeship," points out that intimacy and trust among friends in communist China has been eroded by fear of disclosure to the authorities of casual heterodoxy by one of the partners to a conversation.[36] The second study reports the use of informants by the Soviet Union and the communist regimes of Eastern Europe as a means of controlling the population and vesting prosecutorial powers in the public; the result was that each person held the fate of his or her friends in his or her hands. In both cases suspicion took the place of intimate human relations.[37]

Following Karl Polanyi, Marshall Sahlins, Stanley Diamond, Marcel Mauss, and other anthropologists (and industrial psychologist Fritz Roethlisberger), we would conclude that compared to market societies, primitive societies, and to some extent also peasant societies, have warmer and less exchange-oriented human relations, less competitiveness, and more cooperation. Following Oscar Lewis (on Tepoztlán), Margaret Mead (on the Manus), R. F. Fortune (on the Dobus), Cora Dubois (on Alor), and A. I. Hallowell (on the Ojibwa), we would doubt the allegations about warm, trusting, and cooperative human relations in less developed economies. Robert Redfield's study of Chan Kom reports that the transformation from subsistence agriculture to cash crops did not injure the society's trusting internal relations and made its treatment of strangers much more hospitable.[38] The ethnog-

---

[35] Richard Sennett, *The Tyranny of Intimacy* (New York: Knopf, 1976).

[36] Ezra F. Vogel, "From Friendship to Comradeship: The Change in Personal Relations in Communist Societies," *China Quarterly* 21 (1965): 46–70.

[37] Jan T. Gross, "A Note on the Nature of Soviet Totalitarianism," *Soviet Studies* 34 (1982): 367–76. Of course, socialism as originally conceived is not indicted, but those command economies speaking in the name of socialism are; it is a question whether concentrated, centralized economic power does not always risk such results.

[38] Robert Redfield, *A Village That Chose Progress: Chan Kom Revisited* (Chicago: University of Chicago Press, 1950).

raphy on the Canadian Eskimos, encountering "civilization" in the persons not of priests and soldiers but of traders employed by the Hudson Bay Company, reveals a benign change from precarious to secure existence without identity problems or social disintegration, although with increased individuation and materialistic values.[39] On the basis of this report, it seems that introduction of commerce among the Canadian Eskimos has not disrupted their traditional social relations.

The evidence from both command economies and primitive and peasant economies certainly does not give much confidence in the validity of the market critics' indictments, but neither does it wholly refute them.

Holding ideology and anger in suspension as best we can, it is along such lines that we might investigate the allegations of the market critics that markets commodify human relations – and the proud boasts of market defenders that the market releases people to make their own friends wherever they choose.

One other set of comparisons: Are soldiers and priests and academics less competitive, less materialistic, less exchange oriented, and less selfish than businessmen? In some ways, yes. But fellow academics, do look around you.

Summary

Because of their opportunity costs nonmarket choices generally reflect most of the characteristics of market exchanges: their implicit pricing, their materialism, and their selfishness. But the market's explicit pricing, the narrowing of criteria in market exchanges, the market's invitation to use price information as a substitute for other information, and the more frequent incidence of desperate exchanges in economic life make market choices different from others. It should be apparent, however, that the main problem for the development of the human personality is the character of the choices made and not the exchange of goods and services for money in the market.

The risk that market patterns of extrinsic rewards will infect social relations whose value depends on intrinsic rewards at first seems substantial, for we know circumstances where behavior learned in one domain is applied to other domains. But some reasons for believing that friendship and love may resist infection include the different degrees of specification, trust, moral obligation, property, and transmissibility that characterize social and commercial exchanges. In the contrast between love and money, we noted that love is particularistic and slow to develop, whereas money is universalistic and instantly available for use. Also, verbal rewards such as may be found in social exchange do not seem to imply the same degree of control as tangible rewards; rather, to use a distinction important in accounting for the failure of extrinsic rewards to erode intrinsic interests, verbal rewards are more informational than controlling.

In contrast to market relations, where the only option available for changing one's circumstances is "exit," in social relations both of Hirschman's options, exit

[39] Nelson H. H. Graburn, "Traditional Economic Institutions and the Acculturation of the Canadian Eskimos," in George Dalton, ed., *Studies in Economic Anthropology* (Washington, DC: American Anthropological Association, 1971).

and voice, are available and the appeal of loyalty may make the circumstances more acceptable.

The evidence for anything like the commodification of human beings in market economies is slight. The impressionistic observations of historians is contradictory and the more systemic evidence from surveys seems to refute the allegation. Alleged causes in market exposure, changing roles, and geographic mobility are not well supported by evidence, nor is the comparison with other economic systems supportive, and the evaluative implications are much more complex than has been presented by the criticisms.

We now turn to other facets of human relations in the market: invidiousness and the value of friendly relations compared to material gain.

12 Invidiousness and the friendship or income choice

If the market does not substantially erode friendship and warm relations, perhaps it changes the nature of these relations, making them more invidious. This result would follow from what is said to be the market's encouragement of "conspicuous consumption," rivalry, and other forms of invidiousness so vividly described by Veblen. In the first section of this chapter we will discuss the market's invitation to social comparison and its alleged consequences for the way we perceive each other. Whether or not rivalrous relations in the market are worse than elsewhere, friendships might still be disvalued when a choice must be made between friendly relations and material gain. As we shall see in the second section of this chapter, there is reason to believe that this devaluation would bring about the wrong choice: The quality of life studies show that anyone maximizing happiness should probably give friendship (and family relations) *higher* priority, for satisfaction with family life and actual numbers of friends contribute more to overall life satisfaction, and especially to happiness, than anything the market has to offer.[1] If people followed this set of social priorities, however, they would have to defy the market to do so. The implications of this choice between friendship and income and the various hedonic standards to guide the choice are explored in this second section.

Social comparisons: the effect of the circumstances of others on the self

Montesquieu, Tocqueville, Smith, Veblen, and others have variously claimed that modern society encourages social comparison, Smith attributing it to human nature, Tocqueville to democratic egalitarianism, but both Montesquieu and Veblen attributing this tendency to market institutions. In modern thought, the market society is believed to encourage social comparisons rather than self-reference, because in the absence of ascription, people are uncertain of where they stand, how well they are doing, and who around them are peers, who are subordinates, and who are superordinates. They need to anchor their self-evaluations and hence their sense of well-being in selected others. In ascriptive societies comparisons may be equally or more frequent, but their reference marks are more or less objective and permanent. In market achievement-oriented societies, social standing is more fluid. People have more different dimensions than are provided by the simple stigmata of status – as many dimensions as there are grounds for striving. And most important, the criteria for rank are more subjective, more easily manipulated to the advantage of the comparing person. In comparison to ascriptive societies and probably to bureaucratic

[1] Angus Campbell, Philip E. Converse, and Willard L. Rodgers, *The Quality of American Life* (New York: Russell Sage, 1976), 76, 368, 374.

220

societies, the more ambiguous social standings of a market society permit social comparisons to contribute to feelings of well-being.

There are two interrelated ideas in the discussion of how social comparisons affect subjective well-being. One of them deals with *how people decide:* conformity, other directedness, and Bem's self-perception theory that, as we will see in more detail in Chapter 18, says that people consult social norms to explain both how they feel and why they feel that way.[2] The other deals with the *standards employed* for evaluations: Compared to what or whom is a person doing well or poorly? The first idea is a sufficient but not necessary condition for the second: I cannot evaluate my own well-being by asking what others think about me without incorporating their comparative standards, but I can decide for myself that I am not doing well by comparing myself to others. It is this use of standards for judgment that concerns us here.

The humanistic ideal (cf. John Dewey) for setting standards is that these should be based in each case on the capabilities and performances of the self, not on the capabilities or performances of others. This is possible and operable within certain human limits, the limits being the tendency to assess "good" and "bad" in terms of the social norms of a person's associates. Just as the value of an object must be anchored in comparison with other similar objects simply to give meaning to the idea of value,[3] so the value of a trait or performance is assessed by the individual in the light of what he or she considers good and bad traits or performances by members of their groups. It is doubtful if individuals *can* assess anything without at least unconscious reference to community norms. The concept of reference group is a key term in this line of analysis; it may be extended to include reference individuals, with the record and ideals of the self as the appropriate "reference individual."

Social comparison in production and consumption

The use of comparative standards carries a meaning in productive enterprise very different from the meaning in consumption.

Production. In production (artistic or commercial) setting one's goals by the best work of another might be called *rivalry* (or in the language Adam Smith used, *emulation*), meaning "striving to equal or excel." The dictionary treats rivalry as a synonym for *competition,* but this is not the way economists use these terms. Contemporary economists use *competition* to mean only "the presence of alternatives" and *rivalry* to mean the "desire to best another," which, as we shall see in a later analysis (Chapter 15) has been used as an operational definition of competitiveness. We find the following lexicon useful: *Rivalry* means the desire "to equal or excel the work of another," *competitiveness* means the desire to get the better of another, and *competition* means the presence of alternatives.[4] Both rivalry and competitiveness clearly involve social comparison and equally clearly violate the hu-

[2] Daryl J. Bem, "Self-Perception Theory," in Leonard Berkowitz, ed., *Advances in Experimental Social Psychology,* vol. 6 (New York: Academic Press, 1972).

[3] Ralph Barton Perry, *General Theory of Value* (New York: Longman's Green, 1926).

[4] Compare Anatol Rapoport, *Fights, Games and Debates* (Ann Arbor: University of Michigan Press, 1960).

manist preference for self-comparison, but they are quite different in their ethical implications.

The reward for competitiveness is the feeling of having humbled or beaten the other, whereas the reward for rivalry, as we defined it, is the sense of having done as well as or better than another. Without reference to how the other feels, the reward for rivalry lies in having met a standard *defined* by the work of another where the feelings of the other are irrelevant. This distinction between competitiveness and rivalry is one of *intentions* and thus enlists ethical criteria. The intentions in rivalry, as we defined it, helps to rob of its force the humanist criticism of the use of social comparison in rivalry.[5]

Competitiveness, defined to mean the desire to get the better of others, involves social comparison, but it is not an attribute that leads to success in the market, for in an experiment to be reported more fully in a later chapter, people identified as having the trait of competitiveness did *worse* than those who did not have this trait,[6] and in observational studies competitive persons failed to succeed in market situations. In Darwinian/Skinnerian fashion, competitiveness would not thrive in a market economy because it is not reinforced. On the other hand, *self*-referential qualities such as self-confidence and self-attribution (Chapter 9), the "work ethic," "desire for challenge" (Chapter 16), industriousness (Chapter 7), and the need for achievement (an *internal* standard of excellence)[7] are all related to economic success in a market economy.

Before moving to consumption, note that in the sphere of production there are two important sets of consequences flowing from social comparisons: economic and hedonic. (1) The consequence of rivalry in the market is a set of escalating standards – as in sports where new records are set every year. The fact that self-regulation and self-reference can also raise standards of excellence does not ipso facto mean that social comparison is not also useful in this respect. The experience of mankind with economies where self-regulation is the sole stimulus to higher standards has not, with the exception of religious communities, been successful. (2) The hedonic consequence is more uncertain, as we shall see, but where people's statuses are more ambiguous, as in an achievement society, they tend to be benign.

The point is that it is the *use* of social comparisons that determines their merit, not their presence and not the simple fact of external references to works or persons.

Consumption. In consumption processes the use of social comparison might conceivably be beneficial. In cases of social mobility, the former peasant, the immigrant, and the blue-collar worker learn standards of taste, language, and behavior by processes of social comparison. John Stuart Mill's scalar theory of taste improvement (the test for whether a given utility is better than another is whether

[5] I agree with Bandura that "social comparison is inevitable" but *not* his implication that market economies promote more "competitiveness" and social comparisons than do other economies. Albert Bandura, *Social Learning Theory* (Englewood Cliffs, NJ: Prentice-Hall, 1977), 140.
[6] Jack C. Horn, "The Element of Success: Competitiveness Isn't That Important," *Psychology Today* 11 (April 1978): 19–20, reporting work by Robert Helmreich and Janet Spence.
[7] David C. McClelland and David G. Winter, *Motivating Economic Achievement* (New York: Free Press, 1971).

someone who has tried both lower and higher forms prefers the higher form) relied on social comparison processes of this kind.[8] But what strikes the eye is the *invidiousness* of social comparison in consumption processes: keeping up with the Joneses, fashion, and, of course, conspicious consumption. Whereas invidiousness may increase demand, it undermines the purpose of that increased demand by decreasing utility.

Social comparisons: cognitive appraisal versus envy. Just as willingness and ability to engage in competition does not necessarily imply *competitiveness* (Chapter 16), so, making social comparisons does not necessarily imply *envy*. Envy, of course, implies social comparisons, but it also means "begrudging" the good fortune of another, "resenting" his or her well-being, and "coveting" something of the other's. Social comparisons as a purely cognitive appraisal may or may not increase well-being, but the tendency to compare oneself to others in a spirit of envy measurably decreases it.[9]

In the discussion of the division of labor in Chapter 16 I will point out that the more hierarchical occupational pyramids there are available, the more peaks of achievement there will be, and the more people who, comparing themselves with others in any given hierarchy, can say with satisfaction, "I am at the top." The market, we find, accelerated the division of labor.

And the vulnerability of comparisons to subjective interpretation permits them to serve hedonic needs more easily than in ascriptive societies. As we shall see, this is likely to convert social comparisons from a set of conservative, hierarchy-reinforcing perceptions to a set of flexible, hierarchy-reducing perceptions. But there are limits to the social comparison process in market economies.

The limits of social comparison

Although Diener finds evidence that of all possible comparisons, social comparison is the most frequent standard for assessing one's welfare,[10] in fact, the prevalence of social comparison in the empirical quality-of-life studies is quite limited. (1) Andrews and Withey found that answers to their comparative questions involving comparing self with "the neighbor who lives nearest you, who is of the same sex as you," were less informative than straightforward questions asking people how, without comparisons, they feel about various concerns.[11] (2) Campbell et al.'s study of the quality of life shows that, at least in terms of their housing, people compare their current status more with their own previous best experience than with the housing of others.[12] (3) A recent study of women workers in Massachusetts found,

[8] John Stuart Mill, "Utilitarianism," in *Utilitarianism, Liberty, and Representative Government* (1910; reprint London: Dent, 1944), 8, 10. This treatise was originally published in 1861.
[9] Philip Shaver and Jonathan Freedman, "Your Pursuit of Happiness," *Psychology Today* 10 (August 1976): 27–32, 75 at 75.
[10] Ed Diener, "Subjective Well-Being," *Psychological Bulletin* 95 (1984): 542–75 at 567.
[11] Frank M. Andrews and Stephen B. Withey, *Social Indicators of Well-Being: Americans' Perceptions of Life Quality* (New York: Plenum Press, 1976), 168, 191, 241, 317.
[12] Angus Campbell et al., chap. 6. There is other evidence suggesting that group comparisons are more forceful than individual comparisons. See Serge Guimond and Lise Dubé-Simard, "Relative Deprivation and the Quebec Nationalist Movement: The Cognition–Emotion Distinction and the Personal–Group

to the author's surprise, very few social comparison effects, and what comparisons there were were not affected by the sex of the persons with whom subjects compared themselves.[13] And, by contrast, (4) the original study of relative deprivation and its allied notion of reference groups emerged from a comparison of air corps and military policemen in the American armed services,[14] not from market comparisons. There is very little evidence that, compared to traditional villages,[15] bureaucracies, or academic institutions, markets encourage more social comparisons.

Furthermore, where it does occur, the range of comparisons is limited, for people tend to compare themselves only with people like themselves; cross-status or cross-class comparisons are relatively rare and do not have the same effects as comparisons with similar others.[16] This means that the larger the "gap" between what one has and what some reference person has, the less salient will that gap be – a self-limiting property of social comparison that constrains its potential for creating unhappiness.

Gap theory: comparisons in the process of assessing satisfaction. What is called "gap theory" puts theories of social comparison in perspective. Michalos suggests that it is the gaps between the following pairs that occasion dissatisfaction and malaise, or, alternatively, feelings of well-being:

1. "What one has and what one aims for, an achievement gap."
2. "What one actually has and what is ideal."
3. "What is now the case and what one expects or expected to be the case," embracing the problem of the "frustration of rising expectations" and the economists' "rational expectations."
4. What one has and the best that one had or achieved previously. This is the comparison that Campbell et al. found applied when people assessed their housing.
5. "What one has and what some relevant group or person has," that is, social comparison.
6. What people believe they need and what the environment provides. This is the standard that Andrews and Withey found people consciously thought they applied; it also refers to the failure to achieve a good personality-environment fit.[17]

Social comparisons are only one of six kinds of comparisons that may be made. The gaps are not mutually exclusive and in various circumstances any one or more may apply to any particular evaluation, but the many comparisons that gap theory identifies relieve social comparison of the sole burden of providing standards for evaluating one's own achievements. It is a counterweight to Bandura's statement

Deprivation Issue," *Journal of Personality and Social Psychology* 44 (1983): 526–35. The original distinction between "fraternal" and individual comparisons was proposed in W. G. Runciman, *Relative Deprivation and Social Justice* (Berkeley: University of California Press, 1966).

[13] Faye J. Crosby, *Relative Deprivation and Working Women* (New York: Oxford University Press, 1982).

[14] Robert K. Merton and Alice Kitt Rossi, "Contributions to the Theory of Reference Group Behavior," in Merton, *Social Theory and Social Structure,* enl. ed. (New York: Free Press, 1968), 279–334.

[15] See, for example, Oscar Lewis, *Life in a Mexican Village* (Urbana: University of Illinois Press, 1963).

[16] Runciman, *Relative Deprivation and Social Justice.*

[17] Alex C. Michalos, "Job Satisfaction, Marital Satisfaction, and the Quality of Life: A Review and a Preview," in Frank M. Andrews, ed., *Research on the Quality of Life* (Ann Arbor, MI: Institute for Social Research, 1986), 66–7. For a more extended list see Andrews and Withey, *Social Indicators of Well-Being,* 219–31.

that "social comparison is inevitable" and to the idea that markets foster invidiousness and social comparison.[18]

Do social comparisons increase well-being?

If it were the case that social comparisons are necessary to maximize well-being, instead of criticizing the market for encouraging them (which I have been arguing it does not do), we would have to inquire about the kinds of social comparisons that serve this hedonic purpose. Brickman and Campbell ask the relevant questions:

If we remove all variance from . . . a distribution [of some good], do we thereby destroy that distribution as a basis for satisfaction? If we make all people equal, do we thereby destroy social comparison as a basis of satisfaction? Or do we thereby maximize satisfaction, or minimize dissatisfaction – which may be quite different things? . . . Should distribution be negatively skewed (so that most people lie above the mean, but a few lie far below it), positively skewed (so that most people lie below the mean, but a few lie far above it), or bimodal (haves and have-nots)?[19]

They cannot answer these questions, nor can we. But some current data help form a basis for a future answer.

Felicity and infelicity in social comparisons. Andrews and Withey found that their comparative questions, although less adequate for scientific purposes, tended to produce *higher* satisfaction scores than the same questions made without comparisons. The social comparison question was calculated to prevent subjects from selecting people better off or worse off than the self, yet the effect was to *increase* the sense of well-being.[20] One reason was already suggested: People subjectively place themselves higher on any scale of values than objective criteria would suggest. Asked where they stand relative to other Americans, 62 percent thought that they were better off than others, whereas only 13 per cent thought they were worse off.[21]

A second reason why status-neutral social comparisons produce higher satisfaction scores is that we are poor judges of other people's feelings and moods: "Even people who the respondents felt knew them pretty well were in fact relatively poor judges of the respondents' perceptions. This suggests that perceptions of well-being may be rather private matters. . . . The inference is strong that *we as a people do not really know how each other feels.*"[22] This finding reinforces what was said earlier: The market's erosion of gemeinschaft, where people are known in their

[18] Within the range of *self-comparisons*, there are many alternatives not mentioned above: (1) a range of temporal comparisons (now versus an hour ago, a year ago, etc.); (2) the pace of change comparisons: Am I advancing too slowly compared to expectations? (3) satisficing comparisons, actuality versus "good enough"; (4) role comparisons: What should a person in my position have, be, feel? (5) identity comparisons: What sentiments, beliefs, feelings are congruent with my self-image? (6) deserts: What is owing to me? and (7) noncomparative intrinsic responses: What do I actually feel? Andrews and Withey, *Social Indicators of Well-Being*, 219–31.

[19] Philip Brickman and Donald T. Campbell, "Hedonic Relativism and Planning the Good Society," in M. H. Appley, ed., *Adaptation-Level Theory: A Symposium* (New York: Academic Press, 1971), 299.

[20] Andrews and Withey, *Social Indicators of Well-Being*, 240.

[21] Ibid., 317. This is congruent with our discussion in Chapter 22 on the objective and subjective double ratios of achievements to aspirations.

[22] Ibid., 191.

multiple roles and therefore in greater depth, tends to make persons happier because they do *not* know others so well. Ignorance lets the positivity bias (Chapter 4) favor the self unhindered by too much knowledge of others.

Downward comparisons: the restoration of felicity. Perhaps the most important limit on, and also substantiation of, the importance of social comparison is the fact that comparisons with others who are less well-off or similarly bereft tends to be prevalent only among those who are themselves not very happy. Research and theory on *downward comparison* substantiates the view that people are likely to feel better if they compare their lot either with those who are worse off than they are or who are "in the same boat" as they are, suffering in the same way. "People who are unhappy like to see others who are unhappy. They may not necessarily go out of their way to produce unhappiness in others, but sometimes they do. . . . The psychological benefit from these processes is enhancement of subjective well-being." The already happy are less likely to enhance their own well-being by this device, rather "downward comparison processes are most prevalent among those persons who are the most unhappy and least fortunate."[23]

Creating reference points that increase well-being. Although the process of downward comparison may be most prevalent among the already unhappy, wherever attention is drawn to unfortunate others, people in all states of mind improve their perceptions of their own circumstances. In one experiment, subjects who wrote essays on the "hedonically negative events" seventy years ago at the turn of the century and on various personal tragedies known to them, then evaluated their own quality of life higher than did controls.[24]

Ethics and justice in social comparisons
If downward comparisons increase a sense of satisfaction with one's portion in life for the already unhappy (those whom Rawls would call the "least privileged"), and if any reference to unhappy circumstances makes one's own circumstances seem more felicitous, could it be said that the market's tendency to create a few miserable, unemployed people serves the utilitarian purpose: "the greatest happiness of the greatest number"? The point is part of standard criticisms of utilitarianism.[25] The idea is repulsive because it extracts from other people's misery a satisfaction that is unethical and "undeserved" (recall W. D. Ross's statement that happiness is a good only when it is deserved [Chapter 1]). It also violates the general rule that, except for some standard setting, self-comparisons are better than social comparisons.

To complicate this last point, consider the comparative nature of assessments of justice. Those who find social comparison invidious and prefer self-comparisons

---

[23] Thomas Ashby Wills, "Downward Comparison Principles in Social Psychology," *Psychological Bulletin* 90 (1980): 245–71 at 264, 265, 268.
[24] Marshall Dermer, Sidney J. Cohen, Elaine Jackson, and Erling A. Anderson, "Evaluative Judgments of Aspects of Life as a Function of Vicarious Exposure to Hedonic Extremes," *Journal of Personality and Social Psychology* 37 (1979): 247–60.
[25] Amartya Sen, "Utilitarianism and Welfarism," *Journal of Philosophy* 76 (1979), 463–89.

must somehow explain how justice may be done without some reference to other's outcomes or treatments. In fact, distributive justice *always* involves social comparisons (although procedural justice may follow abstract rules without comparisons). Equality, for example, is defined by social comparison. I emphasize the point made earlier: Social comparison per se is not bad; the goodness and badness of social comparison depends on the uses made of that comparison.

Hedonic equality versus income equality

The market is no friend of equality. Neither the justification of its distribution by the justice of deserts, nor the machinery for assigning rewards according to contribution to profitability favor equal distributions. But in hedonic matters, as contrasted to economic matters, market economies seem to create hedonically more equal societies.

Subjective hedonic equality. The difference between ascriptive or bureaucratically assigned ranks and the more ambiguous ranks of market societies was seen earlier to favor self-definitions that permitted people to give themselves higher ranks than objectively indicated. For the same reason people are hedonically more equal than they are equal economically. As matters stand, subjective well-being is much more evenly distributed than income, and, as I have said, is relatively insensitive to income levels.[26] Economic egalitarianism will not, therefore, greatly affect hedonic egalitarianism and the market's inegalitarianism is not a major stumbling block to hedonic egalitarianism. Moreover, given the tendency to misperceive one's objective situation and thus to raise one's relative level of income above others, like Brickman and Campbell we cannot be sure that "the greatest happiness for the greatest number" may not be positively enhanced by at least *some* degree of income inequality. Partly on these very social comparison grounds, economic equality has little support among members of the working class, for they do, indeed, find satisfaction in seeing themselves as better off than they are and are thus in a position to engage in the delights of downward comparison.[27]

Objective income distributions. Nevertheless, the hedonic effect of income inequality must be more complex. Thus, Morawetz found that in Israel, "other things held constant, the more unequal the income distribution the lower the individual's self-reported happiness," but this is confounded with the ideologies of the moshavim where the subjects lived.[28] In the European studies, Greece, which has the most inegalitarian, polarized income structure in the group of European nations, has a polarized but low average sense of well-being.[29] For a variety of reasons,

[26] Angus Campbell, *The Sense of Well-Being in America* (New York: McGraw-Hill, 1981), 234.

[27] Robert E. Lane, "The Fear of Equality," *American Political Science Review* 53 (1959): 35–51; Lee Rainwater, *What Money Buys: Inequality and the Social Meaning of Income* (New York: Basic Books, 1974).

[28] David Morawetz et al., "Income Distribution and Self-Rated Happiness: Some Empirical Evidence," *The Economic Journal* 87 (1977): 511–22.

[29] Ronald Inglehart and Jacques-Rene Rabier, "Aspirations Adapt to Situations – But Why Are the Belgians So Much Happier than the French? A Cross-Cultural Analysis of the Subjective Quality of Life," in Andrews, *Research on the Quality of Life*, 44.

hedonic inequality is unlikely to be as great as income inequality, but we cannot dismiss income inequality as a possible source of hedonic loss, even by those with average incomes.

Rendering social comparison less invidious

Multiplying social roles. As already mentioned, on such public matters as income, prestige, status, and praise the usual recommendation to enhance self-esteem is to facilitate multiple standards of comparison so arranged as to permit more pyramids and therefore more peaks.[30] The argument applies to different domains of life and their social roles as well as occupational pyramids. Social comparisons in different domains may permit an individual to find satisfying comparisons in one domain to balance the unsatisfying ones in another − and a freedom of choice wherever the market's imperial tendencies do not monopolize the accepted standards. Thus, the role specificity (Parsons) of market society where people are known narrowly in their specialized roles, rather than broadly in their multiple roles, offers multiple opportunities for more favorable social comparisons. The good family man, the good friend, the good civic leader, as well as the good violinist, pianist, and cello player, may each have honor in his or her own country.

Privatizing social comparisons. Inasmuch as life satisfaction is more influenced by family felicity and feelings of efficacy and achievement than by economic matters, it is the distribution of these goods to which we must turn if we wish to move toward some version of "the greatest happiness of the greatest number." Since family life and self-referential pride in achievement are more private than economic life and status, they invite fewer social comparisons than do situations with a more objective and public character. For example, as mentioned, there is evidence that in evaluating their housing and communities, people employ more self-referential standards than in evaluating their incomes.[31] The goods in these more private situations have the advantage of being pieces in "variable sum games," that is, games where one person's gain is not necessarily another's loss. Such games are less hospitable to invidiousness; they deal with the kinds of goods that might even invite that most felicitous of all social comparisons: The happiness of others means the happiness of the self. And only to a minor extent are they market goods.

To summarize this discussion of social comparison we may say that the hedonic benefits of social comparisons in market societies derive substantially from the looseness with which rank is defined in such societies, as contrasted to the public, more or less objective ranks in ascriptive and bureaucratic societies. This looseness permits people to see themselves as higher in rank and social benefits than more

[30] Robert E. Lane, "Government and Self-Esteem," *Political Theory* 10 (1982): 5–31. This article owes much to an unpublished manuscript by Morris Rosenberg.
[31] Compare Campbell et al., *The Quality of American Life,* chap. 6, with the treatment in Yuchtman (Yaar), "Effects of Psychological Factors on Subjective Well-Being," in Burkhard Strumpel, ed., *Economic Means for Human Needs: Social Indicators of Well-Being and Discontent* (Ann Arbor: MI: Institute for Social Research, 1976).

objective standards would indicate. Such misperception, in turn, permits them to compare themselves with others whom they imagine to be less well-off than they are and to get the unearned benefits of downward comparisons. This is particularly beneficial to the already unhappy, but others benefit from reference points created by the poor fortune of others – or their own poor fortune at an earlier time.

Occupational choice between money and friendship

In occupational life one often has to choose between the hedonic benefits derived from investment in social relations and those derived from investment in earning money. How does a person decide which investment yields greater satisfaction?

Friendship and income make major contributions to life satisfaction, but in different ways: *Satisfaction* with income yields a greater return in life satisfaction than does *actual* income, whereas, as mentioned, *actual number* of friends yields more life satisfaction than *satisfaction* with friends. Furthermore, what one does with one's income, as indicated by "standard of living," and what one does with friends ("the things you do and the times you have with your friends") make contributions independent of satisfaction with income and number of friends.[32] In this situation, if a person were confronted with a choice between a job with high pay but uncongenial workmates, and one with lower pay but congenial, friendly workmates, which should that person choose and how would the market help to maximize his or her happiness?

Occupational choice

To answer this question we must anticipate the principle of choice to be developed at greater length in Chapter 25 on the structures of happiness. In brief, the resolution of two principles, *maximizing satisfaction* and *minimizing dissatisfaction,* is solved by a third principle, *maximizing net contribution to life satisfaction.* This third principle derives from the quality-of-life studies where it was found that, given a measure of overall satisfaction with life-as-a-whole, feelings about particular aspects of one's life raise this overall measure if the feelings are more positive than average and lower it if they are less positive than average or negative. For example, satisfaction with one's children, or with one's house, or with one's income, each affects overall life satisfaction to some degree. It is that degree, then, that is the measure for our third principle: *maximizing the net contribution to life satisfaction.* The application of these three principles to the problem of satisfaction from workmates or from higher income would look like this:

1. People would behave "rationally" in job selection by giving greater weight to the interpersonal relations involved than to the pay, because job studies show that interpersonal relations are thought by respondents to be more important to them,[33]

---

[32] Campbell et al., *The Quality of American Life,* 76, 368, 374; Andrews and Withey, *Social Indicators of Well-Being,* 124. It should also be noted that "pay" is evaluated more highly than income but is not closely related to happiness; it is income that makes one either happy or unhappy, not pay. Nevertheless, "there is a correlation of about .51 between feelings about income and feelings about job pay," which indicates some independence as well as some association. Andrews and Withey, ibid., 254, 259, 303.

[33] Robert P. Quinn and Linda J. Shepard, *The 1972–73 Quality of Employment Survey* (Ann Arbor, MI: Institute for Social Research, 1974), 67, 69.

     and it has been found that interpersonal relations contribute more to job satisfaction.

2. But the same data might suggest an equally rational policy of minimizing dissatisfaction that would reverse this decision and seek more pay, because job studies indicate there is much less satisfaction with pay than with interpersonal relations.[34]

The dilemma is resolved by using the third principle, *maximizing net contribution to life satisfaction* standard. Relieving job dissatisfaction (or increasing job satisfaction) makes a contribution to life satisfaction that is smaller than that made by improving friendship relations, for neither pay nor job satisfaction (in the Andrews and Withey study) contributes as much to happiness as does friendship. Thus it is the contribution to life satisfaction (or happiness) principle that decides whether satisfaction maximization or dissatisfaction minimization is the better policy. This is a better principle than the income maximization principle of the market because it deals directly with well-being, and it is better than the utility maximization of economists because it refers to a measurable standard. But the decision is made within informational and social contexts that may be distorting.

Informational and perceptual distortions in market economies
The market offers better information on pay than on congenial workmates and more generally makes income more salient than friendship. Under these circumstances, people guided by self-perception processes substituting external for internal standards[35] will probably base their job selections, to the extent they are able, on higher pay rather than on more congenial friendships.[36] This fulfills market criteria, not because pay is preferred to friendship, but because a market culture creates the illusion that preference for pay is normal. In this limited sense, the market frustrates the satisfaction of human wants.

    Of course, there are sources of friends outside the work environment (indeed, compared to other countries, in the United States relatively few friendships are made on the job).[37] But there is a strong indication in the data that by giving up friendship at work for higher pay, people probably will achieve less overall life satisfaction. Furthermore, the satisfaction achieved through higher income may be more chimerical than that gained through friendship, since, as mentioned, *actual* pay is less closely related to income satisfaction than actual number of friends is to friendship satisfaction.[38]

[34] Ibid., 64; Campbell et al., *The Quality of American Life,* 381.

[35] Bem, "Self-Perception Theory."

[36] This would seem to make sense because the difference in "importance" rating, mentioned above, was relatively small in 1973, and in the 1969 study there was no difference between "importance" ratings of friends and of income. Furthermore, as a kind of check on the validity of self-reported "importance" measures, Sheppard and Herrick report that the correlations of these two importance ratings with reported job satisfaction are almost equal. Harold L. Sheppard and Neal Q. Herrick, *Where Have All the Robots Gone?* (New York: Free Press, 1972), 197.

[37] László Cseh-Szombathy, "International Differernces in the Types and Frequencies of Social Contacts," in Alexander Szalai, ed., *The Use of Time: Daily Activities of Urban and Suburban Populations in Twelve Countries* (The Hague: Mouton, 1972).

[38] Campbell et al., *The Quality of American Life,* 358, 382.

Geographic mobility

The decision to leave one's community may also require the weighing of income and friendship advantages and disadvantages. Directly testing the evaluative process is difficult since the reasons given for moving involve many factors, but from *The Geographical Mobility of Labor,* which gives a very complicated and detailed analysis, a picture does emerge.[39] By far the most frequent reasons for mobility preference and the most frequent explanations for moving are economic, and, of these, higher income is more frequent than seeking employment. Somewhat less frequent are reasons related to family, relatives, and, less often, friends. But the "rewards" reverse that order: People rarely improve their income position by moving but often improve their family and friendship positions (they move to where they have family and friends and away from places where they do not). Over a five-year span, friends lost by moving can be replaced (but it does take five years), whereas no significant gain in income is likely to occur over the same period. Except for the managerial and professional classes, the net income satisfaction gained through geographical mobility seems to be minimal or negative.[40]

Without precise information on gains and losses in income and friendship for *each group* of movers (especially the unemployed), little can be said about the trade-off and even less about the "economic" value-weighing involved. But, in an odd sense, the "friendship market" seems to work better than the labor market. Those, except *possibly* the unemployed, who pursue friendship rather than income satisfaction are better off.

Friendship and income as complementary goods

When friendship and income are complementary, not substitute, goods, there is no trade-off. Under these circumstances it would seem to be a matter of indifference whether one pursues satisfaction in the friendship market (receiving income along the way) or pursues income in the labor market (receiving an incidental bonus of friendship). This situation solves several of the problems already mentioned: There is no problem of ordering preferences, for one receives both goods by the same act; there is no substitutability problem, for the two goods are joined; there is no trade-off problem, for the same reason. But common sense and research both suggest that the world is not so constructed. Why?

The reason is that making friends in order to make more money, and making money in order to "buy" friendship both spoil the friendship relationship. Making friends in order to make more money instrumentalizes the friendships; it is a form of interpersonal relations, called "Machiavellianism" in some studies, that leads to

---

[39] John B. Lansing and Eva Mueller, *The Geographic Mobility of Labor* (Ann Arbor, MI: Institute for Social Research, 1967).

[40] Studies of depressed areas have shown that those most likely to benefit economically from geographical mobility are the least likely to move. Chronic unemployment is slightly negatively related to actually moving, even when the unemployed person thinks there are better opportunities elsewhere. Ibid., Appendix D. If the sense of community is so crucially important in Appalachia as it seems to be, there is short-term rationality in the decision to remain in a region with high unemployment.

many acquaintances but few friends.[41] And Machiavellianism tends to lower life satisfaction.[42] On the other hand, making money in order to "buy" friendships often inhibits the friendship relationship because of the nature of the proposed exchange. Only friendly acts and feelings create enduring friendships. They cannot be bought with any other currency.[43] It is true that the rich have more friends than the poor, but the *pursuit* of one good to attain the other is likely to fail. If the market delivers both income and friendship at the same time, so much the better, but the complementarity of the two goods does not ensure this, for the way in which this felicitous bundle is sought makes a difference. Thus, complementarity does not relieve us of concern over the capacity of the market to maximize satisfaction.

Summary

In the sphere of production, we found that social comparisons, once they were stripped of competitiveness, were productive and economically fruitful; they do not suffer greatly by ethical criteria and are essential to evaluations of justice. In consumption, on the other hand, social comparisons are much more likely to be marked by invidiousness with little to recommend them.

Social comparisons are less prevalent than supposed in the market society, because, as revealed in "gap theory," there are so many other ways of establishing standards for evaluating one's relative position. And where they are present, the market society creates more occupational peaks and social roles that serve to multiply favorable comparisons; it also assigns to rank and status such loose associations that individuals are free to assign to themselves much higher social positions than would be assigned by objective criteria. To its shame, the market also creates an underclass of unemployed that gives to all others the ethically dubious pleasure of downward comparison.

The sense of well-being is more equally distributed than is income, largely, again, because in subjective perceptions the hedonic and egocentric biases lead these perceptions to triumph over other perceptions. Market inegalitarianism, therefore, is probably not a major obstacle to hedonic equality, but the issue is unresolved.

If one has to choose between working in a place with congenial workmates or working for a higher wage, one will increase one's satisfactions more by choosing the workmates, and decrease one's dissatisfaction more by choosing higher wage. But the test is which choice contributes more to overall life satisfaction, and in this case that test indicates that congenial workmates is the better choice. Unhappily, the informational and perceptual characteristics of market societies seem to favor choices with lower hedonic payoffs. Analysis of the effects on friendship and income of geographic mobility shows that people who move to seek to be closer to friends and family more often achieve these friendship/familial goals than those who move to increase their earnings achieve their income goals. But, since most

[41] Stanley S. Guterman, *The Machiavellians* (Lincoln: University of Nebraska Press, 1970), 59–62.
[42] Shaver and Freedman, "Your Pursuit of Happiness," 75.
[43] See, for example, George Levinger, "A Three-Level Approach to Attraction: Toward an Understanding of Pair Relatedness," in Ted L. Huston, ed. *Foundations of Interpersonal Attraction* (New York: Academic Press, 1974), 118.

people move for economic reasons, the net effect of geographic mobility in a market society is not felicitous. Where friendship and income are complementary goods, the pursuit of friendship as a product of income or of income as a product of friendship spoils the friendships thus sought.

Work

In Part V the concepts of cognitive complexity, personal control, and self-esteem developed in Parts II and III serve as criteria for assessing the role of work in a market economy. On the one hand, that role may be said to be the scandal of the market. In the world of work, we find uncertainty, anxiety, authoritarianism, waste of talent, and many lost opportunities that could have made work more fruitful. On the other hand, even now work is the market's principal contributor to both happiness and human development.

It is in work, not in consumption and, as research reports show, not even in leisure, where most people engage in the activities that they find most satisfying, where they learn to cope with their human and natural environments, and where they learn about themselves. The economists' ideas that work is the sacrifice or disutility that earns for workers the benefits or utilities of consumption is, I believe, quite false. But the idea that market forces systematically degrade work to increase profits is also false. What is true is that market forces systematically undermine worker satisfactions and learning in order to advance the interest, not so much of owners but of consumers. Consumers may not represent a ruling class, but they are sovereign and those who work are their subjects.

In the name of "efficiency," consumer benefits are purchased by the burdens laid on workers. It is a "purchase" without a purchaser. The implied tradeoff between consumer welfare and worker well-being is not chosen. One reason is that the market cannot weigh many of these sacrifices because they are unpriced. The second reason is that even if (somehow) they were priced in some sense by opportunity costs, there is no "market" wherein individuals may choose between, say, anxiety over cyclical unemployment and the benefits of more consumer durables. People do not buy economic systems or work cultures, they inherit them.

In Chapter 13 I will show how it is that work develops cognitive complexity, personal control, and self-esteem, as well as such qualities as democratic orientations, sympathy for the weaker members of a work force, and an appreciation of self-direction. Chapter 14 deals with allegations that the market systematically degrades work by its focus on the petty details of life, or by exploitation, or by making workers into robots. In Chapter 15 I analyze the allocation of costs of increased work benefits, the way market work contributes to the stratification of a population, how internal labor markets function in situations where they are either more or less sheltered from competition, and how the market rescues people from the world we have (almost) lost, farm work and housework. Finally, in Chapter 16, I analyze the effects on work of three market forces – the efficiency norm, competition, and the division of labor – concluding with a cool appraisal of the *producer economy* where work is given priority over consumption.

13 Learning at work: beyond human capital

The germs of the education of the future are to be found in the factory system. This will be an education which, in the case of every child over a certain age, will combine productive labor with instruction and physical culture, not only as a means of increasing social production, but as the only way of producing fully developed human beings.

Karl Marx, Capital

Introduction

What do working activities contribute to happiness and human development? I must defer the discussion of happiness through work to Part VI, however, in this chapter I will report research showing how selected work practices alter world views, improve cognitive complexity, impart a sense of personal control, and enhance self-esteem. Rather than change occupational values, work experience tends to reinforce those values held prior to work and sometimes to stimulate curiosity about the world outside the work setting, increase empathy for the weaker members of a work team, and lead to more challenging leisure activities. For the sake of simplicity, I will call the acquisition of these values and insights by the simple, but here specialized, term of *workplace learning* or simply *learning*.

The initial discussion of the concept of work is useful as a contribution to clarity, of course, but it has the added advantage that it facilitates dealing with the sometimes vague border between work and leisure, and so will help us later to treat an idea competing with our notion of work as the source of fulfillment, namely, that it is in their leisure, not their work, that people fulfill themselves. The resulting definitions are followed by two features of the current context: declining productivity, on the one hand, and the sense of a "crisis" in the way work influences workers, on the other.

The central contribution of the chapter lies in the second section, which contains empirical analyses on which my claims about the effect of work on personality are based.[1] With the help of this evidence and by enlisting other empirical studies we are then in a position to appraise the humanistic and socialist standards for what work should do to and for a working person, for example, how to engage nature and other people, how to interpret the environment, and, most important, who it is that does and learns these things, that is, the identity of the worker. The successes and failures of market work as judged by these standards is presented in the last section.

---

[1] For reviews of adult socialization putting work learning in context, see Orville G. Brim and Stanley Wheeler, *Socialization after Adulthood* (New York: Wiley, 1965); Jeyland T. Mortimer and Roberta Simmons, "Adult Socialization," in Ralph Turner, ed, *Annual Review of Sociology* 4 (1978).

The concept of work

As always, definitions are normative. Definitions of work sometimes designate a meaning by contrasting "work" to something else: "play," "idleness," "unremunerated activity," "leisure." Each contrast provides a norm: If to "play," the contrast suggests that work is sober, not enjoyable. The distinction between play and work is neither necessary nor logical; for example, this distinction is not present among Australian aborigines. If the contrast is to "idleness," work is given a virtuous connotation; if to "unremunerated activity," as in "paid employment," the importance of extrinsic rewards are exaggerated and the intrinsic value of work is lost from sight; if to "leisure," especially if leisure is defined as "psychologically free time," then, by contrast, obligation or time pressure enters the definition. Work has been defined as "an activity that provides something of value to other people,"[2] thus including unremunerated housework – but not in a household of one as in Robinson Crusoe's household before Friday's entrance converted what Crusoe did into "work." For economists, "labor is usually thought of in an inverted, positive sense as a disutility." The reason is that "labor" is really the sacrifice of some desirable alternative use of one's time and strength.[3] But this reliance on opportunity costs makes every activity "labor," for every activity has an opportunity cost.

Richard Hall suggests the need for the inclusion of a subjective definition. In order to be work 'it must also be considered work by the individual so involved.'[4] There is some merit to this, as an example from the "hidden cost of rewards" literature (to be considered in Chapter 18) makes clear: The same activity produces very different responses among subjects according to whether the experimenter calls it "a puzzle" (when it is regarded as enjoyable and voluntary), "help to another" (when it engages altruism), "a test" (when it arouses mild anxiety and, among middle-class respondents, maximum effort), or "a chore," that is, in the vernacular, "work."[5] Here we adopt Hall's definition, modified to embrace work for the self: "Work is the effort or activity an individual performs for the purpose of providing goods or services of value to others *or the self* and it is also considered to be work by the individual so involved."

The important point is to disengage the concept of work from the concepts of pain or disutility. The difference between work and play turns on the product – the provision of goods and services – not the pain and pleasure involved.

The crisis in work

In a humanistic vein, David Meakin speaks of "a crisis of conscience in the world of work" and of the recent "powerful and vivid indictment of a world that has

[2] U.S. Department of Health, Education, and Welfare (HEW), Special Task Force, *Work in America* (Cambridge: M.I.T. Press, n.d. [c1972]), 31.

[3] Frank Knight, *Risk, Uncertainty, and Profits* (1921; reprint Chicago: University of Chicago Press, 1971), 63.

[4] Richard H. Hall, *Dimensions of Work* (Beverly Hills, CA: Sage, 1986), 13.

[5] Mark R. Lepper and David Greene, "Divergent Approaches to the Study of Rewards," in Lepper and Greene, eds., *The Hidden Costs of Rewards: New Perspectives on the Psychology of Human Motivation* (Hillsdale, NJ: Erlbaum/Wiley, 1987), 238.

degraded work.''[6] The indictment has two principal appeals, a humanistic one and an economic one. (1) The humanistic charge is that the experience of work is both alienating and degrading, or at least fails to develop the talents and personalities of workers; (2) the economic one is that, for these and other reasons, the quality of work products and economic productivity suffer. In this section, except for a brief outline of the economic argument, we will consider mainly the humanistic charge.

The humanistic argument has two main branches: (1) work in a market society is destructive to the human personality, minimally by failing to develop talents and humane values, worse, by eroding the talents, curiosity, ethical codes, spiritedness, and goodwill either given by nature or learned from other experiences; and (2) work has lost, or not achieved, its potential intrinsic appeal, its enjoyable exercise of skill, knowledge, and effort (see Part VI).

A group of specialists on work in the 1970s seemed to confirm these criticisms. They outlined a set of "blue-collar blues": Work frustrations make these workers aggressive (an aggressiveness they take home with them); they feel "locked in," unable to use their hard won credentials and skills, devalued, and, for the lowest in status, they confront an "atmosphere of failure." Nor are the "white-collar woes" much better: Often working in great bureaucracies,[7] white-collar workers resent their impersonal treatment, low pay, repetitive work, and their lack of participation in the decisions that affect them.[8]

These criticisms are held in check by a heightened concern for productivity that is thought to be jeopardized by attention to the intrinsic and educational values of work. The context for this concern, bordering on alarm, is declining economic productivity. Inevitably, it is this economistic version that claims first attention in our market society. By the middle of the 1980s, American (and British) economic productivity had been virtually static for about fifteen years. Furthermore, defective quality and inferior design opened the door to successful foreign competition. Whereas most analysts deprecate explanations relying on a decline of the work ethic, and many alternative, strictly economic explanations have been offered,[9] some observers link the failure to achieve productivity increases to the kind of humanistic arguments just mentioned. As a result of the failure to offer intrinsically satisfying jobs, say two survey analysts, "many job holders are holding back from their jobs, and quality suffers accordingly. . . . Fewer than one out of four jobholders (23%) say that they are currently working at their full potential. Nearly half of all jobholders (44%) say that they do not put much effort into their jobs over and above what

[6] David Meakin, *Man and Work: Literature and Culture in Industrial Society* (London: Methuen, 1976), 1, 182. It should be noted that Meakin is more interested in work enjoyment than in learning at work.
[7] C. Wright Mills called their location a "giant salesroom." C. Wright Mills, *White Collar* (New York: Oxford University Press, 1951).
[8] HEW Task Force, *Work in America,* chap. 2.
[9] See Edward F. Denison, *Trends in American Economic Growth, 1929–1982* (Washington, DC: Brookings Institution, 1985); Robert H. Hayes and William J. Abernathy, "Managing Our Way to Economic Decline," *Harvard Business Review* 58 (1980); Robert B. Reich, *The Next American Frontier* (New York: New York Times Books, 1983), in which Chapter 8 is entitled "Paper Entrepreneurialism." Martin Neil Baily and Alok K. Chakrabarti, *Innovation and the Productivity Crisis* (Washington, DC: Brookings Institution, 1988).

is required to hold on to a job. The overwhelming majority (75%) say that they could be significantly more effective on their jobs than they are now.''[10] Is this lack of commitment and involvement in work, the loss of learning involved, and an apparently low hedonic value of work due in some way to the way the market economy treats work?

Learning at work: effects on cognition and personality

The idea that work is the source of personal development, as contrasted to good character, is generally alien to the history of thought about work, but in recent years that idea has received considerable support. The implied learning may be very broad indeed: "Occupational experience, we believe, helps structure one's view not only of the occupational world but of the social world generally."[11] And it may be deep, in the sense that what is learned becomes part of the worker's personality, establishing a reciprocal relationship between work and personality where each affects the other.[12]

Five studies reveal different facets of the way workers learn from their work experiences. I present the studies briefly before employing their findings in an evaluation of learning from market work.

The effect of task experience on personal and social orientations

In an experimental study, Breer and Locke sought to assess the influence of various kinds of work on social attitudes. Their hypothesis was that "orientations will be generalized to other task situations, and, through the process of induction, to the level of cultural beliefs, preferences, and values."[13] They obtained initial measures of various student attitudes among which an individualism–collectivism dimension was the most important, organized a set of tasks in class and laboratory settings, and remeasured the same attitudes after the task, a week later and again three weeks later. The measures of individualism–collectivism included such items as: "In the ideal society each individual would be willing to put the interests of society as a whole above his personal needs," and "A man's first duty should be to himself and only secondarily to his fellow man." These kinds of statements were developed for a variety of areas of life, such as small groups, the society as a whole, the family, fraternities, and general ways of life (as in the illustrative items). The tasks, in five different experiments, included erector assembly, jigsaw puzzles, crossword puz-

[10] Daniel Yankelovich and John Immerwahr, *Putting the Work Ethic to Work* (New York: The Public Agenda Foundation, 1983), 2–3. The surveys on which these figures are based took place in 1982; the national sample of 845 respondents was composed of people eighteen years of age or older working for pay more than twenty hours a week; it was weighted according to sex and occupational level.

[11] Leonard I. Pearlin and Melvin L. Kohn, "Social Class, Occupation, and Parental Values: A Cross-Cultural Study," *American Sociological Review* 31 (1966): 466–79 at 477.

[12] Greg R. Oldham and J. Richard Hackman, "Relationships Between Organizational Structure and Employer Reactions: Comparing Alternative Frameworks," *Administrative Science Quarterly* 28 (1981): 66–83.

[13] Paul E. Breer and Edwin A. Locke, *Task Experience as a Source of Attitudes* (Homewood, IL: Dorsey Press, 1965).

zles, brainstorming, predicting opinions. Some were designed so that individual performance was more efficient, and others so that collective or group performance was more efficient. The main variation along the individual–collective dimension was rewards for individual performance as contrasted to rewards for group performance.[14]

When the researchers remeasured the orientations of their student subjects, they found that whatever the original individual–collective orientation of the students had been before they participated in the tasks, they tended, when dealing with matters quite irrelevant to the task itself, to move toward the individualistic orientation if they had been rewarded for individual performance, and toward the collectivistic orientation if their groups had been rewarded for group performance. That is, beliefs and preferences that are thought to be the products of early socialization and to reflect long-standing economic interests are, in fact, easily shaped by work experience. With more or less supporting evidence on such other dimensions of thought as theism, egalitarianism, and achievement orientation, the authors conclude that it is work experiences much more than interests or early socialization that shape basic orientations toward life.

The effect of job content on intellectual functioning and personality
In an extensive longitudinal study of a national sample of 785 men employed in civilian occupations, Kohn and Schooler analyzed in detail the work content of their individual occupations and a set of cognitive and attitudinal features of the workers. Their orienting "thesis is that occupational experience has a real and substantial impact upon men's psychological functioning."[15] With respect to the work content, they noted whether the workers worked with things, people, or data (ideas); whether in each case the work was varied or routine, closely or loosely supervised, complex and intellectually challenging or simple, "dirty" or "clean;" whether or not and where it was located in a bureaucratic setting (three or more levels of hierarchy); whether there were job pressures of various kinds, and risks. With respect to the properties of the workers, the researchers measured cognitive performance ("intellectual flexibility"), attitudes toward self-direction, conformity and independence, self-concepts, anxiety levels, attitudes toward change, sense of moral responsibility for one's own acts, respondents' use of leisure time, as well as the usual background variables.

The authors reinterviewed their respondents again ten years later (1974), providing formidable evidence on the causal direction of the association between occupa-

---

[14] To a limited degree this line of thinking is supported by experiments on cooperation and competition, that is, members of groups under the cooperative condition tend to be more egalitarian, and to like themselves and each other better than members of groups in the competitive condition. See Morton Deutsch, *Distributive Justice: A Social Psychological Perspective* (New Haven: Yale University Press, 1985), 158–96.

[15] Melvin L. Kohn and Carmi Schooler, *Work and Personality: An Inquiry into the Impact of Social Stratification* (Norwood, NJ: Ablex, 1983), 55. For a less precise accounting of the same phenomena in a command economy, see Frank Adler, "Work and Personality Development in the German Democratic Republic," *International Social Science Journal* 32 (1980): 443–63.

tion and psychological functioning. With information on job characteristics and psychological functioning in both 1964 and 1974 and background information on both the workers and their parents, it was possible to rule out artifactual relationships. Among other findings, the following are salient:

1. "The substantive complexity of work stands as the keystone of the entire jobs structure – affected by and in turn affecting many other job conditions. . . . [It] is at the core of highly placed, responsible, demanding but rewarding jobs."[16]

2. The substantive complexity of job content (lack of close supervision and routinization of work, and challenging work offering discretion in its execution) has a measured effect on "intellectual flexibility" or, in more familiar terms, cognitive complexity. An occupation that requires self-direction does not merely recruit intellectually more flexible workers, it develops those cognitive powers of the workers as well.[17] That is, the relation between intellectual flexibility and complex work content is "truly reciprocal": People with more flexible and sharper minds are attracted to and select jobs that require intelligence (as has long been supposed) *and* those kinds of jobs actually make people more intellectually alert and flexible.

3. "Self-directedness," the desire to be self-directed in one's work, is caused by (and is a cause of) having a job that permits self-direction; it is associated with intellectual flexibility, lack of distress on the job, self-confidence, and self-esteem. Self-directedness at an earlier time leads to higher income at a later time. It is also associated with nonauthoritarianism, assumption of moral responsibility for one's own acts, trust in others, self-esteem, and lower anxiety.[18] Like the role of substantive complexity in the job conditions, among the psychological variables, self-directedness, not cognitive complexity, is pivotal: "If one of the three dimensions of personality ["ideational flexibility," feelings of distress (e.g., anxiety, low self-esteem), and self-directedness] is pivotal, it is self-directedness."[19]

4. Conversely, "doing work of little substantive complexity is not only associated with but actually causes feelings of alienation."[20]

5. "Men's ways of coping with the realities of their jobs are generalized to nonoccupational realities. Men whose jobs require intellectual flexibility, for example, come not only to exercise their intellectual prowess on the job but also to engage in intellectually demanding leisure time activities."[21]

This sample of findings powerfully reinforces Breer and Locke's conclusions on the effect of actual work processes on social and personal orientations – and adds the important new evidence on mental functioning. As Marx suggested,[22] the factory and other workplaces are schools, offering elements of a stimulating education for some and vacuity for others.

[16] Kohn and Schooler, *Work and Personality,* 136.
[17] Ibid., 77, 118.
[18] Ibid., 142, 148.
[19] Ibid., 150.
[20] Ibid., 18.
[21] Ibid., 81.
[22] Karl Marx, *Capital,* trans. from 4th Ger. ed. (1867) by Eden Paul and Cedar Paul (1887; reprint New York: Dutton Everyman, 1972), 522 (see chapter opening epigraph).

The effect of work experience on occupational values

In a longitudinal study influenced by Kohn and Schooler, Mortimer and Lorence examined the effect of occupational orientations in 1966–7, when their 512 male respondents were in college, on occupational position ten years later in 1976. More importantly, they analyzed the effects of that later occupational experience on the values previously measured when the respondents were in college. The 1966–7 inquiry classified occupational orientation along three dimensions, the first regarded as extrinsic and the second two as intrinsic, that is, related to what a person would actually do on a job. The three dimensions were (1) income-maximizing values; (2) "people-orientation," emphasizing working with or on behalf of other people; and (3) a preference for jobs offering intellectual challenge and autonomy. The content of what the respondents actually did on the jobs they held in 1976 was analyzed along the same three dimensions: (1) jobs whose contents were described by respondents primarily in terms of the high pay; (2) jobs, such as teaching or social work, characterized as primarily dealing with people; and (3) jobs, such as research or sometimes law (depending on what the occupants emphasized), characterized by their "autonomy," innovative thinking, degree of challenge, and latitude in decision making. The respondents again answered questions on their occupational values.

Holding constant background variables (family income and education) these authors found that respondents generally held positions matching their preferences and in two out of the three cases these positions reinforced or strengthened the values they held earlier. But significant differences were found in the way these job experiences seemed to affect the respondents' subordinate earlier values:

1. Having a job with high income increased the value of income but *decreased* a person's previous concern for people and for intellectual challenge.
2. Having a job offering autonomy and challenge increased these values and *increased* a person's previous concern for people.
3. Having a job involving work with people did not affect the strength of any of the earlier values, including the people-oriented values that led to taking the job in the first place.

The authors note that, given this process of value reinforcement, over time people should find the personality–occupation fit more congenial, a fact that helps to explain the positive relationship between job satisfaction and age. They also observe that the common finding that members of the middle class are more interested in intrinsic occupational values than members of the working class is partially explained by the tendency for people to value the qualities of the jobs they have, that is, because middle-class workers already have jobs that offer more intrinsic values, by preferring what they have they will also prefer these intrinsic values.[23] Pushing the analysis back to the parental generation, Mortimer (in another study) found that parental occupational experience, similarly reinforced by their own job experiences,

[23] Jeylan T. Mortimer and Jon Lorence, "Work Experience and Occupational Value Socialization: A Longitudinal Study," *American Journal of Sociology* 84 (1979): 1,361–85.

produced values that were in turn transmitted to the children.[24] Put differently, these findings reveal another way in which the market reproduces itself.

The effect of factory work on personality in less developed countries
In the late 1960s Alex Inkeles, with his coworker David Smith, studied the effect of such modernizing institutions as urbanism, mass media, and, especially, factory work on respondents in six developing countries: Argentina, Chile, East Pakistan (now Bangladesh), India, Israel [Eastern Jews], and Nigeria. Their main premise was that "individuals would incorporate into their own value systems the principles predominant in guiding the operation of the institutions in which they are employed."[25] Modernizing institutions," they say, "need individuals who can keep to fixed schedules, observe abstract rules, make judgments on the basis of objective evidence," have higher aspirations for themselves, are open to new experiences, tolerate diversity, believe that they themselves can partially control their own environments, and have respect for the dignity of others. This complex of attitudes, of which belief in individual efficacy may be the most important, is called *individual modernity*. By comparing the attitudes and values of those working in these modernizing institutions, more especially those working in factories, with the attitudes and values of those "left behind" in the traditional villages from which the factory workers came, the authors were able to infer something about the effects of the institutions.

The authors found that almost all the attitudes and values mentioned were, in fact, enhanced by immersion in modernizing institutions. Although the varied cultures of the countries studied affected levels of individual modernity, they had a negligible effect on the process or·direction of change. Of all the institutions studied, schools and factories made the largest contribution to the development of the values and opinions mentioned. In fact, in each of the six countries studied, factory work contributed more to individual modernity than did level of education.[26] This view is supported by Harold Wilensky's work. Wilensky says, "It is clear that *occupational cultures* (rooted in common tasks, work schedules, job training, and career patterns) are sometimes better predictors of behavior than both social class and pre-job experience."[27]

In Inkeles and Smith's study, unlike the findings of Kohn and Schooler, the kind of work was not important, nor did the findings vary much from plant to plant

[24] Jeylan T. Mortimer, "Intergenerational Occupational Movement," *American Journal of Sociology* 79 (1974): 1,278–99.
[25] Alex Inkeles and David H. Smith, *Becoming Modern* (Cambridge: Harvard University Press, 1974), 4, 307. For a criticism of the methods of this work, see Michael Armer and Dallen Schnaiberg, "Measuring Individual Modernity: A Near Myth," *American Sociological Review* 37 (1972): 301–16. For a (to me convincing) defense, see Alex Inkeles, "Understanding and Misunderstanding Individual Modernity," *Journal of Cross-Cultural Psychology* 8 (1977): 135–76; and Richard M. Suzman, "Psychological Modernity," *International Journal of Comparative Sociology* 14, nos. 3–4 (1973): 273–87.
[26] Alex Inkeles, "The School as a Context for Modernization," *International Journal of Comparative Sociology* 14, nos. 3–4 (1973): 163–79 at 170.
[27] Harold L. Wilensky, "The Uneven Distribution of Leisure: The Impact of Economic Growth on 'Free Time,' " *Social Problems* 9 (1961): 32–56 at 52.

within a country. The process of change, then, was induced by industrial requirements reflected in the norms and practices of factory life itself. As the authors put
it, "Insofar as men change under the influence of modernizing institutions they do
so by incorporating the norms implicit in such organizations into their own personalities, and by expressing those norms through their own attitudes, values, and
behavior."[28]

Significantly, Inkeles and Smith found very little resistance to the industrial order
in their samples of largely factory workers; rather, these third world workers seem
to have decided to work with the new order and use it. In contrast to what might
have been thought to have been a comparable experience by British workers in the
late eighteenth and early nineteenth centuries, the cost in anxiety and well-being
was not high among the modernizing workers; there were, for example, no differences between the modernizing group and the traditional village group in the telltale
psychosomatic symptoms indicating psychic disturbances. Neither the size of the
factory, nor the length of the period worked, nor the migration from village to urban
factory had any systematic effect on these measures of strain.[29]

In line with Kohn and Schooler's reports on self-directedness, we turn to a comparable concept, "sense of personal efficacy," in Inkeles and Smith, modified to
capture the prevalent fatalism in less developed societies. Such questions as the
following were used to assess efficacy: "Some say that getting ahead in life depends
on destiny. Others say that it depends on the person's own efforts. Do you think the
position a man reaches in life depends more on fate or more on one's own efforts?"
"Some say that accidents are due mainly to bad luck. Others say accidents can be
prevented by sufficient care. Do you think prevention of accidents depends: Entirely
on luck? Mainly on luck? Mainly on carefulness? Entirely on carefulness?"[30] For
reasons that seemed to include some inference that because the factory was so powerful its individual members were also powerful, and to point to the use of effective
models among foremen and engineers, length of time in the factory was positively
and strongly correlated with a measure of overall individual modernity embracing
the sense of personal efficacy.[31]

For Kohn and Schooler, as for other students of work in modern society, routinized, closely supervised, repetitive, and dirty jobs are alienating and seem to encourage authoritarianism and moral irresponsibility as well. Although Inkeles and
Smith's study relied on factory norms to educate workers, their failure to find job
content effects is puzzling. One reason that Inkeles and Smith do not focus more
closely on the *kinds* of work people do is because they found that different kinds of
factories did not influence their findings,[32] but this observation does not penetrate

[28] Inkeles and Smith, *Becoming Modern*, 307.
[29] Ibid., 261–4.
[30] Ibid., 328.
[31] Ibid., 158–9, 166, 168. These findings are reported with some hesitancy, since the inference is based
on the high correlation between efficacy measures and the score on the overall individual modernity
measure, which in turn is correlated significantly (.001) with factory experience. Clearly there is room
for much slippage either way in this procedure.
[32] Ibid., 7.

various job contents within these plants, and there is evidence in another study by Inkeles that the kind of work done in the factory does make a difference, at least in attitudes.[33]

For our purposes, the importance of Inkeles and Smith's study is to show that at least in less developed countries, the factory per se is a kind of school for learning such things as temporal discipline, the value of individual initiative and responsibility, the assessment of persons by what they do rather than by lineage, looking beyond parochial horizons, and, it seems, empathic relations with weaker others, and above all, personal efficacy.

Early work experience and adult functioning

A study by two data-conscious psychiatrists, George and Caroline Vaillant, provides us with clues to the influence of early work experience (including studying harder than others) on adult attitudes and functioning. Almost confirming Carlyle's claim that "work is the grand cure for all the maladies and miseries that beset mankind," the Vaillants first report on previous research. "We are continually confronted," they say, "by the fact that prior work history is one of the most powerful predictors of recovery from schizophrenia, from drug addiction, from delinquency, and from alcoholism. . . . At least statistically if not in every case, capacity to work correlates highly with both mental health and capacity to love. . . . Job satisfaction, job stability, . . . employment, and income all appear highly associated with mental health."[34] Compared to welfare, even criminal work contributes more to successful therapy.[35] But, of course, correlational studies do not reveal the direction of causal forces.

In order to remedy this, the Vaillants reexamined (c. 1981) a group of 392 adults about age forty-seven who had been intensively studied more than thirty years earlier when they were about age fourteen. At this earlier period they were tested by measures intended to assess what Erikson has called "Stage Four competence," that is, in Erikson's terms, "the free exercise . . . of dexterity and intelligence in the completion of serious tasks. Such competence," Erikson said, "is the basis for

[33] In an earlier study analyzing the same data, Inkeles reports that a measure of political alienation, political participation, is significantly and positively related to total time spent in a factory and number of factories worked in, suggesting that type of job is not important for political alienation. On the other hand, a reverse indicator of alienation is positively related to objective skill and kind of occupation – the more complex the occupation the more politically engaged (less politically alienated) the worker. We cannot rule out the possibility that those with jobs demanding the least skill, discretion, and autonomy are, even by the surrogate measure employed, the most alienated. See Alex Inkeles, "Participant Citizenship in Six Developing Countries," *American Political Science Review* 63, no. 3 (1969): 1,120–41, especially Table 3. The data further show that being politically active is not consistently related, either positively or negatively, to lack of anomie or lack of group hostility or sense of government effectiveness, that is, to alternative indices of alienation. This leaves open the possibility that other forms of alienation are also related to job content.

[34] George E. Vaillant and Caroline O. Vaillant, "Natural History of Male Psychological Health: Work as a Predictor of Positive Mental Health," *American Journal of Psychiatry* 138 (1981): 1,433–40 at 1,434–5.

[35] See the subsequent report of the uses of work as therapy for drug addiction in *Psychology Today* 16 (April 1982): 18.

cooperative participation in . . . the culture.''[36] The earlier study used a variety of measures to indicate this competence, but the most predictive of later life success were measures of work experience (holding a part-time job or performing regular chores at home) or significant engagement in extracurricular, purposeful activities, or performance in school work (which *is* *work*) beyond what was predicted for a person's measured abilities. These are measures of *activities* requiring a kind of commitment – and not measures intended to assess abilities or attitudes. Intelligence quotients were, over the long period, irrelevant to the outcomes of this study, as were, for the most part, various measured environmental factors. "Of all the childhood measures chosen," report the Vaillants, "the scale reflecting success at Stage Four tasks [i.e., the completion of serious tasks] correlated with adult adjustment most robustly.''[37] In a later interview with a reporter from the *New York Times,* the Vaillants are quoted as saying: "The willingness and capacity to work in childhood is the most important forerunner – more important than native intelligence, social class, or family situation – of mental health.''[38] Whereas the Vaillants' research procedures do not rule out the possibility that underlying personality factors explain both work engagement and success at the earlier stage and personality adjustment at the later stage, their study indicates that whatever these third factors may be, work experience is a valuable mediator for later adjustment.

Six observations on the Vaillants' study are in order. First, observe that in this study no distinctions are made between alienating work and nonalienating work. For the sixteen-year-old, part-time jobs and work chores at home may well seem "alienating," whatever their character. Second, the increase in proportion of youth ages sixteen to nineteen who are both enrolled in school *and* have part-time jobs has recently increased, at least from 1960 to 1979,[39] suggesting that benefits of early work experience are actually increasing. Third, the high and static (at least 1960–79)[40] incidence of unemployment among youth not in school has even more serious long-term effects than have been supposed. Fourth, the low level of challenge and self-direction in entry jobs available to youth may not develop the kind of cognitive skills that Kohn and Schooler have found to be associated with self-directed work, but, compared to those who do not "work" in their youth, it apparently teaches something else: perseveration and a belief in one's own powers to master some of life's challenges. Fifth, although many of the studies focused on

[36] Vaillant and Vaillant, "Natural History of Male Psychological Health," 1,436, reporting on Erik Erikson, "Identity, Psychosocial," *International Encyclopedia of the Social Sciences,* vol. 7 (New York: Macmillan/Free Press, 1968), 61–5.

[37] Vaillant and Vaillant, "Natural History of Male Psychological Health," 1,438. The Vaillants urge various caveats. Leisure uses as well as work are important: " 'Creative vacations' predict mental health as well as work success"; and "capacity for work must be tempered by capacity for empathy." Ibid., 1,438. See also Ellen Greenberger and Lawrence Steinberg, *When Teenagers Work: Psychological and Social Costs of Adolescent Employment* (New York: Basic Books, 1986).

[38] *New York Times,* 10 November 1981, pp. 1, 4.

[39] Victor R. Fuchs, *How We Live* (Cambridge: Harvard University Press, 1983), 93, 100, 254. The proportion of the age group employed who were in school was 37.1% for white males and 23.6% for white females in 1960 and, respectively, 42.2% and 41.7% in 1979, with somewhat fewer nonwhites of both sexes.

[40] Ibid., 99, 253.

males, in general, female workers learn and respond in the same ways.[41] Sixth, a "need to work," although here confounded with the need to earn, gains marginal support from these data.

The process of learning

The process of learning from occupational experience is, like all learning, complex. In the first place, those who set out to learn, rather than merely to perform, develop a self-mastery orientation toward their work as contrasted to a more helpless orientation.[42] Almost none of the process of learning follows the conditioned learning paradigm summarized by the term *stimulus–response,* and almost all rewards operate antecedently through anticipation rather than automatically. The mind, often through the use of verbal symbols, mediates between stimulus and response; learning at work as elsewhere is a cognitive process.[43] Moreover, learning from others is said to be more important than the immediate experience: "Virtually all learning from direct experience occurs on a vicarious basis by observing people's behavior and its consequences."[44] And this is true specifically of work: "Much of the human skill acquisition did not occur in formal education and training, but from one worker to another."[45] The rewards offered by the employer may or may not be salient features of learning, for what is learned depends as much on "self-regulation" as on extrinsic rewards. Self-regulation "refers to a process in which individuals enhance and maintain their own behavior by rewarding themselves with rewards that they control whenever they attain self-prescribed standards. . . . [They] require relational comparisons of at least three sources of information: absolute standards [in this case, employer's or market standards], one's own personal standards, and a social referent."[46] And, at least above the subsistence level, pay or other work rewards are likely to be more important for their informational values than for their material values.

In all of these studies we see the process of *generalization* at work. This process is what makes occupational learning much more than enhancing human capital, for through generalization what is learned at work influences the specific features of human development we have identified. Like Adam Smith, although with a different perspective, Alfred Marshall held that "the business by which a person earns his livelihood fills his thoughts during by far the greatest part of those hours in which his mind is at its best: during them his character is being formed by the ways in which he uses his faculties at work."[47] For example, as in the Kohn and Schooler studies when a worker learns cognitive complexity, a sense of personal control, and self-esteem on the job, these do not evaporate when the worker leaves the job. The

[41] See Joanne Miller, Carmi Schooler, Melvin Kohn, and Karen A. Miller, "Women and Work: The Psychological Effects of Occupational Conditions," *American Journal of Sociology* 85 (1979): 66–94.
[42] Elaine S. Elliott and Carol S. Dweck, "Goals: An Approach to Motivation and Achievement," *Journal of Personality and Social Psychology* 54 (1988): 5–12.
[43] Albert Bandura, *Social Learning Theory* (Englewood Cliffs, NJ: Prentice-Hall, 1977).
[44] Ibid., 12.
[45] Lester Thurow, "Economics 1977," *Daedalus* 106 (Fall 1977): 80. Thurow points out that this kind of learning is hard for the government to foster.
[46] Ibid., 130–1.
[47] Alfred Marshall, *Principles of Economics,* 8th ed. (London: Macmillan, 1938), 1–2.

Breer and Locke study was specifically addressed to this problem. What was learned experientially (and not through precepts) and rewarded at work, shaped attitudes toward things very remote from work: People in cooperative jobs at work thought of the world as more of a cooperative place than those who were rewarded for competitive behavior at work. The Vaillants' study was also specifically addressed to this point of generalization. People who learned qualities of commitment and perseveration at work embodied these qualities in their marital life. In the Kohn and Schooler study again, the preference for challenging, self-directed work "spilled over" into preferences for more challenging leisure activities. This partial cross-domain application of what is learned in one situation to another situation is the definition of that much debated quality, a *personality trait*. But all the studies caution that the work experiences studied make up only one contribution to such trait formation; early socialization and parental values always affect and sometimes dominate trait formation; educational experiences and level are usually equally important. Thus the reverse of these positive findings may or may not be true. If these qualities are undermined on the job they may yet be learned from other socialization experiences, although one can speculate that they will be learned, if at all, with greater difficulty under these circumstances. Like many other studies, Inkeles's work highlights the variation in learning due to cultural variation in the six countries included in his study.[48]

Later we will examine both the psychological and institutional barriers to generalization across domains of life, but at least one contemporary author with considerable evidence at his command supports Marx's view of the effects of work alienation. Melvin Seeman observes, "The price we pay for alienated labor is not simply denial of personal fulfillment, but the further trouble it generates in social life – i.e., political hostilities, frenetic leisure, social movements, race cleavages, and the like." He also notes that "the lack of control in work leads to a sense of low control in political and social affairs; the hostility bred in work situations overflows into intergroup antagonism."[49]

The competing hypothesis that people *compensate* in their leisure time for those qualities of life missing at work (a boring job leads to the search for excitment) also has some support. For example, some French postal clerks with routine jobs engage in especially active leisure activities.[50] Other research reveals how attitudes toward one's work mediates these influences,[51] but the important point for our purposes is that the influence of the market in structuring work reaches into niches and crevices of life themselves protected from direct market influences.

[48] Alex Inkeles, "Nationality Differences in Individual Modernity," in Richard F. Tomasson, ed., *Comparative Studies in Sociology*, vol. I (Greenwich, CT: JAI Press, 1978). See also Ronald Inglehart and Jacques-Rene Rabier, "Aspirations Adapt to Situations – But Why Are the Belgians So Much Happier than the French? A Cross-Cultural Analysis of the Subjective Quality of Life," in Frank M. Andrews, ed., *Research on the Quality of Life* (Ann Arbor, MI: Institute for Social Research, 1986).

[49] Melvin Seeman, "On the Personal Consequences of Alienation in Work," *American Sociological Review* 32 (1967): 273–85.

[50] Michel Crozier, *Petit Fonctionaires au Travail* (Paris: Centre Nationale de la Recherche Scientifique, 1955).

[51] Joseph F. Champoux, "Perceptions of Work and Nonwork: A Reexamination of the Compensatory and Spillover Models," *Sociology of Work and Occupations* 5 (1978): 402–22.

The features of the work experiences explored in the five studies that affected learning varied: In Mortimer and Lorence and in Kohn and Schooler it was the content of the work itself, especially the degree of self-direction at work; in Breer and Locke the individualistic or collective nature of the work for which subjects were rewarded shaped the attitudes that were later generalized to other life domains. The setting is part of the tuition: In Inkeles and Smith the norms of the factory as a whole seemed to be the tutoring feature of work, and in Kohn and Schooler the degree of bureaucracy and the level within that bureaucracy were some of the environmental features of work that affected learning.[52] In the Vaillants' study the setting might be school or out-of-school work, but wherever the work took place it was the experience of perseveration and application to work that formed the basis of later achievements and adjustments. Because the experience of work is manifold, its teachings are also manifold.

Humanistic criteria and learning from work

Most work teaches some skills and basic norms – punctuality, conformity to rules, minimal social competence – but these are not the features of learning that engage the interest of the humanist critics of work. Rather, these critics raise the level of their observations to more fundamental aspects of cognition, attitudes, and values, thereby establishing standards for what work can and should do. Here we undertake a series of evaluations of market work at this more fundamental level. For example: How does the kind of work found in market societies teach people to relate to nature and to each other? How does it help them to understand the world around them and, more especially, their own selves? Profound as these questions are, they often imply stereotypical impressions of market work, impressions that may be corrected or confirmed by the research we have just examined and other cognate studies.

Work is an engagement with nature
The proposition that work teaches people to relate to nature and to each other raises issues of the harmony between man and nature and the value of manual work, each of which offers problems. For William Morris manual work was a way of uniting with nature, creating a harmony between humans and their environment.[53] Farmers enjoy this experience; so may carpenters and, in a different sense, machinists. In Studs Terkel's *Working,* it was a mason who took the greatest satisfaction in the products of his work.[54] For George Orwell working with one's hands was not so much a device for uniting with nature as a means of expanding one's consciousness:

---

[52] In these accounts we miss the group induction of counterproductive norms familiar in American industry ("making out," punishing "rate busters," etc.). See Michael Burroway, *Manufacturing Consent: Changes in the Labor Process under Monopoly Capitalism* (Chicago: University of Chicago Press, 1979); David Halle, *America's Working Man: Work, Home and Politics among Blue-Collar Property Owners* (Chicago: University of Chicago Press, 1984).

[53] Meakin, *Man and Work,* 7–8, citing William Morris, *News from Nowhere.* Note that the ecologists cite the ecological problems of the current "crisis," but not the learning problems.

[54] Studs Terkel, *Working* (New York: Avon, 1975), 17–21.

"Cease to use your hands and you have lopped off a huge chunk of your conscious-ness."[55]

If these inferences are accurate, they apply to a declining part of the American work force, for only about 3 percent of the work force is engaged in agriculture, and manual laborers are declining as a proportion of the labor force. As a conse-quence, work is decreasingly a confrontation with things or with nature; rather, it is increasingly a social confrontation; "Reality is becoming only the social world, excluding nature and things, and experienced primarily through the reciprocal con-sciousness of others."[56]

The problem of the man–nature relationship may be specified as a choice among humans as subordinate to nature, as the beliefs of primitive peoples imply, or mas-ters over nature, which is the market version of the proper relationship between management and the factors of production, or living in a kind of coequal harmony with nature, exemplified by traditional agricultural workers and now recommended again by conservationists. Before accepting the currently popular idea of harmony with nature, consider the benefits of the market's rough version. It is *mastery* over nature, with all its dangers to our fragile ecology, that seems to incorporate more clearly the values of the relief of poverty,[57] which we found to be such an important contribution to cognitive development. Furthermore, those living in circumstances that might be said to be most closely in "harmony with nature," peasants and villagers in traditional societies, are less likely than the urbanized factory workers in these same societies to be tolerant of others' opinions, open to new experiences, to believe in their own efficacy, value scientific opinion or hold any of the other views that Inkeles and Smith incorporate in the measure of "individual modernity." Moreover, in a kind of paradox, it will be an act of exemplary mastery to decide how to conserve, substitute for, and reproduce nature's bounty of raw materials and arable soil.

The second problem dealing with the value of manual labor offers less of a con-flict of values. People who work primarily with things ("nature" in that limited sense) develop lower levels of cognitive functioning, value self-direction less, and have lower senses of moral responsibility than those who work with ideas or peo-ple.[58] Working with things is a poor teacher; William Morris's disdain for "book-ishness" is severely misplaced.

These and like bits of evidence imply an ascending historical sequence in the development of cognitive flexibility, valuing independence over conformity, and sense of personal efficacy: from tilling the soil as a peasant or sharecropper (I do not include farmer-owners) to manual work in collective gatherings (as in factories?) to working primarily with people (as in many of the service indus-tries) to working with ideas. The market has been blamed for contributing to

[55] George Orwell, *The Road to Wiggin Pier*, 173, quoted in Meakin, *Man and Work*, 2.
[56] Daniel Bell, *The Coming of Post-Industrial Society* (New York: Basic Books, 1973), 30–1.
[57] The idea of man's "dominion" over the other creatures of the earth has religious sanction, of course. Recently Pope John Paul II tied this to work: "Man's dominion over the earth is achieved in and by means of work." *Laborem Exercens* (1981).
[58] Kohn and Schooler, *Work and Personality*, 110, n. 8 on p. 64.

this sequence. Should it not be credited for accelerating it and blamed for retarding it?

Work is an engagement with the social world

In learning about and from other people one must, as Piaget points out, observe that the views, opinions, and judgments in one's own head are not the only ones. As we said of exchange, the social experience at work erodes *egocentricity*, by which Piaget did not mean selfishness but rather the belief that only what is in one's own mind is real and valuable, and develops *sociocentricity*, that is, the recognition that others have legitimate perspectives of their own.[59] There is oblique confirmation of this sociocentricity in the finding that the pleasure coworkers derive from their work is a cause of the work enjoyment of each worker.[60] Even in a competitive market economy, almost all work requires cooperation as well as obedience.

There is some evidence in Inkeles and Smith's study that industrial work, as contrasted to rural agricultural experience, increases both the tendency to hold opinions and the tendency to tolerate or even value the opinions of others, even "weaker" others such as (in these underdeveloped countries) a man's wife or son: "The factory may be a training ground which inculcates a greater sense of awareness of the dignity of subordinates and restraint in one's dealing with them."[61] But in their more detailed examination of the features of work that affect such attitudes, Kohn and Schooler find that it is only self-directed work (substantively complex, loosely supervised, and nonroutine) that promotes similar attitudes of tolerance, respect, and trust.[62] Following the guidelines of previous research,[63] we might say that in plants where management treats its workers with respect, workers will treat each other with respect. And within such plants, those whose jobs offer the self-direction that Kohn and Schooler locate as the pivotal feature of work content respect themselves more and will respect others more as well. As the history of capitalist work reveals, there is nothing immanent in the market that compels either management respect or self-directed work, but neither do command economies reveal such immanent tendencies.

The incentive to learn from, adapt to, and be included in a work group is powerful in all societies. In economic groups, "powerful incentives to work lie in the individual's membership in a social group. He dare not relax lest he lose the benefits of membership."[64] But although friendliness is associated with productivity, the

[59] Jean Piaget, "Mental Development of the Child," in his *Six Psychological Studies,* ed. D. Elkind (New York: Random House, 1967).

[60] Barry Gruenberg, "The Happy Worker: Determinants of Job Satisfaction," *American Journal of Sociology* 86 (1980): 247–71 at 269.

[61] Inkeles and Smith, *Becoming Modern,* 24, see also 21–2; but note that some measures of distributive justice failed to discriminate between traditional and modern groups. (p. 23)

[62] Kohn and Schooler, *Work and Personality,* 142, 174; *tolerance* and *respect* are measured largely by items in the F-scale, for example, "The most important thing to teach children is absolute obedience to their parents," and "There are two kinds of people in this world: the weak and the strong." *Trust* is measured by Rosenberg's "Faith in People" scale, including, for example, "Do you think most people can be trusted?"

[63] See Abraham H. Maslow, *Eupsychian Management* (Homewood, IL: Irwin/Dorsey, 1965).

[64] Raymond Firth, "The Social Framework of Economic Organization," in E. E. Clair and H. K. Schneider, eds., *Economic Anthropology* (New York: Holt, Rinehart & Winston, 1968), 79.

tendency to socialize is usually unproductive,[65] creating a tension between social learning and productive work.

Work experience is an instrument for understanding the world

The "understandings of the greater part of men are necessarily formed by their ordinary employments," said Adam Smith, who then went on to say that the person engaged in repetitive industrial work "becomes as stupid and ignorant as it is possible for a human creature to become."[66] This "understanding" is as broad as what Marx (or his translators) call "consciousness." The ideologies, the perspectives on the world that the sociology of knowledge once said emerged from one's social *position,* may, following Breer and Locke, be also assigned to one's work experience. As mentioned, position in the social strata does affect social outlook, but work experience is at least as important in its own right.

According to Inkeles and Smith, in the less developed countries, at least, (and there is evidence that the same general relations apply to developed countries)[67] a factory worker, compared to his village cousins:

is an informed participant citizen, . . . is highly independent and autonomous in his relations to traditional sources of influence, especially when making decisions about how to conduct his personal affairs, . . . and he is ready for new experiences, that is, he is relatively open-minded and cognitively flexible.[68]

In introducing the idea of "cognitive flexibility," these authors refer to the mental operations employed in "understanding the world," and not the content of their understandings. Kohn and Schooler's measure of cognitive flexibility (called "ideational flexibility") merits further examination here: It is based on a respondent's ability to weigh two sides of a problem, a test involving differentiation of figure from ground, measured tendency to agree with whatever point of view was presented (acquiescence set), and interviewer's rating of intelligence.[69] The substantive complexity of the work has the most effect on ideational flexibility and the effect is substantial. At any given time, this influence of job condition on mental functioning is even greater than that of education, but over time, although important, it is somewhat less important than education and social class.[70]

Piagetian findings are relevant in another way here. Piaget emphasized the value of formal operations permitting abstract thought, but his work with adolescents led

[65]Randall Filer, "The Influence of Affective Human Capital on the Wage Equation," in Ronald G. Ehrenberg, ed., *Research in Labor Economics,* vol. 3 (Greenwich, CT: JAI Press, 1981).

[66]Adam Smith, *The Wealth of Nations* (1776; reprint New York: Random House/Modern Library, 1937), 734–5.

[67]See Joseph A. Kahl, *The Measurement of Modernity: A Study of Values in Brazil and Mexico* (Austin: University of Texas Press, 1968); and R. M. Suzman "Psychological Modernity" on the generality of Inkeles and Smith's measure of individual modernity.

[68]Inkeles and Smith, *Becoming Modern,* 291.

[69]Kohn and Schooler, *Work and Personality,* 38, 60. Compare the discussion in Chapter 7 on cognitive development (including a measure of differentiation) and the discussion in Chapter 8 on the dangers of complexity beyond the capacities of people to handle that degree of complexity.

[70]Kohn and Schooler, *Work and Personality,* 168, 170. Compare Robert E. Lane, "Political Observers and Market Participants: The Effects of Markets on Cognition," *Political Psychology* 4 (1983): 455–82; Idem, "Market Thinking and Political Thinking," in Adrian Ellis and Krishan Kumar, eds., *Economy and Society: Studies in Fred Hirsch's "Social Limits to Growth"* (London: Tavistock Publications, 1983).

him to caution against the value of abstraction without the sobering feedback of experience. Although he did not say so, work experience can produce, within its domain of relevance, a corrective tropism toward reality.[71]

Work is a crucial means for achieving a successful identity

Through work, it is said, man realizes his potentials, expresses himself, and partially defines his identity.[72] An identity too closely linked to work is incomplete and destructive of other values, but along with "an intelligible theory of the processes of life," Erikson finds work to be crucial to identity; he says such an identity develops from a " 'conflict free' habitual use of a dominant faculty, to be elaborated in an *occupation;* a limitless resource, a feedback, as it were, from the immediate exercise of this occupation, from the companionship that it provides, and from its tradition."[73] By and large, it is those who *achieve* or forge for themselves their own identities (often after a crisis), rather than those who accept "foreclosed" identities from their various statuses, who have the most fruitful and reliable self-concepts.[74] If occupation *gives* a person an essential ingredient for his or her identity, self-direction at work seems to offer one of the best instruments for *forging* an identity. And occupation must increasingly fill up the empty space left by the evisceration of meaning in a working-class identity.[75]

Anthropologist Sandra Wallman is critical of an identity based exclusively on work: "Where 'over-identification' occurs in industrial society it is diagnosed as pathology: anyone too closely identified with work is 'workaholic,' bound to be neglecting other obligations, and probably suffering from stress." She holds that in smaller societies where roles are diffused (Parsons) and people are known in multiple roles, identities are somehow more healthy.[76] Why the fox should be healthier than the hedgehog, or by what criteria of social contribution, happiness, or self-development the dedicated scholar is a lesser person than the unspecialized family man, is unclear. It is precisely this division of labor that I said created the multiple specialties offering more ladders for superior performances.

Work is a primary source of favorable self-concepts

We turn again to the subject of self-esteem (Chapter 10), a product of several processes, three of which are the way a person thinks he or she is evaluated by others (reflected appraisal), a person's appraisal of his or her own achievements, and a

---

[71] See Jean Piaget, *The Moral Judgment of the Child,* trans. M. Gabin (1932; reprint New York: Free Press, 1965).

[72] We will not explore "self-realization" because of difficulty in defining its meaning and because we have no evidence. For a stimulating discussion, see Jon Elster, "Self-Realization in Work and Politics: The Marxist Conception of the Good Life" (Paper prepared for conference on Marxism and Democracy, 28–31 March 1985).

[73] Eric Erikson, "The Problem of Ego Identity," *Journal of the American Psychoanalytic Association* 4 (1956): 58–121; reprinted in Maurice R. Stein, Arthur J. Vidich, and David M. White, eds., *Identity and Anxiety* (Glencoe, IL: Free Press, 1960), 44.

[74] Edmund Bourne, "The State of Research on Ego Identity: A Review and Appraisal," Part I, *Journal of Youth and Adolescence* 7 (1978): 223–51.

[75] David Macarov, *Incentives to Work* (San Francisco: Jossey-Bass, 1970), 97–8.

[76] Sandra Wallman, "Introduction," in her edited volume, *Social Anthropology of Work* (London: Academic Press, 1979), 17.

person's ability to select favorable dimensions on which to be judged and to judge the self.[77] High status at work and participating in decisions at the workplace increases measured self-esteem. More significantly, workers who are closely supervised and have no occasion to exercise their skills in some routine job see themselves as low in status,[78] deprived of opportunities to achieve, and therefore robbed of an opportunity to select one of the significant dimensions for assessment (although a person has other dimensions at the workplace, such as popularity). No doubt it is for these kinds of reasons that job characteristics have been found to modify self-esteem. Specifically, after statistically controlling other job circumstances and social backgrounds for both men and women, jobs that facilitate self-directed work (jobs with substantive complexity, looser supervision, and nonroutine work) and higher status jobs are found to inspire greater self-confidence and self-esteem for jobholders than jobs without these characteristics.[79]

Work commitment and productive orientation

Work may be said to be the vehicle for expressing what Fromm called "a productive orientation" (as contrasted to hoarding, receptive, and marketing orientations).[80] In one sense, any kind of work will contribute to a productive orientation, and people who have been work-deprived (unemployed) for a long time lose this orientation.[81] But, the escapist themes of blue-collar daydreams, the limited responses of those working in token economies, and our everyday observation raise formidable doubts about the capacity of dull, routine work to elicit a productive orientation. For these kinds of jobs, pay is regarded as the source of motivation, but working for pay is not in any sense a productive orientation.[82] If people believe they are "overpaid," they do work harder,[83] but again this is not a productive orientation. If the idea of "occupational commitment" (measured by an index including an item reflecting a person's assessment of the moral worth of his or her job) approximates this idea of a productive orientation, then we have evidence that opportunities for self-direction do, indeed, encourage such an orientation.[84] More than half of an American national sample report (as mentioned) that they have "an inner need to do the very best job possible." Once more, it is those whose jobs permit them discretion that are most likely to express this opinion.[85]

---

[77] Morris Rosenberg, *Conceiving the Self* (New York: Basic Books, 1979).

[78] Kohn and Schooler, *Work and Personality*, 89, 144.

[79] Ibid., 206.

[80] Erich Fromm, *Man for Himself* (New York: Rinehart, 1947).

[81] Marie Jahoda, "The Impact of Unemployment in the 1930s and the 1980s," *Bulletin of the British Psychological Society* 32 (1979): 309–14.

[82] Frederick Herzberg, B. Mausner, and B. Schneiderman, *The Motivation to Work* (New York: Wiley, 1959).

[83] Edward E. Lawler, "Equity Theory as a Predictor of Productivity and Work Quality," *Psychological Bulletin* 70 (1968): 596–610.

[84] Kohn and Schooler, *Work and Personality*, 62; partial ownership of a firm also contributes to work commitment. Unfortunately, Kohn and Schooler pay no attention whatsoever to the effects of job conditions on productivity (there is, for example, no entry for "productivity" or "efficiency" in their index), but they have one of the few models available providing information on the effect of circumstances of work on psychological functioning.

[85] Yankelovich and Immerwahr, *Putting the Work Ethic to Work*, 21. The "strong inner need to do the

Commitment to work is a function of independence on the job, as evident in the dedication of the self-employed; it is also a function of skill level.[86] In a word, a productive orientation cannot be expected to emerge from "alienated" labor; here is where the Marxist criticism and the criticism in *Work in America* and other sources find their mark. As we shall see in Chapter 18, pay itself is a source of resistance to a productive orientation, substituting the market economist's income maximization orientation instead.

Work is an experience useful in combating boredom and alienation
Whereas Marx found work in capitalist society to be a principal source of alienation (from one's product, the process of production, one's fellow beings, and from the norms of humanity itself),[87] Voltaire argued that "work banishes three great evils: boredom, vice, poverty," and Carlyle (in one incarnation) held that "work is the grand cure of all the maladies and miseries that ever beset mankind."[88] One may find a kind of support for Voltaire and Carlyle in the fact that for people who want to work, work-deprivation is a source of meaninglessness[89] (far worse and more frequent than Durkheim's meaninglessness of frantic striving among workers), and of other maladies of the soul.

Whether work is alienating or a cure for alienation depends on the kind of work. I draw attention again to Kohn and Schooler's findings that "doing work of little substantive complexity is not only associated with, but actually results in, feelings of alienation."[90] But Kohn and Schooler disagree with Marx on the relationship of work alienation to ownership of the means of production; Kohn and Schooler find it almost irrelevant.

If ownership is irrelevant, interpersonal relations are not. Thus, a study of women in repetitive, low complexity, clerical jobs in Chicago found that the social relations at work, not only among themselves but also in "managing" their managers, were sufficiently engaging to make up for the lack of complexity in the tasks assigned to them.[91]

Work *can* combat boredom and alienation, but may not. Whether the market encourages systematic reduction of skill as a cost-reducing measure will be treated in the next chapter.

very best I can regardless of pay" varies substantially across cultures: from 17% in Britain to 57% in Israel and 51% in the United States. Public Agenda Foundation survey reported in Daniel Yankelovich et al., *The World at Work: An International Report on Human Values, Productivity and its Future* (New York: Octagon, 1984), 393.

[86] John H. Goldthorpe, David Lockwood, Frank Bechofer, and Jennifer Platt, *The Affluent Worker in the Class Structure* (Cambridge, UK: Cambridge University Press, 1971), 160–5.

[87] Karl Marx, *Economic and Philosophical Manuscripts of 1844,* trans. T. Bottomore, in Erich Fromm, ed., *Marx's Concept of Man* (New York: Unger, 1961), 99–103.

[88] Voltaire, *Candide,* chap. 30; Thomas Carlyle, *Rectoral Address at Edinburgh,* 2 April 1786.

[89] E. Wight Bakke, *Citizens Without Work: A Study of The Effects of Unemployment Upon the Workers' Social Relations and Practices* (New Haven: Yale University Press, 1940); HEW Task Force, *Work in America;* Jahoda, "The Impact of Unemployment."

[90] Robert Blauner comes to similar conclusions. See his *Alienation and Freedom* (Chicago: University of Chicago Press, 1964), chap. 2.

[91] Helen Z. Lopata, Kathleen F. Norr, Deb Barnewolt, and Cheryl A. Miller, "Job Complexity as Perceived by Workers and Experts," *Work and Occupations* 12 (1985): 395–415.

Work gives structure to a day and a life

It is hard to conceive of a "rational life plan" that does not involve devotion to an occupation; at least some occupations qualify for what even the most critical humanist would call "work." People without work miss "the rhythm and meaning" of the work day as much as the pay and the respect flowing from work.[92] People who report that they would work even if they did not have to, give as their reasons: "to keep occupied" (32%), "warding off boredom and loneliness" (36%), and because they would "feel lost" without work.[93]

The obvious point is that this implied fear of leisure hardly fits the market concept of a tradeoff between the pleasures of leisure and the painful yet profitable experience of work, but this leads to the further question of whether the market is in any way responsible for the evident fear of leisure. Perhaps the market erosion of community, if only the temporary community of the village post office, bears some responsibility, or perhaps leisure *guilt* prowls in our lives as a companion to the work ethic, but more likely, in any age, many people lack leisure competence. Bertrand Russell is probably right in saying that "to be able to fill leisure intelligently is the last product of civilization, and at present very few people have reached that level."[94] One cannot appraise market effects on work without also appraising market effects on work's principal alternative, leisure.[95]

Work is the source of feelings of competence

Here I focus directly on one of the three elements defined as essential for human development. Inkeles and Smith report that compared to traditional agrarian life, working in a factory is related both theoretically and empirically to "a marked sense of personal efficacy," meaning that the individual believes that he or she and others can learn partially to control their environments (including "nature").[96] But, again, we learn from Kohn and Schooler that this sense of efficacy, or lack of fatalism, is a product of certain specific job experiences. In this case, the important job experience is not substantive complexity of work but rather lack of work routinization. Another, and more surprising, aspect is that time-pressured work leads to *less* fatalism and a greater sense that what happens to a person is largely his or her own doing.[97] Self-attribution of this kind is certainly market doctrine, the source of both initiative and self-help on the one hand, and of people's rationalizations for the unhappy fates of the unemployed and the poor on the other.[98]

[92] Special Task Force, *Work in America*, chap. 1; see also Jahoda, "The Impact of Unemployment."
[93] N. C. Morse and R. S. Weiss, "The Function and Meaning of Work and the Job," *American Sociological Review* 20 (1955): 191–8. These answers were predominantly from working-class persons; the 9% who said they worked because they "enjoyed their work" were largely middle-class.
[94] Bertrand Russell, *The Conquests of Happiness* (London: Allen & Unwin, 1930), 208. Russell also accepts the view that work structures the day: "It fills a good many hours of the day without the need of deciding what to do."
[95] Robert E. Lane, "The Regulation of Experience: Leisure in a Market Society," *Social Science Information* 17 (1978): 147–84.
[96] Inkeles and Smith, *Becoming Modern*, 22, 290
[97] Kohn and Schooler, *Work and Personality*, 203.
[98] Adrian Furnham, "The Protestant Work Ethic and Attitudes Towards Unemployment," *Journal of*

Work experience contributes to mental health and social adjustment
In the Vaillants' research report we saw not only that early work experience could be beneficial, but also that people who had had any kind of work experience were better candidates for a cure of mental illness than those who had not. It seems that for the normal population, work, even factory work, can contribute to mental health. The work experiences of early industrialization in England (and the United States, to a lesser extent) were such that they must have contributed to higher rates of mental disturbance, as well as misery, within the working population of all ages. However, the same seems not to be true of the transition to industrialism in the less developed world today. At least by the measure of psychosomatic symptoms widely used as a surrogate measure of mental health by the Public Health Service in the United States, those men who experienced the drastic changes involved in moving from a village boyhood to an adult factory job revealed no more psychosomatic complaints than those protected by the continuity and security of their village life or those born "modern."[99] There is complementary, if equally surprising, evidence in American data.

As part of a general survey of the nation's health, in 1970 the National Health Center conducted a survey, *Selected Symptoms of Psychological Distress,* including such self-assessed symptoms as: "Do your hands ever tremble enough to bother you?" "Have you ever felt you were going to have a nervous breakdown?" "Have you ever been bothered by your heart beating hard?" and so forth. In the past the answers to these questions have been predictive of maladjustment or, when serious, of breakdown. With respect to work, the authors report: "Symptom patterns by occupation appear to differ somewhat from what might commonly be supposed. Thus professional, clerical, and *operative* [i.e., factory worker] occupations tended to have *lower* symptom rates, while farmers and farm managers, and private household and service workers tended to have *higher* rates."[100]

Similarly, market work by married women seems not be be deleterious to their mental health even though they must work longer hours, for their husbands rarely pick up their share of the housework or child care. Compared to married women without market jobs, they show fewer signs of stress and distress.[101] In a market society unemployment is not simply the absence of work but the absense of function and dignity, as well; unemployment is associated with serious mental strain and increased ill health.[102]

Occupational Psychology 55 (1982): 277–85; Idem, "Why Are the Poor Always With Us? Explanations for Poverty in Britain," *British Journal of Social Psychology* 21 (1982): 311–22.

[99] Inkeles and Smith, *Becoming Modern,* 296.

[100] U.S. Department of Health, Education, and Welfare, National Health Center, *Selected Symptoms of Psychological Distress, United States,* Health Statistics, ser. 11, no. 37 (Rockville, MD: Public Health Service, 1970), 9–10.

[101] Richard Hall, *Dimensions of Work,* 204. See also Pamela K. Adelman, "Occupational Complexity, Control, and Personal Income: Their Relation to Psychological Well-Being in Men and Women," *Journal of Applied Psychology* 72 (1987): 529–37.

[102] See, among many studies, D. Dooley and R. Catalano, "Economic Change as a Cause of Behavioral Disorder," *Psychological Bulletin* 87 (1980): 450–68.

Summary

This chapter points out that many facets of learning have a work locale, and that much of the learning that takes place is only partly related to occupational skills. Second, the concept of human capital that seems initially to fulfill the criteria of and provide the incentive for learning at the workplace rather shrinks in scope in the perspective of the humanist critics of work in market societies. Third, whereas the humanist criticism rarely mentions ethical criteria for work, in fact, Kohn and Schooler's data show that self-directed work increases a sense of moral responsibility. Fourth, the emphasis on the benefits of self-directed work reminds us of the frequency of work directed by others, work that is routine, closely supervised, and unchallenging – with due allowance for the studies showing that what is "unchallenging" to academics is, in fact, often difficult and challenging to workers. The rule is: initiative in the market, obedience at work, including, of course, market work. Mill put it this way: "It is not sufficiently considered how little there is in most men's ordinary life to give any largeness either to their conceptions or to their sentiments."[103] Mill thought that an interest in politics would broaden workers' horizons; today we know that it is at the workplace that a person's mind is more likely to be trained and broadened. Finally, and most important, with the exception of cognitive flexibility derived from the exercise of choice, the kinds of things learned at work cannot be learned in the consumer market.

If market work rarely has the damaging consequences alleged by humanistic critics, neither does it offer to many the full benefits of fulfilling experience. In the next few chapters we will examine in more detail some of the more serious allegations, but here, by way of summary, let us contrast the generally benign character of factory work emerging from Inkeles and Smith's study of modernizing nations with the more conditional findings of Kohn and Schooler's study of work in contemporary Western economies. Inkeles and Smith's account gives a positive hedonic tone toward work, but the effects of nonself-directive work in Kohn and Schooler's account embraces a large proportion of the labor force. That kind of work *fails to develop* cognitive complexity and a sense of personal competence, intellectually demanding uses of leisure time, liberal democratic ideology (as contrasted to authoritarian conservatism), moral responsibility, receptivity to change, self-confidence, self-esteem, and protections against anxiety.

[103] John Stuart Mill, "Representative Government," in *Utilitarianism, Liberty, and Representative Government* (London: Dent, 1910), 216.

14 Degradation of work in the market?

> *To the Greeks work was a curse and nothing else. Their name for it – PONOS – has the same root as the Latin POENA, sorrow. For them PONOS was colored with that sense of a heavy burdensome task which we feel in the words FATIGUE, TRAVAIL, BURDEN. The turn of phrase which in English is restricted to down-right drudgery, the Greeks applied to physical work of every sort. . . . Close contact with the material world seemed to them a painful and humiliating necessity, to be reduced to the lowest possible minimum, if possible to be eliminated altogether.*
>
> Tilgher, Work: What It Has Meant to Man Through the Ages

In the previous chapter I quoted Meakin's comments on "a crisis of conscience in the world of work" and his references to "a powerful and vivid indictment of a world that degraded work."[1] One of the main themes of this book is that most work is not degrading; rather, under certain circumstances, it is a major source of both happiness and human development. Consequently it is crucial that we assess these criticisms of work in the light of the evidence in Chapter 13 and of other empirical studies illuminating the various aspects of the degradation thesis.

There are four principal headings employed to organize the discussion: (1) degradation of purpose – the loss of the transcendent value of work in the dailiness of life and the dominance of materialistic and selfish purposes; (2) degradation because working people are exploited and fail to receive the value of their products; (3) degradation because machines reduce the unique value of humans to machinelike processes; and (4) degradation because work in a market society reduces the use of available or potential skills – the "deskilling" argument.

Degradation of purpose

Transcendence

Immanence and transcendence. Work can be caught up in the dailiness of things, not necessarily routine, but lodged irredeemably in here and now, self and survival. In that sense it is *immanent* in life. "It is not so much that man makes his life through work as that his life largely coincides with his work," said Peter Anthony.[2] But many scholars believe that to fulfill its function work must link the individual to the larger community, the larger society, and especially the larger self. Bertrand Russell points in this direction when he speaks of the *constructiveness* of work: "Something is built up which remains as a monument when the work is completed."[3] In interviewing the unemployed, Marie Jahoda found that they missed

[1] David Meakin, *Man and Work: Literature and Culture in Industrial Society* (London: Methuen, 1976), 1, 182.
[2] Peter David Anthony, "Work and the Loss of Meaning," *International Social Science Journal* 32 (1980): 416–28 at 419.
[3] Bertrand Russell, *The Conquest of Happiness* (London: Allen & Unwin, 1930), 212. Russell adds the

this link, turning inward in its absence. She called their search for purposes larger than those implied in simply meeting the demands for existence a search for *transcendence*.[4] William Leiss says that in the market "the sphere of material exchange is not *transcended*, but rather extended ever more deeply into the 'psychological' domains. The needs for self-esteem and self-actualization are expressed through the purchase of commodities."[5]

The concept of transcendence has many meanings. For the Christian, transcendence might mean: "To work is to cooperate with God in the great purpose of the world's salvation."[6] The undisillusioned Communist might once have found a "moral impetus through collective aspiration and idealism."[7] Or it may be found in a kibbutz or brudderhoff or in any collective enterprise where workers believe they are building a movement or exemplifying a moral tradition.

The transcendental qualities of work in the market are by no means obvious; certainly no market economist refers to them. Those who speak in this vein find support in religious or historical movements, and refer to "the spirit" of work, or its historical or potential "meaning." Thus it is said that Protestantism was "the moving force in the profound spiritual revolution which established work as the base and key to life" (a transcendence that itself was transcended). Or the idea that work is the source of changing the unhappy circumstances of all people's lives, and not just that of the workers themselves, has been invoked to give work a transcendant quality.[8] Marx said work is the source of "the development of the social individual which appears as the great foundation stone of production and wealth."[9] As a sample of the kind of transcendence a romantic writer can invest in those ideas, I quote Tilgher once again:

It is in work that the man of capitalist civilization finds his nobility and worth. His whole code of ethics is contained in one precept, "work." [And] the holiness of work is reflected upon wealth and sanctifies it. . . [wealth does not derive its value in consumption, but from its ability] to create new wealth, new work, new activity.[10]

One is tempted to disregard these poetic expressions and give work the prosaic meanings that most workers express when they talk about their work, but there are indications and glimpses of something else latent in the mundane material world the economists analyze. As in Jahoda's sample, transcendence may refer to more mundane matters, focusing on the idea of transcending the most narrow and self-centered

proposition that "the most satisfactory purposes are those that lead indefinitely from one success to another without coming to an end." (p. 214) Thus purposiveness will be a stable and chronic state.

[4] Marie Jahoda, "The Impact of Unemployment in the 1930s and the 1970s," *Bulletin of the British Psychological Society* 32 (1979): 309–14. An alternative term might be *meaningfulness*, but as Peter Anthony points out, this concept seems to be different from that of *purpose*, which I wish to specify.

[5] William Leiss, *The Limits to Satisfaction* (Toronto: Toronto University Press, 1976), 57, emphasis added.

[6] Andreano Tilgher, *Work: What It Has Meant to Men Through the Ages*, trans. D. C. Fisher (1930; reprint New York: Arno/New York Times, 1977), 16. Tilgher gives as an example Hemmelrich's flight to the Soviet Union to find fulfillment in his work, as narrated in Malraux's *La condition humaine*.

[7] Meakin, *Man and Work*, 56.

[8] Ibid., 3.

[9] Karl Marx, *Grundrisse: Foundations of the Critique of Political Economy*, trans. M. Nicolaus (1939; reprint Harmondsworth, UK: Penguin, 1973), 705.

[10] Tilgher, *Work*, 131, 135, 137.

version of the self. After hours of describing his deep frustration, a Swedish steel-worker suddenly discovered that he had omitted to mention his basic feelings about work and he insisted on adding:

I want to work, I like to work. I don't want to sit at home . . . I want to work in manufacturing industry, make things . . . to make the thing itself, to stand there in the centre, that is something special. . . . I like to work with machines. . . . All workers . . . want to do something useful, do a good job.[11]

Market doctrine is deaf to such voices; market practice tolerates but does not know how to enlist transcendence of any kind.

As the criticisms in this section will reveal, the humanist view of modern work is by no means universally eulogistic. Tilgher himself has doubts. Toward the conclusion of his book, he says: "At the end of the road followed by the civilization of labor, there may thus be a supreme irony of history, a total denial of work as having any spiritual value whatsoever."[12] In Arendt's vivid language, *homo faber* becomes *animal laborans*.[13]

Transcendence in a market economy. Basically, the market is on the side of immanence, the lodging of work in the mundane calculations of making a living. For the purposes of learning cognitive complexity and personal control, this is probably a strength, though self-esteem might flourish from association with a cause larger than the self. But there are allied considerations: The market seems ill conceived to bring out the latent pride and transcendent vision of the Swedish steel-worker – though it does not stamp them out. Consider, however, some alternatives that the market's stress on immanence forecloses.

1. Whereas both Greeks (Homer, Xenophon) and Christians believed that work was a curse placed by their deities upon mankind for hubris, in the Christian version, but not the Greek, work as penance was a means of atonement. But penance was usually achieved through self-mortification rather than through work, a circumstance that leads Kenneth Burke to observe how market work contrasts with religious observation of this kind: The market "convert[ed] a religious psychology of 'retribution' and 'penance' into a commercialist psychology of ambition."[14] Burke does not say so, but one might interpret this as harnessing guilt to work, and from any point of view, frutiful work is a better expression of guilt than is penance. From the modern perspective, however, guilt is an unfortunate source of motivation.

2. One interpretation of the degradation of work in a secular age is that nothing has taken the place of the religious purpose that, it is said, once gave work its dignity. This failure to replace religious meanings would undermine the idea of the dignity of man; it would suggest a kind of Sartrean *nothingness* where humans had failed to discover their own secular sources of purpose and meaning. For want of something else, the Protestant ethic has, according to Weber, survived the demise of its religious source and "the idea of duty in one's calling prowls about in our

[11] Jahoda, "The Impact of Unemployment," 312, quoting research by Palm (1977).
[12] Tilgher, *Work,* 155. Writing in Fascist Italy in the late 1920s, Tilgher may have been torn between Fascist romanticism and the realities of work life he saw around him.
[13] Hannah Arendt, *The Human Condition* (Chicago: University of Chicago Press, 1958).
[14] Kenneth Burke, *A Grammar of Motives* (Berkeley: University of California Press, 1969), 114.

lives like the ghost of dead religious beliefs."[15] Some believe that the market does more to erode than to support the derivative work ethic,[16] but others, with more data at their command, find the work ethic strong, though transformed, in the modern market economy.[17] The work ethic can serve to fill the void of "nothingness," or simply "empty lives," as a form of minimal transcendence. Russell, again, points out that work, in contrast to leisure, solves the problem of what to do with oneself and provides "continuity of purpose [which] is one of the central ingredients in happiness in the long run, and for most men this comes chiefly through work."[18]

3. As members of a society priding itself on its individualism, we may find many forms of transcendence uncongenial. Consider the Fascist version of transcendence: "Work constitutes the sovereign title which legally gives men full and useful citizenship;" and: "The Nation is above individuals, categories, classes. Individuals, categories, classes are the instruments which the Nation uses to achieve its highest development."[19] The market protects us from transcendent claims of community, which, even without the Fascist distortion, can result in groupthink – or indeed, in less thinking altogether.[20]

4. There is also a logical or semantic problem in an exclusive emphasis on transcendence. Could there be any transcendence if there were no mundane world to be transcended? This is not simply asking whether there could be a "top" if there were no "bottom." Rather, the question points to the way the immanent and the transcendent need each other. Work must do its daily mundane acts in order for it to perform its transcendent roles, whatever they may be. Christian economics, it will be recalled, presided over poverty, which has its own forms of degradation. In any event, the mundane, if not exactly a base for these superstructures is, in its immanent form, a matter of vital interest for survival. We need the mundane, too.

5. If the market interpreters think of work as a disutility without any elements of transcendence whatsoever, others invest in it the total meaning of life: "As work has been the lot of man from time immemorial, man has invested work with something of the significance which he believes inheres in life. . . . If life has any meaning, work has meaning because life is work."[21] Yet if work contains "the meaning of life," is that meaning somehow reduced as work hours shorten and leisure, the market analyst's good, expands? The claims of the sociology of leisure stating that it is in the unstructured domains of leisure that people achieve their full potentials would be destroyed.[22] If the identification of work with life itself were eroded by the market (something that some critics find implausible), we should not mourn.

[15] Max Weber, *The Protestant Ethic and the Spirit of Capitalism*, trans. T. Parsons (New York: Scribner's, 1958), 182. From articles first published 1904–6.

[16] Daniel Bell, *The Cultural Contradictions of Capitalism* (New York: Basic Books, 1976).

[17] For example, see Daniel Yankelovich and John Immerwahr, *Putting the Work Ethic to Work* (New York: Public Agenda Foundation, 1983).

[18] Russell, *Conquest of Happiness*, 210.

[19] "Declaration of the Fascist Cooperative Convention," 24 June 1922, quoted in Tilgher, *Work*, 120.

[20] See accounts of the effect of "community" on prejudice and parochial acceptance of village views in Clyde Z. Nunn, Harry J. Crockett, Jr., and J. Allen Williams, Jr., *Tolerance for Nonconformity* (San Francisco: Jossey-Bass, 1978).

[21] Anthony, "Work and Loss of Meaning," 419–20.

[22] See Joffre Dumazedier, *Sociology of Leisure* (Amsterdam: Elsevier, 1974).

The goals for which people work are trivial or valueless
The main theme of the criticism of work in the comments under this heading is that market work serves mainly ignoble purposes, namely to increase earnings intended for consumption and personal wealth. Since this is the acknowledged purpose of work in market economics, we are invited to derail the discussion of the market experience in order to justify consumption and wealth – an invitation we must decline. Instead, let us examine some of the underlying assumptions of the criticism.

Meaningless consumption. Passing over the general criticism of "materialism" (working for money), we turn to the idea that work loses its value when people spend their earnings in valueless or pernicious ways. If work has its claims to larger purposes and transcendent goals, consumption seems bereft of such claims; there is no transcendental purpose for consumption. There are several ways in which the emphasis on consumption might be thought to degrade work. In the first, the purpose of work is trivialized and the work itself therefore lacks dignity when people buy junk with their earnings. If the end is worthless, the means cannot be worth much – unless we accept that work contains within it the two ends, happiness and human development, that are its independent sources of worth.

Alternatively, the rationality of work is undermined if the purpose is irrational, if the earnings are spent irrationally, the irrationality of the ends is communicated to the means. Erich Fromm puts the matter this way: "The act of buying and consuming has become a compulsive irrational aim, because it is an end in itself."[23]

If working in order to buy more goods were, indeed, a defect, the market rationale would receive a fatal blow. But closer examination shows that the criticism is not so much of working for consumer goods (the criticism does not include the poor), but of the *choices* made by people with discretionary income. Setting aside the implied arrogance (paternalism) of taste, we turn to the latent criticism of discretion itself. If one focuses less on *what* people buy and more on the *buying process,* the critics' dilemma comes into view. Among children, good buying habits are directly related to cognitive development;[24] there is no reason to believe that consumer choices do not serve the same developmental purpose. The critics' dilemma, then, is this: Discretion, self-direction, in work is a positive good, improving, as we have seen, people's cognitive skills; but discretion in consumption, which might equally improve cognitive skills, is scorned because the subjects of the choices made are disapproved of. Why is discretion on the settings of a machine screw healthy but discretion in the purchase of domestic machines unhealthy?

Working for wealth instead of for the good of the services performed. In his continuing argument favoring *function* (the services to society that work renders) over *possession,* Tawney expresses this view: "Degradation follows inevitably from the refusal of men to give the purpose of industry the first place in their thought

---

[23] Erich Fromm, *The Sane Society* (New York: Rinehart, 1955), 134–5.
[24] Scott Ward, Daniel B. Wackman, and Ellen Wartella, *How Children Learn to Buy* (Beverly Hills, CA: Sage, 1977).

about it . . . [for] when the criterion of function is forgotten, the only criterion which remains is that of wealth.''[25]

The problem here is whether one should indict the work people do because the workers' *purposes* are ignoble, or, instead, look at the consequences. The consequential argument is best stated in verse:

> The root of evil, avarice,
> That damned ill natur'd baneful vice,
> Was slave to prodigality,
> That noble sin; whilst luxury
> Employ'd a mission of the poor,
> And odious pride a million more:
> Envy itself and vanity
> Were ministers of industry.[26]

The consequential argument is recapitulated in modern economics in the concept of demand for labor as "derived demand" – derived, that is, from the consumption imperative. Keynsianism states the public advantages of the "consumption function" or "propensity to consume" less elegantly than Mandeville but more persuasively. This consequentialist view is focused on a moral end: full employment.

As shown in our discussion of "meaningless consumption," it is easy to show that *what* is consumed is a matter of ethical concern, but apparently it is not easy to devise a way of ennobling work either by enlisting effort dedicated to the public good or to persuade the public to purchase only noble things. Yet Tawney's criticism of the subordination of the intentionalist idea of service to the motives and institutions of profit survives as a criticism of the market's system of rewards:

The idea that there is some mysterious difference between making munitions of war and firing them, between building schools and teaching in them when built, between providing food and providing health, which makes it at once inevitable and laudable that the latter are conducted by professional men who expect to be paid for service but who neither watch for windfalls nor raise their fees merely because there are more sick to be cured, more children to be taught, or more enemies to be resisted, is an illusion.''[27]

The mysterious difference is, however, demystified in one case: Whereas the soldier, teacher, and doctor have scoring systems not measured by money, the entrepreneur has no such alternative. Like the others, he seeks rewards in self-esteem and the esteem of others.

Work as pain – a disutility. Little further need be said under this heading. In this view, as mentioned, a person's desire to work is measured "by the sum [of money] which is just required to induce him to undergo a certain fatigue.''[28] Are both transcendent values, the linking of the individual to a larger purpose, and

[25] Richard H. Tawney, *The Acquisitive Society* (New York: Harcourt Brace, 1920), 35.
[26] Bernard de Mandeville, *The Fable of the Bees: or Private Vices, Public Benefits,* ed. with commentary by F. B. Kaye (Oxford, UK: Oxford University Press, 1924).
[27] Tawney, *The Acquisitive Society,* 96.
[28] Alfred Marshall, *Principles of Economics,* 8th ed. (London: Macmillan, 1938), 15. The economist and the romantic historian seem hopelessly at odds on this point. Recall Tilgher's idea of work as "the summing up of all duties and virtues . . . [where] the man of capitalist civilization finds his nobility and worth.''

immanent values, the earning of a living for one's family, degraded – or are they ennobled – because they are born (or borne) in pain?

The ennobling argument is to see in the transcendence of pain the virtue and nobility of work – a Kantian view of moral worth in conquering disinclination. By this interpretation, measures of work dissatisfaction are measures of the moral worth of workers who continue working; the more dissatisfied, the nobler are the workers. In contrast, market doctrine holds that work is necessarily aversive and suggests that only fools engage in more work than required. Both arguments are not only perverse but run contrary to the pervasive humanist doctrines now urging that work should be positively engaging, that people should find in their work intrinsic pleasure – and the efficiency doctrines that suggest such intrinsic pleasures stimulate initiative.

Market activities are themselves degrading. Certain kinds of market work, like buying and selling, are particularly vulnerable to criticisms of market activities themselves. Buying and selling often imply dissimulation or deceit; they may involve salespersons in inauthentic relations; the criteria for success have no necessary ethical components; buying and selling imply the use of others as means and not as ends. Marx expressed this in characteristically colorful language: "Every product is a bait by means of which the individual tries to entice the essence of the other person, his money. Every real or potential need is a weakness which will draw the bird into the lime."[29] One form of enticement is suggested by Fromm's concept of the "marketing orientation" whose theme is "I am as you desire me";[30] in selling themselves, individuals alienate part of themselves. In short, the universal "propensity to truck, barter, and exchange" is a corrupting propensity.

If it were both universal and corrupt, the charge would be that human beings are corrupt, and the particular criticism of the market would lose most of its force. Polanyi reports that economies employing the self-regulating market are unique in their emphasis on profit from trading,[31] but the broader scanning of human societies in the Human Relations Area Files reveals a very widespread tendency for "economic exchanges involving money," which, in turn, are correlated with "individuals display of wealth" and with property rights: "full time entrepreneurs," "work organization on a contractual basis," and "individual ownership of significant property."[32] Working for profit (especially in praise and esteem) is very widespread, indeed; perhaps the market expands the incidence of working for material profit, but it did not invent it and there is no reason to believe that material profit is in any way morally or developmentally inferior to working for profit in social exchanges. I know of nothing in the psychological literature to suggest that economic exchange is in some manner a corrupting experience.

[29] Karl Marx, *Economic and Philosophical Manuscripts of 1844*, trans. T. Bottomore, in Erich Fromm, ed., *Marx's Concept of Man* (New York: Unger, 1961), 141.
[30] Erich Fromm, *Man for Himself* (New York: Rinehart, 1947). Political leaders campaigning for election ingratiate themselves as a matter of necessity. Fromm, a socialist, is silent on ingratiation as a standard practice of the instrument he would employ to make the decisions that markets now make.
[31] Karl Polanyi, "Our Obsolete Market Mentality," in his *Primitive, Archaic, and Modern Economies*, ed. G. Dalton (Boston: Beacon, 1971).
[32] Robert B. Textor, *A Cross-Cultural Summary* (New Haven: HRAF Press, 1967).

Among these several criticisms, I conclude that well-being and development are found more in the immanence (dailiness) of work than in transcendent purposes, that the consequentialist argument of the hidden hand dominates intentionalist arguments, that is, the dinner produced by grocers is more important than the lack of benevolence involved, and that market activities of buying and selling are not inherently degrading. But the relation of the value of what is produced to the value of the acts of production is a more complicated question.

Until it is recognized that work has values other than production for consumption, work will always be vulnerable to criticism based on what people consume. Mandeville sought to break that connection by pointing to employment per se as the greater value. For Smith, and economists more generally, the question of the quality of taste is irrelevant, because the fact that someone wants and can pay for a good – demand – is a sufficient condition to establish the worth of the work involved in producing it. And yet consumer values and work values are not irrelevant to each other. At the margin, one might agree that the hedonic and developmental values of work for the hairstylist who follows the fashions of the rich to provide them with eternally new variants in elegant coiffures and the counter clerks selling junk food to children in need of a different diet, are not seriously undermined by the low ethical, health, or aesthetic worth of their products. Beyond that margin, the dealer in crack or heroin may be happy in his work and may develop cognitive complexity of high order, but these work values are overwhelmed by the damage he does to others. Neither market economics nor humanist criticism provides us with the criteria needed to differentiate these cases; nor can we do so here. As a starter, we must recognize that the value of work is not exhausted by the economic or ethical values of the goods and services the work produces and that, consequently, the humanist criticism of the worth of the commodities produced is insufficient to make the value of the work that made these things also valueless. Such antisocial acts as dealing in drugs pose a separate problem.

The selfishness argument

Work is degraded in a market economy because people are working exclusively for themselves. We know that when a market economy is introduced into a primitive economy, people share less of their wealth with their kin and community.[33] Although this allocation of rewards to the self and the household rather than the extended family is not experienced as degrading, nevertheless, intuitively one finds the idea of sharing more attractive. If one prefers the justice of equality or of need to the justice of deserts, the market case is lost from the beginning.

There are seven answers to this point about market selfishness (a point too large to be developed at length here):

1. Recent ethical concern for the effects of gifts on their recipients makes sharing something less than wholly beneficent: What happens to the autonomy and sense of personal control of the nonproductive brother-in-law who becomes dependent on

---

[33] George Dalton, "Theoretical Issues in Economic Anthropology," *Current Anthropology* 10 (1969): 63–102 at 77–8.

his wife's productive brother for his dinner? And empirically, one of the obstacles to economic development in the less developed countries has been the inability of the enterprising person to benefit from his or her enterprise. This is a defensive answer; there are more positive ones.

2. Work is not degrading when it benefits other people, even though it also, and primarily, benefits the self (cf. Mandeville's poem). In market societies, this is achieved by the invisible hand

By directing [a businessman's] industry in such a manner as its produce may be of the greatest value, he intends only his own gain, and he is in this, as in many other cases, led by an invisible hand to promote an end which was not part of his intention. . . . By promoting his own interest he frequently promotes that of the society more effectually than when he really intends to promote it.[34]

Ethicists who limit moral credits to benevolence and goodwill must disapprove, but consequentialists will find redeeming social merit in acts that benefit others while also, and intentionally, benefiting the self.

3. Self-benefits that enlist and enhance the learning processes outlined in Chapter 13 are not degrading because they develop the self. They cannot be both enriching and degrading at the same time.

4. Working for the self is an incentive to work harder and to learn more, reinforcing the material benefits to others and psychological benefits to the self mentioned in items 1 and 2. The self-employed generally voluntarily work longer hours than firm employees; the solo lawyer works longer hours than the firm lawyer.[35] Furthermore, the initiative and pleasure individuals get from work that they find intrinsically interesting derives in substantial part from their concept of the task as their own.[36] *That* kind of self-interest can only be benign; indeed, it represents the consummation of certain important humanist standards for superior work situations. A blanket indictment of self-interest in work is absurd.

5. The self, as William James pointed out, encompasses all that can be termed "mine," as in "my family," "my community," and "my employees!" In the next chapter we will see that managers who can afford to do so, pay their workers more than market wages; for the manager of a firm, these workers are "*my* employees."

6. The idea that self-interest corrupts or degrades the work that serves that interest rests on the economistic assumption that self-interest is necessarily addressed (to cite Smith again) to "augmentation of fortune." There is ample evidence that self-interest is equally enlisted in motives that have more attractive reputations: the need for achievement,[37] high standards of workmanship,[38] reputation for fair dealing.[39]

7. In a capitalist market economy it is difficult to divorce the reward system from the work system, for the same act of reward both allocates individuals to their work

[34] Adam Smith, *The Wealth of Nations* (New York: Random House/Modern Library, 1937), 423.

[35] Harold L. Wilensky, "Work, Careers, and Social Integration," *International Social Science Journal* 12 (1960): 543–74.

[36] Edward L. Deci, *Intrinsic Motivation* (New York: Plenum Press, 1975); Mark R. Lepper and David Greene, eds., *The Hidden Costs of Rewards: New Perspectives on the Psychology of Human Motivation* (Hillsdale, NJ: Erlbaum/Wiley, 1978).

[37] David C. McClelland, *The Achieving Society* (Princeton, NJ: van Nostrand, 1961).

[38] Richard DeCharms, *Personal Causation: The Internal Affective Determinants of Behavior* (New York: Academic Press, 1968).

[39] Robert H. Frank, *Passions Within Reason:: The Strategic Role of the Emotions* (New York: Norton, 1988).

positions and rewards them for their work. But it is not impossible, and, indeed, it happens all the time. As we shall see in Chapter 15, although "economics emphasizes the role of markets in allocating resources, . . . in practice, markets play only a limited role in allocation decisions within organizations."[40] Within the somewhat loose constraints of the external labor markets, the firm is able to reward labor with one hand and allocate labor with the other; the two can be divorced. It is this practice that might make market socialism viable: market constraints on efficiency and product selection combined with internal, possibly ethical, constraints on the reward system within the organization.[41] That is, firms could be as selfish as always; individuals in the internal labor markets of worker self-managed firms might – or might not – choose to maximize individual material self-interest. (Unfortunately, this does nothing to relieve *market* socialism of its inability to shed the market's inherent priority given to consumers over workers, as will be shown in Chapter 16.)

These interpretations of work must be put in context. The trend from working for subsistence to working for those things that discretionary income will buy has led to a *discovery* of the frivolity of mankind—a discovery of a human quality rather than a creation of that quality. Discretionary income in primitive, household, and command economies has always led to conspicuous display or monuments to self-aggrandizement: jewelry, ornaments, pyramids, and statues such as Ozymandias erected in his honor. Transcendent purposes, such as national or religious glorification, do take on the character of self-abnegation, but often at the cost of pursuing goals with no great ethical or cultural value – and often, too, at the cost of individual freedom as the "greedy" transcendent institutions absorb their more or less willing victims.

As discretionary income becomes more widespread and people become adjusted to it, there are signs of consumption-fatigue (not Durkheim's feverish search for more) and of a desire to work both for the intrinsic pleasure of working[42] and for purposes with a "post-materialist" content: the benefit of community, of freedom, and participation, and for a very few, cultural and scientific development.[43] These tendencies depend for their nourishment upon market-induced economic growth; the question is whether the dominant market culture will allow these fragile tendencies, made possible by market wealth, to prosper.

Pay is incommensurate with work contribution: exploitation

If the multiple purposes and motives of market work create problems of evaluation that defy easy analysis, so does the question of "exploitation," basically an issue

---

[40] Martin Neil Baily and Alok K. Chakrabarti, *Innovation and the Productivity Crisis* (Washington, DC: Brookings Institution, 1988), 91.

[41] The evidence on the success of group payments, such as group bonuses, is not very promising. See Edward E. Lawler, III, "Using Pay to Motivate Job Performance," in Richard M. Steers and Lyman W. Porter, eds., *Motivation and Work Behavior* (New York: McGraw-Hill, 1975). But profit sharing might work better. See Martin Weitzman, *The Share Economy: Conquering Stagflation* (Cambridge: Harvard University Press, 1984).

[42] Yankelovich and Immerwahr, *Putting the Work Ethic to Work;* Deci, *Intrinsic Motivation.*

[43] Ronald Inglehart, *The Silent Revolution* (Princeton: Princeton University Press, 1972).

of who should get more and who should get less in the market. This is the second major issue for analysis in this chapter.

The monetary value of work in a market economy

The resolution of the problem of economic value is beyond the scope of this treatment,[44] but certain themes must be exposed to present a proper picture of the market experience. Tawney's criticism of the failure to reward service has this further aspect: "The . . . consequence is the degradation of those who labor but who do not by their labor command large rewards; that is, of the great majority of mankind."[45] In confronting the problem of who should get what, we deal with the usual difficulties of joint costs and joint products, difficulties not easily resolved even without the emotional distortions of concepts of "exploitation."[46]

The classic definition of a fair wage gives a frequently used standard for measuring exploitation. As set forth by Pigou, the concept of a fair wage relies on marginal productivity and says in effect that if all similar occupations were paid the values of their marginal products, and if the net private and net social products are equal [no externalities], and if this arrangement maximized the national dividend, then everyone is paid a fair wage.[47] This view is unsatisfactory since it does not take into account earlier circumstances (such as women's earlier relegation to housework, or black's handicapped start in the competition) and because it gives no account of the historical contribution of science and invention on which all productivity rests.[48] In any event, the thesis seems to be circular: "Factors are paid their marginal product, but wages or prices determine marginal products *rather than the reverse*. . . . Substantively, marginal productivity does not help much in specifying economic equity."[49] That is, the marginal product of any employee must be measured in such a way as to take into account the marginal products of all other employees, using their current, possibly "exploitative," wages as part of the measure.

But surplus value fares no better; it ignores the contribution to value of demand and the marginalist school of analysis, and it can be located in many different places. Intuitively, one senses that capital has more market power – it can outwait labor's greater urgency – so capital is overpaid. But intuitively, again, it seems that labor would not be employed in any enterprise at all had not some entrepreneur launched the enterprise in the first place. So labor is overpaid. And it is well known that invention and entrepreneurship rapidly lose their advantages by reason of the imitation of others. If entrepreneurs are underpaid, managers must be getting something owed to entrepreneurs, so management is overpaid.

[44] For a summary discussion, see Paul A. Samuelson and William D. Nordhaus, *Economics*, 12th ed. (New York: McGraw-Hill, 1985), 416–17, 457.

[45] Tawney, *The Acquisitive Society*, 35.

[46] See Andrew Reeve, ed., *Modern Theories of Exploitation* (London: Sage Publications, 1987).

[47] Arthur C. Pigou, *The Economics of Welfare*, 4th ed. (1932; reprint London: Macmillan, 1948), 549.

[48] See Leonard Trelawney Hobhouse, *The Elements of Social Justice* (London: Allen & Unwin, 1922), 161–3.

[49] Lester Thurow, "Toward a Definition of Economic Justice, *The Public Interest*, no. 31 (Spring 1973): 56–80 at 71, 75, emphasis added.

In the end, "exploitation" means returns to someone that are unjustifiably low. All justifications imply a criterion value, such as honor or wealth, and an argument regarding the distribution of that value. Economists specify their proximate criterion value as the maximal production of goods and services within the resources available, but their ultimate criterion is maximization of utility or satisfaction. The perfect market, they say, serves justice and efficiency by the same device: Justice and efficiency will be maximized if, within specified constraints, each agent receives as its reward its contribution to marginal product. Over the long run, the behavior of markets can be *explained* by immanent tendencies to find equilibrium where each factor of production, including labor, of course, is paid its marginal productivity.

There are three things wrong with this formula: (1) Maximal utility is not served by maximum production of goods and services because life satisfaction is more responsive to work enjoyment and achievement than levels of goods and services; (2) the attempt to justify wages by reference to the marginal productivities of various classes of labor is circular because the current marginal productivities of any one class of labor to be assessed depend upon the current wages of all other classes of labor – thus, the attempt at any explanation of the exploitation of labor as a whole is circular, assuming what is to be accounted for; and (3) *justifications*, depending, for example, upon the assignment of "pain" or "disutility" to work, in the case of labor and "waiting" in the case of interest are confounded with *explanations* of why labor and savings are paid their current levels of pay. Except in a world where justice is the only criterion for behavior, justifications and explanations are very different.[50] In his defense of the single utilitarian standard, John Stuart Mill comes close to this same position.[51]

If this line of reasoning is accepted, the argument that labor is degraded because it is exploited comes down to opposition to wages that perpetuate poverty *if* the wages might be improved without making poverty worse for the "underpaid," the Rawlsian "difference principle."[52] People need to believe that they are fairly paid, of course, but if people are not prepared to seek "reflective equilibrium" or accept the rationale of the "original position," the multiple grounds for more strictly economic arguments are available to justify almost any solution that is compatible with opportunity costs. The degradation of work from low wages cannot be addressed without a systemic account of the sources and consequences of low wages.[53]

Whereas exploitation deals with who should get what income share, the argument

[50]Robert E. Lane, "Market Justice, Political Justice," *American Political Science Review* 80 (1986): 383–402.
[51]John Stuart Mill, "Utilitarianism," in *Utilitarianism, Liberty and Representative Government* (London: Dent, 1910), 54 and passim.
[52]John Rawls, *A Theory of Justice* (Cambridge: Harvard University Press, 1971), sec. 13. But at that point the unhappy relationship between unemployment and inflation, which is briefly discussed in Chapter 15, serves as a reminder of what Samuelson and Nordhaus called a "tragic flaw in the capitalist system."
[53]It is for this reason that the fact that wages are lower in most command economies than in advanced Western nations cannot be taken as evidence that command economies "exploit" labor rather more than do market economies.

over the effects of machines on those who work with them returns us to the intrinsic character of work quite irrespective of levels and distribution of pay. We turn to this "man–machine" relationship next.

The man–machine relationship

There are two issues that must concern us in treating the way the man–machine relationship influences the market experience: (1) What is the effect of working with machines on those who use them at work? (2) What is the relationship of markets to mechanization? This second issue is closely related to the question of the autonomy of technology – the "technological fix" to be discussed.

The effects of machines on human personality

Under the guiding influence of a productivity conscious society, said Lewis Mumford, "man becomes a machine, reduced as far as possible to a bundle of reflexes; rebuilt at the educational factory to conform to the needs of other machines."[54] Earlier, Marx said pretty much the same thing, but confounded mechanization with the market system. More recently, from a very different quarter, Erik Erikson points out: "Psychiatric enlightenment has begun to debunk the superstition that to manage a machine you must become a machine, and that to raise masters of the machine you must mechanize the impulses of childhood."[55] The following evidence favors Erikson over Marx and Mumford.

Technology and humane learning. Concerning what is called *the man–machine relationship* (although more women than men work with machines), the evidence is fairly persuasive that "the large majority of people working with machines, even those who have little control over them, like their machines and are satisfied with their work. This finding," says Form, "suggests that the alleged link between the spread of machine technology, work routinization, and worker alienation may be a myth waiting to be exposed."[56] In addition to the "ideological issues" that Form had in mind – perhaps themselves a legacy of Marx's writing at a time when "dark satanic mills" were abundant – the reason for the persistence of the myth may lie in the prevalent image of the assembly line, where the myth does have foundation. The myth is undermined, first, by an appreciation of the fact that less than 5 percent of the American labor force work on assembly lines, and, second, by a closer look at the machines recently introduced: a shipping clerk is given a forklift, saving his back and requiring new motor skills; a radio repairman employs new miniaturized equipment that challenges his ingenuity; a physical therapist finds she can tend more patients with her new self-help machinery; a manual glass cutter acquires new precision equipment requiring greater coordination. After a comprehensive examination of a variety of technological changes, Eva Mueller finds

[54] Lewis Mumford, *The Transformation of Man* (New York: Harper Torchbook, 1972), 129.
[55] Erik H. Erikson, *Childhood and Society,* 2d ed. (New York: Norton, 1963), 324.
[56] William Form, "Resolving Ideological Issues on the Division of Labor," in Hubert M. Blalock, Jr., ed., *Theory and Research in Sociology* (New York: Free Press, 1981), 155.

that not only does the introduction of new machinery offer new challenges to the work force but that, contrary to expectation, it often increases opportunities for sociability at the plant as well.[57] Mueller reports: "There seems to be very little validity in the stereotype which sees mechanization and automation as making jobs increasingly dull, requiring nothing but 'robots' to interact with competent and self-sufficient equipment."[58] Further support for both Mueller's rate of job changes due to technology and the effect of those changes is found in the Gallup Poll's report that 44 percent of jobholders say that over their lifetime their jobs have been changed by technology and that of this group three-quarters say that these changes made their work more interesting.[59] Finally, about three-quarters of the workers sampled in the United States, Sweden, and Israel agree that "as a result of technological changes, my work has become more interesting," and about three-fifths of the workers in West Germany and Japan also agree.[60]

I am not aware of precise studies of the effect of machines on learning, but subject to modification by other studies, Mueller's findings hold. They suggest that the effect of machines may be both substantial and beneficial (at least for men):[61] (1) Those workers equipped with new technology believe that their skills are more fully used, and (2) whereas job *dissatisfaction* is generally closely associated with monotony, less advancement, less learning, and less planning of one's own work, those with new machines reported *more* job satisfaction after receiving the new equipment.[62] Obviously machines vary in their demands and contributions to learning. The introduction of machinery requiring greater skill and more variety, physical mobility, and permitting control over pace and intensity of work offers benefits from the person–machine relationship not available to others. But today, unlike the situation in Detroit in the 1920s, it is the least skilled and least educated who are excluded from the new technology.[63] Thus even the modestly skilled may find their promotions blocked by the increased requirements for knowledge adequate to handle the new technologies.

Markets and mechanization

Ellul suggests an autonomous "technological imperative" quite independent of the market,[64] a theme expressed in the words of an engineer as: "If something *can* be

[57] Eva Mueller, *Technological Advance in an Expanding Economy* (Ann Arbor, MI: Institute for Social Research, 1969). An earlier study suggests that one form of machine technology, automation, *reduces* interaction with peers, but increases it with supervisors. See William A. Faunce, "Automation in the Automobile Industry," *American Sociological Review* 33 (1958): 401–7.
[58] Mueller, *Technological Advance in an Expanding Economy*, 122, 123–5.
[59] Quoted in Yankelovich and Immerwahr, *Putting the Work Ethic to Work*, 2.
[60] Daniel Yankelovich et al., *The World at Work: An International Report on Human Values, Productivity and its Future* (New York: Octagon, 1984), 397.
[61] But see R. L. Feldberg and E. N. Glenn, "Technology and Work Degradation: Effects of Automation on Women Clerical Workers," in J. Rothschild, ed., *Machina ex Dea: Feminist Perspectives on Technology* (New York: Pergamon Press, 1983). For a broader view, see D. F. Noble, *Forces of Production: A Social History of Automation* (New York: Knopf, 1984).
[62] Mueller, *Technological Advance in an Expanding Economy*, 15, 18.
[63] James L. Baron and William T. Bielby, "Workers and Machines: Dimensions and Determinants of Technical Relations in the Workplace," *American Sociological Review* 47 (1982): 175–88.
[64] Jacques Ellul, *The Technological Society*, trans. J. Wilkinson (London: Cape, 1965).

made, it *must* be made."[65] Yet it is inconceivable that the economic system within which technology works is helpless in the face of a technological imperative. It is this machine–market relation to which we now turn.

For contemporary observers looking at what can only be called tractor worship in the early days of communism in the USSR, and at later beliefs that machinery was the tool of inevitable progress (a Soviet reports says "automation improves all the basic characteristics of work content"),[66] the link between market economics and mechanization seems seriously impaired. Something of that link is restored, however, in reports that it takes the Soviet economy twice as long to go from invention to application as it takes the American economy.[67] In this respect, at least, markets are accomplices to technology. But it is a two-way relationship.

The effects of technology on markets. For Karl Polanyi the principal evil of technology lay in its contribution to the industrial revolution, which then contributed to the hypertrophy of a market economy. The market economy, in turn, then dominated culture and society.[68] More specifically, in the early days of industrialization, the machine contributed to the development of a *labor* market, which in turn transformed the family relations developed around cottage industries. To his criticism of the machine per se, mentioned earlier, Marx added that the machine led the head of a household to sell his wives and children as well as himself: "He has become a slave dealer."[69] In a sense, Adam Smith agreed, calculating that in North America the value of each child before he or she leaves home "is computed to be worth a hundred pounds clear gain to [the parents]."[70] For William Morris, the evil of machines lay both in their effects on craftsmen's skills – the deskilling argument we shall examine – and in the ugliness of the products produced in the spirit of commercial gain, the latter arguments linking technology, markets, and aesthetics.[71]

Technological developments in one area of the economy influence the distribution of wages and labor markets in all areas. This is illustrated by the difference between labor-saving and capital-saving changes. Labor-saving technology in one sector tends to depress wages in that sector, perhaps increasing wages in another sector, a redistributive influence evident in the relative pay in agriculture and industry during the nineteenth century.[72] Similarly, the effect on general wage levels by

[65] Dennis Gabor, *The Mature Society* (New York: Praeger, 1972), 43. Gabor says that viewed from the outside, technology appears "autonomous." (p. 40)

[66] V. I. Ussenin and associates, "Soviet Workers and Automation of the Production Process," in Jan Forslin, Adam Sarapata, and Arthur M. Whitehill, eds. *Automation and Industrial Workers: A Fifteen Nation Study*, vol. 1, pt 1 (Oxford: Pergamon Press, 1981), 170.

[67] Zbigniew K. Brzezinski, *Between Two Ages: America's Role in the Technetronic Era* (New York: Viking, 1970).

[68] Karl Polanyi, *The Great Transformation* (New York: Rinehart, 1944).

[69] Karl Marx, *Capital*, trans. Eden Paul and Cedar Paul, ed. G. D. H. Cole (1867; reprint New York: Dutton Everyman, 1974), 497–8.

[70] Smith, *The Wealth of Nations*, quoted in Peter Gay, ed., *The Enlightenment: A Comprehensive Anthology* (New York: Simon and Schuster, 1973), 591.

[71] May Morris, ed., *The Collected Works of William Morris*, vol. 23 (London: Longman, Green & Co., 1915), 24.

[72] For an analysis of how this difference in technology in different sectors leads to greater or lesser

technological advances affects levels of demand and prosperity. "The advance in knowledge," said Denison, "is the biggest and most basic reason for the persistent long-term growth of output per unit of input."[73] And as we shall see in the next chapter, technologically advanced sectors of the economy tend to offer better wages and better opportunities for challenge and personal development. Thus technology both accelerates the general development of markets and changes the ratios of effort-to-pay between market sectors.

The effect of markets on technology: the importance of competition: When we reverse the causal relation and ask about the effects of markets on technological change, we begin to see limits to the autonomy of technology, for the market helps to *release* technology from the forces of tradition, habituation, and especially from the cohesive loyalty of groups to the practices that bind them together. In one version, the bourgeoisie released the forces of technology against the ancien régime to consolidate bourgeois power, but then technology became independently powerful because of its contribution to production.[74] In another version, the spirit of *rationality* (with its correlate, *change*) informs the market system and this spirit independently sponsors technological revolutions.[75] A third version finds in *competition* the market element that fosters technological change by attacking the comfortable group relations and habits of bureaucracy encrusting any current technique.

For example, Schon shows the resistances to innovations by great corporations *when firms are not threatened by competition.* The corporation, he says, seeks stability above all else: "Uncertainty, which is the heart of innovation is taboo" – unless it is enforced by market competition.[76] Even without the research budgets of the giants, it is small, competitive firms that introduce a very large proportion of the new products and new techniques – small firms, highly vulnerable to competition and stimulated by the desire to "beat the competition."

Like public bureaucracies, industrial bureaucracies suffer from inertia, routine, and habit. Baily and Chakrabarti indict the failure of management of American firms to innovate, blaming it for the relatively greater slowdown in American productivity in the 1980s compared to that in the industries of America's competitors. In the main, their arguments deal with a failure to apply available technology fast enough to match foreign competition. In confirmation, one of their worst cases of failure to adapt was the notoriously uncompetitive electricity generating industry, and one case in which American management did apply technology was the highly competitive textile industry that retained its market shares.[77] There can be little doubt that competition from Japan and Germany is serving as a stimulus to renewed

---

inequality, see Jeffrey G. Williamson and Peter H. Lindert, *American Inequality: A Macroeconomic History* (New York: Academic Press, 1980).

[73] Edward F. Denison, *Accounting for United States Economic Growth 1929–1969* (Washington, DC: Brookings Institution, 1974), 79.

[74] Jurgen Habermas, *Toward A Rational Society,* trans. J. J. Shapiro (Boston: Beacon, 1970).

[75] David S. Landes, "Technological Change and Industrialization," in Tom Burns, ed., *Industrial Man* (London: Penguin, 1969), 69–89.

[76] Donald A. Schon, *Technology and Change: The New Heraclitus* (Oxford, UK: Pergamon Press, 1967), 110.

[77] Baily and Chakrabarti, *Innovation and the Productivity Crisis.*

concern for technology. Competition is an uncertain stimulus to technological innovation, but without it, such innovation is likely to be slower.

Whereas the general causal effect of markets on technology is a favorable one, it is nevertheless true that market power, the *absence* of competition, can also be a source of technological innovation. For example, it is said that nine out of ten new products fail; without the cushion of profits derived from market power, the new products might never be tried. Without the protection of the kind of market power gained by differentiated products, firms would experience the same reluctance to innovate that is said to inhibit their in-house training: The products, like the trained experts, might be poached. Since one of the characteristics of firms with market power is higher expenditures for research and development, this seems to belittle the role of market competition in developing technology.

If the relationship between innovation and competition between firms in particular industries is sometimes unclear, the overall market record is more nearly what Marx and Engels said it was: "All fixed, fast, frozen, relations, with their train of ancient and venerable prejudices and opinions are swept away, all new-formed ones become antiquated before they can ossify. All that is solid melts into air."[78]

We may relate these findings and arguments to the quality of work by a set of causal patterns that reveal the conflicting tendencies in the way technology and competition combine to influence quality of work in a market economy. Over the long run,

> Competition→ technology→ better jobs

> Competition→ technology→ more affluent society→ better jobs

But in the short turn,

> Competition→ lower profits→ poorer jobs.

Within the overall beneficial effects of the market–technology synergy on quality of work, there are pockets of costs borne by workers in the most competitive industries.

Technological progress: mechanization to automation. Of the larger technological trends that may affect learning, for example, the shortened time span from invention to application, advances in agricultural technology releasing much of the farm labor force to work in the cities, increases in information technology in clerical work, and so on, one of these, ambiguously treated in a fifteen-nation study of the effects of new production technology, has aroused recent attention: the introduction of "automation," chiefly in continuous process manufacturing. Blauner has analyzed the technological movement from (1) crafts to (2) stationary machines, to (3) assembly lines, to (4) automated plants. He finds a kind of inverted U curve in alienation among the workers of industries representing these various stages: low alienation in the period of craft industries leading to high alienation in the "first industrial revolution" to even higher alienation in the period of assembly lines to lower alienation again in the "second industrial revolution" based on automation.

[78] Karl Marx and Friedrich Engels, *Manifesto of the Communist Party* (New York: International Publishers, 1932), 12.

The point is important for learning because alienation is known to inhibit exploratory behavior.[79] Although partially supported by subsequent American studies,[80]
and challenged by studies of French and British automation,[81] Blauner's research
may most plausibly be interpreted at the moment as holding that the introduction of
such technology *can*, if properly managed, reverse the learning-inhibiting earlier
stages of stationary machines and assembly line processes. But to the degree that
the market is responsible at all, it is as responsible for the earlier and unhappier
forms of mechanization as for the later and more felicitous stage of continuous
process automation.

Looking for evidence of "progress" in the circumstances conducive to humane
learning at work, we find that neither the market nor technology exhibit any immanent progressive unfolding program. Technology offers new possibilities and
both the market and centrally planned economies offer means – but the capitalist
economies put consumer needs first and the command economies have put defense
needs first, although the intrinsic problem of their system of coordination was the
lack of consumer (market) guidance on what to put first. In both socialist and capitalist economies, technology must be guided by human intelligence endowed with
humane values; the title of the Yugoslav report to *Automation and Industrial Workers* offers a lead: "Man—Not the Machine Alone—Can Change the World."[82]

Technological change and trauma. Markets accelerate technological change,
largely because of the force of competition. To that extent, the traumas of change
are assignable, in part, to markets. There is substantial evidence that major life
changes damage not only mental health but physical health as well. Holding firm to
the "ancient and venerable prejudices" that so appealed to Burke, as well as to a
job, a mortgaged home, and a salary, working persons might well experience trauma
when these things are swept away. In a study of life events very like that of Holmes
and Masuda (cited in Chapter 8), F. T. Miller and associates found that on a scale
of life events (death of spouse, divorce, minor violations of law, etc.) marked off
in forty standardized levels of severity of subjective stress, a West Coast urban
sample placed "fired from work" in eighth place, just below "major personal injury or illness" and "detention in jail"; they placed "retirement from work" tenth,
followed by "gain of family member" and "sexual difficulties." A less drastic
"change to different work" is well above the mean of stressful life events at a rank
of sixteen, just below financial troubles and just above "pregnancy" and "death of

[79] Salvatore R. Maddi, Marlin Hoover, and Suzanne C. Kobasa, "Alienation and Exploratory Behavior," *Journal of Personality and Social Psychology* 42 (182): 884–90
[80] Frank M. Hull, Nathalie S. Friedman, and Theresa F. Rogers, "The Effect of Technology on Alienation from Work: Testing Blauner's Inverted U-curve Hypothesis for 110 Industrial Organizations and
245 Retrained Printers," *Work Occupations* 9 (1982): 31–57.
[81] "It is extremely doubtful whether automation leads to the overcoming of alienation in work in any
profound sense." Duncan Gallie, *In Search of the New Working Class: Automation and Social Integration Within the Capitalist Enterprise* (Cambridge, UK: Cambridge University Press, 1978), 296. See
also David Halle, *America's Working Man: Work, Home and Politics Among Blue-Collar Property
Owners* (Chicago: University of Chicago Press, 1984).
[82] Valentin Jez, "Man – Not the Machine Alone – Can Change the World – The Yugoslavian Report,"
in Jan Forslin, Adam Sarapata, and Arthur M. Whitehill, eds., *Automation and Industrial Workers: A
Fifteen Nation Study*, vol. 1, pt 2 (Oxford, UK: Pergamon Press, 1981).

a close friend."[83] Job changes were less stressful for a comparable rural popula-tion.[84] As the agent that breaks tradition and disrupts the solidarity of social groups, the market offers no relief for change – except more changes in the worker's own life: mobility, flexible changes in skills, relocation, and sometimes changed expec-tations.

Without minimizing these costs, we should also observe their incidence and con-sequences. In developing countries, those who migrate from traditional villages to factory jobs in cities show no more symptoms of stress or psychological dysfunc-tions than those who remain in the traditional villages.[85] In advanced countries migration is generally economically and occupationally good for people (they do better if they migrate to new areas than matched others at the place of departure or place of destination),[86] but these net benefits to the workers themselves must be weighed against the costs arising from the strain of adaptation and do not take account of the strain on family cohesion and spouses. In two-career families these strains can be severe.[87] Whereas geographic mobility has probably remained con-stant for well over a hundred years, in part because migration westward was com-mon before technological changes became so frequent, the distances have in-creased.[88] The intuitively plausible idea that technology and the market that accelerates adaptation of technology to industry increase mobility and migration is probably true, but the effect of the market is less than appears on the surface. Studies of seventeenth- and eighteenth-century England reveal much greater migration than had been suspected,[89] and other studies show that behind the facade of stability in French villages there has always been high geographic mobility.[90] In recent decades geographic mobility in the United States has been constant. One out of six people changes residences every year and one out of fourteen moves across county lines, that is, moves beyond the local community – but more frequently because of hous-

---

[83] F. T. Miller, W. K. Bentz, J. F. Aponte, and D. R. Brogan, "Perception of Life Crisis Events," in Barbara Snell Dohrenwend and Bruce P. Dohrenwend, eds., *Stressful Life Events* (New York: Wiley, 1974). The basic measure and concept were developed by Thomas H. Holmes and R. H. Rahe and reported in "The Social Readjustment Rating Scale," *Journal of Psychosomatic Research* 11 (1967): 213–18.

[84] Thomas H. Holmes and Minoru Masuda, "Life Change and Susceptibility to Illness," in Dohrenwend and Dohrenwend, eds., *Stressful Life Events*. The power of even benign changes to disrupt established life patterns is revealed in the income-maintenance experiments where it was found that a governmentally provided income for a three-year period led to an *increase* in the dissolution of marriages. See Peggy Thoits and Michael Hannan, "Income and Psychological Distress: The Impact of an Income-Maintenance Experiment," *Journal of Health and Social Behavior* 20 (1979): 120–38.

[85] See Alex Inkeles, "Personal Adjustment and Modernization," in his *Exploring Individual Modernity* (New York: Columbia University Press, 1983).

[86] Peter M. Balu and Otis D. Duncan, *The American Occupational Structure* (1967; reprint New York: Free Press, 1978), 256–9.

[87] See Jeylan T. Mortimer, "Dual Career Families: A Sociological Perspective," in Samiha S. Peterson et al., eds., *The Two-Career Family – Issues and Alternatives* (Washington, DC: University Press of America, 1978).

[88] See Victor F. Fuchs, *How We Live: An Economic Perspective on Americans from Birth to Death* (Cambridge: Harvard University Press, 1983), 138.

[89] Peter Laslett, *The World We Have Lost*, 2d ed. (New York: Scribner's, 1971).

[90] Lawrence Wylie, *Chanzeaux: A Village in Anjou* (Cambridge: Harvard University Press, 1966); Idem, *Village in the Vaucluse: An Account of Life in a French Village* (1957; reprint New York: Harper/Colophon, 1964).

ing circumstances than because of job changes.[91] The increase in job changes over a lifetime – from about six in 1900 to about twelve now – is more attributable to the declining proportion of the work force engaged in farming (itself a product of massive improvements in agricultural technology), necessarily tied to a place, than to changes in industrial technology. Accepting all these caveats, it is nevertheless fairly certain that markets increase geographical mobility and so the stresses (and benefits) of change.

Market-accelerated technological changes also cause occupational changes, although perhaps more slowly than generally believed. During the 1962–7 period, a prosperous period and therefore one conducive to changes in technology, technological advances "changed relatively few jobs to a significant degree – about 2 or 3 percent a year." The reason is that changing a machine often does little more than change what the individual does *in the same job* and usually in the same department as well as the same firm.[92] But the incidence of the effects of technological change are uneven: Although in general the people who get new machines benefit from them and the direct effect is upgrading for the already skilled, the indirect effect for blacks and the unskilled is likely to be job displacement.[93] Whereas the technology of the factory originally served the unskilled, especially those moving from agriculture to industry, today it seems to serve the already skilled. Once again the Matthew Principle ("For to every one that hath shall be given . . .") and the malign cycle prevails.

Technological unemployment. We cannot trace the multiple relations among markets, technology, and unemployment. But it will be useful to point out one important difference between technological unemployment and other kinds, notably those related to the business cycle and to changes in taste (to the extent that these kinds are separable). Unemployment created by the business cycle and by changes in taste or product demand have few if any social benefits, whereas advances in technology imply an increase in our knowledge and power over nature. As mentioned, technology is a source of national and individual wealth – 38 percent of the growth in national income from 1929 to 1969.[94] Thus, we approach the problem of technological unemployment[95] in a mood to tolerate some transient unemployment costs, if they are not too high.

[91] Sar A. Levitan, Garth L. Mangum, and Ray Marshall, *Human Resources and Labor Markets* (New York: Harper and Row, 1972), 9.

[92] Mueller, *Technological Advance in an Expanding Economy,* 10–12, original emphasis.

[93] Richard H. Hall, *Dimensions of Work* (Beverly Hills, CA: Sage, 1986), 22–3.

[94] Denison, *Accounting for United States Economic Growth 1929–1969,* 80. There is later evidence, however, that the rate of national income increase attributable to technology is decreasing. See Denison, *Trends in American Economic Growth, 1929–1982* (Washington, DC: Brookings Institution, 1985).

[95] Among economists, the role of technology in creating unemployment, once thought to be a dominant factor, is sometimes minimized and it is assimilated into the general categories of unemployment (frictional, cyclical, and structural) without special attention to its causes: "Technological unemployment is sometimes referred to as a separate and distinct category. However, the concept adds very little to our understanding of unemployment in that technological unemployment can easily be slotted into the other types of unemployment." James J. Hughes and Richard Perlman, *The Economics of Unemployment: A Comparative Analysis of Britain and the United States* (Brighton, UK: Wheatsheaf/Harvester, 1984), 32.

Mueller's estimate that technological change affects only 2 or 3 percent of the jobs each year gives an outside measure of the maximum incidence of technological unemployment, but it fails even to suggest the cumulative effect or its concentration. In ordinary industry and commerce, "the decline in traditional production industries, coupled with the introduction of new technology, has led to a marked decline in employment in manufacturing and production industries." It is a decline whose results are made worse by the "spread of new technology to the service sector," which must now accept the responsibility for employing those whose jobs have been lost in manufacturing.[96] Whole industries may be sharply eroded, as in the decline of the railroads due to the rise of motor and air transportation, and large geographical regions affected, as in the case of Appalachia when oil displaced coal as the preferred fuel.[97]

The market's relief for pain is adaptation, and its expression in the market is seen in workers' adaptation to frictional unemployment. But structural unemployment is different: "Because the structurally unemployed generally have a large investment in their skill and location, they are less likely than young mobile workers to find new jobs quickly." As Levitan and associates say, unemployment of this kind "requires vigorous efforts at retraining or relocation."[98] Without an agency that might profit from these "vigorous efforts," the market is devoid of any remedial instrument. But if there is no easy market remedy, there is a market or market-mediated cause. In addition to constant efforts to reduce the cost of labor, the "dominant source" of structural unemployment, says Hall, "is the move by organizations to reduce costs . . . through technological change in the form of mechanization, automation, and computerization."[99] Thus, the market is a mediator; technological changes that the market did not cause in any ultimate sense, and whose pains it cannot easily remedy, nevertheless are mediated by market mechanisms in such a way as to make their proximate causes and consequences fairly attributable to the market.

Although command economies are subject to the same problems of frictional unemployment (estimated at about 0.4% in the USSR) and to the same technological changes (rather slower than in the West), they have been said *not* to be subject to the same consequent unemployment. The reason is that "the typical Soviet enterprise's insatiable demand for additional labor is sufficient to ensure both a general regime of job security and aggregate full employment." But, less creditably, the cause of this insatiable demand is that "the more inputs [labor or capital goods] the enterprise can have allocated to it, the better, so far as the management is concerned. If these inputs are incorporated in the production plan, they will be covered in the enterprise's financial plan, even if planned losses are involved. . . . [And] the larger the enterprise labour force, the higher the basic pay scales of management."[100] The productivity costs of this arrangement are high, involving a lower

[96] Hughes and Perlman, *The Economics of Unemployment,* 153.

[97] Levitan et al., *Human Resources and Labor Markets,* 36; see also Curt Tausky, *Work and Society: An Introduction to Industrial Sociology* (Itasca, IL: Peacock, 1984).

[98] Levitan et al., *Human Resources and Labor Markets,* 35.

[99] Hall, *Dimensions of Work,* 21.

[100] Philip Hanson, "The Serendipitous Soviet Achievement of Full Employment: Labour Shortage and

standard of consumer living in return for economic security and the avoidance of the severe pains of prolonged unemployment. We are told: "The ending of mass unemployment in the USSR, which occurred in the course of a mere eighteen months in 1929 and 1930, has a strong claim to be considered one of the most important events in twentieth-century world history,"[101] but with the arrival of glasnost, the picture changes. After years of assertion that there is no unemployment in the Soviet Union, recent news stories uncover regional unemployment of substantial proportions.

Technological changes are bound to reduce employment in one area while increasing it in another. The market's way of handling the problem of technologically induced changes in employment opportunities, is, as mentioned, improving individual adaptation, especially by increasing people's dispositions to move from one job to another. But at the same time, the market accelerates changes so that these adaptations are too slow and too expensive for those redundant in one area or occupation to move and retrain for the new jobs elsewhere. Market instruments to ease the pains of transition are almost totally missing; relief must come from outside the market. In this respect, the market experience under circumstances of rapid technological change may be quite unhappy.

The mediating role of culture

Cultural differences, both within and between nations, influence the market–technology relationship. Inasmuch as markets are part of culture, the domestic market may inadvertently help adaptation to technological change in at least three aspects. As Touraine points out, technological changes will be more readily accepted by those already "participating in modern consumption norms," for their interest in technology and its products have been aroused. These consumption norms, of course, are urged upon society by markets. Also, "the stronger the consciousness of community, the more difficult it is to accept technological change." Thus, the market's dissolution of the bonds of community, a theme stressed by Tönnies, may help to prepare a population for technological change. Finally, the contribution of the labor market to the movement from farm to industry helps this process of adaptation to technology, for according to Touraine, urban workers (who are already in a changing structure) accept change more easily than rural workers.[102]

Cultural differences between nations are at least as strong. Two illustrations will

Labour Hoarding in the Soviet Economy," in David Lane, ed., *Labour and Employment in the USSR* (Brighton, UK: Wheatsheaf/Harvester, 1986), 88. A detailed discussion of Soviet labor statistics (pp. 36–49) accounts for some of the anomalies in the data underlying the various accounts of unemployment in various chapters.

[101] R. W. Davies, "The Ending of Mass Unemployment in the USSR" in D. Lane, *Labour and Unemployment in the USSR*. For an alternative view stating that the end of unemployment in the USSR was part of a plan to "defeat the working class" by atomizing it and thus to prevent rebellion against the unfavorable working conditions and "harsh labor laws" imposed by the regime, see Donald Filtzer, *Soviet Workers and Stalinist Industrialization: The Formation of Modern Soviet Production Relations* (Armonk, NY: Sharpe, 1986).

[102] Alain Touraine, with Claude Durand, Daniel Pecaut, and Alfred Willener, *Workers' Attitudes to Technical Change* (Paris, OECD, 1965), 119, 133–4.

demonstrate the mediating roles of national cultures – and in the first illustration, of freedom of inquiry and speech, as well.

Mechanization in market and command economies. In the fifteen-nation study (Forslin et al.) of the effects of "automation" (actually a confounding of assembly lines, new machines, and, very rarely, continous process technology called *automation* in the United States) on worker attitudes and behavior, the command economies found benign effects whereas the Western nations found virtually no effects. The East German socialist contributors state: "The results of the investigation stress anew that scientific-technological progress in the GDR means . . . the establishment of working conditions under which people feel well, have opportunities for deepening collective relations and can express their creative potential."[103] And their Soviet counterparts claim:

Judging by the estimation of workers directly affected by technical progress . . . automation improves all the basic characteristics of work content. It increases the variety of work, makes it more independent, provides the chance to use a greater degree of accumulated knowedge, increases the possibility of creative work, [and so forth].[104]

But in the American contribution the authors state: "workers [both operators and maintenance men] attached to automated departments differ little in attitude and behavior from those doing similar work in nonautomated plants."[105] The British and the West German reports in the same multinational study came to the same conclusions.[106] How can we account for the victory of the null hypothesis in the West and the triumph of the machine in the socialist countries? One hypothesis is that the ideology of progress under socialism has so captivated socialist scholars that their interpretations reflect this ideology. In the Soviet case this is made more plausible by the reported incidents of Luddite behavior by workers seeking to stop the use of automated machines. In a news story titled "The Soviet Luddites" Mark Frankland reports:

Industrial robots at the prestige Tolyatti car plant are now protected from vengeful workers by strong cages following a series of "accidents" which put them out of commission. The motive, the Communist Party newspaper, *Pravda,* reports, is not only that the machines are "efficient and tireless," but that they are also "uncompromisingly demanding" of their human assistants. The robot simply cannot adjust itself to "an unskilled or lazy assistant," the paper says.[107]

The Yugoslav experience, closer in practice to the Soviet experience than to the Western experience, but reported under more relaxed circumstances, finds mechanization of this kind truly alienating.

[103] Erhard Ulrich and Gerhard Dörfer, "The Influence of Automation on Workers in the Automobile Industry – Results of the Case Study in the Federal Republic of Germany," in Forslin et al., *Automation and Industrial Workers,* vol. 1, pt 2, p. 161.
[104] V. I. Ussenin and associates, "Soviet Workers and Automation of the Production Process," 170.
[105] Betty M. Jacob and associates, "Automation and the American Automobile Worker: Routes to Humanized Productivity," in Forslin et al., *Automation and Industrial Workers,* vol. 1, pt 1, pp. 65–94 at p. 69.
[106] There is, in fact, no conflict between these Western findings and the favorable effects found in the Mueller and Blauner studies discussed, for both agree on the effects of assembly line on workers; Blauner is talking about continuous processing plants and Mueller about technological products used by individuals in advanced work.
[107] Mark Frankland, (London) *Observer,* 5 June 1983.

Automation in Britain and France. Duncan Gallie studied the effects of genuinely automated processes in England and France. Both these experiences differ from those studied almost twenty years earlier by Blauner in the United States.[108] Blauner argues that the blurring of blue-collar/white-collar differences, the development of teamwork, the introduction of variety and responsibility at work, and especially the increased autonomy on the job and freedom from personal supervision all lead to a reduction of alienation and increased identification by workers with the manufacturing process. In contrast, Mallet, and other French writers following his lead, argue that as workers learn of their indispensability in continuous process plants and develop a sense of control, they seek ever larger degrees of control and become the vanguard of a new workers' movement to seize control over industry. Control, rather than wages, becomes the fulcrum of conflict.

Examining the effects of automation in several continuous process oil refineries in Britain and France, Duncan Gallie found that the effects of automation on worker attitudes, alienation, and worker–management relations were not different from the effects of other industrial processes, but that the differences between British and French workers' attitudes were substantial. He concludes "that the nature of the technology *per se* has, at most, very little importance" for the social integration of the work force in the industrial process. "Instead, our evidence indicates the critical importance of the wider cultural and social structural patterns of specific societies for determining the nature of social interaction within the advanced sector."[109]

Our interest is captured by the fact that, holding constant the degree of marketization and levels of technology, nevertheless, worker response patterns to the same major technological changes varied greatly between cultures. As mentioned in the discussion of the systematicity of social analysis in Chapter 2, Gallie's findings remind us of the interacting character of economic and social systems, with the latter sometimes dominating the former.

Deskilling

The criticisms of market work because of its failure to offer any form of transcendent purposes, the allegations of economic exploitation, and the belief that work with machines tends to degrade work, are often accompanied by a fourth line of criticism: Market forces tend systematically to deskill workers, depriving them of the opportunities for work satisfaction and personal development that is possible in modern industry and commerce. We turn to this last criticism here.

The changing level of worker skills required
Workers develop cognitive complexity, self-esteem, and social responsibility at work primarily if their jobs are substantively complex, that is, if their jobs require complex skills. Any assessment of the market's role in the process of human development, therefore, must rely on some estimate of the way the market encourages or

---

[108] Serge Mallet, *La Nouvelle Classe Ouvrière* (Paris: 1969), as reported in Duncan Gallie, *In Search of the New Working Class*, 16–21. Except for the comments on market effects, the following discussion relies substantially on Gallie.
[109] Gallie, *In Search of the New Working Class*, 296.

discourages the use of these complex skills. One criticism of industrial work in a market economy is that it relies on work where "the *absolute* level of skill of all but the very highest jobs is – to say the least – minimal."[110] We have rejected this view as incongruent with the more probing studies, cited in Chapter 13, of what workers actually do, and, in any event, the evidence from command economies suggests that to the extent that the criticism bears weight, it applied even more to command economies than to market economies.[111] It is a criticism of industrialism, not markets.

The criticisms of the market that we wish to examine are diachronic; they allege that there is an inherent tendency in the capitalist "labor process" to simplify work and to degrade skills as much as possible, as Frederick Taylor proposed.[112] Their arguments take two forms. Harry Braverman argues that a "capitalist class" devises machines and routinizes skills in order to gain control over labor. Control is facilitated by depriving workers of knowledge.[113] On the other hand, without doubting the process of deskilling Richard Edwards argues that the motivation is only partly to control (so as to inhibit collective organization); more importantly, it is the normal profit motive, leading to arranging work so that training costs are minimal and the least skilled, and therefore the cheapest, labor is employed.[114]

Before dealing with the substantive question of actual deskilling, we turn to the prior question of whether the alleged drive by owners and/or managers to reduce work to the simplest operations is motivated by a desire to maximize short-term control over labor or to maximize short-term profits. The question might further be interpreted as drawing a distinction between conceptions of capitalist society and conceptions of a market economy. A brief answer is that in societies where power is the main currency, maximizing control would be the most important motive, whereas in societies where money is the main currency, profits would be most important. Following this line of thought I suggest a curious inversion of the current "deskilling" argument. In both the Soviet Union and the Republic of China there is reported a widespread recognition of the need to improve the profitability of state enterprises by letting market calculations play a larger part in decision making. Inevitably, this process deprives party-appointed managers of some of their discretion and the party itself of power and patronage. As matters stand, managers and party officials do not gain personally from increased profitability; thus the profit

---

[110]R. M. Blackburn and Michael Mann, *The Working Class in the Labour Market* (London: Macmillan, 1979), 280.
[111]See Peter Rutland, "Productivity Campaigns in Soviet Industry," in D. Lane, *Labour and Employment in the USSR*.
[112]Frederick W. Taylor, *Scientific Management* (1911; reprint New York: Harper, 1947).
[113]Harry Braverman, *Labor and Monopoly Capital* (New York: Monthly Review Press, 1974). Marx's original argument along these lines spoke of the alliance of "the man of knowledge" with capital against the "productive laborers."
[114]Richard Edwards, *Contested Terrain: The Transformation of the Work Place in the Twentieth Century* (New York: Basic Books, 1979). We take Braverman's and Edwards's arguments to refer to "deskilling" in an absolute sense, rather than to "underemployment of skills" – the meaning of deskilling used by Hall, *Dimensions of Work*, 23. Given the rising level of skills flowing from increased education, underemployment is an additional serious problem. One solution to the rising level of skills is job molding, but Kohn and Schooler (*Work and Personality*) find this solution to be infrequent and of limited usefulness.

motive is minimal, but the power motive is considerable.[115] Managers and party officials are, therefore, reluctant to introduce changes expanding market controls that would make their enterprises more profitable but deprive them of power. This is essentially what Filtzer says happened in the Soviet Union where "the Stalinist elite," having crushed the peasants, "had to defeat the working class, all the while hiding its attack behind a rhetoric of building socialism."[116]

But in capitalist market societies money is the main currency and therefore the profitability of the enterprise is the main consideration. Managers are sensitive to profits in small part because their jobs are at stake.[117] More generally, short-term company profits are the criteria by which managers are judged and judge themselves, at least in the American economy.[118] I conclude, therefore, that the alleged deskilling in capitalist, but not communist systems, is, or would be if true, only another aspect of attempts by managers to reduce costs and thereby to improve their profit scores – and nothing more. With many exceptions,[119] management in market economies follows principles of profit maximization rather than power maximization.

There is no immanent tendency in a market society to match jobs to expectations, or to educate only enough people so that there will be jobs enough to fulfill their expectations. Their expectations are, of course, based on the past levels of education required for each job level; upgrading educational levels in the population generally will frustrate these expectations. Scitovsky points out that although the proportion of total jobs classified as managerial and professional steadily increased for the 1952–54 period, the "ratio of professional and managerial jobs to college graduates" steadily declined over this period.[120] In terms of hedonics, this leads to frustration and the sense that one is not called upon at work to use one's faculties, but in terms of cognitive development and its associated sense of personal control, one must thank the blind forces of the market for offering a supply of talent that is good for industry but that had not been demanded before it was available. That is, society benefited in this case by having a system of supply *not* dependent on prior or even anticipated demand.[121]

---

[115] As Weber pointed out, parties are defined by their power. Thus, it is relevant that in the USSR "the director of an enterprise of any size will invariably be a Party member, and he himself will therefore be under effective Party supervision." Elizabeth Teague, "The USSR Law on Work Collectives: Workers' Control or Workers Controlled?" in D. Lane, *Labour and Employment in the USSR*, 243.

[116] Filtzer, *Soviet Workers and Stalinist Industrialization*, 254.

[117] James Soref and Michael Soref, "Profit Constraints on Managerial Autonomy: Managerial Theory and the Unmaking of the Corporation President," *American Sociological Review* 46 (1981): 1–18.

[118] Robert B. Reich, *The Next American Frontier* (New York: New York Times Books, 1983), chap. 8.

[119] Harvey Liebenstein, *Beyond Economic Man: A New Foundation for Microeconomics* (Cambridge: Harvard University Press, 1976).

[120] Tibor Scitovsky, "Excessive Demand for Job Importance and its Implications," in Scitovsky, ed., *Human Desire and Economic Satisfaction: Essays on the Frontiers of Economics* (New York: New York University Press, 1986), 139. Original essay published 1981.

[121] Ibid., 140. Scitovsky's criticism of the narrow vocationalism of the education is congenial to most humanists, but the prodemocratic, pro–Bill of Rights, and protolerance attitudinal changes that *any* higher education produces do some of the things that Scitovsky believes flow only from liberal arts education. And these higher educational effects are noticeable even after the major effects of recruitment are accounted for. See Herbert Hyman, Charles R. Wright, and John Shelton Reed, *The Enduring Effects of Education* (Chicago: University of Chicago Press, 1975).

Evidence on deskilling

Has there been a process of deskilling in factories – and among clerical workers?[122] One recent analysis says the net effect of the introduction of machines to do work previously done by skilled workers depends on which group of workers are employed to service and repair the machines. If the servicing and maintenance of the machines is performed by former craftspersons unable to find jobs employing their special skills, some deskilling has taken place. If, on the other hand, the servicing and repairing of these machines is performed by formerly less skilled workers, there has been a net upgrading of skill requirements.[123] Another, similar analysis includes in the evaluation the nature and number of people in an occupation as well as what members of that occupation actually do. Thus Spenner points out that although the occupation of *engineer* may have been downgraded in the actual skills required, there are proportionately more engineers in the work force, thereby upgrading the work force.[124]

Trend figures are somewhat more conclusive. In gross terms, we may note that in 1900 the proportion of the work force labeled "operatives and kindred" was 13 percent; by 1970 this had grown modestly to 18 percent. "Professional, technical and kindred" in 1900 was 4 percent, which had grown three and one-half times to 14 percent by 1970. "Clerical and kindred" were 3 percent in 1900, but by 1970 they had increased their proportion five and one-half times to 18 percent.[125] The categories are gross; William Form provides a more detailed account of changes in job content of U.S. manual workers over the 1870–1970 period and concludes: "The most striking trend is the slow rise in male skilled workers since 1900 and the rapid decline of unskilled workers. For women, the percentage of skilled, operatives, and laborers remained constant, but service workers have increased as domestic workers declined." Cautiously, Form comments on these research reports: "We can conclude that skilled work has not declined over seventy years. . . . To sustain his position, Braverman must prove that today's skilled workers are less skilled than they used to be. His attempt is not convincing."[126]

In his 1979 article Kenneth Spenner, obviously influenced by the work of Kohn and Schooler (treated in Chapter 13), analyzed the substantive complexity of work and the closeness of its supervision among those working with data, people, and things. He found that whereas some jobs have been downgraded, a larger proportion

[122] Evelyn Glenn and Rosalyn Feldberg, "Degraded and Deskilled: The Proletarianization of Clerical Work," *Social Problems* 25 (1979): 52–64.

[123] Charles Sabel, *Work and Politics: The Division of Labor in Industry* (New York: Cambridge University Press, 1982).

[124] Kenneth I. Spenner, "Prometheus Deciphered: Temporal Change in the Skill Level of Work," *American Sociological Review* 48 (1983): 824–37.

[125] U.S. Bureau of the Census, *Historical Statistics of the United States; From Colonial Times to 1970*, pt 1, Series D 182–232 (Washington, DC: U.S. Government Printing Office, 1975), 139. By another set of estimates, in 1900 the labor force included 13% "unskilled"; by 1982 this group had declined to 4%. Tausky, *Work and Society*, 59.

[126] William Form, "Resolving Ideological Issues on the Division of Labor," 149.

of jobs has been upgraded and requires more complex skills and greater worker independence from supervision.[127] In the subsequent (1983) report mentioned before, Spenner added an estimate of the "autonomy" or self-direction of workers permitting initiative and control over the content, manner and speed with which their tasks may be performed. He found few important changes in the past few decades in the balance between more and less autonomous jobs.[128]

What is *not* at issue here is the desire of management to cut costs; rather the issue is whether firms, responding largely to profit incentives in an atmosphere of competition, find it to their advantage to cut costs by routinizing work, simplifying tasks, and thus reducing the need for skilled labor. If they did and do, we would be left with the conclusion that although, compared to traditional villagers, industrial (and service) workers may develop superior cognitive processes and greater feelings of control over their own destinies, the further learning involved in the kinds of discretion Kohn and Schooler discuss would be systematically undermined by market processes. Form found that between 1870 and 1900 the market seemed to respond to cost indices in precisely this manner, but that since 1900 the combined forces of technology and economics operated to increase the demand for skill and hence for more discretion at work.

Evidently the market is neutral on the character of work; it responds to consumer demands as a matter of intrinsic propensities, but responds to workers needs only when workers raise the costs of indifference. In the relatively more class-conscious British setting, Blackburn and Mann found that ordinary factory workers did not assess the constraints on the kind of jobs offered in the 1970s, for "they are not felt by the workers as constraint, in the sense of an active alien force imposing itself on their lives. They have internalized the constraint and identify it as reality itself. . . . For the most part the constraints are not subject to evaluation – they are the 'given' context of action."[129]

In the American setting the market circumstances are even more likely to be identified as "reality itself"—and yet the evidence, at least so far as *change* is concerned, seems to be quite the opposite: Workers are more dissatisfied even if the objective features of work have not declined. After an exhaustive review of the literature, Mortimer reports:

There is little support in the survey data for the contention that changes in the objective features of work have deteriorated so much that they cause the widespread decline in job satisfaction. It suggests little dramatic change in economic rewards, health and safety hazards, or in the time demands of the jobs. . . . [But] we do know that workers are now less satisfied with the intrinsic features of their jobs.[130]

There has been no deskilling for any group; indeed quite the opposite is true for men. There has been failure, however, to develop jobs with the levels of chal-

[127] Kenneth I. Spenner, "Temporal Change in Work Content," *American Sociological Review* 44 (1979): 968–75.
[128] Ibid.
[129] Blackburn and Mann, *The Working Class in the Labour Market*, 287, 297–8.
[130] Jeylan T. Mortimer, *Changing Attitudes Toward Work: Highlights of the Literature* (New York: Pergamon for American Institute Studies in Productivity, 1979), 10.

lenge and self-direction appropriate to a better educated labor force. Before blaming the market, note that Yanowitch says the same thing has happened in the Soviet Union.[131]

Summary

By and large, I have rejected the idea that workers are degraded because they are paid less than their "true value" – on the grounds that neither marginal productivity nor any other current measure can be called a true value. There are economic grounds for thinking workers are overpaid and similar grounds for thinking they are underpaid. The justice arguments that count are consequential; the persuasive economic arguments are those that weight productivity consequences of paying workers less as against other productivity consequences of paying workers more. The criteria, I believe, are more likely to be economic advantage than power or status advantages.

We have found that technology and machines are, with the exception of assembly line technology, more likely to increase the challenge of work than to decrease it. Thus, for the critics the point of establishing market responsibility for technological advance is greatly diminished, but for others it is important. Our main finding is that, because of the pressure of competition, markets are more likely than other economies to accelerate the *pace* of change, and although this has beneficial direct effects on the kinds of jobs offered and on the levels of wages affordable, it has deleterious effects on the market experience of those forced out of the labor market. The experience of change itself is stressful, but within limits it seems to increase cognitive and other capacities – and beyond those limits it reduces them, as I argued in the chapter on environmental complexity (Chapter 8).

In spite of the new emphasis on human capital, there is nothing immanent in market principles or practices that leads to more jobs that demand more skills – or jobs that demand fewer. History shows periods of both trends. For the past ninety years the trend has been toward increasing the demand for skills for men, but not for women. As women enter jobs that have traditionally been occupied by men, this will change.

Transcendence – a discovery in work of purposes beyond one's own survival and wealth – and immanence – the inherent quality of work that provides immediate utility and intrinsic enjoyment – are polar magnets tugging in opposite directions. Some reconciliation may be found in the middle ground where persons enjoy the work itself, and sustain themselves in reasonable comfort while working, on or off the job, for ideals that transcend the worker's own immediate benefits. Since immanence inheres in the work, the market gives it priority; transcendence is not a market property and must be forged by each individual without help from the market. By its failure to recognize and enlist transcendence the market loses a source of energy, but at the same time it protects its population from appeals that will only lead to disappointment.

[131] Murray Yanowitch, *Work in the Soviet Union: Attitudes and Issues* (Armonk, NY: Sharpe, 1985).

15   Distributing workplace learning

Introduction

The market does not and, as I shall argue in the next chapter, cannot give to work the priority that it merits on the grounds of its hedonic and developmental potentials – but neither does it systematically degrade work. What it does is to award to some the advantages of challenging, self-directed work and to others the disadvantages of routine, closely supervised, and unchallenging work. In this chapter we explore the market's distribution system for these kinds of satisfying and unsatisfying work.

The chapter has four principal sections. First, I ask, Who is likely to pay for improving workplace enjoyment and learning? We will find that the market system allocates costs in such a way as to make almost impossible any provision for workplace learning that does not also improve productivity. The second section treats the contribution of family, technology, and market to the stratification of workplace learning. We will discover that the major proportion of the explanation for stratification lies in family and technological processes, not in the market. In line with the argument of Part V, we construct an alternative stratification hierarchy based on work rather than consumer utilities. Third, analysis of the assignment within firms (internal markets) of opportunities for workplace learning shows again how disadvantageous product competition is to workers. And finally, we find in farm work and housework that these facets of the world we have lost need not be mourned. Together this information should help us answer a modified version of the question that has been said to typify political science: Who gets what features of development through work activities, when, and how?

Throughout the discussion two things stand out: the way so many features of the labor market are chronically dependent on changes and trends in the consumer market, and the way competition in the consumer market impinges on and limits the freedom of employers to give worker benefits priorities over consumers.

Who pays for improving learning?

Prior to our attempt to assign costs for the improvement of workplace learning in a market society, we need to understand why employers are not free to alter their labor costs as they please. An important part of that understanding lies in appreciating that source of the demand for labor.

The demand for labor is a derived demand

Market systems are consumer-driven systems; the wants they are devised to satisfy are consumer wants. How, then, shall we think of the problem of raising the relative priority of work to foster full employment and improve learning at work?

289

Full employment. The demand for labor, significant because of its effect on employment and unemployment, is derived from the demand for the things labor is employed to make. As Mandeville observed, the demand for luxuries by the rich, or as Keynes observed, for funeral pyramids by ostentatious and superstitious rulers, may be as useful to full employment as the demand for necessities by the poor and far more useful than the wants of the impecunious. If we allow consumer preferences to govern the system, we may achieve fuller employment at the cost of making foolish and humanly wasteful things. On the other hand, if we were to seek a work-driven as contrasted to a consumption-driven economy, we would give priorities to those products or services that had high labor/capital ratios – to relieve unemployment – rather than to produce socially useful products.

But in so doing, we would be faced with a paradox. If, as unions seem sometimes to believe, the function of industry is to provide jobs rather than products, then increased productivity (doing more with less labor) would be ''inefficient.'' Moreover, we would undermine many of the processes that have contributed to the development of wealth and so to the relief of daily drudgery of the kind that Markham said ''blew out the light within [the] brain'' of *The Man With a Hoe*. It is not a fruitful solution.

The appropriate priority for learning at work. To foster the circumstances favoring learning at work, we would promote those products or services whose production involved the most substantively complex, unsupervised, varied, egalitarian (no one has a ''low'' rank), ''unheavy'' work processes.

Those most likely to favor the uses of work for purposes of personality development are likely to express disdain if not disgust for a materialist consumer society.[1] But it is the maintenance of aggregate demand by these very consumption hungry materialists that sustains the derived demand for labor; and it is the very policies of growth, said to threaten our fragile ecology, that make possible the resources for such job enrichment.

One of the values of a consumption-driven economy is *efficiency* (Chapter 16), which has been said to have outgrown its high value in Western societies.[2] Before we conclude that the emphasis on efficiency and productivity represents too high a cost in fulfillment at work, joining the ''no-growth'' chorus, we should note some economic effects. Without productivity increases, the young will have difficulty in finding jobs, the working population will have trouble meeting their (rising?) expectations, and the surplus to permit Pareto optimal egalitarian income redistributions will be absent. Modest productivity increases may pose a choice between two

[1] See, for example, E. J. Mishan, ''The Wages of Growth,'' *Daedalus* (Fall 1973): 63–87 and other articles in this issue devoted to a discussion of ''no-growth'' policy. The postmaterialists share this disdain for the consumer society. See Ronald Inglehart, *The Silent Revolution* (Princeton: Princeton University Press, 1972); and Idem, ''Post-Materialism in an Environment of Insecurity,'' *American Political Science Review* 75 (1981): 880–900.

[2] John Kenneth Galbraith, *The New Industrial State*, 2d rev. ed. (New York: New American Library/ Mentor), 382; Arthur Okun, *Equality and Efficiency: The Big Tradeoff* (Washington, DC: Brookings Institution, 1975). As late as 1965 a distinguished sociologist (not an economist!) defined ''the problem of labor'' as the problem of maximizing efficient production. See Wilbert E. Moore, *The Impact of Industry* (Englewood Cliffs, NJ: Prentice-Hall, 1965).

syndromes: lower wages with lower unemployment (U.S. in the 1970s) and higher wages with higher unemployment (Germany in the 1970s). Following this line of evidence, not only are we obligated to increase productivity, but we are obligated to increase it greatly, perhaps even to *maximize* it. Unless it can be shown that increasing self-direction, challenge, and the intrinsic enjoyment of work also increases productivity, we are confronted with a genuine dilemma.

Assigning costs

The main cost of improving the kinds of human capital (discussed in Chapter 1) is the income foregone when individuals choose education rather than paid work whenever the latter is available to them.[3] But since these costs usually increase an individual's lifetime earnings by more than their discounted costs, they are investments rather than costs, investments that generally return more to society than to the individuals themselves. In the following assessment of the incidence of costs for improving learning conditions at work, bear in mind that the individual workers have already paid something toward the total cost.

Policies designed to increase the educational and intrinsic value of work, such as those now offered in work-redesign proposals, have three possible effects on the cost of, and therefore the demand for, labor: (1) Work-redesign policies may increase the direct costs of each unit of product, or (2) they may increase the productivity of labor, making it *less* expensive per unit of product, perhaps, as in Sweden, chiefly by reducing absenteeism and labor turnover.[4] And/or (3) the policies may increase the supply of labor by making work more attractive, thereby reducing the cost of and increasing the demand for labor. As many observers have noted,[5] the effects on productivity of these experiments are often mixed, although continuing to offer an educated workforce simple routine jobs seems to sacrifice both potential productivity gains and opportunities for learning at work.

Following market principles, increased costs for labor have two main likely outcomes, depending on the elasticity of demand for the product: If the demand is elastic, the immediate costs are borne by labor, either by directly or indirectly reducing employment or, less likely (for reasons to follow), by decreasing money wages. If the demand for the product is inelastic, the cost is likely borne by the consumers in increased prices for the product. The machinery for this is familiar[6] and will not be explicated here.

In the real world wages rates are "sticky" and do not change quickly, with the consequence that employment levels are more likely than wage levels to be varied.

[3] Theodore W. Schultz, *Investment in Human Capital: The Role of Education and Research* (New York: Free Press, 1971).
[4] Richard H. Hall, *Dimensions of Work* (Beverly Hills, CA: Sage, 1986), 284.
[5] See, for example, E. A. Locke, D. B. Feren, V. M. McCaleb, K. N. Shaw, and A. T. Denny, "The Relative Effectiveness of Four Methods of Motivating Employee Performance," in K. D. Duncan, M. M. Gruenberg, and D. Wallis, eds., *Changes in Working Life* (Chichester, UK: Wiley, 1980).
[6] A fuller elaboration of the forces at work would include (1) the substitutability of other factors for labor, (2) the elasticity of supply for these other factors, (3) the proportion of labor costs to total costs, (4) current levels of unemployment, (5) the firm's competitive position (see below). See John R. Hicks, *The Theory of Wages* (London: Macmillan, 1935). We return to this problem in Chapter 21, "The Economics of the Intrinsic."

For example, a study of the British labor market found that wages did not vary with net changes in level of employment.[7] In fact, as Samuelson and Nordhaus point out, the two expected effects, substitution of labor for leisure and, as wages increase, the use of higher income to purchase more leisure, just about cancel out. The consequence is that the labor supply curve is "close to vertical with income effects just balancing out substitution effects."[8] This means that an increase has its effect on unemployment rather than on real wages.

Who pays for improved conditions of learning, then, depends on (1) the effect on productivity influencing net unit costs, (2) the elasticity of demand for the product, and (3) ease of entry into the industry. For many reasons, productivity is crucial. Under certain conditions, even in the short run, improving the quality of work life can improve productivity,[9] but when the quality of work life is cast in the form of increasing learning, the more general benefits of education on productivity may be enlisted. Inasmuch as increased education contributes about a fifth of productivity gains, the appeal to the standard "satisfaction-does-not-change-productivity" arguments[10] must be reconsidered, for satisfaction from learning is different from other forms of satisfaction. Whether giving priority to work experiences is compatible with market economy is an open question to be addressed in the next chapter.

As we shall see, there is another reason for believing that the costs of improving the circumstances for learning often devolve on the consumer or on labor outside the firm (who lose potential jobs). The firms that offer the most favorable circumstances for learning at work usually have a degree of market power, shifting the cost to the consumer or to labor outside the plant. Market power, evading the forces of the market, is the key.

Improving learning versus increasing wages? Increasing the circumstances favoring learning is different from increasing wages in one important respect. Improving these learning circumstances does not offer the same market system benefits as does improving wages: If you increase wages at the same time that you increase costs, you also increase aggregate demand for a variety of market products; if you increase the quality of work life (profitability remaining the same),

[7] D. I. Mackay, D. Boddy, J. Brack, J. A. Diack, and N. Jones, *Labour Markets Under Different Employment Conditions* (London: George Allen & Unwin, 1971), 389

[8] Paul A. Samuelson and William D. Nordhaus, *Economics,* 12th ed. (New York: McGraw-Hill, 1985), 618. In general, the elasticity of demand for labor increases with the proportion of capital costs to total costs, the difficulty of substituting other factors for labor, and the elasticity of supply for those factors whose increase involves the need for matching labor. One solution to "sticky" wages is to make wages depend on profitability; see Martin Weitzman, *The Share Economy: Conquering Stagflation* (Cambridge: Harvard University Press, 1984).

[9] Edward E. Lawler, III, "Strategies for Improving the Quality of Work Life," *American Psychologist* 37 (1982): 486–93; David J. Cherington, H. Joseph Reitz, and William E. Scott, Jr., "Effect of Contingent and Non-contingent Rewards on the Relations Between Satisfaction and Task Performance," in Daniel Katz, Robert L. Kahn, and J. Stacy Adams, *The Study of Organizations* (San Francisco: Jossey-Bass, 1980), 257–64.

[10] Victor H. Vroom, *Work and Motivation* (New York: Wiley, 1964); compare U.S. Department of Health Education and Welfare (HEW), Special Task Force, *Work in America* (Cambridge: M.I.T. Press, n.d.), 2.

there is no such increase in aggregate demand and therefore no increase in employment for other workers elsewhere. We have returned again to the system characteristics with which we started this discussion.

Costs of slow response to changed incentives. Some (e.g., Likert) estimate that it takes as much as seven years for a work force habituated to obedience
and reliant on money rewards to learn how to appreciate and take advantage of
increases in self-direction and nonmonetary values. As Kohn and Schooler point
out, much of the effect of self-directed jobs on personality is lagged – in their case
over a ten-year-period.[11] Time in the market is measured by compound interest
rates, for example, 10 percent compounded doubles in seven years. If, where the
appropriate interest rate is 10 percent, the benefits of work redesign do not emerge
for seven years, a firm has to calculate the benefits to be double the present benefits
in order for the improvement in work conditions to be worth the cost. It is in such
forms as this that the indifference of the market to improvements in "human capital" that do not imply short-run increases in productivity is registered.

Of the three market assignments of costs under conditions of no or low productivity increases, two have ethically defensible solutions: The beneficiaries pay, the
consuming public pays. One solution is indefensible: those made unemployed by
the increased costs of labor pay. It is at this point that the market fails.

Stratification

The principal concern of those worried about social stratification is usually whether
the benefits of any process go to the poor or to the rich. As we shall see, this focus
is a reflection of our market tendencies to make income the main dimension of
concern. Later in this chapter I will introduce the idea of "privileged classes"
where engagement in enjoyable and fruitful work is the dimension along which
people are graded. But in the meantime, we cannot evade more traditional questions
on the distribution by income strata of opportunities for workplace learning.

As everyone knows, the better educated and those from more prosperous families
receive more of the benefits of self-directed, nonroutine, relatively unsupervised
work than do the less well educated and the children of the less prosperous. Our
task, then, is to assess the influence of the market, as compared to family and
technology, on this underlying stratification. The well-rehearsed arguments on the
effects of markets or, more loosely, capitalism, on social stratification and social
classes and the relationship between market economies and social classes cannot be
entered here.[12] I offer, instead, a modest introduction to the way in which markets
influence the way social stratification affects learning at the workplace. What we

[11] Melvin Kohn and Carmi Schooler, *Work and Personality: An Inquiry Into the Impact of Social Stratification* (Norwood, NJ: Ablex, 1983), 141.
[12] In addition to Marx and the classical sociologists, some recent works include Ralf Dahrendorf, *Class
and Class Conflict in Industrial Society* (Stanford: Stanford University Press, 1959); Anthony Giddens,
The Class Structure of the Advanced Societies (1973; reprint New York: Harper Torchbook, 1975); Frank
Parkin, *Class Inequality and Political Order* (New York: Praeger, 1975); and Richard F. Hamilton,
Class and Politics in the United States (New York: Wiley, 1972).

shall find is that, side by side with the market system, the technological system and the family processes of socialization have a great deal to do with the stratification of opportunities that develop at work.

Unemployment

The first and most tragic problem is that of unemployment, for there can be no workplace learning without a workplace. Is unemployment caused primarily by exogenous forces, such as government and unions, or by endogenous forces such as the business cycle, chronic lack of demand, or transitional problems of adjustment to market-induced change? What proportion is structural, what proportion cyclical, and what proportion transitional? Although these questions are crucial for certain purposes, I have nothing to add to the answers others have given[13] and can only report my conclusion from reading these sources. Endogenous market forces share a substantial portion of the blame, largely because "It was cheaper to give many lower skilled individuals a lifetime income [on welfare] than it was to raise their earning capacity by the same amount."[14]

A second cause of unemployment is the alleged relation between unemployment and inflation, currently reflected in the concept of a "natural rate of unemployment" – that rate at which the pressures for wage inflation are held in check by unemployment – representing some combination of exogenous and endogenous forces. Samuelson and Nordhaus, who accept the validity of analyses confirming this relation and seem also to accept its endogenous character, find it disturbing: "The high natural rate of unemployment, with the accompanying necessity to accept much involuntary unemployment, is a central flaw in modern capitalism. And, indeed, the problem seems to be getting worse over time, as higher and higher unemployment rates are necessary to restrain inflation."[15] In this statement, Samuelson and Nordhaus seem to be assigning responsibility to the market for much unemployment, but this assignment does not mean that exogenous, nonmarket forces (e.g., unions) may not be blamed for the market "solution" to inflation, namely, unemployment. If the trend that these authors perceive prevails, workplace learning declines and the shape of the social pyramid flattens on a broader base, cancelling its previous tendency to resemble a diamond.

Stratification, work, and personality

The principles of the market are ineluctably inegalitarian: Rewards are to be commensurate with contributions to profit. But the same principles are equally opposed

[13] For a classic defense of the "natural rate" suggesting that all government policies to change it are in vain, see Milton Friedman, *A Program for Monetary Stability* (New York: Fordham University Press, 1960); antidotes are suggested in Bertram Gross and Alfred Pfaller, "Unemployment: A Global Challenge," *The Annals* 492 (July 1987). The new evidence on the personal costs of unemployment are available in P. Kelvin and J. Jarrett, *Social Psychological Consequences of Unemployment* (Cambridge, UK: Cambridge University Press, 1985). Samuelson and Nordhaus say: "In the long run, the only level of unemployment consistent with stable inflation rates is the natural rate of unemployment. The long run Phillips curve must therefore be drawn as a vertical line, rising straight up from the natural rate of unemployment." Samuelson and Nordhaus, *Economics*, 253.

[14] Lester Thurow, "Economics 1977," *Daedalus* 106 (Fall 1977): 79–84 at 81.

[15] Samuelson and Nordhaus, *Economics*, 258.

to the formation of social classes, for the same reasons that they oppose community. Barriers to the free flow of the factors of production, including management and labor (that is, people), are hostile to the forces of even an imperfect market. As cohesive self-conscious groups, social classes are market impediments; they imply transaction costs and friction. Whereas inequality is neither good nor bad, social classes are bad. The dilemma for the market is that inequality is inevitable and yet by principles outside those of market economics, inequality will result in stratification systems whose members form social classes.

The relation between social class and personality[16] interacts with the relation between work and personality in complex ways, as any three variables might be expected to do. Assuming that we wish only to explain the effects of work and class on personality, the following propositions will be variously significant.

Social class position→work experience→personality   (1)

Work experience→social class position→personality   (2)

Social class position→personality   (3)

Work experience→personality (see Chapter 13)   (4)

The third proposition is known to be strong. "Of all aspects of social structure," say Kohn and Schooler, "social stratification is by far the most important" in influencing "men's values and orientations."[17] But the first proposition helps to explain that relationship by interposing the mediating influence of work experience. This, too, is confirmed: The influence of social stratification on values and orientations in the United States is substantially reduced (reducing correlations by from half to two-thirds) by eliminating or controlling for the effects of those features of a job that influence self-direction. That is, the low quality of work experience contributes more than do other aspects of the class system to people's self-doubts, lack of trust, authoritarianism, and conformism in their moral standards.[18]

The stratification effect of the first proposition is further enhanced in two ways: (1) a recapitulation of the preentry stratification within the firm reinforces the original premarket effects, and (2) the substantive complexity and hierarchical level of a person's job at a given time will be reflected in the complexity and hierarchical level of that person's job ten years later.[19] One roll of the dice influences the outcome of the next roll. So propositions 3 and 1 are correct, and a fifth proposition emerges:

Social class position→work experience→social class position→ personality   (5)

Proposition 2 puts work experience as the prior cause, that is, work experience

[16]There is an extensive literature on social class and personality; for example, see Alan L. Gray, ed., *Class and Personality in Society* (New York: Atherton, 1969); Charles A. Valentine, *Culture and Poverty: Critique and Counter Proposals* (Chicago: University of Chicago Press, 1968); Margaret J. Lundberg, *The Incomplete Adult: Social Class Constraints on Personality* (Westport, CT: Greenwood Press, 1974); Oscar Lewis, *LaVida: A Puerto Rican Family in The Culture of Poverty – San Juan and New York* (New York: Random House/Vintage, 1966).
[17]Kohn and Schooler, *Work and Personality,* 14, 32.
[18]Ibid., 28.
[19]Ibid., 227–8, 140–1.

has a prior and independent influence on a person's class position that mediates the influence of work experience on personality. This proposition implies a kind of technical fix on class and personality: Whatever work has to be done establishes a hierarchy of positions that will then be reflected as class positions in society and in that fashion influence personality. Thus, "positions within work organizations are [necessarily] structured in a hierarchical way. . . . The distribution of inequality is fixed. There are a set number of positions at particular levels."[20] The organization of work processes determines class; the role of education and character, but not income, is primarily to serve as initial guidelines leading people to their respective levels in the work hierarchy. If prior differences in income and educational levels were lessened, the requirements of work would still stratify people in roughly the same ways and thus influence their personality-shaping experiences on the job.

The role of markets

Our concern is with the influence of the market on these several propositions.[21] To the extent that we are concerned solely with inequality (and not the filling of positions in this unequal structure), the second proposition is the easiest to dispose of. This proposition holds that regardless of other elements of social structure, work assignments determine class position because income and status reflect job complexity (including responsibility); the social class determinants of personality are wholly or largely derivative from the requirements of work. Thus whether the economy is a market economy or not is irrelevant; any advanced society with similar work requirements would have a similar stratification profile.[22] Unless technological and organizational requirements are malleable, any advanced economy would also distribute the opportunities for learning self-direction, acquiring self-esteem, and developing intellectual flexibility in the same hierarchical order.

There is, however, an uncertain degree of necessity in this argument: Technological and organizational requirements may, indeed, be malleable and markets may mold them in ways not fixed by technological requirements. Furthermore, because the determinants of social class are, in fact, prior to work assignment, social class has a set of influences before as well as after work, and we are returned to proposition 5: social class position→work experience→social class position→ personality. Two questions emerge from this analysis: To what extent are meritocratic requirements of technology invulnerable to other influences in a market society? And does the family dominate the market in assigning workers to their social class positions?

Questioning the meritocratic assumption. The implication in the technological fix solution is that we are dealing with a meritocracy: only skills count. But we know that in all organizations politics and connections are likely to enter; the question is *the degree* to which skills determine salary, promotions, and honors.

[20]Richard Hall, summarizing, but not endorsing, this position in his *Dimensions of Work,* 169.
[21]For a review of various cognate positions, see Arne Kalleberg, "Work and Stratification: Structural Perspectives," *Work and Organizations* 10 (1983): 251–9.
[22]See Aage B. Sorenson, "The Structure of Inequality and the Process of Attainment," *American Sociological Review* 42 (1977); 551–93.

Market constraints are intended to limit such factors by the pressure for efficiency. Do they provide such a guardian role?

As pointed out in Chapter 7, the loose relationship between occupational requirements and income weakens proposition 2 (and its repetition as a middle sequence in proposition 5), and suggests that the market is a fragile guardian of meritocracy. The way incomes attach to jobs is influenced by supply and demand and by market-measured merit, to be sure, but as Jencks' found, there remains a large scope for luck, favoritism, inertia, and "ruling class" self-help in these discrepancies.[23] An example of inertia mixed, no doubt, with compassion is offered by Dalton and Thompson in their analysis of the salaries and performances of 2,500 engineers and managers in six technology-based companies. Comparing their performance ratings and the job complexity of their assignments with their annual salaries, these authors found that after the age of thirty-five, the ratings and assignments of those studied steadily declined but their salaries continued to rise to a high plateau at about age forty-two. That is, salaries and job complexity (and performance) were convergent for about the first ten years of employment and then steadily diverged. And if the engineers' divergence could be explained by technological obsolescence, this would not explain why the managers were steadily paid salaries increasingly disproportionate to their assessed "worth."[24]

More generally, as both Broom and Cushing and also Fligstein et al.[25] have noted, there is an arbitrariness to the job–wage relationship that is hard to explain in terms of job complexity or social "importance" – and sometimes in terms of market rationality, as well. For example, given the strong relationship between education and first job, how can it be that as educational differences in the postwar period declined, income differences did not?[26] Income follows a course of its own, and not one ruled exclusively by supply and demand. The market is only a modest guardian of meritocracy in commerce and industry, possibly not so good as the old Prussian army or the Society of Jesus. This situation weakens the technological fix.

Markets and families: assignment to occupational positions. In assessing market influences on the shape of the class structure, it is important to evaluate parental influences on their children's skill levels. And there is reason to be concerned with the fairness and efficiency of assignment to meritocratic roles, as well as with their overall inequality. Market fairness and efficiency unite in their criteria,

[23] Christopher Jencks et al., *Inequality: A Reassessment of the Effect of Family and Schooling in America* (New York: Harper/Colophon, 1972).
[24] Gene W. Dalton and Paul H. Thompson, "Accelerating Obsolescence of Older Engineers," *Harvard Business Review* 49 (Sept–Oct 1971): 57–67, reported in Shlomo Maitel, *Minds, Markets and Money* (New York: Basic Books, 1982), 97.
[25] Leonard Broom and Robert G. Cushing, "A Modest Test of an Immodest Theory: The Functional Theory of Stratification," *American Sociological Review* 42 (1977): 157–69; Neil Fligstein, Alexander Hicks, and S. Philip Morgan, "Toward a Theory of Income Determination," *Work and Occupations* 10 (1983): 289–306; Lester Thurow, "Toward a Definition of Economic Justice," *The Public Interest,* no. 31 (Spring 1973): 56–80.
[26] Census Bureau Report December 1987, in *New York Times,* 3 December 1987; Robert M. Hauser and David L. Featherman, *The Process of Stratification: Trends and Analyses* (New York: Academic Press, 1977).

for fairness in the market has no other criteria than contribution to efficient operations (a self-confirming criterion). Consider the following propositions:

Parental class connections→the child's first job: nepotism   (6)

Parental occupation and education→the child's entry skills through providing the child with superior education   (7)

Parental genes→the child's native intelligence   (8)

Parental occupational values→the child's occupational selection   (9)

Only the first of these intergenerational influences on job assignment, nepotism, violates market norms; nepotism is not only a nonmarket phenomenon, but may be said to be discouraged by the market, as is suggested by French data showing that heirs of founders do worse than both the founders and unrelated managers.[27] Where so much else is for sale, the market firms' instinct for self-preservation seems to inhibit the sale of many managerial and professional jobs – as is further indicated by the low correlation marking a direct path between father's education and occupation, on the one hand, and son's occupation, on the other. Thus, Duncan, Featherman, and Duncan show that father's education and occupation are only trivially directly related (.04 and .12) to son's occupation.[28]

But there is nothing in market doctrine, or certainly in market practice, to discourage the differential benefits of family influence; there is nothing to say that children should start equal. Since we know that those from better educated and more affluent homes have better occupational prospects, from the point of view of market functioning, it would be reassuring to find that the children of these homes *do,* in fact, have superior talents. And this seems to be the case.

If the direct route from father's status to son's occupational status is trivial, Duncan et al. show that the main influence of paternal characteristics is via son's intelligence (.27, .28), as in proposition 8, and son's education (.19, .22), as in proposition 7. Much more important, however, is the influence of son's (respondent's) intelligence and his educational attainment on his occupation (.53). The implication is that the family helps the child in two ways, through nature and nurture to higher (or lower) intelligence, and through influencing the level of education, which is important, and the kind of education, which is not important, that a child receives.[29] But the major determinant is the individual's own intelligence and education – and motivational factors measured separately.[30] This is compatible with proposition 2 and the earlier discussion claiming a close relationship between job requirements and stratification; it reinforces the argument for meritocracy that the market is supposed to protect. In sorting out market influences, the family influence seems to refer to an earlier premarket theme of lineage and patronage, and the (larger) effect

[27] Dean Savage, *Founders, Heirs, and Managers: French Industrial Leadership in Transition* (Beverly Hills, CA: Sage, 1979).

[28] Otis Dudley Duncan, David L. Featherman, and Beverly Duncan, *Socioeconomic Background and Achievement* (New York: Seminar Press, 1972), 103.

[29] Ibid.

[30] Ibid., 116–66.

of intelligence and education on occupational attainment is at least compatible with market premises.

Occupational preferences. In a consumption-driven society, occupational preferences should be derived preferences, not derived from some deep font of skill and inclination, but from the consumer preferences of others. For the market, occupational preferences have no significance other than their role in guiding people toward the niche in production where their talents yield the highest possible marginal product. Perhaps, aside from competence, the most important market criterion for occupational preferences is that they be flexible, to change with shifts in technology and consumer tastes.

In fact, occupational preferences are formed early and rigidify with experience. As mentioned in Chapter 13, Mortimer and Lorence's research shows that early occupational values influence the selection of the first job that then reinforces those early values.[31] Working-class youth seek income rather than autonomy and challenge or service with and for people; within the range of careers for which they are prepared they are likely to select those with initially higher pay but little career promise. Unlike studies devoted entirely to "occupational attainment" or income, our focus on work that offers scope for learning is less concerned with these indicators of "success" and more concerned with circumstances favoring learning at work. Based on work done by Mortimer and associates, Hall suggests the following sequence: "parental occupation→parental occupational values→preadult values and work expectations [of their children]→work settings→ongoing and continuing socialization and reactions to work."[32] In that case, it is the market influence on parents' occupations that would start the chain, moving the inquiry back a generation. This supports proposition 2 (parental occupation/education→child's education→occupational attainment); parental work experience is a source of the occupational values they teach their children.

The influence of social class as a system of stratified values is seen once again in the way a "materialist market ethos" selectively influences those least prepared to resist it (and, because of their circumstances, most in need of money) thus limiting possible future learning of self-direction from substantively complex jobs.

Money, talent, and learning at work

The market works through money; it is not only the "measuring rod" of welfare, but as price the signaling device for household decisions, and as income the means to effectuate those decisions. We are thus prepared to believe that the influence of education on a person's occupational status is a discreet reflection of income. No doubt this is often true, but it seems that other factors, namely home influences on intelligence and values, are greater, the home influencing what is absorbed in school and confounding the correlation between years of education and occupational sta-

---

[31] Jeylan T. Mortimer and Jon Lorence, "Work Experience and Occupational Value Socialization: A Longitudinal Study," *American Journal of Sociology* 84 (1979): 1,361–85.
[32] Hall, *Dimensions of Work*, 117.

tus. This is a familistic pattern more characteristic of gemeinschaft than of a market society.

If it were the quality of schooling that determined a child's ability, we would say that the rich bought better schooling and so prepared their children for jobs requiring cognitive complexity. But as Christopher Jencks and associates report: "Overall, the evidence shows that differences between high schools contribute almost nothing to the overall level of cognitive inequality."[33] This conclusion supports the earlier finding that the most important contributor to cognitive development during school years was a family or individual variable, not a school variable.[34] Significant for our purposes is the further finding that in more egalitarian communist societies, cognitive development is similarly related to parental education and occupation. The authors of a Polish study asked whether in their society, where educational and housing facilities were relatively equal, it was such "extrinsic [factors as] schools, housing, health and welfare services, recreation, and criminality records" or such "intrinsic [factors as] personal attributes of the family members, parental occupation and education, as well as birth order and family size" that accounted for cognitive development among eleven-year-old children. They found that quality of school made little difference, but that the educational and occupational levels of the children's parents made a great deal of difference in the children's cognitive development. These discrepancies in parental endowments, though diminished by the communist regime, still retained their full power to influence children's achievements. As it turned out, family factors were important in Poland to about the same degree as had been found to be the case in the American (capitalist) milieu by Jencks.[35] Such findings are compatible with, but do not prove, the assumption of another nonmarket network: a genetic network.[36]

At the bottom of the income scale, income buys two things: (1) remission of the evil effects of poverty on intelligence (see Chapter 7), and (2) admission to mainstream culture.[37] Although money does not buy leisure, for the working class works shorter hours than the middle class, it buys freedom from anxiety, the "psychologically free time" that goes with leisure; it also buys self-confidence, for income is the best demographic predictor of an internal locus of control;[38] and it buys the appreciation of nonmaterial values that permits the children of even modest wealth to select those values that Mortimer and Lorence showed led to careers marked by

[33] Jencks et al., *Inequality*, 93.

[34] James S. Coleman et al., *Equality of Educational Opportunity* (Washington, DC: U.S. Government Printing Office, 1966).

[35] Anna Firkowska, Antonina Ostrowska, Magdalena Sokolowska, Zena Stein, Mervyn Susser, and Ignacy Wald, "Cognitive Development and Social Policy," *Science* 200 (23 June 1978): 1,357–62.

[36] One must modify the implications of these findings, at least among an elite stratum; in the United States the school that a person attends greatly affects his or her occupational attainment, but this seems to have more to do with credentialism and favoring likeness, which are nonmarket phenomena – unless, of course, one defines market processes as a device for class rule, which is reasonable up to a point but extraneous to the definition of the market used here.

[37] Lee Rainwater, *What Money Buys: Inequality and the Social Meaning of Income* (New York: Basic Books, 1974).

[38] Gerald Gurin and Patricia Gurin, "Personal Efficacy and the Ideology of Individual Responsibility," in Burkhard Strumpel, ed., *Economic Means for Human Needs* (Ann Arbor, MI: Institute for Social Research, 1976).

jobs with autonomy and challenge. When the market distributes wealth it distributes something relevant in a variety of ways to job assignment: Without directly buying jobs, parental wealth buys parental values that parents then use to guide their children into jobs with higher hedonic and developmental yields.

None of this affects the central point made in Chapter 13: Irrespective of economic systems, the substantive content of the work, early work experience, job selection based on earlier occupational values, and to some degree the norms of the factory (or other) workplace, shape important elements of personality. Job content is the most important of these: As a replication of Kohn and Schooler's American study in the somewhat more egalitarian and less class differentiated Polish society revealed, precisely the same job contents affected personality and cognitive functioning in Poland as in the United States,[39] even though parental values and degrees of social inequality in the two countries were quite different. Whatever the antecedents of the person who gets the job, the job content is more important than the jobholder's antecedents.

Characteristics of market stratification

Given human history, it is hard to say that markets are in any way uniquely responsible for stratification or inequality; their main functions seem to be to employ wealth criteria where other systems employ lineage or power and to make strata more porous. They are not more agglutinative (one status base buys others), but, as mentioned at the beginning of this section, they are intrinsically inegalitarian and have no incentive or means to change the "natural" inegalitarian order as it emerges from their system – except, perhaps, by economic growth.[40] We need not enter the argument over the inevitability of stratification[41] (although the technical fix proposition contributes to the inevitability argument) or take sides in the discussion of comparative degrees of inequality in socialist and capitalist countries, a discussion many believe has been rendered moot by recent history. It seems to have been the case that the smaller differences in wages in command economies are enlarged by political favoritism to the point where there is a general similarity to income inequality in at least some market societies.[42] Similarly, the rates of mobility in at least one command economy (Poland) were similar to those in the United States, if one eliminates the agricultural sector where sons succeed to their father's occupation.[43] Apparently, market-induced stratification and the (perhaps lesser) stratifica-

[39] Kazimierz M. Slomczynski, Joanne Miller, and Melvin L. Kohn, "Stratification, Work, and Values: A Polish–United States Comparison," *American Sociological Review* 46 (1981): 720–44.

[40] See Simon Kuznets, "Economic Growth and Income Inequality" (Presidential address), *American Economic Review* 45 (1955): 1–28. For other inherent market effects on inequality, see Jeffrey G. Williamson and Peter H. Lindert, *American Inequality: A Macroeconomic History* (New York: Academic Press, 1980).

[41] Kingsley Davis and Wilbert E. Moore, "Some Principles of Stratification," *American Sociological Review* 10 (1945): 242–9; for a contrary view see Erik Olin Wright, *Class Structure and Income Determination* (New York: Academic Press, 1979).

[42] See Parkin, *Class Inequality and Political Order.*

[43] John W. Meyer, Nancy Brandon Tuma, and Krzysztof Zagorski, "Education and Occupational Mobility: A Comparison of Polish and American Men," *American Journal of Sociology* 46 (1981): 406–21.

tion of command economies influence values and orientations through occupational hierarchies in roughly the same way,[44] although access to these jobs will differ. The important point is that wherever there is hierarchy (vertical division of labor) in work organizations, there will be social stratification, whether in a market economy or not. But, joining with other, more universal forces, the market influences the selection of persons for better jobs, and tends to exaggerate stratification differences by exaggerating the pay differentials associated with different work requirements. But it is the force of familial characteristics, not wealth (and therefore not market), that is mainly responsible for the tendency of higher status parents to have children with higher occupational status. It is this counterintuitive finding that weakens the force of money, and therefore of the market, in that transmission.

The privileged class, the moneyed class, and the ruling class

Those whose jobs offer self-direction, substantive complexity, and challenge, variety, little supervision, and intrinsic satisfaction of excellence or self-determination, may be called members of the *privileged class*. Their privilege lies in doing freely and (usually) with social approval and support[45] what they want to do and usually do best. Whereas people of power may make certain controlling decisions and gratify some of their wants in this way, and wealthy people gratify their wants in the consumer market, those who have the good jobs (in the sense defined) gratify their wants, and perhaps needs, in the processes of producing and not of ruling or consuming. By definition, work is central to these members of the "privileged class."

The class structure in a scheme where a privileged class is defined in this way has a shape that does not correspond to the prevailing conceptions of class hierarchy. The rationale for this structural revision is obvious: Work satisfaction and self-expression has a claim to a ranked order, and to inclusion in Weber's "life chances," quite as strong as consumer satisfaction and expression that is allegedly measured by wealth. Furthermore, to the extent that personal development is a consideration (as it is in formal education, another measure of status), the developmental aspects of working in a good job are certainly greater than in most forms of consumption. In this ranking, for example, owners are ranked according to whether they are themselves members of the labor force. If they are, Kohn and Schooler find that in terms of the hedonic and learning benefits received, they belong alongside other top managers who have discretion and enjoy their work.[46] If they are not part of the work force, they do not qualify for this version of privilege.

At the top of the privileged class hierarchy are the professionals. Strumpel's analysis of work and life satisfaction finds:

Professionals appeared to be best adapted to our economic system. They were more satisfied with their *jobs,* their *education,* and their *living standard.* Their *job involvement* was the highest and they were the most attached to its intrinsic rewards. Together with the managerial workers, they were the most *advancement* minded. Their level of satisfaction with their present standard of living was outstanding, and although they were more likely to expect

---

[44] Kohn and Schooler, *Work and Personality,* 284.

[45] For example, the three highest occupations on a measure of occupational prestige are scientist, doctor, minister – and it is not until we get to the ninth position that we encounter businessman. Harris poll, October 1977, reported in *Public Opinion* 4 (1981): 31.

[46] Kohn and Schooler, *Work and Personality,* 81, 89, 90.

income increases, they would not be significantly more unhappy than others if their standard of living were to *remain the same* over the next five years. They also have the strongest sense of *fate-control*.[47]

With a finer grained analysis and a focus wholly on enjoyment of work, it seems that urban university professors may rank at the top of the professionals, for more than any other group, they would choose the same career if they had a second chance.[48]

Managers also rank high in job satisfaction, but their focus on financial rewards rather than on what they actually do at work leaves uncertain their status in the privileged class, and their desolation at the idea of not being better off in five years leaves them vulnerable to shock, suggesting that it is not the activity itself but success in that activity that is rewarding.[49] Neither white-collar workers nor blue-collar workers enjoyed their work as much as these two privileged groups. From other data we find shopkeepers and small businessmen rather low on two hedonic scales (happiness and life satisfaction), but how much this is attributable to frustrations at work is unclear.[50]

Possibly below (and possibly above) these groups we might expect to find artists and writers. And if we think along a hedonic rather than a learning dimension (because of the limited learning of those who work with things), we would also include craftspeople and artisans, the skilled carpenter, electrician, and plumber. Asked Ruskin's question, "Was it done with joy?" the plumber is more likely than the sales executive to say yes.[51] At the bottom of this particular hierarchy, we might find a janitor ranking higher than a low-level bureaucrat, and a television repairperson higher than a ceremonial leader dressed in gorgeous robes.

Members of the privileged class are not, as Daniel Bell once suggested,[52] necessarily members of the "ruling class," for they do not directly control the fates of others, although some (e.g., J. M. Keynes) would say that it is the power of the ideas generated by a small segment of this privileged class that in the long run control all our fates.[53] As Marx pointed out, men of knowledge often have been the allies of men of power and wealth (Chapter 14), but there is one consideration that

[47] Burkhard Strumpel, Richard T. Curtin, and M. Susan Schwartz, "Economic Life-Styles, Values, and Subjective Welfare," in Strumpel, *Economic Means for Human Needs*, 51–2.

[48] HEW Task Force, *Work in America*.

[49] Strumpel et al., "Economic Life-Styles, Values, and Subjective Welfare," 54.

[50] Ronald Inglehart and Jacques-Rene Rabier, "Aspirations Adapt to Situations – But Why Are the Belgians So Much Happier than the French? A Cross-Cultural Analysis of the Subjective Quality of Life," in Frank M. Andrews, ed., *Research on the Quality of Life* (Ann Arbor, MI: Institute for Social Research, 1986), 22.

[51] A paperhanger I once interviewed at some length described to me the challenge of making the strips of wallpaper join properly at the corners of a room. In the same interviews a locomotive fireman said with rapture in his voice, "Oh, Mr. Lane, if you could only see the [train] yard at night." Robert E. Lane, *Political Ideology: Why the American Common Man Believes What He Does* ((New York: Free Press, 1962).

[52] Daniel Bell, "The Measurement of Knowledge and Technology," in Eleanor B. Sheldon and Wilbert E. Moore, eds., *Indicators of Social Change* (New York: Russell Sage, 1968), 145–246 at 181, 189. But note comments on bureaucratic control of science at p. 236. See also Bell, *The Coming of Post-Industrial Society* (New York: Basic Books, 1973).

[53] Stigler questions Keynes's famous aphorism on the powerful "scribblers" of the past, modestly claiming that economists do not have much influence on policy; economic forces have that effect. George J. Stigler, "Do Economists Matter?" in his *The Economist as Preacher and Other Essays* (Chicago: University of Chicago Press, 1982).

limits this more or less natural alliance: The jobs of the men of knowledge are defined by their *self-direction*. Considering this defining characteristic, we see why it is that people trained to think for themselves and who value independence are, contrary to their economic (i.e., consumer) interests, so often out of harmony with the great and rich and powerful.

There is some suggestion here that the powerful leaders of society do not have "good jobs"; perhaps even like Plato's guardians, they accept their powerful roles as a *sacrifice*. Circumstances vary: The top office may receive gratifying deference, but lack discretion and the ability to do a creative job. On some other dimensions the top office (president or chairman) would rank high, but still not have a "good" job in the sense described here. If Maslow's need hierarchy[54] were a class structure, those with the good jobs would be at the peak of the pyramid. It is the emphasis on consumer satisfaction that blinds people to this alternative system of stratification.

As for the cross-generational perpetuation of the members of this segment of the privileged class, in both Poland and the United States it is the education of the parents that determines success at school and that gives to each individual the characteristics that get him or her a privileged first job.[55] Further, it seems from Mortimer's analysis that occupational preferences are often framed by parental influences derived from their own parental job experience.[56] Like other classes, then, the privileged class has an inherited character that is inegalitarian in its implications.

Dual economy and internal markets

In this section I will show that it is the absent or weakened force of competition and the presence of internal rather than external labor markets (bureaucracy) that favor circumstances promoting learning at work. In addition to thinking of labor markets as specialized by skill, function, and place, we may think of them in two other ways. One of them, no longer considered viable in detail but useful as pointing to differences in the terms of work offered in various sectors of the economy, is the idea of a "dual economy" that divides industrial sectors into *core* and *periphery*.[57] Other authors, employing many of the same criteria, speak of "mainstream" and "marginal" labor markets.[58] The other major way of thinking of labor markets is

---

[54] Abraham H. Maslow, *Toward a Psychology of Being*, rev. ed. (Princeton, N.J.: Van Nostrand, 1968). For criticism of the validity of Maslow's need hierarchy, see M. A. Wahba and L. G. Bridwell, "Maslow Reconsidered: A Review of Research on the Need Hierarchy Theory," *Organizational Behavior and Human Performance* 15 (1976): 210–40.

[55] Firkowska et al. "Cognitive Development and Social Policy."

[56] Jeylan T. Mortimer, "Intergenerational Occupational Movement," *American Journal of Sociology* 79 (1974): 1,278–99.

[57] Barry Bluestone, William D. Murphy, and Mary Stevenson, *Low Wages and the Working Poor* (Ann Arbor, MI: Institute of Labor and Industrial Relations of the University of Michigan, 1973). For a criticism of the idea of a dual economy and a proposal to divide the labor market into a variety of other kinds of divisions, see Robert L. Kaufman, Randy Hodson, and Neil D. Fligstein, "Defrocking Dualism: A New Approach to Defining Industrial Sectors," *Social Science Research* 10 (1981): 1–31. These authors employ a mix of criteria, often dividing a single industry, such as utilities, into core and peripheral sectors. See also Lynne G. Zucker and Carolyn Rosenstein, "Taxonomies of Institutional Structure: Dual Economy Reconsidered," *American Sociological Review* 46 (1981): 869–94.

[58] Sar A. Levitan, Garth L. Mangum, and Ray Marshall, *Human Resources and Labor Markets* (New York: Harper & Row, 1972), 220–2.

more fundamental: It differentiates between the *external* labor market located between firms, and the *internal* labor market within a firm. Both visions have consequences for the development of learning at work. Both of them suggest how protection from product competition benefits learning at work.

The dual economy

Labor markets in core and peripheral segments of the economy. The *core* is composed of those industries that are stable, central to the health of the national economy, capital intensive, often possessed of integrated manufacturing processes, often also able to differentiate their products so as to enjoy a degree of market power, and frequently enjoying the benefits of large government contracts. The firms in this segment are large and employ much of the labor force. Core industries would be well represented among the 5 percent of the large firms employing about 60 percent of the labor force. To the work force their importance lies in their relatively high pay, greater security, internal training programs, and more generous fringe benefits.

The characteristics of the *periphery* are just the opposite. It is composed of small, frequently unstable, labor intensive, highly competitive firms, paying lower wages, offering little security and few fringe benefits. It is here that the approximately 10 million laborers working for wages at the legal minimum may be found. Excluding some uncertain classifications, about a fifth of the labor force is clearly working in these so-called peripheral labor markets.[59] Partly because of their lack of knowledge of the labor market, low skills, disinclination to move (and the high cost of moving), partly because of discrimination, and partly because of available welfare support when without work, workers in this sector infrequently move from peripheral industries to core industries.[60]

What draws our attention to this distinction is the fact that on almost all grounds (except perhaps creation of new jobs, which is more likely to come from small enterprises[61]), the *less* competitive firms enjoying market power are better employers, offering better jobs. This superiority is as great in opportunities for learning and developing on the job as it is in wages and fringe benefits. Consider, then, the implications of the tuitional advantages of firms that are very large, inevitably bureaucratic, relatively less vulnerable to their environments,[62] partially sheltered from competition, and possessed of market power. Where, for both consumers and mar-

[59] Ibid.

[60] Ibid., 222–3. Some also argue that the availability of welfare supports inhibits the search for better jobs. See Victor R. Fuchs, *The Way We Live: An Economic Perspective on Americans from Birth to Death* (Cambridge: Harvard University Press, 1983), 191. The invulnerability of firms with market power should not be overemphasized: Competition among nations is a constant threat. Also the advantages of firms large enough to receive government contracts means that for that very reason these firms are vulnerable to sudden shifts in government policy; core industries are more likely than peripheral industries to be unionized and therefore vulnerable to union pressures; and even the largest are vulnerable to corporate raiders.

[61] David L. Birch, "Who Creates Jobs?" *Public Interest* 65 (1981): 3–14.

[62] See James L. Baron and William T. Bielby, "The Organization of Work in a Segmented Economy," *American Sociological Review* 49 (1984): 454–73.

ket theory, the great advantage of the market is its sensitive adaptation to its social environments, the advantage for employees is the "invulnerability" of the firm to its environment. Where the "norm or ideal" of the perfect market is that no single firm by its decisions affects the prices of goods, these superior employers enjoy market power permitting them to adjust and protect their prices. Where bureaucracy is thought to be an inferior alternative to the market, it is superior for promoting circumstances that favor employee development. The very engine of the market, competition, seems to be the agent that makes better conditions of employment impossible. Taken further, we might say that the competitive market is, in the short run, the enemy of personality development at work.

One can demonstrate by various equations and graphs that oligopoly, "monopolistic competition,"[63] or other forms of market power lead to a "less than optimal" distribution of resources, although it is by no means clear that in the real world even consumer prices are raised above the competitive level by these forms of market power.[64] Now, for the criterial issue at the focus of our discussion, it seems that both workers who "seek to maximize satisfaction from real wages" and those who seek developmental and intrinsic values at work are better off when sheltered from the short run influences of the competitive market. The long run, of course, may be different: In the United States competition among small companies increases employment. The implications of this analysis do not lead to government ownership or command economies, but they do lead to a rejection of the perfect market as a "norm or ideal" for developing human capacities at work.

Internal labor markets: working in a bureaucracy

Since the market is often presented as the antidote to the evils of bureaucracy, note that Kohn and Schooler's analysis of the effects of working in a bureaucracy (measured by levels of hierarchy) are largely benign. Bureaucratization *reduces* feelings of alienation and anxiety, and *increases* the value of self-direction, higher standards of morality, openness to change, self-esteem, and more intellectually demanding uses of leisure time. Although working in a bureaucracy does not increase the cognitive flexibility of bureaucrats, they *are* more cognitively flexible because bureaucracies *select* for that quality.[65] Kohn and Schooler argue that for blue-collar workers greater job security in bureaucracies seems to promote some of these qualities, and for the white-collar workers the substantive complexity of their jobs accounts for the bureaucratic effect.

The credits given to the market for reducing the effects of bureaucracy, to the extent that in a period of giant firms the market really has this effect, are not credits at all, or, at least, are mixed credits.

[63] On oligopolistic competition, see E. H. Chamberlin, *Theory of Monopolistic Competition* (Cambridge: Harvard University Press, 1931). John Robinson, *The Economics of Imperfect Competition* (London: Macmillan, 1933).
[64] See Alfred D. Chandler, Jr., *The Visible Hand* (Cambridge: Harvard University Press, 1977).
[65] Kohn and Schooler, *Work and Personality*, 47, 89, 139, 141. For an alternative interpretation of the effects of bureaucracy, see Michel Crozier, *The Bureaucratic Phenomenon* (Chicago: University of Chicago Press, 1964).

Internal labor markets: protection from outside markets
Core industries achieve their superior employment records by means of their internal markets, that is, after a person has been hired from the external market, his or her work assignments, promotions, training, and wage scales are all administered in the protected sphere of the firm. "The internal labor market," say Levitan and associates, "is controlled more by institutional rules which are not always compatible with assumptions of the competitive labor market."[66] Similarly, Baily and Chakrabarti point out that although "economics emphasizes the role of markets in allocating resources, . . . in practice, markets play only a limited role in allocation decisions within organizations."[67] In a study of British labor markets, it was found that:

Conditions prevailing at plant level may have an effect on wages in a manner which is rigorously excluded from the traditional [economic] model. Economic rationality and competitive forces are not strong enough to result in a situation where each employer pays no more and no less than the market wage.[68]

The insulation from market forces is, of course, incomplete. At the "port of entry,"[69] where the internal market meets the external market, adjustments to the external world are necessary; the norms of the external market influence firm norms; firms watch and copy each other, and so on. But their partial independence *permits* them to consider the well-being of the employees as well as their own profits – which are often substantial.[70]

There are enough accounts of anonymity and impersonality, disregard for the communities in which workers live, surveillance, intrusive management, and authoritarian styles of supervision, to show that permission is by no means obligation. The hiring practices of large corporations have been criticized for the use of credentials with little relation to the task,[71] vague and ambiguous criteria for promotion – allowing for favoritism and premature identification of "stars" whose later promotions serve mainly to validate this early selection.[72] The record is indeed mixed. The "rational," meritocratic virtues of private bureaucracies are as easily overemphasized as the market's claim to rely on productivity related criteria.

Why internal labor markets favor their employees
Before assuming some intrusion of nonmarket altruism and fellow feeling by the managers of large corporations, we must note the purely economic advantages flowing from what is likely to be called "good personnel policy." It reduces turnover; internal recruitment for promotions offers performance incentives to firm employ-

---

[66] Levitan et al., *Human Resources and Labor Markets,* 21.
[67] Martin Neil Baily and Alok K. Chakrabarti, *Innovation and the Productivity Crisis* (Washington, DC: Brookings Institution, 1988), 91.
[68] Mackay et al., *Labour Markets Under Different Employment Conditions,* 393.
[69] Hall, *Dimensions of Work,* 169, reporting on work by Grandjean.
[70] The primary source for analysis of internal labor markets is Peter B. Doeringer and Michael J. Piore, *Internal Labor Markets and Manpower Analysis* (Lexington, MA: Heath/Lexington Books, 1971).
[71] See Ivan Berg, *Education and Jobs: The Great Training Robbery* (New York: Praeger, 1970).
[72] Hall, *Dimensions of Work,* 221–2.

ees; employees are more familiar with internal markets than external ones and can help to place themselves, and employers know the internal candidates for positions better than external candidates; substandard employees can be trained; many firm skills are job-specific and can more easily be trained from inside than recruited from outside, and so forth. By some reports employers are more interested in the cooperativeness and reliability of middle status industrial employees than their skills or intelligence, the former representing matters that can be judged best by experience.[73] Furthermore, although there is much evidence that worker satisfaction is not related to productivity, there is reason to believe that this applies more to degrees of *dissatisfaction,* which is related to extrinsic job circumstances, than to satisfaction, which is related to intrinsic features of work, the work itself.[74] Finally, managers probably do not know the consequences of worker morale and, purely on the grounds of cost, include a margin of safety.

The circumstances favoring the use of internal labor markets help to account for its superior attention to employee concerns. Although sheer size is important, profitability and growth are more important. More important still is the nature of the industry. High-technology industries with less routinized work are more favorable to workplace learning. Industries with personnel departments and internal training programs are, not unnaturally, more concerned with employee development. On the other hand, unionization inhibits internal labor markets and thus discourages one circumstance favoring learning at work.[75] And workers trained at company expense may be hired away by competitors. For example, Britain's government-sponsored National Computing Centre reports that the "root cause" for the intense shortage of skilled information technologists in a society with high unemployment "is the failure of firms to retrain staff and/or recruit trainees. The excuse for that failure," says the report, "is both the cost and "the fear that staff will be poached before the investment in training is repaid."[76] That is, two pillars of the market, competition and mobility, actively *discourage* the development of human capital by individual firms.

Before assigning purely market causes to these phenomena, we should note that there are also powerful reasons for inhibiting labor training in nonmarket societies such as the USSR: "In most factories . . . one or two months training in a narrow skill is adopted. . . . The lack of interest in the quality of output means that there is little incentive to improve training."[77] Furthermore, the fear of poaching may be even greater in command economies because of the premiums on hoarding labor supplies.

Market power permitting beneficial treatment of employees relaxes the con-

---

[73] Robert M. Blackburn and Michael Mann, *The Working Class in the Labour Market* (London: Macmillan, 1979), 280.

[74] HEW Task Force, *Work in America,* 2.

[75] Jeffrey Pfeffer and Yinon Cohen, "Determinants of Internal Labor Markets in Organizations," *Administrative Sciences Quarterly* 29 (1984): 550–72, cited in Hall, *Dimensions of Work, 274.*

[76] *The Guardian* (London), 1 September 1987. The counterforce in the market economy that overcomes this disincentive seems to be job-specific skills and protected, relatively less competitive labor markets.

[77] Silvana Malle, "Heterogeneity of Labour Markets," in David Lane, ed., *Labour and Employment in the USSR* (Brighton: Wheatsheaf/Harvester, 1986), 122–3.

straints of product markets; to a small extent it exemplifies the tendencies of a work-driven model instead of a consumer-driven model, where the work of employees already employed is the motor. As a consequence, as mentioned, the costs of these worker benefits are more likely to be borne by consumers – or by the unemployed. This is most clearly seen when, as in the automobile, shipbuilding, and steel industries, market power is challenged, in these cases by foreign competition.

Modifying the profit motive: weakness of the classical model
These self-interested policies do not account for certain beneficial wage policies that suggest that, contrary to competitive market theory, managers can and do *choose* to share the benefits of firm profitability with their employees. For example, there is a very high correlation between a firm's sales margins and the average hourly earnings of its employees, leading Schlicter to argue "that wages, within a considerable range, reflect managerial discretion, [and] where management can easily pay higher wages they tend to do so."[78] Another study found that there was no correlation between percentage change in wage rates and percentage change in employment for fifty-seven industries in the 1948–60 period.[79] As mentioned, Mackay et al.'s study of employment practices in Britain finds that the profitability of a firm, rather than the "demand and supply conditions for [a] particular type of skill," is the major determinant of increases in wage rates in the industries examined. Finally, when the statutory minimum wage law is periodically increased, few firms discharge their employees, though there is reason to believe that hiring is slowed down.

It has often been observed that the primary beneficiaries of the separation of ownership from management, and the consequent growth of managerial power, are managers themselves,[80] but now it seems that they share their benefits with their employees when they can safely afford to do so. The implied difference between owners and managers in their willingness to share profits lies not only in the difference in personal stakes in profits, but also in management's broader sense of responsibility for the welfare of employees.[81] In a sense, these larger views were not so much "unmarketlike" as they were concerned with the environment within which the market operated and that sustained market institutions. It is ironical that Marx anticipated how it might be that the separation of management from ownership

[78] Sumner Schlicter "Notes on the Structure of Wages," *Review of Economics and Statistics* (February 1950), quoted in Levitan et al, *Human Resources and Labour Markets*, 225.
[79] Lloyd Ulman, "Labor Mobility in the Industrial Wage Structure in the Postwar United States," *Quarterly Journal of Economics* (February 1965): 73–97, cited in Levitan et al., ibid.
[80] For a report on evidence to support this view, see Hall, *Dimensions of Work*, 61. Before it is concluded that managers have been released from the binding principle of profit maximization, however, we should note that a study of the dismissal of chief executive officers among the 300 largest firms showed that in the given year 5% of the films dismissed their CEOs (without regard for their family connections) largely on the grounds of poor profit performance. See David R. James and Michael Soref, "Profit Constraints on Managerial Autonomy: Managerial Theory and the Unmaking of the Corporation President," *American Sociological Review* 46 (1981): 1–18; compare Leonard Broom and Robert G. Cushing, "A Modest Test of an Immodest Theory." Broom and Cushing find no relation between company performance and executive compensation.
[81] Francis X. Sutton, Seymour Harris, Carl Kaysen, and James Tobin, *The American Business Creed* (Cambridge: Harvard University Press, 1956).

implied the beginning step in the reconversion of the benefits of property back to its worker producers.[82]

Household economies

Combined with technology, market forces have contributed to the massive changes from agricultural and household work to industrial and commercial work. Both of these changes are products of the long-term shift from traditional manorial or household economies to market economies, a shift characterized by a reduction in the proportion of the labor force engaged in farming and then in a reduction in the proportion of the population (housewives are not usually counted as members of the ''labor force'') engaged in housework. The effect of the market (and technology) on the distribution of occupations with various opportunities for workplace learning is seen in both instances. And the effect on workplace learning of the various kinds of work to be done in the household reinforces the theory of how job content influences skills and values that emerged from studies of work in industry.

From farm to market: freedom from agricultural employment

Recall that Marx held that it is the formation of a labor market that announces the beginning of capitalism.[83] In addition to the move from cottage to factory, this meant moving from agricultural employment to industrial or commercial employment, a move that raises issues of net gains and losses for what is learned at work. As people have moved from more or less subsistent farms, the development of the labor market has been rapid, even in this century: In 1900, 38 percent of the labor force was agricultural; by 1982 that proportion was 3 percent. About 89 percent of the labor force now work for wages and salaries. At the same time, an increasing proportion of the population have entered the labor force, enlarged in the past few decades principally by the entry of married women with children.[84]

The movement from farm work to industrial or service work involves several of the values of learning at work: (1) ownership versus nonownership of one's own means of production, (2) working for others versus self-employment, and (3) the content of the tasks done. As we know from Chapter 13, each of these features of work and work setting has implications for work learning.

In the Kohn and Schooler study, both (1) *owning the means of production* and (2) *self-employment* are related to higher self-esteem, greater value assigned to self-direction, and greater intellectual flexibility. The job circumstances of self-employed farmer-owners seem to contribute substantially to the development of favorable learning opportunities. But it is not the title of ownership that makes the difference; it is discretion involved in self-employment.

Though relatively unsupervised, the actual content of farm work – (3) *the nature*

[82] Shlomo Avineri, *The Social and Political Thought of Karl Marx* (Cambridge, UK: Cambridge University Press, 1968), 178.

[83] Karl Marx, *Capital*, vol. 1 (Moscow: International Publishers, 1958), 170.

[84] Fuchs, *The Way We Live*.

of tasks performed—is often routine and involves heavy work, both of which are associated with low personality development, as mentioned in Chapter 13. The farm laborer who enters the urban labor market generally does escape from his position as the modern equivalent of *The Man With A Hoe,* but the move from working as an owner on owner-operated farms to working as a nonowner in industrial or service firms offers a combination of favorable and unfavorable working circumstances whose net intellectual and personality benefits are indeterminate.

If the issues were to be referred to hedonic criteria, the choice would be clearer: In a review of quality-of-life data covering nine European nations and the United States, Inglehart and Rabier report:

> In both the 1970s and the 1980s, those who depend on farming for a living had the lowest percentage "very happy." Moreover, in both time periods farmers ranked lowest on overall life satisfaction. The antigrowth school may be right about the low quality of life in big cities, but seems strikingly wrong insofar as it tends to romanticize farming as an attractive way of life.[85]

On the separate issue of freedom or autonomy, opinions regarding entry into the labor market differ. Whereas Marx saw the introduction of the labor market as the instrument introducing "wage slavery" and others have seen it as a means of oppression, Shorter believed that it was a means of escape from the constraints and surveillance in village life and Coser saw it as a means of escape from household service.[86]

Taking into account the two criteria mentioned, happiness and learning, the movement from farm to market is a means of leading people who do work with little opportunity for intellectual flexibility, self direction, and challenge and who are generally unhappy and sometimes feel unfree, to remedy these conditions. At least this is true in periods of prosperity when jobs are available.

Housework

We have partially relieved the market of responsibility for stratification of learning at work and assigned greater responsibility to processes internal to the firm. Studies of housework seem to duplicate this assignment of responsibility to processes internal to an organization. Defining housework as "the work that must be done to maintain a household, work that someone would have to be hired to do if family members did not do it themselves," Kohn and Schooler studied the most meaningful analogs to paid employment in this nonmarket form of work. Once again, they found that compared to noncomplex work (washing, sweeping, preparing meals) and to routinization ("doing the same thing in the same way repeatedly"), substantively complex work (largely keeping accounts, budgeting, and dealing with tradesmen and servicemen) was causally related to more "ideational flexibility" and a greater value for self-directedness.[87] If there is a lesson here, it is that unpaid work, free of the pressures and competitiveness of the market, has no different effects on

[85] Inglehart and Rabier, "Aspirations Adapt to Situations," 20.
[86] Edward Shorter, *The Making of the Modern Family* (New York: Basic Books, 1975); Lewis A. Coser, *Greedy Institutions* (New York: Free Press, 1974).
[87] Kohn and Schooler, *Work and Personality,* 242–3, 253, 255.

cognition and valuing self-direction than paid market employment. The character of the work itself makes the difference; characteristics of the environment are primarily important as they influence what people *do* at work.

Although "closeness of supervision" is relatively meaningless in Western households, in Chinese households the mother-in-law is the supervisor of her son's wife. It is relevant, then, that a study in Taiwan of three-generation households found that "living in a three generation household affects women's values in much the same way that close supervision on the job affects men's values."[88] That is, close supervision of women in their households reduces their enjoyment of their work and their development of cognitive flexibility and the value of self-directedness in the same way that close supervision in market work reduces these skills and values for industrial and commercial employees.

Summary

Whereas the references to the incidence of costs represent responses to market forces (and of market power), there is no market mechanism permitting an individual to choose which outcome is preferred. There is no mechanism for decisions among or within the four groups that might bear the costs of the circumstances favoring learning at work: (1) workers who benefit from the learning, (2) consumers, (3) the unemployed and workers vulnerable to unemployment, and (4) taxpayers. Among the first three, only the market decides—but not by processes where the consequences of the decision are consciously weighed and chosen.

A second cause for this tendency to slight benefits of work redesign to workers is that markets do not register benefits to society unless they are also benefits to firms; learning at work may or may not benefit the firm, but it is a benefit to society. And third, the market information system's concentration on price information tends to elide other considerations that have not been and perhaps cannot be registered in price terms. The market is an imperfect mechanism for registering preferences weighing the values of learning at work against consumption.

The lesson in this chapter is not new. In the early 1970s Mishan observed: "The potential increase in well-being that would come about as a result of providing work that is more creative, more communal, and generally more enjoyable might be worth more than the actual increase in well-being that is provided by yet more goods."[89] We have examined the merits of assigning priority to work at the expense of consumer sovereignty and sought to allocate the costs, noting counterarguments regarding social benefits from wage increases that do not occur from changes beneficial to learning at work. In calculating the costs of work redesign, we observed

---

[88] Nancy J. Olson, "Family Structure and Socialization Patterns in Taiwan," *American Journal of Sociology* 79 (1974): 1,395–417. Douglas and Isherwood point out that the economy of having the same person undertake the repetitive, low-skill jobs of housework and also the care of the children accounts for low pay and low status of women. See Mary Douglas and Baron Isherwood, *The World of Goods: Towards an Anthropology of Consumption* (1978; reprint Harmondsworth, UK: Penguin, 1980). The lower status of women is not exclusively a market product: The Soviet Union exhibits the same pattern. See Janet S. Schwartz, "Women Under Socialism: Role Definitions of Soviet Women," *Social Forces* 58 (1979): 67–88.

[89] Mishan, "The Wages of Growth," 74.

the high likelihood that labor would, through wages foregone or increased unemployment, pay for any benefits that did not increase productivity – except that where a firm has market power, these worker benefits are both more likely to occur and more probably charged to the consumer. Competition, we said, was the enemy of those circumstances favoring worker learning at work.

In assessing the roots of the stratified opportunities for learning at work, analysis indicates heavy responsibilities in technological considerations and in family socialization processes, processes that occur in the absence of markets. Furthermore, we located the hidden hierarchy based on utilities from working activities rather than consumer utilities. In internal markets, we found again the benefits of market power and evidence of managerial willingness to share profits with workers when the firm was not pressed by interfirm competition, noting how this sharing violates standard market theory.

In two analyses dealing in part with circumstances now less characteristic of market economies, we suggested that the rise of the labor market liberated (and liberates) farmers from work that is uncongenial to personal development in the workplace; we found in the household, and by inference in household economies, circumstances that closely duplicated those of market work.

In support of economic analysis, so often criticized, it must be said that even the primitive economics employed here offers a lens through which much that is hidden to the naked eye comes to light. Economists understand systemic analysis better than most.

16 Giving work priority over consumption

The previous chapter's treatment of the way labor markets allocate the costs of improving learning in the workplace and allocate work positions in a stratified society, and how internal markets escape the pressures of the external market, prepares the way for more detailed treatment of the effects of three central aspects of the market: efficiency (the efficiency norm), competition, and the division of labor. We shall see how *economic* efficiency may actually frustrate social efficiency, and how competition, which we said in the previous chapter favored consumers over workers, is unlikely to become internalized by workers as a trait of *competitiveness* – because that trait is not rewarded by the market. The division of labor that favors the development of self-esteem (Chapter 10) has somewhat different implications when applied to knowledge – thus dividing workers between those with brawn and those with brains – but these are not the implications Marx thought he saw in the division of labor. Since the markets accelerate the division of labor, we must also ask whether the consequent specialism is a source of narrowed insight and interest depriving workers of a more wholesome "well-roundedness." I conclude that the consequent specialism does not. The last part of this chapter is devoted to exploring why an economy that gives priority to workplace satisfactions and achievements, that is, a *producer economy,* is incompatible with market forces.

The efficiency norm

Market constraints on behavior are not self-enforcing; they require the kind of cultural support that makes the principles of the market appear both rational and moral. This support, which might once have been served by the Protestant ethic, is now the belief that efficiency, doing more with less effort and fewer resources, is not only a source of greater wealth (for someone) but also a duty or even a moral command for everyone. Because of its effect on economic growth and social wealth, the efficiency norm has long-term benefits for workplace learning; in the short run, it is likely to inhibit provision for this kind of learning.

Source in the profit maximand

Common sense sees profits as the difference between income and costs, a residual sum accruing to ownership.[1] The efficiency norm derives its original force from the

[1] Economists find it useful to separate the components of profits into managerial pay, interest, rent, and risk bearing. See Frank H. Knight, *Risk, Uncertainty and Profits* (1921; reprint Chicago: University of Chicago Press, 1971); Paul A. Samuelson and William D. Nordhaus, *Economics,* 12th ed. (New York: McGraw-Hill, 1985), 538, 660–3. Even if firms do not, in fact, seek to maximize profits, the pressure to show annual profit increases is enough to exert pressure on cost containment, the portion of the efficiency norm that most affects learning at work. Samuelson and Nordhaus, *Economics,* 538; John Kenneth Galbraith, *The New Industrial State,* 2d ed., rev. (New York: New American Library/Mentor, 1972), 171.

fact that owners profit from both increased income and decreased costs. Pleasing customers but not workers (any more than necessary to gain their cooperation) serves the profit maximand. In this way the market process creates an efficiency norm dedicated to the service of consumers. This pressure toward efficiency is almost unique to market systems; it is not exigent in household or command economies, the latter because of managerial devices to deflect such pressure. We address ourselves to a system dedicated to profits derived, with certain qualifications, from high consumption and low cost; the individual benefits of work in all its aspects are subordinate to this end.[2]

Economic efficiency versus physical productivity

In a market economy, economic efficiency is defined in monetary units, not physical units. Physical or engineering efficiency can be very different from economic efficiency. Thus, the crucial human inputs are labor costs, not hours of labor or physical output per hour of labor, for increases in productivity measured by man-hours per unit of output may not increase economic efficiency because of associated increases in wage rates. High-factor costs can mean that the "productive possibility frontier" is not the physical possibility frontier, but the possibility frontier wherein a firm or firms can operate profitably. Because it is measured in money terms, human and physical resources may still be "available" at the economist's "productive possibility frontier" – but they will be employed only if they lower their prices. This is the clue to the problem of costs associated with facilitating learning at work.

Efficiency among firms and economies

The efficiency of an economy is related to, but is not the sum of, the efficiencies of firms. High unemployment is compatible with, or may even be caused by, a set of firms that are 100 percent efficient. Efficiency reaches its maximum when a firm or economy cannot wring more output from the available means or inputs.[3] The definition applies equally to firms and economies, but here I limit the discussion to firms, for compared to firms, economic systems are much more loosely governed by an efficiency norm. If greater learning at work increased the efficiency of the economy but not that of firms, it would not be adopted, for it would then be an externality not registered in the accounting systems of individual firms.

Noneconomic sources of the efficiency norm

In the 1920s it was said that there were three perfectly efficient institutions: Standard Oil of New Jersey, the Prussian Army, and the Society of Jesus. To the extent that this is true, economic efficiency must take its place among other kinds of effi-

---

[2] The subordination is due to the crucial fact that improving the circumstances of learning, cognitive flexibility, and the value of self-direction at work seems not to improve efficiency or productivity. The argument and evidence on this point was presented in the previous chapter.

[3] From an economy-wide point of view, "productive efficiency occurs when society cannot increase the output of one good without cutting back on another. An efficient economy is on its productive possibility frontier." With unemployed resources, an economy is inside this productive possibility frontier. Samuelson and Nordhaus, *Economics, 29*.

ciency and the things that are thought to be essential to efficiency, like competition, may or may not be necessary.

Many noneconomic forces are allied in promoting the efficiency norm: the technological imperative discussed in Chapter 14, the underlying desire to control one's environment discussed in Chapter 9, and possibly some facets of Parson's "inherent directionality" of the trend toward rationality," which he says is like the pressure to "optimize gratification."[4] Beliefs in the supernatural no doubt contributed to the efficiency of the Jesuits, and Tilgher, following Weber, claimed them for economic efficiency as well: "Calvinism," he said, "lays the foundation of the tremendous discipline of the modern factory founded on the division of labor – very different from the easy-going ways of the independent artisan."[5] In economic life, if there is a crystallizing event, it may be the transition from premarket cottage industry (or the putting-out system) with its policy of *satisficing* to the market-accelerated factory industry where a policy of *maximizing* became the goal.[6]

A single maximand (*wirtrationalitat*) such as profits or salvation may contribute to efficiency by enlisting and coordinating all efforts toward the single goal; a single maximand permits maximization because all means must be directed to this one end. As soon as plural ends are allowed, each must be weighed against the others, and the much more difficult process of optimization must be undertaken.[7] Analytically, the single maximand serves as the major premise; since the outcomes of all reasoning therefrom must be compatible with that premise, only those subordinate premises that have valid outcomes are admissable. The multiple premises of multiple goods do not constrain reasoning in that manner.

But all behavior maximizes something; for most individuals (but not firms) the single maximand of material gain sacrifices the very thing it is intended to maximize, life satisfaction. In this respect, the assumption of a single maximand gives only the illusion of efficiency in economic life, and not the substance – unless consumers are thought to be soldiers in the service of the market or priests in a society of consumers. The efficiency norm that takes as its premise the maximization of profit does not serve efficient pursuit of happiness.

If economic efficiency does not necessarily imply engineering efficiency, neither engineering nor economic efficiency necessarily implies social efficiency, that is, the promotion of goals in order of their aggregated preferences. In fact, economic efficiency implies social *in*efficiency whenever it interferes with optimization of other social goals with higher priority. One example of the way the efficiency norm may inhibit other social goals is the tendency for benign qualities of work to reflect back on work in ways that seem to run counter to the efficiency norm. Kohn and Schooler identified a group whose members use leisure in intellectually demanding ways (reading, active pursuit of an avocation); these authors then searched for indications of the causes and consequences at work of such more challenging uses of

---

[4]Talcott Parsons, *The Social System* (Glencoe, IL: Free Press, 1951), 352.
[5]Adriano Tilgher, *Work – What It Has Meant to Men Through the Ages* (London: Harrap, 1931), 60.
[6]William Parker, personal communication, 1978.
[7]The "economic approach," says Gary Becker, "assumes maximizing behavior." *The Economic Approach to Human Behavior* (Chicago: University of Chicago Press, 1976), 5.

leisure. They found a very modest tendency for these more challenging kinds of leisure to be causally related to the increase in substantive complexity of work performed, the chances of becoming an owner, and especially of self-direction at work. But the most significant relation to work of a pattern of more challenging leisure is not causal but *consequential:* It tends to *reduce* the hours of work performed![8] Leisure activities that represent a more worthwhile pattern of living are not only separate from but in opposition to facets of work that are economically and humanly productive.

We turn now to two economic arrangements that are said to contribute to market efficiency: competition and the division of labor.

Competition

Among humanists and psychologists competition is thought to be at the unfavorable end of a single dimension whose favorable end is cooperation. Among economists, competition is the favorable end of a dimension whose unfavorable end is monopoly. These two sets of intellectuals are talking past each other; psychologists understand competition to be a trait of rivalrousness, or *competitiveness,* whereas economists see competition as a circumstance where individuals have a choice among competing alternatives. Thus economists distinguish *between* rivalry and competition, the latter meaning only the presence of alternatives: "A person has competition if the party he wants to trade with has alternative opportunities for exchange."[9] It is this confusion of definitions, in part, that leads market critics to believe that a "competitive economy" implies that people will learn competitiveness as part of their workplace learning. But it would be naive to believe that when an individual innocently presents alternatives to the services you have been rendering your customers and seeks to attract them away from you, that you do not become psychologically competitive. We will deal first with competition in the economist's meaning, and limit the discussion to interfirm competition.[10]

Competition as the presence of alternatives

It is almost always beneficial to be a third party when others offer alternatives, that is, compete against each other. As *consumers,* individuals benefit from enlarged choices because they can satisfy more diverse tastes. They also benefit in the manner described in Chapters 7 and 8: Enlarged choices increase cognitive complexity – unless these choices are too demanding, in which case they reduce cognitive complexity again. As diminished constraint, enlarged choices increase autonomy and self-direction.

As *workers* whose firms vigorously compete against each other, individuals lose. Competitive firms offer fewer work benefits than do firms with market power, as we saw in the previous chapter. Workers are no longer third parties; they are agents

---

[8] Melvin Kohn and Carmi Schooler, *Work and Personality: An Inquiry into the Impact of Social Stratification* (Norwood, NJ: Ablex, 1983), 230. For women, the challenging use of leisure had virtually no effects except, in comparison to men, a more substantial tendency to increase family income. (p. 237)
[9] Tibor Scitovsky, *Welfare and Competition,* rev. ed. (London: Allen & Unwin, 1971), 14.
[10] For want of space, I do not treat competition in the labor market.

of competing units. Thus people's interests are different in the two economic roles they play: As consumers they benefit, as workers they lose. In the market economy we know workers' consumer roles take precedence, even though this does not contribute much to happiness (Part VII) or satisfy their major wants for achievement and satisfying work – major, at least, in an affluent society.

Competition as rivalry and competitiveness

The meaning of competitiveness. There is no standard psychological definition of competitiveness, but there is much overlap in the various definitions. Morton Deutsch says that as a "psychological orientation," competitiveness embraces the following aspects: (1) *cognitively,* as contrasted to the cooperative propositions that "we are for one another," competitiveness implies that "we are against each other" and that "we are linked together . . . so that if one gains, the other loses." (2) *Motivationally,* in contrast to a predisposition to trust the other and wish him or her well, competitiveness implies that "one is predisposed to cathect the other negatively, to have a suspicious, hostile, exploitative attitude toward the other, to be psychologically closed to the other, to be aggressive and defensive toward the other, to see the other as opposed to oneself and basically different. (3) *Morally,* as contrasted to mutual respect and egalitarian feelings toward the other, competitiveness "sanctions inequality and legitimates a win–lose struggle to determine who will have superior and who will have inferior outcomes."[11] But note that trust is both a condition of a market economy and associated with economic growth.[12]

To the economist (and to me) this must seem a somewhat pejorative account of the characteristics of those seeking to win in zero sum games: promotions where only one of several candidates will be chosen, bidding for a contract, and so forth. Definitions are not right or wrong; Deutsch's experimental data lend credence to his list of attitudes that are actually associated with competition in the laboratory. Nevertheless, we will narrow our definition to the dimension used in an experiment by Deci and colleagues to be discussed: "the desire to best others, to be successful in interpersonal competition."

In order to avoid misunderstanding, note that this narrow definition says nothing about purposeful assertion, goal directedness, or desire to achieve the object for which people are competing.

Competitiveness and developmental learning. Kohn and Schooler report that "the competitiveness of [a worker's] relations with fellow employees, and his

---

[11] Morton Deutsch, *Distributive Justice: A Social Psychological Perspective* (New Haven: Yale University Press, 1985), 84–6.

[12] Alex Inkeles and Larry Diamond, "Personal Development and National Development: A Cross-Cultural Perspective," in Alexander Szalai and Frank M. Andrews, eds., *The Quality of Life: Comparative Studies* (Ann Arbor, MI: Institute for Social Research, 1986), 73–109 at 97; Ronald Inglehart and Jacques-Rene Rabier, "Aspirations Adapt to Situations – But Why Are the Belgians So Much Happier than the French? A Cross-Cultural Analysis of the Subjective Quality of Life," in Frank M. Andrews, ed., *Research on the Quality of Life* (Ann Arbor, MI: Institute for Social Research, 1986), 52.

participation in union or other work-related group activities, prove to have little independence relevance'' to their dependent variables, self-directedness, cognitive flexibility, and self-esteem. Furthermore, "on-the-job interpersonal relations do not greatly affect off-the-job psychological functioning; it is the structural imperatives of the job that affect men's ways of dealing with the larger world.''[13]

In an experiment comparing the effect of competition on intrinsic interest in solving a puzzle, one group was set competing against other groups while a control group was told to work as quickly as it could so as to finish in the allotted time. Compared to the group working against time, the competitive group rather quickly lost interest in the puzzle, implying decrements of associated learning.[14] As we shall see in Chapters 18 and 19, such extrinsic factors as pay and competitive scores reduce learning about the work itself because of the distracting attention to rewards and scores.

Going far afield, we report Margaret Mead's finding from a study of societies with three dominant modes of interaction: competition, cooperation, and independence. Mead found very few differences among the three kinds of societies in their capacities to develop strong, effective personalities.[15]

I conclude tentatively that competitiveness either has no effect on developmental learning or, when salient, may actually decrease it. One component of that learning, self-esteem, is jeopardized for those who need help most, those with low self-esteem. An additional value, subjective sense of well-being, is undermined by the social comparisons necessarily implied by competitiveness.[16]

Does the market foster competitiveness?

Competitiveness does not lead to success. In modern economic thinking, rivalry is a distraction from the serious work at hand: "The Economic Man neither competes nor higgles – nor does he cooperate, psychologically speaking; he treats other human beings as if they were slot machines.''[17] As a psychological disposition, competitiveness does not favor economic success. In a study of college students, business school students and graduates, and a national (mail) sample of scientists, two traits – (1) *work ethic,* a desire for hard work, and (2) *mastery,* "a preference for challenging tasks, a drive toward internal standards of excellence'' – showed clear relationships to success: academic success for the students, frequency of citation for the scientists, and income for the business graduates. But (3) *competitiveness,* defined as "the desire to best others, to be successful in interper-

[13] Melvin L. Kohn and Carmi Schooler "Occupational Experience and Psychological Functioning: An Assessment of Reciprocal Effects," *American Sociological Review* 38 (1973): 97–118 at 105.

[14] Edward L. Deci, Gregory Betley, James Kahle, Linda Abrams, and Joseph Porac, "When Trying to Win: Competition and Intrinsic Motivation," *Personality and Social Psychology Bulletin* 7 (March 1981): 79–83.

[15] Margaret Mead, *Cooperation and Competition Among Primitive Peoples* (1937; reprint Boston: Beacon, 1967).

[16] Philip Shaver and Jonathan Freedman, "Your Pursuit of Happiness," *Psychology Today* 10 (August 1976): 27–32, 75.

[17] Frank H. Knight, *Risk, Uncertainty and Profits,* 66.

sonal competition," showed no relationship by itself, though combined with the first two traits, it showed a modest contribution to success.[18]

Psychologists have discovered another behavioral syndrome whose defining characteristics include highly competitive and manipulative behavior; these characteristics are derived, not from Freud but from Machiavelli's *The Prince*. Machiavellians' operating premises and practices include beliefs that trusting others leads to trouble, "cutting corners" is necessary to get ahead, people should always be told what they want to hear, honesty is not always the best policy, people should dissemble when it is to their advantage, and similar principles related to taking advantage of others and beating them wherever possible.[19] Machiavellians generally win in experimental games where there is both a lack of continuity of relationships, such that the participants will not likely see each other again, and some ambiguity about the rules. But they do not "win" in the larger market society. To the surprise of Christie and Geiss, who developed and tested the Machiavellianism syndrome, "high Machs" are *less* successful in their occupational careers than are "low Machs."[20] Thus, at least in those many situations relevant to career advancement, Machiavellian competitive manipulation is not effective.

Departing some distance from the ordinary affairs of the market, there is evidence that compared to Mexican-American children, Anglo-American children pursue self-defeating competitive strategies in games where cooperation is necessary to win. In explanation, it is suggested: "The environmental milieu in which U.S. children develop during the early school years, given the high value placed on individual achievement through competition, may lead to a strong 'I' orientation by age 7 which masks any potential for behaving on the basis of an autonomous morality of cooperation."[21]

Finally, in prisoner's dilemma games, those with competitive orientations anticipate that their partners will compete and therefore tend to lose more often than noncompetitive players.[22]

On the basis of this fragmentary evidence, I conclude that competitiveness is (1) not rewarded or reinforced in a market economy, and is (2) dysfunctional for many economic "games" where cooperation is necessary.

[18] Jack C. Horn, "The Element of Success: Competitiveness Isn't That Important," *Psychology Today* 11 (April 1978): 19–20, reporting work by Robert Helmreich and Janet Spence.

[19] Richard Christie and Florence L. Geis, *Studies in Machiavellianism* (New York: Academic Press, 1972), 3–4.

[20] Using a familiar measure of socioeconomic status the authors found that "there was not only no correlation with Mach but, contrary to our prediction, there was no relationship between upward social mobility (the change from father's SES to respondent's SES) and Mach. . . . [But] it is also possible that low Machs got ahead by hard work, while highs advanced by combining manipulative skills with less arduous labor." Ibid., 354.

[21] S. Kagan and M. C. Madsen, "Co-operation and Competition of Mexican, Mexican-American, and Anglo-American Children of Two Ages under Four Instructional Sets," *Developmental Psychology* 5 (1971): 32–9. The quotation is from a summary of this and related research by D. R. Price-Williams, "Cultural Psychology," in Gardner Lindzey and Elliott Aronson, eds., *Handbook of Social Psychology*, vol. 2 (New York: Random House, 1985), 993–1,042 at 1,013.

[22] H. H. Kelley and A. J. Stahelski, "Social Interaction Basis of Cooperators' and Competitors' Beliefs about Others," *Journal of Personality and Social Psychology* 16 (1970): 66–91. The authors distinguish between market competition and competition in prisoner's dilemma games.

Cross-cultural evidence on the sources of competitiveness. Following the study of the degrees of competitiveness among Anglo-American, Mexican, and Mexican-American children, many other studies under a variety of circumstances pursued the matter further. Studies in Korea, Israel, and Germany found that the rural–urban dimension was a crucial determinant: In a review, Price-Williams says that "competition is one of the inevitable concomitants of the worldwide trend toward urbanism." Beyond that, there seems to be an even more general "modernity" factor: Canadian Indians are less competitive than Canadian Caucasians, Australian aborigines are more cooperative than rural Australians, and Polynesian and Maori children are more cooperative than matching Caucasian groups.[23] The urban–modernity factor does not exclude a market influence, however. Since all rural and "native" populations are less exposed to the market than urban Caucasian groups, we cannot say whether marketization has contributed to competitiveness or not.

On the basis of current evidence, I believe that market *practice* does little to teach or reinforce competitiveness. In the preceding reports on the relative economic failure of those marked by competitiveness, we see some evidence for failed reinforcement. Most people are employees in firms where individual competition often leads to Liebenstein's "X-inefficiency"[24] and is therefore discouraged, though there are exceptions, for example, where bonuses are awarded on the basis of relative performance.[25] In their internal labor markets, employees are sheltered from the competition between firms (Chapter 15). Tönnies made this point a hundred years ago: "Competition in trade and elsewhere . . . is only metaphorical; [the competing individual] is faced not with another individual, either in selling or giving, but with the calculable circumstances of fate, with fortune."[26] I know of no evidence showing that markets foster competitiveness more than bureaucracies, with their "competitive examinations," or science laboratories, with their partially concealed but powerful rivalries for priority, or law schools where grades determine class standing and membership on a prestigious Law Review.

But the market affects competitiveness indirectly through its influences on social structure and through its ideology. Perhaps it does so by increasing urbanization, though this is uncertain, but it almost certainly does so by reducing the power of *primary groups:* "In studies of the determinants of cooperative and competitive behavior, [research reports] have demonstrated that an important factor leading to cooperativeness is primary group identification. . . . The presence or absence of primary support groups was the major predictor of cooperativeness."[27] In Chapter

---

[23] Price-Williams, "Cultural Psychology," 1,013.
[24] Harvey Liebenstein, *Beyond Economic Man: A New Foundation for Micro-economics* (Cambridge: Harvard University Press, 1976); see also George J. Stigler, "The Xistence of X-efficiency," *American Economic Review* 66 (1967): 213–16; Liebenstein, "Inefficiency Xists–Reply to an Xorcist," *American Economic Review* 68 (1978): 203–11.
[25] Edward E. Lawler, III, "Using Pay to Motivate Job Performance," in Richard M. Steers and Lyman W. Porter, eds., *Motivation and Work Behavior* (New York: McGraw-Hill, 1975).
[26] Ferdinand Tönnies, *Community and Society,* trans. C. P. Loomis (New York: Harper Torchbook, 1963), 186. First published as *Gemeinschaft und Gesellschaft,* 1897.
[27] Richard W. Brislin, "Cross-Cultural Research in Psychology," *Annual Review of Psychology* 34 (1983): 363–400 at 371–2, citing research by Madsen and Lancy in New Guinea.

15 the power of competition to accelerate technological change damaging to established industrial group relations reveals one way in which the market erodes primary groups at the workplace. But the major effect is through its polar pull against family and community.

The *ideology* of the system confounds firms and individuals, circumstances and dispositions. Thus, when the market system is called "the competitive system," people may well infer that as individuals they are called upon to compete. The Lynds reported in the 1930s that residents of Middletown believed that "competition everywhere insures everything's being done that literally *can* be done. . . . That competition is what makes progress and has made the United States great."[28] In the 1970s most Americans (88 percent of a national sample) believed that "it is having to compete with others that keeps a person on his toes" and 81 percent held that "competition, whether in school, work, or business . . . leads to better performance and a desire for excellence."[29] Adam Smith, too, had no doubt about the value of rivalry: "Rivalship and emulation render excellency, even in mean professions, an object of ambition, and frequently occasion the very greatest exertions."[30] Since the elites in the cited national sample believed these things as much as the nonelites, it is apparent that the beliefs are taught, reinforced by public opinion, and made part of an untested axiomatic cultural code. When the United States is economically challenged, the appeal is not to basic economic defects, but to inadequate "competitiveness."[31] It seems to me that in a simple transformation of meanings and linguistic extensions, the desire for competition-as-alternatives is translated into the belief that to create alternatives people must have the personality trait of competitiveness or rivalry. But those who do have it are actually more likely to fail.

Competitiveness in the market versus cooperation in the workplace. The apparent conflict between competitiveness in the labor market and cooperation in the workplace disappears if the personality orientation called competitiveness is actually dysfunctional for ordinary market success. The traits that do relate to market success – work ethic, a sense of mastery, desire for challenge, and "industriousness" (Chapter 7), which is strongly correlated with "cooperativeness"[32] – are not in conflict with those qualities that facilitate work in most work settings. What seems from the doctrine and ideology of the market to promise a "contradiction," or at least a set of incompatible qualities, does not do so. The real conflict between market and workplace is between initiative and obedience.

At the institutional level, I reaffirm my belief stated in Chapter 15 that interfirm competition favors consumers at the expense of workers and inhibits firms from

---

[28] Robert S. Lynd and Helen M. Lynd, *Middletown in Transition: A Study in Cultural Conflicts* (New York: Harcourt Brace, 1937), 63, 409.

[29] Herbert McClosky and John Zaller, *The American Ethos: Public Attitudes Toward Capitalism and Democracy* (Cambridge: Harvard University Press, 1985), 122.

[30] Adam Smith, *The Wealth of Nations* (1776; reprint New York: Random House/Modern Library, 1937), 717.

[31] Robert B. Reich, "The New 'Competitiveness' Fad," *New York Times*, 14 January 1987.

[32] Christopher Jencks et al., *Who Gets Ahead? The Determinants of Economic Success in America* (New York: Basic Books, 1979), 222–3.

attending to the development of their work force. But it does not have the effect on personality attributed to it. For one thing, individual competitiveness is not important in the processes of workplace learning examined by Kohn and Schooler; it is not, therefore, part of the schooling of the factory. Nor is it rewarded by other market processes: Because it impedes creative work processes and for other reasons, competitiveness as a trait is not a desirable characteristic for those who aspire to succeed in the market; competitive people are less successful than others. Consequently, the alleged conflict between competition in the market and cooperation at work is not severe. On the other hand, competitiveness may be indirectly fostered by the market's erosion of the kind of social solidarities that inhibit competitiveness, and the ideology and language of the market leads people to believe that competition is necessary in order to achieve excellence. Nevertheless, since other institutions such as schools and professions seem to create situations stimulating competitiveness just as much as the market does, we find that competitiveness as a personality trait is not a market product. Competitiveness has many nonmarket sources and is more likely to be reinforced by urbanism, individualism, and social anonymity, than by the market itself.

The division of labor

Although the division of labor is largely a product of work technology, the market accelerates the process of dividing work into specialties. How do these specialties influence what is learned and enjoyed at work? Marx differentiated between (1) the division of labor for the "detail worker" who is "split up [and] transformed into the automatic motor of some partial operation," and (2) the division between "the man of knowledge and the productive laborer."[33] Although Marx believed that all division of labor "entails some crippling both of mind and body,"[34] in fact, the differences between these two types are enormous. Here we will examine both kinds of division of labor, noting trends that greatly modify Marx's conclusion.

The effects on developmental learning of the detail worker

Adam Smith both admired the division of labor for its efficiency and recognized that it tended to brutalize labor. As mentioned in Chapter 13, Smith saw the effect of factory specialization as follows:

The man whose life is spent performing a few simple operations, of which the effects are, perhaps, always the same, or very nearly the same, has no occasion to exert his understanding, or to exercise his invention in finding expedients for removing difficulties which never occur. . . . The torpor of his mind renders him not only incapable of relishing or bearing a part in any rational conversation, but of conceiving any generous, noble or tender sentiment.[35]

[33] Karl Marx, *Capital*, trans. from 4th Ger. ed. (1867) by Eden Paul and Cedar Paul (1887; reprint New York: Dutton Everyman, 1972), 381, 382, 383.
[34] Ibid., 384.
[35] Smith, *The Wealth of Nations*, 734–5. Smith was not alone; Ferguson (quoted in Karl Marx, *Capital*, 383) and Steuart and Montesquieu joined the chorus, although the latter were more likely to criticize the effects of commerce than of industry. Marx, *Capital*, 383, criticized Smith for minimizing the effects of division of labor on the worker.

Smith's German opponent, Schiller, said of the division of labor:

Everlastingly chained to a single fragment of the Whole, man himself develops into nothing but a fragment; everlastingly in his ear the monotonous sound of the wheel that turns, he never develops the harmony of his being, and instead of putting the stamp of his humanity upon his own nature, he becomes nothing more than the imprint of his occupation or of his specialized knowledge.[36]

Recent evidence supports Smith, Schiller, and Marx in this respect. With reference to the detail worker, Kohn and Schooler confirm these effects of simple repetitive tasks on learning. As the cognitive complexity of those with substantively complex tasks *develop* through work, so the cognitive capacities, the thinking ability, of those with simple repetitive tasks *deteriorate*.[37]

The problem of the effects of the division of labor on the detail worker plagued the former command economies just as much as it did market economies. Concepts of reform are similar: redesign work so as to eliminate the effects of routinization.[38] If economic efficiency is reduced, however, the market will reject reforms.

Market responsibility for detail work. To the extent that the market's efficiency norm, the pressure to produce more at less cost, is responsible for the division of labor into repetitive, routine, unchallenging tasks, it seems to take away all the benefits the human capital thesis endows in it. As is well known, Marx thought this was the case: "The manufacturing division of labor is a development peculiar to the capitalist method of production."[39] We now know that command economies follow the same routes and "the capitalist method of production" has both extended "detail work" in assembly lines and gone a little distance to reduce it in higher technology firms or to obviate it in the enlarged service sectors. (Neither Smith nor Marx would have thought of a waiter as a "detail worker.") The efficiency norm presses blindly toward least cost methods; but what the market imposes on workers, technology may (or may not) relieve.

But the division of labor prompted by the efficiency norm working through industrialization is only one of several kinds of specialization.

[36] Friedrich von Schiller, "On the Aesthetic Side of Man," quoted in Robert Eccleshall, "The Undivided Self," in Bikhu Parekh, ed, *The Concept of Socialism* (New York: Holmes and Meier, 1975), 96.

[37] Routinization of work has effects less powerful than those of lack of substantive complexity, but they are substantial. By itself, with other job conditions held constant, routinization increases alienation – feelings of powerlessness, self-estrangement (or self-rejection), and normlessness – distrust, conformity, self-deprecation, and anxiety. Kohn and Schooler, *Work and Personality,* 89, 144. There is some irony in the further fact that mechanically paced work actually increases one element of the job conditions that favor self-direction: It reduces close supervision by a foreman.

[38] For analysis of redesign of work in the American capitalist world, see the works of Argyris, Likert, Maslow, etc.; U.S. Department of Health, Education, and Welfare, Task Force, *Work in America* (Cambridge: M.I.T. Press, n.d.), largely influenced by Herzberg, offers a review of the criticism of the time. For the socialist world see Radovan Richta, *Civilization at the Crossroads* (Prague: Arts and Sciences Press, 1968); and the East German and Hungarian reports in Jan Forslin, Adam Sarapata, and Arthur M. Whitehill, eds., *Automation and Industrial Workers: A Fifteen Nation Study,* vol. 1, pt 2 (Oxford, UK: Pergamon Press, 1981).

[39] Marx, *Capital,* 380. Durkheim, on the other hand, found the source in the increased need for efficient production following the rise of urban living. Emile Durkheim, *The Division of Labor in Society,* trans. G. Simpson (New York: Free Press, 1964). Original work published 1893.

Specialization of knowledge

There are three relevant issues in the matter of the specialization of knowledge: (1) the character of specialization, (2) market effects on specialization, and (3), if the market accelerates specialization, how shall we appraise specialists as contrasted to the "well-rounded personality"? As in the discussion on competition, our concern goes beyond workplace learning to the broader effects of specialization on personality.

Kinds of division of labor. Anthropologists distinguish among various kinds of specialization:[40] *Specialization by decree* may be seen among the Indian castes and in South African apartheid; not only is this devoid of the efficiency payoffs that attracted Smith, it prevents society from benefiting from these payoffs. *Specialization by custom,* as may be seen in the concept of "women's work," has similar disadvantages. In these two senses the division of labor is not even modern, let alone industrial, and rather than being fostered by the market, it is eroded by market norms of which the efficiency norm is an important element.

But the third form of specialization, *specialization by choice,* is in some degree a market-favored variety, and has many efficiency advantages if people are good at doing what they like to do.[41] One could hardly say that assembly-line workers like to do what they have "chosen" to do for a living; but even for these jobs selected faute de mieux the basis of selection is better than bases of caste, color, or paternal occupation. (My Detroit taxi driver was waiting for a job to open up on the assembly line – because the pay was better!) For most occupations modern principles of division of labor is an alternative to archaic forms of the division of labor.[42] At any level, *choosing what one does* contributes to commitment and, whenever circumstances permit, to developmental learning at work.

The changing role of the man of knowledge. Marx's criticism of the division of labor as knowledge specialization occurred in a society where knowledge could still be considered a unified whole. Smith was a contemporary of the *encyclopedists* whom Henry Adams cites as a benchmark for the time when all significant knowledge could be encompassed in a single mind. At the time science and technology had not yet merged, education was still in the classical tradition, and the knowledge industries that Machlup says (rather generously) employ a quarter of the American work force had barely begun to develop.[43]

---

[40] This classification is taken from Sandra Wallman, "Introduction," in Wallman, ed., *Social Anthropology of Work* (London: Academic Press, 1979), 14–15.

[41] Ibid. Wallman points out that specialization by choice extends beyond *what* one does at work to the degree of effort and excellence invested in the work, something that no doubt prevails in all forms of economy.

[42] See Jack P. Gibbs and Dudley L. Poston, "The Division of Labor: Conceptualization and Related Measures," *Social Forces* 53 (1975): 468–76.

[43] Fritz Machlup, *The Production and Distribution of Knowledge in the United States* (Princeton: Princeton University Press, 1962).

The rise of the "knowledgeable society"[44] has greatly increased the proportion of the "men of knowledge" (as they were then called) in the work force and increased the knowledge requirements of many, though by no means all, "productive laborers." Today indeed Marx's criticism, though still partially valid, must be modified by seven altered circumstances.

1. RISING LEVELS AND CHANGING RATIOS. Society has tried to raise the level of knowledge of the simplest laborer to a level commensurate with increased job requirements. Instead of men of knowledge and capitalists allying themselves against the worker, they have allied themselves in a joint effort to persuade, even to beg, young candidates for work to stay in school, to get as much education as they can. The offensive inegalitarian implications of the original division of labor are modified at the margin by this new coalition. When the baseline rises, the dialogue across the strata changes dramatically.

2. PROFESSIONALISM OF THE MEANS OF PRODUCTION. Specialists with modest intellectual qualifications, like nurses and forest rangers, seek professional status, that is, status where the members of a specialty assume collective responsibility for a body of theoretical knowledge and the control of its interpretation, training, and admission to an occupation.[45] Professionals seek control of the "means of production" in their own fields. In this sense, recognition of the division of labor by middle-strata (as well as high-strata) members of the work force is eagerly sought as a step toward recognition and collective self-determination.

3. DISTRIBUTED OWNERSHIP OF HUMAN CAPITAL. As mentioned in Chapters 1 and 13, with the expansion of the division of labor into knowledge specialties, *human capital* has become an increasingly important force in production such that today the return on human capital is estimated to be larger than the return on physical capital.[46] Four-fifths of U.S. national income is derived from earnings (the yield of effort plus human capital) and only one-fifth from property – a great reversal since Adam Smith's day.[47] As John Locke said, each person owns himself, therefore each person owns his own human capital and this form of the means of production.

4. KNOWLEDGE AND KNOWLEDGE CENTERS AS POWER BASES. The rise of specialized knowledge creates alternative, coordinate power bases. The division of labor divides men of knowledge (scientists and scholars) from men of money (capitalists, managers, and entrepreneurs), each group with characteristic institutions, codes, and loyalties. Of course, men of knowledge serve men of money and the firms they control – this service is a source of profit to each and a source of eco-

[44]Robert E. Lane, "The Decline of Politics and Ideology in a Knowledgeable Society," *American Sociological Review* 31 (1966): 649–62. In a five-part definition, the knowledgeable society is characterized as one based on extensive inquiry, objective truth standards, allocation of large resources to gathering and interpreting knowledge, and use of inquiry and knowledge in reexamining the values of the society. (p. 650)

[45]Harold Wilenski, "The Professionalization of Everyone?" *American Journal of Sociology* 70 (1964: 137–58.

[46]Jeffrey G. Williamson and Peter H. Lindert, *American Inequality: A Macroeconomic History* (New York: Academic Press, 1980), 202.

[47]Theodore W. Schultz, *Investing in People: The Economics of Population Quality* (Berkeley: University of California Press, 1981), 140.

nomic prosperity for all. And, no doubt, the relation invites "perversion" of knowledge to exploitative uses, as well. But as Lipset and Dobson point out, the university is the source of heterodoxy and criticism in all societies, market and socialist, first, second, and third worlds. It provides, these authors say, the functional equivalent of a dissenting proletariat.[48] The university becomes, in a modest way, a power base alternative to both unions and citadels of wealth.

5. SPECIALIZATION REDUCES ANONYMITY AND SUBSTITUTABILITY. It has been suggested that the market's preference for anonymous and impersonal "units" of labor leads to substitutability of persons for one another, a loss of uniqueness, anomie, and "moral neutralization."[49] On the other hand, the division of labor among specialists represents an *impediment* to substitutability, for there can be no substitution of one kind of specialist for another kind. It is the unspecialized workers, left outside the division of labor, who are most substitutable one for another.

Hierarchy in a knowledgeable society has two opposing effects, the second dominating the first.

6. KNOWLEDGE VERSUS STATUS. There is a division of labor by *level of decision* that forms a gradient of the general importance of decisions taken. In a minor sense, the efficiency norm is now said to transcend that hierarchy: Where expertise and superior status in an organization conflict, the efficiency norm means that expertise trumps status. In this sense, the efficiency norm does the opposite of what Marx said it did: In the interest of profits, it pits knowledge against power.[50]

7. BUT HIERARCHIES MONOPOLIZE COGNITION. The division of labor by level of decision generally prevails. Although the market is said to be an alternative to hierarchy, dispersing and decentralizing decisions in autonomous units, it has nevertheless generated ever larger corporations with fewer autonomous units. It was this that led Mannheim to worry about the usurpation of cognition at the higher levels of business (Chapter 8).[51] Centralization of strategic decisions may not mimic Marx's division between brains and brawn, but it has the same effect on developmental learning.

Kohn and Schooler's research might be interpreted to support this view. Experience in self-direction on the job improves cognitive capacities and leads to valuing self-direction itself, the latter point being especially relevant to Mannheim's thesis. Furthermore, Kohn and Schooler report that the higher a person's rank in a bureaucracy, the more that person values self-direction and the more he or she learns to think in cognitively complex ways. Whereas the problem is even more acute in command economies, it is nevertheless true that as the market generates increasingly large hierarchical units, it contributes to a division of labor by level of decision that frustrates learning at the bottom.

---

[48] Seymour M. Lipset and R. B. Dobson, "The Intellectual as Critic and Rebel: With Special Reference to the United States and the Soviet Union," *Daedalus* 101 (Summer 1972): 137–98.

[49] Paul Diesing, *Reason in Society* (Urbana: University of Illinois Press, 1962), 23–4.

[50] Warren G. Bennis and Philip E. Slater, *The Temporary Society* (New York: Harper Colophon, 1969). These authors report a tendency for tasks to be assigned to teams of experts created for the occasion, rather than to an officer in a departmental hierarchy.

[51] Karl Mannheim, *Man and Society in an Age of Reconstruction*, trans. E. Shils (New York: Harcourt Brace, 1948), 60–6.

Demoralization of the unspecialized. One clear disadvantage of the knowledgeable society is an unhappy concomitant of the advantages: To be unskilled in the world of the skilled is as degrading as to be poor among the rich. But this is not a problem unique to the market; bureaucracies and schools offer the same problems. In any event, excellence in family and friendship roles offer relief.

For the skilled and partly skilled, the division of labor offers multiple ladders for excellence, the multiplicity providing individuals more opportunities to be "the best" or "high" on one of these ladders and insulating them from unfavorable comparisons across ladders.

I conclude that specialization of knowledge, very likely accelerated by the efficiency norm of market economies, has very few of the characteristics of the specialism of function, as in the detail worker. On the contrary, specialization has within it an immanent tendency to include ever more members of society, to broaden rather than narrow power bases, and to give specialists a sense of worth as the multiplication of occupational status pyramids increases the number of "top rank" positions in society (Chapter 12). At the same time, it excludes and demeans the unspecialized, and in the developed market economies, widens the gulf between the very large numbers of "men of knowledge" and all the others.

Specialization and personality

The term *narrow specialist* is a cliché, almost collapsed into one word. The opposing term of opprobrium is *shallow*. If the efficiency norm increases specialization, does it make people narrow or shallow?

Work versus nonwork roles. There is a division of labor among roles such that the work role is only one of several. Anthropologist Sandra Wallman favors the well-rounded person: "The normal balance in any society would seem to be to spread identity investment across all of livelihood so that each role gets and gives its due."[52] What is "its due"?

On the one hand, one might assume that the market-accelerated separation of work from family would make it easier to develop work roles and family roles without confabulating them: separate but equal. On the other hand, Wallman reports:

Very likely this balance [of roles] is easier to maintain in those settings – usually small scale but not necessarily rural – in which role frames tend to be overlaid and relationships "multiplex," a person brings all his identities to bear in each context, or finds them relevant by others who "know all about him" willy-nilly.[53]

I know of no evidence showing that roles learned separately and practiced separately, as is the case in advanced market economies, are less healthy than those learned together and integrated in practice, as in less advanced, mainly household economies.

[52] Wallman, "Introduction," 17.
[53] Ibid.

Specialization versus generalism. Perhaps colored by an anthropologist's concern with kinship, Wallman fears work specialization (Chapter 13).[54] Almost by definition work specialists are bound to be neglecting other obligations; time is more or less inelastic. How shall one resolve the dispute? The self-employed lawyer who works late into the night, the nurse in the ghetto who takes on more than she can easily manage, or the scientist who gets up at dawn to see the results of an experiment serve one set of purposes; the family man and civic leader another set. The more people "throw themselves into their work," the more they learn from it.

The market has a criterion. If a person is earning more money by his or her devotion, and if the money is worth more than leisure given up, the devotion is justified. If one earns less than the leisure is worth, then not. By assigning a money value to the uses of their "leisure" (i.e., what they do beyond their specified paid duties), this criterion systematically disvalues the nurse and the scientist; it is not a good one.

There are three weaknesses in this criterion. (1) It assesses a voluntary, intrinsically worthwhile and worthy activity in monetary terms. In Part VI we will see how money payments (in this case, offered but not accepted) depreciate voluntary activities and make them less enjoyable. (2) It fails to appreciate the value of *choosing,* which has value regardless of which options are chosen. Where one can *choose* the role to be assessed, for example, parent, good friend among friends, or skilled or professional worker, one can improve one's self-esteem.[55] And (3) by implication, the criterion devalues the learning that takes place in an activity, placing the weight entirely on utility. As pointed out in Chapter 1, even to individuals, personal development and hedonic rewards are different criteria. We might say that the guiding principle is the benefit derived from *choice* (giving a larger meaning to the "specialization by choice" already mentioned), not balanced diversity nor the ratio of income earned to the value of the leisure given up.

The value of work experience in a market economy is often sacrificed on the altar of efficiency, which in turn is enforced by the profit maximand where profits derive from maximizing consumer interests and minimizing worker interests. Similarly, worker interests are sacrificed by competition for customers, a competition that makes expenditures on workplace learning impossible unless that learning also serves productivity. Both of these tendencies operate to hinder the development of worker priority that would give worker welfare a value commensurate with consumer welfare. We explore these implications in the next section.

Is the market compatible with worker priority?

Stripped of its spurious economics and history, Marx's critique of capitalist society was focused on what work did to individuals. As noted in the opening quotation to Chapter 13, he hoped that "the germs of the education of the future are to be found

[54] Ibid.
[55] See Morris Rosenberg, *Conceiving the Self* (New York: Basic Books, 1979).

in the factory system,"[56] but believed that this would not be possible in a market economy. To some extent, he was right. In the discussion that follows, I refer to an economy that favors enjoyment and learning at work as a *producer economy,* to distinguish it from the *consumer economy* that we have been calling a market economy.

As pointed out earlier, the basic problem with the consumer economy is that anything that increases costs to a firm without increasing revenue (and thus income and profits) cannot be chosen in a genuinely competitive economy. That is why the firms with market power offer work circumstances that are more favorable than can be offered by competitive firms. In the previous chapter we asked who should pay for such improvements in the quality of work life that did not increase productivity: the workers who benefit? consumers? owners? or the persons displaced from their jobs because the cost of labor has risen, that is, the unemployed? As mentioned in that chapter, market mechanisms in consumer economies solve this question in complex economic ways, depending on various alternatives and elasticities. A producer economy, therefore, must face the following problems.

Competition prohibits costs in one firm not incurred by another. We already know that the superior terms of employment in firms with market power are, because of that market power, paid for substantially by consumers and to a lesser extent by the displaced or unemployed workers. But, in a genuinely competitive market economy, *no-one will pay;* the costs will not be incurred and the workers will have to get along as best they can (which is better than they used to do, thanks to changes in technology rather than to market influences). The market economy is a consumer economy. Competition, the very agency that polices efficiency, is hazardous to the value of a producer economy.

The difficulties of giving priority to worker well-being

Problems in workplace improvements that reduce national or worker income. The producer economy may be *more* efficient than a consumer economy; if so, so much the better. If it is less productive of consumer values and incurs some loss of commodities, the humanist critic will say that the cost buys goods of higher immediate value. There are two responses to that: (1) Sacrificing the larger *affluence effect* (Chapter 1) to immediate gains for workers not only undermines their standard of living, as this is conventionally conceived, but also the economic basis of the producer economy itself. It nibbles at the goose that laid the golden egg. It is cavalier to examine only the short-term benefits. (2) The second response is that there is no machinery in a (consumer) market economy to make that tradeoff. It would not matter whether workers demanded that worker welfare be given priority or whether managers give the workers what they asked for, the results would be the same: loss of competitive advantage.

The dilemma is illustrated by two proposals for improving the quality of work life. One proposes government intervention. Lawler points out that if firms were required to report on employee well-being as they now report on their financial

[56] Karl Marx, *Capital,* 522.

statuses, and if government were to employ tax incentives similar to those used to increase investments (accelerated depreciation, etc.) or even fine companies for higher rates of worker dissatisfaction and illness,[57] the quality of work life would be improved. The proposals are inviting, but they do not address the problem of cost: If a firm must increase its costs, perhaps to avoid fines and taxes, in order to maintain or increase man-hour *physical* productivity, the firm does not thereby increase *economic* productivity. The advantages of Lawler's proposals rapidly vanish in an internationally competitive world.

Another proposal suggests that the problem can be solved by voluntary reduction of wages by the workers whose work life is to be improved. After reviewing the "product flow attributes," "assignment attributes," "incentive attributes," of a variety of ways of organizing production (putting out, federated, communal, inside contracting, etc.), Oliver Williamson finds that "worker cooperatives do approximate the radical ideal for work organization." They meet the economic criteria for efficiency partly because workers in worker-owned cooperatives "will presumably work for lesser wages, since the oppressiveness of the Authority Relation is removed, and the greater profitability which thereby results should provide the necessary funds for such organizations to grow from retained earnings."[58] Thus, Williamson finds that it is "possible for work to contribute positively to individual development" if workers themselves are willing "to tradeoff material rewards for personal development."[59] Under these circumstances it is not necessary for the firm to have market power or for the final incidence of costs to be levied on consumers. But in the consumer economy, the market culture hinders the development of the appropriate values and the rise of the consensual social support to induce workers to accept lower pay. One might imagine that in a producer economy workers would be willing to accept the tradeoff, but the problem of how to get from here to there remains unsolved.

The double duty of pay: rewarding and allocating labor by the same act. In the consumer economy, pay is thought to do double duty: The same payment both rewards the worker for his or her performance and allocates labor to its economically most productive uses. That is, the level of payment offered is "compensation" to the recipient and incentive for recruiting "the best person" to a job with that given level of payment. In the producer economy both functions of pay are depreciated. Self-regulation and the process-benefits of work might conceivably police standards and reward people for their performances, but under no circumstances could self-regulation allocate workers to their economically most productive employments. The underlying theory of marginal productivity says that labor at all levels of competence will be employed up to the point where their marginal productivities just equal marginal cost. Granted that this theory is rarely reflected in practice in a world with unions, government regulations, impediments to mobility, and

[57] Edward E. Lawler, III, "Strategies for Improving the Quality of Work Life," *American Psychologist* 37 (1982): 486–93, especially 487.
[58] Oliver Williamson, "The Organization of Work: A Comparative Institutional Assessment," *Journal of Economic Behavior and Organization* 1 (1980): 5–38 at 33.
[59] Ibid., 37.

so forth, but it is nevertheless better than nothing and the producer economy offers nothing.

The dilemma is apparently made somewhat less severe by the current mixed pattern of job selection. As reported in Chapter 13, Mortimore and Lorence studied the job selections and experiences of three groups: (1) those who valued income most, (2) those who valued "the chance to work with people and to be useful to society," and (3) those who valued intrinsic rewards, chiefly "the use of abilities, expression of interests, and creativity." They found that the members of each group selected the kinds of jobs that served their values and were then generally reinforced in those values by their work experiences in their first jobs.[60] That is, the problem of allocating the labor force whose members are possessed of multiple motives, including but not limited to pay, already exists and the self-selection of people according to the kinds of rewards they prefer works reasonably well. If the producer economy increased the number of people with Mortimore and Lorence's two non-pecuniary motivational preferences, the economy might work almost as well. But by saying that the producer economy will work if only small, though beneficial changes in motivation are made, we are saying, in effect, that the producer economy shares the advantages of a market economy only to the extent that it does not succeed in replacing the incentives of the market economy. This is correct, but there is a long way to go before the desire for intrinsic work benefits and the desire for the autonomy and learning that comes from self-direction at work actually *replace* the desire for material benefits.

Security of tenure favors learning but reduces market flexibility. The two major disutilities of work life are routine, unchallenging jobs and job insecurity. They are independent of each other. Both the least and the most challenging jobs may be insecure; we do nothing to relieve one by relieving the other. A producer economy, therefore, might pursue job redesign without attempting to improve job security, but the two prime values to be maximized in the producer economy, intrinsically enjoyable work and opportunities for self-development, strongly suggest the value of job security. This is so for the obvious reason that enjoyment of work is undermined by the stress and anxiety of job insecurity, and also because people learn less when they are anxious and insecure.

As we shall see in the next chapter, security of job tenure reduces management flexibility and makes pay a fixed rather than a variable cost, very much like seniority systems but without the flexibility allowed by shedding a firm's more recent recruits. Inasmuch as the strength of the market lies in its adaptability to changing circumstances, job tenure throughout a firm undermines this market strength. Job security is an infringement on the market system; it exists in spite of market forces and is resisted everywhere by management (at least for lesser employees).

The limits to exchange in a producer economy. There remains the issue of the salience of exchange in a producer economy, the central concept in market

[60] Jeylan T. Mortimore and Jon Lorence, "Work Experience and Occupational Value Socialization: A Longitudinal Study," *American Journal of Sociology* 84 (1979): 1,361–85, quotations at 1,362.

economics. It is also a major contribution to sense of personal control. But the producer economy does not jeopardize exchange in most of the arenas where the consumer economy relies upon it. Inasmuch as the producer economy produces goods for market exchange, exchange retains its central position in the consumer and interfirm markets. And because labor is hired in the external labor market, labor services in exchange for employment also keep exchange central, however modified they will be by the depreciation of the monetary motives. Within firms, however, the exchange of work for pay is depreciated; it no longer forms the dominant nexus of the work relationship tying workers to their employment. Rather, when work is regarded as a positive utility, pay is not the reward for work but is more of a fringe benefit. This is not so different from current consumer economy practices, where medical insurance, vacations, contributions to pension funds, and so forth are important rewards for work. Gradually to increase the interpretation of pay as more of a fringe benefit than the reason for working does not represent so radical a challenge to the market ideology or to cognitive reorganization as does Williamson's suggestion of voluntary loss of income.

Worker ownership and self-management is not a solution to the problem of worker well-being

One common answer to the dilemmas mentioned is to make workers owners, or part owners.[61] For many people this is thought to be beneficial in itself; it may be, but the evidence seems to suggest that the benefits of learning at work and enjoying work depend much more on what workers *do* at work than on whether they share in the title of ownership or share the firm's profits.[62] As Kohn and Schooler put it, "The central fact of occupational life today is not ownership of the means of production; nor is it status, income, or interpersonal relationships on the job. Instead, it is the opportunity to use initiative, thought, and independent judgment in one's work – to direct one's own occupational activities."[63]

In a market economy, if workers own their own firms there are some benefits of morale, a modest sense of increased control, and new incentives to care about the productivity of the firm, the last of these reinforcing the efficiency norm that undermines a priority for worker well-being. Whatever the benefits and costs, worker-owners are faced with the same (or enhanced) exigent efficiency norm backed up by competition as are shareholder-owned firms. Although there is nothing whatsoever in market principles that is violated by workers' ownership of the firms that employ them,[64] the temptations for workers to indulge their preferences for quality of work life at the expense of conventional efficiency is substantial. Experience with employee ownership is mixed,[65] but whatever the outcome of continuing ex-

---

[61] Martin Weitzman, *The Share Economy: Conquering Stagflation* (Cambridge: Harvard University Press, 1984).

[62] Corey Rosen, Katherine K. Klein, and Karen M. Young, "When Employees Share the Profits," *Psychology Today* 20 (January 1986): 30–6;

[63] Kohn and Schooler, *Work and Personality,* 81.

[64] Robert E. Lane, "From Political Democracy to Industrial Democracy?" *Polity* 17 (1985): 624–48.

[65] Cornell Self-Management Working Group, "Toward a Fully Self-Managed Industrial Sector in the United States," in G. David Garson and Michael P. Smith, eds., *Organizational Democracy* (Beverly

perimentation may be, two things are clear: (1) Self-direction on the job is an un-mixed blessing for most workers, and (2) if there are costs incurred in improving the quality of work life, the worker-owners must confront the implications of the efficiency norm. In a worker-owned firm the best solution might be acceptance of the countermarket idea of lower profits, and the worst would be to load the costs on the unemployed, including the former workers in the worker-owned plants.

Marx was right, the market economy is unfavorable to worker priority, not be-cause it undermines the processes of exchange, but because any costs devoted to improving work life in the competitive part of the economy make a firm vulnerable to reduced sales and profits because of the violation of the efficiency norm.

Summary

Driven by the profit maximand and reinforced by competition, the firms in a market economy seek to increase their efficiency; they favor the customers who provide them with revenue and disfavor workers whose wages represent costs. Efficiency in other institutions has many sources other than profit maximands and competition, but these are not available in a system with a profit maximand.

Competition as alternatives among firms has positive effects on individuals in the marketplace but is the source of the inability of competing firms to yield economi-cally "inefficient" benefits to their employees. Competitiveness as a trait impedes fruitful learning, but is probably not more encouraged by a market economy than many other modern institutions. This is partly because it is associated more with individual failure than with success, that is, competitiveness (but not assertion and dreams of empire – Schumpeter) is not rewarded by the market.

The division of labor has two manifestations: (1) As detail work, it impedes learning as well as work enjoyment; it is encouraged by the efficiency norm, but is dependent more on technology than market forces other than the efficiency norm itself. (2) As specialization, the division of labor has almost opposite effects. For a growing number of workers, specialization increases their self-esteem, incentives to learn, and sense of competence and power, but for those without specialties in a world of specialists, it is a human disaster.

A (consumer) market economy, driven by the efficiency norm, is hostile to all expenditures that do not increase profits. As a consequence firms will not undertake programs to improve the quality of work life unless these programs also increase economic efficiency, making provisions for workplace learning a hostage to the profit maximand. Proposals to enlist the government in forcing firms to do other-wise run against the basic problem of increased costs in an internationally compet-itive economy; proposals to pay for the changes by reducing wages run into the resistance of workers whose values are formed in a consumer economy.

The producer economy is not all roses. It risks the prosperity that makes it pos-

Hills, CA: Sage, 1976), 96–101; J. Vanick, *The General Theory of Labor-Managed Economies* (Ithaca, NY: Cornell University Press, 1970).These experts in worker self-management advise a separation of ownership from control in worker-owned firms similar to the pattern that now exists in the standard capitalist firm.

sible to change priorities to favor worker well-being rather than consumer interests; its legitimacy is threatened because there is no forum where it can be chosen; pay loses its double function of reward and allocation of labor where pay is depreciated; and although any economy needs job security for workplace learning to prosper, that security reduces the adaptive capacities of firms.

And to our great regret, the many advantages of worker-owned and/or worker-managed firms in a market economy do *not* include avoidance of the penalties and disadvantages of investments in workplace learning that do not also serve the dominant interests of consumers.

Codicil on work in a market economy

Whereas the first four parts of this book dealt with new ways of thinking about the hedonic and developmental payoffs of a market economy, in Part V we have come across a fundamental defect apparently inherent in market processes themselves. Unhappily, we cannot say that the more realistic accounts of cognitive and emotional processes in market behavior discussed in the first four parts help with this particular problem, although I believe they help with other aspects of market analysis and give an account of the market experience that is superior to any known previous accounts.

What we have found in this discussion of work is that working activities are the best agents of well-being (see Part VII) and the best sources of cognitive development, a sense of personal control, and self-esteem available in economic life, better than a higher standard of living, and, I believe, better than what is offered by leisure. Well-designed work does not, of course, serve as a panacea, but not only does it favor human development in the terms given, it helps people to learn about certain aspects of nature, to engage with other people more satisfactorily, and to cope with their environments with greater success. We have examined the theory that markets degrade work and found that whereas in the past this has been true, it seems for the moment not to be true at least with respect to the dominant "deskilling" argument. Nor is the theory valid with respect to machines and other technology and only ambiguously, if at all, on the grounds of economic "exploitation." The market offers little in work that can satisfy the need for transcendent values, but this is as much a protection against distracting (and exploitative) appeals as it is a defect in the way the market works.

In asking how the benefits of workplace learning are distributed, we found that where a firm had market power, any net costs associated with these benefits might be assigned to consumers or to other workers (as unemployment), or where market power is missing, to the benefited workers themselves (perhaps also as unemployment for some). In the larger question of the market's role in stratification, where the "best jobs" went to the top strata, we located much, but not all, of the responsibility for stratified benefits in familial and technological processes. Assignment of benefits within firms, the internal market, was also partly determined by technology, but the main point in that discussion was the severe constraints imposed on these internal markets by the competitive pressure for lowered costs, with the results that only the firms with market power were able to, and did, share the fruits of their market power with their employees. In this they violated market theory.

In passing we relieved the market of responsibility for encouraging the trait of competitiveness among its participants and, except for the detail worker, of making specialists who lacked the human qualities one associates with a whole personality.

We concluded that giving worker well-being the same status as consumer welfare is not feasible in a competitive market economy unless workers choose to sacrifice their income for that purpose. This outcome is difficult to achieve in an economy where money is the measure of dignity and success. Although the producer economy that would result from the suggested change in priority offered a variety of benefits, it also incurred many problems of its own that makes it less of a utopian solution for the times than a single-minded view of workplace learning would suggest. The benefits of worker-owned and managed firms, even in market socialism, do not include complete freedom to give workplace learning and worker well-being priority over the sources of the profit that serves as its guarantor of the future, that is, the difference between income from consumers and the costs of production, including, of course, labor costs. If we move in the direction of a producer economy, as I think we should, we will at least do so with our eyes open.

PART VI

Rewards

People do not work for "nothing," but what they do work for is often not just the pay they receive. Rather, they may work for the pleasure they find in their working activities, a pleasure that Juster has found to be generally greater than people's pleasures in their leisure activities.[1] They may work because meeting the challenges at work increases their sense of personal control, or out of a sense of duty, or because of a pressing need to achieve some high standard of excellence. Wherever their motives may be, people evade the market's focus on exchange, for these motives are satisfied by internal rewards that do not depend upon exchanging money for work. When people work for these self-rewards and not for any apparent external rewards, they are said to be working because of *intrinsic* motivation and thus working for intrinsic rewards.

Part VI is devoted to an exposition of the nature of such motivation, the kinds of internal self-rewards enlisted, and the consequences for the market of work not motivated by market rewards. These consequences are substantial. In the first place, they destroy the formula on which economists rely: The utility of pay is compensation for the disutility of work. Where work is a positive utility, this formula clearly will not do. Then, substantively, these intrinsic rewards make it impossible for levels of pay to serve as the allocators of human resources, thus upsetting the calculations that are the guarantors of efficiency in the market. And, as we have seen earlier, giving priority to utilities derived from work instead of utilities derived from commodities and leisure, upsets the rationale of the market as the best device for satisfying human wants and thus for maximizing human happiness.

Chapter 17 is devoted to an exploration of the validity of the hypothesis that people work, by and large, to maximize their pay. Not surprisingly, we find this a totally inadequate account. Chapter 18 begins an analysis of intrinsic rewards with a report on research on *The Hidden Costs of Rewards,* a counterintuitive body of research and theory showing that where people enjoy what they are doing, pay actually *decreases* their enjoyment. This fascinating research, however, has a limited, though important, application to market work; Chapter 19, therefore, points out these many limits after first showing how devastating this theory would be if it were more extensively applicable. Then, in Chapter 20, I seek to balance the books on the value of intrinsic motivation, honored by humanists and philosophers but despised or more likely ignored by economists. We will find that the health, happiness, and learning benefits accruing to those who enjoy their work for its intrinsic rewards rather than for the pay received are very great indeed. But reliance on intrinsic benefits to workers cannot guide an economy and may not extend to others any benefits at all. Finally, with the benefit of this analysis of intrinsic rewards

[1] F. Thomas Juster, "Preferences for Work and Leisure," in Juster and Frank P. Stafford, eds., *Time, Goods, and Well-Being* (Ann Arbor, MI: Institute for Social Research, 1985), 348–9.

337

behind us, we return in Chapter 21 to the subject of Chapter 16: What happens to the market under these altered circumstances? The answer lies in a series of changes in price, mostly benefiting those motivated by extrinsic rewards, and in a set of changed formulae incorporating the pleasures of work and the pains of pay, and due to the intrinsic ethical motives, the pleasures and pains of altruism. In the end, we find that intrinsic and extrinsic motivations and their respective rewards each contribute something to a market or indeed any other kind of economy.

17 Maximizing pay: costs and consequences

It is surely not to be assumed without investigation or inquiry that production is a means only. . . . We are impelled to . . . to give thoughtful consideration to the possibilities of participation in economic activity as a sphere of self-expression and creative achievement.

Frank Knight, The Ethics of Competition

In the labor force of the mid-1980s almost everyone, except the roughly one-ninth who were either self-employed or in the agricultural sector, was an industrial or commercial employee working or seeking to work for pay. Here we examine the hypothesis that working people seek to maximize their pay. It is well known that, having other values and other considerations in mind, people who work rarely do adopt such a maximizing strategy, but it will be useful to explore the implications and limits of *the pay maximization hypothesis,* a hypothesis common among critics and defenders of the market alike. The hypothesis is not merely an economist's device employed for analytical purposes, for it is also a managerial belief actively guiding the government of firms.[1] As part of the partially unconscious market ideology,[2] the pay maximization hypothesis also affects a variety of behaviors and attitudes of which market participations are often unaware.

The main reason why the pay maximization hypothesis fails is that it does not take into account the relation between an external *incentive* such as pay and internal rewards based on the desire for personal control and self-esteem, desires whose objects are not always served by increased pay. The desire for pay is a proxy for these other motives. Of course, people generally want more pay, but that is true only if they make the connection between pay and these internal rewards. Thus pay is not always an appropriate reinforcement for economic behavior. When it is, the quality of work often suffers, for then a person does only what increases pay and not those things that advance the task on which a person is working. Both the quality of work and workplace learning suffer.

As we proceed with this inquiry, we will first explore the nature of the pay maximization hypothesis and its relation to more general theories of motivation. Then we consider the relation between pay and the two motives for personal control and self-esteem, the role of the desire for more security as an alternative to the desire for higher pay, the hidden premises in the pay maximization hypothesis, and, finally, the relation between effort contingent on specified pay increments and effort contingent on earning a living.

[1] Edward E. Lawler, III, "Using Pay to Motivate Job Performance," in Richard M. Steers and Lyman E. Porter, eds., *Motivation and Work Behavior* (New York: McGraw-Hill, 1975), 535–6.
[2] See Herbert McClosky and John Zaller, *The American Ethos: Public Attitudes Toward Capitalism and Democracy* (Cambridge: Harvard University Press, 1985).

The pay maximization hypothesis

Macarov states the hypothesis clearly: "From the theory of the free market [we learn] that men *should* try to maximize their economic positions; from the vision of the economic man – that men *will* try to maximize their economic positions . . . and from selective observation that men do try to maximize their income."[3] In a more relaxed form, the hypothesis states that people are always motivated to seek more pay and more income. Why should this be so?

"Monks traded for religious reasons, . . . Kula trade is mainly an aesthetic pursuit, . . . a Feudal economy was run on customary lines, . . . the Kwakiutl [economy] on honor," and more recently, the mercantile economy was motivated among elites by the desire for power and glory. In capitalist society, says Polanyi, the motives are "hunger and gain," both, I may add, summarized in the pay maximization hypothesis. Closer examination shows the usual mixed motives, including duty to others and work enjoyment. "However," says Polanyi, "we are not concerned with actual, but with assumed motives, not with psychology but with the ideology of business. Not on the former, but on the latter, are views of man's nature based." As the market reinforces this view, "man is divided into economic and non-economic; . . . material [motivation] is rational; to act otherwise [than on these material motives] is not only immoral, but also mad."[4]

The pay maximization hypothesis does not claim that pay is the only motive in the work situation, but rather that all other "desires, aspirations and other affections of human nature" relevant to work can be measured by desire for pay.[5] After stating their purpose as an "attempt to find an exact description of the endeavor of the individual to obtain a maximum of utility, or, in the case of the entrepreneur, a maximum of profit," von Neuman and Morgenstern say: "We shall therefore assume that the aim of *all* participants in the economic system . . . is money, or equivalently a single monetary commodity."[6] To the humanistic critics of this materialism, Hall says: "Extrinsic motivations, such as money, are no less moral or of a 'lower order' than more intrinsic motivations such as making maximum use of one's talents."[7]

Pay and the formula for motivation

The motivational formula

A person is motivated to perform a certain act when (1) the person has an enduring disposition favoring some goal or value, (2) the person perceives something he or she might do to approach or achieve that goal or value, (3) something is of sufficient

[3] David Macarov, *Incentives to Work* (San Francisco: Jossey-Bass, 1970), 139.

[4] Karl Polyani, "Our Obsolete Market Mentality," in his *Primitive, Archaic, and Modern Economies*, ed. G. Dalton (Boston: Beacon, 1971), 68, 69.

[5] Alfred Marshall, *Principles of Economics*, 8th ed. (London: Macmillan, 1938), 14.

[6] John von Neuman and Oskar Morgenstern, *Theory of Games and Economic Behavior*, 3d ed. (Princeton: Princeton University Press, 1953), 1, 8, emphasis added.

[7] Richard H. Hall, *Dimensions of Work* (Beverly Hills, CA: Sage, 1986), 91. Alfred Marshall makes the same point: "The desire to make money does not necessarily proceed from motives of a low order . . . [for money is] a means to all kinds of ends." *Principles of Economics*, 22.

worth to the person to serve as an incentive overriding other current incentives, (4) the *means* to achieve the goal are cogenial (not immoral nor too unpleasant or costly), (5) the person believes the means are within his or her competence and will achieve their purpose, and, finally, (6) any accompanying fear of effort or achievement is not a sufficient deterrent.[8] We will call this test against which the pay maximization hypothesis must be measured the *motivational formula test*.

Internal rewards: a motivational hierarchy

There is also a hierarchy of motives such that in cases of conflict, dominant motives defeat subordinate ones, and subordinate motives, often in disguise, serve the dominant ones. As we have observed, Adam Smith commented that behind the apparent drive to "augment one's fortune" or to "better one's condition" was something else: "It is the vanity, not the ease or pleasure, which interests us."[9] In line with much psychological theory, we will claim that three interrelated motives are dominant: (1) the desire for a feeling of psychological competence, that is, the belief that when one acts the environment responds, (2) the desire for self-esteem, Rawls' chief primary good, and (3) the desire for a sense of self-consistency, that is, a sense of continuity with past experience, and an integrated identity. These are *self-rewards*, internal to the person. To be a powerful motive, a particular desire must, among other things, serve one or more of these dominant motives. The protean character of money makes pay a strong candidate for such service. We will call acknowledgment of these internal rewards *the motivational hierarchy test*.

The pay maximization motive is seriously qualified

The pay maximization hypothesis meets the motivational formula test in most respects, but not uniformly. Without recapitulating the arguments and evidence against economic man, consider the following two modifications of the original "enduring disposition:" The enduring disposition may be concerned with *security* of income, not its size (to be discussed). Another modification has to do with variability of the disposition; in the case of pay (or income), these dispositions are, in fact, variable. There are three grounds for questioning the constancy of this disposition:

1. The market assumes correctly that people have a disposition for money, but is assumes incorrectly that there is no declining marginal utility for money. We know that there is from studies of the quality of life, recent studies of "post-material attitudes," and observations by economists, including both Schumpeter and Galbraith.[10] Schumpeter called the concept of declining marginal utility more of a logic

---

[8] John W. Atkinson, "Motivation for Achievement," in Thomas Blass, ed., *Personality Variables in Social Behavior* (New York: Halsted/Wiley, 1977); David G. Winter, *The Power Motive* (New York: Free Press, 1973). On the relationships between attitudes and behavior, see Icek Ajzen and Martin Fishbein, *Understanding Attitudes and Predicting Social Behavior* (Englewood Cliffs, NJ: Prentice-Hall, 1980).

[9] Adam Smith, *The Theory of Moral Sentiments*, ed. D. D. Raphael and A. L. Macfie (Indianapolis: Liberty Press, 1974), 50. Original text published 1759.

[10] Over the 1950s and 1960s the relationship between income and self-reported feelings of well-being declined for the more affluent third of a national sample. See Angus Campbell, Philip E. Converse, and Willard L. Rodgers, *The Quality of American Life* (New York: Russell Sage, 1976), 28. The evidence that people who have had security and reasonable affluence in their childhood are less materialistic is

than a psychological proposition;[11] so long as one does not believe that *everything* has a shadow price (a clear conscience? friendship? maternal care?), there is no reason to exempt money from the force of the "logic." Like most, but not all, enduring dispositions, the urgency of the desire for pay wanes with the success a person (or nation) has in increasing pay (Chapter 26). The enduring disposition is often a waning disposition.

2. The opposite hypothesis proposing an *increasing* marginal utility of pay is also true. As we have seen (Chapter 13), those who enter occupations to make money find this original desire reinforced by their experiences in their first jobs (and those who enter the labor force with different motivations are likewise reinforced in their lower priority for pay).[12]

3. The more one knows about a job, the weaker is the enduring disposition for pay. For example, one study of desirable job characteristics finds that "the combined effect of nonmonetary job characteristics on job ratings is more than twice that of earnings. Equating a job's overall desirability with its pay is therefore likely to be quite misleading." People are misled because they have observed the attention given to pay for jobs in the abstract, or for jobs that the respondents do not hold; in those cases the rated importance of pay is much higher than it is for the jobs people actually hold: "Workers are likely to rate jobs they have not held on the basis of characteristics that are easy to ascertain in advance, like pay and occupational title. As a result, they probably put more weight on pay when making prospective judgments than when making retrospective ones."[13] This changing perspective as one learns more about a job offers grounds for unstable dispositions along the lines of the *approach/avoidance* formula, which says that as people approach a goal their fears may become greater than their original desires, thus leading to vacillation (Chapter 23), only very likely in reverse. At a distance a goal, say a job with lower pay, seems more to be avoided than approached, but the closer one gets, the more attractive it seems. At some point the approach gradient crosses the avoidance gradient and reluctance gives way to eagerness.[14]

provided in Ronald Inglehart, *The Silent Revolution* (Princeton: Princeton University Press, 1972) and subsequent articles. Schumpeter acknowledged that there must be a declining marginal utility for money, but argued that no one knew the slope (hence progressive income taxes are not necessarily justified); see Joseph A. Schumpeter, *History of Economic Analysis,* ed. Elizabeth Boody Schumpeter (New York: Oxford University Press, 1954), 1,072. John K. Galbraith was less cautious; he said: "The paradox of pecuniary motivation is that, in general, the higher the amount the less its importance in relation to other motivations." *The Affluent Society,* 2d ed., rev. (Harmondsworth, UK: Pelican, 1970), 144.

[11] Schumpeter, *History of Economic Analysis,* 1,058. Harrod avoids the problem of such "noneconomic goods" by limiting the field of economics to what "is concerned only with the goods and services of which the constituent items can be made alternatively available to one or other of different persons. Thus goods like friendship or mystical experiences are excluded." Roy Harrod, *Sociology, Morals, and Mystery* (London: Macmillan, 1971), 64.

[12] Jeylan T. Mortimer and Jon Lorence, "Work Experience and Occupational Value Socialization: A Longitudinal Study," *American Journal of Sociology* 84 (1979): 1,361–85.

[13] Christopher Jencks, Lauri Perman, and Lee Rainwater, "What is a Good Job? A New Measure of Labor-Market Success," *American Journal of Sociology* 93 (1988): 1,322–57 at 1,328, 1,343.

[14] See John Dollard and Neal E. Miller, *Personality and Psychotherapy* (New York: McGraw-Hill, 1950), 355–63.

The second and fifth elements in the motivational formula refer to the belief that there is something a person can do to reach a goal, that is, to increase pay, and the belief that the acts will be effective. Where these beliefs are missing, as is often the case, the mental set of the desiring person is not called a *motive*, which implies at least an urge to action; rather, it is a simple desire, an *inoperative* disposition. People who question the efficacy of unions or the fruitfulness of a job search are deprived of motivation to join unions or look for jobs. Inactive dispositions have statuses and consequences very different from active ones. They exert no economic pressure; reason enough for economists, interested in the operant system, to limit their attention to motives and not to include mere desires. These unmotivated workers are like impecunious consumers who do not affect demand.

To anticipate the following discussion, behind any discounting of available means may be people's beliefs that their environments are not responsive to their own acts. These people lack internality (Chapter 9) – a necessary ingredient in motivation but unspecified in the formula.

The third element in the motivational formula refers to the power of a particular goal to enlist the enduring disposition. *Any* pay increase meets this criterion; but the cost (item 4 in the motivational formula) is the likely deterrent. If the disposition is weak, small costs will deter. Thus the pay maximization hypothesis implies a cost–benefit analysis as a necessary ingredient. If the outcome is uncertain, risk acceptance and risk aversion enter the formula. The pay maximization motive is subject, like almost all economic acts, to qualifications dealing with the actor's attitudes toward risk. Risk bearing is certainly not the monopoly of the entrepreneur and is not limited to the category "profit."

The final element of the formula (fear of or ambivalence about the goal) is the last of the provisos: The worker may not attach conventional meanings to money or work, often because of some experiences lost to consciousness.[15] The grounds for questioning the acceptance of conventional meanings are provided in the discussion of money symbolism in Chapter 6: People bring to their earnings a surprising variety of idiosyncratic memories and associations. To some, pay is associated with "shameful failure" or "inadequacy," whereas to others pay is a fair measure of effort and ability and adequacy.[16] These perspectives must modify wage bargaining in ways that confound economic rationality. Those who have more money are believed to be more healthy and wholesome personalities than those who have the

---

[15]The fourth condition (acceptability of means) was added to the basic formula because scholars found that without including it, attitudes were very likely to live a life quite separate from their related behavior (as attitudes toward work often do), and the last of these conditions (avoidance) was added to help account for the behavior of those who want to achieve but who also fear achievement. For example, women seeking business or academic success might fear to win contests against men lest they be thought "unfeminine." See David W. Tresemer, *Fear of Success* (New York: Plenum Press, 1977). To further complicate the analysis, one must consider the psychoanalysts' view that for various reasons some people do not fear failure but rather *seek* it. See Edmund Bergler, *Money and Emotional Conflict* (Garden City, NY: Doubleday, 1951), 24.

[16]See Adrian Furnham, "Many Sides of the Coin: The Psychology of Money Usage," *Personality and Individual Differences* 5 (1984): 501–9; Paul F. Wernimont and Susan Fitzpatrick, "The Meaning of Money," *Journal of Applied Psychology* 50 (1972): 218–26.

least,[17] greatly enhancing the value of pay beyond what it will buy in the market and again making the wage bargain unequal quite out of proportion to the respective economic strengths of the bargaining parties. The symbolism may itself be "income." "Whatever symbolism money has for the individual, and whatever presumptions and illusions he has about how added money would affect the way he lives, are as much a part of the increment for him as is the money itself."[18]

Comment. The simple pay maximization hypothesis is really quite complex: (1) Because the act of receiving pay affects the desire for pay in a reflexive manner (declining or increasing marginal utilities), the motive is inherently unstable. (2) Because the means may seem inappropriate or ineffective, what might have been a motive remains only a desire. (3) Because acting on the basis of the motive implies costs, a cost–benefit analysis is implied; (4) because of risks, risk aversion or acceptance must be included. (5) Because pay and money are loaded with connotative values, the amount of money may be irrelevant.

The formula can be stated in B. F. Skinner's learning theory terms: Money is a general reinforcer; once people learn that they can get what they want by working, they acquire the habit of working for pay.[19] The "pay-for-work" reinforcement theory is also a market theory, expressed by Marshall in terms similar to Skinner's.[20] But reinforcement theory is both retrospective and mindless and therefore incompatible with market theories depending on rational expectations. For example, "A reinforcer could conceivably strengthen a response beyond the point of maximization of utility or could fail to strengthen a response sufficient to maximize utility."[21] Although it may be shown that the logic of the utility maximization hypothesis and the reinforcement mechanism often arrive at similar interpretations, the processes and the practices are likely to be sufficiently different as to produce quite different outcomes. Victor Vroom, borrowing from general motivation theory, offers a cognitively sophisticated interpretation of work motivation in which pay is only one of several goals; he says that the *valence* (strength of the goal's attraction) times *expectancy* (expectation that the individual can achieve his or her goal) equals the power of motivation to prompt action.[22] In practice, with proper specifications Vroom's theory has predicted choice of occupation, duration of work, and work effort.[23] With plural valences the theory is an optimization, not a max-

[17] Joseph Luft, "Monetary Value and the Perception of Persons," *The Journal of Social Psychology* 46 (1957): 245–51.
[18] Wernimont and Fitzpatrick, "The Meaning of Money," 144.
[19] B. F. Skinner, *Science and Human Behavior* (New York: Macmillan, 1953), 78. In his *Social Learning Theory,* Bandura also points to money as a general reinforcer and a means of deferring gratification: "Money, which can be exchanged for countless things that people desire, is also widely used on a deferred basis as a powerful generalized incentive." (Englewood Cliffs, NJ: Prentice-Hall, 1977), 103.
[20] Marshall, *Principles of Economics,* 331.
[21] Howard Rachlin, "Economics and Behavioral Psychology," in J. E. R. Staddon, ed., *Limits to Action: The Allocation of Individual Behavior* (New York: Academic Press, 1986), 222. Rachlin "indicate[s] that (with respect to steady state behavior) a maximization mechanism and a reinforcement mechanism are indistinguishable" in their outcomes, but this depends upon identifying utility maximization and pay maximization, a position rejected here.
[22] Victor H. Vroom, *Work and Motivation* (New York: Wiley, 1964).
[23] See Steven E. G. Lea, Roger M. Tarpy, and Paul Webley, *The Individual in the Economy* (Cambridge, UK: Cambridge University Press, 1987), 151.

imization, theory, and only as the values of the workers dictate is it an income
theory at all. Nevertheless it is dependent on extrinsic rewards and lacks a concept
of self-rewards necessary for a link between these extrinsic rewards and personal
control, self-esteem, and self-concept.

The links between pay and self-rewards

The motivational hierarchy test
People's favorable attitudes toward themselves are their most treasured property; in
many ways, these are the maximand on which all their other values and motives
rest. Plural motives draw their force from these favorable attitudes. The expected
utility formulation of work motives (see following), which is the currently dominant
doctrine, is a proxy for these more powerful internal rewards. In the end, all economic behavior is energized and guided by the pursuit of a sense of personal effectiveness, self-esteem, and self-consistency.

Social learning theory is an appropriate theory for interpreting these kinds of
internal rewards. It holds that the evident effectiveness of external reinforcement is
due to the information the reinforcement provides to the rewarding or punishing
self. Without such an internal screening process people would be helpless pawns of
circumstances – a view directly challenging Skinner's formulation. Social learning
theory goes beyond Vroom's theory of rational expectations to propose that external
rewards can motivate a person *only* if those rewards prompt confirming internal
rewards. "In social learning theory," says Bandura, "interest grows from satisfactions derived from fulfilling internal standards and from perceiving self-efficacy
gained from performance accomplishments and other sources of efficacy information."[24] These self-rewards include feelings of competence, satisfaction with striving, achievement of internal standards of excellence[25] or morality, the belief that
others approve of the self, and similar gratifying beliefs. Unlike those things learned
by rote or by pure contingent reinforcement, for example, a habit of working for
pay, "practices derived from social learning theory are well suited for cultivating
competencies that serve as a genuine basis for exercise and perception of self-
determination."[26] Self-rewards deal with the invisible world of the self; my thesis
is that unless a connection is made between an external motive, such as the desire
for pay, and internal rewards dealing with personal control, self-esteem, and self-
consistency, the rewarded practice will be only superficially learned and the reward
itself will be only transiently motivating.

External rewards have the "advantage" of being perceptual and can therefore
appeal to those at the Piagetian stage of "concrete operations," a stage when abstractions and logical transformations are not yet within reach – as they will be for

---

[24] Albert Bandura, "Self-Efficacy Mechanism in Human Agency," *American Psychologist* 37 (1982):
122–47 at 133.
[25] David C. McClelland and David G. Winter, *Motivating Economic Achievement* (New York: Free
Press, 1971).
[26] Bandura, *Social Learning Theory*, see p. 21 for comments on reinforcement, and p. 113 for comments
on self-determination.

those who have arrived at the higher stage of "formal operations."[27] To some unknown extent, therefore, reliance on external rewards may inhibit cognitive growth, substituting the seen for the merely possible or imagined. Internal rewards have another advantage over external rewards: They limit the use of external rewards by authorities to manipulate their publics; the stronger the power of internal rewards, the less people behave like puppets. Internal rewards are the companions of the internal locus of control, the belief that one can influence one's environment. And they are the rewards of self-direction. To the extent that the market can be identified with either classical or operant reinforcement theory, it loses sight of the better part of human motivation.

Personal control: having versus earning. Pay is easily linked to feelings of personal control, as we saw in the discussion of internality in Chapter 9, for money is a major source of power over things and a frequent source of influence over others. As mentioned, level of income is the best single demographic predictor of a sense of internal control.[28] Inquiry into the gratifications yielded by the possessions that money buys (or that are otherwise acquired) finds that "the central feature of possessions – its principal defining characteristic, as well as the major motivational force behind it – is causal efficacy or control over aspects of one's environment."[29]

These comments deal with the consequences of having money. I would like to propose that there is a difference between *having* money and *earning* money, that is, a distinction between income and wealth, on the one hand, and pay-for-work, on the other.

In the quality-of-life studies, the hedonic value of family income is lower than the hedonic value of pay, although there is considerable overlap. The authors of one such study believe this difference is attributable to the fact that income is evaluated in the context of budgets and costs, and pay in the context of what the work is worth.[30] An alternative or supplementary hypothesis is that pay is valued because of its closer connection to personal control; pay is almost always thought to be earned money. In any event, since the contribution of *actual income* to life satisfaction is low, whereas the contribution of *satisfaction with income* is high,[31] the hedonic yield of income does not come from what it buys but from what it represents,

[27] Jean Piaget and Barbara Inhelder, *The Psychology of the Child*, trans. H. Weaver (1966; reprint New York: Basic Books, 1969).

[28] Gerald Gurin and Patricia Gurin, "Personal Efficacy and the Ideology of Individual Responsibility," in Burkhard Strumpel, ed., *Economic Means for Human Needs* (Ann Arbor, MI: Institute for Social Research, 1976.

[29] Lita Furby, "Possessions: Toward a Theory of Their Meaning and Function Throughout the Life Cycle," in P. B. Baltes, ed., *Life-Span Development and Behavior* (New York: Academic Press, 1978), 322.

[30] Frank M. Andrews and Stephen B. Withey, *Social Indicators of Well-Being: Americans' Perceptions of Life Quality* (New York: Plenum Press, 1976), 303. Most people in the United States and especially in Britain (but not in Germany) believe that they are fairly paid. see Daniel Yankelovich et al., *The World at Work: An International Report on Human Values, Productivity and its Future* (New York: Octagon, 1984).

[31] Andrews and Withey, *Social Indicators of Well-Being*, 302.

its symbolic value, including the manifest evidence of economic competence that earned income provides.

Aristotle comments: "Everyone feels a stronger affection for those things which have cost him some effort to acquire; e.g., those who have made their money love it more than those who have inherited it."[32] It is the outsider, not the owner, who believes that "old money" or inherited money is better than earned money; the self-made man has no contempt for his nouveaux richesse, whatever his wife may think. Wives' own earnings, however, are especially prized by the women who earn them; they are peculiarly "her own."[33] Because it is more precious, earned money is more likely to be saved, whereas windfall money, with lower value, represents an immediately expendable sum.

What is "earned" may be a subjective matter and by a series of psychological processes outlined in "just world" theory,[34] people are likely to think that whatever they have acquired is earned. In this, market theory confirms their belief, for the definition of fairness in the market is a procedural one: If the transactions were fairly conducted, the outcome is ipso facto fair – and fairly earned.[35] A further justification is supplied by the market theory that earnings are an appropriate yield for the earner's human capital. Thus the earner, compared to the mere owner, is doubly rewarded – rewarded for both earning and owning. The increment in a sense of personal control when a person earns his or her rewards in the market is thereby ethically justified.

Self-esteem If pay does not serve to enhance a person's self-esteem, it will prove to be a transitory and inefficient motivator. As mentioned, Rawls gives to self-esteem great importance as the most valuable of the goods he designates as "primary;" he hopes that it will not flow from differential income but rather will come from equal civic rights.[36] That hope is vain,[37] for self-esteem in the market society flows more from achievement than from such ascriptive qualities as citizen or person (Chapter 10). It follows that it is *earned* income, and not just wealth, that more certainly yields self-esteem – a point congruent with Tawney's emphasis on earned versus property income.[38] Marshall's comment to the effect that self-respect is a condition for "true happiness"[39] has now received empirical validation: As mentioned in Chapter 10, in some quality-of-life studies self-respect has the strong-

[32] Aristotle, *The Nichomachean Ethics*, trans. J. A. K. Thompson (Harmondsworth, UK: Penguin, 1976), 30; In *The Conduct of Life*, Emerson makes the same point: "The farmer is covetous of his dollar, and with reason. . . . He knows how many strokes of labor it represents." *Bartlett's Familiar Quotations*.

[33] Carin Rubenstein, "Money and Self-Esteem, Relationships, Secrecy, Envy, Satisfaction," *Psychology Today* 15 (1981): 29–44; Viviana A. Zelizer, "The Social Meaning of Money: 'Special Monies,' " *American Journal of Sociology* 95 (1989): 342–77.

[34] Melvin J. Lerner, *The Belief in a Just World: A Fundamental Delusion* (New York: Plenum Press, 1980).

[35] John Rawls, *A Theory of Justice* (London: Oxford University Press, 1972), 86.

[36] Ibid., 440.

[37] Robert E. Lane, "Government and Self-Esteem," *Political Theory* 10 (1982): 5–31.

[38] Richard H. Tawney, *The Acquisitive Society* (New York: Harcourt Brace, 1920).

[39] Marshall, *Principles of Economics*, n. 1, p. 17.

est correlation with overall life satisfaction of any of the attitudes or circumstances measured.[40]

The pay maximization hypothesis has the support of one of our dominant values – the sense of control – and in the process acquires the second – self-esteem. Other sources of self-esteem might be the sense of being admired because one is rich (reflected appraisal) or from one's perception of the self as at least richer than others (social comparison).[41] These rewards are not given in the pay-for-work situation, however, for they depend on the variable grounds on which people choose to judge themselves; they are given by the internal processes that reward and punish the self.

Self-concept. For reasons of parsimony, I have hitherto treated self-esteem as an ultimate desideratum, but this must be modified to make room for the idea that people sometimes sacrifice self-esteem in order to preserve the continuity of their selves. Thus, to avoid a sense of personal disintegration, they will give priority to acts and beliefs that are consonant with their identities even when these reflect poorly on the self.[42] This is relevant here as an explanation of the relation between the *value* of pay and *attitudes* toward other features of the situation.

For psychologists, a value is a cognitive representation of a motive; the "enduring disposition" in the motivation formula may thus be restated in cognitive terms as a value. Attitudes, on the other hand, are more topical and situationally specific. Since values of this kind are both more "fundamental" and more abstract than attitudes, logically, values should dominate attitudes, but in fact the constraint is weak. In competition with the attitudes they should inform, values survive only if they are better reflections of the *self-concept* than are those theoretically "subordinate" attitudes. People's self-concepts, not their values, are sovereign.[43] Thus, in our case, a person's high evaluation of money (avarice) would not necessarily predict behavior if some attitude toward, say, the person offering the money, were more closely related to the self-concept. A disposition favoring more money, represented by the (cognitive) value of money, will be dominant only if in any given situation, this disposition or value is closer to the self-concept than any competing attitudes. The maximization of pay hypothesis has the self-concept to contend with, for many will not enjoy conceptions of themselves as avaricious. People protect their self-concepts by referring to consequences, not motives. A person is not "avaricious" – he or she is a "business success," a "good breadwinner," or, more simply, rich.

We know from the literature on volunteering, and less certainly from the evidence on working when it is not economically "necessary,"[44] that people work

[40] Angus Campbell, *The Sense of Well-Being in America* (New York: McGraw-Hill, 1981).

[41] Morris Rosenberg, *Society and the Adolescent Self-Image* (Princeton: Princeton University Press, 1965).

[42] Eric Erikson, "The Problem of Ego Identity," *Journal of the American Psychoanalytic Association* 4 (1956): 58–121.

[43] Milton Rokeach, *The Nature of Human Values* (New York: Free Press, 1973).

[44] See O. Hawrylshyn, "The Economic Nature and Value of Volunteer Activity in Canada," *Social Indicators Research* 5 (1978): 1–72; Kenneth Boulding, *The Economy of Love and Fear: A Preface to Grants Economies* (Belmont, CA: Wadsworth, 1973), 30. On working when not necessary, see H. Roy Kaplan, "Lottery Winners and Work Commitment: A Behavioral Test of the American Work Ethic,"

without pay, thus skipping the mediating instrument of pay in achieving internal rewards. We also know that people work harder if they believe they have been "overpaid," again because of internal rewards and punishments.[45] Pay helps, especially during the period when skills are being learned,[46] but it not a necessary condition for feeling rewarded by work. Is it a sufficient condition? We turn to that next.

Experience with contingent rewards

In Chapter 9 we saw that the market's reliance on contingent reinforcement, as contrasted to benefits due to ascriptive characteristics, contributed to a sense of personal control. Here, as foreseen, we must modify that view to show that the kind of contingent reinforcement that narrowly specifies the character of the act producing the reward, as in experiments with animals, does not generalize in humans to a sense of personal control. Instead, the learning is purely stimulus specific. At the end of this chapter we shall compare the learning involved in unconditional pay and unconditional income. Here we examine some of the implications of contingent rewards of the specific kind and inquire into the nature of the pay-for-work contingency where internal rewards seem to be minimal. Why is it that pay narrowly contingent on particular work responses actually undermines interest in work and craftsmanship?

The market assumes, along with economists (and the Soviet Constitution of 1936 that states: "He who does not work shall not eat."), that if people were not paid they would not work. We know this to be partially false from the evidence of volunteering,[47] and to be partially true from the evidence of the effects of the "iron rice bowl" in China and of the guaranteed income experiments in the United States, some of whose subjects failed to enter the labor market[48] (Chapter 9). We can learn something from reinforcement theory and research, the lessons from "payment by results," and the experiments with token economies in various institutions.

External reinforcement

The kind of operant conditioning identified with B. F. Skinner has offered an active version of the earlier Pavlovian concept of conditioning; it seems to yield research evidence for the effectiveness of pay in producing, among other things, desirable work behavior. In this version, the organism must first act (press a lever, discriminate among shapes) to receive the reward. Associating the reward with the act, the rewardee repeats the act and it becomes a habit, reinforced by the reward. The

The Journal of the Institute for Socioeconomic Studies (Summer, 1985), reported in *Woodrow Wilson Quarterly* 10 (1986): 24–5.

[45] Edward E. Lawler, "Equity Theory as a Predictor of Productivity and Work Quality," *Psychological Bulletin* 70 (1968): 596–610.

[46] Albert Bandura and Dale H. Schunk, "Cultivating Competence, Self-Efficacy, and Intrinsic Interest Through Proximal Self-Motivation," *Journal of Personality and Social Psychology* 41 (1981): 586–98.

[47] See note 44.

[48] Philip K. Robins, "Labor Supply Response of Family Heads and Implications for a National Program," in Robins, Robert G. Spiegelman, Samuel Weiner, and Joseph G. Bell, eds., *A Guaranteed Annual Income: Evidence from a Social Experiment* (New York: Academic Press, 1980), 63.

theory holds that "the rate of performance will increase when valued outcomes (reinforcers) are made contingent on performance."[49] Nothing so "ghostly" as "preference" or "enjoyment" is admitted, let alone "internal rewards." Like food pellets to animals, "money is a general reinforcer" to humans – in work as elsewhere.[50] Research supports the theory that improved performance follows improved reinforcement – at least within a narrow time and behavioral range.[51] Moreover, the general learning from contingent relations is a necessary condition of effectiveness, that is, a condition for avoiding "learned helplessness." For example, one study finds that children's "perception of . . . noncontingency, causal understanding, and expectations of future contingencies are all likely to influence the process where children of all ages manifest learned helplessness."[52] Not to understand contingent relations is to misunderstand causality including the causes of the things that one attempts to change. At the minimum, pay contingent on work contributes to a narrow understanding of contingent, causal relations.

Pay contingent on performance. Income contingent on contribution to the economy is the central moral justification of the market's reward system. This justification runs into difficulties with income derived from rent and interest and shareholder's dividends, but for workers a consequential analysis of "payment by results" (PBR) can make the justification plausible.[53] For nonmanagerial employees, PBR is that form of remuneration that most closely corresponds to this moral justification. It is one of the two main forms of remuneration: "The main distinction among contemporary pay systems," say Granovetter and Tilly, "is between payment by time ('daywork') and payment by results ('PBR', or 'piecework')."[54] A study by the International Labor Office gives the rationale of PBR in almost Skinnerian terms:

PBR is based upon a simple, widely held belief about human motivation, namely that if workers value money then the offer of more money conditional upon more effort being expended will call forth that effort. In other words, PBR is a way of harnessing the money motive so as to get work done more speedily or better.[55]

[49] Skinner, *Science and Human Behavior*. For a discussion of reinforcement theory in economics, see Lea et al., *The Individual in the Economy*, 148. The theory has historical roots in the associational psychology of Locke and Condillac.

[50] Skinner, *Science and Human Behavior*.

[51] See Herbert C. Kelman, "Compliance, Identification, and Internalization: Three Processes of Attitude Change," *Journal of Social Issues* 21 (1965): 31–46. But not until social learning theory was modified to include "self-rewards" was there any way of explaining either the work ethic or intrinsic work satisfaction. See Bandura, *Social Learning Theory*.

[52] Frank D. Fincham and Kathleen M. Cain, "Learned Helplessness in Humans: A Developmental Analysis," *Developmental Review* 6 (1986): 301–33.

[53] Managers may be held to account for their performance and in spite of very loose connections between company performance and managerial pay, there is a little evidence that some accountability is maintained. See David R. James and Michael Soref, "Profit Constraints on Managerial Autonomy: Managerial Theory and the Unmaking of the Corporation President," *American Sociological Review* 46 (1981): 1–18; compare Leonard Broom and Robert G. Cushing, "A Modest Test of an Immodest Theory: The Functional Theory of Stratification," *American Sociological Review* 42 (1977): 157–69.

[54] Mark Granovetter and Charles Tilly, "Inequality and Labor Processes," in Neil Smelser and R. Burt, eds., *Handbook of Sociology* (Beverly Hills, CA: Sage, 1987). The quotation is from p. 86 of the manuscript version: Research Paper No. 939, New School for Social Research.

[55] ILO (International Labor Office), *Payment by Results* (Geneva: ILO, 1984), 4.

PBR has been effective: "There are many studies that have shown that after the installation of individual or group PBR schemes output has gone up substantially, at least in the short run."[56] A review of fifty-six studies by F. A. Locke and associates examined the effects on productivity of goal setting, participation in decisions, job enrichment, and monetary incentives in various PBR schemes. These authors found that "clearly money emerges as the most effective motivator, followed by goal setting and job enrichment."[57]

Nevertheless, piecework and payment by results declined in almost all Western countries since its peak in the late 1940s (when PBR accounted for 30% of pay in the United States and 50% in Sweden).[58] This is because changed production methods made it harder to identify the contributions of individual workers, the value added by labor became smaller relative to that of capital in some industries, other concepts of work motivation more congenial to workers came into prominence, and for reasons that follow – it taught the wrong lesson.

Contingent reinforcement: token economies

There is some evidence that token economies behave in many respects like market economies. Comparing token economy behavior in a psychiatric hospital in Australia with market patterns, one study found that the behavior of residents in a token economy was consistent with basic principles of consumer demand theory in three areas: (1) the relationship between income and total expenditure; (2) the relationship between income and purchases of luxuries versus necessities; and (3) the price elasticity of luxuries versus necessities."[59] Another study found that when there was an increase in token wages the labor supply from high income subjects slightly declined and from the low income subjects slightly increased in a manner very like that of increases in market wages.[60]

A token economy was introduced into the Anna State [mental] Hospital in Illinois in the 1960s to bring order and voluntary compliance into a disorderly, confused, primarily custodial situation. "The general philosophy," say the experimenters, "may be summarized as eliminating the negative aspects of behavior by emphasizing the positive."[61] The subjects were hebophrenics, mental retardates, schizophrenics, paranoids, and others with similar disabilities; the average age was fifty and the average previous tenure in the hospital was sixteen years. The experimenters first sought to find out the character of the wants of the patients; these were

[56] Ibid., 28.

[57] F. A. Locke, D. B. Feren, V. M. McCaleb, K. N. Shaw, and A. T. Denny, "The Relative Effectiveness of Four Methods of Motivating Employee Performance," in K. D. Duncan, M. M. Gruenberg, and D. Wallis, eds., Changes in Working Life (Chichester, UK: Wiley, 1980), 374–5.

[58] ILO, Payment by Results, 121–2.

[59] Robin C. Winkler, "Behavioral Economics, Token Economies, and Applied Behavior Analysis," in J. E. R. Staddon, ed., Limits to Action: The Allocation of Individual Behavior (New York: Academic Press, 1980), 271–2.

[60] J. H. Kagel, R. C. Battalio, R. C. Winkler, and E. B Fisher, "Job Choice and Total Labor Supply: An Experimental Analysis," Southern Economic Journal 44 (1977): 13–24, reported in Lea et al., The Individual in the Economy, 164–5.

[61] Teodor Ayllon and Nathan Azrin, The Token Economy; A Motivational System for Therapy and Rehabilitation (New York: Appleton-Century-Crofts, 1968), 23.

things like privacy, certain kinds of clothing, eating particular meals at a particular time, more counseling, opportunities for religious services, and bits of freedom (walks on the grounds, a trip to town). Each of these "goods" was given a price in tokens, for example, 1 for choice in an eating group, 4–30 for a choice of room, 100 for a trip into town, 5 for a private audience with the chaplain, 1–5 for certain consumables at the commissary, and so forth. In this particular experiment the tokens could not be hoarded or exchanged, thus there was no market in tokens, and the transactions were limited to an exchange of tokens for work in a preferred task.

Knowing the job preferences of the patients, the experimenters first reinforced (paid tokens for) work on the preferred job. On the eleventh day it was explained that the subjects could continue in that job if they wanted to, but because of other patient's needs, tokens would only be paid for another job known to be disliked. In a particular experimental group of eight, all patients except one switched to the disliked job for which they were to receive tokens. One compliant patient explained: "No, honey, I can't work at the laundry (her preferred job) for nothing. I'll work at the lab. I just couldn't make it to pay my rent if I didn't get paid." Another who preferred the lab said, "You mean if I work at the lab I won't get paid? I need tokens to buy cigars for my boy friend and to buy new clothes so I'll look nice like the other girls."[62]

The results showed that the tokens produced the desired behavioral changes but only when they were given immediately after a person performed the specific acts desired, not in advance and not for generalized "good behavior." Over the 1960s and 1970s many institutions of many kinds (including prisons and homes for delinquents) adopted similar programs; similar experiments in schools for normal children have also multiplied. By the late 1970s it was clear that "the history of token economies . . . has been one of virtually unmitigated success."[63] Whatever the characteristics of the persons involved, whether the behavior modification was directed at aggression, or deportment, or, of special interest to us, of *work productivity,* and whether rewarded by food, or privileges (including special freedoms), or money, the token economies produced "dramatic increases in desired behavior." But "in a vast majority of studies, removal of the token program led to a rapid return to baseline rates of response." Moreover, "behavior outside the immediate setting remained unaffected by the program."[64]

PBR, tokens, and markets

The two examples of contingent payments, PBR and token economies, have in common the close relationship between performance and rewards. The success of the token economies tempts us to observe that "market rationality" works exceptionally well in a madhouse, but more specific inferences from the two forms of

[62] Ibid., 233

[63] Mark R. Lepper and David Greene, "Divergent Approaches to the Study of Rewards," in Lepper and Greene, eds., *The Hidden Costs of Rewards: New Perspectives on the Psychology of Human Motivation* (Hillsdale, NJ: Erlbaum, 1978), 225.

[64] Ibid. But these authors observe that later experiments, exercising greater care in the instructional program, showed "some evidence of persistent or generalized gains." (p. 26)

payment are more helpful. Experience with both PBR and tokens reveals the very limited, situationally specific kinds of learning produced by contingent rewards. The value of reinforcement is said to be that it offers feedback on one's behavior, contributing to learning and cumulatively developing expertise. It is the innoculant and therapy for helplessness, teaching the individual that when he or she acts the world responds. It develops in the individual that *internality* that psychologist's prize, the belief in one's own competence.[65] But the contingent reinforcement so perfectly modeled by PBR and token economies does none of these things. Why not?

In the first place, the internality, or belief in one's own effectiveness, that was learned is deliberately narrow, limited to a previously specified set of acts; it does not lead to confidence in one's ability to cope, to self-direction, for there was no reinforcement for self-direction. The beneficiaries of PBR and tokens do not learn initiative, self-reliance, thinking for themselves. As it fails to lead to self-direction, it fails by a larger measure to lead to Emerson's "self-reliance: I appeal from your customs. I would be myself. I cannot break myself any longer for you. . . . I will not hide my tastes or aversions."[66]

What the token economy and PBR research uncovered is the degree to which tokens or payments preempt self-determination, making moot many of the opportunities to exercise control. Like a philosopher-king, the paymaster seems to absolve the individual from the duty to exercise his or her independent conscience, inviting, on occasion, "malignant obedience."[67] Second, the process of reinforcement by pay offers no means for thinking about alternatives, let alone weighing them; they include no causal models other than their own – a naked post hoc propter hoc inference on the source of hedonic value. The informational feedback is on how to achieve pay, not on how to get the work done or improve the processes the worker employs. In some cases these methods teach how to "make bonus with a pencil," how to fake it. Reinforced by pay, people do not learn about work itself; it this sense, pay reinforcement is very unlike the reinforcement of solving a problem in a problem-solving exercise; pay rewards are very unlike the intrinsic rewards of work. Payment has an anesthetizing effect on curiosity, on the learning of skills apparently tangential to the particular task at hand, and even on conscience. It narrows the focus of attention to those kinds of behavior that have a visible "payoff."[68] The messages people hear are "conditioned responses"; these messages do not educate, for to educate is to give reasons and *rewards give no reasons*.

One of the most salient and attractive features of Skinnerian social learning is that rewards, as distinct from punishment, draw people into the field to learn more,

---

[65] See Martin E. P. Seligman, *Helplessness* (San Francisco: Freeman, 1975).
[66] Ralph Waldo Emerson, "Self-Reliance," in *Essays of Ralph Waldo Emerson,* ed. Irwin Edman (New York: Crowell, 1951).
[67] See Stanley Milgram, *Obedience to Authority: An Experimental View* (New York: Harper & Rowe, 1974). Whether the malignant obedience that Milgram found to characterize the behavior of persons instructed by someone clothed in the appurtenances of science was also prompted by the fact that *subjects were paid* for their participation in the experiment has, so far as I know, not been investigated.
[68] Kenneth O. McGraw, "The Detrimental Effects of Reward on Performance: A Literature Review and a Prediction Model," in Lepper and Greene, *The Hidden Costs of Rewards,* 54–5.

whereas punishment encourages escape[69] (Chapter 9). While it is true that the captive subjects of the token economies like the reward system in contrast to the rules and punishments that preceded it, most workers do not like PBR and instead of being drawn to work by it, they are more likely than those paid by time to be absent from work. By definition, the rewards themselves are not aversive, but the PBR reward system is. Work, then, loses some of its potential hedonic value.

Learning materialist values by contingent reinforcement? As mentioned, what people learn from their reinforcement by pay is exactly what they are rewarded for learning and nothing more: They learn to work for pay, that pay is the value of work. Do they also learn a more general materialism? On the one hand, the very limitations of contingent learning inhibits generalization and what generalization there is may never go beyond the kinds of things for which one has in the past been rewarded. On matters of work discipline and responsibility no genuine dispositional set is created in the token economies. So little has been internalized, indeed, that in making these institutions into more rational and orderly places, the measured character structures (cross-situational dispositions) of their populations seem to remain unchanged.[70] This suggests the important point that the materialism that market critics fear is developed by the market's pay maximization hypothesis may remain isolated and local to work. What prevents the payees in token economies from learning what they need to learn to function in the outside world also prevents them, and perhaps the payees of PBR systems as well, from developing the character traits of the selfish materialist.

Yet, on the other hand, we cannot say that working for pay does not reinforce the value of pay and perhaps of money more generally. In the Mortimer and Lorence study discussed in Chapter 13 college students who valued high paying jobs, rather than jobs with intrinsic challenge or that involved working with people, were likely to have first jobs that paid well, which then *reinforced and augmented* their high evaluation of money. Their appetites grew by what they fed on.[71] Not one, but at least four psychological theories suggest ways in which earning money might increase the value of pay: (1) contingent reinforcement ("do again what you have been rewarded for in the past"); (2) post-decisional dissonance reduction ("reduce conflict by seeing the merit of what you are now committed to");[72] (3) the love of the familiar ("the devil – or saint – you know is better than the one you don't know");[73] or (4) self-perception theory ("I must like money since I have been

---

[69] Skinner, *Science and Human Behavior.*

[70] It should be noted that learning theory based on contingent reinforcement also has a record in therapeutic contexts of genuine personality change. See, for example, J. Wolpe, *Psychotherapy by Reciprocal Inhibition* (Stanford, CA: Stanford University Press, 1958).

[71] See Mortimer and Lorence, "Work Experience and Occupational Value Socialization."

[72] Jack W. Brehm and Arthur R. Cohen, *Explorations in Cognitive Dissonance* (New York: Wiley, 1962). But note that if the pay is insufficient, the individual may persuade himself that he acted out of conviction. See Leon Festinger and J. Carlsmith, "Cognitive Consequences of Forced Compliance," *Journal of Abnormal and Social Psychology* 58 (1959): 203–10.

[73] Robert B. Zajonc, "Attitudinal Effects of Mere Exposure," *Journal of Personality and Social Psychology* (1968): Monograph Supplement, Pt 2, 1–27.

working for it").[74] Which of these theories is operative does not matter, for the result is that working for money, as in PBR and the token economies, enhances the value of money. For these reasons the lack of internalization of the work discipline or sense of responsibility for people's work by contingent token reinforcement fails to convince us that the general value of money is not enhanced by the experience.[75]

This learning takes place in the context of obedience to instructions and to authority. As Bandura has pointed out, contingent reinforcement, illustrated by these examples, are not acts of mechanical responses to stimuli, but are mediated by internal rewards – in this case the internal rewards are not for self-direction, craftsmanship, initiative or creativity, but for obedience to instructions. This implies a paradox. Personal control is achieved by obedience – and by manipulating the paymasters into thinking a reward is earned. Perhaps self-esteem is also earned by successful manipulation of paymasters and by living up to a self-concept of either a loyal, trustworthy employee (inmate), or a successful manipulator of alien rules. But the more a person values self-direction at work, the less influence pay will have as a determinant of that person's decisions, and the less effectively will pay offer grounds for these internal rewards of personal control, self-esteem, and congruence between behavior and self-concept. The paradoxical use of obedience combined with manipulating the manipulator to feed personal control and self-esteem is limited by the very meaning of personal control.

Security of pay versus pay maximization

Marginal utility of money and security for poor and rich
The desirable qualities of pay are quantity and *security,* the latter representing a dimension of supreme importance to many.[76] It is also important to society, for the insecure are more vulnerable to group pressure and less principled in their moral commitments.[77] In some sense amount and stability of income are tradeoffs – which the maximization hypothesis ignores. The need for security usually precedes the demand for more pay, with the consequence that the poor are least likely to be pay maximizers. Thus, the better off, for whom the marginal utility of income is less

[74] Daryl J. Bem, "Self-Perception Theory," in Leonard Berkowitz, ed., *Advances in Experimental Social Psychology,* vol. 6 (New York: Academic Press, 1972).

[75] This interpretation seems to be at variance with the findings by Kohn and Schooler to the effect that interests and skills learned at work by people working on self-directed and cognitively complex tasks transfer to their leisure time activities. The difference is accounted for by Kohn and Schooler's attention to *what people did* at work, not *how they were paid.* See Melvin L. Kohn and Carmi Schooler, *Work and Personality: An Inquiry into the Impact of Social Stratification* (Norwood, NJ: Ablex, 1983). On the question of transfer of interests and skills from work, the null relationship is the strongest. See René Bergermaier, Ingwer Borg, and Joseph E. Champoux, "Structural Relationships Among Facets of Work, Nonwork, and General Well-Being," *Work and Occupations 11* (1984): 163–82.

[76] In the United States, about two-thirds of all employed workers, regardless of age, think of job security as "very important," only a few percentage points fewer than those ranking "good pay" as similarly important. See Harold L. Sheppard and Neal Q. Herrick, *Where Have All the Robots Gone? Worker Dissatisfaction in the '70s* (New York: Free Press, 1972), 198. The data were collected by the Department of Labor and the Michigan Survey Research Center in 1969 and the early 1970s.

[77] David C. McClelland, *Human Motivation* (Glenview, IL: Scott, Foresman, 1985), 381, citing research by Ward and Wilson (1980).

than it is for the poor, are more likely to be pay maximizers, a reason for believing that the curve for the marginal utility of money is, indeed, "kinky": The marginal utility of income is highest for the poor but they seek security rather than more income, thus at least flattening out the demand for pay increases, and the marginal utility of money is lower for the rich, but because they already have security their demand for more money will be greater. To the extent that circumstances permit, the poor will seek low-pay–high-security jobs and some of the rich will seek low-security–high-pay jobs. And, ironically, the more these risks pay off, the more secure the rich will be and the more confident their attachment to the social order: "The feeling of personal security that the possession of money gives is perhaps the most concentrated and pointed form and manifestation of confidence in the social-political organization and order."[78]

Job security and earned income
Security of pay is a social signal to which employees are sensitive. Dwight Bakke (as mentioned in Chapter 13) puts it this way: "Economic security is one of the major goals of workers . . . but [security] is desired chiefly as an advantage in the attempt to perform in a socially respected role and to gain control over one's own affairs."[79] Again, income from pay is not so much a means of exchange as it is a symbol, in this case a symbol of acceptability, and as Bakke puts it a dichotomous value (working or not – a little like Rainwater's "mainstream" below which is an abyss[80]). Under these circumstances the offer of a job is the incentive, and the amount of pay is secondary. But note that the firm and social costs of job security in loss of flexibility of adjustment are high, especially if the consequence is increased unemployment. Samuelson and Nordhaus called the unemployment-inflation relationship the "central flaw" in the market;[81] we now see that the flaw also frustrates the search for security at work, a supreme desideratum for many.

Materialistic monism versus human pluralism
Because the market works exclusively through prices, work motives other than wages are not responsive to market signals. Thus, the desire for excellence (craftsmanship), or the desire for approval, or the search for solidarity or companionship at work, or any of the other common motives that prompt people to take a job, are insensitive to variations in pay. This plurality of motives poses three problems.

Pay versus plural motives. These alternative motives seem to contribute to economic *in*efficiency both by failing to evoke increased labor supplies when

---

[78] Georg Simmel, *The Philosophy of Money,* trans. T. Bottomore and D. Frisby (1907; reprint London: Routledge & Kegan Paul, 1978), 179.

[79] E. Dwight Bakke, *Citizens Without Work: A Study of The Effects of Unemployment Upon the Workers' Social Relations and Practices* (New Haven: Yale University Press, 1940), 280–1.

[80] Lee Rainwater, *What Money Buys: Inequality and the Social Meaning of Income* (New York: Basic Books, 1974).

[81] Paul Samuelson and William D. Nordhaus, *Economics,* 12th ed. (New York: McGraw Hill, 1985), 258.

there are increases in demand for labor and by failing to place members of the work force in the economically most fruitful jobs – as these are defined by the market.[82] On the other hand, plural work motives offer opportunities to invite into the work force those who are not interested in higher wages, or at least are more interested in something else. A larger work force may not increase efficiency or (as it is currently defined) productivity, but it does increase production and wealth – it makes society economically more productive.

In addition to the motive for job security, two other motives illustrate the implied market dilemma. (1) The relation between *prestige* and pay is by no means iso-morphic; even in our wealth-conscious society rankings of occupational prestige do not correlate highly with income rankings.[83] The economic consequence is that those seeking prestige will not be placed according to market criteria for they will not respond to pay signals. (2) People value having congenial workmates and some-times seek work to avoid loneliness; but the *affiliative motive* has at best an ambig-uous relationship to the desire to earn more money. As mentioned, the market, as distinct from household economies, opposes the use of kinship and friendship as criteria for employment. Thus, the affiliative motive works in opposition to market criteria. But, like prestige, it may increase the size of the work force and the size of the national product. Where market efficiency is at odds with societal productiv-ity, something is wrong.

Utility maximization with plural motives. The presence of plural motives in people's arsenal of energizers is clearly an advantage. It permits them to draw on various emotional resources to meet various work circumstances, to find satisfac-tions in work when the wages do not satisfy.

Efficiency norms and freedom of choice. Most efficiency criteria may be defended on the grounds that they lead to a larger social product (with the excep-tions noted in Chapter 16) that, in turn, enlarges both consumers' choices and, because of the jobs created, workers' choices as well. What is missing in a system dedicated to pay maximization is freedom of choice of a motive. The philosopher Harry Frankfurt said that it is a condition of being human that one must be able by an act of will deliberately to alter one's schedule of values;[84] it is this freedom that is threatened by exclusive reliance on pay maximization criteria.

An autocephalic, self-regulating, cybernetic system like the market is efficient only to the extent that feedback from its operations signal lag and gain, permitting the system to correct its course as it goes along. Wages and prices offer such feed-back signals; prestige, affiliation, and other noneconomic motives do not. As Frank Knight said: "In a social order where all values are reduced to the money measure,

---

[82] Inasmuch as the income elasticity of the labor supply is already close to zero, these losses are much smaller than might be supposed. See ibid., 618.

[83] See Donald J. Treiman, *Occupational Prestige in Comparative Perspective* (New York: Academic Press, 1977).

[84] Harry G. Frankfurt, "Freedom of the Will and the Concept of a Person," *Journal of Philosophy* 68 (1971): 5–20.

in the degree that this is true of modern industrial nations a considerable fraction of the most noble and sensitive characters will lead unhappy and futile lives.''[85]

The hidden premises in the pay maximization hypothesis

The pay maximization hypothesis is nested in a variety of hidden premises that we accept because of the familiarity of the hypothesis. When we question the hypothesis, we expose these premises to closer scrutiny, with the result not only that the hypothesis itself seems less well founded, but that the familiar world it reflects seems strangely implausible.

If people are not maximizers economic values lose their justification

The assessment of economic values is conditioned by the way they are determined. The market criteria for assessment are wholly procedural. If the procedures are those of a perfect market, the values assigned to labor or other factors of production are correct, no matter what they are.[86] The explicit correctness of the values included in any given pay schedule, therefore, is determined by the nature of the transactions that produced them. But the *implicit* assumptions of explicitly correct procedures include the maximization hypothesis, for transactions where one party does not exert itself, or settles for less than what others would get, does not fulfill the requirements of a competitive transaction, and the justification of the system is undermined. If one party to a transaction is not an income maximizer, the evaluative part of economic analysis leads rather quickly to the notion that people are rich because they want to be, not because they contribute anything equivalent to the wealth of the economy.

Dominant employer, dominant currency assumptions

In Marshall's treatment pay represents the reward for undergoing ''a certain fatigue''[87] (Chapter 14); in other treatments pay represents the reward for giving up leisure. In either case the tradeoff might logically be expressed in reversed terms, that is, in terms of the value of the thing given up. One might say that workers seek to maximize rest or leisure, and the amount of fatigue or sacrifice of leisure the worker ''pays'' to his or her employer is just sufficient to induce the employer to pay the worker for his or her work.

This logically identical but reversed formulation reveals the implicit, and probably accurate, assumption that workers want pay more than employers want their work; things might be different in a market where workers were in short supply and jobs plentiful. The reversal also undermines the *income* maximization hypothesis and suggests in its place a subjective welfare maximization hypothesis that would reflect people's own concept of the values they seek to maximize.

By putting the matter as a tradeoff between work and rest or, in Marshall's term,

---

[85] Frank Knight, *The Ethics of Competition and Other Essays* (New York: Augustus M. Kelley, 1935), 66.
[86] Compare Rawls, *A Theory of Justice*, 84–6 on the theory of pure procedural justice.
[87] Marshall, *Principles of Economics*, 14.

the relief of fatigue, another facet of the business ideology comes to light: the assumption that the natural state of a work force is a state of rest from which the offer of payment calls workers forth. In fact, for some people the rise of "leisure centrality" makes work itself a form of respite from the activities in which they invest their emotional life, for example, bowling clubs, gardening, or moonlighting. Not only is the assumption wrong, but it seems to license a jaundiced view of workers common among employers – their workers are lazy.

The limited success assumption

The pay maximization hypothesis does not assume that people will all be successful in maximizing their pay, but rather that in the process of trying to get more money, people will make the economy prosper, that is, the community will benefit even if many of the striving individuals do not. But this formulation might mean that *none* of the employees engaged in this effort will be the beneficiaries, for the benefits may all go to owners of physical capital, or money, or land, or their allies in management. If that were the general case, however, the habit of striving would soon extinguish – on the grounds of failure of reinforcement. Some, perhaps many, workers would have to be rewarded for their striving if the hypothesis were to have any plausibility over any period long enough for people to learn the consequences of their acts. These successes, in turn, put pressure on the general wage level that might be expected to rise under such pressure. At this point certain features of the labor market are relevant.

For all factors of production except land, increasing the price increases the supply and increasing the supply decreases the price. Yet because of the counteracting forces of income effects and substitution effects of a change in wages, the consequences of a change in the price of labor is unpredictable. In fact, the substitution effects seems dominant: An increase of 10 percent in real wages seems to lead to a 1 to 2 percent *reduction* in the labor supply.[88] Similarly, the increased supply of labor reflected in unemployment should lower wage rates, but, in fact, wage rates are insensitive to unemployment except as it reduces the size of wage *increases* negotiated by unions. Rather than representing the normal positive slope, the price elasticity of labor is closer to vertical, that is, zero.[89] It is for reasons of this nature that studies of the effect of wages on the use of nonmarket time show minimal results: "Results for men have often been disappointing: Data on their labor market hours suggest relatively minor responses either to their own wage rates or to the growing labor market income of their wives."[90]

In a competitive market, the consequences of a successful pay maximization hypothesis for labor as a whole is that it increases prices without increasing supply

[88] Samuelson and Nordhaus, *Economics*, 616.
[89] Ibid., 618. Note that the failure of wages to decline with unemployment is in direct conflict with the Marxist argument that capitalists deliberately produce unemployment to keep wages down.
[90] G. Cain and H. Watts, "Toward a Summary and Synthesis of the Evidence," in Cain and Watts, eds., *Income Maintenance and Labor Supply* (Chicago: Rand-McNally, 1973), reported by Frank P. Stafford and Greg J. Duncan, "The Use of Time and Technology by Households in the United States," in Juster and Stafford, eds., *Time, Goods, and Well-Being* (Ann Arbor, MI: Institute for Social Research, 1985), 245–88 at 246. Market wages also have only minor effects on both male housework and child care.

and therefore (unless the incomes of other factors decline) produces inflation. To make economic sense of the pay maximization thesis one must assume that (1) it is directed at individual workers who gain only as other workers lose, or (2) it is directed at a firm's labor force willing to reduce the profitability of their firm and hence (very likely) the security of marginal workers, or (3) it is directed to the nation's labor force, where the employed gain at the cost of the unemployed. Other possibilities, including consumer payments through higher prices are suggested in Chapter 15, but given the powers of the forces opposing labor wage maximization efforts, and the unhappy results for employees just outlined, the "best" economic outcome for these competitive strivings is for workers to strive and *fail to improve their position* – except as productivity justifies success. Put differently, success in improving pay schedules is constrained by the "production frontier," limiting what any factor of production may earn if other factors do not yield some of their share of the national product (which they, indeed, have done in the United States in postwar years – but perhaps at the cost of investment). In the short run, players in the market are playing a zero sum game. Only in this framework can pay maximization be reconciled to economic equilibrium and growth. "Maximization," therefore, has a very special meaning: " 'Maximize,' but not more than anticipated productivity increments of, say, 2 to 4.5 percent each year (U.S.)." Since labor has relatively little influence over productivity (Chapter 15), the maximization hypothesis is constrained to limits beyond worker control.

Given the nature of the market as an ecology, these meanings are not surprising. Nature says to each species: Maximize your survival characteristics or some other maximizing species will occupy your niche.

Contingent income versus contingent pay

Our review of the narrowing and inhibiting effects of *pay* directly contingent on performance seems to clash with two other findings in this book: Personal control is the product of acting and seeing the environment respond, and guaranteed *income not* contingent on effort has been found to be demoralizing. I pointed out earlier that learning a sense of personal control from contingent responses depends, as Kohn and Schooler show (Chapter 13), on the discretion involved in choosing among possible acts; otherwise the actor learns no more than a pigeon does when rewarded for pecking a lever. But the relation between contingent pay and contingent income has not been explored and requires exploration. Why is directly contingent pay bad and contingent income good?

There are three principles at stake: (1) Individuals learn more and are happier when they *earn* what they receive; (2) *discretion* and *choice* are necessary concomitants of freedom, a sense of personal control, and learning from experience; (3) in assigning rewards, society requires some degree of *accountability* to others for benefits received (one is always accountable to oneself). In applying these principles it is convenient to draw a distinction between *molar contingency,* as in earning a living, and *molecular contingency,* as in working for pay. The molar life context refers to the framework of a life within which such molecular activities as marriage, civic activities, child-rearing, and work take place. The norms and activities useful in creating a life framework include winning one's own way in the world, that is, *earning,* and *accountability* to one's spouse, children, community, and so forth. The key to the difference between the molar and the molecular contexts lies in the scope of *discretion* remaining within the contingent relations. A person required to work for a living has many choices of just how to go about it; a person required to turn out so many units of an identical product or rewarded by tokens for a specified behavior has no discretion left.

Within the context of work, *earning* is assumed (except for economic rent and interest, of course), but methods of *accountability* differ. We welcome payment by performance (PBR) by managers as a means of assuring accountability and do not grieve that their legitimate discretion has been stifled – for it has not. In the interest of accountability and earning, it is possible to hold with Tawney that income should be contingent on performing a useful function in society[91] and to reject the molecular application of that principle to payment by results for workers.

The lessons we draw from the income maintenance experiments, therefore, are radically different from those inferred from the experience with PBR and the token economies. Noncontingent income teaches the value of income without anything further, not even the narrow learning of the token economies and PBR (and the work discipline in market work reimbursed by PBR). Its messages are no less materialistic, and they are solipsistic, with no cooperative effort, no union with others, no social benefits in return for the individual benefits conferred. Like unemployment, a guaranteed income offers no structure to the daily life and nothing conveying to others the message Bakke said was essential to dignity: "to perform in a socially respected role and to gain control over one's affairs." The evidence reported in Chapter 9 on the relation of a guaranteed income to job satisfaction is telling: Security of income did not increase job satisfaction for those who continued working, and for some actually decreased it. This is consonant with the finding in one of the life satisfaction studies that "meeting life's challenges" contributed more to overall happiness than anything else.[92] At the molar level where people are creating a life framework, noncontingent income does not yield satisfaction, or personal control, or self-esteem. Work loosely contingent on pay often does.

Summary

All economies are based on energies released by the master motives for personal control of people's immediate environments and self-esteem (as modified by the desire for self-consistency). The motive for maximizing pay is a proxy for these motives. It serves the master motives as well as most proxies serve their principals – with a variety of delinquencies. As a master motive itself, the pay maximization motive fails.

An unrealistic assumption, wrongly assuming invariance in a disposition whose

[91] Tawney, *The Acquisitive Society.*
[92] Frank M. Andrews and Stephen B. Withey, "Developing Measures of Perceived Life Satisfaction: Results from Several National Surveys," *Journal of Social Indicator Research* 1 (1974): 1–26.

force varies with its success and with the costs and risks incurred, ignorant of the dominant internal rewards of personal control and self-esteem, misunderstanding the meaning of money, comprehending only external reinforcements, satisfied with conditioning rather than complex learning, overlooking conflict between security and size of income, grounding itself on maximizing rather than optimizing or satisficing assumptions, blind to the alternative "currencies" implied in the reciprocal relations of leisure and money, anticipating widespread failure – such an assumption has somehow persuaded people of its worth.

The persuasion is strong, but only partial: "The desire to seek other satisfactions from work may partly offset the effectiveness of financial inducements. . . . Material welfare is not always the paramount concern of those whose standard of living is very low."[93] "The obvious economic variables [rates of pay, rates of taxes] affect the hours that people work, but they are not overwhelmingly important. Conventions, and perhaps social pressures, are probably the strongest determinants."[94] "It is quite evident . . . that individual profit is not the only, and often not even the main, motive for working."[95]

Drawing on the distinction between the contingency involved in the molar process of earning a living and in the molecular process of working for pay, we might say that the *self-reliance* learned in the molar process might be matched by the *self-direction* learned in a "good job" by the *privileged classes* (Chapter 15) who have such jobs, but others receiving pay contingent on results do not learn self-direction.

We can also see the difference between a "good job" and "good pay." From their pay, people learn the "earning principle," but if the pay is too closely tied to particular performances they do not learn the larger lessons of person control, self-esteem, and consistency of the self with an image of the self as a creative, autonomous person. Learning to earn a living and then learning from the flow of pay received is not unimportant or trivial; but, on balance, the *potential* learning from a complex job is richer, more complex, and more satisfying.

For most nonmanagerial jobs, the information derived from pay is less meaningful than the information learned from work.

Information about the pay of self and others tells us, through its default values (stereotypical inference), of the worth and character of an individual, but it is false information.[96] Information about the nature and quality of a person's work is more informative and will almost certainly have better default values.

Attention to pay has been found, in the token economies and elsewhere, to distract people from the work itself, since their attention is focused so substantially on what pays. Workmanship loses out.

Maximizing pay is self-reinforcing; it tends to make materialists of us; attention to work might, on the other hand, make craftsmen of us. On the other hand, as reported in Chapter 16, there is no reason to believe that internal rewards will lead people to produce the goods that others want. We are not, therefore, free to create

[93] ILO, *Payment by Results*, 28, 30.
[94] Lea et al, *The Individual in the Economy*, 164.
[95] R. C. Kwant, *Philosophy of Labor* (Pittsburgh: Duquesne University Press, 1960), 153.
[96] Luft, "Monetary Value and the Perception of Persons."

a model of rewards for work according to the values of a work situation alone; there is the economy to consider as well.

The pay maximization tenets of economic theory have been reinforced by the experience of history, for the pay maximization hypothesis has presided over a remarkable achievement: In terms of income we are four times better off than our grandfathers, and some multiple of superiority survives when a number of the disamenities and regrettable necessities that have accompanied economic growth are taken into account.[97] Somehow under the pay maximization hypothesis, poverty, illness, and other sources of misery decline. But money promises to make people happier than it actually does; it is misleading (Chapter 26). The dilemma is illustrated by a physical index, health. It is people's job satisfaction, not their incomes, that best predicts their health,[98] but measures of job satisfaction are less closely linked to health and life expectancy than are measures of *national* income.

[97] William D. Nordhaus and James Tobin, "Is Growth Obsolete?" in Milton Moss, ed., *The Measurement of Economic and Social Performance,* vol. 38 of *Studies in Income and Wealth* (New York: National Bureau of Economic Research, 1973).

[98] Robert Karasek, Bertil Gardell, and Jan Lindell, "Work and Non-work Correlates of Illness and Behavior in Male and Female Swedish White Collar Workers," *Journal of Occupational Behavior* 8 (1987): 187–207.

18 Hidden costs of rewards and intrinsic satisfaction

The concept of the intrinsic

In this chapter we depart from the market's central, some say defining, characteristic,[1] *exchange,* and deal with a cluster of concepts of a different order: *intrinsic motivation, process benefits, internal rewards, satisfaction with procedures,* and the enjoyment of activities that happen also to be *means* in any standard ends–means relation. What these have in common is their focus on activities that are not undertaken for the usual categories of observable rewards but rather because they are rewarding in themselves. The particular focus of our attention is the enjoyment of working per se and the effect of payment on this enjoyment. Counterintuitively, it seems that payment for doing something one enjoys does not add to its utility or pleasure, but *detracts* from it. This undermining of economic utility has been called *The Hidden Cost of Rewards,*[2] and we shall adopt this term.

By definition, activities that are satisfying in themselves do not depend for their full worth upon exchange value (how much the activity is worth in the market), nor from their "use value" in the conventional sense of the usefulness of the activities. Rather they derive their *value in use by the actor.* The satisfaction derived from intrinsically satisfying activities is yielded by an act of consumption, not production. Acts of consumption are not acts of exchange; rather they are normally the ultimate purpose of exchange and follow from exchange or from prior labor. But consumption of enjoyable work activities is different. Employees sell their labor and talent in the labor market and incidentally acquire the opportunity to consume the pleasure of working. To the extent that markets are limited to exchange phenomena, they cannot cope with intrinsically satisfying activities, of which there are a large number.

The idea of the intrinsic is uncongenial to the reinforcement theory explicated in the previous chapter as well as economic theory. Both are outcome oriented, whereas theories of intrinsic pleasure or motivation focus on what, from an outcome point of view, is a process. Both rely on extrinsic rewards to explain behavior, whereas theories of the intrinsic rely on processes internal to the person (or in the case of aesthetics on qualities of an object, or in the case of truth on qualities of logic or inquiry.) Therefore reinforcement theory and economic theory are inevitably consequential, whereas theories of the intrinsic may be intentional.

A number of lines of thought and research come together to illuminate the concept of activities that are satisfying in themselves without apparent benefits or in-

---

[1] "At the center of the economist's stage is market . . . exchange. That act of exchanging is the source and proof of all economic gain, which explains the economist's preoccupation with it." Tibor Scitovsky, *The Joyless Economy* (New York: Oxford University Press, 1977), 133.

[2] Mark R. Lepper and David Greene, eds., *The Hidden Costs of Rewards: New Perspectives on the Psychology of Human Motivation* (Hillsdale, NJ: Wiley/Erlbaum, 1978).

centives from external rewards. One is Fried's analysis of means and ends in which he points out that an end is not just a goal, but rather is "a structure of ordered complexity" that includes the necessary means for its achievement. Every activity, whether or not it is rationally linked to an end, has some positive or negative hedonic value and to that extent it *is* an end, though often transitory and subordinate to other ends.[3] The force of this argument has been borne out in attitude research where it has been found that unless respondents specify their feelings about both the object or policy in view *and* the means to achieve it, respondents' attitudes do not predict their behavior.[4] The intrinsic value of ends, then, borrows much of that value from their implied means and, as with ends, that value is intrinsic.

A different but related way of conceiving of the intrinsic value of means is to consider the process whereby the hedonic value of an activity may change. As Allport has pointed out, initially unattractive activities pursued for some desired goal, perhaps learning to read, become attractive as one acquires the skill necessary for the original end. Allport calls this the *functional autonomy* of acts that "can become intrinsically interesting."[5] To some extent this process rests on the more general principle of enjoying the exercise of a learned skill.[6]

The idea of *process-benefits* also contributes to our understanding of activities that are enjoyable in themselves. Juster and associates have inquired into the enjoyment people receive from engaging in various activities, without considering their usefulness or their products. "People have preferences for what they do, and these preferences can be thought of as distinctly different from the satisfactions obtained from the tangible products of activity." This is true of both market work and of household, nonmarket work; and, of course, true of various leisure activities.[7] Preferences are precisely what markets cater to, but economic analysis tends to stop short of the actual consummation of preferences in both labor and consumer markets, dealing instead with observable choices. "Many of the outputs conventionally associated with well-being are actually instrumental outputs, and are not themselves ultimate components of well-being." Food and clothing bought in the market offer opportunities for satisfaction, but aside from the satisfaction of ownership, it is the eating of the food and the wearing of the clothes that constitute the activities that

---

[3] Charles Fried, *The Anatomy of Values* (Cambridge: Harvard University Press, 1970). At a simple physiological level, it seems that ends and means are reversible in the sense that any activity can be made to serve as a means to another more desired (end) activity – and these ends–means relations can then be reversed: water to the thirsty animal as a reward for running a treadmill, running to the exercise-deprived as a reward for drinking. Research by Premack (1965) reported in Albert Bandura, *Social Learning Theory* (Englewood Cliffs, NJ: Prentice-Hall, 1977), 103.

[4] Icek Ajzen and Martin Fishbein, *Understanding Attitudes and Predicting Social Behavior* (Englewood Cliffs, NJ: Prentice-Hall, 1980).

[5] Gordon Allport, *Personality and Social Encounter: Selected Essays* (Boston: Beacon Press, 1960), 141.

[6] John Rawls calls this "the Aristotelian Principle." See *A Theory of Justice* (Cambridge: Harvard University Press, 1971), 426. His extension of the principle to include a desire to acquire the skill of another person who has demonstrated that skill (p. 428) is of less certain validity, though supported by social learning theory.

[7] F. Thomas Juster and Paul N. Courant, "Integrating Stocks and Flows in Quality of Life Research," in Frank M. Andrews, ed. *Research on the Quality of Life* (Ann Arbor, MI: Institute for Social Research, 1986), 150.

yield the intended satisfaction. "The psychological satisfaction from activities are a different element [different from purchasing] in the well-being function, and can be thought of as the intrinsic 'process benefits' attached to time uses."[8] Our analysis of intrinsic motivation in work, therefore, treats but a small segment of the internal, little studied, world of intrinsic values.

A converging line of thought and research comes not from the area of work but rather from the study of leisure. Leisure activities are autotelic in some degree; they embrace as Huizinga says, "activities that are ends in themselves";[9] they include, says Csikszentmihalyi, *"the flow experience,"* where

action follows upon action according to an internal logic that seems to need no conscious intervention by the actor. He experiences it as a unified flowing from one moment to the next, in which he is in control of his actions, and in which there is little distraction between self and environment, between stimulus and response.[10]

Csikszentmihalyi reports that this flow experience was present among surgeons and musicians in their work as well as among basketball players, chess players, and rock climbers in their play.

Strangely, recent research on justice also shows how it is that procedures can be more important to a person than outcomes. The test for the quality of *procedural justice* was long confined to its capacity to yield substantive justice, the fair allocation of benefits and punishments. Recent research, however, shows that most often claimants and defendants in courts (and parties to justice proceedings elsewhere) care as much, or more, about procedures as about outcomes, especially whether they feel that they were treated with consideration or have had a fair and full opportunity to present their cases before a tribunal in which they have confidence.[11] Illustratively, people judge the common experience of being stopped for a traffic offense more by how the policeman treated them than whether or not they were fined.[12] Summarizing these findings one might say that people care more about how they are treated than what they get.[13] The benefits from procedures that participants rate as fair are *process benefits;* the satisfactions they receive from their participation are not contingent on outcomes, they are *intrinsic* features of the processes involved in their experiences, often depending on their opportunities to express their side of their cases.

The final line of research that contributes to our understanding of activities that are enjoyed in themselves is the main one we shall examine: intrinsic motivation, that set of motives that is said to account for the enjoyment of these activities.

---

[8] F. Thomas Juster and Frank P. Stafford, "Introduction and Overview," in Juster and Stafford, eds., *Time, Goods, and Well-Being* (Ann Arbor, MI: Institute for Social Research, 1985), 3–4.

[9] Johan Huizinga. *Homo Ludens: A Study of the Play-Element in Culture,* trans. R. F. C. Hull (Boston: Beacon Press, 1955).

[10] Mihalyi Csikszentmihalyi, *Beyond Boredom and Anxiety* (San Francisco: Jossey-Bass, 1975). See Robert E. Lane, "The Regulation of Experience: Leisure in a Market Society," *Social Science Information* 17 (1978): 147–84.

[11] See E. Allan Lind and Tom R. Tyler, *The Social Psychology of Procedural Justice* (New York: Plenum Press, 1988).

[12] Tom R. Tyler and Robert Folger, "Distributional and Procedural Aspects of Satisfaction with Citizen–Police Encounters," *Basic Applied Psychology* 1 (1980): 281–92.

[13] Robert E. Lane, "Procedural Justice in a Democracy: How One Is Treated Versus What One Gets," *Social Justice Research* 2 (1988): 177–92.

"Intrinsically motivated activities," said Edward Deci, "are ones for which there is no apparent reward except the activity itself, . . . activities [undertaken] for their own sake. The activities are ends in themselves, rather than means to an end."[14] He illustrates this with examples of curiosity and exploratory behavior in animals whose physiological needs have been satisfied; for the observer this behavior is apparently not motivated by any expectations of rewards other than the activity itself. Since it is unsatisfactory to say that an activity is its own reward, Deci and the others we shall examine postulate an internal reward: "Intrinsically motivated behaviors are behaviors which a person engages in to feel competent and self-determining."[15] Here Deci is building on a substantial body of theory and research showing that a desire to feel effective by controlling, or at least influencing, one's environment is part of our biological inheritance, useful for all animals in a Darwinian world.[16] This feeling of competence is the reward that satisfies the intrinsic motive, the reward latent in pursuing an activity undertaken for no publicly apparent instrumental reason. The desire to feel competent and self-determining is the motive for the cognitive assessment of self-attribution discussed extensively in Chapter 9.

Theories of intrinsic motivation depend upon rewards internal to the self. Thus social learning theory, accounting for behavior largely in terms of the abilities of human organisms to reward themselves, is one source of theoretical interpretation. Although all species are dependent upon observed contingency relations – else they have no way of knowing what causes what – "At the highest level of development, individuals regulate their own behavior by self-evaluative and other self-produced consequences." The knowledge that they have done well is a reward in itself, though of course it is pleasant to have this confirmed by someone else. And at certain stages in learning, external rewards are useful and sometimes necessary, for "without the aid of positive incentives during the early phases of skill acquisition, potentialities remain undeveloped."[17] But ultimately the external reward must prompt internal rewards for any behavior to persist.

Distinguishing intrinsic and extrinsic rewards
To illustrate the problem of discriminating between external and internal rewards, one might note the distinction between the *need for achievement* and the *success drive*. The need for achievement is considered an intrinsic motivation[18] because it

[14] Edward L. Deci, *Intrinsic Motivation* (New York: Plenum Press, 1975), 23. In addition to Deci, I am indebted to the following for my understanding of intrinsic motivation, although the interpretations and extensions are wholly mine: Richard DeCharms, *Personal Causation* (New York: Academic Press, 1968); Lepper and Greene, eds., *The Hidden Costs of Rewards*; William W. Notz, "Work Motivation and the Negative Effects of Extrinsic Rewards: A Review with Implications for Theory and Practice," *American Psychologist* 30 (1975): 884–91; Barry M. Staw, *Intrinsic and Extrinsic Motivation* (Morristown, NJ: General Learning Press, 1976); Thane S. Pittman and Jack F. Heller, "Social Motivation," in *Annual Review of Psychology* 38 (1987): 461–89.
[15] Deci, *Intrinsic Motivation*, 61.
[16] Robert W. White "Motivation Reconsidered: The Concept of Competence," *Psychological Review* 66 (1959): 297–333.
[17] Bandura, *Social Learning Theory*, 103. A cognate line of theory and research stresses the role of the intrinsic in socialization. See J. McV. Hunt, "Intrinsic Motivation and its Role in Psychological Development," *Nebraska Symposium on Motivation* (Lincoln: University of Nebraska Press, 1965).
[18] Bandura, *Social Learning Theory*, 34. See also Heinz Heckhausen, Heinz-Dieter Schmalt, Klaus

relies on an internal standard of excellence and is not dependent for its strength on outside rewards, but the success drive, as it is commonly conceived, is likely to depend upon recognition or wealth (external rewards). Here as elsewhere, the intrinsic and extrinsic are hard to separate, for the "reward" for intrinsic motivation is the inner feeling, but the information that produces that feeling is often extrinsic – and, indeed, may be manipulated by another. We are dealing with what Kenneth Burke called the "paradox of substance," the tendency of the intrinsic to be judged by extrinsic standards while the extrinsic is apprehended by intrinsic qualities of the observer.[19] "Indeed," he says, "the question as to what a thing is 'in itself' is not a scientific question at all . . . but a philosophical one."[20]

Nevertheless, research has found ways of coping with this "philosophical" question. Juster's research required him to sort out the enjoyment derived from the activities themselves from the enjoyment of the products of those activities; he reports that in most cases ordinary people are capable of this discrimination. The test case is housework, where he found that "in marked contrast to the data for market work, . . . having a clean house" is confounded with intrinsic enjoyment of cleaning house.[21]

It will be useful at this stage to summarize the various interpretations of *why* people enjoy activities irrespective of their outcomes. The discussion of means and ends provides no clue, but the concept of "functional autonomy" tells us that people enjoy using a skill once is has been learned. Process benefits are more protean; their satisfactions include the physiological and sensory satisfactions of eating and drinking, the social satisfactions of associating with friends, and the rest and relaxation that comes from certain leisure activities. Our concern is with the satisfactions of work activities, where Juster finds that people most often mention enjoying the company of the people they work with, enjoying (or regretting the absence of) the challenge and learning associated with their work, (regretting) boring and repetitious work, and the responsibilities (or lack thereof) in their jobs, a finding that applied to men only. Less often they mention their pay, which although certainly an extrinsic factor, seems to generalize to and thus to contaminate their perceptions of their work activities, although as an indicator of status pay has certain intrinsic qualities as well.[22] The discussion of play brought out the enjoyments of loss of conscious purposiveness, of merging the self with the environment, and of a sense of control over one's activities. In the analysis of judicial and other legal proceedings, the opportunity to be heard, to state one's case, and the sense that one was

Schneider, Margaret Woodruff, and Robert Wicklund, *Achievement Motivation in Perspective* (New York: Academic Press, 1985).
[19] Kenneth Burke, *A Grammar of Motives* (1945; reprint Berkeley: University of California Press, 1969), 32–4.
[20] Ibid., 469.
[21] F. Thomas Juster, "Preferences for Work and Leisure," in Juster and Stafford, *Time, Goods, and Well-Being*, 348–9. Those respondents who confounded the two have much higher process benefits scores than those who did not, suggesting "that the intrinsic rewards from housework are actually a good bit lower than even the low values recorded for the raw process benefit scores" of cleaning house. (p. 350)
[22] Juster and Courant, "Integrating Stocks and Flows in Quality of Life Research," 155–8.

treated with dignity seemed to contribute most to the satisfactions of justice procedures. Finally, Deci subsumes all intrinsic enjoyment under a single motive: the satisfactions derived from feeling "competent and self-determining." We will return later to these satisfactions derived from intrinsically enjoyable activities.

The intrinsic in other domains

We have explored these convergent bodies of theory and research to suggest the scope of the wide domain where theories of market exchange seem inappropriate. Some idea of the role of intrinsic satisfaction in other domains may contribute to this picture. Ethics, religion, and epistemology show the high road to the intrinsic; everyday life and interpersonal relations take the low road; happily, the two are confounded.

In ethics the high value placed on the intrinsic draws something from Kant's concept that only human beings have intrinsic worth or *dignity,* for all other goods are subject to exchange – suggesting a barrier between the exchangeable and the intrinsic that is paralleled by the hidden cost findings of incompatibility between exchange and the intrinsic. We all experience the conflict between intrinsic and extrinsic in one guise or another. The "prudential moralist" who's "virtue" and sense of justice is prompted by fear that his victims might retaliate has eviscerated the intrinsic qualities of virtue and sense of justice. In a parallel sense intrinsic work motivation also loses its value when the work is paid for. The religious dilemma, weighing fear of extrinsic consequences against intrinsic piety is quite similar, but in this case the extrinsic may be God and the devil: Aquinas observes that "the extrinsic principle inclining to evil is the devil. . . . But the extrinsic principle moving to good is God who both instructs by means of his Law, and assists us by Grace."[23] The love of the good for itself is the intrinsic foundation of religion, as it is of ethics. Similarly, the belief that there is a truth with intrinsic validity independent of the authority of the speaker is said to come late both in historical development and in child development.[24]

In everyday life the intrinsic is often threatened by extrinsic rewards. "Whereas some social exchange occurs in love relations, the expressive orientations characteristic of intrinsic attachments contrast with the orientation to obtain extrinsic benefits in calculated exchange."[25] In that contrast, "true love," at least, is thus subject to the threat of calculations of extrinsic benefits. The intrinsic pleasure of play or sports[26] is subtly corrupted by concern for extrinsic awards, although only a purist (spoilsport) would say that concern for victory contaminates the intrinsic spirit of any game. As one can easily imagine, filial devotion to powerful and rich

---

[23] Thomas Aquinas, *A Treatise of Law* (Chicago: Gateway Press, n.d.), 1. Similarly, Burke points out that "men's abilities and habits were said to be 'intrinsic' principles of action – the 'extrinsic' motives were fear of God and the Devil." Burke, *A Grammar of Motives,* 467.

[24] On socialization, see Peter L. Berger and Thomas Luckman, *The Social Construction of Reality* (Garden City, NY: Doubleday Anchor, 1967), 171ff.

[25] Peter Blau, *Exchange and Power in Social Life* (New York: Wiley, 1964), 8.

[26] See Mihaly Csikszentmihaly, "Play and Intrinsic Rewards," *Journal of Humanistic Psychology* 15 (1975): 4–24.

parents, marrying into a wealthy family, creative drama where box office receipts must be watched, dedication to one's students in freely elective courses – all lend themselves to such conflict.

The history of concern for the circumstances of work reveals a gradually increasing, though episodic, attention to intrinsic satisfaction in work. Bentham's views, cited in an earlier chapter, are representative: The "desire for labour for the sake of labour – of labour considered in the character of an end, without any view to anything else, is a sort of desire that seems scarcely to have place in the human breast."[27] The early factory legislation, the wages and hours and child labor laws, all testify to nineteenth-century and early twentieth-century concern with work, but that concern was focused on the extrinsic burdens of industrialization. Some isolated spokesmen pointed to the possible enjoyment of work. At the beginning of this period, Fourier's utopia (but not Owen's experiments in New Lanaark) emphasized the value of making work itself enjoyable, and by the middle of the nineteenth century, Ruskin and William Morris criticized work that was not done "with joy," finding that the intrinsic pleasure in one's work was undermined by the industrial revolution's attack on crafts and destroyed by the market's formula of wholly extrinsic motivation. From an entirely different direction Marx's criticism of work, which in the end was much more about the intrinsic satisfactions of work than about equality and justice,[28] is the major nineteenth-century statement, with echoes in communist literature and Soviet justifications of policy that survive the failure of Marx's economic diagnosis.

The first major modern conceptualization of a basic distinction between the *intrinsic* values attached to the work itself and the *extrinsic* values of pay and working conditions was made by Frederick Herzberg and his colleagues.[29] In this formulation, the intrinsic features of work, what people actually do at work, satisfies "the need to grow psychologically" and the extrinsic features satisfy the "need to avoid pain."[30] What struck Herzberg and his colleagues was the fact that whereas job *dis*satisfaction was a function of the extrinsic features of the job, job *satisfaction* was almost exclusively a function of the presence of the intrinsic factors.[31] Thus it is possible to think of intrinsic work enjoyment as a modern, or perhaps "post-industrial" concept – but an ancient reality.

Opposed to these formulations is the theory of contingent reinforcement discussed in the previous chapter. In this theory motivation is always directed by anticipation of extrinsic rewards and is directly the product of the individual's history of such rewards. But the research on intrinsic motivation that I will report is defined

[27] *Jeremy Bentham's Economic Writings,* vol. 3, ed. W. Stark (London: Royal Economic Society by Allen & Unwin, 1954), 427.
[28] Robert Tucker, *Philosophy and Myth in Karl Marx* (Cambridge, UK: Cambridge University Press, 1961).
[29] Frederick Herzberg, B. Mausner, and B. Snyderman, *The Motivation to Work* (New York: Wiley, 1959). See also Frederick Herzberg, *Work and the Nature of Man* (1966; reprint New York: New American Library/Mentor, 1973) for a review of later research "confirming" his findings. The Hawthorne studies were silent on intrinsic work enjoyment. See Fritz J. Roethlisberger and W. Dixon, *Management and the Worker* (Cambridge: Harvard University Press, 1939).
[30] Herzberg, *Work and the Nature of Man,* 91.
[31] Ibid., 91–111.

by the apparent *absence* of extrinsic rewards. As mentioned, reinforcement theory and economic theory are both in conflict with this theory of intrinsic motivation; it is the implications of this conflict that pose our problem for analysis.

The hidden costs of rewards

When one works for pay, one seems to be working for whoever offers the payment. Under capitalism, said Marx, "The external character of work for the worker is shown by the fact that it is not his own work but work for somebody else, that in work he does not belong to himself but to another person."[32] By contrast, work that is self-determined and intrinsically interesting not only relieves workers of their alienation and passivity, but is thought to release great new energies and imaginations for the productive system. What stands in the way of the release of these new energies? It seems not to be private property, since private employment appears to enlist more intrinsic motivation than public employment.[33] Strangely, research on "the hidden costs of rewards" implies that the market itself interferes with the release of these self-generated energies, for paying people to do work they enjoy not only detracts from that enjoyment, as mentioned, but also reduces effort,[34] degrades quality, decreases work commitment, and may even increase premature mortality.[35] These findings have a limited but important application to the world of daily work. The research that supports them has been qualified so that its provenance is limited, but for our purposes the findings represent an important entry into the problem of locating the occasions when workers identify with their work, when they think of the work they have to do as somehow "my work." We turn here to a brief sampling of the research that supports these counterintuitive propositions.

Calder and Staw offered forty students two jigsaw puzzle assembly tasks, one consisting of plain puzzle pieces without pictures and with numbered parts to match numbered positions, the other task was to assemble puzzles on which pictures from *Life* and *Playboy* magazines emerged when put together. Pretests showed that the first was considered boring and the second challenging and enjoyable, that is, intrinsically interesting. Half of the subjects for each task were paid (with the payment prominently displayed) and the other half were not. The measures of the effects on "intrinsic motivation" were ratings of the tasks on their degree of enjoyability and the students' willingness to volunteer for future experiments of a similar nature without payment. The experimenters found that "for the low intrinsically motivat-

[32] Karl Marx, *Economic and Philosophical Manuscripts of 1844*, trans. T. Bottomore, in Erich Fromm, *Marx's Concept of Man* (New York: Ungar, 1961), 99.

[33] Michael P. Smith and Steven L. Nock, "Social Class and Quality of Work Life in Public and Private Organizations," *Journal of Social Issues* 36 (1980): 59–75.

[34] For example, Pittman et al. found that compared to those receiving only intrinsic rewards, the extrinsically rewarded selected simpler and less challenging tasks. Thane S. Pittman, Jolee Emery, and Ann K. Boggiano, "Intrinsic and Extrinsic Motivational Orientations: Reward-Induced Changes in Preference for Complexity," *Journal of Personality and Social Psychology* 42 (1982): 789–97.

[35] Stanley E. Seashore and Thomas D. Taber, "Job Satisfaction Indicators and Their Correlates," in Albert D. Biderman and Thomas F. Drury, eds., *Measuring Work Quality for Social Reporting* (Beverly Hills, CA: Sage, 1976). These authors found that people working for extrinsic rewards have "higher rates of premature death from chronic heart disease" whereas intrinsic work satisfactions "induce lower death rates." (p. 102)

ing blank puzzle the enjoyable ratings increase with the introduction of the extrinsic monetary reward. However, for the high intrinsically motivating picture puzzle task, the enjoyable ratings decrease [with the reward]." What is striking is that the payment for the intrinsically interesting task reduced enjoyment *below* that of the boring task. The amount of time volunteered for future similar experiments "exactly parallels those of the enjoyable ratings." Further questioning revealed that "the payment of money decreased the perception of trying" on both kinds of tasks.[36] Observe that for the dull task, reinforcement theory is apparently the best explanation, but only hidden cost theory can explain the reduction in intrinsic interest by the payments – a point important to the issue of the market consequences of hidden costs.

In a series of experiments, Deci explored the various aspects of this alchemy. Generally his test of whether payment decreased intrinsic motivation was whether or not the subjects continued to work on their puzzles rather than read the magazines available in the ostensibly unobserved free-time breaks provided. In order to avoid the "social approval" motive, the experimenters left the room during the breaks but unobtrusively watched through one-way mirrors. In every case those not paid were more likely to continue to work during the breaks or to volunteer for further work more often than those who were paid.

Kruglanski and associates invited a group of adolescents to volunteer for a set of tasks that they found intrinsically interesting, offering one group a reward for participation and another no reward. The rewarded subjects were less satisfied with the tasks and were less likely to volunteer for a subsequent occasion than the unrewarded subjects.[37]

In a quasi–field study where the subjects were unaware that they were being studied the same "hidden cost of rewards" was observed. In a college newspaper office, after a four-week trial period (permitting pretreatment assessment of each individual) one group was paid during the fifth, sixth, and seventh week, but another group was never paid over the sixteen-week observation period. In the eighth week the two groups reported their enjoyment of their work: Members of the paid group enjoyed their work less than the unpaid group, and at the end of the sixteen-week period after both groups had returned to the usual unpaid status, members of the briefly paid group still liked their work less than the others.[38]

The draft lottery during the Viet Nam War offered a natural test of the effect of extrinsic rewards on college students' motivation. When college students were not rewarded by draft deferment for staying in school, they liked their studies better. The same was true for members of the ROTC (Reserve Officers Training Corps) in college: When ROTC no longer served as a vehicle for draft deferment, these apprentice soldiers (the same ones) liked their ROTC programs better.[39]

---

[36] Bobby J. Calder and Barry M. Staw, "Self-Perception of Intrinsic and Extrinsic Motivation," *Journal of Personality and Social Psychology* 31 (1975): 599–605 at 602–3. Calder and Staw note that their results could be explained by either self-perception theory or dissonance theory.

[37] Arie W. Kruglanski, I. Freedman, and G. Zeevi, "The Effects of Extrinsic Incentives on Some Qualitative Aspects of Task Performance," *Journal of Personality* 39 (1971): 606–17.

[38] Reported in Staw, *Intrinsic and Extrinsic Motivation*.

[39] William W. Notz, "Work Motivation and the Negative Effects of Extrinsic Rewards," 887.

The indicated studies report a loss of interest and liking for the intrinsically attractive activity when it is extrinsically rewarded; there are also *performance decrements*. When subjects are paid for performance on such "concept attainment" tasks as discovering what there is in common in a set of examples or what is the rule governing a set of cases, the rewarded students do less well than those from the same pool who are not rewarded.[40] When subjects are given nonverbal tasks requiring imagination, such as making a platform for holding a candle that must be attached to a vertical board when the only material available is a candle and a box of thumbtacks, "rewarded subjects consistently took longer to find the correct solutions to the . . . problem and, in addition, made more errors than nonrewarded subjects, even though their reward was contingent upon recording a correct answer."[41] The same pattern holds for other creative tasks, such as writing stories from given lists of words and thinking up story titles.

The hidden cost effect starts young. Performance on the Peabody Picture Vocabulary Test and the Goodenough-Harris Draw-a-Man test among preschool children again revealed "performance decrements" but "when rewarded subjects were shifted to nonreward [tasks], their performance improved dramatically." Although it reinforces the main findings of hidden cost research, the study implies a limit to the duration and generalization of the inhibiting effects. The authors of this study suggest that "material rewards can produce a *temporary* regression in psychological functioning," but the skills and attitudes are later restored to normal by habituation.[42]

When the task involves the interpersonal relations and consideration for others, the same performance decrement following pay takes place. Garbarino found that when older children were tutoring younger children, compared to unpaid tutors paid tutors had a more negative attitude to the subject matter and to their tutees, and the tutees learned less.[43]

Cash payments also discourage altruistic acts. Upton interviewed a sample of the public to find out their attitudes toward giving blood. One group was then offered a cash inducement to give blood and another was not. Among those who had indicated an interest in giving blood, those offered cash inducements were *less* likely actually to give blood than those who were not offered cash inducements. Among those who showed little initial interest, the cash inducement made little difference.[44]

The performance decrement also seems to hold across species:

Two chimpanzees, Alpha and Conga, painted organized patterns without the stimulation of any reward or social approval for their work; they threw tantrums when deprived of their pigments, paper, and brushes before they felt the picture was finished. When the chimpanzee

---

[40] Kenneth O. McGraw, "The Detrimental Effects of Reward on Performance: A Literature Review and a Prediction Model," in Lepper and Greene, *The Hidden Costs of Rewards,* 34–5.

[41] Ibid., 37.

[42] John C. McCullers, Richard A. Fabes, and James D. Moran, "Does Intrinsic Motivation Theory Explain the Adverse Effects of Rewards on Immediate Task Performance?" *Journal of Personality and Social Psychology* 52 (1987): 1,027–33 at 1,027, emphasis added.

[43] J. Garbarino, "The Impact of Anticipated Rewards on Cross-Age Tutoring," *Journal of Personality and Social Psychology* 32 (1975): 421–8.

[44] Reported in John Condry and James Chambers, "Intrinsic Motivation and the Process of Learning," in Lepper and Greene, *The Hidden Costs of Rewards,* 72

was bribed with a food reward, and learned to draw for its supper, it lost interest in the organization of the picture. Any old scribble would do, and then the animal would immediately hold out its hand for the reward. Its previous careful attention to design was gone, to be replaced by a simian form of commercial art.[45]

It is even less intuitively plausible that the *withdrawal* of rewards previously promised would improve either the attractiveness of the task or its performance, but under certain limited circumstances this has occurred. A group of students was promised academic credit for a course but halfway through the course half of these students had the credit withdrawn. For the remainder of the course this no-credit group worked harder, performed better, and enjoyed the course more than those who continued to believe that they would receive credit, although, not surprisingly, subjects in this experimental condition liked the experimenter less than did the control group.[46]

Under a variety of circumstances, with many kinds of rewards, both laboratory and field studies show that paying people for their work may reduce their motivation, initiative, learning processes, and performances.[47] "Neither the age of the subjects, the method of presenting the reward (trial-by-trial or upon completion of the task), the contingency of the reward on performance, nor the type of extrinsic reward . . . appears for the moment to be a critical variable in producing a detrimental effect" on performances.[48] As mentioned, these findings are in direct and dramatic conflict with market theory and practice, as well as the theory and results of token economies;[49] they seem to undermine the theoretical foundations of both economic theory and psychological contingent-reinforcement theory.

To assess this conflict we need to analyze the psychology of the hidden costs of rewards more closely, identifying the basic theories that explain the counterintuitive findings. We also need to locate the flaws in the research and its application to economic life in order to find out how much of a challenge to economic theory the theory of hidden costs represents.

The interpretation of intrinsic motivation

The theory of motivation mentioned in Chapter 17 is an "expectancy x value" theory, that is, the strength of motivation to strive toward a goal is the probability of achieving that goal multiplied by the value given to the goal itself (with the

[45] René Dubos, *Man Adapting* (New Haven: Yale University Press, 1965), 28.
[46] DeCharms, *Personal Causation*, 333, reporting research by K. E. Weick.
[47] McGraw, "The Detrimental Effects of Reward on Performance," 40.
[48] Lepper and Greene, "Divergent Approaches to the Study of Rewards," in Lepper and Greene, *The Hidden Costs of Rewards*, 237. These authors report on the "limits to the generality of any particular approach."
[49] See ibid. for analysis of differences between the findings on token economies and the hidden cost research. These differences have many sources: (1) The populations studied are often different (normal vs. disturbed); (2) the behaviors studied differ, with more complex tasks often assigned to the hidden cost subjects; (3) the dependent variables in the token economies are behavioral rather than attitudinal, for example, at least in the early token economy studies, there was no interest in intrinsic motivation; (4) in the token economy research, too, the rewards were tailored to the purposes of the program, namely, compliance; (5) although in the later studies, an effort was made to produce longer term effects (with some evidence of success), the earlier ones abruptly terminated the program to see the immediate effects.

qualifications mentioned).[50] Although acknowledging the power of the market's direct reward for work, it does not explain the counterintuitive hidden cost effects seen in the experiments sketched here. There are two main interpretative theories of hidden costs: cognitive evaluation or *self-perception* theory, and a branch of cognitive balance (or congruity) or *dissonance-reduction* theory. There are other explanations as well.

Self-perception and the drive for self-determination

The theory of self-perception initiated by Daryl Bem[51] builds on the discovery that people tend to attribute their own behavior to environmental rather than dispositional factors.[52] Whereas past scholars (and philosophers) have assumed that each person was privy to his own decision-making process, Bem suggested, and much research has found, that people often interpreted their own acts as outside observers would interpret them, reasoning backward from behavior to inference about sources of causation. Their explanations are drawn from those generally available in their communities, not from insight.[53] Nor are scholars particularly insightful about themselves. As Bentham was writing that "the desire for labour for the sake of labour . . . seems scarcely to have place in the human breast,"[54] did it cross his mind that he was enjoying that laborious, creative moment? Similarly, one wonders what magnitudes of royalties can justify to economists themselves the "disutilities" of their work.[55]

Cognitive consistency and dissonance reduction

The second main body of theory that helps to account for a person's intrinsic motivation derives from dissonance reduction (balance) theory, which says that a person

[50] See Victor H. Vroom, *Work and Motivation* (New York: Wiley, 1964). Although the dominant theory of work motivation is bound to extrinsic goal values, others have made provision for intrinsic values in the theory with the following result: Task motivation = intrinsic values associated with performing and completing the task + extrinsic value anticipated × the perceived probability of accomplishing the task and of receiving the extrinsic rewards. See research by R. J. House and others reported in Staw, *Intrinsic and Extrinsic Motivation*, 4–5.

[51] Daryl J. Bem, "Self-Perception Theory," in L. Berkowitz, ed., *Advances in Experimental Social Psychology*, vol. 6 (New York: Academic Press, 1972).

[52] More precisely, people tend to offer environmental explanations of their own behavior but dispositional explanations for the behavior of others. See E. E. Jones and Richard E. Nisbett, *The Actor and the Observer: Divergent Perceptions of the Causes of Behavior* (Morristown, NJ: General Learning Press, 1971).

[53] For supporting evidence, see Chapter 27 in this text. A hidden assumption in Bem's theory is that in order to preserve their good opinions of themselves, people feel under pressure to justify their acts to themselves. The pressure is only intermittent; much behavior is unjustified. For a cognitive interpretation of this tendency to arrange evidence to favor the self, see D. T. Miller and M. Ross, "Self-Serving Biases in the Attribution of Causality," *Psychological Bulletin* 82 (1975): 213–25. For a restoration of motivational factors to cognitive theories, see Miron Zuckerman, "Attribution of Success and Failure Revisited, or: The Motivational Bias is Alive and Well," *Journal of Personality* 47 (1987): 245–87. Zuckerman points out that both cognitive and motivational forces are at work; he also notes many occasions when it is either self-serving or proper protocol to attribute success to another; see also Mark L. Snyder, W. G. Stephen, and D. Rosenfield, "Attributional Egoism," in J. H. Harvey, W. Ickes, and R. Kidd, eds., *New Directions in Attributional Research*, vol. 2 (Hillsdale, NJ: Erlbaum, 1978).

[54] *Jeremy Bentham's Economic Writings*, 427.

[55] According to Stigler, economists do tailor their publications to fit what the market will "buy," although few would likely say so. See George J. Stigler, *The Economist as Preacher and Other Essays* (Chicago: University of Chicago Press, 1982), 13, 32–3.

is likely to select or adjust his or her opinions in such a way as to cluster together the things he or she likes in one set and the things he or she dislikes in another set so that they are congruent with each other, like-signed things going with like-signed things.[56] Here, to self-perception theory's motive of the need for justification another motive is added: the desire to remove the discomfort of dissonance and to make one's beliefs and attitudes harmonious. A grossly simplified version might be set forth as follows: Imagine a sentence with two elements with emotional loadings and a connection established between them, such as, "My friend Joseph has cheated." The positive valence $(+)$ of "my friend Joseph" is positively connected $(+)$ to the negative valenced $(-)$ term "cheated," or, symbolically, $(+)(+)(-)$. This is uncomfortable or *dissonant*. Whenever "good" things are associated with "bad" things dissonance occurs.[57]

An experiment with training school students for a task showed that those students who were paid low rewards ($.25) for attending each day, compared to those paid $2.00 for attending, had better attendance records after the payments stopped. This is because "low reward students . . . have enhanced their intrinsic motivation for the work experience."[58] According to self-perception theory, students observing their hard work for low wages infer that they like their work. According to balance theory, the sentence, "I $(+)$ work hard for a positive connection to $(+)$ low wages $(-)$," is unbalanced and psychologically dissonant; it is, therefore, changed to "I $(+)$ work hard because $(+)$ I am learning something $(+)$."

Of course, the circumstances are unusual; it would be a travesty of the workaday world to claim that low pay usually leads people to define the content of their work more favorably. But there will be some areas of work life where insufficient justification mechanisms are likely to apply. For example, people working on relatively poorly paid, dull jobs in charitable and artistic settings commonly explain their work as more interesting than it is, or more interesting than they would report it to be if the jobs were well paid. If steelworkers are skeptical, librarians will be poignantly reminded of their long hours cataloging acquisitions.

Our concern is with the relation between explanations of behavior relying on

[56] See Robert P. Abelson, E. Aronson, W. J. McGuire, T. M. Newcomb, M. J. Rosenberg, and P. J. Tannenbaum, eds., *Theories of Cognitive Consistency; A Source Book* (Chicago: Rand McNally, 1968); Leon Festinger, *A Theory of Cognitive Dissonance* (Stanford: Stanford University Press, 1957). In a sentence with two affectively loaded terms and one connection, there are eight possibilities, half of them congruent and half incongruent: i.e., where $(+)$ means either "like" or "positive association," and $(-)$ the opposites, the following are incongruent: $(-)(-)(-)$, $(-)(+)(+)$, $(+)(+)(-)$, and $(+)(-)(+)$. The remaining four possibilities are congruent.

[57] The classic experiment by Leon Festinger and J. M. Carlsmith, "Cognitive Consequences of Forced Compliance," *Journal of Abnormal and Social Psychology* 58 (1959): 203–10, has been interpreted both as proof of dissonance theory (people reported a boring task as interesting because they were paid so little for it and needed to reconcile their act with their perception) and as proof of self-perception theory (seeing themselves working for low payments, subjects interpreted the task as intrinsically interesting). D. J. Bem, "Self-Perception: An Alternative Interpretation of Cognitive Dissonance Phenomena," *Psychological Review* 74 (1967): 183–200.

[58] Deci, *Intrinsic Motivation,* 167–8. The experiment that Deci is commenting on is: K. Bogart, A. Loeb, and I. D. Rothman, "A Dissonance Approach to Behavior Modification" (Paper presented at the meeting of the Eastern Psychological Association, Philadelphia, April 1969.) Deci also observes that this is a better example of the overjustification phenomenon because here, but not in Festinger and Carlsmith, subjects were paid for their work, and not for the way they described it.

Table 18.1. *Intrinsic and extrinsic justifications of work behavior*

		Level of extrinsic rewards	
		Low	High
Level of intrinsic rewards	Low	(1) Insufficient justification (unstable)	(2) Perception of extrinsically motivated behavior
	High	(3) Perception of intrinsically motivated behavior	(4) Overjustification (unstable)

extrinsic (environmental) rewards and those relying on intrinsic (dispositional) rewards. Following Staw,[59] we may present the results in a fourfold table (Table 18.1). Where levels of intrinsic rewards are low and extrinsic rewards are high (2), people know why they are working – to get the extrinsic rewards. Where the extrinsic rewards are low and the intrinsic rewards are high (3), as when working on a hobby, people also know why they are working – because it is enjoyable. The various theories are tested in the two other combinations. Where both extrinsic and intrinsic rewards are low (1) people are faced with *insufficient justification*. Finding themselves in this position, they must somehow justify it, and according to cognitive balancing theory, they reinterpret their enjoyment of the task and find that, after all, it cannot be so bad or they would not be doing it, thus *increasing* the sense of intrinsic motivation.[60] In the fourth possible combination (4), extrinsic rewards are high, or at least sufficient, and intrinsic rewards are also high; people are faced with *overjustification*. This is the hidden cost situation. Because of the salience of the extrinsic rewards, the conventional mercenary interpretation of why people work, the inaccessibility of their own reasoning and even feelings, and the preferences for disjunctive (this *or* that) rather than conjunctive explanations, people tend to find that they are then working *for* money and not because of their enjoyment of the task.[61]

With the help of these two theories of self-perception and dissonance reduction, we can explicate the hidden cost mechanism more specifically. When a person is paid, the individual asks, Did I do it for payment? The following sequence of interpretations then sometimes (but with many lapses) occurs:

[59] Staw, *Intrinsic and Extrinsic Motivation*, 11.
[60] When people find themselves working in a boring job for little pay, they account to themselves for this anomaly by finding that, after all, they do enjoy the work. In a more familiar language, we would call this a *rationalization*, prompted more by the advantages to self-perception of a particular occasion than by a reference to inner feelings. Would such a rationalization have worse consequences than the rational but illusionary belief that greater income would make a person happier?
[61] Staw, *Intrinsic and Extrinsic Motivation*, 11–12.

If people are adequately paid for an activity, they will tend to assume they did it for pay, whatever their other motives were, because according to self-perception theory, they borrow the prevailing economic theory of work. For this case, self-perception theory carries the burden because there is no dissonance to be reconciled. But from this point on, the inference that implies hidden cost begins and Deci's theory of the drive for self-determination is used to explain the behavior.

If workers are (had to be?) paid for the activity, that activity, they reason, must not be particularly enjoyable, or they would not have been paid to do it.

If they engaged in an activity, enjoyable or not, *because* someone was willing to pay to have it done, then that someone was the master, the "primary locus of causation" or "locus of control" has shifted and the paid persons have lost their autonomy.

If they have lost their control over that activity, the activity is less attractive to them; they become less likely to volunteer for it on a subsequent occasion, to perfect their skills beyond any level that has an obvious payoff, and to believe that it is *their* tasks for which they are responsible (except as they are paid to be).

More important than task perception is the way the individual then *perceives the self,* and this is where rewards (market or otherwise) may have systematically undermined feelings of self-determination. It has been said:

From an early age, people's behaviors are so strongly governed by extrinsic rewards and controls that behavior becomes strongly governed by extrinsic rewards rather than a means of satisfying interest or curiosity. I suspect that as rewards continue to co-opt intrinsic motivation and preclude intrinsic satisfaction, the extrinsic needs – for money, for power, for status – become stronger in themselves.[62]

If the market incubates these habits and values, the costs are substantial.

Over- and underjustification. Overjustification decreases the perception of intrinsic rewards (as excessive and unnecessary), whereas sufficient justification increases the perception of intrinsic rewards – of enjoying the activity itself – as necessary to explain one's behavior.

Additivity. The relationship between extrinsic rewards and intrinsic rewards is generally considered not to be additive but rather interactive. It is the essence of the theory of hidden costs that high extrinsic rewards *detract* from intrinsic motivation and rewards, for that is the meaning of "cost." If they were additive the following simple formula would prevail: Task motivation = intrinsic value + extrinsic anticipated value × the perceived probability of receiving the extrinsic rewards.[63] The evidence presented is conclusive on the point: Sometimes extrinsic rewards reduce the intrinsic pleasure of doing something.

The idea that pay may *reduce* enjoyment in an activity seems so dissonant with market practice and our own unguided reflection that it is implausible without further qualification. One of these qualifications derives from the processes of internalization.

[62] Edward L. Deci, "Applications of Research on the Effects of Rewards," in Lepper and Greene, *The Hidden Costs of Rewards,* 202.
[63] Formulation by R. J. House as reported in Staw, *Intrinsic and Extrinsic Motivation,* 4–5.

Internalization. The contrast between responses to "money" in the token economies (Chapter 17) and in the studies of hidden cost reveals an important point: There is a fundamental difference between the *internalization* of a requirement, as when people in hidden cost situations convince themselves that their work *is* enjoyable, and contingent reinforcement's *compliance* with rewards for reasons that have nothing to do with conviction. We would say that the internalized act is voluntary, willing and willful; it is "caused" by the *dispositions* of the acting person.[64] The compliant act was caused, we would say, by the *circumstances* of the situation. The introduction of pay into a task situation, then, moves, or seems to move, the locus of causality from disposition to circumstance, from internal to external; it alters the task from chosen to unchosen, and since people do not work without motives, it transmutes intrinsic motivation into pecuniary motivation. Strangely, it *creates* Skinnerian man where he was missing earlier.

Changing John Doe's behavior may not be difficult, but to go beyond behavior to persuasion, or even conviction, requires a strategy enlisting Doe's values and beliefs in the change process. It can't be forced. Like the work ethic, intrinsic work motivation, being internalized, operates without supervision, crosses frontiers of role specialization, and does not stop at the place where "what I am paid to do" stops. Except as shall be noted, money rewards do not form the basis of internalization, but rather enlist compliance and invite doing only that for which one is paid and nothing more. "Extrinsically motivated workers act in accordance with a minimax strategy: They minimize their performance of a task by restricting it to aspects deemed indispensable to attainment of the contingent reward."[65]

Dissonance reduction and liking one's job

One interesting economic implication of dissonance reduction relates to the theme of intrinsic motivation. Observe the difficulty it imposes on the conventional economic reading of the sentence, "I like my work." Conventionally, work is a disutility and the sentence reads, "I like something that is a pain," or $(+)(+)(-)$. In the economists' world, "I dislike my work" is the only formula that does not produce the pain of dissonance.[66]

Hidden gains: inadequate justification revisited

Since insufficient justification sets in motion a process with effects opposite to those of hidden costs, we may call them *hidden gains,* or, more fully, *the hidden gains of inadequate rewards.* These gains, of course, represent increases in people's sense of enjoying work by those who are inadequately rewarded – to justify lack of rebellion, involuntary accommodation to the boss, hard work, and the work ethic

---

[64] Richard Nisbett and Lee Ross, *Human Inference: Strategies and Shortcomings of Social Judgment* (Englewood Cliffs, NJ: Prentice-Hall, 1980), 122–5.
[65] Arie Kruglanksi, "Endogenous Attribution and Intrinsic Motivation," in Lepper and Greene, *The Hidden Costs of Rewards,* 95.
[66] There is a solution to this, however, in dissonance reduction theory itself. The positive association of pay with work makes work itself attractive, for "a reward's protracted association with an activity promotes the development of positive affect toward that activity." Ibid., 99, citing 1975 work by S. Reiss and L. W. Sushinsky.

itself. By this theory, wages below expectations protect the employer from resentment that "exploitation" might be expected to create, because the worker must account to himself, or more likely herself, for this dedicated working behavior. In place of the Protestant ethic, whose message was attention to somber duty and certainly not that one secretly *enjoyed* one's work, comes the theory of hidden gains to explain work behavior not explainable by wages.

Is it so implausible? Juster found almost no differences by occupation in reported work enjoyment, the house painter and the executive sharing pleasures in what they do at work.[67] But, of course, it is a prescription for exploitation.

Hidden costs and self-determination

One of the underlying premises of Deci's hidden cost interpretation is the desire to feel competent and self-determining that he added to his analysis of intrinsic motivation. In a sense hidden cost theory could work without this desire for self-determination, but the assumption that this is "man's primary motivational propensity"[68] makes it plausible to infer that this desire to be a cause operates in this as in many cognitive processes. Some of the machinery for this motive is supplied by the theory of *locus of control*[69] explicated in Chapter 9. The desire for competence and self-determination that Deci added to self-perception theory is a desire for internal locus of control. Assigning this single, broad motive for self-determination in accounting for intrinsic enjoyment of working activities is a mistake.

Distinguishing work enjoyment from self-determination

There are other reasons for intrinsic motivation,[70] as we saw in the review of the interpretations of intrinsic satisfaction in the first part of this chapter, for example, physiological and sensory satisfactions, enjoyment of social intercourse, rest and relaxation, loss of conscious purposiveness, and satisfaction in the expression of one's case in judicial proceedings. More broadly, catharsis, the expression of one's feelings, and compliance with a sense of duty are not easily comprehended under the title, "feeling competent and self-determining." Fourier's concept of "work as potential joy" led him to assign jobs in his utopia to those who naturally enjoyed those jobs, for example, dirty jobs for children who loved to play with dirt. In this scheme there was nothing suggesting the feelings of competence or self-determination. Empirically, the experiments assessing intrinsic motivation by measures of enjoyment and willingness to volunteer rely on inferences that are not

[67] "Contrary to what most would expect, there is virtually no association between the process benefits from work and the intrinsic characteristics of the job as reflected by its occupational status." Juster, "Preferences for Work and Leisure," 341.

[68] DeCharms, *Personal Causation*, 269.

[69] See, for example, Herbert M. Lefcourt, *Locus of Control: Current Trends in Theory and Research* (Hillsdale, NJ: Erlbaum, 1976).

[70] Staw gives the following list of reasons for enjoying one's work: task variety, task uncertainty (or challenge), social interaction inherent to the job, task identity (identification with the product), task significance, responsibility for results, (overcoming) barriers to task accomplishments, knowledge of results. See Staw, *Intrinsic and Extrinsic Motivation*, 7–8.

convincing. I am inclined to believe that enjoyment of an activity is likely to be produced by feelings of competence and self-determination,[71] but there are exceptions.

In fact, as we shall see in Chapter 19 on the limits of hidden cost, there are sources of intrinsic motivation and its gratification in work enjoyment that do not incur hidden costs, such as a variation of the need for achievement and the satisfaction of conscience.

Maximizing pay versus self-determination

Although the desire for self-determination is not the only motive accounting for hidden cost phenomena, it is an important one. Consider how that motive compares with the standard motive for more pay, the pay maximization hypothesis discussed in the previous chapter.

There are a number of similarities. Avarice (I use the term without prejudice as shorthand for the income maximizing motive) is the basic motivational propensity in market doctrine. Like avarice, the "need for feeling competent and self-determining . . . is [said to be] a basic motivational propensity which is continually present and will be the primary motivator unless some other factor interrupts the process."[72] Like avarice (in economic theory but not in practice), the desire to feel competent and self-determining is not subject to satiation (declining marginal utility), although one may tire of any particular expression of either motive. Like avarice, the desire to feel competent is thought to be "a relatively stable personality characteristic"[73] contributing to transitivity of preferences. And, finally, like avarice, the desire to feel competent is considered to be the norm, deviations from which must be explained.

There are many differences between the two motives and between their respective reward systems: differences in the ways they are learned, the probability that the rewards will produce satisfaction, their roles in the psychic economies of individuals, and their consequences for the person and the society, including their effects on productivity. (1) Avarice is usually an instrumental motive with the consummation of its gratification deferred until something is purchased, whereas the consummation of the desire to feel competent is immediate and almost indistinguishable from the act itself. (2) The greater immediacy of the need to feel competent means that avarice is more likely to be misleading about its capacity to gratify than is the desire to feel competent.[74] That is, the longer the chain of inference regarding acts and their gratification, the more opportunities there are for misinterpreting the he-

---

[71] Theories of work and life satisfaction do find that the experience of control makes a substantial contribution to those kinds of satisfaction. See, for example, Robert I. Sutton and Robert L. Kahn, "Prediction, Understanding, and Control as Antidotes to Organizational Stress," in Frank M. Andrews, ed., *Research on the Quality of Life* (Ann Arbor, MI: Institute for Social Research, 1986).

[72] Deci, *Intrinsic Motivation*, 100.

[73] Ibid., 107. The reference here is to the need for achievement regarded as a "special case of intrinsic motivation."

[74] Angus Campbell shows that feelings of competence are, indeed, better predictors of life satisfaction than is income. See his *The Sense of Well-Being in America* (New York: McGraw-Hill, 1981), chap. 13.

donic consequences of an act. (3) The internality of feelings of competence makes their rewards invisible and therefore less vulnerable to comparison, envy, and competition.[75] In contrast, the rewards of greed and avarice are to be found in external goods and so to invite comparison and invidiousness. In this sense, intrinsic rewards are not "status goods" whose advantages erode when others have them, too.[76] Avarice is more easily channeled by outside influences such as advertising, but the desire to feel competent, partly because its very essence is *self*-determination, is more resistant to manipulation.[77]

The two motives are not symmetrical in their relationships: Avarice may serve the need to feel competent, but the need to feel competent is unlikely to serve avarice. This asymmetry is reflected in the biological standing of the two motives. Avarice and acquisitiveness have no direct biologically programmed elements[78] (Chapter 27), but it is thought that the need to feel control over one's own environment is shared with other species and therefore has some biological substrate prompting the human disposition.[79] In this sense the desire to feel competent is likely to be more universal, harder to change, and dominant in any conflict of motives.[80] Without considering their effects on productivity, the economy of competence is more attractive.

Summary

In this chapter I have reported on a world of satisfaction and motivation that is certainly economic, yet lies outside the boundaries of exchange. I have also suggested that it represents a source of energy and initiative that not only may not be enlisted by the market but, through the mechanism of hidden cost, is discouraged by exchange. Hidden costs are explained by the two theories of self-perception and cognitive balancing (or dissonance reduction); but the case of insufficient justification (where people find themselves working hard for low pay) is not, from the market's point of view, a case of hidden *cost* at all, but rather a case of *hidden gain*,

---

[75] The rewarding feelings of competence are not available for Veblen's "conspicuous consumption"; we do not keep up with the Jones's in our intrinsic satisfactions; there is no bandwagon effect; nor is there the "Pufendorf effect." "The ambition of mortals esteems those things most which few men have in common with them; and thinks meanly of those which are seen in the hands of everyone." Samuel Freiherr von Pufendorf, *Of the Law of Nature and Nations,* trans. B. Kennett (London, 1710), bk. 2, chap. 3, p. 115.

[76] Fred Hirsch, *Social Limits to Growth* (Cambridge: Harvard University Press, 1976).

[77] Jack W. Brehm, *Responses to the Loss of Freedom: A Theory of Psychological Reactance* (Morristown, NJ; General Learning Press, 1972).

[78] See Stephen E. G. Lea, Roger M. Tarpy, and Paul Webley, *The Individual in the Economy* (Cambridge, UK: Cambridge University Press, 1987), 165; Ernest Beaglehole, *Property: A Study in Social Psychology* (London: Allen & Unwin, 1931).

[79] White, "Motivation Reconsidered;" Martin E. P. Seligman, *Helplessness* (San Francisco: Freeman, 1973).

[80] This poses a problem in characterizing the desire to feel competent as "intrinsic," since the biological components represent a source of satisfaction external to the motive itself. Deci solves this problem as follows: Whereas thirst, hunger, and sex drives derive their satisfactions from changes in non–nervous system tissue, making them extrinsic to the central nervous system, the satisfaction derived from mastery and feeling self-determining remains in the brain and does not generally alter non–nervous system tissue. Deci, *Intrinsic Motivation,* 61–2.

that is, a case where the worker invests in dull work more energy and more commitment than the pay seems to justify. Hidden costs deprive workers of intrinsic motivation and satisfaction by robbing them of feelings of personal control and responsibility for their own work. These feelings do not emerge from the experience of loss of discretion so much as from a cognitive construction placed upon their experience. Hidden gains increase intrinsic motivation and satisfaction, though not because the feelings spring from their joy at work but because the "logic" of the situation implies that they *must* feel that way. Both hidden costs and hidden gains are to some degree "intellectualized"; they take initial feelings associated with working experiences and increase or decrease these feelings by cognitive processes.

The effects of working for another person or agency do not, it seems, have the effects that Marx and others have thought, for it is the *content* of the work, the discretion and challenge and not its ownership or the allocation of surplus value, that determines feelings of control. The economy of self-determination is more attractive than the economy of pay – but for its economic effects you must wait for the discussion in Chapter 21.

19 The limits of hidden costs in the market

In this chapter I create a straw man with real bones and then produce a bonfire that disfigures him but does not wholly destroy him. The straw man is created in the first section by spelling out the full economic implications of hidden costs and intrinsic motivation; he is a horrid figure. Even in his charred condition he may be considered to be the modern version of the "spectre" that Marx thought he saw haunting Europe. The bonfire is represented by an item-by-item undermining of the force of the theory of hidden costs. We start by examining the difference between pay as information, which does not incur hidden costs, and pay interpreted as control, which does. We then look at some quite powerful self-rewards, other than desire for self-determination, that motivate work without either extrinsic rewards or hidden costs: for example, desire for excellence and desire to deal fairly. Unlike the situations where the intrinsic motivation is the desire for self-determination, when persons with these motives receive their pay, their work motives are not undermined. This section on self-rewards is followed by an examination of the role of choice in voluntarily work, an inquiry regarding just how much the desire for intrinsic rewards informs work motivation, and an exploration of other situations where pay is welcomed without producing a sense of being controlled.

The market costs of hidden costs

Some astonishing market implications follow from the idea that money rewards reduce enterprise in the free enterprise economy. Let us review these implications before drastically reducing their strength:

DEENERGIZING THE PRODUCTIVE SYSTEM
1. Emphasis on money payments deemphasizes work and work achievement (as contrasted to money achievement) by focusing attention on money rewards.
2. It reduces the initiative, activity, and enterprise people invest in their work. When work becomes less enjoyable, by contrast, other activities are relatively more enjoyable.

REDUCING THE QUALITY OF WORK PERFORMED
3. Emphasis on money rewards reduces the *quality* of performance at work. Not only do hidden costs reduce commitment, they also impair the quality of work.
4. It reduces the breadth of learning on the job and hence the capacity of each worker to improve his or her own productivity. When people believe they are working only for money, they learn only those things that seem relevant to increasing their pay, not those other things that would only improve their products.

IMPAIRING DISTRIBUTION OF FACTORS AND TALENT TO THEIR MOST PRODUCTIVE USES
5. Emphasis on money rewards impairs the capacity of the market to allocate talent according to its best, most productive, uses. In Chapter 17 we said that nonmone-

384

tary motives, blind to market signals, impair proper market allocation; here, the perverse process appears again when wages no longer reflect degrees of commitment or willingness to learn. This is so, of course, because it is through price (money) signals that the market allocates the factors of production.

6. Money rewards and intrinsic rewards make up a dual currency with strange unmarketlike effects. The *dual currency* refers to the two kinds of rewards: intrinsic work satisfaction and money wages. For example, in recognition of the value of intrinsic satisfactions at work, creative labor accepts less than its marginal return, in effect asking the other factors kindly to accept some portion of its own earned economic remuneration. (See Chapter 21.)

7. By themselves, money rewards fail to bring forth increased labor supplies when they are needed. That is, wages do not reward for intrinsically enjoyable work and they do not attract creative people to the jobs that need to be done.

DISTORTING THE RATIONALITY OF INDIVIDUAL LIFE PLANS

8. The market's exclusive attention to money rewards confounds individual calculations of utility. For example: (a) in any mixed motive game, exclusive attention to money payoffs encourages people to conceal their intrinsic satisfactions so as to get more extrinsic rewards. Then, by interpreting their desires on the basis of their acts (in accordance with self-perception theory) they risk the loss of these intrinsic satisfactions that have thus been displaced. (b) Inadequate extrinsic rewards invite workers to believe that there *must be* intrinsic satisfactions or they would not be working for such poor extrinsic rewards. This is the phenomenon of hidden gains mentioned in the previous chapter.

9. Emphasis on money rewards discourages people from seeking intrinsic work satisfactions, persuading them that they are content with extrinsic rewards. The partial incompatibility of extrinsic and intrinsic satisfactions found in hidden cost research leads to devaluing the major source of satisfaction in work.

DISTORTING JUSTICE

10. The market's exclusive attention to money rewards distorts justice in the market by embracing only one of the rewards for work. This is true not only for the obvious reason that the market's justice of deserts considers only extrinsic rewards, but also because, according to hidden cost theory, money payments not only crowd out intrinsic satisfactions but actually detract from them for no reason related to justice. It is also true because of the inherent difficulty in allocating and measuring the intrinsic.

11. Exclusive attention to money rewards distorts the tax burden by levying taxes only on one kind of "income" from work. Thus, the ability-to-pay doctrine of progressive taxation no longer corresponds even in the principle to equality of sacrifice.

If these implications are in any degree true, they imply that the market is in subtle ways undermining its own purpose, a condition that has, in other connections, been called a "contradiction."[1] The hidden cost contradiction is, I repeat, only a minor force in the market, standing for a wider range of phenomena tending to undermine

[1] The Marxist "contradiction" implies an explosion such that the "centralization of the means of production and the socialization of labor reach a point where they prove incompatible with their capitalist husk . . . [and] burst asunder." Karl Marx, *Capital*, vol. 1 (New York: Dutton/Everyman, 1974), 846. More recently other critics have claimed that the market undermines its own foundations in other ways: "A system that depends for its success on a heritage that it undermines cannot be sustained on the record of its bountiful fruits." Fred Hirsch, *Social Limits to Growth* (Cambridge: Harvard University Press, 1976), 12. Capitalism "exhibits a pronounced proclivity toward undermining the moral foundations on which any society, including the capitalist variety, must rest." Albert O. Hirschman, "Rival Interpretations of Market Society: Civilizing, Destructive, or Feeble?" *Journal of Economic Literature* 20 (1982): 1,463–84 at 1,466.

people's identifications with their work. It implies only an erosion of the energy of the system; it is more like the problems of a meritocratic bureaucracy: The very procedures it employs to guarantee a standardized product often inhibit the effective delivery of that product; but the services *are* delivered.

The impact of hidden costs is broad but thin. It is broad because most jobs and job settings have some intrinsically attractive features that might be affected by "hidden cost,"[2] that is, the intrinsic motivation to control one's own work is extensive. The impact is thin because in most work situations there are usually available so many work motives other than intrinsic enjoyment, so many ways of thinking about self-determination other than those available when working for oneself, and so many other messages contained in the pay packet (or profit-and-loss statement of the self-employed), that the erosion of commitment is probably only a modest, though important, impediment to market functioning.

I have stated these market costs baldly; they must be qualified. We will examine the limits of this "contradiction," and the limits of hidden cost more generally.

Explaining why people like their paid work

Extrinsic rewards as information, not control

There are two ways whereby the desire for a sense of one's own competence can be consummated and intrinsic motivation enhanced: (1) Under circumstances of insufficient justification people increase their perceived intrinsic motivation in order to account for their behavior and to reduce dissonance; and (2) information derived from praise or success directly tells people that they have conquered the challenge presented by the task (or, alternatively, that they have failed). The second is important and sometimes undermines the "hidden cost effect."

Following this second line of thought on pay as information, we see that it is just as plausible that payments should be interpreted as evidence of success, thereby as evidence of personal control, reinforcing a person's sense of competence and self-determination. And, indeed, self-perception theory provides for this second route: "Every reward has two aspects, a controlling aspect and an informational aspect. . . . The relative salience of the two aspects will determine which process will be operative."[3] The information, of course, may not be encouraging, but "if a person's feelings of competence and self-determination are enhanced, his intrinsic motivation will be increased,"[4] that is, the motive for undertaking this activity purely to increase a personal feeling of competence will increase. Praise increases intrinsic motivation; criticism and blame decrease it. But success without praise will serve as well. Those who succeeded in anagram tasks were more willing to play again

---

[2] Recall (from Chapter 18) that Deci believes that the impact of hidden costs is "pervasive." Edward L. Deci, "Cognitive Evaluation Theory and the Study of Human Motivation," in Mark R. Lepper and David Greene, eds., *The Hidden Costs of Rewards: New Perspectives on the Psychology of Human Motivation* (Hillsdale, NJ: Wiley/Erlbaum, 1978), 174.

[3] Edward L. Deci, *Intrinsic Motivation* (New York: Plenum Press, 1975), 142.

[4] Ibid., 141. As pointed out in Chapter 17, social learning theory agrees on this point: Interest is the product of "perceiving self-efficacy" gained from performance. Albert Bandura, "Self-Efficacy Mechanisms in Human Agency," *American Psychologist* 37 (1982): 122–47 at 133.

and actually did better in the second round than those who had failed.[5] In passing we may note how this new version of the old story of cumulative advantages of success, especially in a competitive economy, increase inequality.

When are rewards merely informational and when are they controlling? And, since feedback of some kind is necessary to improve performance and, indeed, to feel competent, why cannot money serve this purpose? The matter is crucial for appraising the importance of hidden costs for the market economy. Deci, again, provides a relevant study. After a task was completed, subjects of both sexes were given the competence-enhancing message: "Very good, that's the fastest this one has been done yet." Boys who were thus praised *increased* their intrinsic motivation whereas girls *decreased* theirs. This puzzling sex difference was found to be due to the fact that boys interpreted the praise as information on their performance, whereas the girls, more sensitive to interpersonal relations, interpreted the praise as a form of control.[6] It is not the presence of a contingent reward that matters, but the construction put upon it, and that construction can be modified by the way the individuals think of themselves and their acts. For example, Bandura reports that "when material rewards for each task completion are accompanied by self-verbalization of competence, children sustain high interest in the activity."[7] The self-verbalization of competence seems to convert the extrinsic material rewards into a message containing information on whether the competent child has done well or not; the failure to receive the reward does not then undermine feelings of competence. It is how the receipt or failure to receive a reward is construed that is important.

The question of interpreting rewards might be put another way: For whose use is the feedback on performance desired? If for the performer, self-determination is protected (though self-esteem may be wounded by evidence of low competence). If for a paymaster, self-determination is threatened and control passes to others. Since prices have the dual function of controlling and informing people, there is some hope that given a "masculine" callousness to control, wage information will be interpreted as purely informational and not controlling. The point is important, for the construction put upon price information is influenced as much by a market culture of self-reliance and self-attribution (Chapter 9) as by market practices.

Interpreting contingent extrinsic rewards as information rather than as control solves a fundamental puzzle. Throughout this book we have generally held that the experience of contingent rewards contributed to understanding causality and that a sense of mastery or self-determination was learned through a history of acting and finding that the environment responded. The alternative is learned helplessness. The theory of hidden costs, on the other hand, says that the experience of contingent

---

[5] N. T. Feather, "The Relationship of Persistence at a Task to Expectations of Success and Achievement Related Motives," *Journal of Abnormal and Social Psychology* 14 (1969): 522–61; Idem, "Effects of Prior Success and Failure on Expectations of Success and Subsequent Performance," *Journal of Personality and Social Psychology* 3 (1966): 287–98.

[6] Deci, *Intrinsic Motivation*, 146–7. These sex differences were also supported by Richard Koestner, Miron Zuckerman, and Julia Koestner, "Praise, Involvement, and Intrinsic Motivation," *Journal of Personality and Social Psychology* 52 (1987): 383–90.

[7] Bandura, "Self-Efficacy Mechanisms in Human Agency," 134.

rewards of pay *reduces* the sense of self-determination. The difference lies in whether or not one sees the contingency as informational or as controlling.

The information conveyed to the self and others by wage information extends beyond the workplace, of course, and tells a story of its own. British anthropologist Geoffrey Gorer puts it in this way:

Dollars can be considered as adult equivalents of marks and grades which signified the school child's relative position in regard to his fellows. . . . This "rating" aspect of money is for Americans . . . at least as important as any of the uses to which it can be put. . . . Until you know the income bracket of a stranger, and he knows yours, your mutual relationship is unsatisfactory and incomplete.[8]

The interpretation of money payments as information rather than control may have the advantage of preserving intrinsic motivation in the immediate situation, but it has other implications. In the longer term, the controlling aspects of money cannot be avoided. Moreover, the more a person believes that income contains the information about his or her worth, the more the intrinsic value of life is supplanted by a money value. In Kant's term, a person's *dignity* has evaporated into exchange value. Most Americans deny that they evaluate people according to income,[9] but we know that wealth information represents a kind of "default value," that is, failing other information, people use income and wealth to assess personality – and the rich are thought to have more wholesome personalities than the poor.[10]

The two interpretations of income: *Because I am paid, I am no longer self-deter-mining,* and *Because I am paid, I am competent and* (to some extent) *control my environment,* are obviously in direct conflict. Marx hears only the first message, but many, if not most, workers hear the second more clearly, with the muffled echo of the first not quite out of earshot. Focusing on the workplace, one might find the first interpretation salient; focusing on the market, the second is louder. One might say that the Marxists are like the girls in Deci's experiment – they are more sensi-tive to the questions of who is controlling whom – and the workers, followers of Adam Smith, are like the boys, more sensitive to the informational aspects of money. In the consumer-driven society, the informational aspect of money is more vivid. But it is that kind of society that focuses on money rather than on work itself.

In most cases it is implausible to believe that a sense of being *overpaid* reduces intrinsic motivation for very long, since workers quickly come to believe that they are worth every penny they are paid. The high rewards serve as information telling the workers that they are good at what they are doing and are competent in their work – in both the psychological sense and the commonsense version of compe-tence.

Distinguishing internal standards of excellence from enjoyment and self-determination

An internalized standard of excellence, of high workmanship or of achievement, is as "intrinsic" as the desire for self-determination (or, indeed, conscience) in the

---

[8] Geoffrey Gorer, *The American People* (New York: Norton, 1948), 173–5.

[9] Morris Rosenberg and Leonard E. Pearlin, "Social Class and Self-Esteem among Children and Adults," *American Journal of Sociology* 84 (1978): 53–77.

[10] Joseph Luft, "Monetary Value and the Perception of Persons," *The Journal of Social Psychology* 46 (1957): 245–51.

sense that these motives operate without benefit of visible external rewards.[11] In their different ways, scientists, artists, and entrepreneurs[12] receive rewards for performance that may be described as feelings of competence and self-determination, but they are of a special character that may conflict with other expressions of self-determination. For example, in an analysis of the reasons why subjects of an experiment chose to sacrifice an original Tinkertoy assembly, which they had enjoyed putting together, for a model constructed from a blueprint, whose assembly had not been an enjoyable task, DeCharms distinguished *task-involvement* (with its intrinsic pleasures) from *ego-involvement* (with its intrinsic pride in achievement). These subjects sacrificed the construction that was a pleasure to make to save the construction that they thought was a superior product. One is not always most proud of the activities that are either the most freely creative (self-determined) or the most enjoyable.[13] Ruskin, whose principal concern was excellence in art, says: "I believe the right question to ask, respecting ornament, is simply this: Was it done with enjoyment – was the carver happy while he was about it? It may be the hardest work possible, . . . but it must have been happy too, or it will not be living."[14] The proposition is glib: Was it ever true that the happier the artist the better his or her work?[15] Ego-involvement with its standard of excellence and task-involvement with its standard of pleasure are different. And both are different from feelings of self-determination.

The market is sensitive to high standards of excellence, for they have cash value, but not to the desire for self-determination. By divorcing the two we release the desire for self-determination once again to its uncertain fate in the market. Moreover, judging by the economic records of those with the need for achievement, an internal standard of excellence or accomplishment is fully compatible with, and may be subjectively measured if not stimulated by, financial rewards.[16] Money

[11] "Achievement motivation is a special case of intrinsic motivation, that is, achievement motivation differentiates out of the basic motivational propensity of needing to feel competent and self-determining in relation to the environment." E. L. Deci, *Intrinsic Motivation*, 107.

[12] On entrepreneurs, see Joseph A. Schumpeter, *The Theory of Economic Development: An Inquiry into Profits, Capital, Credits, Interest, and the Business Cycle*, 2d ed., trans. R. Opie (Cambridge: Harvard University Press, 1936).

[13] Richard DeCharms, *Personal Causation: The Internal Affective Determinants of Behavior* (New York: Academic Press, 1968), 341–52. In another experiment, college students worked on a hidden figure test under two conditions, one a testlike, ego-involving condition, the other a gamelike, task-involving condition. As was the case in the Tinkertoy experiment, intrinsic motivation (as measured by volunteered free time selection) was more stimulated by the task-involving (gamelike) condition than the ego-involving (testlike) condition, but in this study the more enjoyable task turned out to be the one on which later tests of performance showed improvement. Koestner et al., "Praise, Involvement, and Intrinsic Motivation."

[14] John Ruskin, *The Seven Lamps of Architecture*, in Kenneth Clark, ed. *Ruskin Today* (Harmondsworth, UK: Penguin, 1982), 235. Original work published 1849. Later Ruskin adds: "You cannot get the feeling by paying for it – money will not buy life." (p. 236). The Koestner et al. study (notes 6 and 13) supports Ruskin's hypothesis.

[15] See Walter Kaufmann, "The Inevitability of Alienation," in Richard Schact, *Alienation* (Garden City, NY: Doubleday/Anchor, 1970), xv–xvii.

[16] David C. McClelland, *The Achieving Society* (Princeton, NJ: van Nostrand, 1961). We are not here concerned with the question of the relationship between measures of the achievement motive and economic growth, which has been subject to substantial criticism. See Allan Masur and Eugene Ross, "An Empirical Test of McClelland's 'Achieving Society' Theory," *Social Forces* 55 (1977): 769–74. I believe the relationship of individual achievement motive to individual behavior rests on stronger evidence.

rewards for the intrinsically motivated whose *need for achievement* is expressed in the pursuit of excellence suffer no hidden costs and no loss of self-determination.

Justice motives and other interpretations of the relationship of pay and intrinsic motivation

Hidden cost doctrine says that when people believe they are not only well paid but even *overpaid* for their work they will interpret this as control and will, for this reason, do only what is necessary to receive their pay. In fact, when workers are led to believe that they are overpaid on an hourly basis they work *harder,* and when "overpaid" on a piece rate basis they improve the quality of their work. This greater effort is not attributable to increased feelings of self-determination but rather to the fact that people have a sense of what is *fair,* as in the common workers' phrase, A fair day's work for a fair day's pay. Here equity theory, not hidden costs, offers the relevant theoretical interpretation.[17]

Both market ideology and market doctrine justify market distribution by the justice of deserts. And they both tell the individual that effort and skill are reflected in each individual's level of pay; one gets what one deserves – and most people believe it.[18] Those who believe the market justification will first tell themselves: "If I work harder or more skillfully, I will be paid more," and then: "If I am paid more, I must in all fairness work harder or more skillfully." The market ideology has thus provided an intrinsic reward alternative to enjoyment: the satisfaction of conscience.

Other limits to hidden costs

Choosing one's own work

Within the theory of hidden costs there is a contradiction, one internal to the theory itself. Both self-perception theory and cognitive balance theory are importantly influenced by the worker's sense that he or she has *chosen* the work personally. In the case of self-perception, the worker might say: (1) "If I chose the task, I must be interested in it"; and (2) "If I chose the task, it is *mine* and therefore I am not merely the pawn of the paymaster."

Experimental research shows that the sense of having *chosen* to do what people are doing is a partial innoculent against hidden cost.[19] The market is partly successful in persuading people that their choice of a job and a career is voluntary. About two-thirds of the American population believe (1975–7) that "getting ahead in the world is mostly a matter of ability and hard work" in contrast to the roughly one-

[17] Edward E. Lawler, "Equity Theory as a Predictor of Productivity and Work Quality," *Psychological Bulletin* 70 (1968): 596–610.

[18] Wesley H. Perkins and Wendell Bell, "Alienation and Social Justice in England and the United States: The Polity and the Economy," in Richard F. Tomasson, ed., *Comparative Social Research,* vol. 3 (Greenwich, CT: JAI Press, 1980); Faye J. Crosby, *Relative Deprivation and Working Women* (New York: Oxford University Press, 1982).

[19] D. E. Linder, J. Cooper, and E. E. Jones, "Decision Freedom as a Determinant of the Role of Incentive Magnitude in Attitude Change," *Journal of Personality and Social Psychology* 6 (1967): 245–54, reported in Deci, *Intrinsic Motivation,* 166–7. In laboratory experiments this sense of having chosen the task – even if one is a volunteer for the experiments – is missing.

eighth who believe it is a matter of "getting the breaks."[20] But the market process stops at the boundaries of the firm; as we have said, within the firm hierarchical processes take over and that sense of voluntary choice is necessarily more constrained (Chapter 15).

Desire for intrinsic satisfaction

Many, perhaps most, manual workers are said not to seek or to value intrinsic work satisfaction; they simply want payments to sustain their lives outside the workplace. To the extent that this is true, there are no hidden costs as these are conventionally defined, because there is nothing in the original motivational package against which a decrement of motivation can be a charge.[21] But lack of intrinsic interest in the work itself *is* nevertheless a human and economic cost.

On the other hand, it cannot be the case that workers do not *prefer* to enjoy their work, and it is unlikely that most do not also prefer autonomous, nonroutine, discretionary work within the bounds of their competences. One reason why they say they are satisfied with their work and do not express this preference is that they think of the alternative as unemployment. For example, compared to workers in prosperous areas, workers in depressed areas report *higher* job satisfaction.[22] The strictly work-for-pay "orientation toward work is quickly abandoned if intrinsic returns become more available: intrinsic rewards undermine the importance of extrinsic rewards."[23]

One cannot, therefore, accept at face value the claims of workers or their interpreters that workers are "satisfied" with extrinsic rewards. In any event, it is unclear how much of this indifference to "self-expression" there is to explain: 50 percent of a national sample of American workers said "that what they did at work was more important to them than the money they earned."[24] Hidden costs are certainly limited by the extrinsic work-for-pay orientation of many workers, but current expressions of satisfaction with purely extrinsic rewards must be discounted.

Socialization for extrinsic rewards.

Socialization for extrinsic rewards. If part of the problem is the lack of jobs with objectively intrinsic possibilities, another part is the source of the dispo-

---

[20] Herbert McClosky and John Zaller, *The American Ethos: Public Attitudes Toward Capitalism and Democracy* (Cambridge: Harvard University Press, 1984), Table 5.9.

[21] International Labor Office (ILO), *Payment by Results* (Geneva: International Labor Office, 1984), 29. Similarly, "repetitive, short-cycle work attracts those whose attitude to work is in fact instrumental." John H. Goldethorpe, David Lockwood, Frank Bechhofer, and Jennifer Platt, *The Affluent Worker: Industrial Attitudes and Behavior* (Cambridge, UK: Cambridge University Press, 1968). And, referring to manual workers in the Detroit automobile factories, Kornhauser reported: "When the working men were questioned about what they really want in life, their answers overwhelmingly specify financial and material goods. . . . There are strikingly few expressions of interest in personal achievement, self-development, and self-expressive activities." Arthur W. Kornhauser, *Mental Health of the Industrial Worker: A Detroit Study* (New York: Wiley, 1965), 268.

[22] Norman M. Bradburn and David Caplovitz, *Reports on Happiness* (Chicago: Aldine, 1965), 68. Professional and managerial employees did not reveal this improvement in work satisfaction because of the economic depression of their districts.

[23] Barry Gruenberg, "The Happy Worker: Determinants of Job Satisfaction," *American Journal of Sociology* 86 (1980): 247–71 at 269.

[24] Daniel Yankelovich et al., *The World at Work: An International Report on Human Values, Productivity and Its Future* (New York: Octagon, 1984), 322, reporting on data in Quinn and Staines, *Quality of Employment Survey, 1977.*

sitions and learned habits of the working class. Fisher and Pritchard found that intrinsic work motivation was partially dependent upon the worker having an initially high sense of personal control.[25] But, as we said, a sense of personal control has to be learned by the experience of acting and having the environment respond, an experience less frequent in the working class.[26] Income, indeed, is the best demographic predictor of the sense of personal control and level of parental income is an excellent predictor of intrinsic work values.[27] Neither family socialization nor the schooling of working-class children encourages self-determination or anticipation of intrinsically interesting jobs.[28]

Circumstances frustrating hidden costs

Where rewards are part of a contractual relation they do not incur hidden costs. Kruglanski compares the feelings of payer and payee when, on the one hand, the passenger pays a taxi driver for driving him to the airport, and, on the other, when a guest pays his host for driving him there. For taxi driver and passenger payment for services is, as Kruglanski says, *endogenous* to the activity, whereas both host and guest might feel uncomfortable in a payment for a friendly service; payment is *exogenous* to that relationship. Kruglanski tested his theory by comparing the effect of winning money in a coin-tossing game with "winning" money in amateur athletic contests; in the first case the intrinsic pleasure in the game was not reduced by money rewards, but in the second case it was reduced.[29] Similarly, Staw, Calder, and Hess found "an interaction of norms and payment such that the introduction of an extrinsic reward decreased intrinsic interest in a task *only when there existed a situational norm for no payment.*"[30] Across cultures there are

[25] Cynthia D. Fisher and Robert D. Pritchard, *Effects of Personal Control, Extrinsic Rewards, and Competence on Intrinsic Motivation.* U.S. Air Force Human Relations Laboratory, Technical Report no. 20 (July 1978), quoted in Richard Hall, *Dimensions of Work* (Beverly Hills, CA: Sage, 1986).

[26] "Developmental changes in perceptions of noncontingency, causal understanding, and expectations of future noncontingency are all likely to influence the process whereby children of different ages manifest learned helplessness." Frank D. Fincham and Kathleen M. Cain, "Learned Helplessness in Humans: A Developmental Analysis," *Developmental Review* 6 (1986): 310–33 at 301; see also John Condry and James Chambers, "Intrinsic Motivation and the Process of Learning," in Lepper and Greene, *The Hidden Costs of Rewards,* 72; and Lepper and Greene, "Overjustification Research and Beyond: Toward a Means–Ends Analysis of Intrinsic and Extrinsic Motivation," in Lepper and Greene, *The Hidden Costs of Rewards,* 131.

[27] For the relationship between income and personal control, see Gerald Gurin and Patricia Gurin, "Personal Efficacy and the Ideology of Individual Responsibility," in Burkhard Strumpel, ed., *Economic Means for Human Needs* (Ann Arbor, MI: Institute for Social Research, 1976). For evidence on the influence of parental income on occupational values, see J. T. Mortimer and J. Lorence, "Work Experience and Occupational Value Socialization: a Longitudinal Study," *American Journal of Sociology* 84 (1979): 1,361–85.

[28] Samuel Bowles and Herbert Gintis, *Schooling in Capitalist America: Educational Reform and the Contradictions of Economic Life* (New York: Basic Books, 1976).

[29] Arie W. Kruglanksi, "Endogenous Attribution and Intrinsic Motivation," in Lepper and Greene, *The Hidden Costs of Rewards.*

[30] Barry M. Staw, Bobby J. Calder, and R. Hess, "Intrinsic Motivation and Norms about Payment" (Working Paper, Northwestern University, 1975), reported in Staw, *Intrinsic and Extrinsic Motivation* (Morristown, NJ: General Learning Press, 1976), 16.

often similar interpretations of the kinds of things appropriately exchanged for money.[31]

Note how currencies differ in their exogenous status: Where money is not acceptable, deference and affection may be, and where these are exogenous, money may be the endogenous currency. When they are exogenous rewards, deference and affection will then seem to be controlling and exact hidden costs.

The market extends the boundaries of the endogenousness of money in many ways, as many as may be embraced by the centuries long drift from status to contract.

Who is controlling whom: a culture of job scarcity. Although there are variations, the basic process in transforming intrinsic interest into extrinsic, instrumental interest is simply construing "working *and* receiving pay" to mean "working *for* pay." The reasoning is not the fruit of logic or evidence, however, but of culture. For example, the causal attribution might be reversed: *They* are forced to pay *me* because I do a good job at work. If the level of pay is unimportant to me or if I have alternative employments, then *I* am in a position to control *them*.[32] Recall Marshall's statement reported in Chapter 14: A person's desire to work is measured "by the sum [of money] which is just required to induce him to undergo a certain fatigue." In Chapter 17 we noted the reverse of this version of the bargain: The worker "pays" the employer by yielding up just enough energy to induce the employer to pay "a certain amount of money." In the current work culture, the stereotype is of a shortage of work, not of workers. The construction is bound by the culture of work shortage: Where there are great labor shortages – divers on oil rigs, carpenters in a frontier boomtown, doctors in an epidemic – it is doubtful if monetary rewards would be construed as controlling.

Hidden costs are partly under management control. There is a difference in the degree of actual control authorities allow their subjects. Deci and associates examined the differences in responses between children taught by control-oriented teachers and by "teachers oriented toward supporting autonomy." Compared to the latter, the control-oriented teachers reduced the intrinsic motivation of children in their learning tasks – and also reduced their sense of self-esteem and their sense of internal control.[33] There are similar differences in the effects of employers' policies on workers' sense of self-determination: Cross-national studies show that American and Israeli management styles give their workers a greater sense of self-determination than do Austrian, or Italian, or even Yugoslavian styles.[34] Thus managers have

---

[31] Harry C. Triandis, "Culture Training, Cognitive Complexity, and Interpersonal Attitudes," in Richard W. Brislin, Stephen Brochner, and Walter J. Lonner, eds., *Cross-Cultural Perspectives on Learning* (New York: Halstead/Wiley, 1975).

[32] There are unverified reports about a science among rats based on the contingent reinforcement of humans to produce pellets whenever a rat presses a lever, and better reports of experiments where students conditioned their lecturers to move to the extreme left of the platform by apparently attending to the lectures only when the lecturers spoke from these leftward positions.

[33] Edward L. Deci, John Nezlek, and Louise Sheinman, "Characteristics of the Rewarder and Intrinsic Motivation of the Rewardee," *Journal of Personality and Social Psychology* 40 (1981): 24–30.

[34] Arnold S. Tannenbaum, Bogdan Kavcic, Menachem Rosner, Mino Vianello, and Georg Wieser, *Hierarchy in Organizations* (San Francisco: Jossey-Bass, 1974).

the power to mitigate the influence of hidden costs, or more generally to give to their workers the sense that a variety of important decisions regarding the shopfloor are within the control of workers themselves. After all, this was the situation in Kohn and Schooler's crucial study of what people learned at work (Chapter 13).

Management can pay for participation to reduce workers' sense of being controlled. To pay for intrinsically motivated work is to risk hidden costs, but to pay for other forms of "self-determination" in industrial enterprises seems to work fairly well, even though the idea of someone else paying for any individual's *self-determination* appears at first to be a contradiction. Thierry, defining participation as "giving employees, whose work . . . [is] affected by organizational decisions . . . , a say in one or more phases of the cycle of taking decisions," surveyed the various forms of participation in industrial enterprises and found, not unexpectedly, that participation increased with level of pay but also that paid participation, although not "always affecting performance," had the informational and motivational effects of *unpaid* participation. It appears that if self-determination cannot itself be bought, the participation that favors it can be increased by pay.[35]

Pay is often a successful motivator when not contingent on performance

Noncontingent rewards by themselves not only fail to produce hidden costs but may enhance performance. Pittman et al. found that compared to the contingently rewarded *and to the unrewarded* controls, those who were *rewarded irrespective of their performances* showed the greatest interest in more complex work on a second trial.[36] Here, pay gives almost no information on performance and offers only the loosest kind of control. By itself, then, noncontingent pay is very likely favorable to performance. Where rewards are free of any taint of contingency, they do not incur hidden costs, a fact that has led one commentator to suggest: "Wages could be paid noncontingently to attract people to the job and keep them satisfied, and then [within the firm] intrinsic factors would be the dominant motivators."[37]

Unanticipated payments do not incur hidden costs. Payment by itself seems not to incur hidden costs. This point is most clearly shown in an experiment where the subjects were their own controls. Kruglanski and associates used deception to make the point, as follows: (1) Without prior notice the experimenters paid subjects

---

[35] Henk Thierry, "Rewarding Participation," in *Sonderdruk aus Betriebswirtschaftliche Forschung und Praxis*, vol. 1 (Berlin: Verlag Neue Wirtschafts-Brief, 1986), 2–15. Like Thierry, Vanderslice et al. found that participation increased satisfaction but could find no effect on productivity. Virginia J. Vanderslice, Robert W. Rice, and James W. Julian, "The Effects of Participation in Decision-Making on Worker Satisfaction and Productivity: An Organizational Simulation," *Journal of Applied Social Psychology* 17 (1987): 158–70.

[36] Thane S. Pittman, Jolee Emery, and Ann K. Boggiano, "Intrinsic and Extrinsic Motivational Orientations: Reward-Induced Changes in Preference for Complexity," *Journal of Personality and Social Psychology* 42 (1982): 789–97, emphasis added.

[37] Deci, *Intrinsic Motivation*, 227. Because people are vulnerable to "the illusion of control," they will interpret their acts as controlling even if they must distort the facts to do so. See Ellen J. Langer, *The Psychology of Control* (Beverly Hills, CA: Sage, 1983).

after they had completed their experimental tasks; (2) this post hoc payment in no way affected the subjects' attitudes toward their task, willingness to volunteer, or intrinsic interest in their work; (3) the experimenters then persuaded subjects that they had, in fact, been told *in advance* of the proposed payment; (4) whereupon subjects reinterpreted their early feelings about their intrinsic interests, downgrading the tasks.[38] This is powerful proof of the way payments interpreted as *contingent* on performance undermine intrinsic enjoyment of work. But since payment by itself does not have this undermining effect – where wages, or more likely salaries, lose this contingent connection in the context of habitual payments – payment for market work will not incur these hidden costs.

Summary

The implications for market economics of an incentive system that not only denies the value of pay but claims that it *reduces* motivation are fundamental and corrosive. They are best viewed both as cautions against glib assumptions of the pay maximization hypothesis and as glimpses into the effects of intrinsic motivation, even without further reliance on the hidden cost mechanism. The hidden cost threat to the market, however, is undermined by the following considerations:

Where pay is interpreted as information rather than control, the sense that pay undermines self-determination is greatly weakened.

At least two intrinsic motives other than self-determination override the effects of hidden costs: a desire for achievement, interpreted as pride in excellence, and feelings of equity – the latter working against the overjustification source of hidden costs in a manner that leads people to work harder when they feel they are being exceptionally well paid.

The perception that the work is self-chosen undermines the effects of hidden costs – and the market facilitates this perception.

For hidden costs to operate, the desire for intrinsic rewards must be salient – and the market dampens this desire undermining the effects of hidden costs. In this respect, the social preparation of working populations for a life of extrinsic rewards is supportive of the market's reliance on this kind of reward.

Intrinsic work satisfaction and money rewards are compatible and hedonically additive in situations where making money is so intimately connected with the very nature of the job (endogenous) that intrinsic work enjoyment involves making money. In this respect, the market undermines hidden cost effects by making so much of life endogenous to money payments.

Where the contingent relation of rewards to performance is veiled or very loose, the rewards will not seem to be controlling and hidden costs will be avoided. This is the corollary of the basic principle: The more obvious it is to workers that their "engagement in the activity [is] *a means to some extrinsic goal*," the less interest and affection do they have for the activity itself.[39] On the other hand, it is the

---

[38] Arie W. Kruglanski, S. Alon, and T. Lewis, "Retrospective Misattribution and Task Enjoyment," *Journal of Experimental Social Psychology* 8 (1972): 493–501, reported in Lepper and Greene, "Overjustification Research and Beyond," 116–17.

[39] Lepper and Greene, "Overjustification Research and Beyond," 116, emphasis added.

essence of market exchange that with the same act of exchange, the market "apportions tasks [control] through the apportionment of rewards";[40] the market cannot therefore avoid, though it may attempt to conceal, the controlling aspect of pay.

Where the main reward is reputation, as among scientists, or affection, as in gemeinschaft and family relations, money rewards will seem to be less controlling.

Reinforcement theory is valid: "A reward's protracted association with an activity promotes the development of positive affect toward that activity."[41]

When pay is interpreted as informational feedback rather than as control, extrinsic rewards fail to extract hidden costs. As mentioned, price is both information and control; market effects therefore are ambiguous.

The sense that pay is controlling is not inherent in the wage bargain, but rather is a partial artifact of the high ratio of applicants to jobs. The labor market's chronic state of underemployment of labor is an important source of this artifact; where jobs are plentiful, there are fewer, if any, hidden costs.

The conversion of extrinsic to intrinsic rewards (reversing hidden costs and applying the principles of *under*justification) also follows from the increased liking for an object or an activity when it becomes familiar,[42] and from the reverse operation of Allport's functional autonomy of motives: Disliked activities initially undertaken purely for their instrumental value become intrinsically attractive when the skills involved are learned.

We shrank the world of hidden cost to a rather small, though still important, sphere within the market economy. That sphere casts a reflected light on many of those malaises that surface with various names from time to time: *acidie*, apathy, alienation, anomie, inner migration of the soul. Often these are various expressions of the loss of intrinsic work satisfaction and failed opportunities to express intrinsic motivations of the kinds described.

[40] Frank Knight, *Risk, Uncertainty, and Profits* (1921; reprint Chicago: University of Chicago Press, 1971), 56.
[41] S. Reiss and L. W. Sushinsky, "Overjustification, Competing Responses, and the Acquisition of Intrinsic Interest," *Journal of Social Psychology* 31 (1975): 1,116–25.
[42] Robert B. Zajonc, "Attitudinal Effects of Mere Exposure," *Journal of Personality and Social Psychology* 9 (1968): Monograph Supplement, Pt 2, 1–27.

20 Intrinsic values: a balance sheet

Whereas the intrinsic domain challenges the market's central concept of exchange, it is the darling of humanist thought. The humanist devotion to the intrinsic flows from a philosophy of individualism and freedom that prizes self-determination, autonomy, the dignity of man. This philosophy embraces an approach to life that emphasizes the value of things in themselves, of *being,* as contrasted to *doing,* of appreciation as contrasted to performance. In this approach it is right that individuals should be guided more by self-rewards than external rewards that make them dependent on their environments. As in aesthetics and ethics and the contemplative religions, a special value is placed on the intrinsic, without reference to costs, causes, or consequences.

But in a social *system,* it is impossible to value things in themselves and to avoid dependence on the environment; everything has costs, causes, and consequences both for the self and the society. From a social scientific approach the idea of the intrinsic seems ghostly – a quality, substance, or state that is valued in itself without reference to its effects on the individual or society. In the previous chapter we sought to explain how this antieconomic quality could be accounted for; here we examine its effects or consequences.

The first of these sets of probable consequences is wholly benign; it is amazing to see the positive correlates (and probable consequences) of intrinsic work enjoyment. And as we move on to question its effects on learning and to the stimulation of creativity, the results are also favorable to the intrinsic. But then the balance changes as a closer examination shows the moral, social, and psychological deficiencies of intrinsic value of work, the way this value displaces other values and, in the end, the risks of so hedonistic an approach to value.

Benign consequences of intrinsic work satisfaction

Associated benefits

Mental and physical health. Compared to others, the person who has learned self-directed values and enjoys the intrinsic satisfaction of work is more likely to have better physical and mental health[1] and to live longer.[2] Inasmuch as an individual's ill health is a social cost (through its effect on insurance premiums and lost manpower), we might say society also benefits from the contribution that intrinsi-

---

[1] Robert Karasek, Bertil Gardell, and Jan Lindell, "Work and Nonwork Correlates of Illness and Behavior in Male and Female Swedish White Collar Workers," *Journal of Occupational Behavior* 8 (1987): 187–207.

[2] L. E. Hinkle, Jr., et al., "Occupation, Education and Coronary Heart Disease," *Science* 161 (1968): 238–46.

cally motivated work makes to each person's good health. Since those who enjoy their work are also less likely than others to have drinking problems,[3] there is an additional social and personal gain from intrinsic pleasures at work.

Contributing to others' enjoyment of work. "Job satisfaction tends to increase among members of occupations in which the average level of intrinsic satisfaction is high, irrespective of the individual's level of [intrinsic] satisfaction. . . . To be among workers who derive pleasure from their work has an independently enhancing effect on one's own job assessment."[4] Beyond job satisfaction is (again) group mental health: The "quality of the social environment [measured by coworkers' estimates of their own sense of well-being] is related to the mental health of employees," reducing depression and anxiety.[5] Laugh and the world laughs with you; weep and you weep alone.

The support of "high" culture. We know (Chapter 13) that the set of things associated with intrinsic satisfaction (challenge, discretion, self-direction) actually contributes to the use of leisure time in intellectually more demanding ways. The major determinant of cultural tastes, of course, is education and especially parental tastes, but to some minor extent, the support of high culture derives from this "spillover" from work of a preference for intellectually challenging leisure forms.

Socialization of children in work culture or money culture? Many people "take their work home with them." In a minor (though statistically significant) way, people who enjoy the actual process of working are more likely than others to talk about their work at dinner.[6] The matter is probably little different in centrally planned economies.[7] One alternative, talking about money at home, has the effect of making the children "money conscious." Later, as adults, "such people are least likely to be involved in a satisfactory love relationship. . . . They also tend to be sexually unsatisfied, report worsening health, and almost half of them are troubled by constant worry, anxiety, and loneliness."[8] Taking work home may or may not add to family enjoyment,[9] but if favorable talk about work at home makes children

---

[3] Richard H. Hall, *Dimensions of Work* (Beverly Hills, CA: Sage, 1986), 110.

[4] Barry Gruenberg, "The Happy Worker: An Analysis of Educational and Occupational Differences in Determinants of Job Satisfaction," *American Journal of Sociology* 86 (1980): 247–71 at 269.

[5] Rena L. Repetti, "Individual and Common Components of the Social Environment at Work and Psychological Well-Being," *Journal of Personality and Social Psychology* 52 (1987): 710–20 at 710.

[6] F. Thomas Juster, "Preferences for Work and Leisure," in Juster and Frank P. Stafford, eds., *Time, Goods, and Well-Being* (Ann Arbor, MI: Institute for Social Research, 1985), 347.

[7] Aleksandra Jasinska and Renata Siemienska, "The Socialist Personality: A Case Study of Poland," *International Journal of Sociology* 13 (1983): 3–87 at 46–7. These authors do not report on talking about work at home, but they point out that "60 percent of the workers studied in 1974 said that they often thought about their work in their spare time, 32 percent said that they thought about it sometimes, and only 8 percent said they did not think of work after hours." Of these thoughts more were "practical and businesslike," one-third were pleasant, and one-tenth were unpleasant.

[8] Carin Rubenstein, "Money and Self-Esteem, Relationships, Secrecy, Envy, Satisfaction," *Psychology Today* 15 (May 1981): 29–44 at 42.

[9] For a discussion of the relation between work and family life, see Rosabeth Moss Kanter, *Work and*

work conscious, rather than money conscious – with its destructive effects – this spillover of intrinsic interest in work offers benefits to children and a bonus to the worker: pride in children inducted into the work milieu on more favorable terms.

Reciprocal relationship between intrinsic work satisfaction and life satisfaction. Overall life satisfaction and enjoyment of one's work must each contribute to the other, but which causal direction is the more important? In order to answer this question, Chacko employed methods that indicate causal directions; he found that "job satisfaction has a greater influence on life or nonwork satisfaction than vice versa and [the findings] are consistent with research indicating that work attitudes and experiences are major determinants of nonwork behaviors and attitudes."[10]

A good that prolongs a healthy life, contributes to the work enjoyment of others, supports (however tangentially) high culture, helps to socialize children in a work rather than a money culture, and contributes to life satisfaction is a good worth cultivating.

Learning and the intrinsic

Intrinsic motivation facilitates learning in many ways: Curiosity is the exemplar for discussion of the biological foundations of intrinsically rewarding activities[11] – and curiosity is the foundation of learning. Intrinsic motivation has been found to facilitate creativity. For educators, intrinsic motivation is the preferred motive and a sense of *mastery* and of excellence are the preferred rewards: "Children are intrinsically motivated to learn; they want to understand themselves and the world around them; they want to feel effective in dealing with their environment." Extrinsic rewards discourage this intrinsic desire to learn.[12] From the beginning to the end, intrinsic motivation is regarded as superior to the extrinsic: "At each stage of the learning process, self-initiation, self-direction, self-disengagement, and later self-interest in returning to the activity are diminished in the extrinsic context when compared to the intrinsic context."[13]

Learning from extrinsic motivation, as in the token economies, is situationally specific and ceases when no longer rewarded. As we saw in Chapter 17, after removal of the reward in the token economies, there was a rapid return to the kinds of behavior prevailing before the tokens were instituted and there was almost no generalization to other situations of the behavioral patterns followed when re-

---

Family in the United States (New York: Russell Sage, 1977). Juster found no relation between his measures of process benefits and overall life satisfaction; the relation reported in the text must be regarded as tentative until this relationship is clarified. See F. Thomas Juster and Paul N. Courant, "Integrating Stocks and Flows in Quality of Life Research," in Frank M. Andrews, ed., *Research on the Quality of Life* (Ann Arbor, MI: Institute for Social Research, 1986), 165.

[10] Thomas I. Chacko, "Job and Life Satisfaction: A Causal Analysis of Their Relationships," *Academy of Management Journal* 26 (1983): 163–9 at 163.

[11] Dan E. Berlyne, *Conflict, Arousal, and Curiosity* (New York: McGraw-Hill, 1960).

[12] Edward L. Deci, *Intrinsic Motivation* (New York: Plenum Press, 1975), 210.

[13] John Condry and James Chambers, "Intrinsic Motivation and the Process of Learning," in Mark R. Lepper and David Greene, eds., *The Hidden Costs of Rewards: New Perspectives on the Psychology of Human Motivation* (Hillsdale, NJ: Wiley/Erlbaum, 1978), 75.

warded. Learning under the stimulus of intrinsic motivation is much more likely to generalize to other situations because the learning is initiated and maintained by the self; what one has learned, then, is one's own.[14] Nor will the behavior cease with the cessation of the reward, for the reward is the feeling of competence and self-determination that satisfies a motive regarded as insatiable – if not prepotent all the time.

The intrinsically motivated, when they have successfully completed a task, choose subsequent tasks more complex than those chosen by the extrinsically motivated.[15] They exercise their minds rather than filling their purses. Drawing on the Breer and Locke experiments, for example, showing that working on cooperative tasks generalized to make workers see the world as a cooperative place and competitive tasks induced perceptions of a competitive world (Chapter 13), we see how the reward of a sense of self-determination following an intrinsically motivated task is likely to lead to an ideology whose actors are self-determining.

Further, in searching for "the solution to the mystery," rather than simply "seeking for an answer,"[16] the intrinsically motivated search for an understanding of what they are doing; as Ruskin said of the craftsman who has been taught to understand the principles of his work, "You have made a man of him. . . . He was only a machine before, an animated tool."[17]

So much may be said of the contribution of intrinsic motivation to life and learning. What, then, may also be said of those who go to night school in their pursuit of promotions and higher salaries, of the high school teachers who seek a master's degree to increase their salaries, and the secretaries who learn business management after hours? Is it not the genetic fallacy to discount this learning because of its genesis in a desire for extrinsic rewards? And given the principles of the *functional autonomy of motives* pointing out that the original motive is often not the final one, should we not anticipate an accretion of intrinsic motivation when a basic skill is learned under the stimulus of extrinsic rewards? It may well be true that intrinsic and extrinsic satisfactions "are sometimes not additive," but that may merely mean that they are sequential, that is, the state of mind that resents payment of enjoyable tasks as a method of control may wane once the skills required for tasks for which a person was paid have been learned.[18] Schools, too, often find that working for grades produces perverse incentives that change as students learn the skills that were

---

[14] On the use of self-monitoring and self-imposed standards, see Albert Bandura, "Self-Efficacy: Toward a Unifying Theory of Behavioral Change," *Psychological Review* 84 (1977): 191–215; on the lack of experimental evidence for believing that intrinsic motivation generalizes, see Mark R. Lepper and David Greene, "Divergent Approaches to the Study of Rewards," in Lepper and Greene, *The Hidden Costs of Rewards,* 226.

[15] Thane S. Pittman, Jolee Emery, and Ann K. Boggiano, "Intrinsic and Extrinsic Motivational Orientations: Reward-Induced Changes in Preference for Complexity," *Journal of Personality and Social Psychology* 42 (1982): 789–97.

[16] Condry and Chambers, "Intrinsic Motivation and the Process of Learning," 69.

[17] John Ruskin, *The Stones of Venice,* vol. 2 in Kenneth Clark, ed., *Ruskin Today* (Harmondsworth, UK: Penguin, 1982), 282.

[18] See Albert Bandura and Dale H. Schunk, "Cultivating Competence, Self-Efficacy, and Intrinsic Interest Through Proximal Self-Motivation," *Journal of Personality and Social Psychology* 41 (1981): 586–98.

rewarded;[19] as Bandura points out, "Most of the things that people enjoy doing for their own sake originally had no reinforcing value."[20] On life's larger stage extrinsic rewards for knowing more do prompt important forms of learning.

Do they also contribute to the cognitive complexity that makes complex learning possible (Chapter 3)?

Cognitive complexity and intrinsic motivation. Rational calculation has been associated with monetary rewards but it is the intrinsically rewarding tasks and the people drawn to them that seem to be more adequately characterized as cognitively complex. There was a strong association between the self-directed work that makes work intrinsically enjoyable and cognitive complexity in Kohn and Schooler's research discussed in Chapter 13. And in Chapter 18 we learned from the hidden cost experiments how people interested in the tasks, as contrasted to those who were interested in rewards, learned more about the work itself, were more open to peripheral cues, and were more likely to pursue these cognitive interests once the task was completed. Conversely, those pursuing money or other external rewards seemed to proceed under more cognitively simple rules. In comparison to intrinsic motivation, material "interests" may be said to be *less* under the guidance of cognition and *more* vulnerable to a "simple" pattern of responding to a presenting money stimulus. This simplicity is more apparent than real, but compared to the evidence of learning where the rewards are intrinsic, learning from extrinsic rewards is, indeed, less complex.[21]

In a brilliant analysis Hirschman reviewed the reinterpretation of avarice from a "passion" to a cognitively controlled "interest" as an intellectual preparation for capitalism. With the discovery that money motivation is often less rational (i.e., yields less utility than intrinsically motivated work) and proceeds from cognitively simpler understandings, "the passions and the interests" have now reversed themselves in the presence of intrinsic work motivation. This is so because the *interests,* which the theory identified with money, seem more stimulus bound, and the *passion* for self-determination that makes self-determined work even more valuable than money is more cognitively complex. (Or at least with a little semantic sleight of hand, we can see the problem that way.)

---

[19] Three sociologists lived among their students, like anthropologists in an alien tribe, and found that these students had developed the most refined calculations for maximizing their grade point averages at minimum effort, quite irrespective of what they learned. The students understood all too well that life rewards, such as acceptance at their preferred law schools, were distributed for high grade point averages – and not for intrinsic love of learning. Howard S. Becker, Blanche Geer, and Everett Hughes, *Making the Grade: The Academic Side of College Life* (New York: Wiley, 1968). But, as we understand the term, they got an education.

[20] Albert Bandura, *Social Learning Theory* (Englewood Cliffs, NJ: Prentice-Hall, 1977), 106.

[21] This characterization of avarice as relatively more simple than responses to motives for self-determination is almost certainly a true characterization of much economic behavior, but it is not an explanation, and references to theories of stimulus response behavior tell us little about the complexities involved. Recall from Chapter 1 the discussion of the seeming simplicity but actual complexity of the Basic Economic Sequence (BES), the calculations involved in any straightforward avaricious behavior. And recall further the complexity of money symbolism discussed in Chapter 6.

Creativity, productivity, and intrinsic work motivation

In general, like job satisfaction,[22] intrinsic work satisfaction has no close relations with productivity, although that kind of intrinsic satisfaction dependent on the pursuit of excellence very likely does.[23] In summarizing a variety of findings, including those dealing with intrinsic satisfaction, Richard Hall says, "Seeking productivity gains through improving job satisfaction would be a mistake."[24]

Research on motivating workers to higher productivity in the short term usually finds that extrinsic rewards are the best motivators.[25] An apostle of the intrinsic, E. L. Deci says: "The introduction of extrinsic rewards often improves performance. . . . So, if one is primarily interested in performance and is not concerned with intrinsic motivation, then extrinsic reward systems, if properly administered, may be quite effective," especially, he adds, "on a one-shot basis."[26]

But where creativity is desired, intrinsic rewards are usually necessary. McGraw makes the distinction between, on the one hand, tasks where an *algorithm* (a set of rules for calculation) is useful, for example, in serial learning, paired associative learning, and perceptual recognition, and, on the other hand, those tasks where a *heuristic* (a model serving to stimulate investigation) is needed, for example, in concept formation and problem solving. There are no hidden costs in algorithmic tasks for there is no intrinsic motivation, but there are many in tasks guided by heuristics. The point is made by Glucksberg's experiment. He devised two versions of the same basic problem: In the heuristic-type task, inventing a candle platform from a matchbox and thumbtacks, the task took imagination and inventive skill and, when rewarded, produced hidden costs. In a much simpler version of this same task where the matchbox was emptied and placed on the table in such a way as to suggest its use, there were no hidden costs because there was no challenge. Routine tasks that can be achieved by following a formula or algorithm lack the challenge necessary to incur hidden costs of rewards, and payment in these cases will motivate people without eroding creativity – for there is no creativity involved. Where creativity is required and the latitude of a heuristic provides the guiding principles, payment reduces creativity, thus incurring hidden costs.[27]

Protecting creative occupations from hidden costs. Scientists, artists, and writers all seek payment for their work, of course, without any apparent loss of their creativity. This seems to create a wide hole in the theory of hidden costs. Because

[22] Victor H. Vroom, *Work and Motivation* (New York: Wiley, 1964); D. C. Cherington, *The Work Ethic* (New York: AMACOM, 1980).

[23] See Edward E. Lawler, III, and Lyman W. Porter, "The Effects of Performance on Job Satisfaction," *Industrial Relations* 7 (1967): 20–8.

[24] Hall, *Dimensions of Work*, 92–3.

[25] See, for example, F. A. Locke, D. B. Feren, V. M. McCaleb, K. N. Shaw, and A. T. Denny, "The Relative Effectiveness of Four Methods of Motivating Employee Performance," in K. D. Duncan, M. M. Gruenberg, and D. Wallis, eds., *Changes in Working Life* (Chichester, UK: Wiley, 1980).

[26] Deci, *Intrinsic Motivation*, 207, 208.

[27] S. Glucksberg, "Problem Solving: Response Competition and the Influence of Drive," *Psychological Reports* 63 (1962): 36–41, reported in Kenneth O. McGraw, "The Detrimental Effects of Reward on Performance: A Literature Review and a Prediction Model," in Lepper and Greene, *The Hidden Costs of Rewards*, 54.

hidden costs apply largely to creative tasks, we would expect these tasks to be most vulnerable to such costs. The reason these creative tasks do not suffer is that they are protected by several features of their situations. Take the case of scientists: In the first place, their salaries are rarely contingent on their discoveries or inventions. Also, for academic scientists, at least, "the substantive findings are a product of collaboration and are assigned to the community" rather than to the scientists themselves.[28] Furthermore, scientists receive payment in a currency not dependent upon their financial paymasters, *recognition;* they are independent of their paymasters (but not of their colleagues or journal referees). And finally, this extrinsic reward of recognition is, or may be, interpreted as information, feedback endogenous to their calling, not as control (Chapter 19). It is for these reasons, among others, that scientists report no relationship between amount of control over their jobs and intrinsic motivation.[29]

But in an age when creative application of the principles of science moves rapidly to engineered invention and then to more mundane tasks on the shopfloor, the need for creativity diffuses downward in the job hierarchy.[30] Working just for pay then will stifle creativity. Quite irrespective of the theory of hidden costs, identification with *pay* instead of the *work* itself erodes not only work enjoyment but also the productivity of manufacturing and commercial enterprises.

Moral, social, and psychological deficiencies

The incidental and systematic benefits of intrinsically motivated work must be balanced against certain countervailing deficiencies.

1. INTRINSIC WORK SATISFACTION IS SELF-CENTERED. The beneficiary of intrinsic satisfaction is the worker himself or herself; neither community nor family directly shares the benefits. The rewards of intrinsic motivation, feelings of competence and self-determination, cannot be divided with others, exchanged, or given to one's children. Although it may be true that the happy creative worker is a better community and family member, the argument is morally weak, for its message is: Make me happy and I will be better to you. Moral appeals where the benefits to others are entirely externalities to the self lose their moral value. We know of no hidden hand that makes beneficial to society those things sought by intrinsic motives; to paraphrase an eighteenth-century moral philosopher: "It is not from the intrinsic motivation of the butcher, the brewer, or the baker, that we expect our dinner." In contrast, pursuit of that paramount extrinsic good, money, yields rewards that *can* be shared with others, given to children or, as Marshall pointed out, to philanthropies, or exchanged for something else – where exchange is reciprocally beneficial. And there is evidence that in this case the hidden hand does contribute to social wealth that others may share.

[28] Robert K. Merton, *Social Theory and Social Structure*, rev. ed. (New York: Free Press, 1968), 610–12.
[29] Edward E. Lawler and D. T. Hall, "Relationship of Job Characteristics to Job Involvement, Satisfaction, and Intrinsic Motivation," *Journal of Applied Psychology* 54 (1970): 305–12.
[30] Warren G. Bennis and Philip E. Slater, *The Temporary Society* (New York: Harper Colophon, 1969).

2. THERE ARE NO INSTITUTIONALIZED CONSTRUCTS FOR INTRINSIC SATISFAC-
TION. In the market one person's extrinsic interest serves to check another's, thus
limiting the fruits of his or her own avarice to the individual. This is the purpose of
competition and the hidden hand. One consequence is the reduced necessity of
overt, public control. But intrinsic motivation and its satisfaction have no such
social machinery for regulation; rather the regulators must be internal, the internal
rewards and punishments that social learning theory proposes: rewards of pride or
punishments of shame, a good or bad conscience, a sense of achievement or of
failure. If these features of "character" fail, however, public agencies or public
opinion must take over the job. My decision to be self-determining may conflict
with your decision to be self-determining, and without a market in these commodities, government must reconcile our conflicting interests.

3. INTRINSIC SATISFACTIONS MAY TAKE UGLY FORMS. If intrinsically motivated
activities are defined as those "for which there is no apparent reward except the
activity itself . . . [or] behaviors which a person engages in to feel competent and
self-determining," then vendettas, acts of racial intolerance, masculine chauvin-
ism, and self-aggrandizement must stand alongside puzzle solving as intrinsically
motivated activities. The need for power has the same footing as the need for
achievement. In the sphere of work, bureaucrats have been found to enjoy their
work more and to feel more competent (in control of their own fates) when they
follow the rules irrespective of the consequences.[31] There is nothing in the reference
to those self-rewards making an activity intrinsically satisfying that says the self-
rewards are benign.

4. THE SOCIAL VALUE OF EXCHANGED GOODS CONFLICTS WITH THE SOCIAL VALUE
OF INTRINSIC GOODS. Knight pointed out that making something that would sell
was no guarantee of its moral value,[32] but at least it has the value that someone else
wanted the item. Enjoying one's work does not even have that value.

5. INTRINSIC MOTIVATION RELIES ON A WEAK THEORY OF ATTRIBUTION. For
cognitive psychologists, the usual attribution of cause to individuals, instead of to
circumstances, in most situations is a "fundamental attribution error" to which we
are prone, perhaps, because of our need to believe in intrinsic motivation.[33] And
B. F. Skinner, the apostle of the extrinsic, tells us:

We recognize a person's dignity when we give him credit for what he has done. . . . If we
do not know why a person acts as he does, we attribute his behavior to him. . . . We admire
people to the extent that we cannot explain what they do. . . . What may be called the
literature of dignity is concerned with preserving credit.[34]

But, he says, it is all an illusion because the causes of behavior are extrinsic to the
individual. Without accepting Skinner's learning theory, we may still believe that

[31] See, for example, Samuel Bacharach and Michael Aiken, "The Impact of Alienation, Meaninglessness, and Meritocracy on Supervisor and Subordinate Satisfaction," *Social Forces* 57 (1979): 853–70.
[32] Frank Knight, *The Ethics of Competition and Other Essays* (New York: Augustus Kelley, 1935).
[33] See E. E. Jones and R. E. Nisbett, "The Actor and the Observer: Divergent Perceptions of the Causes
of Behavior," in E. E. Jones, D. E. Kanouse, H. H. Kelley, R. E. Nisbett, S. Valens, and B. Weiner,
eds., *Attribution: Perceiving the Causes of Behavior* (Morristown, NJ: General Learning Press, 1972).
[34] B. F. Skinner, *Beyond Freedom and Dignity* (New York: Bantam/Vintage, 1972), 55.

the apotheosis of the intrinsic stems partly from our desire that it should be so, and perhaps partly from a historical thrust to emancipate humankind from divine control. Kenneth Burke says: "Humanists assign to man an *inherent* or *intrinsic* dignity, whereas supernaturalists assign to man a *derived* dignity. Any motive humanistically postulated in the agent would be a *causa sui* insofar as it is not derived from any cause itself."[35] *Causa sui* in the self implies personal control, but no one claims that personal control is an uncaused cause. That is an epistemological monstrosity, the end of inquiry itself.

6. SELF-DETERMINATION IS SOUGHT THROUGH WEALTH. There is a market route to feelings of control quite independent of the route through self-directed tasks. Two British psychologists observe: "Wealth is (quite correctly) seen as the basis of economic independence."[36] Thus, one cannot appropriate the desire for feeling competent and self-determining only to the work experience, for it has an alternative expression in the pursuit of money. Indeed, one wonders at the short-sightedness of workers (if there are any) who pursue self-determination at work without considering how they and their families will be self-determining in life outside of work. Surely a rational Life Plan is not so limited. The meaning of material self-interest changes when it becomes a proxy for the desire for competence and self-determination.

Both the market and intrinsic motivation, where it has not been inhibited by hidden costs, express and rely upon the value of self-determination. As we have seen, intrinsic motivation often depends for its reward upon the feeling that the motivated individual is personally in control of his or her own work and is responsible for its perfection. And as the advocates of the market explain, the purpose of the market is not only to maximize wealth but to free each individual for the pursuit of his or her own happiness in his or her own way. The implied contradiction – the market encourages people to maximize their own happiness in their own ways but deprives them through hidden cost of a feeling of self-determination at work – is paradoxical, for it seems that the market thus encourages self-determination by voluntary work but threatens self-determination by fulfilling the contract in paying its workers. The paradox is resolved by our understanding that everyone freely makes contracts of which some feature is unpleasantly constraining: Both the free choice and the experience of constraint are real.

If intrinsic work satisfaction suffers from its apparent selfishness, lack of institutions for resolving conflicts, lack of any inherent goodness, uncertain usefulness to society, weak psychological basis, and apparent ignorance of the prudential concern for independence outside the workplace, it may also suffer by comparison with other values foregone. Inherent satisfaction in working activities themselves may have opportunity costs that are too high. Economists would say that this is true because of the lack of relationship between work satisfaction and productivity, but when this important point is allowed, there may be other values given up as well. We turn to these in the following section.

[35] Kenneth Burke, *A Grammar of Motives* (Berkeley: University of California Press, 1969), 50.
[36] Peter Kelvin and Joanna E. Jarrett, *Unemployment: Its Social Psychological Effects* (Cambridge, UK: Cambridge University Press, 1985), 104.

Intrinsic work satisfaction: the conflict with three other values

The important conflicts between intrinsic motivation and economic productivity will be treated in Chapter 21; here we turn to three of the less familiar conflicts: distribution of intrinsic rewards and selected concepts of justice, deferred versus immediate gratification, and the conflict between the expression of one's personality and the constraining demands of social institutions, a conflict referred to as the *personality–environmental fit*. We will find genuine sacrifices in catering to hidden costs, and genuine risks in failing to do so.

Justice problems in distributing positive work utilities

We understand fairly well the justice problems of distributing income and wealth and the difficulties markets have in satisfying many of the justice criteria suggested for these distributions.[37] Although it may seem that the distribution of any good follows similar lines of argument and counterargument, there are certain differences in the matter of intrinsic work enjoyment that deserve attention.

Substantively, it is impossible to distribute *satisfaction* – only the goods and opportunities that yield satisfaction. In the labor market where workers are free to choose, there is poor information on quality of work life, the default values of money are strong, family benefits flow from money but not for intrinsic satisfaction, and the strength of anxiety about security are often dominant (Part VII). Thus, the labor market only partially reflects the relative values of intrinsically enjoyable work and money.[38]

In the hope of finding cues within two forms of justice, we turn to each of them briefly.

Justice of equality. Money has the great virtue that within equal income brackets, subjective equality of satisfaction is facilitated. Since there is no similar way of distributing jobs equally to achieve equal satisfaction, except perhaps by some auction that paid no attention to skill or merit, this device is ruled out.[39] In any event, to look to a free market for outcome equality is to look in vain.

Empirical evidence cannot give us the right principle, but it can suggest the magnitude of the problem. Two opposite kinds of findings reveal the dilemma: First, subjective well-being is, in general, more equally distributed than is income. This is because of the low correlation of income to overall subjective well-being and the contribution of nonmarket domains to this sense of well-being. Between 1957 and

[37] For an overview, see John Chapman and Roland Pennock, eds., *Markets and Justice*, NOMOS 31 (New York: New York University Press, 1989); Robert E. Lane, "Market Justice, Political Justice," *American Political Science Review* 80 (1986): 383–402. In the postwar period Rawls, Sen, Nozick, Ackerman, Dworkin, Rae, Walzer, Rescher, Goodin, Barry, Hayek, Thurow, Okun, and many others have treated market justice in a variety of ways.

[38] Christopher Jencks, Lauri Perman, and Lee Rainwater, "What Is a Good Job? A New Measure of Labor-Market Success," *American Journal of Sociology* 93 (1988): 1,322–57; Daniel Yankelovich and John Immerwahr, *Putting the Work Ethic to Work* (New York: Public Agenda Foundation, 1983).

[39] For discussion of the auction device see Ronald Dworkin, "What is Equality? Part 1, Equality of Welfare," *Philosophy and Public Affairs* 10 (1981): 185–246.

1978 this relatively greater equality of "happiness" increased.[40] Put epigrammatically, people are less unhappy than they are poor and less happy than they are rich.

But second, the distribution of intrinsic enjoyment of one's work is reversed. For example, a measure of the value of (largely) nonmonetary characteristics associated with "good jobs," including autonomy, and lack of repetitiveness, finds that the overall inequality for these (largely) intrinsic goods is 2.8 times as great as earnings inequality alone.[41] Whereas happiness is *more* equally distributed than income, intrinsic work enjoyment is *less* so. The relation between income equality and the equality of intrinsic work satisfaction borrows the market's inegalitarian tendencies and magnifies it. The failure of the labor market to provide adequate information on the features of work that contribute to intrinsic work satisfaction merely exacerbates a more fundamental problem.

The justice of need is irrelevant to ordinary market distributions, but the justice of deserts, or equity, as it is called in psychology, is directed relevant.

Justice and equity. Let us suppose that justice requires us to offer intrinsic work enjoyment on the same principles as income, which is thought to be a surrogate measure of consumer enjoyment. In that case we would turn to the justice of deserts (or equity or proportionality): to each according to his or her contribution. In the current market arrangement we can define *contribution* as contribution to profit at the margin, or marginal productivity. But we cannot use this as the criterion for distributing intrinsic rewards because to do so would be to subvert the purpose of intrinsic enjoyment of work.

Could we, instead, say that a person *deserves* intrinsic rewards to the extent that he or she contributes to the intrinsic rewards of work of others – on the grounds that "we have no more right to consume happiness without producing it than to consume wealth without producing it?"[42] By good fortune, that obligation seems to take care of itself; as mentioned, "to be among workers who derive pleasure from their work has an independently enhancing effect on one's own job assessment."[43] One person's intrinsic satisfaction radiates to others, making the benefit to others a by-product of one's own selfishness – the very definition of the workings of a hidden hand, a hand well hidden in connection with the distribution of intrinsic rewards up to this point.

But the hidden hand is not the servant of the justice of deserts, since intentions, rather than consequences, often serve as the grounds for the justice of deserts. Inadvertently making people happy is unlikely to qualify. And because the benefits to others are such a small fraction of the benefits to the self, even consequential justice might not apply. Serendipity is not justice.

If we shift our attention from the market to taxes, a point relevant to justice

---

[40] Angus Campbell, *The Sense of Well-Being in America* (New York: McGraw-Hill, 1981), 234.

[41] Jencks et al., "What Is a Good Job" 1,350, 1,353. Gender inequalities among intrinsic working benefits were the same as income inequalities – men benefited about twice as much as did women in both respects. The method employed for the analysis used here does not permit weighting individual preferences.

[42] George Bernard Shaw, *Candida,* act 1.

[43] Gruenberg, "The Happy Worker," 269.

emerges. Tax policy based on "ability to pay" is premised on the notion that ability to pay is a rough measure of sacrifice. But the sacrifice refers only to extrinsic rewards, income, and not to intrinsic rewards, chiefly a sense of competence and self-determination. The utilities derived from these intrinsic rewards are not taxed; compared to people who derive their satisfactions from consuming the goods and services earned at work, people who derive their satisfactions from the work itself are free from government levies on their source of satisfaction. This has two implications: (1) inasmuch as the working class derives its satisfaction largely from extrinsic rewards, the working class is more heavily taxed than the people with what we called earlier "the good jobs," that is, the professional, artistic, and entrepreneurial classes. (2) The poorly paid artistic professions are compensated in some measure for their poor pay by the fact that *their* benefits derived from work are untaxed.

The transfer of income from the creative occupations to the mercenary occupations is an unjustified transfer. It is, however, a gift that is Pareto optimal, at least in its modified, trading version, hurting the giver less than it benefits the receiver.

Hidden costs raise havoc with equity theory, which says that people feel equitably treated if their ratios of inputs (costs, sacrifices) to outcomes (benefits, losses) are the same as others' ratios.[44] By redefining work from the category of costs or sacrifices in the denominator of the ratios to the category of benefits in the numerator, the equity of any set of ratios will be drastically disturbed.

Deferred versus immediate gratification

There is a quality of immediate gratification in the hidden cost formula (payments for current work reduces my current self-determination) that is disturbing. Taking a longer view, we could say that hidden costs of rewards can be legitimate charges, not against self-determination but against the future of a self-determining life. That is, even where money payments give individuals the sense that they are no longer their own bosses (because they are not), this unease, this hidden cost, is worth incurring. These costs, then, are the expenses necessary to buy longer term self-determination. Extrinsic rewards of all kinds (money, praise, esteem) are then counters to invest in larger life enterprises. Is a person undermining self-determination if he or she submits to these controlling rewards? No more than the student who submits to the controlling curriculum and examination system to win the later freedom of professional practice.

But the acceptance of loss of self-determination now for more later is also disturbing and certainly incurs risks. Consider the destinations in life of those who substitute the American success motive for an internalized standard of excellence embodied in the achievement motive. From the individual's own mature point of view, this substitution represents an inferior self-chosen "life plan." Arriving at the destination could be empty of satisfaction and filled with unappeased appetites. The policy of money now for work enjoyment later incurs a risk captured by Philip

---

[44] Elaine Walster, Ellen Berscheid, and G. William Walster, "New Directions in Equity Research," in Leonard Berkowitz and Elaine Walster, eds., *Advances in Experimental Social Psychology*, vol. 9 (New York: Academic Press, 1976), 1–42.

Slater's slogan applied to the work ethic: "the postponed life."[45] Commenting on Keynes's idea that we must bear the indignity of avarice until our GNP is large enough to support us all comfortably, Schumacher points out that in the meantime we become habituated to our vices and when the time comes we cannot live without them.[46] Allport's "functional autonomy" certainly offers reasons for undertaking disliked tasks now with the understanding that as they become familiar we will like them better later. In this case the argument seems to be saying that if one does not like working for money now, one will learn to like it later, a view partially confirmed by Mortimer and Lorence's discovery that first jobs reinforced the values inherent in those jobs.[47] One learns to accept inferior sources of satisfaction.

Inevitably the extrinsic overlaps the intrinsic; in any life plan there will be, as mentioned earlier, dilemmas inviting self-deception, especially in intellectual, artistic, and scientific fields. Self-deception is a form of unconscious dissonance that may be relieved by conversion to open materialism. Referring to the creative artists mentioned earlier in this chapter, the writer who, responding to this dissonance, says frankly, "I write novels to make money," has lost some of the fruitful tension that promises better work.

No doubt there is an unpleasant immediacy about the drive for intrinsic work satisfaction and, if that is all there is to it, the hedonic costs to the individual and the productivity costs to the society are high. We have cautioned against an alternative unpleasantness: the postponed life.

Intrinsic work satisfaction and the personality–economy fit

The normative idea of a personality–economy fit is that society is best served when people can receive the rewards *they* want and these are the same as the rewards that *firms* want to offer.[48] If there is a discrepancy, both workers and firms suffer. We know that firms want to offer money rewards and that many people want precisely these kinds of rewards. In these terms, are there not "hidden costs" in offering intrinsic rewards to those who prefer extrinsic ones? Quite apart from economic considerations (e.g., the depreciation of pay standards when people want to work for intrinsic rewards), the imposition of uncongenial standards on working people who simply want more pay and an expanded freedom away from work is a hidden cost of the intrinsic. Humanistic social scientists cannot *will* that people should find intrinsic work satisfaction more rewarding than pay because the very heart of intrinsic motivation is the desire for autonomy and *self*-determination.

To define "hidden cost" along these lines is to propose that firms, and perhaps whole economies, whose workers are motivated by extrinsic motivation, that is, by

---

[45] Philip Slater, *The Pursuit of Loneliness* (Boston: Beacon Press, 1970), chap. 6.

[46] E. F. Schumacher, *Small Is Beautiful: Economics as if People Mattered* (New York: Harper/Colophon, 1973), 29.

[47] Jeylan T. Mortimer and Jon Lorence, "Work Experience and Occupational Value Socialization: A Longitudinal Study," *American Journal of Sociology* 84 (1979): 1,361–85.

[48] John R. P. French, Jr., Willard L. Rodgers, and Sidney Cobb, "Adjustment as a Person–Environment Fit," in George V. Coelho, David Hamburg, and John E. Adams, eds., *Coping and Adaptation* (New York: Basic Books, 1974). See also Elchanan I. Meir and Samuel Melamed, "The Accumulation of Person–Environment Congruences and Well-Being," *Journal of Occupational Behavior* 7 (1986): 315–23.

money rewards, should make performances contingent on pay, whereas firms or economies whose workers are motivated by such intrinsic rewards as self-determination, the desire for excellence, or the enjoyment of challenging and creative tasks should offer *these* rewards. Both self-perception theory and theories of cognitive congruence would find this result congenial.

Yet there is a patent cost in accommodating to the best personality–economy fit in this way: the benefits in health, sobriety, and longevity, the socialization of children into a work culture rather than a money culture, the improved quality of leisure pursuits, the improvement of learning skills and creativity, and, indeed, the real (as contrasted to the imagined) contributions to life satisfaction of intrinsic motivation and rewards all discourage this relativistic solution. Important as it is, a good personality–economy fit is not a primary good; intrinsic enjoyment of *productive* activities comes closer.

Intrinsic values in historical perspective

Interest in intrinsic satisfaction, process benefits, and self-determination at work continues to increase.[49] Is this evidence of some progression in industrial and post-industrial societies? Could we say, for example, that for most of human history solidarity was the goal and social approval the currency of most societies? that in the early and middle phases of the industrial revolution economic gain was the goal and money was the currency that was most universally used and sought? that in the postindustrial society, with traces of a postmaterialist orientation emerging among those socialized in security and affluence,[50] exchange of material goods for money loses its primacy and intrinsic motivations and intrinsic work satisfactions emerge as stronger forces – even in a market society? As a consequence, human time becomes more valuable because there are two competing hedonically satisfying uses of that time, consumption *and* production. Theodore Schultz's analysis of the increased value of human time roots this increase in the rise of knowledge and the need for more time for consumption.[51] Our analysis roots this increased value of human time in the recognition that working has a positive utility that sometimes is greater than consumer utilities.

Even when hidden costs have been limited to their smaller sphere, the effects of hidden costs and of a concern for the intrinsic more generally are substantial and still growing. Compared to some unspecified higher standard, these costs include the erosion of initiative and of concern for quality; decline of peripheral learning at the workplace; misallocation of talent; inhibition of growth of the labor force; mis-

[49] Jeylan T. Mortimer, *Changing Attitudes Toward Work: Highlights of the Literature* (New York: Pergamon for American Institute Studies in Productivity, 1979), 10; Daniel Yankelovich and John Immerwahr, *Putting the Work Ethic to Work* (New York: Public Agenda Foundation, 1983).
[50] Ronald Inglehart, *The Silent Revolution* (Princeton: Princeton University Press, 1972); and Idem, "Post-Materialism in an Environment of Insecurity," *American Political Science Review* 75 (1981): 880–900.
[51] Theodore W. Schultz, *Investment in Human Capital: The Role of Education and of Research* (New York: Free Press, 1971); Idem, "Fertility and Economic Values," in his *Economics of the Family* (Chicago: University of Chicago Press, 1974).

interpretation of individual utility, leading to a consequent pursuit of relatively unrewarding goals; and certain selective injustices in the economic domain.

Summary

Whereas the intrinsic offers much that is congenial to any humane appreciation of the quality of life, in placing intrinsic values within the context of a social system, the causes and consequences of any set of intrinsic values must be considered. Having examined the causes in earlier chapters, we turn to the consequences, among which are:

Satisfaction of intrinsic work enjoyment is associated with mental and physical health, higher life and work satisfaction, contributions to the work enjoyment of others, a tendency to choose more challenging leisure activities, and socialization of children into a culture of work rather than of money.

Intrinsic enjoyment of work facilitates a variety of forms of learning, including those we have associated with human development: cognitive complexity, self-attribution, and self-esteem.

Intrinsic satisfaction with work is especially important in, and probably crucial to, creativity on the job. Thus, partly because hidden costs only occur where the jobs have challenging and creative features, intrinsic work enjoyment is closely associated with invention, discovery, and creativity. The point is not tautological, however, for it seems that pay sometimes actually reduces creativity and high standards of performance in jobs where these qualities are called for. Scientists are protected from.hidden costs by the separation of their extrinsic rewards from the sources of their self-esteem.

But intrinsic values are marked by genuine social defects: they cannot be so easily shared and therefore are more ''selfish''; unlike material values, they are less constrained by opposing interests; they may take ugly forms of revenge or cruelty; unlike market values, they do not necessarily lead to the production of something someone wants; they rest on misleading theories of dispositional and personal attribution; and, to challenge the chief virtue that Deci has said inheres in them, they do not provide greater scope for self-determination than does a secure income or money in the bank.

The distribution of intrinsic rewards incurs justice problems that are at least different from those in distributing income and possibly more serious. Although overall life satisfaction is more equally distributed than income, ''good jobs'' yielding intrinsic rewards are less equally distributed. For this, there is no corrective machinery in the market. The market's criterion for distributing income rests on the justice of deserts, contribution to productivity (profits) and thus to national wealth. This criterion is not available for distributing intrinsic rewards, however, for whereas workers' contributions to productivity may be substantial, to use productivity criteria is to violate the very concept of the intrinsic. Another source of injustice lies in the lack of taxation of the psychic income from intrinsic work enjoyment, making equality of sacrifice impossible. For equity theory based on the market's idea that work is an "input" or cost, recasting work as a benefit disturbs the cost-benefit ratios on which the theory depends.

Whereas the immediacy of intrinsic rewards implies a kind of carpe diem, deferring the gratification of intrinsic motivation may mean relying in the present on extrinsic gratification, thus risking habituation to extrinsic rewards.

If one attempts to perfect the personality–economy fit so that those who prefer extrinsic rewards get their wishes and those who prefer intrinsic rewards also get their wishes, one deprives the extrinsically rewarded of the benefits associated with intrinsic rewards, for example, longer life, a greater probability of long-term happiness. A better solution is to seek to promote intrinsic rewards in work that is socially productive. (But this may not be possible in a market economy – see Chapter 16.)

But the humanist proponent of intrinsic motives and rewards need not despair, for there is (fragile) evidence of a long-term historical movement: from reliance on social support to reliance on economic gain to reliance on intrinsic motivation and rewards in the changing economies of the world.

21 The economics of the intrinsic

In previous chapters of Part VI and in Part V we have been concerned mainly with the effects of the market on learning and enjoyment of work (or of the personal and social consequences of market behavior). Here we reverse the causal flow and focus on the effects *on* the market of giving priority to intrinsic work enjoyment, but quite without benefit of the straw man with genuine bones discussed in Chapter 19. There are four sections: For an appraisal of the comparative advantages of giving work satisfaction priority over consumer satisfaction, we turn first to some problems of comparing consumption of *work* pleasures with acquiring money to provide for the subsequent consumption of *commodities* (and leisure). The second section is devoted to the problems of market allocation of the factors of production, particularly labor, when intrinsic work enjoyment rather than pay is the major attraction of work. We then consider the implications for the usual market formula where work is a disutility of assigning positive utilities to work, devising formulae for net utility (1) when work is a pleasure, (2) when there are hidden costs, and (3) when the sense of duty is satisfied by work. Finally, we offer a brief comment on the symbiotic quality of intrinsic and extrinsic rewards in the market.

In concluding the chapter we complete our discussion of intrinsic and extrinsic rewards with a glance back at the main lessons learned in Part VI.

Producer versus consumer values

"The difference between liking and disliking one's work" said Tibor Scitovsky, "may well be more important than the differences in economic satisfaction that the disparities in our income lead to."[1] We are accustomed to positive utilities for income but not for work (Chapters 13 and 14). Here we explore the consequences of thinking of a job as a commodity or a cluster of commodities.[2] The main question concerning the assignment of jobs to the same commodity status as cars and cornflakes is the usual one in such cases of classification: What is gained by this recategorization? And what is lost? For our purposes, there is a gain in bringing together for comparison two sources of utility that have rarely been thus compared. What is lost, for the moment, is the causal connection: Whether pleasurable or not, paid work is a condition for purchasing cars and cornflakes.

Comparison of these partially unlike goods cannot rely on the single dimension of price, but that poses no difficulty since we frequently handle without difficulty

---

[1] Tibor Scitovsky, *The Joyless Economy* (New York: Oxford University Press, 1977), 104.
[2] There is an irony in proposing that jobs be considered in a manner similar to that of commodities, for Samuel Gompers's insistence that "labor is not a commodity" always struck a sympathetic chord among noneconomists, although it never changed the economists' concept of "labor" as one of several factors or production.

413

preference orderings for such unlike goods as friendship, reading books, and market work.[3] Even in the market, price is only one of a variety of considerations taken into account.[4]

Comparing proximate ends and means

A greater difficulty is posed by comparing consumption of a good, in this case the enjoyment of work, with acquisition of a good, in this case money, representing only the means of consumption. This is the problem of comparing proximate ends with means to ends. The latter is inevitably more complex:

CONSUMING WORK
1. What satisfactions does working in a certain job offer?

ACQUIRING MONEY
1. How much money does a certain job offer?
2. How much of that money should be saved to purchase future commodities?
3. What commodities can I buy with that money?
4. What satisfactions do those commodities yield?

In the more complex decision on consumer satisfaction the likelihood of misjudging one's genuine satisfactions is probably greater. On the other hand, the perils of instant gratification implied by a choice of consuming the pleasures of working now and the advantages of greater freedom of choice yielded by money, leave the issue of genuine ego-syntonic satisfaction over time quite unsettled.

Comparing work identities and consumer identities

Economic value is, of course, only one kind of value: Consider a more important value, the value of the self in the eyes of the self, self-esteem. A person who builds self-esteem on income or consumer goods is generally considered in some sense less estimable than one who bases self-esteem on craftsmanship, skills, work, or even independence from control by others. The grounds for this intuitive judgment are complex, but they have something to do with the greater value of creating rather than consuming, of doing rather than having, of something more integral to the person than what might be acquired by gift or luck.

Property in the self versus property in goods

As tenants of their jobs, workers do not enjoy the sense of competence and self-determination that comes with ownership,[5] but long after Blackstone the claims of

---

[3] Jencks et al. created a measure of combined extrinsic and intrinsic qualities of a good job. These authors point out that "a realistic scheme for comparing jobs must use some common metric to value both monetary and nonmonetary characteristics and must sum these values." They identify those job characteristics that exert the greatest influence on workers' judgments about a job's desirability and weight them to assess the average weights given in the job ratings. This permits them "to predict how 'good' workers will say a job is and, ultimately, how workers with perfect information would choose among the jobs available to them." (p. 1,324) But this goes only a small distance toward giving consumer and worker utilities a common metric. Christopher Jencks, Lauri Perman, and Lee Rainwater, "What Is a Good Job?" *American Journal of Sociology* 93 (1988): 1,322–7.

[4] See Peter Earl, *The Economic Imagination: Towards a Behavioural Analysis of Choice* (Armonk, NY: Sharpe, 1983); K. J. Lancaster, *An Introduction to Modern Microeconomics,* 2d ed. (Chicago: Rand McNally, 1974); George Katona, *Psychological Economics* (New York: Elsevier, 1975), chaps. 13–14.

[5] See Wesley N. Hohfeld, *Fundamental Conceptions of Property* (New Haven: Yale University Press, 1923).

property ownership are no longer those of "exclusive dominion"; rather property is considered a bundle of rights that can usually (but not always) be enforced through claiming elements of this assigned, but revocable, bundle of rights.[6] In any event, the main source of intrinsic satisfaction does not come from ownership but from the pleasure of workmanship or achievement or of demonstrating excellence. That pleasure is exclusively for the person working the job, whether tenant or owner. More significantly, it is the owner of human capital, rather than the owner of physical capital, who enjoys those rewards. Just as the economic yield on human capital is now higher than the yield on physical capital[7] (Chapters 1, 16), so also (but not because of its productivity) the yield in utilities to owners of human capital is likely to be greater than the yield to owners of physical capital. This follows from the idea that it is the sense of meeting life's challenges and exercising one's skills that yields more utilities than does the usufruct of one's own property.

Market allocation where rewards are intrinsic

Changing the function of price: the case of labor

In the labor market, as in other markets, the function of price is to allocate resources to their best, that is, most profitable, uses. What is the effect of intrinsic rewards on a market system relying on price information for self-regulation? We will find that "pricing" intrinsic rewards runs into unusual difficulties, but before entering upon that analysis, consider the difficulties in the ordinary process of using the price of labor as a guide to allocating it to its best use. Among the determinants of the price of labor such exogenous factors as birth rates and rates of immigration, changes in technology (and whether it is labor saving or capital saving),[8] the conflicting influences of the income effects (the higher the wage, the more attractive the job and the greater the supply) and substitution effects (the higher the wage, the more it is possible to substitute leisure for labor), the demand for and price elasticity of the products of any particular class of labor, unionization and the vulnerability of firms to short-term stoppages, proportion of labor costs to total costs, current levels of unemployment (often curiously irrelevant), the firm's competitive position and much else. From this matrix the final resolution is both complex and often indeterminate.[9] As a partial consequence of this complexity, both general levels of wages and wage differentials are surprisingly sticky, that is, unresponsive to the usual play of market forces.[10]

All of this suggests that the most hallowed of theories of economic determinants

[6] See Lita Furby, "Possessions: Toward a Theory of Their Meaning and Function Throughout the Life Cycle," in P. B. Baltes, ed., Life-Span Development and Behavior (New York: Academic Press, 1978).
[7] Jeffrey G. Williamson and Peter H. Lindert, American Inequality: A Macroeconomic History (New York: Academic Press, 1980), 202; Theodore W. Schultz, Investment in Human Capital: The Role of Education and Research (New York: Free Press, 1971).
[8] Because savings are not sensitive to interest rates, and since the supply of land is more or less fixed, and the supply of time is absolutely fixed, none of the factors of production is absolutely price elastic – only relatively so.
[9] John R. Hicks, The Theory of Wages (London: Macmillan, 1935). See also Chapter 14 in this text.
[10] Paul A. Samuelson and William D. Nordhaus, Economics, 12th ed. (New York: McGraw-Hill, 1985), 621.

of wages, marginal productivity, is seriously hedged about with a variety of modifying influences, as noted in Chapter 14. Like the concept of utility maximization, the marginal productivity theory of rewards is difficult to test, depends on the prices of any given status quo for these tests (making circular Pigou's arguments based on marginal productivity),[11] and where it can be tested, the "factors of production do not seem to be paid their marginal products."[12]

It is in this matrix of forces that the problem of pricing intrinsic satisfactions must be placed. In theory, intrinsically attractive work would be discounted, but since unattractive work does not command a premium,[13] in practice this is unlikely. If disamenities do not add to the price of labor,[14] we are not likely to find amenities subtracting much. Within this small margin, some few forces are discernible.

Effects of prices in allocating human resources
The discussion on the *information* system of a market suggests that pay is likely to be "overpriced" and the intrinsic to be underpriced in a system that does not provide appropriate information on the intrinsic merits of work. People demand the qualities they know something about.

Entry into occupations that invite the exercise of talents that people may learn to enjoy in school or as a hobby in their youth, for example, jobs for jazz musicians and Shakespearian actors, will attract more candidates than economic demand can accommodate, thereby depressing wages. The supply of amateur (volunteering) musicians and actors will depress the wages in those occupations.

Occupational prestige invites entry into politics and science, two areas where people rate higher in prestige rankings than in economic rankings. This condition tends to depress political and scientific salaries compared to business salaries.[15]

Entrepreneurs (as contrasted to managers) do not get the full market value of their creations,[16] in part because they are said to be driven by nonpecuniary motives.[17]

[11] Arthur C. Pigou, *The Economics of Welfare*, 4th ed. (1932; reprint London: Macmillan, 1948).
[12] Lester Thurow, "Toward a Definition of Economic Justice," *Public Interest*, no. 31 (Spring 1973): 56–80 at 70.
[13] R. S. Smith, "Compensating Wage Differentials and Public Policy: A Review," *Industrial and Labor Relations Review* 32 (1979): 339–52 at 347. For a somewhat different conclusion, see R. E. B. Lucas, "Hedonic Wage Equations and Psychic Wages in the Returns to Schooling," *American Economic Review* 67 (1977): 549–58. I am indebted to F. Thomas Juster for these citations: See his "Preferences for Work and Leisure," in Juster and Frank P. Stafford, eds., *Time, Goods, and Well-Being* (Ann Arbor, MI: Institute for Social Research, 1985), 333–4.
[14] Juster, "Preferences for Work and Leisure," 334.
[15] Donald J. Treiman, *Occupational Prestige in Comparative Perspective* (New York: Academic Press, 1977). Rewards in prestige or status are as easily classified as extrinsic as they are intrinsic, but as "reflected appraisal" these rewards share in the intrinsic satisfactions of self-esteem.
[16] "For markets to work well, the prices facing individuals and companies when they make decisions must be representative of the values of the products or services to the economy as a whole. When appropriate prices are not known or when decisions are based on private values that differ from social values, then productivity, particularly measured productivity, will suffer." Martin Neil Baily and Alok K. Chakrabarti, *Innovation and the Productivity Crisis* (Washington, DC: Brookings Institution, 1988), 92.
[17] Joseph A. Schumpeter, *The Theory of Economic Development: An Inquiry into Profits, Capital, Credits, Interest, and the Business Cycle*, 2d ed., trans R. Opie (Cambridge: Harvard University Press, 1936); Michael Maccoby, *The Gamesmen* (New York: Bantam, 1978).

The intrinsic pleasure of "running your own business" will lead to more bankruptcies than rational (but inevitably fallible) calculations would suggest, especially in easy entry businesses like restaurants and boutiques.

Liking one's job for nonfinancial reasons implies less interest in moving to another job because the pay is better, a situation that leads employers to exercise what has been called the "rational selective exploitation" of the less mobile.[18]

From the Mortimer and Lorence study discussed in Chapter 13, we learn of a reinforcing effect: Those who at an early stage want jobs offering higher pay tend both to get these kinds of jobs and then to value their income even more after they hold them, making them ever more likely to seek and find higher pay. Those who at an early stage want jobs working with people or with other intrinsically satisfying qualities were also more likely to get those kinds of jobs and were also reinforced in their choices, making them ever less likely to demand more pay or to move to jobs offering them more.[19]

At the same time, the tendency of markets to ignore the pleasantness or unpleasantness of work will tend to offer those with pleasant work a form of economic rent in payments beyond what is necessary to induce them to enter the labor force.

The effects of self-perception and dissonance reduction theory
To help complete the picture of the determination of both money wages and intrinsic work enjoyment where the rewards of work are largely intrinsic, we refer back to the discussion in Chapter 18 on the definition of the intrinsic and the theories of hidden cost. Recall that we pointed out that the theory of self-perception changed the order of a person's assessment of his or her market worth. Instead of saying, independently, "I am worth X and should receive X (or more likely, X + something)," an individual looks at the salary and decides that whatever it is, it must be the correct assessment of his or her worth: "Because I am paid X, I must be worth X." Similarly, if lowly paid in a disliked job, an individual changes that dislike to a more favorable assessment to explain to himself or herself why he or she is working there: hidden gains. Both of these devices serve to reinforce the status quo and to quiet restless spirits who might otherwise believe that they are worth more than they are paid.[20]

All of this suggests that the calculations people make under the income maximization hypothesis, where work is a disutility for which pay is compensation, will be considerably different from those in the situations we have been describing where intrinsic satisfactions are given priority. We turn to an explication of that difference.

[18] Charyl E. Rusbult, David Lowery, Michael Hubbard, Orly J. Maravankin, and Michael Neises, "Impact of Employee Mobility and Employee Performance on the Allocation of Rewards Under Conditions of Constraint," *Journal of Personality and Social Psychology*, 54 (1988): 605–15.

[19] Jeylan T. Mortimer and Jon Lorence, "Work Experience and Occupational Value Socialization: A Longitudinal Study," *American Journal of Sociology* 84 (1979): 1,361–85.

[20] An alternative explanation of worker quiescence is provided by Sherry Cable in her "Attributional Processes and Alienation: A typology of Worker Responses to Unequal Power Relationships," *Political Psychology* 9 (1988): 109–27; see also Barrington Moore, Jr., *Injustice: The Social Bases of Obedience and Revolt* (White Plains, NY: M. E. Sharpe, 1978).

The calculus of the intrinsic

The difference may be shown by three additions to the conventional formula: (1) adding the pleasures of work to the pleasure of pay; (2) adding the hidden cost effect, that is, subtracting the pain of pay from the pleasures of work; (3) adding the pleasures and pain of duty (work ethic). In the first stage we move from the simple economist's concept of net utility (NU) equalling the pleasures of pay less the pains of work, to a three-term formula allowing for the pleasure of work. Thus:

$$NU = Pleasure(pay) - Pain(work) \tag{1}$$

$$NU = \{Pleasure(pay) + Pleasure(work)\} - Pain(work) \tag{2}$$

Now, if we add considerations of hidden costs, we must think of pay as also a pain, since it detracts from the pleasure of work. The most sensible version is one that adds the utilities derived from both pay and work but discounts for the negative effects of pay on work pleasure. This might be written as:

$$NU = \{Pleasure(work) - Pain(pay)\} - \{Pain(work) + Pleasure(pay)\}, \text{ or} \tag{3}$$

$$NU = \{Pleasure(work) + Pleasure(pay)\} - \{Pain(work) + Pain(pay)\} \tag{4}$$

Of course, there could be no Pain(pay) if there were no Pleasure(work), in which case the economists' two-term version (1) would prevail.

There is an additional source of intrinsic satisfaction that we have given little attention to: the pleasures of a rewarded conscience. Experience with service credit programs in several cities is illuminating. These programs provide for a kind of credit bank whose credits are earned by voluntary social service work, such as baby-sitting for the poor, delivering meals to the elderly, or teaching English to new immigrants. The credits thus earned can be "cashed" by the earners when they, in turn, need help, thereby mixing altruistic motives with self-help motives. Experience with this program shows that such intrinsic satisfactions as the "satisfaction one gets from doing the job . . . [and] the value attached to altruism" are *not* undermined by the fact that one may benefit oneself by claiming services in return; rather these satisfactions are additive.[21] An economist, starting with the proposition that for any act, marginal cost (MC) must equal marginal return (MR), suggests that in the case of service credits the "marginal value placed by the supplier of caring services on the service credit he or she earns (MVSC), plus the marginal psychic benefit of supplying such services (ALT)" must equal marginal cost, or: $MC = MVCS + ALT$.[22] But altruism, I should add, is rarely costless, so there should be a term for "Pain(alt)." To make the idea of altruism in ordinary work life more general, we might think of the moral element of altruism as more of a sense of doing one's duty, thus enlisting the work ethic that survives in various forms.

Thus, to add to the previous formulae, we should consider the following:

$$NU = \{Pleasure(work) + Pleasure(duty) + Pleasure(pay)\} - $$
$$\{Pain(work) + Pain(pay) + Pain(duty)\} \tag{5}$$

[21] Edgar Cahn, *Service Credits: A New Currency for the Welfare State* (London: Suntory Toyota International Centre for Economics and Related Disciplines, London School of Economics, 1986), 21–2.
[22] Nicholas Barr, "Comments," in ibid., 38.

And if we convert these from average gains and costs to marginal gains and costs we get the same formula in balance where $MR = MC$.

The failure of wages to behave in the fashion predicted by conventional price theory may have its source in the oversimplified version of motivation employed by that theory. The alternative mentioned might go further in accounting for the observed relationships between levels of pay and labor supply.

There is a suggestion here that those who enjoy their work get their rewards in intrinsic work enjoyment, which permits those who enjoy pay to get more pay. This serendipitous solution, however, is undermined by evidence that intrinsic motivation is not substituted for avarice but merely added to it.[23]

As mentioned, the actual market does not credit intrinsic motivation and does not acknowledge intrinsic rewards. With the possible exceptions of certain occupations such as actors, artists, scientists, and entrepreneurs, those with intrinsically interesting jobs are, in general, paid more than those with less interesting jobs, as one would expect from the evidence on the failure of the market to pay more for disamenities at work. It is not only that intrinsic values are irrelevant to market considerations, but there is often a perverse relationship between what is enjoyable and what is well paid. Thus, people are paid for their skills in the use of discretion that is itself rewarding. To repeat an earlier caution, the analysis of the effect of the intrinsic on wages is important within a very small margin; larger forces are likely to swamp these effects.

Intrinsic/extrinsic symbiosis

In a sense, those with intrinsically valuable jobs who make up the privileged class are socially parasitic on the extrinsic. This is so because for the members of the privileged class (mentioned in Chapter 15) to exercise their skills and achieve a standard of excellence in a technological society, others must produce an economic surplus. Unless businesspersons go about their business purposefully creating wealth, that wealth will not be created, and the good jobs will not be created, either. And paying workers in money according to their productivity has a better chance of increasing productivity than paying workers in intrinsic rewards. For example, part of the work enjoyment of many workers in command economies is precisely the lack of pressure to produce, an enjoyment threatened by President Gorbachev's market-oriented perestroika.[24]

---

[23] The "post-materialists," with their concern for participation and a society "where ideas count," do not seem to lose their interest in income as they acquire these social concerns – their "higher" interests are simply added to their personal materialism. See Alan Marsh, " 'The Silent Revolution,' Value Priorities and the Quality of Life in Britain," *American Political Science Review* 69 (1975): 21–30; Inglehart's rejoinder is in his "Value Priorities, Life Satisfaction, and Political Dissatisfaction Among Western Publics," in Richard F. Tomasson, ed., *Comparative Studies in Sociology,* vol. 1 (Greenwich, CT: JAI Press, 1978), 173–202.

[24] In the port city of Ilyichevsky, "the port [administration] plays an almost parental role in the life of its workers." Under perestroika market requirements threatened to introduce uncertainty and relocation to port workers. At one point "a third of the talleymen had to be eliminated. . . . Some workers say the cutbacks gave the remaining workers a new attitude toward their jobs. . . . 'You can feel it,' Mrs. Gorozhankina (a worker at the port) said. 'People are more diligent in their jobs and they don't try to

Even economically, the extrinsic is similarly parasitic on the intrinsic: Both scientists and entrepreneurs produce more wealth, as groups, than they receive in income. If even part of the analysis of how intrinsic work enjoyment leads to underpayment is true, there is a surplus in the camp of the intrinsic that is disbursed and dispersed outside that camp.

Where each of two forms of life seems to live off the proceeds of the other, we do not speak of parasitism, but of symbiosis. The intrinsic and extrinsic reward systems are not only characterized by the opposition suggested by hidden costs but, in a larger sense, by their symbiotic relations to each other.

Summary

The comparison between two sources of satisfaction, working and receiving money for one's work (for later consumption of commodities and leisure), compares an instant gratification with one involving a long chain of causes and conditions; inevitably the shorter chain is a more certain route to gratification. Such a comparison also involves a comparison of implied identities, the working identity gaining over the consumer identity by its association with creation and contribution to others. Finally, there is more satisfaction in *doing* than in *having* because the first is more clearly associated with the prime cause of happiness, meeting and mastering life's challenges. Put differently, the hedonic yield from human capital is higher than from physical capital or money.

Although price is only loosely related to changes in the supply and distribution of labor whenever wages are thought to be the reward for work, where intrinsic rewards are dominant, the logic of the situation means that in utility terms pay will be "overpriced." In conventional economic thinking those with creative jobs or prestigious jobs, entrepreneurs, the self-employed, the community-minded, and those who value working with people will be underpriced. In practice, of course, the agglutinative tendencies of the market (each value base gathers to it other values) mean that those jobs offering pleasure through responsibility are also the best paid jobs.

As in medieval times, there are forces reinforcing "the customary wage," but instead of authoritative sanctions, these forces are the tendencies of people to see what they are paid and infer from that their market worth – as predicted by self-perception theory.

The calculus of the intrinsic means that both the pleasures and pains of at least three elements of the work situation must be included: the pleasure as well as the pain of work, the pain as well as the pleasure of pay, and the pleasures and pains of duty. The outcome is more complex than that suggested by the pay maximization hypothesis discussed in Chapter 17.

Because the number of intrinsically rewarding jobs is increased by the wealth

evade work. Maybe people are more afraid, afraid they will be fired if another cutback happens.' This disturbs . . . the director's assistant, who feels people should be working better, not out of fear, but out of a sense that it will bring them a better life. . . . So far, the new thinking has produced widespread anxiety, but little real change in the economic landscape.'' *New York Times*, 10 May 1988, pp. 1, 12.

produced by extrinsically motivated materialists, and because increasing GNP is dependent on the contribution of entrepreneurs and scientists movitated by the intrinsic rewards of their professions, the extrinsic and intrinsic live in a symbiotic relation with each other.

Conclusion to Part VI

We have been getting along pretty well, after all, without much attention to the intrinsic, relying on pay to motivate and allocate human resources but also allowing each person to derive such intrinsic rewards from work as he or she may find. The intrinsic is a private matter, hidden like the costs it is said to incur, from public view and assessment. Why not let Marshall's concept of the "net force," of various motives reflected in what people are willing to accept for their work carry the burden of this intricate, often subjective analysis?

The answer is to be found in the analysis of these five chapters. Perhaps most telling are the data reported in the balance sheet given in Chapter 20: People who are intrinsically motivated and rewarded at work live longer, learn more, and are more creative and happier than those who are primarily motivated by pay. But behind that answer is the more fundamental one: The valued product of an economy is a combination of happiness and human development. If pay serves to maximize wealth but not happiness and certainly not human development, it is pure convention and ease of analysis that preserves the priority of pay and its associated goods of commodities and leisure.

But assume that increasing wealth carries with it, as it does, an occupational roster with ever greater opportunities for intrinsic rewards, the evidence presented here in Part VI reveals that the motives for individual wealth are not, at least by themselves, those that prompt the most intelligent, creative, and productive effort. That kind of effort comes from people who are intrinsically motivated by a desire for excellence, or who are sufficiently self-directed to make the work, not the pay, the focus of their attention. And self-direction, in turn, is invoked in jobs where the contingent rewards of pay are not controlling. The pay maximization hypothesis, we found, fails to motivate and therefore fails to explain market behavior. Therefore, purely in its own economic terms, the market and its interpreters cannot maximize their own final value of wealth without attention to intrinsic motivation and rewards.

Turning to our own criteria of happiness and human development, we may rely on the chapters of work in Part V to explain the failure of market rewards to maximize happiness. Part II on cognition and emotion further explained why the market fails to maximize that feature of human development we have called complex cognition. Here that explanation is complemented by the discussion of creativity, so dependent on intrinsic motivation with its focus on the work rather than on pay for the work. Also, in Part VI we have evidence on the two features of human development discussed in Part III: personal control (self-attribution) and self-esteem. Both are central self-rewards of work where workers feel they can control their own work, as was clear in the discussion of hidden costs in Chapter 18. And both enter the credit side of the ledger in the evaluation of intrinsic values in Chapter 20. Yet on the other side of the ledger, neither the sense of personal control nor self-esteem helps to guide a market economy toward efficient allocation of resources and the maximization of wealth.

The market's central defining feature is exchange, but for the reasons given, the intrinsic cannot be exchanged. One cannot exchange or buy or sell a sense of self-determination, satisfaction with an internal standard of excellence, or a conscience appeased by the performance of duty.

We seem to arrive at the same unhappy conclusion as was forced upon us in Chapter 16: The market is as uncongenial to intrinsic motivation and rewards as it is to a priority for the utilities of working activities over those of consumer activities. Given the fact that the satisfactions from work are substantially derived from intrinsic rewards, the parallel conclusions are not surprising.

Within the interstices of a market economy we may find many opportunities for happiness and for personal development, but we must do these things without any direct help from the market. The indirect help through the *affluence effect* must suffice until better institutions are devised.

PART VII

Utility and happiness

I have suggested two maximands for the market: human development and happiness. Our discussion up to this point has focused more on the conditions of human development (specified as cognitive complexity, personal control, and self esteem) than on happiness, although inevitably hedonic states have entered the analysis. It could not be otherwise. Even though the two goods are separate, the discussion of each implies acknowledgment of the other. When they conflict, that conflict must be noted and the usual alternative basis for support, ethics, must be shown to be supportive. When they are congruent, the hedonic rewards of developmental processes are important incentives for engaging in those processes.

It is for these reasons that there have been many references to hedonic moods in the interpretations of the market experience. Thus, the development of cognitive complexity by the market was placed in the context of joy and sorrow as well as such emotions as pity, guilt, or anger. The hopes and fears stimulated by money symbols are freighted with hedonic implications; insecurity obviously influences happiness as well as the thinking processes noted; one protects one's sense of personal control and self-esteem because one feels unhappy at their loss; we do not object to unemployment solely because of the waste of human resources but also because it makes people miserable; the inability of a system of exchange to comprehend intrinsic motivations is a defect because it deprives people of important pleasures; the frequent failure of money to promote happiness is itself a failure whether or not it also distorts market choices. Over the long journey to this point we have inevitably touched on happiness, the subject of Part VII.

The previous focus on human development, however, has left unanswered many questions of crucial importance to the claim that the market is the primary agent for satisfying human wants. In the last analysis, these are questions of happiness and satisfaction with life-as-a-whole. Up to this point, however, we have not defined and explored concepts of happiness, life satisfaction, or utility, together representing the second of the two elements in our explananda. This analysis is made more difficult by the fact that there is no developed theory of happiness, although fragmentary theories of positive and negative affects and massive studies of the quality of life have made important contributions on which we rely. In analyzing market claims to maximize utility, we are, almost by accident, contributing to this still defective theory of what may be called *hedonics*.

The first task, undertaken in Chapter 22, is to understand some of the meanings of happiness and its companion, satisfaction with life-as-a-whole, to show the difference between these two cognate concepts, to strip them of their ineffable, tautological qualities, and to give an example of how they may be assessed. In this same chapter we will examine the differences between objective accounts of the conditions of happiness and subjected accounts of the moods themselves. (In Chapter 28

I will show how the elements of objective accounts are best conceived as hedonic assets whereas the subjective accounts alone deal with hedonic *income*, that is, happiness itself.) Chapter 23 gives a direct assessment of the economists' claim that the market is the principal agent for satisfaction of wants in human society. For this purpose it is necessary to analyze both wants and satisfactions and the various solutions to ratios of wants to satisfactions available in the market, an analysis that deals with two claims: (1) The market is itself the source of wants that cannot be satisfied, and (2) the market is inimical to the reduction of wants whose reduction might ease people's states of dissatisfaction. From time to time I have referred to the economists' use of the term *utility*, but only in the context of this chapter are we able to deal in detail with the utility theory of the market that Stigler says has now come to dominate the field. Like others, I find it empty.

In the studies of the quality of life, the question of the balancing of pleasures and pains, joys and sorrows (affect balance) mirrors and extends Bentham's original scheme of hedonic accounting. In Chapter 24 I take up this question, finding on the way that most of the pleasures and pains that Bentham mentions have only remote relations to market affairs. Whether or not that relation is closer, there is an obstacle to the influence of the market on the experiences of pleasure and pain in the set of more or less fixed dispositions with which people confront their market experiences. Other obstacles to market influence have more to do with the difficulty of switching from market pursuits to familial or contemplative pursuits, for in this set of choices the market's equilibrating responsiveness to choice is not very helpful. Yet internal equilibrating devices, such as the adaptive-level phenomenon, partially make good this deficiency.

Chapter 25 introduces several hedonic *structures* (by which I mean both patterns of thought and of institutional behavior) to help explain the way the *market* structure interacts with these hedonic structures. The most important is the *psychocentric* structure where we place human behavior rather than price behavior at the center of things. Others are scalar structures of needs and their satisfactions, cybernetic feedback loops to match the market's own cybernetic system, concentric circles of satisfaction where intimate relations form a core surrounded by other sources of satisfaction, each psychologically more distant as we move outward from the core, the domain and concern matrix that lies at the heart of Andrews and Withey's analysis of subjective well-being, and a patterned way of thinking about hedonic choices that permits the contribution to life satisfaction to take the place of those monetary measures that less adequately reflect subjective well-being.

Taking up a major theme of this book, Chapter 26 shows how new evidence reveals that differences in collective wealth are strongly related to happiness (the *affluence effect*) but that individual differences in income show little relation to either happiness or life satisfaction. The affluence effect is explained substantially by the effect of economic growth on poverty and by certain inhibitions to the adaptation process that perpetually creates new and higher standards. The failure of money to buy happiness in any given society is explained by the nature of the things that give daily pleasures, the failure of many pleasure-yielding activities to go through the market, and the way individual dispositions resist market influences on sense of well-being. But if income *levels* are not hedonically significant, income *changes* are. The discussion concludes with an analysis of why some people are condemned to walk the hedonic treadmill and others are not.

Any concern for the satisfaction of human wants will necessarily give priority to the way those wants relate to the genuine ego-syntonic needs of the wanting person rather than to the subsequent and more superficial aspects of rational calculation dealing with whatever wants a person may have chosen. Chapter 27 explores this problem of interpreting the self and therefore of locating the difficulties people have in interpreting the sources of their own happiness. I treat this first as a problem of *authenticity,* then as a problem of *compensatory choices,* then as a problem of interpreting the sources of *emotional arousal,* and finally as a problem of expressing *biologically programmed* needs and behavior. The market, it seems, is an inadequate instrument for dealing with these problems and market analysis ignores them. They cannot be successfully ignored, however, for the problems of choice implied by each of the prior discussions, whether of work, the intrinsic, or the selection between pursuit of money or pursuit of friendship, depends upon the way people interpret the sources of their own happiness.

Finally, in the last chapter of Part VII, we will deal with the problem of summing of satisfactions or utilities, showing the necessity of sorting out the *assets* that yield the psychic *income* from that "income" itself. We find that contribution-to-happiness (or to satisfaction with life-as-a-whole) offers the cardinal properties necessary for summing as well as a much closer approximation to genuine utility than does the usual money calculation. But even then, the problems posed by the relationships among the goods whose utilities are to be summed is complex and must take into account current versus future yields, interlocking dependencies, incompatibilities, and other interaction effects. The specific problem of adding moral and commercial utilities is solved by the contribution-to-happiness device. Lacking knowledge of the sources of utilities, markets again prove to be inadequate aids to this process of summation.

As Aristotle said, "whereas all other goods are necessary preconditions of happiness or naturally contribute to it and serve as its instrument . . . [happiness] is the highest good."[1]

[1] Aristotle, *Politics,* trans. William Ellis (New York: Everyman/Dutton, 1943), 81.

22 Understanding happiness

In this penultimate Part VII we explore the concepts of utility, satisfaction, and happiness. Our target is the relation of these moods and thoughts to market institutions and practices. Koopmans reports that economists study "the satisfaction of human wants in human society," and "the best ways of satisfying human wants."[1] Mises claims that there are no boundaries to economics, for "economic action consists in the endeavor to remedy the state of dissatisfaction" wherever it is to be found.[2] Pigou states: "In the deepest sense, economic reality comprises states of mind – the satisfactions and dissatisfactions of human beings – and nothing else."[3] To this may be added the catechism of an economics text: "What is the economic system supposed to do? The answer that it should contribute to human happiness is as good a start as any."[4]

Certainly the market makes a contribution to the satisfaction of human wants, but as pointed out in the introduction to this part, there are reasons to doubt the effectiveness of the market in maximizing happiness. In order to clarify both the contributions and the failures of the market in these respects, we must first examine the nature of happiness and utility, explore their relationships to each other and to the market, and only then can we assess the claims of the economists.

I start this chapter with an exploration of the conditions necessary for the development of a theory of happiness as a contribution to understanding the strange association between economics and what we may call *hedonics*. The second major theme in this discussion deals with skepticism about both the possibility of happiness and the possibility of our knowing anything about it. The relationships between objective and subjective accounts and the special problems of the achievement–aspirations ratio arising from subjective estimates are then explored. In the final section I give a brief outline of the main methods and findings of the quality-of-life studies on which I rely for my interpretation of market effects.

[1] Tjalling C. Koopmans, *Three Essays on the State of Economic Science* (New York: McGraw-Hill, 1957), 169.
[2] Ludwig von Mises, *Epistemological Problems of Economics*, trans. G. Riesman (Princeton: van Nostrand, 1960), 61.
[3] Arthur C. Pigou, *The Economics of Welfare*, 4th ed. (1932; reprint London: Macmillan, 1948), 19. Here Pigou may have been following Jevons's belief that economics was basically an investigation of "the condition of the mind." Jevons, *The Theory of Political Economy*, R. D. C. Black, ed. (New York: Penguin, 1970), 15. Joan Robinson quotes Stalin's definition of the purpose of socialism as "securing the maximum satisfaction of the constantly rising material and cultural requirements of the whole society," Joan Robinson, *Economic Philosophy* (Harmondsworth, UK: Penguin, 1964), 11.
[4] R. S. Eckaus, *Basic Economics* (Boston: Little Brown, 1972). This quotation is borrowed from David Morawetz et al., "Income Distribution and Self-Rated Happiness: Some Empirical Evidence," *The Economic Journal* 87 (1977): 511–22 at 511 n. 3.

Toward a theory of happiness

Freud once proposed that the cultural superego, embedded in social norms and ethical theory, had, of necessity, imposed upon mankind such a burden of guilt that happiness was not possible. In culture, as among individuals, conscience "troubles too little about the happiness of the ego, and it fails to take into account sufficiently the difficulties in the way of obeying it."[5] In general, he thought, scholars had paid too little attention to happiness – and too much attention to morality. This point of view seems to ignore the Greeks, the Enlightenment, Bentham, and the utilitarians, but there is something in it. If happiness is at least one of the supreme goods, as so many scholars from the Greeks to contemporary philosophers (such as Ross, Russell, and unreconstructed utilitarians like J. J. C. Smart) claim, why has a separate theory of happiness been so late in developing – so much later, for example, than theories of knowledge?

Setting aside for the moment the Greek idea of the happy life, we may find some of the reasons for the delayed appearance of a separate theory of hedonics in the following considerations. In the process we see, in a preliminary way, the close association of economics with hedonics at the very beginning of both disciplines.

Common origins of economics and hedonics

Relief from economic exigency. For the development of a theory of happiness an economic surplus for enough people must remove the priority of economic matters, for people are unlikely to think about happiness when they are busy thinking about hunger or distracted by the poverty around them.[6] Thus, just when it was becoming apparent that the wealth, or poverty, of nations is not given in the nature of things we find elements of a new branch of philosophy that was to develop into economics, focusing on both happiness and economics: for example, Turgot and Condorcet in France like Smith and Bentham in England emerge at the same time from the same set of circumstances. Both groups followed Montesquieu's explicit statements to the effect that in his account of the spirit of commerce he is moved by the idea that poverty is not a necessary condition of the human species. The change in technological possibilities opened a new frontier of thought to cope with the new possibilities.

The malleability of people and institutions. The idea that human nature was malleable (Condillac) and that people were generally educable (Locke) was a further condition for the development of both economics and hedonics. It is necessary for hedonics, as Mill explains because people must choose among the oppor-

[5] Sigmund Freud, *Civilization and Its Discontent*, trans. J. Riviere (1930; reprint London: Hogarth Press, 1951), 139.
[6] This argument has much in common with theory and research on postmaterialism reporting that a high value placed on nonmaterial goods is disproportionately supported by those brought up in more affluent and secure circumstances. See Ronald Inglehart, *The Silent Revolution* (Princeton: Princeton University Press, 1972); Idem, "Values, Objective Needs, and Subjective Satisfaction Among Western Publics," *Comparative Political Studies* 9 (1977): 429–58.

tunities available to them those that will give them a greater share of happiness. And it is necessary for market economics because the market requires of people that they be able to learn from experience and that they calculate their interests with care. For market economics to develop, as Hirschman reports, the ungovernable "passions" had to give way to the calculating "interests."[7] Hirschman also points out that "only in the modern age, particularly in the eighteenth century . . . [emerged] the novel idea that happiness could be engineered by changing the social order."[8] Engineering of happiness and rational economic calculation again had a common origin.

Liberation from moral intellectual hegemony. The moral reasoning that holds that (1) intention is more important than consequences, and (2) only merited happiness is a good, is an obstacle to both economics and theories of happiness – partly because it devotes itself wholly to the question of merit. The Greek idea that happiness and "virtue" must be joined was a distraction for an empirically based theory of what makes people happy, especially when virtue is given its later exclusively moral content. Moreover, the ethical idea that only intention, not consequences, are ethical would have completely blocked Smith's hidden hand, which explicitly excludes "benevolence" so as to examine the benign consequences of self-interested actions. Both economics and hedonics were also liberated by Mandeville and Vico's moral paradox of social good derived from private "vice," a paradox showing the social benefits of employment and material well-being to be derived from the selfish expenditures of the rich (or anyone else). And then later the liberation was greatly favored by the consequentialist view of utilitarians, where the hedonic outcome of behavior for all concerned became the test of the value of that behavior. These doctrines may not make for good ethics,[9] but confounding ethics with economics and hedonics tends to undermine clarity in all three fields.[10]

Liberation from religious hegemony. As is well known, emerging concepts of capitalism had to overcome Christian objections to "usury"[11] and ideas about "fair prices." In a parallel but different fashion, hedonics had to overcome the idea that happiness was a matter of the Divine will. For example, Spinoza's geometry of happiness had very little to say about the nature of happiness (except

[7] Albert O. Hirschman, *The Passions and the Interests: Political Arguments for Capitalism Before Its Triumph* (Princeton: Princeton University Press, 1977). In the process "happiness" also gave way to "want satisfaction."

[8] Albert O. Hirschman, "Rival Interpretations of Market Society: Civilizing, Destructive, or Feeble?" *Journal of Economic Literature* 20 (December, 1982): 1,463–84. It is interesting to note that the subtitle of Spencer's *Social Statics,* the American nineteenth-century free-enterprise bible, is *The Conditions of Human Happiness* (New York: D. Appleton & Co., 1878).

[9] Amartya Sen and Bernard Williams, "Introduction," in Sen and Williams, eds., *Utilitarianism and Beyond* (Cambridge, UK: Cambridge University Press, 1982).

[10] For an effort to integrate ethics with economics, see Amitai Etzioni, *The Moral Dimension: Toward a New Economics* (New York: Free Press, 1988).

[11] The effectiveness of the Church's prohibition of usury was undermined by various rental schemes that the church itself employed. See Karl Marx, *Capital: A Critique of Political Economy,* vol. 3, *The Process of Capitalist Production as a Whole,* ed. Friedrich Engels (London: Lawrence & Wishart, 1974), 611, 613. Original work published 1894.

its ethical quality) and nothing about the human sources of happiness; rather it was an exploration of the proposition that if a person desired happiness for the self he or she would also desire happiness for others if human knowledge were in accord with "a greater knowledge of God."[12] In passing I note that, given human suffering, knowledge of God might equally turn to theodicy, explaining not happiness but evil and misery. Economics, with its secular accounts of ways to increase this-worldly welfare, had to make its way against interpretations of God's Will and the explanation of evil.

Neither market economics nor primitive hedonics make room for concepts of duty embedded in the Protestant ethic, but economic life borrowed energy from this source. Since the Protestant ethic justifies wealth but not happiness, hedonics was in the position Freud complained of: the claims of duty had to be tamed and put into perspective.

This sketchy account of common obstacles to the development of both economics and hedonics seems to omit the Greeks. But if one defines happiness as the good life, as the Greeks did and as Russell comes close to doing – "The happy life is to an extraordinary extent the same as the good life"[13] – a theory of happiness is part of a more general theory of conduct and behavior and therefore embraced by moral, religious, and even economic thought. Under these circumstances happiness is likely to be folded into those departments of thought without strain – as I believe has been the case. But that makes a theory of happiness captive to a theory of the good life, again confounding ethics and hedonics.

Economics and hedonics

These glimpses into the historical and intellectual circumstances obstructing the development of both economics and hedonics do not explain why the two should continue to be so closely related. Two points help to make that connection a trifle clearer, one dealing with utilitarianism, and the other with the current uses of utility in economic theory. With respect to the first of these, both hedonics and economics borrow heavily from Bentham's utilitarian theory, hedonics obviously from Bentham's focus on happiness as not only the supreme good but in fact the only good for which men do or should strive. The use of the term *utility,* meaning something between satisfaction and happiness, reveals economists' debt to Bentham. In the next chapter we will distinguish utility from happiness, but for the moment must accept the pursuit of utility maximization as reasonably close to the *pursuit* of happiness and treat utility accordingly.[14]

Where Smith developed a market theory of productivity and wealth, Bentham, almost by accident, developed a rationalization of the market in terms of pain and

---

[12] Baruch Spinoza, *Ethics Demonstrated in Geometrical Order,* in Monroe C. Beardsley, ed., *The European Philosophers: From Descartes to Nietzsche* (New York: Random House Modern Library, 1960), 197, 209. Original work published 1677.

[13] Bertrand Russell, *The Conquest of Happiness.* (London: Allen & Unwin, 1930), 245.

[14] One of the limitations on this identification of happiness with utility is that only "that part of social welfare which can be brought directly or indirectly into relation with the measuring rod of money" is fairly considered. Pigou, *The Economics of Welfare,* 11.

pleasure. For two hundred years, utilitarianism has dominated discussion of happiness, often as the foil for other theories. As the heirs of Bentham, an inheritance ignored by Malthus and Ricardo, incorporated by Jevons and Edgeworth, and then, shedding the term "happiness" but clinging to "utility," embraced by Marshall, economists, perhaps to their own surprise, have often been the principal interpreters of pain and pleasure, converting these terms into utilities and disutilities, wants and want satisfaction. It seems that Smith's idea of wealth as a sufficient explanandum was insufficient for his successors to serve as a justification of economic behavior. Economists must have wanted a justification that would give greater credit and wider scope to the behavior they were accounting for; striving for wealth must have seemed insufficient for that purpose.

The second point in explaining the contemporary relation of hedonics to economics is that utility theory, with its Benthamite origins, has been found to be essential to microeconomic analysis. Stigler explains the relatively late, nineteenth-century adoption of utility theory by economists as due to the early status of economics as a set of policy prescriptions rather than as an academic discipline [which might be said to begin with the appointment of Senior to the faculty at Oxford]. An academic discipline, he suggests, seeks general explanations in contrast to a nonacademic subject seeking immediate policy applications for which utility theory was apparently not useful.[15]

There are good reasons why economists focus on want satisfaction and utility, for "utility theory allowed a unified explanation of behavior: everyone was a utility maximizer, and all economic problems became simply problems of taste and obstacles (so, Pareto)." As the science developed, utility theory was to "become a part of the working equipment of the competent practitioners of the science." As a consequence, we now find the "adoption of the marginal utility theory by the ruling theorists of economics . . . [for] there does not appear to be any serious rival explanation."[16] Thus, shedding the term "happiness" but retaining the concept of "satisfaction," economists now explain their discipline in the ways cited by Koopmans, Mises, and Pigou: the study of the satisfaction of wants in human society. In many ways, utilitarianism has triumphed, a triumph at least as great in public policy as in the market; thus, it can be claimed that "social policy in our country is based on implicit utilitarianism."[17]

The common origins of economics and hedonics and the usefulness of a theory of utility to microeconomic analysis helps to account for their union in modern thought. What is now needed is a separate analysis of hedonics that is not linked to economics, a link that inevitably tends to justify one or another economic or political system. It is no more appropriate for study of "the satisfaction of wants in human society" to be attached to the study of income and wealth than for the study of health to be lodged in a Department of Pharmacology.

[15] George J. Stigler, "The Adoption of the Marginal Utility Theory," in his The Economist as Preacher and Other Essays (Chicago University of Chicago Press, 1982).
[16] Ibid., 78, 82, 83.
[17] Norman Bradburn, The Structure of Psychological Well-Being (Chicago: Aldine, 1969), 233.

Economists and psychologists

Today, as I shall show, the study of happiness, like the study of other moods, is firmly attached to the discipline of psychology, which is free to look for its sources in any corner of behavior where moods are important. But this interest by psychologists is relatively recent.

Although happiness is clearly a psychological concept, this did not lead economists to examine the way psychologists treat happiness or satisfaction. Schumpeter explains that "economists have never allowed their analysis to be influenced by the professional psychologists of their times, but have always framed for themselves such assumptions about psychological processes as they thought it desirable to make."[18] Robbins agrees.[19] In defense of Schumpeter, one might say that the late development of psychology as an empirical discipline left the field open until quite recently to scholars to make such psychological assumptions as they pleased without violating the canons of good scholarship.[20] Psychology itself passed through two phases of development uncongenial to an interest in happiness. In the words of the originator of psychoanalytic theory: "What is called happiness in its narrowest sense comes from the satisfaction – most often instantaneous – of pent up needs which have reached great intensity, and by its very nature can only be a transitory experience."[21]

A second resistant school of psychological theory in the recent past, dominant for twenty years in academic psychology, was the "learning theory" of classical or operant conditioning (e.g., Watson and Skinner), a theory that excluded *ab initio* the epistemological validity of internal feelings.

But all that has changed. After extended attention to other emotions, one wing of social psychology, chiefly inspired by work at the University of Michigan, gave massive attention to moods of happiness as a complement to the very considerable work previously done on depression. The growth of the study of happiness, outlined in this chapter, has led to discussions that have been criticized as theoretically un-

[18] Joseph A. Schumpeter, *History of Economic Analysis,* ed. Elizabeth Boody Schumpeter (New York: Oxford University Press, 1954), 27. Schumpeter not only based economics on logic but claimed that logic itself was based on "the pattern of economic decision." See his *Capitalism, Socialism and Democracy* (London: George Allen & Unwin, 1950), 122.

[19] "Professional economists, absorbed in the exciting task of discovering new truth, have usually disdained to reply [to psychologists]; and the lay public, ever anxious to escape the necessity of recognizing the implications of choice in a world of scarcity, has allowed itself to be bamboozled into believing that matters, which are in fact as little dependent on the truth of fashionable psychology as the multiplication table, are still open questions on which the enlightened man, who of course, is nothing if not a psychologist, must be willing to suspend judgment." Lionel Robbins, *The Nature and Significance of Economic Science,* 2d ed. (London: Macmillan, 1935), partially reprinted in Daniel M. Hausman, ed., *The Philosophy of Economics: An Anthology* (Cambridge, UK: Cambridge University Press, 1984), 122–3.

[20] One effort toward an integration, based in part on the psychology of MacDougal, failed, as it was bound to. See A. W. Coats, "Economics and Psychology: The Death and Resurrection of a Research Programme," in S. J. Latsis, ed., *Method and Appraisal in Economics* (Cambridge, UK: Cambridge University Press, 1976), 43–64.

[21] Men's search for happiness, said Freud, is bound to end in disappointment; it's methods include reducing demands, withdrawal from the world, intoxication, renunciation of the instincts, an immersion in art or science (available to only a few), love (which makes us defenseless against disappointment), and flight into neurosis. As a consequence, "the goal towards which the pleasure-principle impels us – of becoming happy – is not attainable." Freud, *Civilization and Its Discontents,* pp. 27–39.

sophisticated; it is only in the 1980s that a theory of happiness or well-being seemed to be emerging, and that theory is still considered to be in a primitive state.[22]

I have attempted to account for the late development of a discipline of hedonics, the union of hedonics with economics, and the usefulness to economics of the derivations of Benthamite theory surviving as utility theory. The main element of that usefulness is the way it has permitted, without examination, a generalized theory of economic behavior. The idea that there can be a separate theory of hedonics, or that economists can ever go beyond the tautological concept of utility, assumes that we can know something about happiness or life satisfaction. This has been questioned by both philosophers and economists. We now turn to the set of problems raised by these questions.

What can we know of happiness?

There are two forms of skepticism relevant to our purpose, one that doubts that mankind can be happy (hedonic skepticism); and another that doubts that we can ever know much about happiness (epistemological skepticism). The "worldly philosphers" (Heilbroner's term for economists)[23] and the other philosophers differ in their skepticisms. The worldly philosophers doubt that we can know anything about another's happiness but are content with self-knowledge; they never suffered from hedonic skepticism at all. The other philosophers sometimes expressed more extensive epistemological as well as hedonic skepticism.

Certain Enlightenment philosophers, like Voltaire and d'Alembert, and some nineteenth- and twentieth-century pessimists (e.g., Schopenhauer, Nietzsche, and Spengler) have expressed their skepticism about the possibility of widespread happiness. From this hedonic skepticism, epistemological skepticism may seem to follow, for we cannot know much about what we cannot experience. But since the relief of suffering is vivid and real, knowledge of our own inner states is not at issue (but see Chapter 27), that is, epistemological skepticism seems to follow from hedonic skepticism, but with exceptions, as we shall see.

These various interpreters of skepticism, however, have other agendas. As is the case with ideologies, the skeptical position of the philosophers is functional for certain purposes: for Voltaire, skepticism about universal happiness was useful in challenging Leibnitz's naive optimism and also for Voltaire's own thesis that "philosophy, universally diffused, will give some consolation to human nature for the calamities it will experience in all ages";[24] for Schopenhauer that skepticism served to challenge his lifetime enemy, Hegel, and for establishing his theory of the will; for Nietzsche, skepticism about happiness helped in challenging the Christian ethic and in bolstering his theory that happiness is a form of power.[25] On the other hand, the market theorists' optimism about the satisfaction of human wants in the market has been useful in warding off both mercantilism on one side, and socialism on the

---

[22] Ed Diener, "Subjective Well-Being," *Psychological Bulletin* 95 (1984): 542–75.
[23] Robert L. Heilbruner, *The Worldly Philosophers*, rev. ed (New York: Simon & Schuster, 1961).
[24] John B. Bury, *The Idea of Progress* (1920; reprint New York: Macmillan, 1932), 150 and passim.
[25] Walter Kaufmann, *Nietzsche: Philosopher, Psychologist, Antichrist*, 4th ed. (Princeton: Princeton University Press, 1974), 192.

other. And their skepticism about knowing another's level of satisfaction has been useful in avoiding interpersonal comparisons that weaken the power of a deductive theory possessed of two psychological assumptions: avarice and rationality. (The usefulness of avoiding utilitarian implications of equality applies only to a minority of market theorists.) Ideas have functions other than mirroring reality.

But there is a deeper reason: It is the business of philosophy to understand a faith, and understanding a faith requires examining the flaws that the faith necessarily conceals, as MacIntyre has persuasively argued; for that reason understanding and belief are incompatible.[26] The market, of course, is a set of institutions as well as a faith, but the faith is essential to make the institutions work: belief that wants can be and are satisfied through market mechanisms, belief that market values are fairly calculated, belief that rewards are commensurate to effort and skill, belief in the social value of private gain. Philosophers need not be skeptical about happiness, but they can be, whereas the official ideology of markets cannot. Ethical philosophers, at least, cannot easily be skeptical about assuming that others are like oneself, but economists find that this form of skepticism is convenient, if only to limit the costs of data collection.

There is contemporary skepticism about the likely fruit of the pursuit of happiness that is more difficult to dismiss. It is based on research on "adaptation level" theory that says that people adapt to whatever level of benefit or pain they currently experience so that, after a relatively brief period with an increment or decrement of these benefits or pains, their senses of subjective well-being (or ill-being) return to where they were before the change. For example, Brickman and Campbell ask whether "the relativistic nature of subjective experience means there is no true solution to the problem of happiness. . . . The pessimistic theme is that the nature of AL [adaptation level] phenomena condemns men to live on a hedonic treadmill," but, they add, there are nevertheless "wise and foolish ways to pursue happiness," both for societies and individuals.[27] One study, for example, shows that as incomes increase, it takes more and more money to "buy" the degree of expressed happiness experienced before the increase.[28] The answer to this form of skepticism lies in the quality-of-life studies I will explicate in this part.

The "possibility" of happiness is not really in doubt, but the grounds for hedonic skepticism do challenge aspects of market theories of utility and want satisfaction, although not the idea that happiness is a proper subject of study in its own right. On the other hand, epistemological skepticism challenges the idea that a theory of hedonics is even possible. We turn, therefore, to the epistemological doubts about our knowledge of happiness. Later we shall see that there are grounds for doubt regarding our knowledge of our own happiness, as well (Chapter 27).

[26] Alisdair MacIntyre, "The Idea of a Social Science," in Bryan R. Wilson, ed., *Rationality* (Oxford, UK: Blackwell, 1970), 112–30.
[27] Philip Brickman and Donald T. Campbell, "Hedonic Relativism and Planning the Good Society," in M. H. Appley, ed., *Adaptation-Level Theory: A Symposium* (New York: Academic Press, 1971), 289, 299–300.
[28] Otis Dudley Duncan, "Does Money Buy Satisfaction?" *Social Indicators Research* 2 (1975): 267–74.

Happiness is too vague a concept to study empirically
As Galbraith put it: "To have argued simply that our present preoccupation with production of goods does not best aid the pursuit of happiness would have got nowhere. The concepts to which one would have been committed would have been far too vague."[29] Galbraith's own vagueness has two parts: First, the relation between production and happiness is particularly ambiguous, since it is just at the point of production that the disutilities of the market system are thought to occur. Thus, the happiness of the market, if we may call it that, is supposed to arise from subtracting the disutilities of work from the utilities of leisure and consumption, leaving a net utility that makes each person's enterprise worthwhile. Second, if Galbraith has in mind the *utility* that goods and services (and leisure) yield the individual, he is turning to a concept that is quite empty of empirical content. Ironically, whereas Galbraith's identification of production and happiness rests on what he believes is the superior precision of "production," that is, income and wealth, a group of Israeli economists report that "we prefer to use the concept of self-rated happiness rather than utility because the former is more easily measured empirically."[30]

The study of "self-rated happiness," or subjective well-being, has a brief history. In 1946 George Gallup had the novel idea of asking people whether they were happy (and has continued to do so for forty years), but it was not until Gerald Gurin and his colleagues (in 1960) studied people's reports on their sense of well-being, followed five years later by the work of Norman Bradburn and David Caplovitz and of Hadley Cantril, that the sources of a general sense of well-being, happiness, or life satisfaction were systematically explored.[31] Since the mid-1960s, prompted in part by the social indicator movement, there have been literally thousands of studies (cross-sectional, cross-cultural, and historical) of the nature and sources of reported work, marital, and life satisfaction.[32] In our discussion we shall rely heavily on four works: Campbell, Converse, and Rodgers, *The Quality of American Life* (1976); Andrews and Withey, *Social Indicators of Well-Being* (1976); Campbell, *The Sense of Well-Being in America* (1981); and Freedman, *Happy People* (1980).[33]

---

[29] John Kenneth Galbraith, *The Affluent Society,* 2d ed., rev. (Harmondsworth, UK: Penguin, 1971), 278.

[30] Morawetz et al., "Income Distribution and Self-Rated Happiness," 512 n. 3.

[31] Gerald Gurin, Joseph Veroff, and Sheila Feld, *Americans View Their Mental Health* (New York: Basic Books, 1960); Norman M. Bradburn and David Caplovitz, *Reports on Happiness* (Chicago: Aldine, 1965); and Hadley Cantril, *The Pattern of Human Concerns* (New Brunswick: Rutgers University Press, 1965).

[32] Michalos reports a review of 2,545 studies on work, marital, and life satisfaction during the fifteen years up to 1986. See Alex C. Michalos, "Job Satisfaction, Marital Satisfaction, and the Quality of Life: A Review and a Preview," in Frank M. Andrews, ed., *Research on the Quality of Life* (Ann Arbor, MI: Institute for Social Research, 1986). See also Richard A Easterlin, "Does Economic Growth Improve the Human Lot? Some Empirical Evidence," in P. A. David and M. W. Reder, eds., *Nations and Households in Economic Growth* (New York: Academic Press, 1974); Inglehart, "Values, Objective Needs and Subjective Satisfaction."

[33] Angus Campbell, Philip E. Converse, and Willard L. Rodgers, *The Quality of American Life* (New York: Russell Sage, 1976); Frank M. Andrews and Stephen B. Withey, *Social Indicators of Well-Being: Americans' Perceptions of Life Quality* (New York: Plenum Press, 1976); Angus Campbell, *The Sense*

One might plausibly question the validity of self-reports on such a subject as happiness; there might, for example, be a tendency to say what would make the interviewer happy. Apparently this is not so; social desirability effects are notably missing within national accounts, although they are discernable when one compares answers to questions about well-being cross-culturally. Nor is there any evidence of inauthenticity, that is, of "faking good" or "faking bad" in these reports. On the contrary, by such objective criteria as degrees of laughing and smiling, interviewers could detect no inconsistencies between how the respondents seemed to feel and their reports of how they felt.[34] All of these studies have been tested for their validity in commonsense terms: If a person reports headaches, sleeplessness, few friends, money worries, and ill health, he or she reports himself or herself as unhappy. If a person is satisfied with his or her housing, neighborhood, family life, work, and friendships, he or she scores high on an Index of Well-Being. Thus, by a variety of internal statistical and external validational tests, the measures of perceived life satisfaction and happiness survive reasonably well.[35]

Happiness as a conscious goal

There is an apparent conflict between the idea that happiness cannot be pursued directly and happiness as a conscious goal. The psychologist Gordon Allport points out that: "The state of happiness is not itself a motivating force but a by-product of otherwise motivated activities"[36] On the other hand, Max Lerner says of Americans: "If asked to reflect on what was their main aim in life, most Americans would probably shrug the question away, since they tend to take life goals as given; but if pressed, they would probably say, 'To be happy,' or 'To lead a happy life.' If asked what they want for their children, their answer would again be happiness."[37] Lerner was largely wrong. Asked to rank their terminal values, American national samples ranked "happiness (contentedness)" fourth in 1968 and sixth in 1971, behind "a world at peace," (first), "family security (taking care of loved ones)" (second), and "freedom (independence, free choice)"

[34] Diener, "Subjective Well-Being," 551. John P. Robinson and Philip R. Shaver, *Measures of Social Psychological Attitudes*, rev. ed. (Ann Arbor, MI: Institute for Social Research, 1973), report: "In this review we have found a number of constant relationships when respondents in social surveys were asked to report on their general satisfaction with life." Among other reassuring properties was the fact that "people who express satisfaction at one time period are quite likely to express satisfaction if interviewed some months later." (p. 34)

[35] Frank M. Andrews and Rick Crandall, "The Validity of Self-Reported Well-Being," *Social Indicators Research* 3 (1976): 1–19; Robinson and Shaver, *Measures of Social Psychological Attitudes*, 12–44. But the National Research Council's Panel on Survey Measurement of Subjective Phenomena, *Surveys of Subjective Phenomena: Summary Report* (Washington, DC: National Academy Press, 1981) found that single items on global happiness, but not specific questions about marital or work happiness, were subject to contextual influences. On the other hand, in the quality-of-life studies the answers to the specific questions predicted answers to the general questions about feelings on life-as-a-whole.

[36] Gordon Allport, *Becoming* (New Haven: Yale University Press, 1955), 68.

[37] Max Lerner, *America as a Civilization: Life and Thought in the United States Today,* (New York: Simon & Schuster, 1957), 693.

(third), but well ahead of "a comfortable life (a prosperous life)" (ninth and thirteenth).[38]

It is possible to have as a goal, and certainly as a value, a state of mind that is a by-product of other activities. Whereas the pursuit of happiness is never an adequate explanation of one's actions, happiness (or even utility) may be a conscious aim while pursuing more concrete ends, just as the satisfaction of claims of duty may be a conscious aim in other actions.

Consciousness of happiness is incompatible with happiness

One impediment in discovering the existence of happiness goes back to Sartre's problem of consciousness; consciousness of consciousness, he says, inhibits our spontaneous feelings of happiness; focusing on the self, one cannot be happy.[39] In more prosaic terms, Mills makes the same point: "Ask yourself whether you are happy, and you cease to be so?"[40] In the same vein, two students of perceived life quality comment that: "Happiness is like an orgasm: if you think about whether you have it, you don't."[41] But if we cannot be conscious of a state of feelings without destroying it, one source of information is denied us.

In a survey in the 1970s Dalkey asked his respondents whether they were ever conscious of evaluating their lives from time to time, and concluded that "some evaluation is kept by most people."[42] Andrews and Withey inferred from their data that such evaluations often occur when major decisions on marriage, changing jobs, or moving to another community forced a consideration of past and future. When people are giving up something and looking forward to something "parts and pieces and incidents in one's life do not tend to be evaluated in isolation but rather in a larger context that encompasses a span of life concerns and a span of time." Almost all of these authors' respondents had made assessments of their lives at some time previous to their survey interviews.[43] Global attitudes toward the felicity of their lives, then, did not make up a "new issue" for these respondents, the kind of issue on which attitudes tend to be unstable, but rather they were familiar, "old" issues with roots and branches in other ideas. In their somewhat better educated sample, Shaver and Freeman, found that "almost eight in ten think about happiness weekly or daily."[44] Finally, incidental to his study of whether positive and negative moods

[38] Milton Rokeach, "Change and Stability in American Value Systems, 1968–1971," *Public Opinion Quarterly* (1974): 222–38 at 226.

[39] Jean-Paul Sartre, *Existentialism and Human Emotion* (New York: Wisdom Library, 1957).

[40] John Stuart Mill, *Autobiography* (Oxford, UK: Oxford University Press, 1969), 86.

[41] Philip Shaver and Jonathan Freedman, "Your Pursuit of Happiness," *Psychology Today* (August 1976): 27–32, 75. Note the distinction between consciousness of a condition and the capacity to will that condition – which is the burden of Elster's arguments about the need for indirection in certain situations. "Some mental and social states can only come about as the by-products of actions undertaken for other ends. They can never, that is, be brought about intelligently and intentionally because the very attempt to do so prevents the state one is trying to bring about." Jon Elster, *Sour Grapes: Studies in the Subversion of Rationality* (Cambridge, UK: Cambridge University Press, 1983), 43.

[42] Norman C. Dalkey, *Studies in the Quality of Life: Delphi and Decision-Making* (Lexington, MA: Lexington Books, 1972), 97.

[43] Andrews and Withey, *Social Indicators of Well-Being*, 309.

[44] Philip Shaver and Jonathan Freedman, "Your Pursuit of Happiness," *Psychology Today* 10 (August 1976): 28.

affected willingness to help others, Berkowitz found that his manipulations of "self-awareness" affected this relationship but did not by itself influence moods.[45] We have then, not only "privileged information" on our own happiness or life satisfaction that economists acknowledge, but information on the happiness of others, indeed, of national populations – and experimental evidence where (unlike the Heisenberg effect) observation does not change the nature of the phenomenon.

I stress this point because it might be assumed that the market (like economists and behaviorists) would train attention on the external world and encourage people to shun introspection. Market encouragement of the calculation of pleasure might, indeed, inhibit the broader view implied by these introspective evaluations of a whole life. In this, it would follow its utilitarian base. As Sen and Williams point out: "Essentially, utilitarianism sees persons as locations of their respective utilities – as the sites at which such activities as desiring and having pleasure and pain take place. Once note has been taken of the person's utility, utilitarianism has no further direct interest in any information about them."[46]

Whereas the market's focus on the externals of life seem to tolerate, at least, hedonic introspection, we may observe that Eastern European socialist societies seemed to prefer objective indicators for evaluating the quality of life,[47] and traditional societies have been found to lack "psychological mobility" to reflect on their own lives compared to alternatives, a condition necessary for appraising life satisfaction.[48] Impressions of this kind lead one to reject the idea that the market inhibits the kind of self-examination or intraceptive thinking that is involved in reflection on one's happiness, as distinct from momentary pleasure or satisfaction.

Objective elements in subjective accounts

Philosophically, the evaluation of objective well-being and the validity of subjective reports of well-being turn on several considerations. One deals with the actual present and future well-being of the person whose preferences and wants are under consideration. Whether a person's well-being is served by fulfilling personal desires or wants depends in good measure on whether he or she is informed of both the implications and consequences of that fulfillment – for others as well as for himself or herself, hence Griffin's emphasis on *informed* desire accounts.[49] That information cannot be wholly subjectively appraised but must meet the objective standards of the outside world; the information must be objectively realistic.[50]

[45] Leonard Berkowitz, "Mood, Self-Awareness, and Willingness to Help," *Journal of Personality and Social Psychology* 52 (1987): 721–9. Other research has found that self-awareness makes people uncomfortable. See Robert A. Wicklund, "Objective Self-Awareness," in L. Berkowitz, ed., *Advances in Experimental Social Psychology*, vol. 8 (New York: Academic Press, 1975).

[46] Sen and Williams, "Introduction," 4. To this Bentham adds that people have no hedonic gain in exploring their own motivation. W. Stark, ed., *Jeremy Bentham's Economic Writings*, vol. 3 (London: Royal Economic Society by Allen & Unwin, 1954), 425.

[47] Rudolf Andorka, "A Long-Term Development of Hungary, Measured by Social Indicators," *Social Indicators Research* 8 (1980): 1–14; Elemér Hankiss, "Structural Variables in Cross-Cultural Research on the Quality of Life," in Alexander Szalai and Frank M. Andrews, eds., *Quality of Life: Comparative Studies* (Beverly Hills, CA: Sage, 1980), 41–56.

[48] Daniel Lerner, *The Passing of Traditional Society* (New York: Free Press, 1958).

[49] James Griffin, *Well-Being: Its Meaning, Measurement, and Moral Importance* (Oxford, UK: Clarendon Press, 1986), 32.

[50] Griffin also holds that a person's values are objective in that they must be anchored in objective

Second, quite apart from the good judgment and moral implications of the wants at stake, there is the distinction between wants and needs. The satisfaction of wants has no moral standing in itself; it might be mere indulgence; it might be perverse, antisocial, and cruel. For moral purposes, then, Griffin turns to what he calls *need accounts,* where the needs, as a subcategory of wants, represent variations on the roster of "things that we aim at simply as normal human beings rather than as the particular human beings we are, things that are both necessary and sufficient for recognizably human existence."[51] Needs, says Griffin, are more objective than wants in that it might be possible in any given society for people to agree on what was "necessary and sufficient for recognizably human existence." It is partly because of this quasi-objectivity that a person's needs may represent an objective moral claim on society where wants do not.

Wants and the origins of value

We are inquiring into the differences between objective and subjective accounts of happiness as a contribution to our understanding of what can be known about that felicitous state. Although Griffin suggests that needs have a more objective (inter-subjectively testable) status than do wants, there is another aspect of the objectivity of needs that focuses on the very origins of value. The origins of value lead to recondite questions of whether the chooser determines the value of a good, or whether the value of the good is what makes the chooser want it. The circularity of the issue is shared with the idea of utility (Chapter 23). (Actually, the question itself is easily solved by partitioning various meanings and allowing for interaction. As in any perception, e.g., the beauty of an object lies not alone in the object nor in the eye of the beholder but in their interaction.) The answers to questions about the location of value, however, have consequences that directly concern us. The idea that the chooser or consumer determines value "works well with ideas of choice and free-dom. . . . Subjective utility allows us to measure usefulness in a particular way, because it makes all objects commensurate in the minds of their owners or prospective owners. We measure objects by their degree of usefulness to us, which reflects the intensity of our desire."[52] Economists prefer subjective utility because it fits their concept of want satisfaction and economic demand. On the other hand, the idea that value is more or less dictated by the properties of the object, which are generally the same for everyone, is attractive for other purposes: "The objective notion of utility works well with our idea of need." If the utility of objects "is defined for us and whose use by us provides directly for social recognition because that is not contingent on our personal preferences," our moral claims upon the object may receive external validation.[53] Thus it serves the purposes of those who seek a more egalitarian distribution of goods – "to each according to his need."

conditions, but this seems to me to confound the public acceptance of values with their private functions for individual thought. Ibid. See also R. M. Hare, "Ethical Theory and Utilitarianism," in Sen and Williams, *Utilitarianism and Beyond,* 23–38.
[51] Griffin, *Well-Being,* 53. Griffin struggles mightily with the problem of criteria for needs, but in the end, when he gives such criteria, they seem only a variation on the lists others have drawn up. See for example, David Braybrooke, *Meeting Needs* (Princeton, NJ: Princeton University Press, 1987), 34–6.
[52] David Levine, *Needs, Rights, and the Market* (Boulder, CO: Lynne Rienner, 1988), 36.
[53] Ibid.

In any event, wanting something may be a necessary condition for finding satisfaction in that something, but it is not a sufficient condition for value, for a thing might be valuable even if no one wanted it, perhaps for lack of courage, or foresight and knowledge. For example, there is value to a fair deal even if neither of the parties to the deal wanted fairness.[54] Nor are any of the variants of utility the sole criterion for value; rather, utility is one among several criteria for choosing among values, such as freedom, knowledge, justice, and especially the elements of human development we have been at pains to examine in previous chapters. Utility is not an end in itself.[55] Thus even summing utilities across persons does not produce a final assessment of value for those persons or for their community.

The distinction between subjective and objective accounts of well-being

If we take subjective accounts at face value we risk accepting the wantlessness of the poor and the acquiescence of the exploited. We also risk accepting the inauthentic self-reports that, although reported to be infrequent, are unacceptable: the housewives who do not like their status but, because they think they should, report themselves as "pleased" with their lives; the abused subordinate who has learned to fear expressions of dissatisfaction. We examine these later, and here remind ourselves that want satisfaction begs the question of the manipulation of wants by the market, and the ambiguity of dissatisfaction (Chapter 23); the objective accounts may not adequately imply utility, but they at least avoid most of these genuine perils.

The rival to subjective accounts is, of course, objective accounts, especially those fitted to the requirements of economic studies. Objective and subjective accounts measure different things; one cannot be substituted for the other.[56] This is illustrated by the controversy over the quality of life in the 1760 to 1815 (or 1830) period. Scholars have reanalyzed data on diets and mortality in this period, discovering that over these decades people were in fact living longer and eating better. (Moreover, they say, whatever deterioration of living standards may have occurred during the middle part of this period was attributable to the influence of the Napoleonic War on the price of food, and not to the industrial revolution.)[57] To this, E. P. Thompson has sensibly replied that misery could not be reflected in such data on diet and longevity: "It is neither poverty nor disease but work itself which casts the blackest shadow over the years of the Industrial Revolution."[58]

Here Thompson is distinguishing between the two concepts, *level of living* and *quality of life*. "The level of living concept," said the Scandinavian scholar, Erik Allardt, "refers to material and impersonal resources with which individuals can master and command their living conditions." "Quality of life" refers to the sat-

[54] Sen and Williams, "Introduction," 6.
[55] Griffin, *Well-Being*, 32.
[56] Erik Allardt, "The Relationship Between Objective and Subjective Measures in the Light of Comparative Study," in Richard F. Tomassen, ed., *Comparative Studies in Sociology*, vol. I (Greenwich, CT: JAI Press, 1978).
[57] See T. S. Ashton, *The Industrial Revolution, 1760–1830*, rev. ed. (London: Oxford University Press, 1962).
[58] E. P. Thompson, *The Making of the English Working Class* (London: Golanz, 1963), 211.

isfaction of "social needs, such as needs for love and self-actualization . . . not defined by the material resources an individual can command but [by] how he relates to other people and to society."[59] Quality of life can be assessed only from subjective sources. Looking at data from four Scandinavian countries, Allardt finds that except for a weak relationship between actual income and income satisfaction, the "relation between objective welfare components [of the measures used] and subjective satisfaction . . . are zero or close to zero." Income itself is the main ingredient in level of living; experiences at the workplace are central to the idea of quality of life; neither measure predicts scores on the other.[60] Other studies support Allardt in this general lack of relationship at any one time, but as we shall see in Chapter 26, there are reasons to believe that level of living has a considerable effect on the quality of life over time through what I have called the *affluence effect*.

Efficiency refers to the relation between means and ends. If quality of life, including work life, is the end and level of living is the means, the zero correlation between them at any one time suggests that, to say the least, the means are poorly fitted to the task. By this reading, increasing levels of living is an inefficient way of increasing quality of life. For example, by manipulating wages and salaries the market seeks to allocate labor to "its *economically* best uses" and so to increase levels of living, but apparently these "best uses" have only a weak relationship to quality of life, or more particularly, quality of work life. Similarly, maximizing gross national product raises levels of living but may or may not improve quality of life for any particular generation.[61]

Objective accounts of well-being

Although Allardt's findings regarding the separation of level of living and quality of life refer to survey research, one might assume that a fortiori the aggregative economic statistics would suffer the same problems of measuring happiness. On the most famous of these statistics, GNP, Kenneth Land points out that:

the more specific limitations of economic indicators . . . are that: (a) such measures as the GNP cannot be equated with psychological satisfaction, happiness, or life fulfillment; (b) market valuations of goods and services (i.e., their observed or imputed prices) are not necessarily related to their contributions to social well-being; (c) nonmarket activities and impacts of market activities tend to be excluded from consideration; (d) distributional considerations tend to be obscured in the GNP averages.

Land further points out that (e) GNP fails to evaluate the social rules that lie behind the market system and that have in themselves considerable effects on both our objective and our subjective well-being.[62] As Joan Robinson says, "In national

[59] Allardt, "The Relationship Between Objective and Subjective Indicators," 205–6; Edward E. Lawler, III, "Strategies for Improving the Quality of Work Life," *American Psychologist* 37 (1982): 486–93.
[60] Allardt, "The Relationship Between Objective and Subjective Indicators," 207. But see Bradburn and Caplovitz, *Reports on Happiness*, for a different interpretation of the effects of work satisfaction on other forms of satisfaction.
[61] Even efforts to develop broader measures of economic well-being fail to include work satisfaction. See William D. Nordhaus and James Tobin, "Is Growth Obsolete?" in Milton Moss, ed., *The Measurement of Economic and Social Performance*, vol. 38 of *Studies in Income and Wealth* (New York: National Bureau of Economic Research, 1973).
[62] Kenneth C. Land, "Social Indicators," *Annual Review of Sociology* 9 (1983): 3.

income accounting, goods have to be entered in terms of their exchange values, not their utilities."[63] To this Juster, Dow, and Courant note that GNP-type measures do not account for changes in product quality, fail to make appropriate distinctions between capital and current accounts in households and governments, and do not include the value of increased human capital added by education and health expenditures.[64]

Addressing themselves to some of these issues, Nordhaus and Tobin propose a partial solution in a measure of net economic welfare (NEW), which includes the values of leisure and imputed household production and subtracts for expenditures on the disamenities that economic growth itself produces (e.g., pollution and the unattractiveness of metropolitan living.[65] On this point, Samuelson and Nordhaus say:

> By relying more on comprehensive measures of national output like NEW, society does not need to be chained to mere material growth unless it wants to. The economy can serve broader goals – such as an appropriate balance between work and leisure, or a better use of resources to protect our environment – if these are what people hold most important.[66]

But even NEW does not include the satisfactions from work – intrinsic rewards and human development – and does not give utility an objective epistemological standing.

There are additional reasons why objective accounts of market income are inadequate to the task of assessing well-being. In a discussion of the impact of economic growth and well-being, Shin finds that such indicators as those measuring health, time spent working, leisure and recreation, educational levels, and freedom of expression have reasonably close relations with his measures of sense of well-being but not with per capita GNP; they substantially modify interpretations of the benefits of rapid economic growth in South Korea.[67] Juster and his associates point out that the matching of actual time use with preferred use of time makes a major contribution to a sense of well-being, but even time-use diaries do not say anything about preferred uses of time, without subjective assessments that require additional questions for inferences about well-being.[68] D'Iribarne reveals the difference in construction placed upon being cold because of the expensiveness of fuel and being cold because one has chosen to go skiing. It is how we think about events or circumstances that determines their contributions to our sense of well-being and not

[63] Robinson, *Economic Philosophy*, 132.

[64] F. Thomas Juster, Paul N. Courant, and Greg K. Dow, "A Conceptual Framework for the Analysis of Time Allocation Data," in Juster and Frank P. Stafford, eds., *Time, Goods, and Well Being* (Ann Arbor, MI: Institute for Social Research, 1985), 114–15.

[65] Nordhaus and Tobin, "Is Growth Obsolete?" Eisner has developed an even more sophisticated system of income accounts that includes unpriced household production, capital formation by governments and households, human capital; Eisner treats police and defense expenditures as intermediate outputs. See Robert Eisner, *The Total Incomes System of Accounts* (Chicago: University of Chicago Press, 1989).

[66] Paul A. Samuelson and William D. Nordhaus, *Economics*, 12th ed. (New York: McGraw-Hill, 1985), 119. Tibor Scitovsky points out the limitations of this measure of welfare in his chapter, "The Place of Economic Welfare in Human Welfare – 1973," in his *Human Desire and Economic Satisfaction: Essays on the Frontiers of Economics* (New York: New York University Press, 1986), 22–3.

[67] Doh C. Shin, "Does Rapid Economic Growth Improve the Human Lot? Some Empirical Evidence," *Social Indicators Research* 8 (1980): 199–221.

[68] Juster, Courant, and Dow, "A Conceptual Framework for the Analysis of Time Allocation Data."

the circumstances alone.[69] But the most cogent evidence of the difference between subjective and objective accounts lies in the finding by all the studies of subjective well-being that it is satisfaction with family life and feelings of self-confidence and self-esteem that contribute most – far more than income – to a sense of well-being or to happiness, however measured.

The differences in objective data, such as actual wages or changes in educational opportunity, and subjective feelings about these things show that there is only a very modest relationship between actual income and satisfaction with income, and, for the same reasons, there is a much smaller relationship between income and a sense of well-being then there is between *satisfaction with income* and a sense of well-being.[70] During the 1960s the educational and occupational opportunities for American blacks increased substantially, but the sense of well-being, especially among the better educated blacks who might be thought to have benefited from these objective changes, actually declined.[71]

Observing these differences, most scholars point out the need for both objective and subjective data, but caution against confounding their meanings, especially against what we may call "the Galbraith fallacy": believing that income and production statistics are surrogate measures of happiness. Because the data omit work satisfaction, they are not even good measures of economic satisfaction. (Indeed, they may not even be good measures of economic production, for by some estimates they include only about half of the economic production in the American economy.)[72]

Knowledge constraint on interpersonal comparisons

Economists' prohibition against interpersonal comparisons is grounded on humanistic and epistemological assumptions: Each individual is different, and we have no way of knowing whether my subjective satisfaction for some particular good is the same as yours.[73] The logic that permits inferences about satisfaction maximization within this restriction rests on the mutual and reciprocal advantages accruing to each "trader" in a free exchange price system that encourages exchanges (buying and selling) until each individual has the bundle of goods that is most satisfying.[74]

The reasoning is unpersuasive. Other disciplines, no less humanistically and epistemologically well grounded, do without that prohibition. For example, in the law,

---

[69] Philippe d'Iribarne, "The Relationship between Subjective and Objective Well-Being," in Burkhard Strumpel, ed., *Subjective Elements of Well-Being* (Paris: OECD, 1974).

[70] Campbell et al., *The Quality of American Life*, 381–2.

[71] Andrews and Withey, *Social Indicators of Well-Being*, 7. An alternative interpretation of the same phenomena relies on the concept of *relative deprivation*, a concept that "has been used to explain why people may become less satisfied, rather than more satisfied, as their objective condition improves – because the improvement of their condition raises their comparison AL [adaptation level] at an even faster rate." Brickman and Campbell, "Hedonic Relativism and Planning the Good Society," 295.

[72] Andrew S. Harvey and Stephen Macdonald, "Time Diaries and Time Data for Extension of Economic Accounts," *Social Indicators Research* 3 (1976): 21–35 at 33.

[73] For an explication and justification of this self-imposed limit, see Frank H. Knight, *Risk, Uncertainty and Profits* (1921; reprint Chicago: University of Chicago Press, 1971), 77–8.

[74] Abba Lerner, like many other economists, calls this the "principle of diminishing marginal substitutability." *Economics of Control* (New York: Macmillan, 1944), 10. Knight prefers a broader term, "the fundamental law of conduct." See his *Risk, Uncertainty and Profits*, 65.

deterrence theory assumes equal disutilities across the population for equal punishment; psychology discovers daily that, along with individual differences, equal stimuli tend to produce roughly equal reactions among similar sets of respondents. John Rawls finds no difficulties in assuming interpersonal similarities in developing the principles for his theory of justice.[75] "Every man," say Clyde Kluckhohn and Henry Murray, "is in certain respect: (a) like all other men, (b) like some other men, (c) like no other men."[76] No one choice is more "scientific" than another. It is not so much science as experience and research that argue against the prohibition. Abba Lerner, after stating that "to obtain a criterion for the optimum division of money income we must assume that different people enjoy similar satisfactions," goes on to comment: "There are no men whose behavior does not suggest the acceptance of the assumption [that others have feelings like those of the self]. To reject it would in fact deny meaning to the assertion that anyone other than myself is capable of feeling any kind of pain or pleasure."[77] Nor is the use of Pareto optimality to avoid interpersonal comparisons successful, for it's validity is based on circular reasoning. If people do assess their own welfare by comparing their situations to others, any gain to another is ipso facto a loss to the self. To avoid invidiousness by assuming that there is no invidiousness is to beg the question.

The research that erodes the value of this prohibition is, once again, provided by the studies of life satisfaction. Although self-assessments of life satisfaction obviously vary somewhat from person to person, it is the *similarity* of responses, especially the similarity across class and other demographic lines, that have struck most observers as so remarkable. Thus, in summarizing their ability to predict a global sense of well-being from their several measures of concerns and situations, Andrews and Withey report: "All in all, the figures show that there are *no* large and stable differences between subgroups in the extent to which their feelings about general well-being can be predicted on the basis of these concern measures." As they summarize their success in predicting global well-being from more local experiences, these authors add: "In short, results presented seem widely applicable throughout the American population."[78] This finding is shared by most studies of subjective well-being.[79]

In conclusion, the solipsistic profession of ignorance of how anyone, other than

---

[75] John Rawls, *A Theory of Justice* (Cambridge: Harvard University Press, 1971).

[76] Clyde Kluckhohn and Henry A. Murray, eds., *Personality in Nature, Society, and Culture* (New York: Knopf, 1949), 35.

[77] Abba P. Lerner, *The Economics of Control*, (New York: Macmillan, 1944), 23.

[78] Andrews and Withey, *Social Indicators of Well-Being*, 147.

[79] In Campbell et al., *The Quality of American Life*, the authors summarize their findings on the relationships between various aspects of life satisfactions and their Index of Well-Being. After recording some differences among social groups, they say: "While all these differences seem quite intelligible, and are large enough to be statistically significant, they remain fairly modest in absolute magnitude. . . . We gain very little in our capacity to account for variations in global well-being from the structure of domain satisfaction by such a descent to more homogeneous subgroups." (p. 82) In an article looking at similar data, Frank M. Andrews and Stephen B. Withey report: "It is of considerable interest to note that these 12 domains explained about half of the variance in *each* of these [demographic] groups, suggesting that these domains have rather broad relevance to different sub-cultures in the United States." See their "Developing Measures of Perceived Life Quality: Results from Several National Surveys," *Social Indicators Research* 1 (1974): 1–26.

the self, feels about the satisfaction of wants has enormous substantive consequences: (1) It inhibits egalitarian inferences from the theory of declining marginal utility (such as the progressivity of income tax policy);[80] (2) it makes utilitarian summing of utilities an arbitrary – and most misleading – way of thinking about community welfare (Bentham would have been horrified); (3) it inevitably exaggerates market sources of want satisfaction, as contrasted to other forms of satisfaction, since its assessment is dependent on "revealed preferences" in market transactions; and (4) in denying access to information on subjective well-being, the omission of direct measurement of want satisfaction (let alone any more general sense of well-being) makes the market itself a rather blunt instrument for satisfying even economic wants.

And (5), as mentioned, an empirically empty theory of utility makes the interdependent theory of utility an unmeasurable, and therefore unattractive, instrument for economic analysis.[81] Market maximization of satisfactions, as Marshall and Pigou have pointed out, and as Koopmans explains, "requires that the satisfaction of each consumer is affected only by his own consumption and work."[82] Knowledge of consumer satisfaction from measures independent of information on transactions, frees analysts of these unrealistic assumptions. The possibility is thus created for a more fruitful discussion of income distribution effects on human satisfaction, repairing a long-standing deficiency in economic discourse.[83]

Even at this preliminary stage we now know something about happiness: We know that neither hedonic skepticism nor epistemological skepticism pose obstacles to our knowing more, that happiness is not so vague a subject as utility in that it lends itself to empirical investigation, that empirical investigations dispose of the ineffable quality of happiness or any other mood, that from time to time people do appraise their own happiness with results that they find informative, that subjective accounts must supplement the prevailing objective accounts for an adequate understanding of happiness. We have seen, too, that in the pursuit of happiness the want satisfaction of the market is not enough but that need satisfaction is not a substitute. And finally like others, we found the restriction on comparison of utilities or states of satisfaction is an absurd limit to the study of happiness, which may be studied comparatively like anything else.

Now, partly as a complement to the discussion of objective and subjective ac-

---

[80] Schumpeter observes that the idea of decreasing marginal utility of income does not necessarily imply a progressive income tax if the aim is to take money away from individuals so as to leave them with more nearly equal amounts of satisfaction. The only valid inference, he says, is that people with higher incomes should pay absolutely more but not necessarily *proportionately* more, with the implication that, as a consequence, the tax structure might be only proportional. Schumpeter, *History of Economic Analysis,* 1,072.

[81] See Kenneth E. Boulding, "Economics as a Moral Science," *The American Economic Review* 59 (1969): 1–12; J. S. Deusenberry, *Income, Saving, and the Theory of Consumer Behavior* (Cambridge: Harvard University Press, 1949). For social scientific research on reference group behavior, see Herbert E. Hyman and Eleanor Singer, eds., *Readings in Reference Group Theory and Research* (New York: Free Press, 1968); and W. G. Runciman, *Relative Deprivation and Social Justice* (Berkeley: University of California Press, 1966).

[82] Koopmans, *Three Essays on the State of Economic Science,* 41.

[83] I. M. D. Little, *A Critique of Welfare Economics,* 2d ed. (London: Oxford University Press, 1957), 53.

counts, we turn to a special problem in the study of happiness: the relationship between objective ratios of achievement–aspirations and subjective ratios.

Objective and subjective worlds: the double ratio

Consider the difference between the modest relationship between *actual income* and life satisfaction and the much stronger relationship between *income satisfaction* and life satisfaction. True of the United States and Europe, it is also separately true of Scandinavia, where, as mentioned, Allardt reports only a weak relation between measures of level of living and quality of life. The discrepancy suggests that the frequently cited formula for self- or life satisfaction,

$$\frac{\text{achievements}}{\text{aspirations}}$$

is actually more complex and involves four terms and two ratios, one for subjective and another for objective relationships. Assigning values to each term, these might be represented as follows:

Subjective	*Objective*
(a) Perceived achievement (Top 25% income bracket)	(c) Actual achievement (Median income)
(b) Aspirations (Top 10% income bracket)	(d) Life chances for individual X (.5 to achieve median .10 to achieve top 25% .01 to achieve top 10%)

As is common in certain life positions, in this example the individual meets increasing resistances to upward mobility (d). Although that person has an average (.5) chance of achieving a median income, he or she has somewhat diminished chances of actually moving into elite positions. Like others, the individual tends to upgrade his or her own position, seeing the self as better off than is actually the case and misjudging the chances of rising even higher. The subjective ratio (a/b) makes the individual dissatisfied with an average status, although, true to form, he or she has perceived the situation to be better than it actually is (a versus c). Perceptually, the person has improved his or her life status and the chances of satisfaction rather substantially. Objectively (c/d), the individual has done what he or she might be expected to do, neither better nor worse. The sources of dissatisfaction lie in the relationship between aspirations and actual life chances (b versus d), where the individual has aspired to a situation beyond all likely success.

Had this representative individual managed to misperceive his or her achievements even more, he or she might have reduced the sources of personal dissatisfaction. The common tendency of those above the very bottom to believe that they are higher in the income scale than they actually are tends to reduce dissatisfaction. The two psychologically adjustable terms (a and b) both tend to exceed reality with opposite hedonic consequences: Aspirations tend to exceed objective life changes with negative hedonic effects, and perceptions of rank (in the lower and middle ranks) tend to exceed actual achievements with positive hedonic effects.

The historically determined probability of success, the objective life chances, are a measure of social structure, of actual mobility and not merely of the hope of mobility. Although people are notoriously poor at estimating probabilities, such as life chances (particularly when the self has stakes in some particular outcome), they remember the vivid case and use it quite haphazardly as representative of a large set of cases (the "representativeness heuristic").[84] Thus, the particular upward mobility pattern of the United States, similar to other Western countries in most respects but distinguished from them in the higher probability that some people of working-class origins will become members of the professional and managerial elites,[85] provides the most tempting and misleading heuristic: the vivid, memorable case (Abraham Lincoln, Andrew Carnegie) representing a skewed, improbable outcome. Such a pattern might be expected to produce a chronically low level of satisfaction, but, for several reasons, that is not the case. One reason for this failure of alienation lies in that complex of things called the "happy consciousness" of the American people.[86] Another reason may be an almost universal "positivity bias" (Chapter 4). The most important reason is most certainly because of the way people adapt to situations persisting over a period of time (Chapters 23 and 26).

Satisfaction and happiness

Satisfaction and happiness are closely related but different kinds of experiences; consequently the market might satisfy all our conscious wants and still leave us unhappy. The two states are different both conceptually and empirically, with different causes and consequences. Among the many analyses of happiness, the work of the Polish scholar Wladislaw Tatarkiewicz offers the most comprehensive review. In the end, Tatarkiewicz defines happiness as the "lasting, complete and justified satisfaction with life, or it is a life which yields lasting, complete and justified satisfaction."[87] In elaboration, Tatarkiewicz says that although "satisfaction" is "the core meaning" of the concept, "even complete satisfaction does not

[84] Daniel Kahneman, P. Slovic, and Amos Tversky, eds., *Judgment Under Uncertainty: Heuristics and Biases* (New York: Cambridge University Press, 1982).

[85] "It is the underprivileged class of manual sons that has an exceptional chance for mobility in this country. There is a grain of truth in the Horatio Alger myth." Peter M. Blau and Otis D. Duncan, *American Occupational Structure* (1967; reprint New York: Free Press, 1978), 435. But, to the contrary, see Robert Erikson and John H. Goldthorpe, "Are American Rates of Social Mobility Exceptionally High? New Evidence on an Old Issue," *European Sociological Review* 1 (1985): 1–22.

[86] Herbert Marcuse, *One Dimensional Man* (Boston: Beacon, 1964). In one ranking [1973] Americans were the third happiest people among eleven economically developed nations; in a ranking a few years later they were fourth. Whereas in no country does income or social class account for much of the variance in life satisfaction, the effect of social class on life satisfaction is the least (of nine countries) in the United States: 6 percent compared to 13 percent in Britain, where it is the most significant. Inglehart, "Values, Objective Needs, and Subjective Satisfaction," 429–58 at 441. See also Ronald Inglehart and Jacques-Rene Rabier, "Aspirations Adapt to Situations–But Why Are the Belgians So Much Happier than the French? A Cross-Cultural Analysis of the Subjective Quality of Life," in Andrews, *Research on the Quality of Life,* 38.

[87] Wladislaw Tatarkiewicz, *Analysis of Happiness,* trans. E. Rothert and D. Zielinskn (The Hague: Martinus Nijhoff, 1976), 16.

necessarily add up to happiness. Satisfaction with particular things, however important – health or an untroubled conscience [note that these are not market goods], success or position – falls short of happiness. . . . Happiness requires . . . *satisfaction with life as a whole."* This is the meaning employed by the studies of the quality of life.

Completeness and duration

In Tatarkiewicz's conceptualization, *completeness* implies a focus on life-as-a-whole such that "the happy man is one in whose life the good has outweighed the bad and who has been granted the goods which he needed and which he has known how to enjoy." Since a person cannot be satisfied with all parts of his life, satisfaction with the parts he thinks most important will do, for these radiate from the part to the whole and color his hedonic feelings about the whole.[88] The quality-of-life findings that satisfaction in one area compensates for dissatisfaction in another seems to question the idea of "most important areas," but the question must remain open. The main thrust of Tatarkiewicz's analysis, however, is to separate partial, ephemeral, and superficial joys, pleasures, and satisfactions from the concept of happiness. And in this he is joined by empirical research on subjective well-being, as when Andrews and Withey ask the question that defines the concept of well-being: "How do you feel about your life as a whole?"

A focus on life-as-a-whole inevitably also implies a longer *duration* for the feelings that we may associate with happiness compared to the transient pleasures or joys of the moment. The idea is cognate to Rawls's idea of "life plans," as contrasted to short-term enterprises that give pleasure but may not be related to any enduring project. An emphasis on duration also has basis in the concept of the self as embracing a continuity of feelings, beliefs, memories; and in the concept of identity or self-concept, with its associated evaluation of self-esteem. Psychologists distinguish between *states,* which are dispositions prompted by particular circumstances, and *traits,* which are enduring, cross-situational properties of the personality. For Tatarkiewicz it is the trait, and not the state, that defines a happy person enjoying a happy life.

Affect and cognition

To what extent is happiness a thought and to what extent is it a feeling? Tatarkiewicz points to the cognitive components of happiness in his reference to "justification," emphasizing the significance of a cognitive appraisal in which illusion is unacceptable.[89] Thus appraisals of life-as-a-whole are a mixture of cognitive assessments and affects. The affects (or emotions), in turn comprise two separable elements, pains and pleasures, joys and sorrows, positive and negative affects. Factor analysis reveals these three factors: cognition, positive affect, and negative affect,[90] each substantially independent of the other. Studies asking separate questions on satisfaction with life-as-a-whole and overall happiness find that satisfaction ques-

[88] Ibid., 6, 9, 11.
[89] Ibid., 8, 10.
[90] Andrews and Withey, *Social Indicators of Well-Being,* 18, 105.

tions elicit answers with more judgmental, cognitive content, whereas happiness questions elicit more emotional content, although the two have a considerable overlap.[91] They serve slightly different purposes and the contributions of various experiences to life satisfaction are different from those contributing to happiness.

Andrews and Withey asked the following questions about global evaluations of or feelings toward life: "How satisfied are you with your life these days?" and, "How do you feel about how happy you are?" The evidence presented shows that whereas fun and family may contribute more to *happiness* than satisfaction, money, economic security, one's house, and the goods and services bought in the market contribute to *satisfaction* far more than to happiness.[92] The market is a most incomplete instrument for satisfying human wants, but it is an even less adequate instrument for promoting happiness.

Happy people versus satisfied people

If the two criterial concepts of well-being are different, they should have a different incidence in different populations. Thus, in Campbell et al.'s study, the young tend to be happier than the old, but less well satisfied with their lives, whereas among the old these tendencies are reversed.[93] One might say that happiness-oriented persons will be less pleased with the market than satisfaction-oriented persons, and it does seem to be the case that, for the young, money is a less important contribution to well-being than for the old.[94] As mentioned, substantial income increments increase happiness but not satisfaction; substantial income losses increase dissatisfaction much more than unhappiness.[95] Happiness, but not satisfaction, applies to substantial gains, but dissatisfaction, and not unhappiness, applies to substantial losses.

People trained in the tradition of market rationalism, or academicians generally, will place their faith in the cognitive evaluations more characteristic of market satisfactions than in the more affective evaluations of other domains. Yet, to repeat a quotation employed in Chapter 4, of the two partially independent cognitive and affective systems, "affective reactions to stimuli: are often the very first reactions of the organism, . . . can occur without extensive perceptual and cognitive encoding, are made with greater confidence than cognitive judgments, and can be made

---

[91] Campbell et al., *The Quality of American Life*, 34, found that their measures of satisfaction and happiness were correlated at .50, a figure just halfway between total identity and total independence. The connotative meanings of satisfaction and happiness have been examined by a semantic differential measure: Happiness and satisfaction are about the same on a positive–negative dimension, but happiness is above average on an arousal dimension whereas satisfaction is below average. See work of J. A. Russell (1978, 1980) reported at p. 312 in Susan T. Fiske and Shelley E. Taylor, *Social Cognition* (New York: Random House, 1984).

[92] Andrews and Withey, *Social Indicators of Well-Being*, 169; Inglehart and Rabier, "Aspirations Adapt to Situations," 8, find that "satisfaction" is a better measure than "happiness" for tapping the aspiration–adaptation model. By partialing out the two sets of evaluations, Michalos showed that evaluations of all the ten measured domains (health, financial security, family life, self-esteem, etc.) were more closely related to life satisfaction than to happiness, a relationship especially marked in the one question on the market domain, financial security. Alex Michalos, "Satisfaction and Happiness," *Social Indicators Research* 8 (1980): 385–422 at 399 and 402.

[93] Campbell et al., *The Quality of American Life*, 156–69.

[94] Bradburn and Caplovitz, *Reports on Happiness*, 11.

[95] Inglehart and Rabier, "Aspirations Adapt to Situations," 28.

sooner.''[96] And because it is harder to rebut their "premises," they will persist in the face of disconfirming evidence when cognitive assessment might be unseated. We need not subscribe to claims of market rationalism to appreciate the facts that market phenomena are more closely linked to cognitively based satisfactions than to emotionally based happiness and that market evaluations are more vulnerable to disconfirmation, change, and, indeed, "rational" displacement. This is an advantage, for the weaker, slower processes of reasoned assessments (compared to affective responses) permit conscious changes of direction to alter misguided pursuits of life goals.

Satisfaction is a mixed and qualified blessing whereas happiness is a good qualified, if at all, *only* by degrees of ethical merit.[97] And whatever may be the extent to which the market succeeds in satisfying human wants, it is not an *adequate* instrument for making people happy.

Concerns and domains: a linear, cumulative model of subjective well-being

Answers to the question posed early in this chapter, What can we know of happiness? are largely provided by two kinds of studies: quasi-experimental studies of the causes and consequences of "positive affect" and "good moods" on the one hand, and the survey studies of the quality of life we have cited from time to time on the other. Here I give a brief exposition of the methods and findings of two of the main quality-of-life studies, Andrews and Withey's *Social Indicators of Well-Being* and Campbell, Converse, and Rodgers's *The Quality of American Life*. They offer a model of how to think about, as well as how to study, the various aspects of happiness.[98] As we develop this model we may bear in mind the contrast between this method and the axiomatic treatments of utility in economics.

The main substantive purpose of these studies of happiness, life satisfaction, or, more inclusively, subjective well-being is to find out what contributes to making people happy or satisfied with their lives. The overall measures of well-being varied. In Campbell, Converse, and Rodgers's treatment it was an index formed by a direct question about life satisfaction and a semantic differential measure offering ten polarized choices, such as: "enjoyable . . . miserable," "full . . . empty,"

---

[96] Robert B. Zajonc, "Feeling and Thinking: Preferences Need No Inferences," *American Psychologist* 35 (1980): 151–75 at 151. Zajonc's dual systems theory is controversial; for a more comprehensive review of the relations between affect and cognition, see Margaret Sydnor Clark and Susan T. Fiske, eds., *Affect and Cognition* (Hillsdale, NJ: Erlbaum, 1982).

[97] W. D. Ross, *The Right and the Good* (Oxford: Clarendon Press, 1930), 136. Rescher says: "Happiness maximization (or utility maximization) [sic] is not a good in itself – and certainly does not serve the interests of justice – regardless of *how* it is maximized." Nicholas Rescher, *Distributive Justice: A Constructive Critique of the Utilitarian Theory of Distribution* (Indianapolis: Bobbs-Merrill, 1966), 54; Amartya Sen, "Utilitarianism and Welfarism," *Journal of Philosophy* 76 (1979): 463–88.

[98] The methods and data in the quality-of-life studies have been reviewed for their validity and reliability on many occasions and generally pass these reviews, at least with qualified support. I place burdens upon the findings not anticipated by the authors of these studies; my intention is to make as plausible a set of cases as the current state of the art permits, but readers are cautioned that the extensions made here, as well as some of the underlying data, are grounded in a science still very young, at least compared to the older science of economics. See Diener, "Subjective Well-Being."

"rewarding . . . disappointing," "friendly . . . lonely."[99] In Andrews and Withey it was a straightforward repeated question: "How do you feel about your life as a whole?" with answers scored along a scale offering opportunities to respond: "Delighted," "Pleased," "Mostly satisfied," "About equally satisfied and dissatisfied" (the neutral point), "Mostly dissatisfied," "Unhappy," "Terrible."[100] The central proposition was that satisfaction of a variety of "concerns," such as how much fun a person was having, in the several "domains" of life would variously contribute to an overall sense of subjective well-being, with special attention to the variation in these contributions.

The *domains* that were included in these studies dealt with work and family, of course, but also with leisure activities, religion, national and local government, house and neighborhood, friendships and voluntary organizations, and, in the case of Andrews and Withey, with the respondent's selves: How did they feel about themselves, their achievements, their ability to adjust, and so forth? Both Campbell et al. and Andrews and Withey found that satisfactions or feelings about these several domains of life each contributed something to the analysts' ability to predict responses to the question about life-as-a-whole. It might appear that the idea of a "domain" of life is an analyst's tool without resonance with the way people think about their lives, but such is not the case. People can easily divide their perceptions and evaluations of their lives into such categories as leisure, work, family (and within the family: children, spouses, responsibilities, etc.), religion, government, standard of living, the prices they pay, and so forth, apparently without conflating them. It is this partialing of life into conceptually distinct domains that inhibits the infection of family and friendship with market codes and value, a matter discussed in connection with "walls and spheres" in Chapter 2 and to be treated later in Chapter 25 as an important hedonic structure.

The *concerns* or *criteria* proposed to respondents include their feelings about how much fun they have, their security, fairness in the way they are treated, their own contributions to the lives of others, their relative success and achievements, and whether their needs have been met. Many of these criteria are shared by most people: People want "to be loved, liked and accepted, responsible, respected, somewhat independent, somewhat secure, interested in life, comfortable, successful, and to have fun." Andrews and Withey believe "that people diverge more in how much of these attributes they want, and in what domains they want them, than in what the criteria mean to them."[101] In this way our horizons are raised beyond the narrow boundaries of income, pay, commodities, and "standard of living."

Since the findings depend on the questions asked, it is inevitable that we should have somewhat different reports, but certain things stand out. In all studies satisfaction with the family, spouses, and children is one of the best predictors of global life satisfaction and happiness. Where the questions were asked, attitudes toward the self ("How do you feel about . . . yourself?") and toward one's achievements

---

[99] Campbell et al., *The Quality of American Life,* 42.
[100] Andrews and Withey, *Social Indicators of Well-Being,* 18, 66; linearity is discussed on p. 46.
[101] Ibid., 12. One reason for the ready cognitive availability of the concerns is that people were not asked about those concerns that might prove hard to answer, such as the desire for power or revenge.

and adjustments to society are even better predictors. In most studies (but not Andrews and Withey's), attitudes toward work were closely linked to life satisfaction.[102] Evaluations of one's own health, one's religious faith, and attitudes toward government make almost no contribution to a person's happiness. Distinctions between objective reality assessments and subjective assessments vary across domains: Actual number of friends is a good predictor of life satisfaction whereas actual dollar income is a poor predictor, although, as mentioned, *attitudes* toward one's income is a good one.[103] The fact that actual income is a much less important contributor to happiness than attitudes toward income reveals again that Democritus was right: "A happy life does not depend on good fortune or indeed on any external contingencies, but also, and even to a greater extent, on a man's cast of mind. . . . The important thing is not what a man has, but how he reacts to what he has."[104]

In Freedman's study satisfaction or happy feelings toward the following aspects of life were most closely associated with self-reported happiness. For single men and women the four most important aspects were: friends and social life, being in love, job satisfaction, and recognition or success in one's work. For married persons, marital satisfaction took the place of "being in love," and "partner's happiness" and "sex life" (for women) and "personal growth" (for men) entered the list of the most important four.[105]

The dominant pattern of the structure of happiness in most studies, as Bentham foresaw, is linear and cumulative. That is, satisfaction with each aspect or domain of life contributed something to the capacity to predict satisaction with life-as-a-whole or to an index of well-being. Adding weights contributed almost nothing, and if the weights were based on what the respondents said were "important" to them, the results were slightly *worse*.[106] This finding contrasts, for example, with the structure that might have been expected from Maslow's theory of need hierarchy, where certain kinds of satisfaction (meeting deficiency needs in a specified order) must precede other, more advanced kinds of satisfaction.[107] The linear cumulative pattern implies that "dissatisfaction with one aspect of life can apparently be made up for in straightforward fashion with other satisfactions."[108]

---

[102] See, for example, Shaver and Freedman, "Your Pursuit of Happiness."

[103] Campbell et al., *The Quality of American Life*, 76, 374; Andrews and Withey, *Social Indicators of Well-Being*, 112, 124, 127.

[104] Quoted in Tatarkiewicz, *Analysis of Happiness*, 29.

[105] Shaver and Freedman, "Your Pursuit of Happiness," Freedman, *Happy People*, 41. Extending the list to ten reveals that those aspects of life ranking in the top four for one demographic group were included in a slightly lower position in the ranking for other graphic groups. The Shaver and Freedman study was based on the readers of *Psychology Today*. Freedman's later study extended the sample to a somewhat lower SES group comprising the readers of *Good Housekeeping*.

[106] "A linear additive model is quite sufficient." Campbell et al., *The Quality of American Life*, 79. "There was a modest tendency for the concerns that had higher relationships to life-as-a-whole to be judged *less* important." Andrews and Withey, *Social Indicators of Well-Being*, 243.

[107] Abraham H. Maslow, *Toward a Psychology of Being*, rev. ed. (Princeton, NJ: Van Nostrand, 1968). One interpretation of Maslow's theory is that the needs are stratified by social class. See Lynda C. Gratton, "Analysis of Maslow's Need Hierarchy with Three Social Class Groups," *Social Indicators Research* 7 (1980): 463–74.

[108] Campbell et al., *The Quality of American Life*, 79. For comments on and criticisms of the linear cumulative model, see Aubrey C. McKennal and Frank M. Andrews, "Models of Cognition and Affect in Perception of Well-Being," *Social Indicators Research* 8 (1980): 257–90.

There is a difference between liking an activity or satisfaction with a set of circumstances and having that liking or satisfaction contribute to one's happiness. I have been reporting contributions, but positive and negative attitudes toward various facets of life, whether or not they contribute to happiness, are also important. The mean scores in the evaluation of the criteria (not their relationship to happiness) reveal that people are most satisfied with their sincerity and honesty and how they get along with others; they are least satisfied with how others respect their rights, other people's sincerity, and their own safety and security; in between are such matters as achievements and ability to handle stress. As we shall see in Chapter 25, the favorability ranking goes "from intimate values in one's private world to the scene of interaction with others, then to problems of competencies, and finally to rather widespread conditions with which people have to cope."[109] Economic matters regulated by the market are intermediate between the high ranking of certain properties of the self (but not the self, itself) and the low ranking of the public domains.

Summary

The dependent variable for the study of the satisfaction of human wants is not ineffable; satisfaction in the various domains of life, life satisfaction, and even happiness have been studied with some success. Even in a market society, people can and do reflect on their overall feelings of well-being. Reports on these reflections are valuable additions to objective accounts of the circumstances that are thought to promote a sense of well-being; subjective and objective accounts are not substitutes for each other, but felicitous complements. Whereas satisfaction implies a cognitive assessment of something and life satisfaction implies a similar assessment of one's life, happiness is more of an affective mood covering a longer period of time. The market is more likely to influence life satisfaction than happiness. The sources of subjective feelings of well-being are not primarily economic, but, as we saw with respect to cognitive development and shall see with respect to subjective well-being, economic development does sometimes represent a crucial infrastructure for the *successful* pursuit of happiness.

[109] Andrews and Withey, *Indicators of Well-Being,* 274.

23 Markets and the satisfaction of human wants

Armed with a definition of happiness and its allied concepts of satisfaction and a sense of well-being, and further equipped with a model for thinking about happiness and satisfaction, we turn to Koopmans's claim that in studying the market one studies "the best ways of satisfying wants in human society." For this purpose, we must consider the nature of wants and wanting and the concept of satisfaction. It is then possible to assess three central problems: the role of the market in *creating* the wants it seeks to satisfy, the nature of the concept of "utility" that economists employ to express satisfaction, and the important question of the scope of the wants that enter – and fail to enter – market transactions.

Examining the claim: the best ways of satisfying human wants

Wanting and happiness

Psychologists treat wanting as a problem of motivation, economists as a matter of demand, philosophers as a problem of values and their justification. Synthesizing and borrowing eclectically, we might say that wanting is a mental state characterized by: (1) a desired object, (2) a sense of incompleteness or deficiency in the failure to attain that object, and (3) belief that satisfaction would follow from the attainment of the object (though not necessarily a belief that the object is attainable). Wanting is not a motive, but a condition for motivation.

The market analysts' emphasis on the satisfaction of human wants is based on the belief that unrequited wants represent pain that is relieved when these wants are satisfied.[1] By itself, however, wanting is not necessarily a pain; think of boys in front of a motorcycle shop window, enjoying their totally unrequited and unrequitable desire for a motorcycle. Fantasy life is a rich and vivid source of satisfaction from unattainable wants. Approaching the matter from the other side, most people find wantlessness to be a vegetable existence, or, as Callicles said, once a person's sources of supply are assured, "his existence is the existence of a stone, exempt

---

[1] "Economists have avoided questions of wants. Wants are taken as fixed, and their origins left to psychology. . . . Focusing narrowly on expenditure [for purposes of explicating demand] entails unavoidably implicit assumptions about consumption, and there is a great danger of these assumptions being psychological nonsense." Lester D. Taylor, "A Model of Consumption and Demand Based on Psychological Opponent Processes," in Paul J. Albanese, ed., *Foundations of Economic Behavior* (New York: Praeger, 1988), 35. The relatively few attempts by economists to study the nature of wants tend to be deductive from premises that do not correspond to psychological theories of wants, as in the cases of Freidman and of Stigler and Becker; see Milton Friedman, *Price Theory: A Provisional Text* (Hawthorne, NY: Aldine, 1962); George J. Stigler and Gary S. Becker, "De Gustibus Non Est Disputandum," *American Economic Review* 67 (1977): 76–90. Amartya Sen's well-known "Rational Fools: A Critique of the Behavioral Foundations of Economic Theory," *Philosophy and Public Affairs* 6 (1977): 317–45, gives some reasons why the economist's rationalistic, deductive approach is misleading.

alike from enjoyment and pain."[2] And the wantlessness of Nirvana is achieved by wanting Nirvana badly enough to subordinate all other wants.

The concept of want satisfaction in the market gives no status to unrequited wants, or to the *pursuit* of satisfaction; the market focuses instead on the penultimate satisfaction, the satisfaction involved in purchases. But many (including Hobbes) would say the pursuit itself has an intrinsic pleasure, a pleasure not wholly accounted for in final consumption nor dissipated by later disappointment. Tatarkiewicz quotes Gracian on this point: "There must always be some desire unfulfilled if we are not to be unhappy in our felicity."[3] This is certainly Bertrand Russell's view[4] and the views of happiness reflected in the heavens of earlier northern and Greek peoples – Valhalla and the Elysian Fields.

Having and wanting. Several studies find that happiness does not have much to do with *having* things but a great deal to do with *wanting* them.[5] It is appetites and not possessions that determine wanting, and in some of these studies the appetites grew by what they fed on; for example, the promoted employee was more interested in advancement *after* he was promoted than before.[6] If increased having does not reduce wanting, we are confronted with another gross violation of the "law" of declining marginal utility.

Reducing wants. Happiness as the *ratio* between achievements and aspirations, or wants[7] (Chapter 22), implies that satisfaction can be achieved either by increasing achievements or by reducing wants. *Reducing* wants (1) is likely to reduce dissatisfactions more than it increases satisfaction, yet quite possibly leaving a larger Bentham-type net balance in one's hedonic account. (2) Except in periods of inflation, any decline in wants implies an insufficient demand, threatening lower economic growth, or even for a time disequilibrium, or if equilibrium persists, it will be one well short of the possibility frontier. Reducing wants, therefore, threatens efficiency as well as the pain of unemployment. Thus, if wantlessness is a vegetable existence and wanting much more than one can possibly achieve is to build up a negative balance in one's hedonic account, only the narrowest scope is allowed for developing a satisfactory achievement–aspirations ratio. And within that narrow scope, the market ethos permits adjusting only one of the two terms in only one direction, that is, increasing achievements. Theoretically this restriction blocks one of the most promising routes to happiness: scaling down wants to match achievements. In practice, as we shall see, people devise their own ways to reduce their wants to manageable proportions.

[2] Plato, *Gorgias,* trans. W. Hamilton (Harmondsworth: Penguin, 1971), 94. Original work written 494.
[3] Wladislaw Tatarkiewicz, *Analysis of Happiness,* trans. E. Rothert and D. Zielinskn (The Hague: Martinus Nijhoff, 1976), 10.
[4] Bertrand Russell, *The Conquest of Happiness* (London: Allen & Unwin, 1930).
[5] George Caspar Homans, *Social Behavior: Its Elementary Forms* (New York: Harcourt, Brace & World, 1961), 272–3; Philip Shaver and Jonathan Freedman, "Your Pursuit of Happiness," *Psychology Today* 10 (August 1976): 27–32, 75.
[6] Homans, *Social Behavior,* 275.
[7] William James, *Psychology: The Briefer Course,* ed. G. Allport (New York: Harper Torchbook, 1961), 54. Original work published 1892.

Dimensions of wanting

Whether wants are reduced or efforts are mounted to achieve the desired level of satisfaction, to assess the role of the market we must understand their character in more detail. Like attitudes, wants have properties of intensity, duration, centrality in a person's psychic constitution, breadth, and so forth, but instead of a catalog of the dimensions of wanting, we will find it more profitable to offer only a sample of market-related problems.

Ordering wants. Wants have a structure not dictated by the Maslow need hierarchy[8] but not haphazard, either. Lionel Robbins said:

The main postulate of the theory of value is the fact that individuals can arrange their preferences in an order, and in fact do so. . . . We do not need controlled experiments to establish their validity: they are so much the stuff of our everyday experiences that they have only to be stated to be recognized as obvious.[9]

Since, in fact, the ordering is usually incomplete and uncertain, the sense that they have order and certainty is most likely due to postdecision dissonance reduction – the tendency after a decision to select and marshal all the evidence and arguments one can think of to defend that decision. We turn to a few of the sources of defective ordering of wants.

Rational ordering of preferences depends in theory on *costing* the various alternatives and choosing the most efficient one, but people do not seem to think this way when they are thinking of their various likes and dislikes and what is missing in their lives. Thus, Andrews and Withey find that the self-reported determinants of preferences have much to do with what people think they need and what they think is fair, but very little to do with what the cost might be. These authors found that in the various domains of life, evaluations of activities and objects rarely referred to costs of "money, time, or energy" and that when made, the references were only trivially related to levels of satisfaction.[10] Wants have structures, but not the ones that make preference ordering the rational, transitive structure that satisfies market rationality.

Urgency or intensity. Cassel claims that even if market analysts must use the objective measures of price instead of subjective measures of wanting and sat-

---

[8] See Edward E. Lawler, III, and J. Lloyd Suttle, "A Causal Correlational Test of the Need Hierarchy Concept," in Richard M. Steers and Lyman W. Porter, eds., *Motivation and Work Behavior* (New York: McGraw-Hill, 1975).

[9] Lionel Robbins, *An Essay on the Nature and Significance of Economic Science*, 2d ed. (London: Macmillan, 1935), selections reprinted in Daniel M. Hausman, ed., *The Philosophy of Economics: An Anthology* (New York: Cambridge University Press, 1984). But, says Frank Knight, "we must beware of the temptation to judge the nature of our conduct by the way we think about it." *Risk, Uncertainty and Profits* (Chicago: University of Chicago Press, 1971), 54. "Economists have had little to say about the source of preference functions or the source of change in preferences over time." Martha S. Hill and F. Thomas Juster, "Constraints and complementarities in Time Use," in Juster and Frank M. Stafford, eds., *Time, Goods, and Well-Being* (Ann Arbor, MI: Institute for Social Research, 1985), 443. Compare Stigler and Becker, "De Gustibus Non Est Disputandum."

[10] The questions were: "Considering what your house/apartment [accomplishments, national government, etc.] takes in money, time, and energy, how do you feel about your house/apartment, etc.?" Frank M. Andrews and Stephen B. Withey, *Social Indicators of Well-Being: Americans' Perceptions of Life Quality* (New York: Plenum Press, 1976), 231–3.

isfaction, at least their measures take account of intensity of desire – by indicating how much a person will pay (sacrifice) for a desired object.[11] Obviously, this measure does not work well for comparing intensity of desire among individuals with different size budgets. Within the budget constraints of an individual it is assumed to work reasonably well for commodities, but not for the unpriced satisfactions that escape the market network (see following).

Even for commodities, however, willingness to pay a certain price is not a good measure of intensity of desire. In addition to (1) the problem of consumer rent (price paid is often less than anticipated utilities), (2) discounting the future leads to a disjunction between cost and intensity of desire because the satisfactions that are bought by paying the required costs do not occur at the same time as the sacrifice; to compare costs or prices and satisfaction across time leads to a looseness between prices and satisfaction that does not support Cassel's belief that price is a measure of intensity of desire – and this, again, occurs without interpersonal comparisons.

(3) Intensity of desire for money is said to be a market creation, but this is qualified in three ways. In the first place, the criticism is directed only at those who already have money; we do not speak of the "avarice" of the poor. Second, empirically, it is not in market societies but in traditional societies that people are most likely to identify possessions and money with happiness.[12] And third, the intensity is much more directed at the fear of *loss* of money than at the desire for gain. For example, as explained in greater detail in Chapter 26, a composite European sample over the decade of the 1970s revealed a loss (from a neutral point) of 26 points in their life satisfaction when their financial situation over twelve months had become "a lot worse" compared to a gain of only 3 points when their situation had become "a lot better."[13] A small decrement has a greater effect on feelings of satisfaction–dissatisfaction than the same size increment (the scale intervals are psychometrically equivalent). That is, we are emotionally more sensitive to loss than to gain – as Tversky and Kahneman have shown by other measures.[14] It is hard to see how price, except perhaps through insurance, can reflect the fact that people feel their losses more intensely than their gains (see following).

Ambivalence. Well short of neurosis (defined as wanting and not wanting the same object at the same time), there is a common pattern of wanting something and also not wanting it according to the proximity of the goal (Chapter 13). In this form, illustrated in Figure 23.1, a person wants the goal more and fears it less when the goal is at some distance. As he or she approaches it, however, fear increases and want decreases, causing the person to retreat to the point where again the goal

[11] Gustav Cassel, *The Theory of Social Economy,* rev. ed., trans. S. L. Barron (New York: Harcourt, Brace, 1932), 49.

[12] Alex Inkeles and David H. Smith, *Becoming Modern* (Cambridge: Harvard University Press, 1974), 326.

[13] Ronald Inglehart and Jacques-Rene Rabier, "Aspirations Adapt to Situations–But Why Are the Belgians So Much Happier than the French? A Cross-Cultural Analysis of the Subjective Quality of Life," in Frank M. Andrews, ed., *Research on the Quality of Life* (Ann Arbor, MI: Institute for Social Research, 1986), 28. See also Andrews and Withey, *Social Indicators of Well-Being,* 28–9.

[14] Amos Tversky and Daniel Kahneman, "The Framing of Decisions and the Psychology of Choice," *Science* 211 (30 January 1981): 435–58.

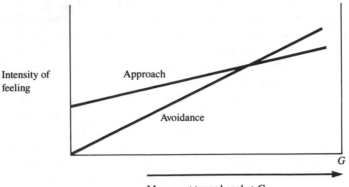

Figure 23.1. *Approach–avoidance gradients*

seems less fearful and more attractive. For example, a person might anticipate the advantages of a job but as he or she gets closer to it the fear of the responsibilities become ever greater. This pattern produces a rhythmic oscillation of wanting and not wanting as the individual approaches and draws back from the target of mixed desires and aversions.[15] The consequence is an intransitive schedule of preferences.

Attainability of a goal. It is the business of the market to make people believe that as many goals as possible are within their reach, for it is not their wanting something that is useful to the market but their motivated striving for it. And all versions of motivation theory claim that people are motivated only by what they think they might attain. Among the many things that might be said about this market-induced sense of scarcity,[16] that is, shortage of attainable wanted things, consider the following:

1. HEDONIC GAINS IN WANTING THE UNATTAINABLE. There are pleasures in wanting the unattainable, as illustrated by the boys in front of the motorcycle shop. Wanting does not necessarily include the belief that one will ever attain the object, even though it includes imagining the satisfactions that possession might bring. There are some hedonic gains in stimulating unrealizable longings to set against the major deficits of frustration and disappointment.

2. ATTAINABILITY MAY BE SELF-FULFILLING. Referring again to Figure 23.1, we can imagine an opposite situation. As a goal becomes increasingly attainable it becomes increasingly desirable, following general attitude and motivational principles that include attainability as part of the formula accounting for their strength.[17] Katona employs this principle to explain why saving does not decrease with social

[15] John Dollard and Neal E. Miller, *Personality and Psychotherapy* (New York: McGraw-Hill, 1950), 355–63.

[16] See, for example, William Leiss, *The Limits to Satisfaction* (Toronto and Buffalo: University of Toronto Press, 1976).

[17] Icek Ajzen and Martin Fishbein, *Understanding Attitudes and Predicting Social Behavior* (Englewood Cliffs, NJ: Prentice-Hall, 1980).

security: The goal of retirement and comfort in old age is brought nearer by social security, leading people to work harder (save more) for this goal.[18] In this way, attainability is a kind of self-fulfilling prophecy: Thinking it attainable, it becomes so.

3. ATTAINMENT INCREASES DEVELOPMENTAL LEARNING. There is wisdom in wanting what is attainable, for the rewards of learning that the world responds to one's efforts (a sense of personal control), that one can achieve what one sets out to achieve (self-esteem), and the tangible rewards accompanying successful striving in the market flow from attainment, not from wanting. But the market is all sail and no anchor; it can induce motivated striving, but it cannot discourage it to tailor wants to possibilities, aspirations to potential achievements, although reducing aspirations to match achievements and inflating perceptions of achievements to flatter self-esteem are common devices (see following).

4. A MORE DIFFICULT ATTAINMENT ADDS TO SELF-ESTEEM. Meeting challenges is a genuine source of global life satisfaction. In Andrews and Withey's study, there is evidence that it was not just the satisfaction of wants but the hurdles overcome and the challenges met in getting what they wanted that made people happy. Of all the questions asked in one of several partially overlapping surveys, the questions comprising a "Self-Adjustment" scale were collectively the second best predictors (.63) of self-reported happiness. Those questions were: "How do you feel about . . ."

The extent to which you are tough and can take it.
The way you handle the problems that come up in your life.
The extent to which you can adjust to changes in your life?[19]

Surmounting obstacles may be as important as satisfying the wants to which the obstacles presented an impediment. Because the uncertainly attainable is challenging, the market might be pardoned for mistaking unattainability for marginally attainable, particularly since what is just marginally attainable for one is just unattainable for another. (See level of aspirations in the next section.)

5. ATTAINABILITY AND THE VALUE OF THE OBJECT SOUGHT. Democracies have also been criticized for their emphasis on unattainable ideals – inviting, it is said, *alienation;* markets are criticized for raising expectations and aspirations beyond any possible level of attainment – inviting *anomie.* Nevertheless, we applaud the high standards of democracy in setting goals toward which we must strive, and we deplore the market's invitation to raise living standards ever higher. The difference is not in setting standards beyond likely attainment, but in the perceived worth of the goals: The worth of achieving a higher standard of living is high for the poor and lower for the rich.[20] Focusing on intentions, striving for ever greater democracy

[18] George Katona, *Private Pensions and Individual Saving* (Ann Arbor, MI: Institute for Social Research, 1965).
[19] Andrews and Withey, *Social Indicators of Well-Being,* July Survey, p. 112. In the May Survey, a similar index of "efficacy" was the best predictor; in addition to the "handling problems" question, that index included "What you are accomplishing in your life?" and "How do you feel about. . . . yourself?" (p. 127)
[20] Adam Smith observed that "if the trappings of wealth are viewed philosophically . . . [they] will always appear in the highest degree contemptible and trifling." Adam Smith, *The Theory of Moral Sentiments,* ed. D. D. Raphael and A. L. Macfie (Indianapolis: Liberty Press, 1974), 183. Original work published 1759.

is always noble, but striving for ever greater wealth is ignoble. Focusing on consequences, both are valuable, wealth only so long as the hidden hand retains its power.

Thus in each wanting person, wants have an order, though not necessarily a transitive one; their levels of intensity are much greater in circumstances of loss than in those of gain; they have a direction that varies with distance from the goal, a probability of attainment in the face of hurdles that, if surmounted, give satisfaction that extra piquancy of flavor, and, withal, an incentive value that contributes to learning. The satisfaction of these wants, however, is not a simple matter.

Satisfaction

If the ''satisfaction of wants in human society'' is the principal purpose of the market, that purpose is underspecified, misleading, and often at war with longer term happiness. Unlike happiness, satisfaction may not be a good in itself, and, as we shall see, unlike unhappiness, dissatisfaction may not be a bad. Happiness is a mood but satisfaction is a judgment, and like other judgments it is to be evaluated according to certain criteria: ethical, cognitive, the breadth of phenomena covered, and the standards applied. The market helps individuals meet some criteria and hinders their meeting others.

Ethical components of satisfaction. Let us bypass the virtues (honesty, loyalty, truthfulness, etc.) and concentrate on the way the market structures satisfaction according to three moral issues.

1. HELPING OTHERS. Like evolutionary processes, market processes provide help to others without intention, the hidden hand again. But without intention or benevolence, this implies no moral credits – and even a consequentialist would have trouble making the search for personal gain a creditworthy issue.

2. SELF-REGARDING PLEASURES. A person wants heroin, wants to gamble with meager savings, wants violent revenge. The enduring self is not to be sacrificed to the wants of the temporary self. All too often, however, the market is the ally of the temporary self against the enduring self.

3. JUSTIFICATION. The idea that everything that happens is justified and victims are always thought to have brought their miseries on themselves, leads to a deplorable form of satisfaction, but it is encouraged by the market's circular reasoning on justice, mentioned in Chapter 17: There is a correct or fair procedure such that the outcome is likewise correct or fair, whatever it is, provided that the procedure has been properly followed.[21] Market procedure is the ''just and fair procedure''; whatever the market does, then, is just – the just world.[22] Thus it is that even a cursory glance at the moral components of satisfaction alert us to its ambiguous standing as a good. There are cognitive components as well.

Cognitive components of satisfaction. As mentioned in the preceding chapter, recent utilitarian philosophers have stipulated that to qualify as a good, satisfaction

---

[21] John Rawls, *A Theory of Justice* (London: Oxford University Press, 1972), 86.
[22] See Melvin Lerner, *The Belief in a Just World: A Fundamental Delusion* (New York: Plenum Press, 1980).

must be *informed* about the satisfying event or object and the consequences of attaining it.[23] Illustratively, consider the problems of informed transactions, and information on the system, itself.

1. JOBS AND COMMODITIES. Employers and vendors have incentives to provide reasonably accurate information about those features of jobs and commodities that might attract employees and customers to apply for work or buy goods in their establishments if and only if the workers or customers have sanctions against deceit. Where they do not, as in the discreet hazards of work or of some purchases such as medicines and some foods, informed satisfaction is not encouraged by market structure.

2. INFORMATION ON THE CONSEQUENCES OF ONE'S OWN ACT: MARKET VERSUS GOVERNMENT. Satisfaction with one's behavior is incomplete without a knowledge of its consequences. Within its own sphere the market helps people to know the consequences of their acts by the feedback in experience with purchased goods or chosen jobs. This is a major contribution to informed satisfaction. Schumpeter's preference for market distributions, compared to public distributions, rests on the feedback from experience that daily informs people on the consequences of what they, themselves, have chosen in the market.[24]

3. THE MARKET SYSTEM. Whereas people do not choose an economic system, their levels of satisfaction with what they get from that system depend on their acceptance of the system they have. Satisfaction with the market itself would qualify as informed if a person knew how it worked. Katona reports that people are far better informed about certain market phenomena, like inflation and interest rates, than they used to be,[25] but a study seeking to assess popular knowledge of the way the system works found that fewer than 2 percent could describe a plausible set of relations among the five elements of the system specified: business, labor, consumers, investors, and advertising.[26] Market agents have no incentive to provide full and accurate information on the way the system works; that is provided, if at all, by economists and by (mostly) apologists in media and textbooks (see following).

4. MARKET GOODS VERSUS NONMARKET PRIVATE GOODS. The merit of Schumpeter's argument applies somewhat narrowly to commodities; not, I think, to the choices between wanting and taking satisfaction, say, in income compared to family life, where the feedback might be greater and better informed – irrespective of the economic system. The quality-of-life studies, not the market, provide information that might be considered crucial to the selection of a life plan devised purely as a pursuit of life satisfaction. For example, time and energy invested in family and friends will, if the person is like others, yield more happiness than time and energy invested in making money – nor will making money help much in improving family

---

[23] For example, see James Griffin, *Well-Being: Its Meaning, Measurement, and Moral Importance* (Oxford, UK: Clarendon Press, 1986), 14–15.

[24] Joseph A. Schumpeter, *Capitalism, Socialism, and Democracy*, 3d ed. (London: Allen & Unwin, 1950), 256–7.

[25] George Katona, *Psychological Economics* (New York: Elsevier, 1975), 32.

[26] Compton Advertising, Inc., *National Survey of the U.S. Economic System: A Study of Public Understanding and Attitudes*, vol 1 (Compton, New York, 1975, Photocopied), 279, Table 22b.

life.[27] Time and energy devoted to developing a sense of accomplishment is more fruitful for life satisfaction than time and energy devoted to foraging for "goods and services you can get in this area."[28]

5. THE SELF. But, as we shall see in Chapter 27, no economic system provides the essential information on what the individual would find satisfying to the enduring person he or she wants to be. In the distinctions made in Chapter 10 on self-esteem, the market satisfies the observed self, rarely the ideal self, usually leaving a gap that remains unfulfilled.

Standards. Another criterion for evaluating satisfaction is whether the standards applied are of the right kind and the right level, as where a person is satisfied with a mediocre performance or a morally questionable act. Satisfaction is a kind of self-reward that should be at least partially independent of external rewards if the individual is to remain an autonomous person. If market standards absorb other standards, the market economy has become a total culture. Market standards of efficiency are high, of ethical conduct they are modest and pliable, of craftsmanship they are no higher than necessary, and so forth.

If market satisfactions may be judged on the basis of their ethical components, their contributions to learning, and the standards they invoke, is the same true of dissatisfaction?

Dissatisfaction

Dissatisfaction has a variety of meanings that are not simply the obverse of satisfaction. Many of these are brought out in Strumpel's analysis of work satisfaction and dissatisfaction. "Economic satisfaction is considered undesirable by many," he says, "if it represents accommodation or acquiescence to a constraining reality. Dissatisfaction may represent an attitude developed in response to opportunity so that it may be concomitant to optimism," and empirically it is the case that dissatisfaction with one's job *is* associated with optimism, for it implies that change is possible. Thus, "dissatisfactions may as often be a symptom of impending success as of maladjustment." Strumpel invokes the issue of standards, already mentioned: The higher the goal, the more likely a person is to experience dissatisfaction, thus where dissatisfaction represents higher aspirations, satisfaction may represent "the stagnation of goals."[29] And he invokes the matter of alternatives, suggesting that no analysis of satisfaction is complete without a review of what is being rejected as well as what is accepted. If the alternative to a poor job is unemployment, a person will likely express job satisfaction, that is, satisfaction may be a measure of desperation. The objective alternatives help to decide the case: An

---

[27] "There is only a low correlation (less than 0.4) between economic and marital concerns, though there is somewhat more of an association among higher-SES persons." Andrews and Withey, *Social Indicators of Well-Being*, 294.

[28] Ibid., 124.

[29] Burkhard Strumpel, with Richard T. Curtin and M. Susan Schwartz, "Economic Life-Styles, Values, and Subjective Welfare," in Strumpel, ed., *Economic Means for Human Needs* (Ann Arbor, MI: Institute for Social Research, 1976), 21 and passim.

otherwise unsatisfactory outcome may be treated as satisfactory if the *alternatives* are worse.[30]

The psychological mechanisms and implications whereby a level of satisfaction is reached are important. In Strumpel's study, "satisfaction appeared to be part of a coping mechanism, a symptom of accommodation, the second-best response of people who found themselves in the role of 'getting ahead' and who were trying to move away from that role."[31] If this way of coping is psychologically satisfying in the short run, in a longer view it represents giving up. Where alternatives are difficult to achieve or costly, satisfaction offers psychological relief: Satisfied individuals are not called upon to do anything about their situations. The matter is as puzzling to philosophers as to social scientists. As Griffin points out: "It is almost impossible to strike the right balance between the two components of happiness – on the one hand, the discontent that leads to better, and on the other, contentment with one's lot."[32]

Under these circumstances we will want to withhold judgment on the merits of the market's capacity to satisfy wants until we know more about the ethical character of the wants, their relation to the genuine, long-term, ego-syntonic desires of the wanting person, their informational bases, the breadth of alternatives outside the market that have been considered, and the criteria employed in those evaluations resulting in "satisfaction." And we will want to know how the market serves the best interests of the wanting person. In some cases, at least, dissatisfaction is a healthier and more socially useful state of mind.

One certain route to dissatisfaction is to want more than one can attain. Thus, the manner in which markets create wants and the degree to which these are beyond attainment is crucial to the satisfaction of wants in society.

Creating wants

It is commonly said that the market creates wants, that the scarcity that evokes these wants is artificial in the sense that it is not necessities that are scarce but rather frivolous things that would not be wanted except for advertising pressure and pressures from the advertisers' allies in trendy publics. Contrasting what they call the "psychological scarcity" of market societies with genuine scarcity of necessary goods in the societies they have studied, certain anthropologists have criticized this want-creation and assigned it to market influences.[33] Similarly, both Rousseau and Durkheim contrasted the relative wantlessness of people in primitive societies with the demands of those in market, or incipient market, societies, with Durkheim holding that the open-ended promise of market societies led to insatiable wants, not just for specific goods but for all goods, indeed, for everything.[34]

[30] Philip Brickman and Donald T. Campbell, "Hedonic Relativism and Planning the Good Society," in M. H. Appley, ed., *Adaptation-Level Theory: A Symposium* (New York: Academic Press, 1971), 228.
[31] Strumpel et al., "Economic Life-Styles," 55.
[32] Griffin, *Well-Being*, 13.
[33] Stanley Diamond, *In Search of the Primitive* (New Brunswick, NJ: Transaction, 1974), 10–11; Marshall Sahlins, *Stone Age Economics* (Chicago: Aldine, 1972).
[34] Emile Durkheim, *The Division of Labor in Society*, trans. G. Simpson (New York: Free Press, 1964). Original work published 1893.

An alternative view is that it is the business of the market to discover latent wants and to provide the means, at a price, for satisfying them. A correlative is that the decisions as to what is a need and what is a want, what is frivolous and what is authentic, are individual decisions, and only a paternalistic society decides these matters for its citizens.

Consider three issues relevant to the allegation that the market creates more wants than it can satisfy: (1) level of aspirations and their latent agendas, (2) adjustment to unattainable wants created by the market, (3) the manipulability of consuming publics.

Level of aspirations and latent agendas. The level of aspirations people set for themselves will determine whether their wants can be satisfied, but these aspiration levels reflect the play of considerations lost to models of rational calculation (Chapter 3). For example, people with internal locus of control, and therefore with more self-confidence, set their goals at challenging but attainable levels of difficulty, whereas externals and self-doubters choose goals that are either very easy or so difficult that their expected failures will not incur censure or self-punishments.[35] What is wanted by these externals is not the apparent goal of the enterprise, but avoidance of blame and humiliation. Children following the examples of models they admire and the precepts they have learned, without coaching and in private, often set standards for themselves that require great effort and risk failure. The self-rewards that they grant themselves if they succeed are their sole sources of satisfaction. As Bandura points out: "These findings are at variance with utility theories that explain behavior in terms of optimal reward–cost balances, unless such formulations include the self-esteem costs of rewarding oneself for devalued behavior."[36] What people want is self-esteem; and *that* is the source of their satisfaction or dissatisfaction.

Strategies of adjustment to the unattainable. How do people respond when the market and its ideology inhibits happiness by creating more wants than it can satisfy, promising more than it can deliver? Merton places this problem in the context of inadequately provided means for the culturally approved goals of success, and suggests that the consequence is cheating.[37] He attributes part of the responsibility for promising more than can be delivered to the idea of equality that implies that success is equally open to all. This is, he says, a democratic idea; it is certainly not a market idea. Nevertheless, the market belief that each person is responsible for his or her own fate combines with the democratic idea that we are all equally worthy of success, to exert pressure to "succeed" on people in democratic capitalist societies – and inevitably to disappoint some portion of the population.

These people are rescued from this invitation to unhappiness by three patterns of

---

[35] In a substantial literature, see, for example, Jerry M. Burger, "Desire for Control and Achievement-Related Behaviors," *Journal of Personality and Social Psychology* 48 (1985): 1,520–33.

[36] Albert Bandura, *Social Learning Theory* (Englewood Cliffs, NJ: Prentice-Hall, 1977), 142–3.

[37] Robert K. Merton, "Social Structure and Anomie," in his *Social Theory and Social Structure,* rev. ed. (New York: Free Press, 1968).

adjustment: (1) their misperceptions of their relative positions in society (Chapter 22), (2) their tendency to anchor their expectations rather more in their own experience than in social comparisons (Chapter 26), and, more importantly, (3) by the very adaptation-level phenomena that seemed to imply a "hedonic treadmill." As previously explained (Chapter 4), the adaptation-level phenomenon says that people adapt to the levels of achievement that they have attained and set their standards accordingly. It is because of this adaptation-level phenomenon that the older are more satisfied with their lives than the younger, who have not yet established in their own minds the level of success they are destined to achieve.[38] And it is for this reason that the more ascriptive or stable a demographic category, the fewer differences in happiness or life satisfaction will be found within those demographic boundaries. For example, levels of income, which are reasonably stable, do not affect global feelings of well-being very much, but *changes* in income do[39] (Chapter 26).

Do the possibilities of income changes create unrealistic expectations? Is there a revolution of rising expectations? Testing the Tocquevillian proposition that improvements in living standards, especially when followed by an interruption of that improvement, create unrealistic expectations, Marylee Taylor found that "none of the [individual past–present] relative deprivation predictions are supported. Expectations seem *not* to be unrealistically dependent on previous experience. The gap between expectations and actual outcomes did not relate to satisfaction in the predicted fashion."[40] Like Glendower, who can "call spirits from the vasty deep," the market may invite people to strive for unattainable goals, but many will not come.

Manipulating consuming publics: autonomy. One issue raised by the market's creation of wants has inflamed certain critics, not so much because it treats of frivolity, waste, superficiality, and degradation of taste, but rather because it raises the question of individual autonomy and systematic, if hidden, coercion. On the matter of who and what creates the wants in the first place, an issue of "taste formation," Lukes asks the pertinent question: "Is it not the supreme exercise of power to get another or others to have the desire you want them to have – that is, to secure their compliance by controlling their thoughts and desires?"[41] Market mechanisms both create and control desires. Marx treats this aspect of the marketing process with hyperbole and scorn:

No eunuch flatters his tyrant more shamefully or seeks by more infamous means to stimulate his jaded appetite, in order to seek some favor, than does the eunuch of industry, the entrepreneur, in order to acquire a few silver coins or to charm the gold from the purse of his dearly beloved neighbor.[42]

---

[38] Angus Campbell, Philip E. Converse, and Willard L. Rodgers, *The Quality of American Life* (New York: Russell Sage, 1976).
[39] Inglehart and Rabier, "Aspirations Adapt to Situations," 28.
[40] Marylee C. Taylor, "Improved Conditions, Rising Expectations, and Dissatisfaction: A Test of the Past/Present Relative Deprivation Hypothesis," *Social Psychology Quarterly* 45 (1982): 24–33 at 24.
[41] Steven Lukes, *Power: A Radical View* (London: Macmillan, 1974), 23.
[42] Karl Marx, *Economic and Philosophical Manuscripts of 1844*, trans. T. Bottomore, in Erich Fromm, ed., *Marx's Concept of Man* (New York: Ungar, 1961), 141.

Galbraith is more sober, but not more cautious:

The individual's wants, though superficially they may seem to originate with him, are ultimately at the behest of the mechanism that supplies them. In the most specific manifestation,
the producing firm controls its own prices in the market and goes beyond to persuade the
consumer to the appropriate responding behavior.[43]

The limit to the "supreme power" of market mechanisms, "eunuchs of industry,"
and producing firms are in some small part formed by the "countervailing power"
(to use another of Galbraith's terms) of other domains. It is sometimes possible to
escape from these persuasive sirens into the family, religion, friendship, or leisure
hobbies.

The issue demands perspective. Both advertisers and the spokesmen for electronic media, where advertisers' wares are so prominently evident, speak of "minimal effects," the main burden of which is that their messages do not *create* preferences but merely evoke and reinforce already existing preferences.[44] Critics of
advertising partially agree when they argue that advertising does not change product
preferences but only changes brand preferences – and that only minimally. If these
two claims are true, there may indeed be waste (advertising is one industry where
the private value of the products clearly exceeds the public value[45]), but there is not
the loss of autonomy that the theory of want-creation implies. A more realistic view
is that advertising *primes* attention, changing the agenda of what is thought about,
making commodities more salient than where advertising is absent.[46]

There are counterforces. Brehm's research on "reactance" as the response of
people whose choices are threatened reveals something of this desire for the expression of one's own autonomous preference (Chapter 18). Those whose preference
ordering among goods is *A,B,C,* and who are told that they cannot have *C,* will
often respond by then preferring *C.* Those whose freedom to choose is threatened
by a "hard sell" in a supermarket respond by avoiding the hard-sell product that
seems to be forced upon them – but an informational "soft sell" campaign has no
such effect.[47]

In any event, most of the population *feel* free, with over half (54%) reporting
themselves as "delighted" or "pleased" with their "independence or freedom –
the chance [they] have to do what [they] want to do."[48] That does not answer
Lukes's question, but suggests only that in contrast to gemeinschaft, where community opinion is *the* source of opinion validation, dominance over consciousness,
even by so powerful a force as the market, is at least sometimes resisted. But there
remains the possibility that our preferences represent Lukes-type expressions of
unfreedom or examples of Marxist "false consciousness," a matter beyond our
inquiry here into subjective well-being.

[43] John Kenneth Galbraith, "Economics in the Industrial State: Science and Sedative," *American Economic Review* 60 (1970): 469–78 at 472.
[44] Joseph T. Klapper, *The Effects of Mass Communication* (Glencoe, IL: Free Press, 1963).
[45] Martin Neil Baily and Alok K. Chakrabarti, *Innovation and the Productivity Crisis* (Washington, DC:
Brookings Institution, 1988).
[46] Shanto Iyengar and Donald R. Kinder, *News That Matters: Television and American Opinion* (Chicago: University of Chicago Press, 1987).
[47] Jack W. Brehm, *Responses to the Loss of Freedom: A Theory of Psychological Reactance* (Morristown, NJ: General Learning Press, 1972).
[48] Andrews and Withey, *Social Indicators of Well-Being,* 269.

Having examined the nature of wants, of satisfaction and dissatisfaction, and the market's tendency to create wants, however they may be resisted, we are now able to turn to the way market analysts assess these matters. In order to do this, however, we must analyze a term I have often mentioned in this discussion, *utility*, and its relation to satisfaction and happiness.

Utility and the satisfaction of wants

Identifying want satisfaction, welfare, and happiness with wealth

In *The Theory of Moral Sentiments* Smith comments on the futility of striving for wealth. The son of a poor man, "whom heaven in its anger has visited with ambition," makes an unhappy discovery: The life of the wealthy "appears in his fancy like the life of some superior rank of beings," but "if in the extremity of old age he should at last attain [wealth], he will find it to be in no respect preferable to that humble security and contentment which he had abandoned for it." Nevertheless, it is "this deception which rouses and keeps in continual motion the industry of mankind."[49]

As reported in Chapter 22, economists have not only followed Bentham rather than Smith, but made utility "a part of the working equipment of the competent practitioners of the science." With many lapses, economists then treat utility as equivalent to welfare, which is identified with happiness, which, in turn, is based on income and wealth. In this analysis, equilibrium of demand and supply may be characterized as the point of maximum utility or satisfaction. The reason, Marshall explains, is that point where economic actions of individuals [have been turned] into those channels in which they will add the most to *the sum total of happiness.*"[50] Galbraith believed that economic production "serves the happiness of most men and women. That is sufficient."[51] Welfare, too, is identified with happiness: "Welfare is used as a synonym for happiness."[52] And, more hypothetically: "In welfare economics we have to infer from objective facts about consumption to states of mind (assuming that 'welfare' *does* refer to happiness, or anything else which could be called a state of mind)."[53] Then, to complete the circle, "welfarism . . . is taken as a function of the respective collection of individual utilities."[54] Utility = Wealth = Welfare = Happiness.

In fact, the idea of utility has very little to do with market experience (What consumer ever went to market consciously to maximize "utility"?), but figures instead in the analysis of that experience. The absence of an empirically based

[49] Smith, *The Theory of Moral Sentiments*, 181. See also R. H. Coase, "Adam Smith's View of Man," *Journal of Law and Economics* 19 (1976): 529–46.

[50] Alfred Marshall, *Principles of Economics*, 8th ed. (London: Macmillan, 1938), 471, 475, emphasis added. But Marshall points out that the inequality of bargaining strength and income among the parties modifies the doctrine, and, indeed, redistribution of income at the cost of lowered productivity might increase satisfaction.

[51] John Kenneth Galbraith, *The Affluent Society*, 2d ed., rev. (Harmondsworth, UK: Penguin, 1971), 279.

[52] E. J. Mishan, "Welfare Economics," *International Encyclopedia of the Social Sciences*, vol. 16 (New York: Macmillan, 1968).

[53] I. M. D. Little, *A Critique of Welfare Economics*, 2d ed. (London: Oxford University Press, 1957), 31.

[54] Amartya Sen, "Utilitarianism and Welfarism," *Journal of Philosophy* 76 (1979): 463–88 at 468.

theory of measurable utility is a serious problem in economic analysis. Even in marketing research the *decision* to buy is the explanandum, the dependent variable, and understanding the nature of satisfaction is useful only as it illuminates that decision.[55] In this context, the concept of utility has been heavily criticized, as the following topics point out.

Circularity. Joan Robinson says, "Utility is a metaphysical construct of impregnable circularity; utility is the quality in a commodity that makes individuals want to buy it, and the fact that individuals want to buy the commodities shows that they have utility."[56] "Satisfaction" is free of that circularity; people do not believe that objects have satisfaction – only the power to give satisfaction.

Location in object or person? Bentham located utility in the object: "By utility," he said, "is meant that property in any object whereby it tends to produce benefit."[57] Sen locates utility in the person: " 'Utility,' " he said, "will be taken to stand for a person's conception of his own well-being."[58] The Sen position is the stronger one. If a person ceases to want something or to benefit from it, that something loses its utility for that person. Utility is not like hardness or lead content that are measurable qualities quite apart from human dispositions. The importance of this subjective treatment of utility is that it leads away from economics to psychology, away from objective assessments toward the subjective accounts discussed in the previous chapter.[59]

Consumer utility is equal to or greater than price. There is a distinction between the utility of an object as represented by its price and the subjective satisfaction an individual receives from the object. "Total utility," which Joan Robinson says represents "satisfaction," is thus distinguished from "marginal utility," which is equal to price. Ordinarily, the price represents the equivalent of the minimum acceptable utility, leaving the consumer with something like "consumer's rent," that is, with an indefinite amount of satisfaction over and beyond that equivalent to the price.[60] In that case, the summing of the marginal utilities of members of a market probably underestimates their levels of satisfaction.

[55] See, for example, James F. Engel, Roger Blackwell, and David T. Kollat, *Consumer Behavior*, 3d ed. (Hinsdale, IL: Dryden Press, 1978).

[56] Joan Robinson, *Economic Philosophy* (Harmondsworth; UK: Penguin, 1964), 48.

[57] Jeremy Bentham, *An Introduction to the Principles of Morals and Legislation*," in Mary Peter Mack, ed., *A Bentham Reader* (New York: Pegasus, 1969), 86. Original work was begun 1778, first published 1780, revised 1789.

[58] Sen, "Utilitarianism and Welfarism," 463. Sen, a severe critic of utilitarianism, also rejects the economists' belief that a hidden hand so orders things that the sum of private utilities represents a close approximation to the public good. There are grounds for thinking of utility as failing to represent the individual's private good as well. James Griffin agrees with Sen. Griffin, *Well-Being*, 14.

[59] For a discussion of the way the same object can have irreconcilably different values to the same individual at the same time, see Nicholas Georgescu-Roegen, "Choice, Expectations, and Measurement," *Quarterly Review of Economics* 88 (1954): 503–34, quoted in Taylor, "A Model of Consumption," 35.

[60] Robinson, *Economic Philosophy*, 123.

The sum of a person's utilities is said to be meaningless. Hayek argued that since utility is a purely relative term and meaningful only when related to something else, no concept of total utility is valid.[61] Here he seems to be arguing against the Greek concept of the happy life and against the validity of the empirical studies that seek to summarize a person's feelings in an "index of well-being" or "satisfaction with life-as-a-whole." Utilities can be summed (Chapter 28), but as mentioned in the previous chapter, even when utility is accepted as meaning satisfaction, the concept of total utility is not equivalent to the concept of happiness.

Utilities are delivered by consumption, not purchase. Identification of utilities with purchase, measured by price, assumes that people are never disappointed with their products; it assumes what must be proven. In fact, it is the consumption of goods (Chapter 18) that provides satisfaction, and purchasing is not in itself regarded as a pleasant act, as we shall see in the next chapter.

Utility is a reactive, not predictive concept. A group of British psychologists examining the psychological foundations of economic behavior report their opinion that utility theory is nearly useless, not only because it is empirically empty but also because "utility theory is reactive rather than predictive."[62] Putting two modifiers, "rational" and "expected," in front of the term "utility" fails to give content to the "impregnable circularity" and emptiness of utility theory.[63]

We may summarize some of the problems arising from utility theory as a theory of want satisfaction: (1) Utility or satisfaction does not derive from transactions but from consumption. (2) In market analysis we cannot know what satisfactions people received from their transactions because we have no independent measure of satisfaction. (3) If we acknowledge that the utility of an object for an individual is wholly dependent on that individual's subjective state, we must turn away from transactions as insufficiently informative and inquire of the individual the degree to which an object of trade is satisfying. (4) Without a predictive, as contrasted to a reactive, theory of utility the market analyst, alone among social scientists, has no measurable dependent variable.

Satisfactions that escape the network of transactions

To provide a conspectus of the kinds of satisfactions that escape the network of market transactions we examine various treatments of the major satisfactions in life to assess their market relevance. Scitovsky sets the stage. "What we lack," says Tibor Scitovsky, "is an understanding of the economy's place in the total scheme of human satisfactions. Only by comparing the economy's contribution with that of all other sources can we attain a balanced perspective." He then proceeds to enu-

[61] Friedrich A. Hayek, *The Constitution of Liberty* (1960; reprint South Bend, IN: Gateway Edition/ Regnery, 1972), 309.
[62] Stephen E. G. Lea, Roger M. Tarpy, and Paul Webley, *The Individual in the Economy* (Cambridge, UK: Cambridge University Press, 1987), 481.
[63] Robinson, *Economic Philosophy*, 48.

Table 23.1. *Index of well-being explained by individual domain satisfaction scores*

Satisfaction with:	Proportion of explained variance (r^2)
Nonworking activities	29
Family life	28
Standard of living	23
Work	18
Marriage	16
Savings and investments	15
Friendships	13
Housing	11

Source: Campbell, Converse, and Rodgers, *The Quality of American Life*, 76.

merate satisfactions "that do not go through the market and [whose] value is not measurable."[64] Scitovsky's list includes: "self-sufficient satisfaction" from the things people do by themselves; "mutual stimulation" from social intercourse; "externalities," mostly from "sensory stimulants" derived from the transactions of others; "nonmarket goods and services," such as those derived around the household; "and the enjoyment of one's work." These are included in the more systematic lists of satisfactions and pleasures in the quality-of-life studies as illustrated in Table 23.1[65] and Table 23.2.[66] They are discussed separately in other chapters of this work.

The indexes in Table 23.2 are more or less self-explanatory. The efficacy index includes items expressing how people feel about the way they handle the problems that come up in their lives, what they are accomplishing, and "yourself." The family index expresses people's feelings about their children, their spouses, and their marriage. The money index includes people's feelings about how secure they are financially, their family incomes, and how well off they think they are. And, at the bottom of the list, the consumer index refers to transportation and access to work and shopping, the medical services in their area, and "the goods and services you can get when you buy in this area – things like food, appliances, and clothes." The report is from a survey conducted in May 1972; there were four such surveys around the same time period; I occasionally refer to the contributions to life satisfaction found in these other surveys where somewhat different questions were asked.

[64] Tibor Scitovsky, *The Joyless Economy* (New York: Oxford University Press, 1977), 80. There are two possible meanings for the concept of "not going through the market": The satisfaction does not arise from a market transaction, and (2) the satisfaction emerges from a market transaction but is not included in the price and may not even be a conscious feature of the exchange. Both are included in Scitovsky's list.
[65] Campbell et al., *The Quality of American Life*, 76.
[66] Andrews and Withey, *Social Indicators of Well-Being*, 124 and appendix.

Table 23.2. *Beta scores for sixteen concerns with high beta*

Index	Score
Efficacy index	.25
Family index	.18
Money index	.15
Amount of fun one is having	.16
House/apartment	.12
Things done with family	.09
Time to do things	.09
Spare-time activities	.08
Recreation index	.06
National government index	.08
Consumer index	.06

Source: Andrews and Withey, *Social Indicators of Well-Being*, 124.

Jonathan Freedman's *Happy People* has a less representative sample and presents its data in a more discursive fashion. The study finds the following are among the principal predictors of their measure of happiness:[67]

Personal growth (1st for married men; 5th–6th for single persons)
Being in love
Happy marriage
Enjoyment of friends
Social life
Job satisfaction
Satisfactory sex life
Gratifying parenthood
Confidence in one's guiding values, lack of cynicism
Belief that it is possible to control the good and bad things that happen to a person.

Important sources of subjective well-being
This sampling of findings serves to reinforce Scitovsky's impression that the most important sources of subjective well-being do not go through the market. A few salient features may be pointed out.

Self. Feelings about the self, a component of the efficacy index, are central to all treatments of happiness; indeed Andrews and Withey suggest that their question, "How do you feel about yourself?" could be a surrogate for their overall question, "How do you feel about your life as a whole?"[68] The market enhances and diminishes the self in many ways, but the most important, as the other items in

[67] Jonathan Freedman, *Happy People* (New York: Harcourt, Brace, 1980), 41ff.
[68] "For some purposes it might be a better assessment of a person's life feelings than a broader one that encompassed feelings about society, the direction of the economy, and so forth." Andrews and Withey, *Social Indicators of Well-Being*, 323.

the efficacy index indicate, is accomplishment and achievement – feelings fed by success in the labor market, not the consumer market.

Self-development.
In another of Andrews and Withey's inventories of the things that contribute most to life satisfaction, "the extent to which you are developing yourself and broadening your life" ranks fifth in importance. This time, instead of the consumer market, the reference is likely to be leisure activities, although a person might think of his or her job as the source of such development. It is hard to think of much broadening from most consumer market activities, although the purchases of books and vacations might qualify, even if the purchases refer mainly to the externals and not their consumption. The important point, however, is not so much the level of satisfaction with these things but that feelings about self and having fun are crucial to happiness, and feelings about having an interesting life and about self-development are also important – more important even than financial security, and far more important than feelings of success and getting ahead.[69]

Family and friends.
The focus on family and friends in all studies is a further reminder of the salience of "things that do not go through the market." (See Chapter 24.)

Leisure time.
Leisure time is a candidate for "going through the market" in the inverted sense of representing an opportunity cost for work. Alternatively it is a form of "income" purchased by work. In their development of a Measure of Economic Welfare, Nordhaus and Tobin give leisure an imputed value calculated on the basis of earnings forgone.[70] On this basis leisure makes up about half of the total calculated consumer income and about 166 percent of actual money income from paid work. In another sense, it represents rest and relaxation that makes work possible, an investment in work, just as work is an investment whose income makes leisure possible. The idea of going through the market, ambiguous in many ways, is least clear with respect to leisure, but it is certainly true that the value of leisure time and its activities do not appear in the measure of GNP.

There is some doubt about the value of leisure activities compared to working activities, at least their average value, if not their marginal value. On the one hand, we have Campbell et al.'s listing (Table 23.1) of satisfaction with leisure activities as the greatest contribution to a sense of well-being. (Andrews and Withey indicate that attitudes toward "things you do with your family," "time to do things," "spare time activities," and a "recreation index" are collectively more important than a combined "income index" in accounting for life satisfaction.[71]) As mentioned in Chapter 18, Juster's studies of what people actually enjoy *doing* reveal that work activities are, on average, preferred to most leisure activities, preferences almost as

[69] Ibid., 135.
[70] Ibid., 517 and § A.3.
[71] Frank M. Andrews and Stephen B. Withey, "Developing Measures of Perceived Life Satisfaction: Results from Several National Surveys," *Journal of Social Indicator Research* 1 (1974): 1–26 at 17.

frequent in working-class as in professional occupations.[72] This latter view seems confirmed by the correlation of hours worked to job satisfaction. Studies indicate the beta coefficient is .04 (or about 8% of variance among fifteen selected items);[73] apparently, giving up leisure for work, within the range measured, is not satisfaction costly. That is, the hedonic value of the two is, by these measures, almost equal. And the fact that actual earnings are only weakly correlated (.30) with satisfaction with earnings does considerably weaken any claim that work satisfaction (leisure foregone) is adequately indexed by market prices and transactions.[74] In Chapter 21 I tried to explicate a model where work has positive utilities whose implication is that the value of leisure measured by work given up would be negative.

Leisure has been defined as "psychologically free time,"[75] suggesting that the market definition of leisure as time free from work is inadequate, for it fails to account for the influence on leisure of the work itself (e.g., worry). Studies indicate that people do bring their work-related attitudes home, so this inference is plausible.[76] If this is the source of "always feeling rushed," a feeling admitted to by about a tenth of the population, leisure satisfaction is not independent of work satisfaction. As a consequence the loss in life satisfaction from "always feeling rushed," which is substantial,[77] strips leisure of some of its attractiveness – but the accounting for it goes back to work. Little wonder that Dale Jorgenson speaks of "the choice between labor and leisure" as "an unsolved problem in the study of consumer behavior."[78]

If satisfactions with the self and its development, with family and friends, and with leisure are clearly not embraced by market transactions, work, money, and commodity transactions seem to be better candidates for such transactions.

Work satisfaction. ''According to Scitovsky:

Work can be pleasant or unpleasant. . . . Those effects of work are completely missing from the economists's numerical index of economic welfare: the net national income or net national product is *not* net of the disutility of the labor that went into producing it, nor does it include the satisfaction of labor. . . . The satisfaction the worker himself gets out of his work is not an economic good because it does not go through the market and its value is not measurable.[79]

---

[72] F. Thomas Juster, "Preferences for Work and Leisure," in Juster and Stafford, *Time, Goods, and Well-Being.* The discussion in this book (Chapter 21) on the economics of intrinsically enjoyable work also leaves uncertain the relative values of leisure and work for various groups in the population.

[73] Campbell et al., *The Quality of American Life,* 302. In Chapter 21 I reported studies showing that work satisfaction *increased* with longer hours.

[74] Ibid., 304. The relationship between income and income satisfaction in each of four Scandinavian countries is only half as large. Erick Allardt, "The Relationship Between Objective and Subjective Indicators in the Light of Comparative Study," in Richard F. Tomasson, ed., *Comparative Studies in Sociology,* vol. 1 (Greenwich, CT: JAI Press, 1978), 205–6.

[75] P. H. Ennis, "The Definition and Measurement of Leisure," in E. B. Sheldon and W. E. Moore, eds., *Indicators of Social Change* (New York: Russell Sage, 1968).

[76] See David C. Glass and Jerome E. Singer, *Urban Stress* (New York: Academic Press, 1972), 18; Rosabeth Moss Kanter, *Work and Family in the United States* (New York: Russell Sage, 1977).

[77] Campbell et al., *The Quality of American Life,* 356.

[78] Dale W. Jorgenson, "Econometrics," in Nancy D. Ruggles, ed., *Economics* (Englewood Cliffs, NJ: Prentice-Hall, 1970), 56.

[79] Scitovsky, *The Joyless Economy,* 90.

Parts IV and V deal with work and its rewards.

Money. The "money index," which fares so poorly in Andrews and Withey's study, does not embrace the considerations set forth in Chapters 5 and 6 on money symbolism. Attitudes toward money itself do, in a sense, go through the market, but they are probably confounded with the prices of the goods and services that they buy. As wages, earned money represents transactions, but the sense of self-determination from the earnings, like other features of work satisfaction, are not entered in objective accounts of the sources of utilities. It is improbable that the love of money per se, the fear and dislike of money, the fantasy life that money elicits, and the sense of control it conveys are fully captured by measures of transactions. It is a matter for further investigation, for we have no measure of the satisfaction people receive from their use of this anything but colorless medium.

Consumption. Market theories identify the point of purchase as the moment when preferences are "revealed" and when utilities are achieved, but it is not the purchase of the good that yields utilities so much as the more private act of *consumption.* Like manufacturing, purchasing is an intermediate step on the way to utilities. As Juster and Stafford point out, many outputs associated with well-being "are actually instrumental inputs, and are not themselves ultimate components of well-being." Food influences both enjoyment and health – but "food itself is an instrumental product while gastronomical enjoyment and health are the real outputs."[80] It is not at all clear that *anticipation* of consumption accounts for the satisfactions of purchasing goods, for time delays usually impose a discount, but it is clear that the main satisfaction lies not in the purchase but in the consumption of a good, and it is this that contributes to well-being; consumption is not a transaction.

Choosing. And yet, what Juster and Stafford miss is that the *choice* that the market facilities is itself satisfying; it is not the "revelation" of preference, but the *expression* of preference that yields utilities. Brehm's research on "reactance,"[81] already described is evidence of the power of the desire to express one's own preferences. Similarly, Csikszentmihalyi and Figurski found that for most people a sense of *voluntariness* contributes a great deal to the satisfactions yielded by any experience.[82] It certainly cannot be said that the expression of choice does not go through the market or even that the satisfaction derived therefrom is not, in some way, priced – if only through the *costs* of the multiplication of shops and products offering more choices. But the value to individuals of the choices made does not register in GNP, of course, nor is there any way in which summing utilities from transactions can reveal the satisfaction received from the voluntariness or the sheer presence of choice.

[80] F. Thomas Juster and Frank P. Stafford, "Introduction and Overview," in Juster and Stafford, eds., *Time, Goods, and Well-Being,* 3.
[81] Brehm, *Responses to the Loss of Freedom.*
[82] Mihalyi Csikszentmihalyi and T. J. Figurski, "Self-Awareness and Aversive Experience in Everyday Life," *Journal of Personality* 50 (1982): 15–24.

There is a darker side to choice. As Mishan pointed out, more choices among commodities may be a burden and not a source of satisfaction,[83] and as the psychoanalyst, Erich Lindeman, observed: "Opportunity [for choice] without capacity will produce stress rather than satisfaction."[84] In Chapter 8 we reviewed the evidence on cognitive regression following information overload. Refuge from stress and overload found in *avoiding* transactions altogether is not priced by the market. By the quirks of hedonic accounting, this preference for avoiding transactions means that fewer transactions mean greater well-being.

Sense of personal control. One aspect of choice (as well as a desired aspect of work) is the sense of personal control over the events that affect one's life (Chapter 9); it is a source of great satisfaction, contributing almost as much as self-esteem to subjective well-being.[85] A sense of personal control (internal locus of control) has a double-edged quality, however. In Strumpel's analysis of the sources of work satisfaction he found that a sense of personal control was a major contributor to that satisfaction for the successful respondents, but contributed to feelings of self-derogation and self-blame among those who were unsuccessful.[86] But the contribution of a sense of personal control to *life* satisfaction, as contrasted to work satisfaction, is unambiguously robust.

Social framework: the market itself. Land's critique of GNP as an indicator of well-being (Chapter 22) points out that the *laws and social framework of the market* itself do not represent an item in any record of transactions and therefore offer utilities or satisfactions – or their opposites – that are unrecorded. By and large, Americans are more favorably disposed to market institutions than any other Western public – and this, not so much because of the standard of living afforded, as because of the *open opportunities* thought to flow from market institutions.[87] Here we return again to the satisfactions of freedom, personal control, and choice. As mentioned, this public support is not based on information about the way the market works or the tradeoffs implied, but it is based on intimate experience with sectors of the market.

The sense of being fairly treated. Fairness may be said to be exogenous to the market; some nearly perfect markets have coexisted with a sense that markets are inherently unfair.[88] The sense of equity, however, contributes a great deal to

---

[83] See E. J. Mishan, *The Costs of Economic Growth* (1967; reprint Harmondsworth, UK: Penguin, 1971), 159–60, 164.

[84] Erich Lindeman, "Mental Health and the Environment," in Leonard Duhl, ed., *The Urban Condition* (New York: Basic Books, 1963), 6.

[85] Angus Campbell, *The Sense of Well-Being in America* (New York: McGraw-Hill, 1981), 214–15. See also Antonia Abbey and Frank M. Andrews, "Modeling the Psychological Determinants of Life Quality," in Andrews, *Research on the Quality of Life.*

[86] Strumpel et al., "Economic Life-Styles," 48.

[87] Herbert McClosky and John Zaller, *The American Ethos: Public Attitudes Toward Capitalism and Democracy* (Cambridge: Harvard University Press, 1985). The stronger support for the market exhibited by Americans, compared to Europeans, is reflected in a Harris Poll commissioned by the Atlantic Institute for International Affairs, reported in *The International Herald Tribune,* 16 May 1983.

[88] See, for example, Hadley Cantril, *The Politics of Despair* (New York: Basic Books, 1958).

overall satisfaction with life, more than any other aspect of interpersonal relations;[89] it also makes a great difference in work satisfaction.[90] If market allocations were regarded as unfair, economic satisfaction would decline dramatically and so would satisfaction with life itself. But they are not; Americans, at least, tend to prefer the justice of equity or deserts that characterizes the market rationale for its distribution system and, if asked to construct a preferred profile of occupational rewards, they lop a little off the rewards of entertainment and sport figures and add a little to the poor but, by and large, they reconstruct the current system intact.[91] In that sense one can say that in the American context the sense of being fairly treated does go through the market.

Among those sources of satisfaction that do not go through the market, three stand out. First, that large unanalyzed reservoir of satisfactions and frustrations represented by public goods that, by their nature, do not go through the market. Second, the most important set of goods escaping the market and one of the most powerful sources of happiness and satisfaction lie within the domain of interpersonal relations that, in fact, are spoiled if they do become part of the market's transactional network. Third, the most important contributions of things that do go through the market are the feelings of achievement and accomplishment that derive largely from the labor market and only secondarily from the consumer market.

Summary

The claim that the market is a study of "the best ways of satisfying human wants" must meet certain arguments about wanting and criteria for the character of the wants, and must further show that the market is a useful instrument for this purpose. My judgment is that the market is useful in this respect, but that usefulness is much more limited than the claim.

Wanting is not necessarily a pain, hence the relief of wanting is not sufficient for life satisfaction. Reduction of wants satisfies many hedonic purposes but is disallowed by the market culture. The ordering of wants requires attention to costs, but people tend to slight this aspect of ordering. Because appetites are not related to having, but rather to wanting, wealth is no insurance against urgent wants.

Intensity of desire is not, as Cassell claimed, accurately measured by economic sacrifice. Ambivalence also interferes with rational ordering of wants. The market exaggerates attainability, but this may be beneficial because (1) it may be self-fulfilling, and (2) meeting more difficult challenges is enjoyable; on the other hand, the exaggeration may frustrate the development of a sense of personal control. The criticism of promising more than can be attained is a masked criticism for the devaluation of the object sought, wealth.

The market does not help guide the pursuit of satisfaction in (1) ethical terms,

[89] Andrews and Withey, *Social Indicators of Well-Being,* 112.
[90] Ephraim Yuchtman (Yaar), "Effects of Psychological Factors on Subjective Well-Being," in Strumpel, *Economic Means for Human Needs.*
[91] Robert E. Lane, "Market Justice, Political Justice," *American Political Science Review* 80 (1986): 383–402; Sidney Verba and Gary R. Orren, *Equality in America: The View from the Top* (Cambridge: Harvard University Press, 1985).

(2) self-regarding pleasures, or (3) appropriate justifications. It often does not provide information for "informed satisfaction," as in the case of certain jobs and commodities, the market system itself, the choice between market and nonmarket goods, and the authenticity of the wants. When the market imposes its own criteria it deprives people of choice and makes efficiency standards dominant over ethical standards. The market feedback is only locally helpful in correcting misunderstandings.

Often dissatisfaction is a superior and healthier state of mind than satisfaction. As a consequence of these various considerations, it is clear that the claims that markets satisfy human wants is only a partial credit to the market.

The market creates more wants than it can supply, frustrating expectations, and manipulating people, but there are psychological counterforces that makes this threat less than has been alleged.

Market analysts' term for satisfaction, *utility*, is generally empty and is analytically useless.

The sources of satisfaction that do not go through the market are substantial and generally make greater contributions to well-being than do those that do go through the market. Of those that may be said to be market related, the important ones relate to the labor market much more than to the consumer market.

24 Pleasure and pain in a market society

The wants whose satisfaction we discussed in the previous chapter are often a source of pain before they are satisfied. Should one then say that the market is primarily a pain-relieving mechanism or is it primarily a ministry of pleasure? Our analysis of satisfaction and dissatisfaction pointed out the benefits and healthy associations of dissatisfaction. But if dissatisfaction is painful, does this not suggest an asceticism (or martyrdom) that Bentham "took pains" to excoriate and that violates the basic utilitarian basis of the market? The unfinished business of the previous chapter leads to a further analysis of how the market deals separately and jointly with the pains and pleasures that fall within its reach.

To complete the discussion in Chapter 23 of the pains and pleasures that do and do not pass through the market we will start with the classic formulations of Jeremy Bentham, as these are supplemented by his modern empirical successors, showing again the limits of the market's reach. Since these formulations deal with the effects of *circumstances* on thought and behavior, they have to be supplemented by a further analysis of the *internal* properties that modify the hedonic effect of what the market presents. We are then ready for the main business of the chapter: How do individuals achieve a balance among these positive and negative stimuli and their internal representations? Toward the end of this discussion we find reasons for assigning the relief of pain to government and the provision of pleasure to the market – and reasons to modify that assignment.

The felicific calculus

Bentham

In market theory there are basically two kinds of pain for which there is, in each case, a remedying pleasure: The pain of work is relieved by cessation of work, or leisure; the pain of unfulfilled consumer wants is relieved, of course, by satisfying those wants in consumer transactions. This seems to correspond to the pain–pleasure calculus outlined by Bentham. In a famous passage, he says:

Nature has placed mankind under the governance of two sovereign masters, *pain* and *pleasure*. It is for them alone to point out what we ought to do, as well as to determine what we shall do. On the one hand the standard of right and wrong, on the other the chain of causes and effects, are fastened to their throne. They govern us in all we do, in all we say, in all we think: every effort we can make to throw off our subjection, will serve to demonstrate and confirm it.

Under these circumstances men not only ought to be but inevitably are governed by *the principle of utility,* "which approves of every action whatsoever, according to the tendency which it appears to have to augment or diminish the happiness of the party whose interest is in question." And, as mentioned in Chapter 23, *utility* means: "that property in any object, whereby it tends to produce benefit, advantage, pleasure, good, or happiness" or reduce pain.[1] There is nothing new in the idea, says Bentham, for "in all this there is nothing but what the practice of mankind . . . is perfectly conformable to.[2]

Bentham is reticent about the complex relationship between pleasure and pain, saying merely that to calculate the merit or value of an act for an individual, one should calculate its tendency to give pleasure and/or pain, and "sum up all the values of all the pleasure on one side, and those of all the pains on the other," and strike a balance.[3] Pleasure and pain have complex relationships to each other that resist simple summing, relationships to which we shall turn after examining the nature of market pains and pleasures. Even the summing of positive utilities is more complicated than Bentham allows.

Hedonic balance sheets

The method chosen for economic analysis employs, discreetly or overtly, a kind of hedonic balance sheet: so much pain for so much pleasure – or relief of wants. The utilities to be bought with wages are earned by the disutility of work; the utilities from saved funds are paid for by the sacrifice involved in "waiting" (Marshall) or "patience" (Fisher); the utility of profits is the reward for bearing risks. (Only the pleasures of rent are not bought by pain of some kind.)

The idea that pleasure must be earned is vaguely Christian, but it is not Puritan nor a reflection of the Protestant ethic, since the object of the pain is pleasure, which is not a Puritan goal, and the object of the Protestant Ethic is fulfillment of duty in one's calling, not pleasure. It seems Benthamite in its form, but Bentham never had the idea that it was necessary, and certainly not desirable, to go through pain to reach pleasure. The doctrine has more of the character of an ethical *justification* than an explanation, and this may be its true source. As Joan Robinson shows in her discussion of the justification for interest,[4] the pain–pleasure sequence adds nothing to causal analysis.

The format for the metaphor, of course, is double entry bookkeeping, which Sombart believed contributed greatly to economic analysis and which Schumpeter called "a towering monument" to "rational cost–profit calculations."[5] The idea of

---

[1] Jeremy Bentham, *An Introduction to the Principles of Morals and Legislation,"* in Mary Peter Mack, ed., *A Bentham Reader* (New York: Pegasus, 1969), 86. Original work begun 1778, first published 1780, revised 1789.

[2] Ibid., 98. In finding utilitarianism the natural expression of human nature, Bentham reflects a general tendency to appropriate human nature for one's cause, a tendency expressed by Adam Smith's concept of "a propensity in human nature . . . to truck, barter, and exchange one thing for another."

[3] Ibid., For communities, which Bentham says are nothing other than collections of individuals, one performs the same calculations for each individual and multiplies the good tendencies by the number of people favorably affected and the bad tendencies by the number of people adversely affected and again strikes a balance. Whereas the applications of Bentham's principles to individuals is criticized because of its apparent indifference to justice and virtue, the criticism of application to communities enlists arguments about rights, minorities, and the quite different outcomes of these applications depending on the way the calculation of "the greatest number" is made. We shall not concern ourselves with these issues here.

[4] Joan Robinson, *Economic Philosophy* (Harmondsworth, UK: Penguin, 1964).

[5] Joseph A. Schumpeter, *Capitalism, Socialism, and Democracy*, 3d ed. (London: Allen & Unwin, 1950). Schumpeter refers to Sombart's emphasis on this device, which he says has been "overstressed."

a ledger in which every credit is balanced by a debit could, then, have been interpreted as a metaphor for life. (For a different balance sheet, see Chapter 28.)

A third possible explanation is the continuation into modern analysis of the experiences of a more primitive society where consumption is a rare good and earning the means of consumption is arduous toil, where postponing consumption is, indeed, painful, and where scarcity makes any risk a threat to life itself. The economy has changed: with institutionalized savings, interest is not a payment for the *pain* of waiting; entrepreneurship is more of a game[6] than a painful bearing of risk, and, as we saw in our discussion of work (Part V), work is sometimes more enjoyable than leisure. Finally, the nature of wants (Chapter 23) is not properly described as only a pain to be relieved.

The metaphor is an impediment to understanding the market experience for several reasons. The idea that pleasures must be balanced by equivalent pains seems most clearly to describe exchanges where something must be given up to gain something else, but it does not help with equilibrium analysis that works more on homeostatic principles than organismic pain–pleasure principles. It stands in the way of the recognition of work as a positive utility, a matter treated in Part VI; it imposes upon reality a causal sequence that is misleading, not least because it understates the role of chance (which is already hard for most people to accept).[7] The pain–pleasure metaphor is at its worst just where it was thought to do some good: It implies that benefits are deserved and that suffering is justified, thus contributing to the insidious belief in a *Just World*[8] mentioned in the previous chapter. Allowing for a transformation from "the other" to "this" world, the doctrine is Calvinist; it sets people searching for the sources of their misfortunes in their own misbehavior rather than in any fault in society.

And yet, rather simply transformed into the concept of contingency (Chapter 9), it is a most valuable heuristic. People are responsible for the consequences of their own acts; gains and losses to them and others may be explained, but not justified, by contingent causal relations.

Market pains

The limits of market pain relief
Bentham lists the following kinds of pains:

(1) The pains of privation. (2) The pains of the senses. (3) The pains of awkwardness. (4) The pains of enmity. (5) The pains of ill-name. (6) The pains of piety. (7) The pains of benevolence. (8) The pains of malevolence. (9) The pains of the memory. (10) The pains of imagination. (11) The pains of expectation. (12) The pains dependent on association.[9]

[6] Michael Maccoby, *The Gamesman: Winning and Losing the Career Game* (New York: Bantam, 1978). Weber referred to business in America as a "sport." The classic work, of course, is Joseph A. Schumpeter, *The Theory of Economic Development: An Inquiry into Profits, Capital, Credits, Interest, and the Business Cycle,* 2d ed., trans. R. Opie (Cambridge: Harvard University Press, 1936). The thrust of Schumpeter's analysis is to undermine the entrepreneur's strictly economic motivation and rely, instead, on the desire to create "a private kingdom."

[7] See Ellen J. Langer, *The Psychology of Control* (Beverly Hills, CA: Sage, 1983).

[8] Melvin J. Lerner, *The Belief in a Just World: A Fundamental Delusion* (New York: Plenum Press, 1980).

[9] Bentham, *Principles of Morals and Legislation,* 99.

The list shows the limits of market relief, for the market is impotent to relieve the pains of awkwardness, enmity, ill-name, piety, benevolence (meaning both costs to the benevolent individual and the absence of benevolence in others), malevolence, most memories, and much imagination. Physical pain, Bentham's "pain of the sense," is only partially remediable by purchasable medicine and care. The cessation of the sense altogether, death, is both inevitable and said by the existentialists as well as St. Augustine, to be the source for conscious beings of lifetime sorrow. The evidence from the quality-of-life research I have been citing shows no such underlying theme and, indeed, life satisfaction increases with age.

Many of the pains in life comprise regrets over opportunity costs, that is, good things given up in order to achieve better things. Bentham's listing of pains seems to exclude such considerations; neither the market nor any other agency is able to relieve this form of regret. On the contrary, by a perverse logic one might argue that by multiplying choices, the market increases opportunity costs so that there are more lost opportunities to regret!

In his *Reflections on the Causes of Human Misery*, Barrington Moore points to the following sources of human misery: (1) war, (2) injustice and oppression, (3) persecution for dissident beliefs, and (4) poverty, hunger, disease.[10] The pains that three of these four circumstances create are generally beyond the capacity of the market to relieve; only poverty, hunger, and disease are directly remediable by economic activity – and here, to refer to a distinction made earlier, it is the market's affluence effect rather than its exchange effect that is at work.

One inference from these limits is that the market is primarily a resource for relatively happy people living in relatively peaceful and democratic societies. It is not much of an instrument for relief of pain or of psychological depression, let alone death, war, and oppression. But the market has its own sources of dissatisfaction, unhappiness, frustration, anxiety, boredom, and depression. Most of these pains are obvious, although their attribution to the market would take some argument: loss of a job, selection among unsatisfying jobs, debt, bankruptcy, buying artificially obsolescent goods, externalities of pollution, and so forth. But some are less obvious.

The pain of shopping. Of course pain comes in a variety of degrees and guises. Taking from Juster's study of process benefits the things people like doing least, a mild degree of pain, we find the following (the least liked first, with the score on a one-to-ten basis): cleaning house (4.18), caring for other people's children (4.53), grocery shopping (4.55), school and work meetings (5.13), other shopping (5.30).[11] These low rankings are little affected by occupational rank, except that the pain of housecleaning declines among the lower ranked occupations. The evidence is mixed on the general public attitude toward shopping,[12] but Juster's

---

[10] Barrington Moore, *Reflections on the Causes of Human Misery* (Boston: Beacon, 1972).

[11] F. Thomas Juster, "Preferences for Work and Leisure," in Juster and Frank P. Stafford, eds., *Time, Goods, and Well-Being* (Ann Arbor, MI: Institute for Social Research, 1985), Table 13.1, p. 336.

[12] "Women report that they enjoy shopping, regardless of social class," but for different reasons. Upper-class women like the pleasant store atmosphere and exciting displays in the stores they frequent. In the middle class, shopping "has taken on the characteristics of a form of recreation." In the lower middle

data have been replicated in two separate years (1975, 1981) and focus specifically on the activity rather than associated pleasures and pains.

These costs are transaction costs and are now revealed to be more pervasive than generally supposed. The pleasure of shopping for the goods that represent the rewards for the "pain" of work may even be assigned to the class of "regrettable necessities" – a strange route to maximizing satisfaction. The levels of pain or pleasure in the act of shopping are, no doubt, reflected in price to the degree that one pays for convenience, deference, and lack of crowding, but the dislike of shopping activities is similar across income groups, suggesting that the general deduction from satisfaction is unlikely to be reflected in prices. Prices are not much more likely to reflect these disamenities than they are to reflect work disamenities, which, as we have seen, are *not* reflected in wages.

Concerns that yield low hedonic scores. Those concerns with average ratings in the "unhappy" and "terrible" ranks of Andrews and Withey's "Delighted to Terrible" scale are as follows (the mode is 5.2): At the very bottom are three political items and one economic item. The political items are taxes (3.2), "what the government is doing about the economy" (3.5), political leaders (3.7); and the economic item is "what you have to pay for the basic necessities" (3.7). In general, political and governmental matters are ranked at the bottom of the satisfaction scale, but they do not detract much from overall life satisfaction because the influence of these assessments on the measurements of life satisfaction is minimal.

Next are a group of items that are ranked in the low end of the scale, but tending more toward displeasure than unhappiness: "your chance of getting a good job if you went looking for one" (4.4), "the amount of pressure you are under" (4.5), family income (4.65), "amount of time you have for doing what you want to do" (4.7), "extent to which you are achieving success and getting ahead" (4.8). These are largely economic and, except for family income, have a common theme: *insecurity, frustration, and stress.* To reinforce this view, note that feelings of financial security are ranked low in satisfaction, much lower than feelings about pay and standard of living, a fact made more important by the relatively close relationship between life satisfaction and sense of financial security or insecurity.[13] As said in Chapter 23, this dimension or cluster is the one where the market creates the greatest pain.

Stress, anxiety, insecurity

Stress. Whereas in the discussion in Chapter 8 I pointed to the regressive effects on cognition created by stress and overload, here we find the same kind of

class, husband and wives often go shopping together. Although there are working-class satisfactions, they are more related to the actual acquisition of needed commodities – less intrinsic to the activity of shopping. James F. Engel, Roger D. Blackwell, and David T. Kollat, *Consumer Behavior*, 3d ed. (Hinsdale, IL: Dryden, 1978), 135–6.

[13] Frank M. Andrews and Stephen B. Withey, *Social Indicators of Well-Being: Americans' Perceptions of Life Quality* (New York: Plenum Press, 1976), 135, 254. Among the thirty-two most predictive items, feelings of financial security ranked eighth.

theft of felicity. The frequent references to the sense of pressure and the shortage of time point to a feature of a market life that has often been noticed ("rat race," "overload," "overcommitted," etc.), but is uncertainly attributable to the market; for example, government bureaucrats have reported the same feelings. But to the degree that these feelings are exacerbated by market competition, they do take a toll on life satisfaction. People who "always feel rushed" rank notably lower on an Index of Subjective Well-Being,[14] and those who report a lot of "hassles" in their daily lives score lower on measures of life satisfaction.[15] Market economies are characterized by innumerable stresses for which there is no market compensation.[16] Both risk and stress (and risk of stress) are pains that filter or modify the pleasures the market offers. Anticipating stress, the individual is frightened and engages in defensive behavior, which "is hard to eliminate even when the hazards no longer exist;" and is extremely resistant to disconfirmation.[17] Thus, in addition to the hedonic loss, there is also a cognitive loss, as reported in Chapter 8.

Anxiety and feelings of insecurity as a learned disposition. The effects of market insecurity are not limited to market activities, for when experiences of insecurity are prolonged and serious, people tend to incorporate what they learn from these experiences into their enduring dispositions toward people and events quite beyond the original experience, though sometimes only when triggered by something similar to what prompted the original disposition. Abbey and Andrews show that a disposition to anxiety and depression affects assessments of life as a whole. Asking themselves, "How is it that people come to feel as they do about well-being?" they examine the personality features that are associated with such feelings. A relatively simple model explains their findings: "Interactions with social world → psychological factors → internal states of depression and anxiety → sense of well-being." In the particular circumstances of their study, these authors found that anxiety and depression were, indeed, associated with prior external stress, and, in turn, were the strongest predictors of assessment of life quality.[18]

Bryant and Veroff found that three out of six of the factors an analysis of the psychological determinants of well-being dealt with were uncertainty, anxiety, and feelings of insecurity. There is no evidence that these characteristics vary with level

[14] Angus Campbell, Philip E. Converse, and Willard L. Rodgers, *The Quality of American Life* (New York: Russell Sage, 1976), 357.
[15] Sheryl Zika and Kerry Chamberlain, "Relation of Hassles and Personality to Subjective Well-Being," *Journal of Personality and Social Psychology* 53 (1987): 155–62.
[16] Although Adam Smith thought disamenities (such as stress) associated with any job would find market compensation, "this proposition has shown surprising resistance to empirical confirmation." Juster, "Preferences for Work and Leisure," 334.
[17] Albert Bandura, *Social Learning Theory* (Englewood Cliffs, NJ: Prentice-Hall, 1977), 62.
[18] Antonia Abbey and Frank M. Andrews, "Modeling the Psychological Determinants of Life Quality," in Frank M. Andrews, ed., *Research on the Quality of Life* (Ann Arbor, MI: Institute for Social Research, 1986). Shaver and Freedman also report that for about a third of their population, worry and anxiety are psychological filters that detract from their feelings of happiness, but in this study the principle source of worry is not economic insecurity and stress but, for parents, their children. See Philip Shaver and Jonathan Freedman, "Your Pursuit of Happiness," *Psychology Today* (August 1976): 27–32, 75.

of income in this sample; the measures are not, therefore, concealed measures of poverty. To the extent that people possessed these characteristics, they were less likely to report a sense of high life satisfaction.[19]

The market's propensity to change the circumstances of people's lives is intrinsic to its successful operation. *Change* is the necessary outcome of competition and rationality; it is both the cause and effect of economic growth.[20] For a considerable number of people, those marked by feelings of vulnerability, lack of self-confidence, a sense of uncertainty about the future, or anxiety in its many nonspecific forms, the pleasures of satisfying their consumer wants and associated market utilities are diminished by these dispositions that are themselves learned from experience in the market.[21]

Money. Where money has the kind of negative associations reported in Chapter 6, the market experience will be painful. For example, where money suggests "painful failure" or "social unacceptability," transactions for money cannot fail to reflect these attitudes.

Disappointment. As mentioned briefly in Chapter 23, a substantial proportion of purchases is disappointing, as the customer complaint departments in large stores testify.[22] Whether the products purchased are themselves enjoyed much more than shopping for them is an open question: People take more satisfaction in their police and fire services than in "the goods and services you get when you buy in this area – things like food, appliances, and clothes."[23] The assumption that it is satisfaction and therefore satiation (and declining marginal utility) that grow with acquisition of a commodity flows from the failure to look beyond the purchase to the process benefits or consumption.[24]

The happy consciousness of the dismal science
Pondering over the persistent use of such phrases as "the object of all economic activity is to satisfy human wants,"[25] one gradually recognizes that such definitions by economists of economic institutions, especially of markets, are always couched in positive language. One does not see the proposition that the function of economic

[19] Fred B. Bryant and Joseph Veroff, "Dimensions of Subjective Mental Health in American Men and Women," in Andrews, *Research on the Quality of Life.* There is, however, a tendency for the educated to worry more about controllable things that they can do something about. See Gerald Gurin, Joseph Veroff, and Sheila Feld, *Americans View Their Mental Health* (New York: Basic Books, 1960).

[20] David S. Landes, "Technological Change and Industrialization," in Tom Burns, ed., *Industrial Man* (London: Penguin, 1969), 69–89.

[21] The market's provision of insurance to remove the terrors of risk do not represent an effective remedy: (1) For the ordinary person the problem is one of uncertainty not risk; (2) insurance usually covers only demonstrable material loss, whereas the most serious losses are usually those of such immaterial things as self-respect, familiar roles and associations, community, family integrity, and so forth; (3) insurance often does not prevent "hassles," but creates them.

[22] Engel et al., *Consumer Behavior,* chap. 22.

[23] Andrews and Withey, *Social Indicators of Well-Being,* 257.

[24] Hirschman bases a theory of market–governmental alternation on disappointment. Albert O. Hirschman, *Shifting Involvements: Private Interest and Public Action* (Princeton: Princeton University Press, 1982).

[25] Gustav Cassel, *The Theory of Social Economy,* rev. ed., trans. S. L. Barron (New York: Harcourt, Brace, 1932), 3.

activity is the relief of misery, or that the advantage of the market economy lies in its superior capacity to relieve *dis*satisfaction. Negative utilitarianism seems to have a place in justifications of governmental activities,[26] but not in market justifications.[27]

The reasons, I think, is that the assumption behind all market transactions is that they represent voluntary choices where each partner chooses whatever is better for him or her; therefore, whatever the character of the alternatives not chosen, the choice satisfies some want – if only to escape from less attractive alternatives. This broadens the concept of want satisfaction, and of the pleasure involved in each transaction, to the point where choosing moldy potatoes over rotten tomatos, arsenic over cyanide, and prison over execution all represent want satisfaction and, in market if not strictly Benthamite terms, degrees of pleasure.

In his fanciful attack on *One Dimensional Man,* Herbert Marcuse speaks of "The Happy Consciousness – the belief that the real is rational and that the system delivers the goods." Marcuse attributes this superficial happiness to the internalization of technological rationality,[28] but perhaps equally fancifully, one might consider whether the widespread and happy acceptance of the market is not due in some small part to its identification in economic analysis with positive feelings of satisfaction rather than with negative feelings of dissatisfaction. In the studies we have reviewed the confinement of expression of "delight" and "pleasure" to the family domain, compared to the more neutral "mostly satisfied" in the economic domain, may represent a distinction parallel to Herzberg's distinction between those things that make work *enjoyable,* compared to those that relieve *dissatisfaction.*[29] Without adequate income, one is dissatisfied; with it, one is satisfied – but not delighted or even pleased. The market relieves dissatisfaction; other domains offer delight and pleasure.[30] Even if we do not find the market primarily a dissatisfaction-relieving mechanism, the want satisfaction offered by the market may be a minimal order of felicity.

Market pleasures

The limits of market pleasure promotion. Bentham's list of pleasures is roughly parallel to his pains: "The pleasures of sense, . . . wealth, . . . skill, . . . amity, . . . good name, . . . power, . . . piety, . . . benevolence, . . . malevolence, . . . imagination, . . . memory, . . . expectation, . . . association, . . . re-

[26] Karl Popper, *Conjectures and Refutations: The Growth of Scientific Knowledge* (London: Routledge & Kegan Paul, 1963), 381–3.

[27] The machinery of economic analysis would undergo some interesting changes if, instead of utility, the central concept became disutility. The marginal disutility curves would slope up as quantity increased, and the indifference curves would be convex instead of concave.

[28] Herbert Marcuse, *One Dimensional Man* (Boston: Beacon Press, 1964), 78.

[29] Frederick Herzberg, *Work and the Nature of Man* (New York: Mentor/New American Library, 1966), 112ff. Herzberg's findings have been widely challenged; see, for example, Richard H. Hall, *Dimensions of Work* (Beverly Hills, CA: Sage, 1986), 119–20.

[30] Expressed feelings about "what you have to pay for the basic necessities, such as food, housing and clothing" are among the least satisfying of all the aspects of life reported. Andrews and Withey, *Social Indicators of Well-Being,* 254.

lief.''[31] Confirming the market's accentuation of the positive, we think of the market as gratifying the pleasures of the senses, but in reviewing pains we did not think of the market as relieving painful sensations. Bentham, too, has a "positivity bias"; he did not mention the pain of poverty but lists in second place the pleasures of wealth. These considerations aside, we quickly see again the limits of the market: The pleasures of amity, good name (to some extent), of piety, of benevolence and malevolence, and of imagination and memory are generally not provided by the market.

Reviewing Andrews and Withey's list of thirteen concerns with the most effect on global life satisfaction (not the list used in Chapter 23), we can see market relevance in several: meeting physical needs (2) and financial security (8) are direct market products, and having fun (1), sense of own worth (3), having an interesting daily life (6), and, with more limited scope, being fairly treated (4) are indirectly relevant. But the remaining seven items (e.g., sense, amity, piety, etc.) are only marginally relevant to the market.[32]

In the previous chapter I listed a variety of pleasures that do not go through the market: self-sufficient satisfactions, social intercourse, leisure activities, enjoyment of work, moral satisfactions, a sense that life has meaning, and so forth.[33] The theme of work enjoyment has a special complexity in the context of market pleasures.

Work: making a pain into a pleasure. As mentioned in Chapter 23, a study by Juster shows that on the average, most people prefer their work activities to any of their leisure activities except talking and playing with their own children, "talking with friends," and "going on trips, outings." Working activities (ranking seventh) were preferred to reading books and magazines, going to church, reading newspapers, playing sports, going to movies, and watching television (the last of these ranking seventeenth).[34] When a "pain," widely regarded as the cost of both leisure and goods, turns into a pleasure, the balance of pains and pleasures in the market (or anywhere) is more difficult to calculate (Chapter 21). This would be especially true if the lower ranking of leisure activities meant that they had crossed some invisible line and were not only relatively less enjoyable than working, but, like "cleaning house," more of a pain than a pleasure.

Pleasures from the market experience

Most of the pleasures the market offers are predictable and obvious: Within budget constraints people buy the food they enjoy, the clothes they believe add most to

---

[31] Bentham, *Principles of Morals and Legislation,* 99.

[32] Andrews and Withey, *Social Indicators of Well-Being,* 135. These remaining items are: self-development (5), coping with change (7), contribution to others (9), religious fulfillment (10), acceptance by others (11), freedom from bother (12), and belief in one's own honesty and sincerity (13).

[33] In order to avoid the difficulty of tracing indirect effects, "not going through the market" is taken to mean two things: (1) The pleasure-yielding satisfaction is unpriced and (2) not flowing directly and intentionally from transactions. There is a further problem with the pleasures yielded by those things that *do* go through the market, namely, the fact that purchases are not the sources of satisfaction; it is the consumption of what is purchased that yields satisfaction. Similarly, it is not leisure that is satisfying (except as surcease from pain) but the consumption of leisure by engaging in pleasurable activities, including rest and relaxation.

[34] Juster, "Preferences for Work and Leisure," 336, 340.

their appearance, the cars that they think suit their needs. Where the market endows people with more money, they find happiness in the things their discretionary income provides: new experiences, novelty, relief from financial constraints (as well as from financial worries).[35] The market is a flexible device for serving these different values. Some pleasures are less obvious. Consider the following.

Choice: market responsiveness to personal rhythms. There are hidden rewards when market rhythms match personal rhythms.

1. LIFE CYCLE. In their youth people value excitement; as they mature, they seek contentment;[36] each can find the forms of pleasure these desires dictate. But the low pay for young married couples when the combination of childbirth and childcare, the expenses of house furnishing, job and marital strains create a peak period of stress is a failure to match demand and supply.

2. WORK AND LEISURE. The market caters to different preferences for work and leisure, although recall that Juster's analysis of marginal and average preferences for working and for leisure activities suggested a lack of accommodation of those who would prefer *more* work;[37] the opportunities for second jobs, such as those available to artisans, are not available to many. The increase of part-time jobs to accommodate (some say exploit) women with children is an indication of (delayed) market responsiveness. For the better off, the income effect of their larger incomes invites greater leisure – an invitation that is generally declined in the United States, for the marginal utility of work fails to decline as predicted. The unemployed do not have that choice.

3. METABOLIC RHYTHMS. There is another rhythm that serves the market well. For those with money, the market satisfies the cyclical, rhythmic pleasures of eating and drinking. Here adaptation-level phenomena are limited by the natural processes of biological rhythms of depletion ever seeking its own renewal.

4. EXCITEMENT AND TRANQUILITY. Mill thought happiness was composed of some combination of excitement and tranquility, with each able to compensate for the other; Berlyne's concepts of optimum arousal offers a similar anabolic–catabolic pattern. Market choices help restore balances. Most people believe that their "chances for relaxation – even for a short time" are at least "satisfactory" and almost as many are "pleased" or "delighted" as are "mostly satisfied" with their opportunities for relaxation. The pain of the market's "rat race" mentioned earlier is limited by the thirty-nine-hour work week – which varies little among Western developed nations. Opportunities for "excitement" might be roughly indicated (if not measured) by responses to Andrews and Withey's questions regarding "How much fun you are having;" the evaluation was only average (5.2). Since the contribution of "fun" to assessment of life satisfaction was very high (.60),[38] the modesty of this rating reduced happiness (more than life satisfaction) by a noticeable measure.

5. MARKET FUN VERSUS SATISFYING FUN. Certainly the consumer market caters

[35] Norman Bradburn, *The Structure of Psychological Well-Being* (Chicago: Aldine, 1969), 231.
[36] Milton Rokeach, *The Nature of Human Values* (New York: Free Press, 1973), 78–9.
[37] Juster, "Preferences for Work and Leisure," 337–40.
[38] Andrews and Withey, *Social Indicators of Well-Being,* 111, 268.

to commercially salable ways of having fun, but it slights those activities that are, in Juster's study, rated as most enjoyable: talking and playing with one's children and social intercourse and visiting. It is uncertain whether market pressures contribute to the amount of fun people have – and therefore to their overall life satisfaction by this route.

Observe, too, that the satisfactions of (6) engaging in a market system liked for its range of freedoms and opportunities, and (7) for its "fairness" reported in chapter 23 are market pleasures.

I have been elaborating here on a theme in the previous chapter: Pleasures and pains that are and are not features of market transactions. Like Bentham's list of pains, most of his list of pleasures find their sources well outside the market, but some others are indeed market-guided pleasures. Among these, we said, was the ability to tailor active and passive pleasures according to the life cycle, but the choice of whether to find pleasure in work or in leisure was not well guided by the market, even when a person wanted to work more than necessary for the income he or she needed or wanted. Similarly, there is reason to believe that the market presses people into those kinds of leisure activities that Juster found were often the least satisfying. But there is one kind of pleasure stemming from an active engagement with life that does, indeed, seem to be encouraged by the market.

The pleasures of feeling effective and of active engagement with life

Feeling effective. To the considerable extent that the market is a device for inviting individual effort and achievement, it can take credit for the contribution to happiness of the previously mentioned efficacy index ("The way you handle the problems that come up in your life?" "What you are accomplishing in your life?" and "How do you feel about yourself?"). In an assessment of contributions to global life satisfaction (different from the one reported), that efficacy index was overwhelmingly the best predictor of satisfaction with life-as-a-whole.[39] Modest evidence from time budget studies suggests that the market invites a more active, engaged life than does a command economy[40] – and that engagement is half of the battle for happiness.[41] It is a concomitant of the act of choosing discussed in Chapter 23.

Active and passive enjoyments. To the extent that markets are instruments for achievement values and help society to shed the trappings of ascription, the market encourages a more active, engaged style of life. Here it seems to conform to Bertrand Russell's belief that the active, engaged life produces pleasant feelings and a more private, introspective life encourages unpleasant feeling. A person may be happy, he says, "provided that his passions and interests are directed outward, not inward. . . . Dwelling on ourselves [invites] . . . fear, envy, the sense of sin,

[39] Ibid., 124.
[40] Philip E. Converse, "Country Differences in Time Use," in Alexander Szalai, ed., *The Use of Time* (The Hague: Mouton, 1972).
[41] Jonathan L. Freedman, *Happy People* (New York: Harcourt Brace Jovanovich, 1978), 30–3.

self-pity, and self-admiration." It does not yield a "sense of the variety of life."[42] Perhaps market experiences represent only a thin slice of that variety, but, for example, comparing women engaged in market work with housewives, one can appreciate Russell's point: Compared to women with market work, housewives "are much more likely to be anxious and worried (46% to 28%), lonely (44% to 26%), and to feel worthless (41% to 24%)."[43]

Further empirical evidence suggests that Russell is only half right: Active engagement is a necessary but not a sufficient ingredient. Among Freedman's sample of magazine readers: "Almost everyone seemed to define happiness in both active and passive terms. . . . The active and passive views of happiness are two aspects of the same state, not two different states. . . . The combination produces or is happiness, either alone is not."[44]

In short, if the actual transactions in the market merely relieve dissatisfactions – but at least that – the market is also a medium where genuinely pleasing experiences can and do take place. It is a place where some people can approach Russell's utopia: "union with the stream of life [in which] the greatest joy is to be found."[45] Observe that it is not in the traditional area of want satisfaction, the purchase of commodities giving a high or rising standard of living, that the market makes its largest contribution, but in the area of work; it is in making, not spending, money.

Like perception, enjoyment of an experience is a subjective phenomenon stimulated by an objective situation. We have been discussing the objective situations offered by the market, but the influences of these situations are severely modified by internal dispositions, interests, and capacities. We turn to them now.

Dispositions and internal rewards

Pleasures and pains are not just given, they are construed; they are part of "the social construction of reality,"[46] part of self-perception that reflects social norms and conventional theories of what pleases and pains an average person in any given society;[47] and they are ingrained features of personality. The ease or difficulty with which the market creates pain and pleasure among its customers and workers is, therefore, not simply a product of market transactions but rather an interaction between these transactions and the dispositions of these people. In hyperbolic form, one might say that like beauty, "utility is in the mind of the beholder." We turn, therefore, to a brief discussion of certain dispositions that facilitate and hinder market pleasures and pains.

[42] Bertrand Russell, *The Conquest of Happiness* (London: Allen & Unwin, 1930), 242–3. A little earlier, another philosopher, John Stuart Mill, inserted a subtext on the value of an active life in his *Essay on Liberty*.
[43] Shaver and Freedman, "Your Pursuit of Happiness," 29.
[44] Freedman, *Happy People*, 32–3.
[45] Russell, *The Conquest of Happiness*, 248.
[46] Peter L. Berger and Thomas Luckman, *The Social Construction of Reality* (Garden City, NY: Doubleday Anchor, 1967).
[47] Daryl J. Bem, "Self-Perception Theory," in L. Berkowitz, ed., *Advances in Experimental Social Psychology*, vol. 6 (New York: Academic Press, 1972).

Ingrained negative and positive affectivity. Unhappiness, or the persistence of negative feelings about what life has to offer, is often chronic and not sensitive to external events: "NA [negative affectivity] is a stable and pervasive personality dimension – high NA individuals report more stress, distress, and physical complaints, even in the absence of any objective stressor or health problems."[48]

The market will run into the same problem of a chronic, nonresponsive mood among the positive affects as well as the negative ones. Freedman calls this unvarying positive mood a "talent for happiness . . . [possessed by] those who manage to be happy . . . more or less regardless of what happens to them. . . . Such people exist and . . . to some extent this talent or capacity plays a role in happiness." It cannot be explained by happy childhood experiences because almost none of these unhappy early experiences "made a great deal of difference" in adult happiness.[49] Apparently want satisfaction in the market or elsewhere makes only superficial differences to those with chronic negative affectivity or this "talent for happiness."

Personal control and efficacy. Deeply embedded tendencies to attribute the causes of events to the self, *internality,* rather than something outside the self, *externality,* is (as we saw in Chapter 9) an important market-related disposition. There is some evidence that internals tend to be happier than externals,[50] largely because they believe that whatever happens to them can be corrected by their own actions and because self-confidence, self-esteem, and a sense of well-being are associated with each other.[51] To the extent that the market does, in fact, encourage internality (self-reliance), it provides a filtering disposition that promotes positive affectivity and life satisfaction.

Conscience. Market "pleasures" filtered through a guilty conscience are not pleasures at all, but there is little evidence that people are in general made less satisfied with their lives because they have not contributed to the well-being of others. People are reasonably satisfied with the "Things you do to help people or groups in this community" and "How much you are contributing to other people's lives," but the answers do little to influence their overall life satisfaction.[52] In spite of the lingering features of the Protestant ethic, the market probably works more through shame than through guilt; but if there is guilt, the focus will more likely be

---

[48] David Watson, James W. Pennebaker, and Robert Folger, "Beyond Negative Affectivity: Measuring Stress and Satisfaction in the Workplace," *Journal of Organizational Behavior Management* 8 (1986): 141–57 at 141. Bradburn, however, finds that his measure of negative affectivity seems to be measuring anxiety and various symptoms of neurotic tendencies and psychic impairment. See Bradburn, *The Structure of Psychological Well-Being,* 231.
[49] Freedman, *Happy People,* 231–2.
[50] Clive J. Robins, "Attribution and Depression: Why Is the Literature so Inconsistent?" *Journal of Personality and Social Psychology* 54 (1988): 880–9.
[51] The "sense of efficacy and accomplishment" mentioned for its contribution to life satisfaction contributed almost as much to overall life satisfaction as did the highest ranking "fun and enjoyment in life." Andrews and Withey, *Social Indicators of Well-Being,* 111–12. This is only one of many measures of internality showing contributions to similar measures of well-being. See, for example, Angus Campbell, *The Sense of Well-Being in America* (New York: McGraw-Hill, 1981), chap. 13.
[52] Campbell, *The Sense of Well-Being in America,* 273.

in line with the market ethos of hard work and achievement than help to others, the latter being a matter on which the market is silent.

Extraversion. As Bertrand Russell predicted, people are happier when they lead "outward looking lives." Argyle and associates find that "one of the best predictors of happiness is extraversion,"[53] partly because extraversion increases friendship, which, as reported, is a major contribution to feelings of well-being.

Neither Bentham's simple addition of pleasures and subtraction of pains nor the linear cumulative quality-of-life model presented in Chapter 22 are easily adapted to the concept of filtering dispositions. The trait + experience model makes for a different kind of assessment, tying predisposition to each incident. For example, for the anxious person the model would look something like this: (job + anxiety), (house + anxiety), and (friendship + anxiety) rather than (job + house + friendships) − (anxiety). The difference lies in the capture of dispositional *states* that are object specific (as well as any generalized *traits* that may be present) as contrasted to reliance on unattached *personality* traits, such as free-floating anxiety.

Internal rewards and punishments

One may think of the disposition to respond in certain ways as part of the system of self-rewards and self-criticisms of social learning theory. The self-evaluation undertaken by internal monitors is partially independent of the rewards and punishments, pleasures and pains of the market or of other social institutions, for they turn on standards that are, insofar as any current experience is involved, antecedent historic creations. "Performance accomplishments build a sense of personal efficacy, increase interest in . . . activities, and produce self-satisfactions." But if the standards are too high, this self-evaluational process creates personal distress.[54] When people watch others who adopt high standards and are self-critical of their own performances, they often adopt these self-critical attitudes for themselves, sometimes when there are no external rewards for their higher standards. For market theory, the tendency to adopt standards that do not promise external rewards, but rather invite self-punishment instead, is an anomaly that cannot be accounted for by utility theory. The puzzle is explained by social learning theory in this way: The self-critical attitudes relieve fear of criticism from others and thus actually reduce worry. Although such self-criticism is a principal source of self-regulation (e.g., stopping smoking), it carries with it a major hedonic disability: "Self-punishment that is successful in averting anticipated threats can prevent reality testing so that it persists long after the threats have ceased to exist."[55] In addition to the hedonic loss there is a cognitive loss in impaired reality testing.

Self-appraisal and self-esteem. Self-punishment and self-reward are reflected in overall measures of self-appraisal. In the life-quality studies, people re-

[53] Michael Argyle, Maryanne Martin, and Jill Crossland, "Happiness as a Function of Personality and Social Encounters," in *Proceedings of the 24th International Congress of Psychology,* vol. 1, ed. J. P. Forgas and M. J. Innes (Sydney: North Holland, Elsevier, 1988).
[54] Bandura, *Social Learning Theory,* 140.
[55] Ibid., 144, 152, 153, emphasis in the original.

sponded to the question, "How do you feel about yourself?" with moderately favorable views but rarely with responses of "delighted" (6%) or "pleased," implying more "satisfaction" than "pleasure." Apparently one is likely to be less pleased with oneself than with one's friends, family, and children. What is important about self-assessment, however, is that it is closely associated with overall assessments of one's life quality: Feelings about one's *life* are only as good as one's esteem for one's *self*.[56] Self-esteem is responsive to actual achievements, of course, and if one fails in the market arena, the erosion of self-esteem is substantial. But self-esteem is more affected by experience in small intimate groups than by achievements in the larger society[57] – and intimate primary groups are uniquely invulnerable to market influences.

Internal conflicts. Internal conflicts are manifested in, for example, projecting the disliked aspects of the self onto others, denial of reality to protect some fragile aspect of the ego, repression of motive that threatens the conscious self-image – and then leaking evidence of the repressed motive in dealing with others. Among the most intense pains of this transient life, these conflicts frustrate the market's effort to satisfy wants and inhibit realistic cognition. The gradual dismantlement of psychoanalytic theory by empirical psychology still leaves something of these psychodynamic processes in place. In the figurative language of psychoanalytic theory one might say that the market allies itself with the id and seeks to give libido a free range; it is, therefore, an enemy of the superego. Such conflicts *use* the material of economic life in their painful struggles,[58] but the market is infrequently the original source of the conflict, for most Freudian scholars attribute the origins of these conflicts to early interpersonal relations. Internal conflicts, however generated, reduce the power of market activities to yield much satisfaction.

The market does not write its credits and debits on a blank slate; it writes where others, including the self, have written before to produce a composite message of pain and pleasure, of red and black figures producing an uncertain balance in the hedonic accounts. We turn to the problems of balancing these accounts in a market economy.

Affect balance

Does the market have a capacity to balance or reconcile or integrate the pains and pleasures it both initiates and responds to? Does it do for pains and pleasures what it does for commodities, equalizing their satisfactions at the margin, or for work and

[56] Andrews and Withey, *Social Indicators of Well-Being*, 135, 265, find that as a predictor of life satisfaction assessments of oneself rank third (in one set of comparisons). Angus Campbell finds that self-esteem is the most important single factor in predicting subjective life quality. See Campbell, *The Sense of Well-Being in America*.

[57] Morris Rosenberg and Roberta G. Simmons, *Black and White Self-Esteem: The Urban School Child* (Washington, DC: American Sociological Association, 1971); Robert E. Lane, "Government and Self-Esteem," *Political Theory* 10 (1982): 5–31.

[58] See Edmund Bergler, *Money and Emotional Conflict* (Garden City, NY: Doubleday, 1951); Walter A. Weisskopf, *The Psychology of Economics* (Chicago: University of Chicago Press/Midway, 1975).

leisure (as it mistakenly sees them), balancing off the utility from earnings against the disutility from the "pain" of work? The ordinal ranking of pleasures, at least within a single breast, is said by at least two philosophers to be possible,[59] and is certainly suggested by the linear cumulative model of the quality-of-life studies. But a finer grained analysis might find that pains are more – or less – commensurable.

In thinking about joys and sorrows, inevitably Tolstoy's concept of the similarity of happy families and the dissimilarity of unhappy families comes to mind. Are pleasures homogeneous and pains heterogeneous? Psychoanalysts, reviewing daily the infinite variety of pains reported to them, would think so, but Maslow suggests otherwise.[60] A linguistic clarification might help: The satisfaction of a need is more likely to be experienced as a relief from pain, the satisfaction of wants or desires is more likely to be experienced as a pleasure. Thus, in Maslow's hierarchy of needs, relief of such deficiency needs as safety and food, belonging and self-esteem, are said to be generally similar, but beyond that, satisfying desires for self-fulfillment are infinitely varied.[61] Of course, there is some sleight of hand in thinking of relief of deficiency needs as devoid of pleasure (and only relief of pain), but the point about the heterogeneity of certain higher satisfactions is valid. Our basic needs are similar, but our wants are infinitely varied. Griffin, for example, defines needs as those "things that we aim at simply as normal human beings rather than as particular human beings we are, things that are both necessary to and sufficient for a recognizably human existence." He contrasts this concept of needs to the things we want for our individualized way of life.[62] In these ways, pains are more commensurable than pleasures, a matter that makes it easier for government, with its invariant rules, to relieve pain than to facilitate pleasure.

In order to clarify these questions of balancing pains and pleasures I propose eight ways of relating pain to pleasure, sorrows to joys, to produce what the literature calls "affect balance."

Intensity and frequency of pains and pleasures

The original theory of balancing affects or emotions is Bentham's: sum the "good tendencies" (pleasures) and "bad tendencies" (pains) and choose the option with the greatest net pleasure or least net pain. In fact, the pleasures and pains have a complex relation to each other. Bentham, of course, was referring to alternative courses of action, not simultaneous experiences, but let us start with the problem of simultaneity. Since it is impossible, except for ambivalence (which is itself a pain), to be happy and sad at the same time, the good tendencies would eliminate the bad ones, or vice versa. One feeling tends to drive out the other; they are simultaneously incompatible. As a consequence, one would expect them to be negatively corre-

---

[59] W. David Ross, *The Right and the Good* (Oxford, UK: Clarendon Press, 1930), chap. 6; James Griffin, *Well-Being: Its Meaning, Measurement, and Moral Importance* (Oxford, UK: Clarendon Press, 1986), 77–83. See Chapter 28 in this book on summing utilities.

[60] Abraham H. Maslow, *Toward a Psychology of Being*, rev. ed. (Princeton, NJ: Van Nostrand, 1968).

[61] "The deficit-needs are shared by all members of the human species. . . . Self-actualization is idiosyncratic since every person is different." Ibid., 33.

[62] Griffin, *Well-Being*, 53. Griffin weakens the distinction between needs and wants by including among the things he calls "needs" those things that an individual might want to fulfill his or her goals in life.

lated. In fact, however, "within a given time period, such as a week or two, one may experience many different emotions, both positive and negative, and . . . in general there is no tendency for the two types to be experienced in any particular relation to one another. . . . To many, this lack of correlation is surprising, not to say unbelievable."[63] But it has been supported by extensive research. Thus, Andrews and Withey in a special analysis asked if their respondents had recently felt "particularly excited or interested in something"; "proud because someone complimented you on something you had done"; and other questions of a similar nature on pleasing aspects of life; and on the painful side, whether they had felt "very lonely or remote from other people"; "bored"; or "upset because someone criticized you"; and so forth. They found that people had usually experienced both "recently" although 70 percent of the respondents had more positive than negative experiences and only about 16 percent had more negative than positive ones.[64]

These findings are puzzling as a logical set of relationships. How can it be that, on the one hand, positive and negative feelings are incompatible and therefore negatively correlated at any one time, whereas on the other, they are independent of each other? The solution to this problem was discovered by Diener and associates. Intensity of feelings of both kinds are *positively* correlated with each other; if an individual feels *very* happy at one time, that individual will likely feel *very* sad at another; volatility compensates for incompatibility. The expected negative correlation is masked by the positive correlations of good and bad intensities of feeling.[65]

In the Andrews and Withey study, the distribution of responses along the "Delighted/Terrible" scale shows more extreme (intense) feelings about family and friends than about most economic matters, suggesting the affective dominance of nonmarket relations – and this is borne out in the correlations of these concerns with overall life satisfaction.[66] The argument might be contested on the basis of other data,[67] but it reveals the main point: For assessing affect balance the affects in a variety of domains must be assessed, regardless of whether one looks at frequencies or intensities. Affect balance in the market alone, or the sum of utilities in the market alone, gives a very poor picture of both balance and sums. Under almost no circumstances could the market maximize the satisfaction of human wants.

Affect balance through domain balance

The "imperial" market is said to penetrate and then convert other domains to its own uses, a process that would, in the case of the family, erode a domain with higher hedonic yields than its own, probably causing a net loss in happiness. The

---

[63] Bradburn, *The Structure of Psychological Well-Being*, 225.

[64] Andrews and Withey, *Social Indicators of Well-Being*, 332. The most favorable balance was among those aged 25–34 and among higher status groups.

[65] Diener, "Subjective Well-Being," *Psychological Bulletin* 95 (1984): 549.

[66] Andrews and Withey, *Social Indicators of Well-Being*, 114, 265.

[67] Veroff, Douvan, and Kulka show that when people report the sources of what makes them happy or unhappy, economic and material themes dominate family and leisure (and certainly national) themes both with respect to sources of happiness and of unhappiness – and more people say that economic and material concerns make them happy than say they make them unhappy. See Joseph Veroff, Elizabeth Douvan, and Richard Kulka, *The Inner Americans: A Self-Portrait from 1957 to 1976* (New York: Basic Books, 1981), 57, 251.

result of this hypothesis is to add to the psychological concept of affect balance a more sociological concept of *domain balance,* which points to the ways societies structure opportunities in the various domains. In gemeinschaft an imperial family might equally well erode the hedonic opportunities of independent work, a process that Shorter says accounts for the flight of the young from French villages to the cities and their new work opportunities in the early nineteenth century.[68] In current industrial America, Andrews and Withey believe that the opportunities for a more favorable affect balance in fact does depend on free choices across domains. As mentioned, they say: "It appears that joys in one area of life may be able to be compensated for by sorrows in other areas; the multiple joys accumulate to raise the level of well-being; and that multiple sorrows accumulate to lower it."[69]

Investing in the domain with the highest hedonic yield. The idea of a balance among the domains requires a criterion to judge "balance." Here the criterion is purely hedonic: What combination of time, effort, skill, and emotional investment in each domain is likely to produce the greatest hedonic satisfaction? Assuming for the moment that one cannot alter the happiness yield in any domain, the strategy would clearly be to invest oneself in the domain with the greatest yield. If domains were commodities, one might count on the declining marginal utility of any particular choice to lead gradually to a different choice, giving a balance to life. But they are activities embracing skills, goods often graced with increasing marginal utilities.[70] In that case, the choice of any one domain becomes increasingly reinforced and the equivalent of workaholism sets in. On the basis of the overall pattern of the Andrews and Withey study (and others), a hedonic maximizer would devote more time to family life, to friendships and begin the slow (and painful) return to gemeinschaft. But at the same time, one would reduce one's civic obligations, reduce one's interest in government, and forsake the republican virtues altogether. But the hedonic value of variety[71] might soon end such concentration and omission. This is the lesson of the economists' experience with cases of marginal rates of substitution.

Positivity makes joys salient. The actual balance of affects is puzzling in another respect: the dominance of positive affect. We are normally conscious only of pain, rather than the absence of pain or feeling good. Moreover, unhappy feelings tend to last longer than happy ones. One would, therefore, expect more consciousness of pain-reducing experiences than of pleasure-inducing ones. But this expectation is not fulfilled because it runs counter to two well established principles: Research on *The Pollyanna Principle* shows that we recall our pleasant experiences more easily than our unpleasant ones,[72] and other research shows that the "positiv-

[68] Edward Shorter, *The Making of the Modern Family* (New York: Basic Books, 1975).
[69] Andrews and Withey, *Social Indicators of Well-Being,* 62.
[70] "One limitation of the law of diminishing marginal utility is that it seems to apply to some things (e.g., money), but not to others (e.g., skills)." Diener, "Subjective Well-Being," 563.
[71] Norman M. Bradburn and David Caplovitz, *Reports on Happiness* (Chicago: Aldine, 1965).
[72] Margaret Matlin and David J. Stang, *The Pollyana Principle: Selectivity in Language, Memory, and Thought* (Cambridge: Schenkman, 1978).

ity bias'' corrects for the tendency to be more conscious of pain than of pleasure.[73] The consequence is that at the unhappy end of the ''Delighted/Terrible'' scale employed by Andrews and Withey, fewer than 2 percent of the respondents chose ''unhappy,'' or ''terrible'' to describe their lives, whereas at the top end, 20 percent chose either ''pleased'' or ''delighted.''[74]

Negative utilitarianism

Karl Popper said: ''Instead of the greatest happiness of the greatest number, one should demand, more modestly, the least amount of avoidable suffering for all.''[75] This reduced agenda, he said, is desirable partly because we do not know how to make people happy and do know something about how to relieve suffering, and partly because he believed that misery has a greater negative hedonic effect than happiness has a positive hedonic effect. Supporting this view, the philosopher James Griffin claims:

It takes a relatively large amount of happiness, as happiness goes (that is, relative to other cases of happiness), to justify a relatively small amount of misery, as misery goes (that is, relative to other cases of misery). . . . A fairly small amount of misery will turn out to make life worse to a greater degree than a fairly large amount of happiness makes it better.[76]

Modest evidence reported in the previous chapter supports this view: Economic losses reduce happiness ratings more than proportionate economic gains increase them.[77] Moreover, induced feelings of unhappiness last longer than induced feelings of happiness. For example, short-term positive feelings induced by a loaded questionnaire produced a sense of general well-being in one sample and a questionnaire with opposite loadings produced a general sense of ill-being in a different but comparable sample. The well-being did not survive an eight-week interval, but the sense of ill-being did.[78] And the proposition is compatible with research in adaptation-level theory: The pain of losing familiar comforts is greater than the pleasure of gaining unfamiliar ones.[79]

If pains are so much more intensely felt than pleasures, then negative utilitarianism makes sense and the utilitarian basis of the market would take on a different, perhaps more somber cast. But the market is surely not a maximin (maximize the

---

[73] David Sears and Richard Whitney, *Political Persuasion* (Morristown, NJ: General Learning Press, 1973). Some of the causes of preference for positive statements lie in the very machinery of the mind. Information is most often held in its positive form; negation thus requires an additional cognitive step. But there are other reasons: see V. S. Folkes and David O. Sears, ''Does Everybody Like a Liker?'' *Journal of Experimental Social Psychology* 13 (1977): 505–19.

[74] Andrews and Withey, *Social Indicators of Well-Being*, 321.

[75] Karl Popper, *The Open Society and its Enemies* (London: Routledge & Kegan Paul, 1966), 284–5, quoted in Griffin, *Well-Being*, chap. 5, n. 22, p. 338. The theme is repeated in different languages in Popper, *Conjectures and Refutations*.

[76] Griffin, *Well-Being*, 84.

[77] Ronald Inglehart and Jacques-Rene Rabier, ''Aspirations Adapt to Situations–But Why Are the Belgians So Much Happier than the French? A Cross-Cultural Analysis of the Subjective Quality of Life,'' in Andrews, *Research on the Qualify of Life*, 28.

[78] Darlene E. Goodhart, ''Some Psychological Effects Associated with Positive and Negative Thinking about Stressful Outcomes: Was Pollyanna Right?'' *Journal of Personality and Social Psychology* 48 (1985): 216–32.

[79] Philip Brickman and Donald T. Campbell, ''Hedonic Relativism and Planning the Good Society,'' in M. H. Appley, ed., *Adaptation-Level Theory: A Symposium* (New York: Academic Press, 1971).

minimum) institution. If it were, it would address itself to *needs,* which it does not do. The market gratifies the wants of those with money, which already excludes the most miserable and impoverished individuals, and among those with money, it gratifies preferences according to the amount of money they have, not according to the urgency of different people's wants and certainly not according to needs. In any event, the evidence is that "money may enable one to increase his joys, but it cannot reduce his sorrows,"[80] which, after all, is the test of negative utilitarianism. Within the market framework, the "happy consciousness of the dismal science" may be warranted, but the framework is very exclusive and small.

The relief of deprivation

The relief-of-deprivation theory is not a case of negative utilitarianism since its thesis is that deprivation is a necessary predecessor to happiness, and happiness, not the relief of unhappiness, is its stated goal. Houston has proposed that "our genetic make-up is such that we are probably happiest when we experience deprivation-based need and are able to satisfy that need."[81] This fits those market, telic theories of happiness and well-being claiming that wanting is painful and that want satisfaction is the relief of that pain.

The deprivation → happiness theory is reinforced by a perceptual theory of *contrast* that says that we selectively notice, pay attention to, and then remember those things that stand out from their contexts or backgrounds. In an unusually prescient manner, Freud made the same point: "We can only intensely enjoy contrast, much less intensely states in themselves."[82] But this theory is dangerous and misleading, dangerous because it is vulnerable to the unwelcome inference that one should solicit pain to create the possibility of pleasure and it risks recruiting Dr. Pangloss and his *Just World* to this version of the utilitarian cause. It is misleading and wrong for several reasons: (1) It fails to take into account the fact that happy people remain happy without those contrasts; (2) prolonged suffering reduces an individual's capacities to relieve that suffering and hence reduces the probabilities that one will ever reap the supposed hedonic future advantages of present malaise; and (3) the quality-of-life studies do not show large differences in subjective well-being by history of deprivation. Moreover, there are strong arguments for thinking of the relief of such pains as boredom as an inferior kind of pleasure; pleasure must have a positive attraction at least as strong as its flight from pain in order to contribute much to happiness.[83]

Nevertheless, because *not* having money may be experienced as deprivation, a pain, acquiring money is a case of the deprivation → happiness theory, for the money is then so much more pleasurable. In the labor market, this means that the

---

[80]Bradburn, *The Structure of Psychological Well-Being,* 226.

[81]J. P. Houston, *The Pursuit of Happiness* (Glenview, IL: Scott, Foresman, 1981), 7, quoted in Diener, "Subjective Well-Being," 563.

[82]Sigmund Freud, *Civilization and its Discontents,* trans. J. Riviere (London: Hogarth, 1951), 28.

[83]Robert E. Lane, "The Regulation of Experience: Leisure in a Market Society," *Social Science Information* 17 (1978): 147–84. In his *Conquest of Happiness,* Bertrand Russell makes the point (p. 208) that leisure is less satisfying than work because most people do not have adequate leisure competences. Thus he reverses the more usual analysis of a flight from work to leisure on hedonic grounds.

deprived will work for less; in ethical terms they are exploitable, but if one were to concentrate on the hedonic, rather than the market, value of money, they are well paid. In the consumer market, the starved (for anything) will be prepared to pay more, with the same distinction between ethical and hedonic evaluations.

The theory is a drive-reduction theory implying that the organism mainly seeks to reduce drives – an unfulfilled drive representing pain. For such a theory, the natural and happiest state of the human species is a state of satiation or of rest, a theory generally discredited in psychology along with its simplistic drive-reduction theoretical source. The theory further implies a naturally passive individual stimulated to pleasure only by deprivation. The concepts of self-initiated activity and of self-regulation and self-reward are missing. Finally, the theory leaves out of account the crucial question of agency: If *I* relieve my deprivations, I gain satisfactions from seeing the world respond to my actions, but the deprivation → satisfaction theory is apparently indifferent to the source of the relief.

Exchange and the relief of deprivation. The two elements in exchange, spending and acquiring, have somewhat ambiguous hedonic characteristics. Is spending, parting with money to make a purchase, a deprivation, followed by the pleasure of acquisition? Or is spending money less of a pain than a positive pleasure, an exercise in power and personal control? And is the acquisition itself a pleasure or a relief of the pain of wanting (which may or may not be an accurate characterization)?

In pointing to the ambiguity of exchange of goods for money we have located the peculiar virtue of exchange – its contingent nature – something gained for something given up, the pain of parting with money matched by the pleasure of acquisition; or, equally accurately, the pleasure of spending money to relieve the pain of wanting something. In each case the exchange proceeds up to the point where pleasures and pains of either kind are equal. And in each case individual variations in interpretation can be accommodated. Under these circumstances, it is reasonable, but not necessary, for economists to think of the market as a source of gratification rather than as a source of relief from pain.

The pleasure of acquisition, the pain of withdrawal

Addicts first seek their drugs to give themselves a charge of synthetic happiness; after dependency sets in they seek the drug to relieve the pain of withdrawal symptoms. Solomon extended this observation to a general principle stating that whenever a major change in motivation takes place, an opposing process emerges to check it. He presents evidence showing that ducklings first seek and follow their mother figure with evidence of satisfaction, but increasingly deprivation of the mother figure arouses what seems to be great distress; among humans, love relationships are first sought for their pleasure and then maintained for fear of loss of the love object. Some physiological changes accompanying strong emotions are compatible with this "opponent-process theory."[84]

[84] Richard L. Solomon, "How the Opponent-Process Theory of Acquired Motivation Came into Economics," in Paul J. Albanese, ed., *Psychological Foundations of Economic Behavior* (New York: Prae-

Whatever the general applicability of the theory, and "initial studies have not been supportive,"[85] one can find confirming illustrations in the hedonic sequences following market purchases: the housewife's initial pleasure at the acquisition of a washing machine is followed by her dependence on a machine that not infrequently greatly pains her by its failures; the pleasure of mobility from an automobile is followed by dependence on it such that its breakdown causes pains out of all proportion to the initial inconvenience of precar reliance on public transportation. Furthermore, the theory is supported by adaptation-level theory: Dependence on an object for satisfaction sets the stage for the pain of withdrawal to an earlier stage that was, at the time, relatively painless. In that sense, the "opponent-process" is worse than the "hedonic treadmill" proposed by adaptation-level theory, for the opponent process is even less felicitous because it is not the search for pleasure but the search for the avoidance of pain that drives the hapless victim in the subsequent phases of the process.

One could find in the cognate *substance abuse* literature[86] many insights into pain and pleasure in a consumer society, most of these reflecting the problems of tempting stimuli in the absence of internal controls. It is the business of the market to tempt; its reliance on budgets to protect against temptation are inadequate in the absence of rational preference scheduling – and that absence is both frequent and well-established; without it or without self-regulation (an unmarketlike concept) people are unable to use a tempting environment to their own advantage. Utility maximization fails under these circumstances.

The effect of income on affect balance

Level of income. One may parcel out the different incidences of joy and sorrow by level of income. As mentioned, among those above the poverty level, money seems to have more of an effect in facilitating positive experiences than in reducing negative ones. In the Bradburn and Caplovitz study reporting this finding, money itself had little separate effect on happiness, but possession of more discretionary income permitted individuals to increase both novelty and sociable relations, each of which is a pleasure in itself. The results are reflected in a separate analysis of the "very happy," "pretty happy," and "not too happy" (= unhappy) responses by income level. Following the proposition that money can increase joy but not relieve sorrow, we would expect each higher level of income to increase the "very happy" responses but to reduce the "not too happy" responses somewhat less. Relatively speaking, that is the case, but not quite as anticipated. In the Bradburn and Caplovitz data (as I have reanalyzed them), at the bottom of the scale the

ger, 1988); Idem, "The Opponent-Process Theory of Motivation: The Costs of Pleasure and the Benefits of Pain," *American Psychologist* 35 (1980): 691–712. The theory also proposes the opposite effect: Self-imposed pain (flagellation in a sauna, parachute jumping) is followed by elation. Note that this part of the theory is similar to the deprivation–happiness theory already discussed.
[85] Diener, "Subjective Well-Being," 564.
[86] See, for example, E. R. Oetting and Fred Beauvais, "Peer Cluster Theory: Drugs and the Adolescent," *Journal of Counseling and Development* 65 (1986): 17–22; Jim Orford, *Excessive Appetites: A Psychological View of Addiction* (New York: Wiley, 1985); C. Bennett, C. Vourakis, and D. S. Woolff, *Substance Abuse: Pharmacological Development and Clinical Perspectives* (New York: Wiley, 1983).

first two increments of $1,000 in income level produce almost symmetrical effects, reducing unhappy and increasing happy answers by half, followed by another smaller symmetrical response with the next $1,000 increase. But for the upper parts of the income scale, the main effects are on the positive "very happy" side, with very little effect in reducing sorrowful "not too happy" responses. For the poor and the lower middle-income groups, the effects on joy and sorrow are almost symmetrical: Money gains its *net* joy-producing balance only for those who are somewhat better off.[87]

Sources of income. As mentioned in Chapter 23, the source of the money might be expected to make a difference, earned money providing double joys (when earned and when spent), but transfer payments offering only a simple pleasure, if it could be called that. There is little joy in a welfare check (and some humiliation), but there is relief from pain.

Roles of government and market

Asked how they feel about governmental leaders and governmental activities, Americans (1976) tend to respond with symptoms of pain, with negative affect. For example, 17 percent of a national sample feel "unhappy" or "terrible" and another 22 percent are "mostly dissatisfied" with governmental attempts to solve U.S. economic problems. In contrast, only about half as many people feel similarly dissatisfied or unhappy or terrible about their incomes, and fewer than a quarter feel that way about their standards of living ("the things you have, like housing, car, furniture, recreation, and the like"). But people's feelings about national government make very little difference to their satisfaction with their lives-as-a-whole (30 items, beta = .07), whereas their feelings about money are twice as important (beta = .15) and feelings about their housing come close to this level of importance (beta = .12).[88] Recommendations on the role of the U.S. government as an agent for influencing people's pleasures and sorrows must recognize that the very instrument is both disliked and perceived to be relatively unimportant.

Perceptions, of course, are often very different from reality; the government plays an important peacetime role in the joys and sorrows of many people, especially (but not exclusively) the poor, sick, unemployed, and undereducated. Popper's proposal to let government relieve sorrow and assign the promotion of joys to civil society of which the market is so prominent a part suggests a division of labor between government and the market in this juncture of pleasure and pain, government relieving pain and the market offering pleasure. As previously noted, Popper has

---

[87] Calculated from data in Bradburn and Caplovitz, *Reports on Happiness*, 9. With some discrepancies at the bottom of the income scale, there appears to be the same tendencies in Inglehart's data. See Ronald Inglehart, "Values, Objective Needs, and Subjective Satisfactions Among Western Publics," *Comparative Political Studies* 9 (1977): 429–58 at 437. With a different set of measures of positive and negative affect (having to do with memories of pleasurable and painful experiences), a different study found the same tendency for increases in income to be associated more with increasing "joy" than with the reduction of "sorrow." Campbell, *The Sense of Well-Being in America*, chap. 5.

[88] Andrews and Withey, *Social Indicators of Well-Being*, 124, 254.

argued the first half of this proposal, the limited role of government, implying, if there is to be happiness, the second half.[89]

There are at least two kinds of difficulties in Popper's solution. One is the evidence that the most important sources of satisfaction are from the family and individual achievement, both of which need government protection, the family through support for schools and provisions for health, and achievement through protecting equality of opportunity and antitrust policy. The second difficulty is the exclusive reliance on the hedonic dimension for guidance. The protection of rights and justice is justified by principles that are only tangentially related to happiness. Relief from pain is not good enough.

Summary

In the previous chapter and this one we have examined the claim that the market is a device offering the best ways of satisfying wants in human society. Without denigrating its magnificent contributions to all the satisfactions that are brought about by increased national prosperity, we must recognize (Parts V and VI) that it fails to give priority to the sources of the greatest happiness, namely, achievement and the meeting of challenges in work, and it fails to acknowledge the intrinsic satisfactions derived from personal control, the performance of duty, and the desire for excellence. Having examined in Chapter 23 the nature of wants and of satisfaction, in this chapter I addressed some problems the market faces in satisfying wants other than self-direction and those embraced by the intrinsic.

In this chapter I have concentrated on the way pains and pleasures relate to each other and to market forces. It seems that the market, and perhaps any economy, is less of a pain-relieving machine than a pleasure machine, well matched to Edgeworth's concept of man as a pleasure-seeking animal.[90] Support for this view, which is also the economists' position, is found in the fact that income tends to increase joys but not to relieve sorrows. Thus, negative utilitarianism, the doctrine of least pain rather than most pleasure, finds little support in the market and, with adjustments, is more characteristic of the government.

Although most of the pains of this world are beyond the market's capacity to relieve, the pains incurred by the market, especially insecurity, are integral to market processes and not easily relieved. Market pleasures, on the other hand, are abundant, stemming partly from the market's capacity to enlarge choices; they include a capacity to cater to individualized wants, a matching of personal rhythms, an invitation to active engagement in life. But the main pleasures are not the want satisfactions of the consumer market but the opportunities for achievement and earning in the labor market.

No stimulus can move an organism that is fixed. The temperamentally happy and

---

[89] Popper, *Conjectures and Refutations*, 381–3. If one believes that pains and sorrows are similar to each other whereas pleasures are more individually variegated, Popper's thesis has the added advantage that the government can handle categorical problems better than individualized problems.
[90] F. Y. Edgeworth, *Mathematical Physics* (1881) quoted in Robert L. Heilbroner, *The Worldly Philosophers*, rev. ed. (New York: Simon & Schuster, 1961), 146. Jevons took a similar view of human nature.

the dispositionally unhappy are relatively immune to market influences, whether because of extraversion or a chronically bad conscience or for some other reason. To the extent that people reward and punish themselves, they are also less vulnerable.

If one finds pleasure in one domain and pain in another, the market is impotent to employ its marginal balancing act, especially when the activities that give pleasure outside the market are likely to have *increasing* marginal utilities, retarding the desire to switch from one domain to another. In order for people to be able to invest in whatever domain offers the highest hedonic yield, the domains themselves must be independent and not undermined by the market. The search for variety may serve as a check against the tendency to invest in only one domain.

There is one internal balancing force: Our tendencies to be more aware of pain than of pleasure are counterbalanced by the Pollyanna Principle and the positivity bias. But the idea that in order for a pleasure to be enjoyed it must have been preceded by a pain is perverse – yet it offers many market exemplars.

25 Markets and the structures of happiness

Processes, such as those we have examined in the two previous chapters, require structures to guide and harness them; they need an organization of ideas, rules, and behavior to implement these guiding and harnessing structures. The market itself guides and harnesses much economic behavior, but it would frustrate our purpose and destroy our perspective to rely on the market structure to channel behavior that often belongs outside the market and often defies its rules. In this chapter I will borrow and invent other structures for our purposes. None are so grand as the market; they are ministructures to guide particular aspects of the analysis.

In this discussion I speak more of satisfaction with life-as-a-whole, or life satisfaction, than of happiness because of the frequent emphasis on cognitive processes (as mentioned, happiness is more of a mood) and because the analyses we rely upon more frequently use life satisfaction as the explanandum. With either happiness or life satisfaction as the focus of attention, it is appropriate that these structures should be psychoeconomic *hedonic structures,* ordering the relation of one pursuit to another, the effects of smaller scale moods and cognitions to overall happiness, the relation of central concerns to more peripheral concerns, the relation of the specific to the general, and the partitioning of the world into domains. We will start with the most important: If we think of persons rather than transactions as the core of the analysis, of human behavior rather than price behavior as the principal components of economic behavior, what sort of a structure would that imply? We start with that question.

Econocentric and psychocentric models

When a domain escapes from the market's network of transactions it avoids direct market control and thereby acquires a kind of autonomy that both market critics and most market supporters have thought impossible. For these scholars, the economy is central, distributing the principal rewards that yield satisfaction; this offers an *econocentric* view of society. An econocentric view of society stipulates: (1) The dominant problem of society is the provision of an economic base to support all other activities; (2) to that end, the dominant social purpose is to maximize material productivity and wealth; (3) the dominant purpose of individuals is to achieve economic security and to increase their individual wealth; (4) therefore the most sought after rewards will be material rewards; (5) other goods, such as prestige, personal control, self-esteem, and social solidarity are based upon the reflections of economic achievements by both societies and individuals. This specification is certainly more Marxist than Smithian, but it is implied both by what market economics states and what it leaves out. The econocentric model may be diagrammed as in Figure 25.1.

503

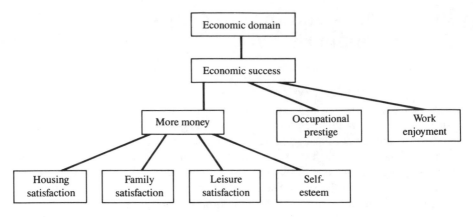

Figure 25.1. *Econocentric model of satisfaction*

I have presented the econocentric model as complete when the satisfactions are located, and in keeping with utility theory, I have not penetrated the nature of the satisfaction (except for self-esteem).

The alternative suggested here is one where the individual is, within powerful constraints, free to choose where to find his or her satisfactions. In this *psychocentric* model, more or less autonomous people move among more or less autonomous domains to select the sources of satisfaction that they believe are most likely to contribute to their happiness. The more internal, psychologically oriented psychocentric model, illustrated in Figure 25.2, takes a further step in specifying possible sources of satisfaction in each domain.

In the econocentric model all satisfactions hinge on success in the economic domain, implying a dependence on the economy that we found was not true in the quality-of-life studies. In the psychocentric model, individuals are placed above and outside the economic system and can choose (within powerful constraints) the domain where they may "back themselves," to use William James phrase, to do well; the chosen areas will reflect the individual's *psychological centrality;* the individual will define his or her identity as peculiarly associated with activities in the chosen areas. The economic area *may* be more important for people's sustenance than for their satisfactions, thus giving expression to the frequent references to the "loss of work centrality" in modern working populations,[1] but, equally, the economic area may well be the major source of satisfaction. Because people can choose, they may choose to invest *more* in the economic domain than any calculation of material rewards would suggest, for we are now free to think of satisfaction as the common denominator of choice, rather than money.

In the psychocentric model, intrinsic motivations and rewards are recognized without difficulty, along with mercenary ones; mutuality of interests is recognized side-by-side with transactions; altruism is restored to its descriptively accurate position, even if, next to self-interest, this position is small; social influence on deci-

[1] See the review of this literature on work centrality and work commitment in Richard H. Hall, *Dimensions of Work* (Beverly Hills, CA: Sage, 1986), 100–3.

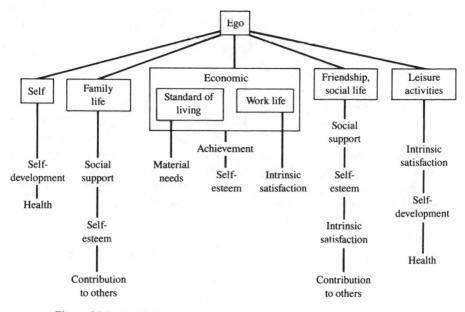

Figure 25.2. *Psychocentric model of satisfaction*

sions and social comparison by decision makers encounter no theoretical difficulties; there are no theoretical obstacles to giving content to satisfaction; collective actions are not burdened with a misleading "logic" apparently demanding free riding (shirking costs when rewards are not contingent on their payment) – yet the free riding and the social loafing (where individuals in joint enterprises did less well than when they acted alone, discussed in Chapter 3) are easily accounted for. If we place the person instead of transactions at the center of things, we are led to focus on human behavior rather more than price behavior.

Scalar, hierarchical concepts of well-being

Scalar analysis helps us to see if certain market products, like feelings of insecurity, prevent the development of other nonmarket attributes, like a sense of belonging or respect for others. Are attitudes and values arising from market activity in some sense prior to other attitudes and values, as eating is prior to thinking? A scale is a series in which it is necessary to achieve the bottom rank before being able to achieve the second one, and the second one before being able to move to the third, and so forth. Learning mathematics (and other subjects) is thought to be scalar: One must learn algebra before one can master trigonometry.[2] The utility of this concept for analysis of the market experience lies in the answer to the question, Does the

[2]In Kohlberg's measures of moral reasoning, one cannot achieve the level of principled reasoning until one has passed through the developmental stages of obedience, instrumental hedonism, orientation to approval, and law-and-order morality. See Lawrence Kohlberg, *The Philosophy of Moral Development* (New York: Harper & Row, 1981).

market facilitate movement from lower scores to higher scores on some selected scalar dimension? We turn to a concept of well-being that has this scalar property, a modified version of Abraham Maslow's concept of "need hierarchy."

The hierarchy of needs

Maslow proposes a hierarchy of needs that meets the scalar test: An individual cannot reach a higher level of needs without satisfying the lower needs. Maslow's hierarchy begins at the low end with safety and physiological needs, belongingness and love needs, esteem needs, and, at the top of the hierarchy, needs for "self-actualization," variously interpreted as growth, personal development, becoming what one can be. Except for the physiologically self-renewing needs, once one of the lower three deficiency needs is appeased in childhood it is more or less undemanding for the remainder of a life. The "need" for self-actualization is different in the sense that, like the development of taste in art or literature, it cannot be appeased but tends to grow by what it feeds on. For our current purposes, the important point is the claim that only the self-actualizing person experiences the full meaning of happiness.[3]

Criticisms of this theory are cogent and damaging, but some at least acknowledge a two-stage scale where self-actualization is a separate, more advanced stage, even if the three deficiency needs do not have genuine scalar properties, but rather press for satisfaction in a variety of orders.[4] Because the need hierarchy has influenced the thinking of many social scientists and humanists, even those who reject it, it is useful as a heuristic of what might be. How does the market relate to this concept of a hierarchy of needs?

The major studies we have been analyzing do not have a scalar structure; there are no crucial concerns that *must* precede others for them to be satisfying. Rather, the structure of happiness in these studies follows a simple, linear, cumulative pattern where "one feeling just seems to 'add on' to another," without weighting or preconditions[5] (Chapter 22). Taking certain questions as rough indicators of the several Maslovian "needs," Table 25.1 indicates the current status of need satisfaction in the United States market society.

These data for assessing Maslow's need hierarchy tell us certain important things about the market. The table includes two kinds of measures: those in the second column represent levels of satisfaction. In order for a need higher in the hierarchy to receive a high score, all the needs lower in the hierarchy must also receive higher scores, indicating that they have been satisfied. For example, for the indicators of belongingness to be satisfied (rank high) security needs must be satisfied. In order for the need for respect to be satisfied, the needs for both belongingness and security must be satisfied. The figures in the third column, contributions to life satisfaction,

[3] Abraham Maslow, *Motivation and Personality*, 2d ed. (New York: Harper and Row, 1970).
[4] See Edward E. Lawler, III, and J. Lloyd Suttle, "A Causal Correlational Test of the Need Hierarchy Concept," in Richard M. Steers and Lyman W. Porter, eds., *Motivation and Work Behavior* (New York: McGraw-Hill, 1975); M. A. Wahba and L. G. Bridewell, "Maslow Reconsidered: A Review of Research on the Need Hierarchy," *Organizational Behavior & Human Performance* 15 (1976): 210–40.
[5] Frank M. Andrews and Stephen B. Withey, *Social Indicators of Well-Being: Americans' Perceptions of Life Quality* (New York: Plenum Press, 1976), 148.

Table 25.1. *Satisfaction ratings and contribution to life satisfaction: need hierarchy*

Need	Index of satisfaction (mean)	Rank contribution to life satisfaction (beta or var. added)
Safety and security		
The extent to which your physical needs are met	5.2, average	2/23, very high
Financial security	4.5, low	8/23, high middle
Belonging		
Acceptance by others	5.4, high average	11/23, middle
Getting on with people	5.7, high average	30/30, very low
Respect: social esteem		
The amount of respect you get from others	5.3, average	23/23, very low
Self-esteem		
How do you feel about yourself?	5.5, high average	3/23, very high
Self-actualization		
Extent you are developing and broadening self	5.0, low average	5/23, high

Note: In the fractions listed in column 3, the first figure indicates ordinal rank, the second the number of items in each ranked list. Because the two tables from which these data derive express "contribution" differently, rank orders are employed to indicate relative strengths of contribution to the measure of overall life satisfaction employed.

Source: Andrews and Withey, *Social Indicators of Well-Being*, Tables 4.2, 4.5; list of Question Means, pp. 249–73. The mean of question means is 5.2.

represent measures of the importance to an individual of the satisfaction of a particular need.[6] If a need, Y, is unimportant (ranks low), the satisfaction of that need cannot be important in influencing the higher needs whose satisfactions are supposed to be conditioned on the satisfaction of Y.

As measured by these questions, Maslow's scalar theory fails for five reasons. First, the satisfaction of security needs is an important predictor of overall life satisfaction, but these needs, especially financial security, are not perceived as well served by the market. The satisfactions derived from them are low, but their low ranks do not prevent other, "higher" needs from achieving higher scores. The market's failure to generate a sense of security does not hinder people from experiencing social solidarity from others or from achieving reasonably high self-esteem.

[6] All but one of the figures are from the April survey where the equivalent of beta weights presented represents the amount of variance explained in a cumulative list of concerns listed by declining significance. After the first four or five items, the figures are small because, as the authors discovered, in almost any list the first items accounted for most of the variance. Out of context they are meaningless. The total variance explained is 62%.

Second, the sense of belonging has just the opposite properties. People are reasonably satisfied with their acceptance by others and very satisfied with the way they get along with other people, but because this satisfaction does not contribute much to their overall sense of life-satisfaction, we would expect it to be relatively unimportant as an influence on the satisfactions of such "higher" needs as respect, or even self-esteem and self-actualization. People's satisfaction of so-called higher needs cannot then be dependent on their satisfactions derived from their sense of belonging, as measured in Andrews and Withey's study. Yet in passing, we should note that the frequent allegation that the market undermines community and solidarity with others receives no support in these data, confirming our analysis in Chapter 11.

Third, the measure of "the amount of respect you get from others" is interesting because it contributes almost nothing to overall life satisfaction. For this reason, no matter what satisfactions people might get from having this need met, we would not want to include it at all in a scalar hierarchy.

Fourth, ratings of self-esteem are ambiguous; most specialists believe that a high, but not excessively high, level of self-esteem is the healthiest[7] and the evidence suggests that this condition is fulfilled. According to Maslovian and other predictions, self-esteem makes a lot of difference in one's life satisfaction (other data show it as the most important of all attitudes[8]) and this, too, is the case. But it is quite compatible with relatively low feelings of security and only average feelings of respect from others.

Fifth, any measure of perceptions of one's own "self-actualization" is also ambiguous. If it is too high, one may simply be satisfied with a very inferior self; if it is too low, one may experience a total lack of development. But it should be a significant factor in one's appraisal of one's life, which it is.[9]

To summarize, the market fails the test of providing a sense of security and, as we have said on the basis of other data, the resulting worry detracts from the want-satisfying capacity of the market. If economic security were a condition for feelings of belongingness, social esteem, and self-esteem at the higher stages, then the failure of the market to provide security would prevent many from ever achieving these goals. But, in fact, it has not turned out this way because people are quite pleased with the way they are accepted and respected by others and with their own selves. In spite of general feelings of insecurity, the ideal of self-development, however much it may fall short in practice, survives, even thrives, in a market society. The missing information is the extent to which this ideal is a real life *goal*, how much it is a consideration in everyday life, how much sacrifice people are willing to make to attain that goal.

[7] Ruth C. Wylie, *The Self-Concept* (Lincoln: University of Nebraska Press, 1974), 127.

[8] Angus Campbell, *The Sense of Well-Being in America* (New York: McGraw-Hill, 1981), chap. 13.

[9] Jonathan Freedman's study of happiness among magazine readers showed that for married men, a sense of "personal growth" made more of a contribution to their happiness than anything else; for single men and women and married women, a sense of personal growth was important, ranking fifth or sixth, but less important than, for example, being in love, marital satisfaction, or enjoyment of friends and social life. Jonathan L. Freedman, *Happy People* (New York: Harcourt, Brace, Jovanovich, 1978), 41.

Feedback loops: homeostasis and cybernetics

Feedback looks

The market may satisfy a person's wants, creating an enduring disposition that, if supplemented by other sources of positive moods, we might call happiness; that happiness then makes the things the market offers more attractive, more want satisfying. We have a feedback loop, as Andrews and Withey observed,[10] a movement first from the specific to the general and then back again from the general to the specific. With a narrow focus on the market, one might say that having satisfied an individual's previous wants, the market is in a better position to satisfy current wants. It is not the case, then, that each transaction is independent of previous transactions, for the want satisfactions of today borrow from those of yesterday and create a ground for the transactions of tomorrow.

Feedback loops of this kind are familiar in many forms of analysis: sociologically, the "vicious cycle of poverty" where the deprivations themselves are the causes of inability to transcend them; psychologically, attributing the causes of events in one's own life to fate, or society, or other people (externality) inhibits the very actions that would give proof to the individual that he or she *is* an effective person. Addiction could be interpreted as a positively accelerated feedback loop.

In the case of the happiness feedback loop we rely on what has been called the "top down or bottom up" problem. The bottom-up theory holds that "happiness is the sum of many small pleasures. . . . The happy life in this view is merely an accumulation of happy moments," a Lockean form of reductionism, or, if the pleasures are well-selected, a hedonist's understanding of happiness. Alternatively, there may be a "global propensity to experience things in a positive way, and this propensity influences the momentary interactions an individual has with the world. In other words, an individual enjoys pleasures because he is happy, not vice versa."[11] We have seen evidence (Chapter 24) that such enduring propensities limit the capacity of the market both to relieve pain and to create pleasure. In the Andrews and Withey study, it appears that a wide variety of domains make about the same contribution to life satisfaction, findings that support the influence of enduring dispositions, the top-down theory. On the other hand, the linear cumulative theory of happiness (Chapter 22) supports the bottom-up theory. If both theories are true, as the evidence suggests, the feedback loop or cybernetic model seems to be the appropriate one. As a consequence, the concept of utility must refer to satisfactions incurred in a continuing "game," a product of history, not just the history of encounters with a certain product but with a much larger range of products, or with the market itself, or with money, or shopping.

One of many similar studies finds evidence of the feedback loop relating work to life satisfaction and life satisfaction to work, but of the two sets of influences "job satisfaction has a greater influence on life or nonwork satisfaction than vice versa." This finding corroborates a body of research showing that "work attitudes and ex-

[10] Andrews and Withey, *Social Indicators of Well-Being*, 15.
[11] Ed Diener, "Subjective Well-Being," *Psychological Bulletin* 95 (1984): 542–75 at 565.

periences are major determinants of nonwork behaviors and attitudes.'' Nevertheless, the reciprocal phase of the loop is important, too, for "satisfaction with work
itself and [with] authority and responsibility were influenced by life satisfaction.''[12]

If the feedback loop is extended to cover a variety of domains, we are faced with
the problem of attribution across domains, a much more difficult task of analysis.
As reported in Chapter 4, people receiving a small gift in a shopping arcade were
thereby put in a happy mood, leading them, quite irrelevantly, to evaluate their
appliances' repair records more favorably.[13] We know that this transfer of affect is
the case in the work–family domains,[14] and it seems to be true that the theory of
spillover in work–leisure relations has considerable support.[15] One of the mechanisms explaining the top-down effect is "priming": "The things that make you feel
good prime more happy memories, while things that get you down prime sad ones.''[16]

The idea that the satisfactions apparently derived from a transaction may be heavily
influenced by the contribution of events in another domain to overall life satisfaction
that, in turn, affects hedonic responses to that very transaction has interesting consequences. Drawing on the evidence from the quality-of-life studies, we remind
ourselves of the importance of two evaluations: (1) hedonic *ratings* of an activity or
mental state, and (2) the *power* of that feeling to affect life satisfaction. Thus, low
rating and high power make a person unhappy; low rating and low power do not
much affect overall happiness. Put differently and more generally, if a domain has
high ratings and high power, it increases global satisfaction and generates a favorable top-down effect, whereas if it has low ratings and high power it generates an
unfavorable top-down effect. Higher power makes a domain or concern a creditor;
lower power makes it a debtor in relation to other domains and concerns. With this
in mind, two illustrative top-down–bottom-up possibilities seem plausible:

*Family felicity increases the capacity of the market to satisfy human
wants.* Because family life is ranked much higher than anything that refers to market activities and because evaluations of that family life, whatever they are, contribute much more to overall life satisfaction (have greater power), it seems likely that
in most cases family life will be the creditor (from which happiness flows to other
domains) and market activities the debtor. On the other hand, although a sense of
efficacy and achievement ("what you are accomplishing," "success and getting
ahead," "yourself") is also a heavy contributor to life satisfaction, in this case the
evaluation of these activities by themselves is ranked about the same as is overall
life satisfaction, and much lower than family life. As a consequence, feelings of

[12] Thomas I. Chacko, "Job and Life Satisfaction: A Causal Analysis of their Relationships," *Academy of Management Journal* 26 (1983): 163–9 at 163.
[13] Alice M. Isen, "Positive Affect, Cognitive Processes, and Social Behavior," in L. Berkowitz, ed., *Advances in Experimental Social Psychology,* vol. 20 (New York: Academic Press, 1987).
[14] Rosabeth Moss Kanter, *Work and Family in the United States* (New York: Russell Sage, 1977).
[15] Melvin Kohn and Carmi Schooler, *Work and Personality: An Inquiry Into the Impact of Social Strat-ification* (Norwood, NJ: Ablex, 1983).
[16] Howard Ehrlichman and Jack N. Halpern, "Affect and Memory: Effects of Pleasant and Unpleasant Odors on Retrieval of Happy and Unhappy Memories," *Journal of Personality and Social Psychology* 55 (1988): 769–79.

achievement are less likely to have creditor status in affecting that overall life satisfaction and are most unlikely to improve evaluations of family life.

Feelings of financial insecurity detract from the contributions of religion and friendship to life satisfaction. Evaluations of financial security are low, and because they are powerful (contributing substantially to overall life satisfaction) they reduce these overall feelings of life satisfaction. On the top-down theory, this depressed overall life satisfaction would then tend to depress the ratings of other domains, such as religion (which has an above average mean rating but is insignificant in its contribution to life satisfaction), and satisfaction with friendship (which is rated slightly higher than religion and also has no power over life satisfaction, although actual number of friends does). There will, however, be many exceptions, for domains have their own powers of bottom-up generation of satisfactions and well-being.[17]

The effect of hedonic ratings and power of one domain on another creates a cybernetic system where every positive and negative contribution to overall life satisfaction feeds back on itself to start another round. Thus, the market is both a creditor and a debtor, borrowing from other more powerful domains and lending to the less powerful ones.

Homeostasis and adaptation levels

The market is an excellent cybernetic, self-regulating system for the production of wealth. But as I have been saying, it is a poor *hedonic* cybernetic system for maximizing pleasure and even worse for maximizing satisfaction with life-as-a-whole. As a hedonic cybernetic system it is out of control, with uncorrected lag and gain leading to cycles of sorrows and cycles of joys and pleasures. It is out of control because the hedonic information in the feedback system does not deal with measurable utility but only with an inadequate proxy, money. The lag- and gain-producing cycles of sorrows and joys follow logically from false information. An empirical example of a cycle of "sorrows" was given in the discussion of self-attribution in Chapter 9: Deprivation in work of self-direction encourages external attribution, which in turn leads people to interpret their successes as due to circumstances and their failures as due to their own lack of ability, which in turn inhibits self-direction, thus completing the cycle. In that chapter I pointed out that this was a better example of the Matthew Principle: "For unto every one that hath shall be given, and he shall have abundance: but from him that hath not shall be taken away even that which he hath." Unhappily, these cycles are partly coincident with social class, exacerbating class differences and possibly contributing to a culture of sorrows disguised as a culture of poverty. The market's celebrated tendencies toward equilibrium seem to offer no cure for these cybernetic failures. An instrument that re-

---

[17] On the other hand, by this line of reasoning the general satisfaction with one's standard of living, which is somewhat influential in affecting global well-being, would create a generally positive disposition that might make people look more kindly on the government. Unhappily for the cybernetic theory, however, it is the poor who seem to get more satisfaction from the government. See Andrews and Withey, *Social Indicators of Well-Being,* 304.

sponds only to supply and demand through price changes is not responsive to hedonic lags and gains that do not register in this calculus.

But there is an alternative cybernetic principle that is genuinely homeostatic, leading the individual to maintain a more constant hedonic equilibrium. This principle is the *adaptation-level phenomenon* that we have previously discussed and will treat in more detail later. It says that after a more or less short time, one adapts to a pleasure or pain, a utility or disutility, so that the new pleasure or the pain is not felt so keenly and one returns to one's previous hedonic level, whatever that may have been.[18] Individual homeostasis and market homeostasis (or tendency toward equilibrium) – by means of which supply deficiencies are remedied by increased prices, thereby increasing supplies and reducing prices – are bound to affect each other. For example, adaptation to rising prices would fail to create the resistance that would tend to lower prices. If adaptation is too rapid, it stifles the signals on which market equilibrium depends.

Second, there is reason to believe that adaptation to pain is slower than adaptation to pleasure (Chapter 24). The lag between adaptations to increased prices (a pain) and equivalent increased wages (a pleasure) may be explained in terms of differential rates in the adaptation phenomena.

Third, the tolerance for delayed gratification, or the "waiting" that once was said to characterize those who saved, is not so painful as has been supposed, providing that the tolerance of delay in gratification is learned in a leisurely fashion. Those now archaic theories of interest as the reward for "patience" or "waiting" have even less justification than supposed.

Fourth, the adaptation-level phenomenon is the antidote to Durkheim's anomie of affluence – and the anodyne for the market's restless tendency to change and grow.

In sum, if the market's reliance on price as the information that will permit self-regulation to maximize satisfaction with life-as-a-whole fails because that kind of satisfaction is not sensitive to changes in price, individuals have within them a counterbalancing force in the way they adjust their sense of well-being to their circumstances.

Asking why victims are so patient in their victimization, Barrington Moore holds that this patience is due to their powerlessness and hopelessness,[19] but it might equally be that they are simply exhibiting adaptation-level phenomena that apply to victims and victimizers alike.

Concentric circles

A fourth structure giving meaning to market patterns of satisfaction and dissatisfaction employs the metaphor of the circle. In their analysis of the pattern of responses to questions about life concerns in various domains of life, Andrews and Withey report that the *domains* form themselves into a set of concentric circles where the

---

[18] M. H. Appley, ed., *Adaptation-Level Theory: A Symposium* (New York: Academic Press, 1971).
[19] Barrington Moore, Jr., *Injustice: The Social Basis of Obedience and Revolt* (New York: Macmillan, 1978).

contents of the inner circle have the greatest power to influence overall life satisfaction and the contents of the outer circle have the least. Fortunately, most (but not all) features of the powerful inner circle also win the most approval and the contents of the outer one win the least. At the core is the self and family, and in the outer circle are governmental policies. "In between these two extremes there is a rough ordering of satisfaction from one's family to one's neighborhood, to community characteristics and services, to characteristics of the economy and media information and entertainment, and finally to the national government."[20] On this map market attributes and activities are near the middle, adjacent to the media and entertainment in the outer fringe, and to community life toward the center.

Like the domains, the pattern of *concerns,* values, evaluations, and criteria that people apply to activities in the several domains of life shows a similar configuration: "from intimate values in one's private world to the scene of interaction with others, then to problems of competencies, and finally to rather widespread conditions with which people have to cope."[21]

Mixing domains and concerns, the map of the things that contribute most to one's happiness or unhappiness, from the most to the least, are: (1) self-efficacy index, (2) family index, (3) money index, (4) amount of fun, (5) house or apartment. And among the least powerful items at the bottom of the list are national government index, local government index, media index, and *consumer index* (!), an index embracing local transportation, medical services, and "the goods and services you can get when you buy in this area."[22]

Three issues concerning the interpretation of the market in this pattern of favored and disfavored concerns and domains affecting happiness stand out. The authors' discussion of the favorableness of the concentric circle of domains gives the first clue: It represents a scale from near to far, from private to public, and especially "from things one might personally influence to circumstances of our common situation" that seem, like the weather, to be beyond the reach of influence.[23] The dimension of degree of influence or "personal control" has been considered crucial to work satisfaction and to life satisfaction more generally.[24] In the transformed language of "voluntariness," "independence," and "freedom," it is also crucial to the defense of the market, as Friedman and Hayek and others have argued.[25] In line with their arguments, people do see their economic activities as more subject to their control than is their democratically elected government, but less than activities in the family, among friends, and in the community and neighborhood. It may plausibly be argued that a market economy and its institutions *teach* self-reliance and independence (I think they do), but people see more intimate fields of endeavor,

[20] Andrews and Withey, *Social Indicators of Well-Being,* 274.
[21] Ibid.
[22] Ibid., 101, 127, 132, emphasis added.
[23] Ibid., 274.
[24] Antonia Abbey and Frank M. Andrews, "Modeling the Psychological Determinants of Life Quality," in Frank M. Andrews, ed., *Research on the Quality of Life* (Ann Arbor, MI: Institute for Social Research, 1986).
[25] Milton Friedman, *Capitalism and Freedom* (Chicago: University of Chicago Press, 1962); Friedrich A Hayek, *The Constitution of Liberty* (1960; reprint South Bend, IN: Gateway, 1972).

rather than economic life, as offering better opportunities to express their control.

Second, there is a kind of *gravitational movement* from outer circles to inner ones. When people do not find satisfaction in one area of life, they compensate by finding it in another.[26] In this compensatory activity they are unlikely to go from the middle circle economic domain outward into the domain of government, civics; this direction neither gives satisfaction nor power to change people's overall enjoyment of life, even though it is the government, and not the family, that can relieve their economic malaise. They will move toward the center, where satisfaction and a sense of control reside. The gravitational pull toward the core implies that some force has to be exerted to travel to the outer rings.

Third, to achieve a fair assessment of global well-being one must span the diameter of the circle. "Any measure of quality of life that focused just on the personal would be too high, or just on the national would be too low."[27] The critics of the market society who focus just on the economic, which occupies a middle circle in the imagined diagram, are unlikely to find an indicator of joys and sorrows that is representative of a whole life. One reason is that level of income (or social class) influences the favorability of ratings in the various domains: The lower the income, the more negative are ratings of economic matters and the more positive are the ratings of government and the media. The lesson is clear. For assessments of the quality of life or even of want satisfaction, study the range of life concerns.

Linear models and the concern–domain matrix

Just as we may place market activities in a pattern of concentric circles with a personal core and a distant circumference, so we may place them in a matrix composed of domains and concerns, as in Figure 25.3. Here we follow Andrews and Withey in the theory that informs their concept of the relationships between human concerns and the application of these concerns to various spheres or domains of life. The basic idea is that there are certain concerns, or criteria, for assessing life events that apply, with varying relevance, pretty much across the board. For example, for such domains as home, work, and leisure activities, people might be concerned with such commonly applied concerns as the freedom and independence enjoyed in that domain, or the amount of fun it permitted. In a special analysis, the investigators ask such questions as, "How do you feel about your house or apartment if you consider only the sense of achievement it enables you to have?" or, "How do you feel about your house if you considered only the standard of living it enables you to have?"[28] Modifying their scheme to fit our needs, we might think of a matrix of domains and concerns as illustrated in Figure 25.3.[29]

In this matrix, $E(ij)$ is the assessment of the sense of achievement that a person's

[26] Andrews and Withey, *Social Indicators of Well-Being,* 306–7.
[27] Ibid, 276.
[28] Ibid., 235.
[29] Ibid., 13, adapted from Exhibit 1.1.

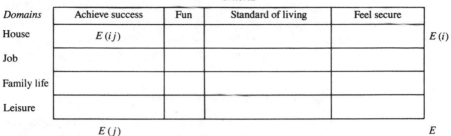

Figure 25.3. *Matrix of criteria by domains*

house permits that person to have, $E(i)$ is the sum of the satisfactions given by the house, and $E(j)$ is the sum of the assessments of achievement felt by that person in all the domains of his or her life. E, then, is theoretically the sum of either the rows or the columns and would be the same as the assessment of the global sense of well-being achieved by a direct measure. As Andrews and Withey point out, this summary figure would not be achieved by simple addition, but rather would require suitable weights.[30] Nevertheless, they found that even without weights the criteria accounted for 58 percent of the variance in their global measure of life satisfaction and conclude that the model "seems to accord well with reality."[31]

Setting aside for the moment the many doubts about the practicality of this simple design,[32] I must be content with pointing out that so many sources of satisfaction are *domain specific* that it is misleading to measure these sources of satisfaction in irrelevant domains. That difficulty also complicates analysis of the interesting problem of substitutable sources of satisfaction; in a market economy one does not, for example, satisfy a desire for a higher standard of living by turning to the family, or, generally, find the satisfactions of gemeinschaft in the factory or office. Rather, one must either look for a given form of satisfaction in the domains where it might be found, or change one's sources of satisfaction and find compensating ones in a more convenient domain.[33]

The fact that people satisfy different concerns in different domains makes the substitution of one domain for another an attractive alternative to the more difficult task of substituting one concern for another. Money is an inadequate substitute for friendship, but friendship in another domain, say, in leisure activities on the golf course, may be a welcome substitute for loneliness at the office. Usually, one looks for what one wants wherever one can find it rather than changing what one wants

[30] Ibid., 14.

[31] Ibid., 239.

[32] For a critique, see Aubrey C. McKennel, "Cognition and Affect in Perceptions of Well-Being," *Social Indicators Research* 5 (1978): 389–426; McKennel and Frank M. Andrews, "Models of Cognition and Affect in Perceptions of Well-Being," *Social Indicators Research* 8 (1980): 257–98.

[33] Questions on the level of satisfaction with one's standard of living applied to family life, for example, might depress both the sum of the criteria across domains and the sum of domains across the criteria. Or, asking questions about satisfactory interpersonal relations at work (satisfying the need for affiliation) might, unless complicated weights were attached, depress both the sum of concern for affiliation and for the domain of work.

in order to stay within a domain; in a mobile individualistic society, people's mental structures are more important to them than their particular social structures – but with exceptions, as where affectionate bonds or fiscal necessities encourage changing goals so as to remain within those bonds or to serve those necessities. (A discussion of the compensatory principle in Chapter 27 supplements this treatment.)

Shadow pricing versus satisfaction currencies

Shadow pricing is the basis of the claim that the market maximizes satisfaction. For both transactions and opportunity costs, exchanging one good for another implies comparison. For market commodities, all of which are priced, such comparisons are facilitated by a common metric, money. Some market theories state that non-market goods are also priced by *shadow prices:* the cost of earnings given up in the case of leisure and the cost of priced goods given up in the case of equivalent nonmarket goods. Because everything has a price, everything can be compared to everything else by the same money metric[34] (see Chapter 5). This is the basis for the most inclusive claim that the purpose of the market is to satisfy wants. I would like to suggest that this argument is false and that a metric other than satisfaction or *happiness yield* is both unnecessary and misleading.

The validity of this claim about the shadow pricing of all goods does not, of course, rest on the actual pricing of satisfaction with family life or friendship; rather, it assumes that rational choices regarding the things that are priced will index the family and friendship values that are not explicitly priced, and that prices will be adjusted in transactions to compensate a "trader" for decrements or increments of the unpriced values. There are four answers to the proposition that all values in a market society have shadow prices:

Shadow prices do not measure process benefits. Dow and Juster point out that in any household the activity of cooking has two products: (1) the meal and (2) the process benefits (and time employed) in the cooking process. The meal has a shadow price, but a distorted one because of deductions of the symbolic value of a home-cooked meal, but the enjoyment of the *process* is not measured by the opportunity costs of the preparer's time in market wages or what it would cost to hire a cook from outside.[35] Similarly, "the shadow price of time [spent on child care at home] has two components: the current foregone wage and the loss of lifetime

---

[34] I believe that Alfred Marshall's idea that economists "take account of differences in real value" through the way they are expressed by "equal economic measures" may be read as support for the idea that the market prices nonmarket goods. See Marshall, *Principles of Economics,* 8th ed. (London: Macmillan, 1939), 17. Labor economist Jack Barbash is more explicit: "Money and non-money are different faces of the same value, . . . economic calculation is only the prism through which other values are filtered. In real work life, accordingly, every point along the [Maslovian] need hierarchy has an inescapable money component." Jack Barbash, *Job Satisfaction and Attitude Studies* (Paris: OECD, 1976), 19.

[35] Greg K. Dow and F. Thomas Juster, "Goods, Time, and Well-Being: The Joint Dependence Problem," in Juster and Frank P. Stafford, eds., *Time, Goods, and Well-Being* (Ann Arbor, MI: Institute for Social Research, 1985), 402, citing R. A. Pollak and M. L. Wachter, "The Relevance of the Household Production Function and its Implications for the Allocation of Time, *Journal of Political Economy* 83 (1975): 255–77.

income associated with reduced labor market time via-on-the-job training.''[36] But even this fails to measure the process benefits of parental care or the improved earning power of the child whose parent, in fact, cared.

Shadow prices do not measure the nonmaterial satisfactions of material success. The monetary values of economic success are only one element of the relevant value of such success; achievement values, intrinsic work enjoyment, and sense of fulfillment are equally or more important, and as self-rewards they are unpriced. Of course, the market does assign valued economic rewards to many kinds of work, but nothing in the studies of life satisfaction implies such shadow pricing, or even a reference to costs or to standards of living or to earning opportunities given up. Success in business is partially measured in money terms, but professional and artistic success is measured in reputation (and internal self-rewards), and many clerical and blue-collar workers measure their success in the coinage of popularity. These satisfactions do not have shadow prices, in part because they are chosen as alternatives to the category of economic rewards.

Shadow prices do not account for the inhibitions against trading unlike goods. The shadow-pricing formulation implies that people are willing to refer to a certain good, money, for a relevant standard when dealing with goods that are very unlike money. Foa set up a series of experimental exchanges where subjects had to pay back a gift or favor received. He provided subjects a variety of six goods represented symbolically by cards: "love," "(material) goods," "services," "information," "status," and "money." When the goods are ordered on two dimensions, particularism (suitability of a good only for particular people) and concreteness, the resulting graph shows, for example, that love and money were similar on the concrete dimension but at opposite polls on the particularism dimension (love is person-specific but money is both fungible and indifferent to persons). Figure 25.4 gives the resulting format.

Foa found that the goods chosen for exchange were either identical to the ones received (status for status, services for services), or adjacent on the two-dimensional scale portrayed in Figure 25.4: money for (material) goods or vice versa, love for status or vice versa, and so on. The principle of exchange of *like for like* was exemplified not only in friendly exchanges but in matters of revenge as well.[37] Since this represents a cognitive classification of goods, it is likely that it applies to calculations of opportunity costs (intrapersonal exchanges) as well. Note that the cognitive classification permits shadow pricing for commodities and (impersonal) services, but not for love or status or personal services. Where the like-for-like principle applies, deriving a monetary standard of value with relevance for satisfactions in the family or friendship domains from goods that happen to be priced in money terms is most improbable.

[36] Martha S. Hill and F. Thomas Juster, "Constraints and Complementarities in Time Use," in Juster and Stafford, *Time Goods, and Well-Being*, 425.
[37] Uriel G. Foa, "Interpersonal and Economic Resources," *Science* 171 (29 January 1971): 345–51.

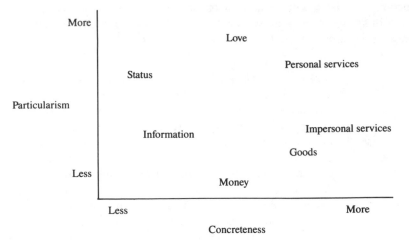

Figure 25.4. *Exchange of disparate goods (Source:* Uriel G. Foa, "Interpersonal and Economic Resources," *Science* 171 (29 January 1971): 345–51. I have added a distinction between personal and impersonal services not present in Foa's account.)

Shadow prices employ as a standard a currency with relatively low hedonic yield. The fourth and main reason why shadow pricing fails is that it is impractical and misleading. Consider again those things in Jonathan Freedman's study that contribute most to the happiness of a married man, in order of importance: (1) a sense of personal growth, (2) being in love, (3) satisfaction with a marriage, and (4) satisfaction with one's job (with minimal reference to wages). Not until tenth place is there a reference to finances, preceded by such things as satisfactory sex life, enjoyable social life, and gratifying parenthood.[38] If these choices relied on the shadow price of finances to assess the value of the preferred good, that would mean that each of them in turn was calibrated by the tenth item chosen and all derived their relative values from comparisons with that low-ranking item. Inasmuch as money value is no more important a common dimension for these goods than is love or personal growth, there is no more reason for money to be the dimension for shadow pricing than for these other higher ranked goods to serve as such a dimension. At this point, the advantage of the use of money stemming from its utility as a *standard of value* has evaporated.

A comparison of answers by the rich and poor offers additional insight. If the money standard prevailed, the poor, for whom money and earnings are more important than they are for the rich, would consider their love life, marital satisfactions, and social life relatively less important than would the rich – because of their belief that money is the source of their happiness and poverty the source of their unhappiness. Money is one of the few things ranked as more important by those who do *not* have it than by those who do.[39] But, in fact, the poor do not differ

[38] Freedman, *Happy People*, 41.
[39] Angus Campbell, Philip E. Converse, and Willard L. Rodgers, *The Quality of American Life* (New York: Russell Sage, 1976), 91–3.

greatly from the rich in the order of things that give them satisfaction or in the kinds of satisfactions that make them happy. A much more plausible explanation of the minimal class differences (and the general principle of valuing nonmarket goods), is the *compensatory principle* that we will discuss more fully in Chapter 27.

The satisfaction-yield metric and the happiness-yield metric perform the job better than the money metric; they directly facilitate utility maximization, as we will discuss.

Structure of domains as a protection against market infection

Shadow pricing is an invitation to "infect" market values in domains where market calculations are usually regarded as inappropriate; thus the limitations to shadow pricing offer a modest protection against the fears of moral pollution expressed by Goodin and Walzer, as discussed in Chapter 2. To that discussion, I add only brief notes from the quality-of-life studies. Specific criteria for satisfaction tend to apply to specific domains. Thus, "freedom from bother" applies most clearly to neighborhood and government, whereas "self-accomplishment" applies best to work and family.[40]

As mentioned in Chapters 2 and 22, the partitioning of the perceptual world into domains makes it possible to employ material incentives in the market without infecting family life; it permits certain desert-based concepts of justice to apply in the market without implying that they must equally apply in, say, the administration of criminal justice. Also, conversely, the partitioning of life into domains protects the market from infection by motives more appropriate to civics or family life: The fact that peoples' belief that they had made a contribution to the life of others was an important influence on their perceptions of their own happiness, ranking ninth among twenty-three measures, but this belief was independent of their belief in their own success and ability to get ahead, which ranked seventeenth in this roster.[41]

There is one further implication of the partitioning of the world into domains, each of which is equipped with its differentiated criteria and values: We are thereby led to a plural valued world. If each domain employed the same criteria, say, piety or wealth, we would risk the tyranny of what Blake called "single vision," and in every domain the proprietors of that vision would govern our lives, if "only" through community censure. For good reason Lasswell defined the democratic personality as one with plural values;[42] the criterion applies a fortiori to the citizen of the market.

The structures we have reviewed include a psychocentric model, a scalar ordering of values, cybernetic feedback loops combined with individual homeostatic adjustments, concentric circles, and the partitioning of the psychic world into domains, each of which has, to some extent, its own codes and values. We now turn to a

---

[40] Andrews and Withey, *Social Indicators of Well-Being,* 237–8.
[41] Ibid., 135. The inference of independence is drawn from the fact that the factor containing "contribute to others" was different from the one containing "achieve success." (p. 418)
[42] Harold D. Lasswell, "Democratic Character," in *The Political Writings of Harold D. Lasswell* (Glencoe, IL: Free Press, 1952).

choice among strategies for maximizing net satisfaction, enlisting a standard different from that of maximizing utilities through monetary calculations.

Investing in happiness: dominant and recessive concerns

Maximizing satisfaction, maximizing happiness, or minimizing dissatisfaction

In general, hedonic criteria suggest three principles to govern a choice of an activity
requiring an investment of time and emotion. (1) The principle of *maximization of
overall life satisfaction* says to choose that set of activities (and their setting) that
gives the greatest yield in overall life satisfaction or happiness. This choice requires
a person to know the happiness yield of any given pursuit, and so is the most
difficult. The other two refer to what is immediately satisfying or dissatisfying. (2)
The *satisfaction maximization* principle says to choose those activities or settings
that yield the greatest satisfaction and pursue them. (3) The *dissatisfaction minimization* principle says to attend to and improve those areas of life that yield the least
dissatisfaction (maximin). The second two principles imply consulting one's feelings (and beliefs) about a given state of affairs and attributing causes to these feelings. And most important, they also require people to make a strategic choice between them – and this choice implies radically different outcomes: to continue
doing what is pleasurable, or to try and make some unsatisfying activity more pleasurable.

The three principles may be illustrated from the data in the quality-of-life studies.
For example, people receive a lot of satisfaction from the "particular neighborhood
in which [they] live" and from "the people who live in the" nearby houses and
apartments, but the "neighborhood index" embracing these items ranks only twenty-
third among thirty factors contributing to happiness [beta .04]. In their pursuit of
happiness, should people spend more time in the neighborhood, which is so satisfying, or should they devote more time to earning money, which is not very satisfying even though the products – a sense of financial security, satisfaction with
family income, and feelings of being well off (items in the "money index," beta
.15) – contribute a lot to people's happiness?

Similarly, attitudes toward the self make a large contribution to happiness, but
people's levels of satisfaction with themselves is only average.[43] Should people then
devote more time to making themselves the kind of person of which they might be
proud? Or, finally, should they attend to their civic duties and seek to reduce taxes
and elect better representatives, since it is this civic sphere of life that is so unsatisfying.

One answer is suggested by efficiency considerations: Invest in those areas where
you can make the most difference in your life satisfaction. This would rule out the
maximin investment in civic affairs, because people do not believe these matters
are subject to their control. Furthermore, since one reason for dissatisfaction with

---

[43] Andrews and Withey, *Social Indicators of Well-Being,* 124, 132, 254, 260, 266. The item, "How do
you feel about yourself?" ranks third out of twenty-three; the increase in variance explained when this
item is added to higher power items is 5.5%.

Table 25.2. *The effect of economic dominance on life choices*

Economic factors	Family/Social life	Economic dominant	Economic recessive
Good standard of living	Empty shell marriage	Happy	Unhappy
Low standard of living	Successful marriage	Unhappy	Happy
High economic achievement	Lonely, without friends	Happy	Unhappy
Low economic achievement	Many friends	Unhappy	Happy

civic affairs is the sense of powerlessness, by the very nature of this particular dissatisfaction, the maximin principle is unlikely to be chosen.

This choice must be made in the context of market offerings but is unguided by price mechanisms, shadow prices, or market criteria. It is clearly a case of using the *contribution-to-life-satisfaction* or *happiness* standard.

Choosing among concerns and domains: the happiness maximization princi-ple. Often people are confronted with paired situations where one of the pair is beneficent and the other malignant. If the contribution-to-life-satisfaction standard is the appropriate hedonic yardstick in these cases of paired choices, some further specificity is given to it by indicating a domain or concern as *dominant* if success in that field contributes more to life satisfaction or happiness than another field, which then might be labeled *recessive*, as in Table 25.2.

The effect of the choice, of course, depends on the independence of family life and economic success, and although we know that subjectively these can be inter-twined (often, in the market economy, to the detriment of family life), nevertheless, in Andrews and Withey's analysis satisfactory family life is at least reasonably independent of level of income.[44] The dominance–recessive characteristics of the domains is subjectively, but not autonomously, determined; it is not autonomous because the culture defines for many people what is dominant, and in a market culture the economic tends to be dominant, though that may be changing in postin-dustrial society.

Cultures vary, of course. In an interesting analysis of the probability of success in what was Communist Hungary, Hankiss says that these probabilities in 1978 were such that those who "set themselves goals relating to education or occupa-tion" will have less chance of attaining their objectives and will suffer more frus-tration than those, for instance, who concentrate on goals in family life or human relations.[45] In capitalist America, educational and occupational successes are easier to attain (perhaps marital felicity is not, though the divorce rates in the two countries

[44] Ibid., 294.
[45] Elemér Hankiss, "Structural Variable in Cross-Cultural Research on the Quality of Life," in Szalai and Andrews, eds., *The Quality of Life: Comparative Studies* (Beverly Hills, CA: Sage, 1980), 54.

are little different), but in the American quality-of-life studies people reveal that family life has a higher payoff even though their behavior implies that they think their happiness lies in successful economic striving.

Resisting the pull toward gemeinschaft. Finally, there seems to be one possible tradeoff that permits the market society to resist the pull of gemeinschaft, made so attractive by the happiness rewards of family life and friendships, and yet to yield up its own store of capitalist happiness. In their study of the psychological factors contributing to happiness, Abbey and Andrews assessed, among other things, the relative importance of a sense of *personal control* (the belief that events were responsive to a person's own acts), and *social support* (the belief that friends and family respected and cared about the person). As substantial literatures predict, both made major contributions to a person's happiness. What is most important, however, is that where one was missing, the other took over the task of making the individual happy. "Internal control and social support work in tandem," say these authors, "for individuals experiencing low levels of either social support or internal control, experiencing a high level of the other . . . increased life quality. Social support somehow compensates for the detrimental effects of lack of internal control, and internal control compensates for the detrimental effects of lack of social support." Furthermore: "Experiencing high levels of both social support and internal control seems to be no more beneficial than experiencing high levels of either one alone."[46] Personal control, as I have said, is taught by the market culture as self-reliance, and rewarded as individualism. Social support is eroded, along with the community and stable family that nurture such support, by the market's demands for occupational, geographical, and vertical mobility. The market's emphasis on individual choice, sometimes called "freedom," contributes to personal control and uproots the seedbeds of social support. Thus the market's encouragement of a sense of personal control may be viewed as a substitute for what the market has taken away: social support and its basis in family and community.

Summary

In a *psychocentric* model I have placed the individual, instead of the transaction, at the center of things, thus replacing the current econocentric model. In so doing we found that many of the problems of analysis of the market are easier to handle.

When the movement up a scale ordering kinds of satisfaction is considered, we found that the market does not inhibit such "higher order" satisfactions as broadening and improving the self in spite of its failure to satisfy the need for security.

There are feedback loops whereby higher satisfaction in one area leads to higher levels of overall life satisfaction, which in turn increases satisfaction in the original area of interest. Those loops represent the combined effects of top-down and bottom-up analyses of market satisfactions. The consequent interdependence of each satisfaction in relation to every other satisfaction alters the piecemeal analysis of the way the market satisfies human wants.

[46] Abbey and Andrews, "Modeling the Psychological Determinants of Life Quality," 108, 110.

Individuals have a kind of homeostatic adaptation process that may obstruct the market's own homeostatic tendencies toward equilibrium.

The gravitational pull toward the center of the concentric circles of concern (locating the self at the center and national affairs at the periphery) tends to make family and friends, rather than civic affairs, the more likely substitute for dissatisfaction in the economy. This is perverse when the things that make the economy unsatisfactory can only be solved by national governments.

If people are dissatisfied with something, they may have to choose between changing domains or changing concerns (goals and values); people are more likely to find satisfaction in changing domains than in changing values.

We do not need or use the money metric, even as shadow pricing, for comparing one source of satisfaction with another. As in the quality-of-life studies, people compare satisfactions without a money standard, even when their concerns are private and do not easily permit comparison with the similar circumstances of others.

The perceptual and evaluative partitioning of the world into domains helps to protect noncommercial domains from infection by the market – and vice versa.

When activities or goods come in packages such that a hedonic good is paired with a hedonic bad, the dominant and recessive properties of a concern (greater or lesser power to influence overall life satisfaction) tend to decide the hedonic outcome.

The market has eroded the basis of a major source of life satisfaction, social solidarity, but according to one study, the grounds of happiness in social solidarity may be compensated for by the grounds provided by personal control over one's own life circumstances.

26 Buying happiness

The purpose of this chapter is to explore the causes and consequences of what seems to be a reversal of the conventional wisdom: Individual differences in income level in any society explain few of the differences in life satisfaction, whereas cross-national differences, reflecting economic growth, account for substantial differences. In Chapter 7 I outlined some of the cognitive consequences of economic development; here, in the first section, we will discuss reasons for thinking economic development also increases the general sense of well-being. In the second section I introduce evidence on the minimal effects of individual higher income on subjective well-being. I try to account for this failed relation in the third section. Recent income changes are the exception to this lack-of-income–happiness relation, so in the fourth section I focus on these changes, especially as they may be caused by recessions. The next section is devoted to an account of why adaptation-level processes do not rob economic growth of its effect on well-being. In the last two sections we will explore further the meaning of money and we will speculate on the future of the "hedonic treadmill."

The effect of economic development on subjective well-being

So far as we can tell at the close of the twentieth century, market economies generate economic growth better than any proposed alternative, but whether or not the resulting increased standards of living make people happier is contested. On the basis of an early cross-cultural study by Cantril, Easterlin says: "In all societies, more money for the individual typically means more individual happiness. However, raising the incomes of all does not increase the happiness of all."[1] Easterlin means that the average measured level of self-reported well-being in poorer countries is not much different from that in richer countries. He explains this failure of increased prosperity to increase subjective well-being by the familiar adaptation-level and social comparison arguments: Evaluations of happiness are inevitably relative to what one has become accustomed to and to the circumstances of others. For example, a study in the Detroit area showed that after a considerable rise in income, people were about as satisfied with their lives as they were before, the only difference being that under the changed circumstances much more money was required to buy the level of satisfaction less money bought before, thus confirming the proposition that the price of happiness increased with wealth.[2] And a cross-

[1] Richard A. Easterlin, "Does Money Buy Happiness?" *The Public Interest*, no. 30 (Winter 1973): 3–10 at 3. See also Easterlin, "Does Economic Growth Improve the Human Lot?" in Paul A. David and Melvin W. Reder, eds., *Nations and Households in Economic Growth: Essays in Honor of Moses Abramovitz* (New York: Academic Press, 1974).
[2] Otis Dudley Duncan, "Does Money Buy Satisfaction," *Social Indicators Research* 2 (1975): 267–74.

national study seemed to show that people in rich nations were no happier than people in poor nations.[3] Easterlin reported the difference between substantial individual income and happiness effects in a static situation and lack of effects over time and across populations as a case of the fallacy of composition: "What is true for the individual is not [necessarily] true for society as a whole." His position has been adopted as the current orthodoxy on the topic.[4]

Later research almost reverses Easterlin's observations on the hedonic effects both of growth and on individual differences in income at any given time. I shall quote from these studies to establish the reversed relationship.

With better data relating per capita income and responses to questions on both life satisfaction and feelings of happiness gathered in dozens of surveys from a number of European countries and the United States, Inglehart and Rabier conclude:

Overall, the more prosperous nationalities tend to be more satisfied [with their lives], but the correlation is not very strong: The top nine nations in life satisfaction have a per capita income that ranges from $3,533 to $10,071, with a mean of $7,162; the bottom nine have incomes ranging from $2,830 to $9,507 with a mean of $6,053. Income and happiness are correlated at the national level, but the linkage is surprisingly weak.[5]

The most sophisticated analysis is that of Inkeles and Diamond, who looked at cross-cultural expressions of subjective well-being *within social ranks and occupations*, thereby eliminating the differences in the numbers of, say, professionals and peasants and extracting a purer measure of the effects of economic growth on sentiments of well-being. Summarizing their research, they say:

The above 10 measures of well-being, from eight different studies, span a rich assortment of nations, samples, and evaluative dimensions. They yield a total of 25 separate tests of our hypothesis – 25 rank order correlations – for this dimension. The median of these correlations is 0.60 – a strong indication, we believe, that personal satisfaction rises with the level of economic development of the nation, even when socioeconomic status is held constant.[6]

Subsequently a cross-cultural study by Gallup has found that, at least at the bottom, "Poverty adversely colors attitudes and perceptions. Although one probably could find isolated places in the world where the inhabitants are very poor but happy, this study failed to discover any area that met this test."[7]

Beyond this general relationship, one can discern another, albeit with similar anomalies: the welfare effect of growth. The two nations that led the happiness

[3] Hadley Cantril, *The Pattern of Human Concerns* (New Brunswick, NJ: Rutgers University Press, 1965).
[4] Stephen E. G. Lea, Roger M. Tarpy, and Paul Webley, *The Individual in the Economy* (Cambridge, UK: Cambridge University Press, 1987), 432.
[5] Ronald Inglehart and Jacques-Rene Rabier, "Aspirations Adapt to Situation – But Why Are the Belgians So Much Happier than the French? A Cross-Cultural Analysis of the Subjective Quality of Life," in Frank M. Andrews, ed., *Research on the Quality of Life* (Ann Arbor, MI: Institute for Social Research, 1986), 45–6.
[6] Alex Inkeles and Larry Diamond, "Personal Development and National Development: A Cross-Cultural Perspective," in Alexander Szalai and Frank M. Andrews, eds., *The Quality of Life: Comparative Studies* (Beverly Hills, CA: Sage, 1980), 94. Of course, meanings of happiness and its opposites vary with culture. For example, Brislin reports that "depression" in Japan tends to have such external, metaphorical referents as "dark," "cloudy," "rain," whereas in the United States people employ internal referents: "sadness," "depression," "loneliness." See Richard W. Brislin, "Cross-Cultural Research in Psychology," *Annual Review of Psychology* 34 (1983), 363–400 at 383.
[7] George H. Gallup, "Human Needs and Satisfaction: A Global Survey," *Public Opinion Quarterly* 40 (1976–7): 459–67 at 463.

roster in Inglehart and Rabier's study were Denmark and the Netherlands; the two laggards were Italy and Greece.[8] The higher the per capita income in a country, the more of its resources it devotes to welfare (with a decelerating turn among the very richest).[9] It is possible that in addition to the income effect there is a social welfare effect that explains some of the hedonic benefits of growth.

Oscar Lewis held that because the culture of poverty was partly based on the capitalist idea that every person is responsible for his own fate, the poor in noncapitalist nations do not suffer as much from their poverty as do the poor in capitalist nations. He reasoned that in noncapitalist nations the poor do not blame themselves – and are not blamed by others – for their poverty.[10] This seems not to be the case.

The individual income–happiness relation

Adam Smith doubted that increased income had much effect on increased happiness. He said, "In ease of body and mind, all the ranks of life are nearly upon a level."[11] Easterlin's opinion on individual income differences disputes Smith,[12] however the number of major studies in partial support of Smith is impressive.

In their major 1976 study Andrews and Withey, after controlling for almost every kind of contaminating factor, said: "The groupings by socioeconomic status show very meager differences [in sense of well-being] . . . and no significant single steps for Life-as-a-Whole." Although there is "a steady progression" in life satisfaction as status increases and "the discrepancies between the top and bottom socioeconomic categories are statistically significant, . . . one tends to note the smallness of differences because many observers of the American scene would have expected larger ones."[13]

In 1978 Jonathan Freedman reported on his research into what makes happy people. On the relation of income to happiness, he says:

The rich are not more likely to be happy than those with moderate incomes; the middle class is not more likely to be . . . happy than those with lower incomes. As long as the family has enough money to manage, which seems to be about ten thousand dollars these days [1976], their reported happiness is at most slightly related to how much money they have. For the majority of Americans, money, whatever else it does, does not bring happiness.

But Freedman adds:

When we survey people with a family income of less than five thousand dollars (and in some studies with less than ten thousand dollars), fewer of them say that they are very happy or moderately happy and more of them say that they are very unhappy than people with higher incomes. [But even this must be qualified:] Even those with the lowest incomes seem to find considerable happiness in life and few of them are miserable.[14]

[8] Inglehart and Rabier, "Aspirations Adapt to Situations," 38.

[9] Harold Wilensky, *The Welfare State and Equality* (Berkeley: University of California Press, 1975).

[10] Oscar Lewis, *La Vida: A Puerto Rican Family in the Culture of Poverty – San Juan and New York* (New York: Random House/Vintage, 1966).

[11] Adam Smith, quoted by Terence Hutchison, "Adam Smith and the Wealth of Nations," *Journal of Law and Economics* 19 (1976): 507–28 at 526.

[12] Easterlin, "Does Money Buy Happiness?" 3.

[13] Frank M. Andrews and Stephen B. Withey, *Social Indicators of Well-Being: Americans' Perceptions of Life Quality* (New York: Plenum Press, 1976), 286–7.

[14] Jonathan Freedman, *Happy People*, (New York: Harcourt Brace Jovanovich, 1978), 138, 136.

In 1981 Angus Campbell reviewed a number of studies of subjective well-being and concluded: "Knowing people's incomes does not tell us a great deal about their general satisfaction with life."[15] In an earlier study by Campbell and associates (1976) the changing relationship between income and self-reported happiness since 1957 was explored. The authors found "the income–happiness relationship has changed quite dramatically between 1957, when a clear positive relationship existed for all [age] cohorts, and 1971, when the relationship had considerably weakened among young respondents but remained intact among older respondents."[16] Over this period the better off third of the population was apparently finding that, for them, money was buying decreasing amounts of happiness.[17] These changes help to explain the discrepancy between Easterlin's report and the later ones.

In 1986 Inglehart and Rabier reviewed a massive set of studies covering eleven European countries and the United States. They said:

As one would expect, the rich are more satisfied with their incomes than the poor, and the highly educated are more satisfied with their education than the less educated. But the differences are smaller than one might expect; and when we analyze satisfaction with one's life as a whole, the explained variance is very modest indeed.[18]

The evidence suggests quite the reverse of Easterlin's thesis: economic growth *does* increase subjective well-being, whereas individual differences at any one time are rather small. Notice, however, that when the effect of money on happiness is examined more closely, the effect on the poor is substantial, as Freedman pointed out; the "minimal effect" thesis applies only to those who are above the poverty level. In advanced countries, for about 85 percent of the population, then, it is true that for the individual "money does not buy (much) happiness," but in less advanced countries the income–happiness relation is substantially larger.[19]

Why does money not buy happiness?

Given the working assumptions of most market participants, the premise of greed in the prevailing interpretations of economic performance, the distinguished utilitarian lineage of the market ideology, and the emphasis on rationality that embraces these views, it is important to understand why it is that money does not buy happiness. Why do these assumptions, premises, ideologies, and this rationality so often fail? In Part VI on pay and intrinsic work satisfaction we saw how much of our pleasure in life derives from intrinsic work satisfaction. In Chapter 23 we saw how many of the sources of pleasure, including economic pleasure, do not go through the market. In Chapter 24 on pain and pleasure we saw how impotent the market is to relieve pain and enhance pleasure, how invulnerable to market stimuli are some dispositions and traits, and how much of our felicity comes from internal rewards and punishments, especially our appraisals of ourselves. In Chapter 11 we saw how

[15] Angus Campbell, *The Sense of Well-Being in America* (New York: McGraw-Hill, 1981), 56–8.
[16] Angus Campbell, Philip E. Converse, and Willard L. Rodgers, *The Quality of American Life* (New York: Russell Sage, 1976), 29.
[17] Ibid., 28.
[18] Inglehart and Rabier, "Aspirations Adapt to Situations," 2–3.
[19] Ibid., 34.

much more effective friendship is than pay in contributing to well-being. And in the chapter to follow this one, Chapter 27 on misinterpreting happiness, we shall find further sources of error deceiving us about the satisfactions we receive from our economic relations.

The case for money – and a rebuttal

It is certainly clear that people want more money, characteristically about 25 percent more than they currently have.[20] Why? The things that money buys are manifold and attractive:

Money is directly or indirectly relevant to all [sic] of man's needs. For example, money can be used to buy tickets to plays and concerts (artistic and aesthetic needs), to take out your spouse (romantic celebration), to go on vacations (leisure needs), to finance your favorite organization (self-actualization needs?). Money can serve to reward you for using your mind effectively and as evidence that you are capable of earning a living and thus related to (though not a cause of) self-esteem.[21]

This impressive roster is deceptive: Artists are poor and aesthetic needs, measured by the way people feel about "the amount of beauty and attractiveness in your world" are, incredible as it may seem, reasonably well met (only 8 percent are dissatisfied). In any event, the satisfaction of these needs contributes less than 1 percent of the variance in explaining overall life satisfaction.[22] "Romantic celebrations" may be expensive or cheap; whichever they are, they do not indicate satisfaction of love or marital relations, which are independent of income.[23] The idea in the passage of "self-actualization" is misconceived; the illustration refers to altruism, which, measured by questions asking how much respondents contribute to the welfare of others, makes only very modest contributions to life satisfaction (ranking ninth in a list of twenty-three, and contributing only 0.3 to the cumulative variance explained).[24] And self-esteem, which *is* most significantly related to a sense of well-being, is almost independent of level of income.[25]

Theory and evidence for the failure of money to buy happiness. The most frequently cited reason why level of income does not relate closely to sense of well-being is that people have simply adapted their expectations and aspirations to their current income level and take that as normal, making their calculations with that level as a starting point. Inglehart and Rabier stress this line of reasoning, and it does bear weight, but there are other causes. In this section we will look at some economic and cultural causes of the failure of money to have a closer relationship to feelings of well-being.

In my opinion, the main reason that money does not yield (much) happiness is

[20] Stanley Lebergott, "Labor Force and Employment Trends," in Eleanor B. Sheldon and Wilbert E. Moore, *Indicators of Social Change* (New York: Russell Sage, 1968), 98.
[21] E. A. Locke, D. B. Feren, V. M. McCaleb, K. N. Shaw, and A. T. Denny, "The Relative Effectiveness of Four Methods of Motivating Employee Performance," in K. D. Duncan, M. M. Gruenberg, and D. Wallis, eds., *Changes in Working Life* (Chichester, UK: Wiley, 1980), 379.
[22] Andrews and Withey, *Social Indicators of Well-Being,* 259, Exhibit 4.5, p. 135.
[23] Ibid., 294.
[24] Ibid., 135.
[25] Campbell, *The Sense of Well-Being in America,* 216.

that the sources of happiness lie elsewhere. But there are other reasons as well. In addition to the considerations that follow, recall (Chapter 24) the hedonic fixity of those who are endowed with either chronic "negative affectivity" or, its opposite, the "talent for happiness." Behind these dispositional resistances to hedonic stimulation there may well lie biological substrates that give a whole life a dominant hedonic tone (Chapter 27). Neither money nor love is likely to change those programmed by nature or experience to be either chronically happy or sad.

Pleasures and concerns that dilute the money–happiness relation
Continuing with the idea presented in Chapter 23 regarding pleasures that escape the market, we turn here to the sources of feelings of well-being for which money is simply not relevant.

The daily pleasures of life. Within the dailiness of life, when given some income security, people draw their satisfactions from things that are not heavily dependent on income. Asked, "What gives you the most personal satisfaction or enjoyment day in and day out?" American respondents say: family (72%), television (48%), friends (47%), music (31%), reading books, magazines, newspapers (28%), house or apartment (24%), the work you do (23%), . . . meals (18%), car (16%), following sports (13%), the clothes you wear (6%).[26] These little anodynes of life are available to most people, depressing the relationship between income and life satisfaction. Income levels, as distinct from changes in income, may be expected under these circumstances to have little effect on these sources of sense of well-being.

Process benefits. Juster and associates' analysis of the activities that people enjoy doing in themselves, quite apart from any extrinsic rewards or outcomes associated with those activities, include a wide range of things: playing with one's own children, socializing with friends, watching television, sports, and other leisure activities – and, be it noted, working at one's job. "Interestingly enough," say Juster and Courant, "differences in income level never appear to have significant impact in any of these data."[27] Part of the reason for this lack of relationship with income is that many of the activities are self-chosen, indicating by their very nature what people like to do. But since this same lack of relationship to income applies to working activities, the further reason, suggested in Part VI on intrinsic work enjoyment, is that people enjoy what they do at work, even if they do not like other aspects of their jobs, such as their subordination to a foreman. And this enjoyment of work activities, too, is relatively independent of income.[28]

[26] Gallup Poll, *Public Opinion* 4 (October–November 1981), 35.
[27] F. Thomas Juster and Paul N. Courant, "Integrating Stocks and Flows in Quality of Life Research," in Andrews, *Research on the Quality of Life*, 165–6.
[28] F. Thomas Juster, "Preferences for Work and Leisure," in Juster and Frank P. Stafford, eds., *Time, Goods, and Well-Being* (Ann Arbor, MI: Institute for Social Research, 1985). Juster does not give a breakdown by income, but, as mentioned in Chapter 15, he says: Professionals, managers, and self-employed respondents do have slightly higher process benefits from work than others, but the differences are not very large and they are by no means systematic across the continuum from professional jobs to unskilled jobs." (p. 341)

The priority of sex and family life. We have found that most studies of the quality of life report that a good marriage and social support (along with personal control and achievement) are overwhelmingly more important than economic matters in contributing to a sense of well-being. Two women respondents explain how these matters make money relatively insignificant: "Money has never been a problem for me . . . I would change lives with anyone who has a decent sex life." "My marriage was painful and unfulfilling and though there was plenty of money it was unbearable. I have no desire to be rich again. I am richer now in my life than I ever could be in cash."[29]

The rise of postmaterialism. As mentioned, for a documented period after 1957, the power of money to increase happiness declined well into the 1980s and, at least during periods of prosperity, may be continuing this downward trend into the next century. This has been explained on the grounds of the declining marginal utility of money relative to such other things as intimate relationships or simply cultivating one's own subjective adjustment to life.[30] Keynes, too, thought avarice would decline when the magical properties of compounded growth had had their effect,[31] and, in his footsteps, Inglehart has shown that the entry onto the scene in the early 1960s of "postmaterialists" contributed to the declining priority of money. Postmaterialists reject the priority of consumerism and the things money buys and show an increased concern for the environment, for participation at work, and for various kinds of freedom. But their heterodox views do not make them happy. As relatively prosperous respondents, they thus dilute the relationship between income level and happiness: "The fact that postmaterialists are a relatively high-income group that does not experience relatively high levels of subjective well-being tends to weaken the relationship between income and happiness."[32]

Pains that increased income does not relieve

Worries. People who say that they worry a lot, or who check more worries than others on a checklist of common worries are less happy than these others. Worries do detract from a sense of well-being, but it is uncertain whether or not money offers much relief from worry. In view of the popular suspicion that the poor are poor because they are careless and do not worry enough, the relationship be-

---

[29] Philip Shaver and Jonathan Freedman, "Your Pursuit of Happiness," *Psychology Today* (August 1976): 27–32, 75 at 27.

[30] During the period 1957 to 1976, there was a "movement from social to personal integration of well-being . . . [and an] increase in self-expressive and self-directive reactions to . . . adjustments." Joseph Veroff, Elizabeth Douvan, and Richard A. Kulka, *The Inner Americans: A Self-Portrait from 1957 to 1976* (New York: Basic Books, 1981), 529, 530.

[31] John Maynard Keynes, "Economic Possibilities for Our Grandchildren," *Essays in Persuasion,* vol. 9 of *Collected Works of John Maynard Keynes* (London: Macmillan for the Royal Economic Society, 1972), 321–34. Original work published 1930.

[32] For example, postmaterialists like to do "interesting and socially useful activities," as well as liking "being esteemed by others, getting along with friends, and leisure activities." Where materialists turn inward toward the family, postmaterialists turn outward toward the society. Inglehart and Rabier, "Aspirations Adapt to Situations," 32.

tween money and worry is not self-evident. Andrews and Withey report that for their measure of worrying, "there are virtually *no* differences associated with socioeconomic status. . . . Higher status people apparently did not reduce the frequency of worrying."[33] On the other hand, a study made fifteen years earlier found that money does buy modest relief from general worry and from such circumstances as holding a job, paying one's bills, and so forth.[34] To the extent that there is *any* relationship between level of income and worrying, the main difference is not the amount of worrying but what people worry about.

Increased income shifts worries from economic matters to more personal concerns, like fulfillment of one's role as parent or spouse.[35] This shift helps to explain some of the waning power of money to buy happiness in rich societies. Over the 1957–76 period, the concerns of Americans shifted from role identities, greatly affected by income, to "a more personalized self-consciousness"[36] where income is less relevant. An increase in national income, like an increase in personal income, shifts the axis of worry to interpersonal and intrapersonal dimensions where money has less power to relieve worries. In this sense, personal and national income first buy happiness through relief of some major worries, but then alter the dimensions of worry toward a field where income loses its significance.

Economic security. In a Canadian study measuring a variety of circumstantial correlates of life satisfaction, "of the 12 domains, satisfaction with financial *security* has the greatest relative impact on satisfaction with life as a whole."[37] One might suppose that income buys economic security, but in several ranges of the economic scale, similar levels of income do not buy similar levels of economic security. Between skilled blue-collar workers and clerical workers there are minimal differences in income, and no differences at all in satisfaction with standards of living, but there are substantial differences in feelings of financial insecurity. In an American study of Baltimore and Detroit by Strumpel, blue-collar workers were found to worry much more than white-collar workers and were " 'very concerned' about societal developments that threatened their standards of living. Their dominant concern was security."[38] At the other end of the economic scale, both managers and professionals were well satisfied with their lives and their standards of living; but for managers, "the idea of a stagnant income made them more unhappy than any other groups except blacks," whereas professionals with equivalent incomes reported that they "would not be significantly more unhappy than others if their standard of living were to remain the same over the next five years."[39] On

[33] Andrews and Withey, *Social Indicators of Well-Being,* 322.
[34] Gerald Gurin, Joseph Veroff, and Sheila Feld, *Americans View Their Mental Health* (New York: Basic Books, 1960), 51.
[35] Ibid., 24–9.
[36] Veroff et al., *The Inner Americans,* 138.
[37] Alex C. Michelos, "Job Satisfaction, Marital Satisfaction, and the Quality of Life: A Review and a Preview," in Andrews, *Research on the Quality of Life,* 75, emphasis added.
[38] Burkhard Strumpel, with Richard T. Curtin and M. Susan Schwartz, "Economic Lifestyles, Values, and Subjective Welfare" in Strumpel, ed., *Economic Means for Human Needs* (Ann Arbor, MI: Institute for Social Research, 1976), 56.
[39] Ibid., 51, 52, 54.

balance, it seems that even though *amount* of money may not buy much happiness, *security* of income seems to buy more of it; to some modest extent the two facets of income define different populations.

Fairness of income. Some studies of economic satisfaction find that assessments of unfairness occur only when people believe that the level of payment is generally too low; then, and only then do they express grievances concerning the fairness of their wages.[40] The two kinds of grievance work together, largely because assessments of what is "good pay" are anchored in what others receive. This relationship, however, might work in the opposite direction: Feelings of justice come first and mediate the effects of income. This makes equity the prime consideration, and is the substance of Liang and colleagues' findings in a community of older people.[41] But other studies, especially those studying workers in metropolitan areas, have found that the sense of equity was different from the sense of receiving a satisfactory amount and is a much better predictor of overall life satisfaction than was either the size of the paycheck or satisfaction with amount of pay.[42] To the extent that sense of fairness of income and actual level of income differ, the income–happiness relation will be further weakened.

The ability to cope

One further reason why money does not buy happiness does not so much explain the lack of relationship as suggest a spurious factor in the small relationship that does exist. Distress or pain eroding life satisfaction is a function not only of the incidence of distress in a person's life but also of the coping skills with which a person deals with distress. From a study of life stress and mental health, examining such adult stresses as physical illness, worries over work and overwork, concern over "getting ahead," lack of close friends, marital difficulties, we learn that these kinds of stresses or pains were only modestly associated with income. Average stressful events scored by social class were: lower class, 5.7; middle class, 5.3; upper class, 4.7. Thus, money buys a little but not much relief from pain, at least for this sample of Midtown Manhattan residents. But the upper- and middle-class mode of coping with such painful stresses was often to undertake actions that might relieve the pain, for example, harder work, whereas the lower-class method included more fighting and drinking, which made the problems worse.[43] Money did not buy much relief from pain, confirming Bradburn and Caplovitz's finding in their sample,[44] but rather that relief came from personal skills and education that were –

[40] Richard T. Curtin, *Income Equity Among U.S. Workers: The Bases and Consequences of Deprivation* (New York: Praeger, 1977), 59. The effect is small: "U.S. workers voiced a widespread and enduring sense of income equity and satisfaction." (p. 55)

[41] J. Liang, E. Kahana, and E. Doherty, "Financial Well-Being among the Aged: A Further Elaboration," *Journal of Gerontology* 35 (1980): 409–20, cited in Ed Diener, "Subjective Well-Being," *Psychological Bulletin* 95 (1984): 542–75 at 554.

[42] Ephraim Yuchtman (Yaar), "Effects of Psychological Factors on Subjective Well-Being," in Strumpel, *Economic Means for Human Needs*, 107–29.

[43] Thomas S. Langner and Stanley J. Michael, *Life Stress and Mental Health* (New York: Free Press, 1963).

[44] Norman M. Bradburn and David Caplovitz, *Reports on Happiness* (Chicago: Aldine, 1965).

Table 26.1. *Satisfaction and happiness following changes in income*

During the past 12 months respondent's situation has become:	% satisfied or very satisfied with life-as-whole	% point difference	% very happy	% point difference
A lot better	85	+4	37	+16
A little better	81	−2	21	+2
Remained the same	83		19	
A little worse	74	−9	14	−5
A lot worse	57	−17	12	−2

Source: Ronald Inglehart and Jacques-Rene Rabier, "Aspirations Adapt to Situations," in Andrews, *Research on the Quality of Life*, 28, Table 1.10.

for our purposes, spuriously – associated with higher income levels. Money did not buy this relief, but because of their endowments, through their own efforts moneyed people achieved relief. It is in some such manner as this that we may understand the very modest influence of money on sorrow reduction reported earlier.[45]

Recent changes in income

Income changes, satisfaction, and happiness
There is a major exception to the "income doesn't buy much happiness" thesis: Recent increments of income buy quite a bit, and recent decrements of income incur a lot of dissatisfaction. Here we will explore some of the ways in which recent changes affect hedonic dispositions. Inglehart and Rabier's analysis of the effects on self-reported life satisfaction and happiness of (also self-reported) recent changes in income can yield insights beyond those explored in Chapter 23 (see Table 26.1). The question was: "How does the financial situation of your household now compare with what it was 12 months ago? Would you say it: got a lot better, got a little better, stayed about the same, got a little worse, or got a lot worse?" The questions were asked in a recession year, 1982.

Gains and losses. First, recall (Chapter 23) that increased income increases happiness more than satisfaction whereas decreases in income detract from satisfaction more than from happiness – suggesting that affect is more responsive to good news and cognition, with its weighing of the consequences, more responsive to bad news.

Notice, second, that small gains have less of an effect on mood than small losses, reinforcing the suggestion made earlier that we are more sensitive to pain than to pleasure, to loss more than to gain. Also the total effect of a loss (−26 satisfaction plus −7 happiness = −33) is larger than the total effect of a gain (+2 plus +18 = 20).

[45] Ibid., as discussed in Chapter 24 in this book.

This is in line with the predictions of four kinds of theories: (1) theories of perception that show losses to be more salient and more keenly felt than gains, that is, theories that chime with the skeptical philosophers mentioned in Chapter 22; (2) theories of declining marginal utility for money that would predict that from any given point on a utility schedule, changes in income below that point would deal with utilities of higher value than changes above that point; and (3) theories of preferred risk showing that people will accept risks to prevent possible losses and reject risks to achieve possible gains.[46] Finally (4), there is the "opponent process" theory that says that things initially sought for their pleasure become objects whose withdrawal is fraught with pain, that is, every enduring pleasure invites pain, loading the pain account at every favorable turn.[47] The first point, then, is the weakness of the adaptation effect with respect to losses and its relative strength in the case of gains.

Past and present. Americans see their futures as somewhat brighter than their pasts, but their "feelings about current state of well-being are quite independent from their expectations about future progress, and only slightly more related to their sense of past progress."[48] Before turning to the hedonic consequences of short-term income changes due to this failed sense of progress, consider some of its other implications. In a sense, this past versus future emphasis reflects two opposing theoretical views: Skinner, who held that it was the "history of reinforcement" and nothing more that determined action; and von Neuman and Morgenstern, who, along with others, put their faith in the rationality of "expected (future) utility." It seems that the person guided wholly by the indicated hedonic calculus would be more likely to follow Skinnerian principles than the von Neuman–Morgenstern theory. Self-perception theory also finds some very modest support in this backward looking posture: Bem's idea that people look back to see what they have done in order to decide how they feel[49] is quite congenial to this notion of backward looking rather than prospective hedonic calculations. But that is a wholly unmarketlike point of view, for the market is no respecter of history (sunk costs, investment in obsolescent talents) and rewards correct anticipations rather better.

Adaptation theory says that people adapt most easily to what they expect; if they expect progress, they will adapt to it with less arousal than if they did not expect it. The very slight sense of future progress (33% saw no change, 40% saw only slight improvement, and only 17% saw the likelihood of important improvements)[50] means

[46] Amos Tversky and Daniel Kahneman, "The Framing of Decisions and the Psychology of Choice," *Science* 211 (30 January 1981): 435–58.

[47] Richard L. Solomon, "The Opponent-Process Theory of Motivation: The Costs of Pleasure and the Benefits of Pain," *American Psychologist* 35 (1980): 691–712. Table 26.1 gives us a clue to one source of satisfaction in safe civil service jobs or jobs in business hierarchies that is missing in competitive jobs; preferences for security in the status quo is rational for the average person, since it avoids risks of losses with their greater hedonic weight than the correlative possible gains.

[48] Andrews and Withey, *Social Indicators of Well-Being*, 106.

[49] Daryl J. Bem, "Self-Perception Theory," in Leonard Berkowitz, ed., *Advances in Experimental Social Psychology*, vol. 6 (New York: Academic Press, 1972).

[50] Andrews and Withey, *Social Indicators of Well-Being*, 315. The weight to be given to these *general* estimates of the future is quite uncertain.

that increases in income will be greeted with more pleasure than if a steady upward gradient were mapped into people's minds. What we have here is evidence for a kind of persistence forecasting theory running counter to the popular "frustration of rising expectations" theory that predicts disappointment if there is no upward gradient. Inasmuch as both persistence forecasting and rising expectations have support elsewhere,[51] the outcome of adaptation processes is uncertain.

Recessions

Recessions offer recurring recent economic losses, and their ensuing economic upswings offer equivalent gains; they would seem to invite some of the short-term changes in mood that escape the adaptation-level phenomenon, even though adaptation is said to be "very fast."[52] There is, indeed, evidence of the effects of recessions on moods that confirms this inference. Andrews and Withey surveyed the American population in May 1972 during relatively good times and again in November of the same year when a recession had set in. In May, 27 percent of the population reported themselves as "very happy" and 9 percent as "not too happy." By November, the growing recession seemed to have decreased the "very happy" responses to 22 percent and increased the "not too happy" responses to 11 percent – not large but, supported by similar changes in other indices of well-being, sufficient to indicate that the direction of change was not a product of chance.[53] Inglehart and Rabier found that in the 1982–3 period their European respondents consistently reported themselves to be two or three percentage points happier and more satisfied with their lives than had been the case in the mid- and late 1970s when the interviews had been conducted during periods of recession.[54]

The importance is not "merely" hedonic; it has other psychological and economic implications as well. Psychologically, well-established learning theory laws state that interrupted benefits increase the time necessary for a habit to "extinguish," in this case for habitual expectations to face reality. Intermittent prosperity, such as the business cycle provides, delays the onset of the adaptation phenomena. (Rapid consumer responses to signals of change in the business cycle further exacerbate the swings of the business cycle.)[55]

Over the mid-term, say, a decade, shorter than would be the case for the relief of poverty in poor countries and longer than the usual recession, a decline in national income may have a disastrous effect on morale. GNP per capita fell considerably in Belgium over the 1973–83 decade, creating high unemployment and greatly deflating postwar expectations. Concurrently the life satisfactions of its members dropped

[51] See, for example, William Watts and Lloyd A. Free, *State of the Nation* (New York: Universe Books, 1973); Marylee C. Taylor, "Improved Conditions, Rising Expectations, and Dissatisfaction: A Test of the Past/Present Relative Deprivation Hypothesis," *Social Psychology Quarterly* 45 (1982): 24–33 at 24.

[52] For example, lottery winners adapt to their good fortune and paraplegics to their bad fortune very quickly. P. Brickman, D. Coates, and R. Janoff-Bulman," Lottery Winners and Accident Victims: Is Happiness Relative?" *Journal of Personality and Social Psychology* 35 (1978): 917–27, cited in Diener, "Subjective Well-Being," 567.

[53] Andrews and Withey, *Social Indicators of Well-Being*, 319.

[54] Inglehart and Rabier, "Aspirations Adapt to Situations," 12.

[55] George Katona, *Psychological Economics* (New York: Elsevier, 1975), chaps 7–8.

precipitously from second or third place in the European rankings to about ninth place, near the bottom. Commenting on this rapid decline, Inglehart and Rabier say: "Unless our indicators are totally erroneous, this phenomenon, in its impact on human happiness, dwarfed most events that make world headlines."[56] There could not be more dramatic illustration of the effect of *changes* of income, as contrasted to levels of income on sense of well-being.

The high hedonic toll taken by psychological insecurity has a basis in the fluctuations of the economy. The effects of recessions on mental health have been well (if somewhat controversially) analyzed;[57] their effects on feelings of well-being seem to be better established and equally disturbing.

Income changes: the benefits and costs of change
There are two theories of the effects of change per se that apply to income changes as they do to other kinds: (1) the benefits of novelty and arousal compared to familiarity and a more passive nonaroused state, and (2) the effects of life events, even benign ones, on well-being.

Novelty and arousal versus familiarity. In an extensive examination of choices of such heterogeneous objects as Turkish letters and Chinese characters, pictures of faces, words, and other objects, Zajonc found that familiarity was a major source of preference for an object. Favorable attitudes toward the objects in one's environment seem to qualify for one version of happiness, contentment. As Zajonc said, "Mere repeated exposure of the individual to a stimulus is a sufficient condition for the enhancement of his attitude toward it." He interprets Berlyne's work on curiosity as evidence of reduction of fear rather than liking the novel. Novelty in general, he says, is aversive.[58]

On the other hand, there is substantial evidence that "novelty" and arousal, *if within the range of tolerance of the individual,* increase well-being. In his analysis of quality-of-life data, Norman Bradburn finds that experiencing "novelty" (meeting a person for the first time, having a novel experience) markedly increases positive feelings (but does not influence negative feelings) and this accounts for some of the greater subjective well-being of the higher socioeconomic groups.[59] The basic theory is that of optimal arousal (Chapter 8), derived from physiological research and experimentation. Berlyne suggests that a prime condition for well-being is optimal arousal: individuals search for greater arousal if they have "time on their hands" and less arousal in periods of overload and excessive stimulation. The paradigm case of arousal of this kind is the instigation to inquiry (curiosity) when some anomaly or threat or dissonant situation appears; the organism then searches its environment to acquire information that, if satisfactory, permits subsidence of the

[56] Inglehart and Rabier, "Aspirations Adapt to Situations," 47.
[57] See M. Harvey Brenner, *Mental Illness and the Economy* (Cambridge: Harvard University Press, 1973); for criticism of Brenner's thesis, see Louis A. Ferman and Jeanne P. Gardus, eds., *Mental Health and the Economy* (Kalamazoo, MI: Institute for Employment Research, 1979).
[58] Robert B. Zajonc, "Attitudinal Effects of Mere Exposure," *Journal of Personality and Social Psychology* 9 (1968): Monograph Supplement 2, 1–27, at 1, 21.
[59] Norman Bradburn, *The Structure of Psychological Well-Being* (Chicago: Aldine, 1969), 133–5.

aroused state. Both arousal and its decline to a minimal state are satisfying; the vegetative state of lack of arousal is not satisfying, as when the bored individual actively seeks arousal.[60] Scitovsky has converted this theory to a critique of American economic behavior, claiming that in the modern American economy people are averse to arousal (which he calls "pleasure"), seeking only "comfort," instead[61] (Chapter 8).

What we would like tentatively to suggest is that income *changes* of all kinds increase arousal; if they are income increases, they will have favorable effects, as might be expected. If they are modest *decrements* of income and within the tolerance of the individual, they may, depending upon circumstances, also induce a pleasurable feeling of challenge, especially if the individual believes he or she can overcome this loss. The strong relationship between Andrews and Withey's "self-adjustment scale" and happiness comes into play in both cases. As mentioned in Chapter 23, that scale asks about "how tough you are," "the way you handle problems," and "adjustment to changes in life." In one survey this was the second most powerful predictor of satisfaction with life-as-a-whole.[62] Here, then, is a very different meaning to the term adaptation – adapting to life's challenges – and it is not satisfied by habituation but rather by active coping.

The costs of life events. Life events, both good and bad, range in their disruptive effects of familiar routine from minor uncertainty involved in taking out a small mortgage or of the marriage of a grown child to the major disturbance of changing jobs, and, at the extreme, the death of a spouse (Chapters 8, 14). These life events, again both good and bad, may be scaled in terms of the disruption of a life. The important point is that the higher the score on this scale, the more likely is a person to be physically ill or mentally disturbed for a short period following the event.[63] A change of income is clearly such an event.

Recall how the guaranteed income experiments discussed in Chapter 9 revealed the disruptive effect of even the benign change in income for the subjects of the experiments: The changed income arrangements *increased* distress and family instability. The rate of family dissolution in the group whose familiar patterns of life were changed by the guaranteed income was significantly higher than in a matched control group at the same poverty level that did not have guaranteed incomes but coped as best they could in the manner familiar to them, often since birth.[64]

[60] Daniel E. Berlyne, *Structure and Direction in Thinking* (New York: Wiley, 1965), 251–5.

[61] Tibor Scitovsky, *The Joyless Economy* (New York: Oxford University Press, 1976), 58 and chap. 4 passim. Scitovsky's theory should be adjusted for Jonathan Freedman's findings to the effect that happiness is a balance of active pleasures and passive rest and security – or comfort. See Freedman, *Happy People.*

[62] Andrews and Withey, *Social Indicators of Well-Being,* 112, 115.

[63] Thomas H. Holmes and Minoru Masuda, "Life Change and Susceptibility to Illness," in Barbara Snell Dohrenwend and Bruce P. Dohrenwend, eds., *Stressful Life Events* (New York: Wiley, 1974). It is not entirely clear whether benign events have the same kind of disruptive effect as do malign events; the literature is conflicted.

[64] "White husbands on the 5-year treatment in Denver and black husbands on the 3-year treatment in Seattle respond with significantly increased distress . . . [and the distress] appears to become larger over time. . . . Among married women . . ., white and black wives on the 5-year treatment in Denver exhibit significantly increased distress at both time points." Peggy Thoits and Michael Hannan, "Income

The stress of adapting to a new situation certainly contributed to the increased distress among the participants in the guaranteed income program, but ancillary effects might come from depriving the recipients of the need to cope as they had learned to do – the satisfactions outlined in the "self-adjustment scale." It would be cruel as well as inappropriate to use Scitovsky's language and say of these members of the poor that they had too much "comfort" (and not enough "pleasure"), but it may be that they missed some of the requisite "arousal" they had learned to accept and use.

In any event, the case seems to relieve the market of some – a tiny fraction – of the blame for failing to provide sufficient financial security. But it would be equally plausible to say that under current circumstances *only* the market can provide the security of *earned* income, the income security that is not aversive – and that it has failed to do so.

If recessions and other shorter term economic changes have these infelicitous effects and yet the *growth effect* (or its consequence, affluence) derived from long-term economic growth is so benign, how may these be reconciled? We turn to that next.

Adaptation to longer term changes in income

Unlike recessions, continuous economic development may invoke adaptation responses just as surely as static levels of income – subject to the caveat on responses to progress mentioned, for people may adapt to a sloping gradient of expectations as they do to a static one. The consequent frustration of rising expectations seems to fit the American case, for, as we have said, Americans are more likely than Europeans to say that they will be severely upset if their incomes do not increase year by year, with almost three-fifths saying they "would be outright dissatisfied" if they are not financially better off in five years.[65]

Lest the problem of rising, and therefore always vulnerable, expectations be attributed to the market's excessive promises and its continuous generation of new wants, we must put the matter in the context of other forces. These rising expectations may well be due to influences more deeply rooted than American economic optimism, for there seems to be a tendency (discovered in an American sample, to be sure) for people to believe that each person's own chances for positive events are above average and his or her chances for negative events are below average. "People are unrealistically optimistic because they focus on factors that improve their own chances of achieving desirable outcomes and fail to realize that others may have just as many factors in their favor."[66] This optimism, part of a larger

and Psychological Distress: The Impact of an Income-Maintenance Experiment," *Journal of Health and Social Behavior* 20 (1979): 120–38 at 131–2, 133, 134–5. The authors are careful to avoid exaggerating their findings; most members of the experimental group were not affected (but none were *relieved* of distress); the guaranteed income was relatively small; most of the distress could be accounted for by other aspects of the subjects lives.

[65] Strumpel et al., "Economic Life-Styles, Values, and Subjective Welfare," 61. This is especially true of managers. (p. 54)

[66] Neil D. Weinstein, "Unrealistic Optimism About Future Life Events," *Journal of Personality and Social Psychology* 39 (1980): 806–20 at 806.

positivity bias,[67] is extremely resistant to rational correction, grossly inflating "rational expectations." Rising expectations have powerful, if misleading, psychological allies.

The point is important for it suggests that the *growth effect,* which Inkeles and Diamond show makes a genuine contribution to well-being, now seems to run into the same adaptation level phenomena that partially impairs the capacity of money to increase individual's sense of well-being over time. Stable growth may simply raise the stakes so that absolute gains less than the anticipated ones add to dissatisfaction. Why, then, contrary to Easterlin's hypothesis, does economic growth improve hedonic ratings when, in the static case, richer individuals do not show much higher degrees of life satisfaction than poorer individuals?

Adaptation: differences between individual enrichment and collective economic growth

The answer must lie partly in the differences in circumstances that the two ways of being economically better off create, and partly in the different psychological processes employed.

1. HEDONIC YIELD AMONG THE POOR. By reducing infant mortality, illness, penury, dependency on relatives and charity, long queues for necessities, and hopelessness, economic growth provides more favorable conditions for more members of the society, the poor as well as the rich. Equally important is the fact that income increases among the less well off have a higher hedonic yield than income increases to the better off.

2. LESS RELIANCE ON SOCIAL COMPARISON. Where differences between the rich and poor rely principally on social comparisons, economic growth can invoke four of the comparisons mentioned in connection with the gap theory: achievement gap, actuality–ideal gap, self-comparisons with previous conditions, and the increased adequacy of meeting needs. Social comparisons are muted by the fact that others' incomes increase along with one's own, and expectations in a constantly growing economy may have been discounted by the adaptation-level phenomena. In the case of growth, social comparisons are often less important than self-comparisons,[68] and with the exception of downward comparisons by the already unhappy, social comparisons do not yield as much life satisfaction.[69]

3. EQUALITY OF INCOMES. Although people do not want enforced equality of income,[70] they nevertheless prefer to live in a society where there are fewer large discrepancies of income, or at least where there are fewer embarrassing poor. There is some evidence for this, but it is not a powerful force.[71] If Kuznets is right, the

[67] David Sears and Richard Whitney, *Political Persuasion* (Morristown, NJ: General Learning Press, 1973); Sears, "The Person-Positivity Bias," *Journal of Personality and Social Psychology* 44 (February 1983): 233–58; Margaret Matlin and David J. Stang, *The Pollyana Principle: Selectivity in Language, Memory, and Thought* (Cambridge: Schenkman, 1978).

[68] Campbell et al., *The Quality of American Life*, chap. 6.

[69] As mentioned earlier, Andrews and Withey found that their battery of comparative questions were not as good predictors of subjective well-being as straightforward questions that did not ask for social comparisons. See their *Social Indicators of Well-Being*, 168.

[70] Robert E. Lane, "The Fear of Equality," *American Political Science Review* 53 (1959): 35–51.

[71] Lee Rainwater, *What Money Buys: Inequality and the Social Meaning of Income* (New York: Basic Books, 1974).

later stages of economic growth accommodate this modest preference by equalizing incomes to a small extent.[72]

4. SELF-ATTRIBUTION FOR GAINS DUE TO ECONOMIC GROWTH. People attribute their socially increased income to their own efforts and in this way meet the conditions of the "achievement gap" already mentioned – and without the pain of sacrifice entailed in winning victories in a static or declining economy.[73] The dark side of this misattribution is that many members of the labor force expect income increases without doing anything to earn them,[74] severing the relation between effort and reward.

5. REDUCING SORROWS. Social wealth reduces the absolute number and severity of sorrows more effectively and across a wider spectrum than individual wealth, and the reduction of sorrow has more hedonic weight than increasing joy.

6. NATIONAL PROGRESS. Some satisfaction is received from a sense of American national progress, a satisfaction that is concealed when, as is usually the case, people appraise their own futures optimistically and the nation's future rather pessimistically.[75] But it *is* only concealed, for American pride in the nation's economic prowess is quite substantial in comparison with pride expressed in other countries.[76]

7. SOCIOTROPIC SATISFACTIONS. There seems to be an influence, however muted, produced by concepts of the public interest on decisions – and of perhaps moods as well. For example, from the voting studies, it appears that (1) "good times" is an independent criterion for vote decisions,[77] and (2) people tend to vote more according to whether the general society is seen to benefit than according to their own benefits from recent policies.[78] These judgments may stem from a belief that what is good for the nation is good for me, but this, in turn, is likely to be based on the opaqueness of personal benefits from public policy.

The affluence effect does not abolish adaptation-level phenomenon; rather, it provides a new and higher standard around which adaptation processes may take place. Whatever the causes, there is marked irony in this hedonistic advantage of social wealth over private wealth in a market society, for social wealth is a public

[72] Simon Kuznets, "Economic Growth and Income Inequality," *American Economic Review* 45 (1955): 1–28.

[73] Robert E. Lane, *Political Ideology: Why the American Common Man Believes What He Does* (New York: Free Press, 1962).

[74] "Higher incomes were impatiently desired. The classic mechanism for coping with high and unfulfilled consumption aspirations is the stepping up of effort – working more or striving for advancement. Yet in the blue-collar stratum, respondents seemed to expect progress in the form of general increases in wage and salary levels rather than from changes in the individual roles within the production set up." Strumpel et al., "Economic Life-Styles, Values, and Subjective Welfare," 59.

[75] Watts and Free, *State of the Nation*.

[76] Eighty four percent of an American national sample expressed pride in their work compared to 43% of Europeans (eleven countries) and 37% of the Japanese. Eighty percent of Americans also expressed "pride in country" compared to 55% of the British, 33% of the French, 30% of the Japanese, and only 21% of the West Germans. Surveys sponsored by the Center for Applied Research in the Apostolate, *New York Times*, 19 May 1920.

[77] Angus Campbell, Philip E. Converse, Warren E. Miller, and Donald E. Stokes, *The American Voter* (New York: Wiley, 1960).

[78] Donald R. Kinder and D. Roderick Kiewiet, "Economic Discontents and Political Behavior: The Role of Personal Grievances and Collective Economic Judgments in Congressional Voting," *American Journal of Political Science* 23 (1979): 495–527.

or collective good, precisely the kind of good that the market is supposed to fail to provide, and is regularly, if reluctantly, turned over to government for nurturance and provision.

Like most environmental circumstances, the social wealth producing the *affluence effect* becomes part of the background to which people adapt. But it is the "figures" in a perceptual field that attract attention, as the research on "the availability heuristic" (the immediate, personal, and vivid dominate the more palid background) shows. Specifically, it is the individual's income and not society's income that is salient. We turn to one aspect of this process, the meaning of wanting money.

The meaning of wanting money

In Chapter 23 I outlined the dimensions of wanting, pointing out that the intensity of desire for an object was not always measured by what an individual was willing to sacrifice (or at least did sacrifice) for that object. This was most obviously true for interpersonal comparisons, but even within a single budget, time lags and consumer rents made the prices paid inadequate measures of intensity of desire. In the case of money, I said that criticisms of the desire for money (avarice) were considered justified only when applied to those who already have a decent sufficiency, that research revealed that the identification of money with happiness was more characteristic of traditional than market societies, and that, in any event, it was fear of loss of money rather than the desire for gain that was most urgently felt. In the context of this discussion of "buying happiness," certain additional features of wanting money are relevant.

Identifying money with happiness

I turn again to Richard Easterlin for my thesis: Is it true that "for many Americans, the pursuit of happiness and the pursuit of money come to much the same thing"?[79] (Chapter 17). Given the slight relationship between money and happiness, how could the American people have been so deceived? To answer that question (more fully examined in the next chapter) we must explore the meaning of wanting money. There are five lines of evidence that support the view that Americans and others in modern economies do not tend to identify money with happiness.

First, we take the occasion provided by Easterlin's reference to Americans to make a larger point on cultural variations in the desire for money.[80] The evidence

---

[79] Easterlin, "Does Money Buy Happiness?" 3. As reported in Chapter 22 on understanding happiness, Max Lerner shared this same view of Americans. Max Lerner, *America As a Civilization: Life and Thought in the United States Today* (New York: Simon & Schuster, 1957), 693.

[80] Cultural norms also influence the emotionality of responses. For example, " 'In Japanese society, people are expected to restrain themselves and express modesty.' It would seem immodest to say that one is *very* satisfied with one's life, or very happy." As a consequence, Japanese responses tend to be limited to "reasonably satisfied," "not very satisfied," and "dissatisfied" with their lives. Inglehart and Rabier, "Aspirations Adapt to Situations," 45. The internal quotation is from Iijima (1982). Americans have no such inhibition. *Within* the American culture, however, tendencies toward more extreme responses do not seem to affect responses: Andrews and Withey assessed individual responses in an effort to get a norm for each person, but found that these did not greatly affect the ranking of their answers or their contributions to overall life satisfaction.

dealing with attitudes in the American culture answers the narrow national question fairly conclusively. The story has a historical dimension. In a predominantly agricultural age, Tocqueville said of Americans: "I know of no country . . . where the love of money has taken a stronger hold on the affections of men." Later evidence suggests that this is a misinterpretation and that money in Tocqueville's France has a much "stronger hold on the affections of men." A 1946 national survey asked respondents in several countries: "Will you tell me in your own words what the word 'happiness' means to you?" Fewer than one-eighth (12%) of a U.S. sample thought of happiness in terms of "money, sufficient money, good wages, and wealth," whereas more than half (52%) of the French defined happiness that way. In contrast, Americans tended (44%) to think of happiness as "contentment, freedom from worry, adjustment to surroundings, peace, quiet," whereas few of the French (12%) shared this view.[81] That this is a genuine cultural difference (and not an artifact of postwar conditions) is suggested by a comparison in the 1970s of the sources of subjective well-being in British Canada and French Canada. "In their evaluation of life-as-a-whole the English-speaking group put greater weight on the quality of leisure, whereas the French emphasized financial considerations. The finding would appear to reflect profound cultural differences in the perception of well-being."[82] (As a further suggestion that *love of money* does not lead to happiness, we note that France ranks at the bottom among the European nations where national feelings of well-being have been measured.)[83] One reason why money does not buy happiness in Anglo-American countries, and perhaps in Protestant countries more generally, is because people in these cultures do not identify happiness with money. Very few Americans at least believe that "the pursuit of happiness and the pursuit of money come to much the same thing." The short answer to the allegation that Americans identify money with happiness, then, is that it is simply wrong; Americans pursue happiness but with more varied goals in mind.

Second, as the data from Rokeach's studies discussed in Chapter 22 reveal, Americans do not rank the value of wealth very high in ordering their values.[84] The data suggest that a prosperous life (money) is seen as either a less honorable goal or a less attractive option than peace, security for one's family, freedom, equality, or self-respect – and at least four other values. Again, it seems that Americans are

[81] Hadley Cantril, ed., *Public Opinion 1935–1946*, prepared by Mildred Strunk (Princeton: Princeton University Press, 1951), 181. The polls were conducted by The American, French, British, and Canadian Institutes of Public Opinion (Gallup) and were all carried out in 1946.

[82] Aubrey McKennel, Tom Atkinson, and Frank M. Andrews, "Structural Constancies in Surveys of Perceived Well-Being," in Szalai and Andrews, *The Quality of Life*, 111–28 at 121.

[83] Ronald Inglehart, "Values, Objective Needs, and Subjective Satisfactions Among Western Publics," *Comparative Political Studies* 9 (1977): 429–58 at 443.

[84] Milton Rokeach, "Change and Stability in American Value Systems, 1968–1971," *Public Opinion Quarterly* 38 (1974): 222–38. In both years "a world at peace" was ranked first, reflecting the war weariness of the later Viet Nam period, followed (1971) by (2) "family security," (3) "freedom," (4) "equality," and (5) "self-respect." "Social recognition" was seventeenth, and "an exciting life" was eighteenth. For a comparable study of Australian values, see Norman T. Feather, *Values in Education and Society* (New York: Free Press, 1975), 209. Since Australians ranked "a comfortable, prosperous life" much lower than Americans, it might be inferred that they were less materialistic than (but equally hedonistic as) Americans, but their first choice, "family security" undermines this interpretation.

not so materialistic as Easterlin (and many, many others) thought; they place personal wealth in a perspective that gives precedence to other values.

Third, from the same study one derives not only a ranking of the value of personal prosperity, but also information on how the two values, prosperity and happiness, are related. The fact that the public had no difficulty in choosing between them is already evidence of the lack of identification of the two in the public mind. Happiness ranks fourth (1968) or sixth (1971) among American values; as mentioned, a prosperous life ranks ninth or thirteenth. The priority of happiness over prosperity is substantial; the correlation between the two is not high; they are different values. Whether this distinction and ranking means (1) some respondents value happiness without earned income – a hedonist's view, or (2) that money is not important to happiness – a humanistic view, or (3) the higher value, happiness, may be pursued in many ways of which wealth is only one, is unclear. What is clear is that happiness is not the first value and it is ranked above and separately from prosperity, both damaging to Easterlin's thesis.

Fourth, the allusion to the identification of happiness with wealth in Chapter 23 may be elaborated here. Studies of developing societies show that it is the traditional villagers and not the modern urban workers who identify happiness with wealth. In Inkeles and Smith's examination of attitudes and beliefs in six developing countries, they found that responses to the proposition that "the more things a man possesses – like new clothes, furniture, and conveniences – the happier he is," were *negatively* correlated with other modern attitudes. Identification of possessions with happiness characterized those who remained in their traditional, largely unmarketized villages, although responses to the proposition that "a man should always strive to make more money, so that he can buy more, better, and different things" were positively correlated with other clearly "modern" attitudes.[85] It is "modern" to believe that more money *contributes* to well-being; it is archaic to believe that money and possessions *constitute* happiness.

Fifth, in one of the quality-of-life studies, very few people ranked money (in this case a savings account) as one of their most important life goals. Two percent of the population think of having "a large bank account so that you don't have to worry about money" as one of two primary sources of their well-being. This 2 percent is largely composed of people who feel *deprived* of money, not those who have it, for money is the only resource that has increased importance for those who *do not* have it. In contrast, compared to the married, the unmarried do not think of marriage as important for a happy life; compared to the educated, the uneducated do not think of education as more important; compared to those with more friends,

---

[85] Alex Inkeles and David H. Smith, *Becoming Modern* (Cambridge: Harvard University Press, 1974), 326. The distinction between wanting more possessions and identifying money or possessions with happiness is uniquely expressed in this study. Others (including Marshall and Schumpeter) have also found the developing countries highly materialistic – at least as materialistic as the more developed market societies. For example, Leonard Doob's analysis of people in modernizing countries finds "the material aspects of [modern] life seem especially attractive. . . . Gains . . . are easily recognizable, although in the long run they may also prove to be in part illusory." Doob, *Becoming More Civilized* (New Haven: Yale University Press, 1960), 247. These findings support the trend expressed in Inglehart's theory of the growth of postmaterialist values, but not his causal theory.

those with fewer do not think friendship more important. It is the *lack* of money that increases its importance. But even in this group the meaning of their interest in money is unclear, for the question confounds financial security with wealth; other evidence suggests that it is the phrase "not have to worry" about finances that is most attractive to them, and this other evidence demonstrates that relief of financial worries and insecurities rather than greater affluence is the major contribution to satisfaction with life-as-a-whole.[86]

The realism of this tiny group of avowed materialists deserves comment. For this small group of subjectively defined "materialists," the larger their actual incomes, the happier they actually were (regression coefficient .33). The religious and the civic minded are not so realistic, for they put their faith in matters that, statistically, do not contribute to life satisfaction.[87]

Economic man

There is little gain in killing economic man again, but to remind ourselves of the symptoms of his mortal illness we will point out the obvious. (1) Jobs are not evaluated primarily in terms of their pay; for example, in one ranking of what makes work satisfying – challenge, friendly coworkers, adequate resources for doing the job, and two other considerations – all had priority over the level of pay.[88] (2) Occupational prestige is not ranked according to income. Thus, in the United States the top ranks are: U.S. Supreme Court Justice, physician, state governor, cabinet member, diplomat, mayor of a large city, college professor, scientist, U.S. Representative in Congress – and then, only in tenth place, is "banker."[89] (3) Over the past fifty years the people in market economies have taken much of their new wealth in leisure – almost as much as they have taken in goods, with the leisure used not to increase earning power but for entertainment, especially watching television.[90] (4) Although income-relevant issues influence voting, no known constituencies in any market society vote straight pocketbook interests; in the United States political choices are decreasingly predictable on the basis of income.[91]

[86] Andrews and Withey, *Social Indicators of Well-Being,* 141.

[87] In the Campbell et al. study the quarter of the population who thought that "having a strong religious faith" was one of the two things in life that contributed most to their happiness were least likely, as a group, to be right, for in fact there was almost no relation between having such a faith and scoring high on the index of well-being (regression coefficient .107). Similarly, the sixth of the population who believed that living in "a country with a good government" was one of the two most important things contributing to their well-being were also wrong, for those who held that belief were not more satisfied with their lives than others (regression coefficient .149). The third of the population who believed that having a good marriage or a good family life was what made them happy were, on the basis of the evidence, almost certainly right. Campbell et al., *The Quality of American Life,* 84–5, 91.

[88] Robert P. Quinn and Linda Shepard, *The 1972–73 Quality of Employment Survey* (Ann Arbor, MI: Institute for Social Research, 1974); Daniel Yankelovich and John Immerwahr, *Putting the Work Ethic to Work* (New York: Public Agenda Foundation, 1983).

[89] See Donald J. Trieman, *Occupational Prestige in Comparative Perspective* (New York: Academic Press, 1977).

[90] On the proportion of new income taken in leisure, see William D. Nordhaus and James Tobin, "Is Growth Obsolete?" in Milton Moss, ed., *The Measurement of Economic and Social Performance,* vol. 38 of *Studies in Income and Wealth* (New York: National Bureau of Economic Research, 1973); on the uses of that leisure, see John P. Robinson, "Changes in Time Use: An Historical Overview," in Juster and Stafford, *Time, Goods, and Well-Being.*

[91] See Donald R. Kinder and D. Roderick Kiewiet, "Sociotropic Politics: The American Case," *British*

The effects of economic growth revisited

The materialist treadmill and the postmaterialist release

Duncan's study showing that as social affluence increased over a fifteen-year period, the amount of money required to provide a given level of financial satisfaction increased in nearly exact proportion[92] seems to be a confirmation of what has been called "the hedonic treadmill."[93] In line with other adaptation theories, this predicts that the consequence of economic growth is to raise the price of satisfaction or happiness by an amount proportionate to that of the increase in real income. Worse, with continued economic growth the hedonic value of money declines, and if one continues to focus on money, it will take proportionately *more* money to buy what any given amount bought before.

There is an escape by changing either or both "concerns" and "domains," as we have seen in Chapters 23 and 25. Inglehart's report that steady economic growth in the postwar period has developed a group of "postmaterialists" whose socialization in circumstances of relative affluence and security has therefore led them to value various forms of participation and freedom more than income and financial security, reveals a shift in both concerns and domains. In no country is the group very large; in the United States it represents about 10 percent of a national sample, but elements of the postmaterialist syndrome infect a much larger proportion of the population.[94] This, and other evidence,[95] suggests two things: (1) For materialists, that is, people who come closer to identifying their life goals and satisfaction with money, the effect of affluence may indeed be to increase the price of life satisfaction at least proportionately to the increases in per capita GNP and possibly disproportionately greater. If materialists do not at least maintain their pace on this treadmill, especially in the United States, they will be bitterly disappointed.

But (2) economic growth has its own remedy: Growth increases the pursuit of values other than money among these postmaterialist (and other)[96] groups for whom level of income has a minimal effect on life satisfaction.[97] In terms of the quality-of-life studies, this means substituting goods offered in the family, leisure, interpersonal, and community domains for goods offered in the economic domain. It is only the materialists, and not the postmaterialists and others who have transcended

Journal of Political Science 11 (1981): 129–61; Kinder and Kiewiet, "Economic Discontents and Political Behavior.

[92] Duncan, "Does Money Buy Satisfaction?"

[93] Philip Brickman and Donald T. Campbell, "Hedonic Relativism and Planning the Good Society," in M. H. Appley, ed., *Adaptation-Level Theory: A Symposium* (New York: Academic Press, 1971).

[94] Ronald Inglehart, *The Silent Revolution* (Princeton: Princeton University Press, 1972); Idem, "Post-Materialism in an Environment of Insecurity," *American Political Science Review* 75 (1981): 880–900, data on the United States at p. 888. Confirming the dependence of postmaterialist values on economic growth, Inglehart further found that as economic growth declined in the 1970s and 1980s, the proportion of postmaterialists in the newest cohorts of adults also declined, but as the older cohort of postmaterialists moved through the life cycle, they retained their value priorities and increased their influence along with their increasing status.

[95] Ronald Inglehart, "Changing Values in Japan and the West," *Comparative Political Studies* 14 (1982): 445–79.

[96] See, for example, Veroff et al., *The Inner Americans*.

[97] Inglehart and Rabier, "Aspirations Adapt to Situations," 32.

market values, who are on a *hedonic treadmill*. Escape from the treadmill comes by pursuing a set of noneconomic interests whose marginal utility is higher than that of the one pursued on the treadmill.

The shrinking of the incidence of urgency

The adaptation-level theory says the demand for income increases more rapidly than the increase in "money supply," that is, disproportionately to increasing per capita GNP. A countertheory relies on declining *urgency* of desire, an urgency that has two components: physiological needs and socially determined aspirations. To the extent that economic growth increasingly meets everyone's physiological needs (which will not occur unless the proceeds of growth are redistributed by governments – itself a product of affluence), only the second source of urgency is operative. The incidence of this reduction of physiological needs is among lower socioeconomic groups. But the upper end of the social spectrum also has causes for declining urgency, for that is where postmaterialism reduces the urgency of desire for money. Only the massive materialist middle remains vulnerable to socially defined urgencies, a group left relatively untouched by these changes at either end of the social scale.

Summary

New evidence shows that economic growth *does* increase a sense of well-being in a national community but being richer than others in any society *does not,* or at least not nearly as much as the ideology and premises of the market would suggest. Money does not buy happiness for individuals because it does not buy the things that make most people happiest, a happy family life, friends, enjoyment of work, and a sense of accomplishment therein. But also, as we saw in the earlier discussion of the capacity of markets to influence pain and pleasure, people's own constitutional dispositions and their abilities to cope with misfortune alter the effects of money stimuli. As it happens, too, many of the ordinary pleasures of life are cheap; perhaps for this reason security of income is often hedonically more important than amount of income. Even in an amoral market economy, priority of equity values sometimes displaces material values.

Recent *changes* in income, on the other hand, do greatly affect well-being, partly because adaptation has not yet set in and because recurring recessions are short enough to escape the adaptation process. These recessions, therefore, inflict great pain on many members of a population. A sharp downturn has major hedonic effects, not least because losses are more important than gains, thus making the increased income of the postwar period less hedonically influential. Sharp changes in income incur the trauma associated with major "life events."

In the longer term, adaptation to rising expectations will set in (especially in the American setting), not only because of market promises, but because the modern human psyche is disposed to expect the self to be favored. The following sets of forces work to reduce rapid adaptation to economic growth: Growth tends to help the poor as well as the rich, and the poor have higher happiness yields from improved income; broad income increases enlist more self-referential standards, whereas individual increases invite more social comparisons that are known to reduce well-being; people attribute their income rises to their own efforts, an attribution that enhances everyone's satisfaction; the nature of growth is to reduce sorrows, which has greater hedonic effect than attempting to increase joys; people take pride in national gains; and people interpret evidence of national well-being as evidence of their own well-being.

With a few final comments on economic man, I offered reasons why it is implausible to believe that Americans, or modern people generally, tend to *identify* happiness with money, although they are likely to believe that money *contributes* to their happiness.

Escape from adaptation theory's hedonic treadmill is possible by adopting values outside of the economic realm; growth tends to shift the values of those socialized in prosperity and security in this direction. The poor are relieved of some of the urgency of their needs for money by economic growth, and rich professionals are relieved by postmaterialist values; only the striving middle class seems unaffected by these forces, reducing the urgency of the demand for more money.

27 Misinterpreting happiness and satisfaction in a market society

Introduction

It is much more important for people's well-being that their preferences genuinely express their authentic values and the deepest, least conflicted elements of their personalities than that their market choices be consistent or meet other formal criteria for economic rationality. On reflection, one finds it astonishing that the analyses of economic choices whose purpose is to maximize satisfaction should devote so much attention to the relatively minor problems of transitivity and consistency when the relation between what is chosen and long-term satisfaction is ignored.

In this chapter we will examine this relationship between the choices people make and their long-term satisfaction. In the process I will put in context the particular problem of the previous chapter: What accounts for the persistent belief that money is so important to happiness? We will look first at some preliminary evidence in the quality-of-life studies suggesting people's misinterpretation of their own moods, and then proceed to explore several sources of misinterpretation, such as the separation of thought and feeling in assessing one's well-being; the pursuit of desires that are compensatory for other, frustrated, primary desires; the way people misinterpret their ambiguous feelings of arousal; and how they may, without realizing it, violate biologically favored programs. Following each of these psychological explanations we turn to market sources and consequences of such misinterpretation.

As mentioned, my principal thesis is that happiness and a satisfying life have much more to do with an accurate assessment of the sources of one's feelings of well-being than with "rational expectations," transitive preferences, marginal equivalences, and objective payoff matrices. The inward-looking assessments of feelings are much more complex and prone to error than seems apparent on the surface,[1] and probably more difficult to achieve than the assessments asked of rational economic man. Assessing our market-derived happiness means, then, that we must interpret our own mood correctly and be able to explain what caused it. Only then can we expect to maximize well-being and minimize ill-being. Our problem is to discern those market forces that contribute to or inhibit these crucial judgmental difficulties and to look at the market consequences of such misinterpretations.

This chapter adds to the analysis of many of the preceding chapters. For example, we can see now a new facet to the systemic analysis of the market suggested in Chapter 2: There are *two* equally important interacting systems involved in the market experience, the personality system and the social system. From time to time I have referred to features of the personality system; this chapter extends those references. The discussion of the failure of rationality assumptions outlined in Chapter

---

[1] Psychiatrist Paul Wachtel reports: "People are not clear about what really makes them happy or what the consequences are of various patterns that are central to their lives." See his *The Poverty of Affluence: A Psychological Portrait of the American Way of Life* (New York: Free Press, 1983), 288.

3 is supplemented here by a new understanding of the prior problem of interpreting what it is that provides one with satisfaction, the satisfaction for which rational processes may then be useful. In Chapter 4 we spoke of the sources of emotional arousal; here I show the difficulty people have in locating those sources. We puzzled in Part V over why people fail to see that it is in their work lives that they find their most satisfactory experiences; this chapter contributes to our understanding of that puzzle. Intrinsic satisfactions treated in Part VI depend upon self-rewards; here I show how difficult it is to know what is rewarding to the self. In short, I deal here with some of the most important clues to the way the market contributes to people's happiness and satisfaction with their lives-as-a-whole.

People do not know what makes them happy

Ignorance of the sources of happiness and the quality-of-life studies. One will not find ready acceptance of the idea that people are ignorant of the sources of their own happiness or their satisfaction with life-as-a-whole because most people are confident that they do know what gives them satisfaction. Yet, satisfaction on particulars and satisfaction with life-as-a-whole (or happiness) are different.

In the first instance, the quality-of-life studies pose questions on particulars, registers of people's feelings (like/dislike, satisfaction/dissatisfaction) on a variety of "concerns" located in various departments of life. For the most part, these questions pose no great difficulty for respondents; I shall mention a few apparently inauthentic responses, but I could not locate many.[2]

The analysis that follows here does not undermine the data I have reported but, rather: (1) helps to account for the remainder of the variance, (2) offers a possible prior set of variables, influencing and perhaps "contaminating," but not invalidating, both the specific and the general questions asked, and (3) supports the following proposition to the effect that observers with superior theories can account for moods better than can the person experiencing the moods.

Importance and inauthenticity. The first bit of evidence to support the claim of ignorance on the sources of one's happiness refers to Andrews and Withey's previously reported finding that there was a slight *negative* correlation between what people thought was important in their lives and what the data said was important; this has been duplicated in other studies.[3] The data will show that, like the

---

[2] The questions focused more on satisfaction than on happiness (although the two are highly correlated). Andrews and Withey: "How do you feel about your life as a whole?" (asked twice in each interview); Campbell, Converse, and Rodgers: an index composed of a straightforward question on satisfaction with one's life combined with the score on a semantic differential covering ten various aspects of life such as "boring/interesting, useless/worthwhile, lonely/friendly." For an assessment of validity, see footnote 35 in Chapter 22 in this text, and Frank M. Andrews and Stephen B. Withey, *Social Indicators of Well-Being: Americans' Perceptions of Life Quality* (New York: Plenum Press, 1976); Angus Campbell, Philip E. Converse, and Willard L. Rodgers, *The Quality of American Life* (New York: Russell Sage, 1976), chaps 2 and 4.

[3] Andrews and Withey, *Social Indicators of Well-Being*, 242–3; Campbell et al., *The Quality of American Life*, 82–93.

erroneous belief that religious fulfillment leads to happiness, the belief in the power of money to induce happiness is similarly misleading.

In the nature of things, examples of choices reflecting conflict between superficial feelings and authentic desires contributing to more deeply felt satisfactions with life-as-a-whole are hard to document, but we can suggest a few instances where the choices seem to be inauthentic." When housewives, who, compared to working women, "are much more likely to be anxious and worried, lonely, and to feel worthless," yet report themselves just as happy as working women, one suspects inauthentic, but not consciously false, responses.[4] When most people speak of their unqualified "delight" with their children but in almost every survey married individuals are happier before the children come and after they leave the home, one suspects that people are thinking of themselves as "delighted" with their children because they feel they *should* experience such delight, but actually have feelings that do not support such very positive thoughts.[5] It is not possible to explain these findings by any general "positivity bias," because these responses contrast with other expressions on matters where obligation and social norms are more ambiguous and yet where very critical and unhappy assessments are frequent.[6] These pressures to think of oneself as happy, or even "delighted," are strongest in the family domain but notably absent when commenting on government in the United States. The difference reflects the tendency to invest more emotion in areas where one can do something about an infelicitous situation, as well as the difference in social norms.

In this preliminary explication of evidence that people misinterpret both their degrees of satisfaction or happiness and the causes of their thoughts and feelings, two things stand out: (1) The separation of thought and feeling is quite common and not necessarily a symptom of pathology (Chapter 4), and (2) like ideologies (of which they are a part), accounts of satisfaction or happiness are not merely reports or neutral explanations but are functional statements that further or retard "extraneous" purposes.

Ego-alien and inauthentic choices

Preferences that genuinely express people's authentic values and the deepest, least conflicted elements of their personality are, as I've said, crucial for market decisions that maximize overall life satisfaction and happiness. Without authenticity, the rationality of people's calculations can only lead to second-best states.[7] Tversky and Kahneman say:

---

[4] Philip Shaver and Jonathan Freedman, "Your Pursuit of Happiness," *Psychology Today* 10 (August 1976): 27–32, 75 at 29.

[5] Andrews and Withey, *Social Indicators of Well-Being*, 265–7.

[6] "Psychologists have long been aware that human subjects, asked to make ratings of almost anything, tend to use the positive side of the rating scale more heavily than the negative side." Campbell et al., *The Quality of American Life*, 99.

[7] James G. March goes beyond the usual concepts of "bounded rationality" to suggest that to the various forms of rationality there should be added concepts of choice mechanisms embracing *future* as well as current preferences. See his "Bounded Rationality, Ambiguity, and the Engineering of Choice," *The*

Consistency is only one aspect of the lay notion of rational behavior. . . . The common concept of rationality also requires that preferences as utilities for particular outcomes should be predictive of satisfaction or displeasure, associated with their occurrences. Thus, a man could be judged irrational either because his preferences are contradictory or because his desires and aversions do not reflect his pleasures and pains.[8]

The discovery of one's most genuinely satisfying preferences seems to refer to the selection of ends while rationality refers to means,[9] but in a more fundamental sense, choosing the best means to poorly selected ends can hardly be thought rational.

I employ two sets of terms to describe different facets of genuinely satisfying choices: "ego-syntonic"/"ego-alien" and "authentic"/"inauthentic." Although the ego terms generally refer to unconscious processes and the authenticity terms refer to more conscious processes, for our purposes these distinctions are not important and I use them to point to various aspects of the same phenomenon.

Ego-syntonic or authentic choices (1) are congruent with the most stable and firmly held *beliefs* of the individual; (2) are resonant with and satisfy the individual's long term *interests;* (3) express the individual's deepest and most keenly felt *emotions;* and (4) serve the individual's dominant *values.*[10] *Ego-alien* choices lack these properties.

One of the psychoanalytic meanings of ego-alien hinges on *repression,* that is, the denial of desires hidden in the unconscious, hidden or repressed because they are unacceptable to the conscious mind. The ego-alien includes choices based on the pursuit of *neurotic gain,* e. g., the temporary and misleading advantages derived, say, by the agoraphobe from staying indoors. Fortunately, there is another psychoanalytic version that does not require the machinery of repression. In this version, ego-alien means intellectual conviction discrepant with characterological preference.[11] Fromm illustrates this concept in a political context. Prior to the rise of the Nazi movement in Germany, he says, the German working class held communist beliefs on the basis of what they conceived to be their interests, but these beliefs were not ego-syntonic, not resonant (*einklang*) with their own authoritarian personalities. Thus, the Nazi movement was quickly persuasive, not so much on

Bell Journal of Economics 9 (1978): 578–608. This fruitful discussion, however, does not come to grips with the intrapsychic processes that give insight into "ego-syntonic" concepts of happiness.

[8] Amos Tversky and Daniel Kahneman, "The Framing of Decisions and the Psychology of Choice," *Science* 211 (30 January 1981): 453–8.

[9] "Rationality should probably include whether values specified are worth pursuing. . . . Rationality is not limited to a choice of means." Abraham Kaplan, "Some Limits on Rationality," in Carl J. Friedrich, ed., *Rational Decision,* NOMOS 7 (New York: Atherton, 1964), 57. Compare Karl P. Popper, *Conjectures and Refutations: The Growth of Scientific Knowledge* (London: Routledge & Kegan Paul, 1963), 380–3.

[10] The ego-syntonic has other, nondefinitional characteristics: It is (1) congruent with the self-concept; (2) generally self-referential (not relying on social comparisons); and (3) the product of experience rather more than of tuition. On the last point, see Robert P. Abelson, "The Psychological Status of the Script Concept," *American Psychologist* 36 (1981): 715–29 at 722.

[11] On the matter of superego-dominated choices, Flugel points to a maturational process from actions taken out of a sense of duty to those taken because of a genuine, thoughtful desire to help another. See John H. Flugel, *Man, Morals and Society, A Psychoanalytic Study* (New York: International Universities Press, 1945).

the basis of its ideological tenets as on the basis of its appeal to something almost inarticulate, an emotional response to the authoritarianism of the movement.[12] For some people (perhaps those describing themselves as "alienated"), support for the market and acceptance of the behavior it requires are, in the same sense, ego-alien.

The ego-alien is largely unconscious, but consciousness is an aid to intelligent and fruitful choice of goals (Chapter 22). To pursue these unconsciously ego-alien goals is to misunderstand the true sources of one's happiness. Since consciousness and self-awareness of all kinds are often painful, ego-alien choices represent the flight from the immediate pain of consciousness toward goals that are likely to prove unsatisfying.

Etzioni uses the concept "authenticity" to mean the unity of thought and feeling, and in contrast to the popular term "alienation." He says: "It is the fate of the inauthentic man that what he knows does not fit what he feels, and what he . . . [feels] is not what he knows or is committed to." Where market institutions may require a person to act without commitment, inauthenticity may be quite common; under these circumstances a person is "unable to participate authentically in the processes that shape his social being."[13] His motives are ego-alien.

Ego-syntonic choices in consumer and labor markets

Consumers have been found to guide their purchases by coherent images of "life styles,"[14] personae on life's stage. If these are masks, the guidance will frustrate rather than implement consumer satisfaction. The secret *sportsman* driving a Volvo because he thinks he should look soberly responsible in the company parking lot, and the *family man* driving an MG because his brother-in-law teases him about his sobriety are equally uncomfortable in their ego-alien roles. No program of information searches, comparative pricing, weighing of desirable and undesirable properties, risk-acceptance or aversion, and probable payoffs will overcome this aspect of misleading choice.[15] These searches and calculations are admirable tactics for achieving a goal, but they do not clarify the relation of the goal to the person's ego-syntonic desires. Yet the capacity of a choice to yield enduring satisfaction depends heavily on this quality.[16] The ego-alien is invulnerable to market feedback because market information is not directed to the problem of genuine desires; it is directed instead at only those things that influence demand.

The theory of misleading choices is likely to apply in the labor market with

[12] Erich Fromm, *Escape From Freedom* (New York: Rinehart, 1941), Appendix, "Character and the Social Process."

[13] Amitai Etzioni, *The Active Society* (New York: Free Press, 1968), 619–20.

[14] Sidney J. Levy, *Marketplace Behavior: Its Meaning for Management* (New York: AMACOM, 1978).

[15] See, e.g., K. J. Lancaster, *An Introduction to Modern Microeconomics,* 2d ed. (Chicago: Rand McNally, 1974); George Katona, *Psychological Economics* (New York: Elsevier, 1975). The interest in "psychographics," and the reaction of a choice to a customer's self-image or life-style comes closer to the questions here at issue. See, for example, Levy, *Marketplace Behavior,* chap. 8.

[16] See Peter Earl, *The Economic Imagination: Towards a Behavioural Analysis of Choice* (Armonk, NY: Sharpe, 1983). Some theories of consumer choice rely on Herbert Simon's concept of *satisficing* (meeting critical requirements on primary dimensions and subordinating consideration of all others); this more veridical description nevertheless looks only at the face value of the desires. See Herbert Simon and Andrew C. Stedry, "Psychology and Economics," in Gardner Lindzey and Elliott Aronson, eds., *Handbook of Social Psychology,* 2d rev. ed., vol. 5 (Reading, MA: Addison Wesley, 1969).

greater force than in the consumer market, for it is there that the ego-alien aspects of career choices will be learned too late for correction, if they are learned at all. A person's self is more directly involved in what he or she does than what he or she eats or wears. Without referring to ego-syntonic properties, research and theory on the personality–economy fit do consider the matching of underlying dispositions with the demands of the job.[17] For example, too few or too many complex demands at work have been found to lead to depression, whereas the right fit between capacities of persons and complexity of jobs minimizes depressive symptoms.[18] Research has found that self-confident people tend to choose tasks with an appropriate level of difficulty; those with low self-confidence choose tasks that are either too easy or too difficult.

When the choice is elevated to the level of domains, as contrasted to commodities and jobs, we are dealing with life plans: whether to invest in work, leisure activities, family, friendship, religion, civics. Here choices made on the basis of what others think (which people discount when explaining the basis of their choices), or of duty, or because of role-appropriateness (which people acknowledge to be important),[19] might well be ego-alien. What is particularly at stake is the decision to make money for reasons that are ego-alien, to serve the market in the fashion dictated by its immanent commands, rather than in one's own ego-syntonic manner.

Compensatory selection of material goods

Many people derive genuine satisfactions from their standards of living, their income, and their material possessions or wealth. The choices they make are authentic and ego-syntonic. But some seek these material things as *compensations* for something else, perhaps to bolster their feelings of self-worth, or to relieve their doubts about their social adequacy, or because they cannot love or cannot win the affections of another.[20]

Choices representing *compensatory* selections may be conscious substitutions of an available object for one that is not available; they may not be ego-alien and, indeed, they may represent a desirable flexibility of goals. But those choices, like the substitution of money for unattainable love, representing a palliative substitute for something still close to the "heart's desire" (an ego-syntonic expression), embrace a large class of ego-alien choices.

What makes one object compensatory for another is a property of the person and

---

[17] See John R. P. French, Jr., Willard L. Rodgers, and Sidney Cobb, "Adjustment as a Person-Environment Fit," in George V. Coelho, David Hamburg, and John E. Adams, eds., *Coping and Adaptation* (New York: Basic Books, 1974). Herzberg and Maslow also deal with the problem of fitting dispositions to tasks. See Frederick Herzberg, *Work and the Nature of Man* (New York: Mentor/New American Library, 1973); Abraham H. Maslow, *Eupsychian Management* (Homewood, IL: Irwin/Dorsey, 1965); Melvin Kohn and Carmi Schooler, *Work and Personality: An Inquiry Into the Impact of Social Stratification* (Norwood, NJ: Ablex, 1983).

[18] Michael Argyle, *The Social Psychology of Work*, 2d ed. (London: Penguin, 1989), 273.

[19] Andrews and Withey, *Social Indicators of Well-Being*, 231–3.

[20] Compensatory theory is burdened with somewhat doctrinaire interpretations of money as feces or penises. These views take exceptional and unusual cases and represent them as typical. See Otto Fenichel, *The Psychoanalytic Theory of Neurosis* (New York: Norton, 1945), 281–2, 389, 490.

not the object,[21] but some objects may invite compensatory choices more than others. The record of compensatory choices that follow suggests that money, because it is the most saleable of all goods (Schumpeter), and because of its prominence in a market society, its easy symbolization (Chapter 6), its glittering attractiveness, is an object that invites compensatory choice more than most. That particular compensatory substitution may be learned very early in life: Parents unable to give love "use money as a substitute for affection."[22] If that is true, the market must invite more compensatory choices than other fields of endeavor.

To the degree that money and possessions are sought as compensations for some personal inadequacy, they are unlikely to provide ego-syntonic satisfactions, for they are not the ego's first choice. In these cases, what is needed and wanted is something else, a reassurance that such material objects rarely can satisfy. If they are psychologically unsatisfactory, so are they economically inadequate, for the "demand" they represent is unstable. In Lancaster's theory of consumer choice, it is not the good itself that is wanted, but its properties;[23] in this case the property desired is reassurance, a property that some substitute object might suddenly offer in greater abundance, or that, with reassurance from another quarter, might no longer be wanted at all.

Examples of compensatory choices in the market
Money and goods are, indeed, pursued for their compensatory value. In her research into the psychology of possessions, Lita Furby reports "that personal possessions provide substitutes where other needs or desires have not been met."[24] The consequences in childhood may be especially damaging. For example, children who are exceptionally acquisitive for material objects are distinguished by their poor linguistic and social development, a condition that tends to be fixed for the remainder of the child's life if not corrected by age six.[25] The material objects seem to be compensations for the childish play and social interactions that most normal children find more satisfying.

From the clinic comes other evidence. People who enhance a deficient sense of integrated wholeness by appropriating to the self external possessions do so to complete themselves and to give themselves a more developed persona in their own eyes.[26] The goods are literally compensations for missing parts. Edward Bergler has specialized in cases of neurosis where money and fantasies of money have played a

---

[21] Kenneth Burke points out: "In the economy of one man, monetary power may be *compensatory* to some other kind of power (physical, sexual, moral, stylistic, intellectual, etc.). That is, he may seek by the vicarage of money, to 'add a cubit to his stature.' But in the economy of another man, monetary power may be *consistent* with one or all of these." Kenneth Burke, *A Grammar of Motives* (Berkeley, CA: University of California Press, 1969), 114–15.

[22] Edith Neisser, "Emotional and Social Values Attached to Money," *Marriage and Family Living* 22 (1960): 132–8 at 133.

[23] K. J. Lancaster, *Consumer Demand: A New Approach* (New York: Columbia University Press, 1971).

[24] Lita Furby, "Possessions: Toward a Theory of Their Meaning and Function Throughout the Life Cycle," in P. B. Baltes, ed., *Life Span Development and Behavior*, vol. 1 (New York: Academic Press, 1978), 320, 329.

[25] Robert White, "Exploring the Origins of Competence," *APA Monitor*, April 1976, pp. 40–5.

[26] Ernest G. Schactel, "Alienated Concepts of Identity," in Eric Josephson and Mary Josephson, eds, *Man Alone* (New York: Dell, 1962), 80–2.

large part; he says the "urge to possession is a compensatory mechanism for narcissism."[27] With greater plausibility, Isaacs says: "In the analysis of both adults and children, we find that their attitudes to material possessions frequently change a great deal during the course of analysis. This change is often in the direction of lessening the wish to own."[28] Relieved of their inner conflicts, these improving patients might then pursue the original and genuine objects of their desires rather than the compensatory objects that could not provide genuine satisfaction.

From the workplace it is reported that, compared to others, those marked by anxiety and low self-esteem are more interested in the pay than in other aspects of their jobs.[29]

Of the "money conscious" who fantasize about money and think about it more than about their work and families, Carin Rubenstein reports:

Such people are least likely to be involved in a satisfactory love relationship [many are unmarried and childless]. They also tend to be sexually unsatisfied, report worsening health, and almost half of them are troubled by constant worry, anxiety, and loneliness. They are dissatisfied with their jobs and feel they earn less than they deserve.[30]

This theme of substituting money for the lost or unattainable affection of friends or family is quite common. Sarason and colleagues find that people with social support in their lives ("people you can count on") are less concerned about "achieving material success" than those without that support, that is, with fewer and less satisfying friends.[31]

Markets and compensatory choices

Markets facilitate compensatory choices as they facilitate a variety of choices; their function is to make choices in economic "transactions" easy and inviting. Making it easy to substitute one commodity for another, exchange, is a virtue in most cases including the case of compensatory choices. The unattainability of an object is not more frustrating because another object is available – usually it is less. But once outside of the range of commodities, this very virtue is a problem. It is easy in a market society to find a substitute in the market for something lying outside of the market; it is harder to go the other way and find a substitute for money and commodities in the "friendship market," "the reputation market," or the "honor market." It is easier to compensate for the loss of love by devoting oneself to making money than to compensate for economic failure by finding a partner.[32] One might indict the failure of these other markets to match the ease of negotiations found in

[27] Edmund Bergler, *Money and Emotional Conflict* (Garden City, NY: Doubleday, 1951), 6.

[28] S. Isaacs, "Property and Possessiveness," in T. Talbot, ed., *The World of the Child* (1949; reprint Garden City, NY: Doubleday/Anchor, 1967), cited in Furby, "Possessions," 324.

[29] Edward E. Lawler, III, *Pay and Organizational Effectiveness: A Psychological View* (New York: McGraw-Hill, 1971).

[30] Carin Rubenstein, "Money and Self-Esteem, Relationships, Secrecy, Envy, Satisfaction," *Psychology Today* 15 (1981): 29–44 at 42.

[31] Irwin Sarason, Henry M. Levine, Robert B. Basham, and Barbara Sarason, "Assessing Social Support: The Social Support Questionnaire," *Journal of Personality and Social Psychology* 44 (1983): 127–39.

[32] Discussing the problem of divorce and marriage, two economists speak of the failure of the "marriage market." See Heather L. Ross and I. Sawhill, *Time of Transition: The Growth of Families Headed by Women* (Washington, DC: The Urban Institute, 1975).

the commodities market, but they may have withered as a consequence of the imperial tendencies of commodities markets.

The result is that compensatory choices tend to substitute things for people, the impersonal for the personal, making money for making love (violating Foa's like-for-like principle, Chapter 25), and leisure for unfulfilling work, the last a market cost as well as a market consequence.

One of the major themes in the preceding accounts of compensatory choices is lack of social support. Reports from psychotherapists and social workers find that deindividuation (the loss of a sense of individual responsibility for one's acts) and loss of community integration and of normative guidance are widespread.[33] Although in Chapter 25 I reported a study showing that it was possible to be happy without much social support if one has a very high sense of personal control, those without that sense of personal control, perhaps the majority, are dependent upon social support for their well-being. To the degree that the market undermines home life (through requiring mobility, creating anxiety, making work life exiguous and unsatisfying, imposing decisional overload), the market shares responsibility for deficiencies in affectionate relations. That may or may not be a burdensome responsibility: In the quality-of-life studies, there is very little evidence of loneliness or dissatisfaction with friends, community, or family relations, but perhaps in these surveys we are asking *The Sorcerers of Dobu* if their neighbors are acting suspiciously.

In perspective, it seems that *it is the focus on money and price* that distracts people from genuinely ego-syntonic choices; wanting something else, many find in money only *compensatory rewards* serving neither market criteria of stable, transitive choices nor principles of subjective well-being. We cannot say how adaptive market institutions may be to these considerations of, shall we say, *false consciousness*. As mentioned, their information systems are not addressed to the problems of compensatory, inauthentic, and ego-alien desires. But whatever these institutions might do to ease these problems remains unexplored because they are currently blinded by the inadequacy of the disciplines that analyze them.

The ambiguous interpretation of arousal

As pointed out in Chapter 4, the market is a cockpit of emotions; it is a device for emotional arousal and pacification of the aroused. We turn here to the problem of explaining why one feels aroused, why one feels happy or sad. As we will see, for the authors to be discussed this is the same thing as explaining *whether* people feel happy or sad. "Whether" becomes "why" when a person has an ambiguous feeling of arousal and must find an explanation to know what the feeling represents. Nisbett and Ross emphasize the importance of lay *theories* of emotion and behavior in people's accounts of their own happiness: "People's characterizations of themselves, like their characterizations of the objects and events that comprise their

[33] Seymour Sarason, *The Psychological Sense of Community* (San Francisco: Jossey-Bass, 1974); National Research Council (National Academy of Sciences), Committee on Child Development, *Toward a National Policy for Children* (Washington, DC: National Academy of Sciences, 1976).

environment, are heavily based on prior theories and socially transmitted preconceptions."[34] Three related theories help to account for the way people explain their emotions and moods.

Labeling and the use of preconceptions. In market affairs people are easily labeled, not only as rich and poor, but also as stingy and generous, prudent and spendthrift, and, in what is called "psychographics," as family men, housewives, sportsmen, brand-conscious elites, and so forth. As mentioned in Chapter 4 on cognition and affect, preconceptions often affix to individuals' unexamined labels that are then uncritically accepted. For example, without use of introspective insight, people often accept stereotypical images of sex-linked traits (females are not good at statistics), of teacher or parental characterizations of their students and children (laziness, moodiness), or peer group definitions ("meatball," "grind"). The social-labeling process shortcuts (and shortchanges) self-knowledge. Moreover, experiments show that even when a person has accepted a self-schema, this view of the self is impervious to disconfirming evidence – following the general disposition to confirm rather than disconfirm a theory.[35] These self-schemas also distort memory and "bias [people's] memories or interpretations of events and thereby influence their expectations and subsequent behavior."[36] In the market as elsewhere people accept labels that distort their genuine interests and desires.

Explaining arousal. With the exception of direct sensory experiences, people have no more direct access to the sources of their feelings than they have access to the working of their optic nerves.[37] Psychologists (of this persuasion) question "the extent to which self-assessments of emotions and attitudes are the product of direct introspection. . . . Once the individual becomes aware of his own state of physiological arousal, the labeling of that state – and the subjective experiences, self-reports, and emotionally relevant behavior that accompany such labelling – is the

---

[34] Richard Nisbett and Lee Ross, *Human Inference: Strategies and Shortcomings of Social Judgment* (Englewood Cliffs, NJ: Prentice-Hall, 1980), 197. The following discussion relies heavily on Chapter 9, "The Lay Scientist Self-Examined," pp. 195–227. The general proposition that people do not have "well-defined" internal knowledge has at least one exception: vivid, personal sensory experience is recalled and used in attitude formation. Where this is missing, people tend to employ their general self-concept as suggested in the discussion of ego-alien attitudes. Alice M. Tybout and Carol A. Scott, "Availability of Well-Defined Internal Knowledge and the Attitude Formation Process: Information Aggregation Versus Self-Perception," *Journal of Personality and Social Psychology* 44 (1983): 474–91.

[35] Susan T. Fiske and Shelley E. Taylor, *Social Cognition* (New York: Random House, 1984), 321 and chap. 11 passim.

[36] Nisbett and Ross, *Human Inference*, 198. The depressed are, however, more realistic in their assessments of how others see them than are nondepressed or normal people – their depression correcting for normal tendencies to exaggerate the positive.

[37] Tybout and Scott hypothesize that "immediately available sensory data" will give a person access to his or her judgmental processes whereas other data are interpreted in Bem's self-perception manner. They confirm this hypothesis by experiments comparing taste data to social consensus data. Tybout and Scott, "Availability of Well-Defined Internal Knowledge."

[38] Nisbett and Ross, *Human Inference*, 199. There is evidence that a person may find reasons for an emotional state and then reject them, preferring to rely on affective "conclusions" without cognitive support. Fiske and Taylor, *Social Cognition*, 334. And it is not infrequent that people do not know *that* they are aroused. (p. 2)

result of a search for a plausible cause of the arousal.''[38] As pointed out in Chapter 4, one discovers first that one is aroused and then searches for a cause, and if that is not readily apparent in the situation, one searches further for something plausible to explain to the self why that arousal is experienced.

This process may be studied experimentally. "By holding constant subjects' emotional arousal but manipulating the source to which it may be plausibly attributed, experimenters have been able to produce either a heightening or lessening of many states, including fearfulness, aggressiveness, playfulness, and sexuality." In one experiment, male students rode an exercycle "with sufficient vigor to induce a high state of physiological arousal." Although physiologically aroused (e.g., elevated pulse and adrenaline counts), after a few minutes this arousal was no longer recognized by the subjects and therefore not used to explain their feelings. "Nudes examined during this period [when a person was aroused but unaware of that fact] were rated as more attractive than those examined immediately after exercise (when subjects knew that they were still aroused from their exertions) or than those examined at a still later period (when there was no extraneous arousal to be misattributed)." Thus, "people's labelling of their emotional states [including happiness] depends on an analysis of evidence conducted in the light of preconceived theories about which antecedents produce which states and which states are the product of which antecedents."[39] The market is rich in preconceived theories of which the misleading income maximization hypothesis analyzed in Chapter 17 is a prime example.

Actor as observer: finding a conventional explanation. As we have seen in Chapter 18, Bem's theory of self-perception is a major source of self-misinterpretation. Because of the frequent lack of privileged information on the causes of a person's own behavior and feelings, that person seeks explanations from the conventional ideas of the culture.[40] (Note the reversal of economic and philosophical assumptions: Outsiders may know more about the causes of an individual's preferences than does the individual concerned.)

Under the influence of these theories, "the question 'What emotion am I feeling?' became 'What stimulus is causing me to feel aroused?' . . . It is clear that people's ability to assess their feelings . . . will turn out to be largely dependent on their ability to perform such causal analysis."[41] But unhappily, the market's causal theory of behavior is a poor theory.

People's inability to explain what influenced their judgment or assessment, in trivial as well as more important matters, has been widely studied. To give some clue to the way in which these false inferences, so important to our analysis of how people assess their own happiness, are supported, I offer here only one of the many available examples of the relevant research.

[39] Nisbett and Ross, *Human Inference,* 200. This discussion is based on the work of Stanley Schacter.
[40] "To the extent that internal cues are weak, ambiguous, or uninterpretable, the individual is functionally in the same position as an outside observer who must necessarily rely upon those same external cues to infer the individual's inner states." Daryl J. Bem, "Self-Perception Theory," in L. Berkowitz, ed., *Advances in Experimental Social Psychology,* vol. 6 (New York: Academic, 1972), 2.
[41] Nisbett and Ross, *Human Inference,* 202.

"Weiss and Brown (1977) studied the accuracy with which women subjects could identify influences on their mood states."[42] Subjects reported daily for a two-month period the quality of their moods and kept track of the various factors that they thought were influencing these moods, such as the amount of sleep the night before, their general state of health, sexual activity, stage of menstrual cycle, the day of the week, and the weather. At the end of the data-gathering period subjects filled out a final form, assessing the importance of the various factors they had been monitoring. Subjects gave great weight to amount of sleep and almost none to day of the week. The investigators then correlated the cooccurrence of mood scores and alleged influencing factors, finding that, in fact, day of the week was most important and amount of sleep had negligible influence. Indeed, there was a slightly negative correlation between what the participants thought was important and what turned out actually to be important. "The more subject's mood covaries with the day of the week or weather, the less likely she was to give weight to these factors in her retrospective report. Thus subjects erred in assessing the impact of various determinants of their mood fluctuations, mistaking strong influence for weak ones or vice versa, and even failing to distinguish between positive influences and negative ones." Later a different group of subjects acted as observers and was asked to make the same assessments of influences on moods, with the result that their ratings of likely influences on moods were nearly identical to those of the actors observing themselves. The evidence suggests again that actors behave as observers, using common theories and benefiting not at all from their privileged insight.[43] Asked why he or she was happy, a person brought up in a market culture would likely say it was because of high income, but we know that this is likely to be wrong, for others with lower income (but not the poor) would give the same answer in otherwise similar circumstances.

If it is the case "that actors' insights into the causes of their behavior and moods are best regarded as inferences rather than as privileged or 'direct' observation of the workings of their mental machinery," when are these inferences most likely to be accurate? In everyday life people are usually "right in their accounts of the reasons for their behavior" because of the obviousness of the relevant theory (hunger as a cause for opening the refrigerator door; a ringing doorbell as a cause for going to the door). Second, since only the actors know the special meanings for *them* of symbols or events (a familiar tune, resemblance to some hated person), only they can report how a particular stimulus will affect these special meanings. Third, people do have privileged information about their own goals and purposes (e. g., saving for a vacation) and sometimes their own decision rules (when in doubt, retreat) that again will give crucial information on why they did what they did or believe what they believe – or feel happy or sad as they do. Fourth, there is privileged access to memory of similar circumstances in the past that helps at least in predicting current behavior and, in a sense, explaining that current action, as well: "I do what I always do in such situations." Similarly, fifth, trained individ-

---

[42] The reference is to J. Weiss and P. Brown, *Self-Insight Error in Explanation of Mood* (Unpublished manuscript, Harvard University, 1977), in Nisbett and Ross, *Human Inference*, 221.
[43] Nisbett and Ross, 221–2.

uals usually have algorithms that guide behavior and judgment, and to the extent that they follow their own professed code, these algorithms can be used later to account for their own behavior and judgment.[44] But no market training will provide the algorithm that informs people that their arousal is stimulated by the flattery or slight received in negotiating a contract – and not the terms of the contract itself.

Thus, the actor has "clues" to what the observer can only infer, but the "clues" are heavily freighted with emotion and distract the individual from more straightforward, perhaps more "rational," interpretations. Under these circumstances the actor might be a better observer of others than of himself.

In short, the actor's unique ability to introspect will aid the goal of self-insight only to the extent that the products of such introspection are roughly as causally relevant as they are available and vivid, and only to the extent that they reflect accurate theories of why people like himself, or people in general, behave as they do. . . . When the actor's data and theories are superior [to those of an observer] he will be more accurate, when either is inferior he may be less accurate. . . . [But] on those occasions when the observer possesses a superior *theory,* it is normally the observer who has the advantage.[45]

The main point, then, is that people's assessments of their own moods are basically inferences about *why* they are aroused; therefore, they are vulnerable to all the common characteristic inferential errors. Taken together, these studies suggest to Nisbett and Ross the following conclusion: "People's guesses about causality for the very most important outcomes are as faulty as their guesses about inconsequential outcomes. Simply put, they suggest that *people do not know what makes them happy and what makes them unhappy.*"[46] Under these circumstances maximizing utility in the market is exceptionally difficult. In fairness to the market, we should add that maximizing utility in other institutions is equally difficult – but no other institution has a doctrine that claims to be the agent for maximizing utility.

Market effects of ambiguous arousal

Markets are arousal mechanisms in at least five respects. One is the dependence on contingency, requiring effort for rewards and alertness to threats and opportunities affecting this contingency relationship. Another is the search for customers or jobs, a search that sometimes generates excessive arousal in the form of stimulus overload. A third is the presentation of novelty as a specific prescription for arousal, novelty in products and in processes that oppose passivity and comfort. Fourth, competition as rivalry (if not necessarily competitiveness) implies a constant state of arousal, lest another get the better of the individual. Fifth, competition as alternatives demands frequent, more or less rational, decisions instead of what Weber called a "traditional orientation" representing references to habit and precedence. Competition focuses the mind in play and work. Csikszentmihalyi reports on "motivational elements which will draw the player into play." He says: "Perhaps the simplest of these inducements is competition. The addition of a competitive element to a game usually ensures the undivided attention of a player who would not be motivated otherwise."[47]

[44] Ibid., 211–12.
[45] Ibid., 223–5, emphasis in original.
[46] Ibid., 223, emphasis added.
[47] Mihalyi Csikszentmihalyi, *Beyond Boredom and Anxiety* (San Francisco: Jossey-Bass, 1975), 41.

The consequence, as mentioned in our discussion of cognitive development and environmental complexity (Chapter 8), is that the market bears responsibility for decisional stress that results not only in strain but, if the decisional requirements lead to overload, also results in a return to more cognitively simple thinking processes. The stressed individual is not only less happy because of the stress but also less able to assess how to relieve his or her distress.

As mentioned in Chapter 24, a person is happiest when he or she experiences the levels and kinds of arousal congenial to his or her own temperament. What is stressful for some is for others an invigorating challenge. The evidence from Freedman's study[48] supports Mill's hypothesis that happiness, for almost everyone, depends upon a mixture of arousal and tranquility or contentment – although Mill erroneously believed that these two states are substitutable for each other.[49] Where the market permits people to choose their level of arousal, it adds one more useful choice, permitting people to achieve the mixture that best suits them. Where it imposes arousal, both choice and contentment are threatened.

Four interpretations of market arousal. If individuals have trouble interpreting their own arousal, social observers rush to fill the void:

1. In the modern, market society, says Arendt, "the ultimate standard of measurement is not utility and usage at all, but 'happiness,' that is, the amount of pain and pleasure experienced in the production or in the consumption of things." As a consequence, she says, we "may end in the deadliest, most sterile passivity history has ever known."[50] For Arendt, passively to accept market happiness is to give up the active struggle for understanding "the human condition." This is a minority view.

2. Marcuse says the market has created a Promethean culture whose price is "perpetual pain." We would be better off, he believes, if we substituted Orpheus or Narcissus for Prometheus, for "theirs is a world of joy and fulfillment; the voice which does not command, but sings; the deed which is peace [the end of arousal] and ends the labor of conquest."[51] Although the language is hedonic, the theme is aesthetic and ideological. The market's arousal is the wrong kind.

3. Simmel believes overstimulation of urban life (which he later extends to commercial life), leads people to build barriers against the world and to turn within for peace and contemplation.[52]

4. Milgram offers some evidence that metropolitan stimulus overload leads people to avoid entangling friendships and to decline opportunities to help others.[53] We

None will deny that the market is receptive to competition. Competition, however, has several modes of expression. As Fromm once suggested, market competition often involves selling the self along with the product and thus *increases* self-awareness, if not self-knowledge.

[48] Jonathan Freedman, *Happy People* (New York: Harcourt, Brace, 1980).

[49] "The main constituents of a satisfied life appear to be two: either of which by itself is often found sufficient for the purpose: tranquility and excitement." John Stuart Mill, *Utilitarianism*, in *Utilitarianism, Liberty, and Representative Government* (London: Dent, 1910), 12. Original treatise published 1861.

[50] Hannah Arendt, *The Human Condition* (Chicago: University of Chicago Press, 1958), 309, 322.

[51] Herbert Marcuse, *Eros and Civilization* (New York: Vintage, 1962), 146–7.

[52] Georg Simmel, "The Metropolis and Mental Life," in *The Sociology of Georg Simmel*, trans. and ed. Kurt H. Wolff (Glencoe, IL: Free Press, 1950).

[53] Stanley Milgram, "The Experience of Living in Cities: A Psychological Analysis," in Frances E.

saw in Chapter 8 that overload tended to prompt a regression to simpler forms of cognition, and elsewhere in this work I have reported that a prime indicator of unhappiness is "always feeling rushed."[54]

However it is expressed, market stimulus overload influences, and probably distorts, the interpretation of one's own long-term hedonic interests.

Market arousal: attributions to the self. One market construction is the attribution to the self for what happens over a lifetime. The undefined arousal then prompts the questions: "What did I do?" "What should I do?" "What can I do?" These are the questions that mastery-oriented children, compared to helplessness-oriented children, ask.[55] The market's reliance on contingency not only requires that benefits be contingent on effort but teaches that events be traced back to causes in the self. I am aroused because of what I did and can do, not just because of what has happened to me.

As noted in Chapter 9, self-attribution is not a very good causal theory; in a sense it is a "noble lie," good for the successful individual (it is associated with hedonic gains) and good for the society (energizing a population to help themselves), but often encouraging activity with individually improbable success.

Consumer arousal and its interpretation

Self-attribution fails to say why commodities yield utilities. For consumers, self-attribution following arousal is misleading in the second stage of a two-stage process. The first stage may be summarized as: "If I chose this myself, it must be satisfying." The stage is correct. Choosing something is normally satisfying; the object chosen is more satisfying *because* it was chosen than the same object would be if it were not chosen. The second stage is misleading: "Because I chose something myself, it must be the means to further satisfaction." But we know from the analysis of people's causal inferences that their causal attributions are extremely fallible and the test of that further satisfaction is not whether the individual chose the object but whether it is an object that serves the purposes for which it was chosen.

Mistaking the source of one's pleasure: failure of market feedback. Returning to the Volvo versus MG illustration mentioned before, misconstruing arousal may come to the same unhappy end as employing ego-alien masks. Why do I get pleasure from the car I just bought? Perhaps I believe that I like it for its reputation for durability, but in fact I like it principally because of its rapid acceleration. If so, I am not informing myself so that the next purchase will be better

Korten, Stuart W. Cook, and John I. Lacey, eds., *Psychology and the Problems of Society* (Washington, DC: American Psychological Association, 1970), 152–73.

[54] Campbell et al., *The Quality of American Life,* 357.

[55] Carol I. Diener and Carol S. Dweck, "An Analysis of Learned Helplessness: Continuous Changes in Performance, Strategy, and Achievement Cognitions Following Failures," *Journal of Personality and Social Psychology* 36 (1978): 451–62; and Idem, "An Analysis of Learned Helplessness II. The Processing of Success," *Journal of Personality and Social Psychology* 39 (1980): 940–52.

suited to my desires. As Schumpeter observed, one of the great market advantages over public goods is that the feedback on decisions is usually prompt and informative, permitting consumers to correct their decisions next time.[56] But not in this case. The market is sensitive to my repeated purchases, not the construction I place on the sources of my satisfactions.

Retrospective accounting for choices. The retrospective assessments of one's motives, mentioned earlier, also applies to retrospective interpretations of one's preferences. Looking at what they did to see how they feel, people will say of a high-priced purchase: "I must have wanted this very much because I paid a lot for it." And, by a process of postdecision dissonance reduction, people will then reduce their worries about having done the right thing by telling themselves that they chose wisely. Both processes interfere with that feedback process that was supposed to have protected people's hedonic yield in the market.

The market is an arousing institution. The fact that the interpretation of arousal is not given in the situation but rather relies on highly fallible processes of interpretation raises new questions about the market's capacity to satisfy human wants. And, because these interpretations often rely on conventional theories of behavior rather than privileged insight into the self, the new questions extend to the capacities of individuals adequately to implement their own ego-syntonic desires in any economy.

Underlying these constructions that the mind places on events is a body whose functions are hidden from consciousness. Is the market well suited to the physiological processes of the human constitution? Although market ideology claims that the market is "natural" to the species (Chapter 3), market doctrine is generally silent on this matter, except perhaps for efforts to support preferred views of economic functioning by reference to some universal "propensity," such as the "propensity to truck, barter, and exchange one thing for another" (but even that, Smith said, flowed originally from our ability to read and write). We turn here to the relation between market processes and values to possible endowed biological programs.

The biological substrates or happiness

Much – we do not know how much – of our behavior and even our thoughts are closely related to our biological endowments. The matter is technical and beyond our capacities, but if, when we speak of our pursuits of happiness we are speaking of something given in our several natures, we are then speaking of pursuits whose outcomes are selectively prejudiced from the beginning. Analysis of the misinterpretation of the grounds of happiness cannot completely avoid the subject.

The theory of happiness as a product of endowed temperament has a long history (e.g., from Hippocrates to Sheldon), and is renewed now in part because of biological and neurological discoveries and in part because demographic variables often explain so little – perhaps 10 percent of the variance. "It is clear," says Diener,

[56] Joseph A. Schumpeter, *Capitalism, Socialism, and Democracy,* 3d ed. (London: Allen & Unwin, 1950), 257–9.

"that at some level hormonal and biological events must mediate mood and Subjective Well-Being."[57] There are two parts to this matter: (1) To what extent is happiness given by various physiological and endocrinological states? And (2) to what extent is happiness, whether given or achieved, the product of satisfying biologically reinforced motives? In neither case, of course, do we assume that nature *determines* outcomes; it merely facilitates or retards the work of culture.[58]

Notice (as mentioned in Chapter 24) that if happiness is in some sense given by physiological states, the role of the market to satisfy the basic human want for happiness is limited. But, on the other hand, if there are biologically reinforced motives congenial to the market, the market's capacities to satisfy human wants are enlarged, not least by giving expression to these very motives. Whereas recent market doctrine is silent on the issue, market ideology, some of it with sources in Herbert Spencer, claims that the market is an extension of natural processes and enlists human nature on its side. (The issue of whether the market violates the natural environment is not here under review.)

These questions are central to the problem of the misinterpretation of the sources of happiness and satisfaction in a market society, for we are even less informed of our physiologcal endowments and internal processes than of our mental processes. Or, more somberly, we know pain as the signal that something violates these processes, but when they are not insulted they tell us nothing. Again, we must rely on those with the best theories of the physiology of happiness because we cannot, of our own knowledge, know the biological sources of feelings of well-being.

The biology of happiness

We turn first to possible clues to the biology of happiness itself. Freedman's inference that some people simply "have a talent for happiness" points in this direction of unknown biological givens. But even if we could fully explicate the physiological bases of happiness, there are limits to the force of such an explanation, for it is unlikely to account for either historical or most cross-cultural differences.

A few clues must suffice: (1) Research on the physiology of the brain has located a "pleasure center" that, if stimulated, gives humans a feelings of euphoria and that animals will self-stimulate to the exclusion of all else when given a chance to do so. The "pleasure center" is the source of norepinephrine and dopamine, two of the neurotransmitters that carry messages between nerve cells and that chemically resemble amphetamines. There is some evidence that the deficiencies in these neurotransmitters are inheritable,[59] a fact that may help to explain why severe depression tends to run in families. (2) Further, the discovery of endorphins, a substance that is secreted by a gland in the hippocampus and that is released in moments of intense action, causing a temporary indifference to pain, suggests a possible chemical basis for optimism or even happiness. (3) Depression of certain kinds may be

---

[57] Ed Diener, "Subjective Well-Being," *Psychological Bulletin* 95 (1984): 542–57 at 561.

[58] "Biological mediation does not invalidate theories that are at a different level of analysis such as the psychological or sociological levels." Ibid.

[59] E. S. Gershon, W. E. Bunnery, J. F. Lecksman, M. van Erwegh, and B. A. DeBauche, "The Inheritance of Affective Disorders: A Review of Data and Hypotheses," *Behavior Genetics* 6 (1976): 227–61, cited in Diener, "Subjective Well-Being," 552.

relieved by a simple chemical, lithium, suggesting the role of diet or dietary deficiencies in mood arousal.[60] (4) Finally, because brain waves differ according to moods of joy and sorrow, the physiology of happiness may be linked to specific stimuli recorded by electroencephalograms.[61]

Money does not stimulate the brain's pleasure center, nor produce endorphins, nor (by itself) introduce lithium in the diet, although it may stimulate brain wave patterns reflecting happy thoughts. To the extent that these findings explain underlying conditions favoring happiness, they represent conditions that influence the effects of culture and human activity on transient and basic moods. If a person has inherited a disposition to be unhappy, or has a dietary or endocrinological deficiency, money will not buy happiness for him or her.

But these are a layman's comments; no doubt the commonsense notion that a baseline for happiness is created by adequate diet and prevention of illness will take us farther in appraising the effect of money on happiness. At the bottom, money buys relief from hunger and illness and cold. That is important.

Biological roots of happiness-yielding activities

As for the biological bases or substrates for the various endeavors that promote happiness, again we can only point to possible areas of confirmation and disconfirmation. The basic proposition is that those strivings for which there are biological substrates (latent programs) are more likely to lead to happiness than those for which there are none. One common inference is that those things that are "easy to learn," such as walking and talking, are more likely than others to have biological programs in the brain that guide behavior.[62] Social learning theorists find experimental reasons for doubting this "easy to learn" hypothesis,[63] however, and we are

[60] I have been guided in some of these comments by the research of Donald Klein, Jan Fawcett, and others reported by Abby Avin Belson, "Studying the Chemistry of Joylessness," *International Herald Tribune*, 17 March 1983. Fawcett says of joylessness, "We seem to be measuring a biological characteristic, like blue eyes, that doesn't change." For an application of similar research to society, see Lionel Tiger, *Optimism: The Biology of Hope* (New York: Simon & Schuster, 1979). Other research shows that it is angry hostile people, not impatient (Type A) people, who are most susceptible to premature death, and that "such toxic personalities can be traced to biological differences that are likely to be present from birth." Sandra Blakeslee citing research by Dr. Redford D. Williams in the *New York Times*, 17 January 1989. This is relevant to happiness because Shaver and Freedman show that misanthropy is also a source of unhappiness. See Shaver and Freedman, "Your Pursuit of Happiness." Roger Masters published an important work in this area too late for my use before going to press; see Roger D. Masters, *The Nature of Politics* (New Haven: Yale University Press, 1989).

[61] Research by Drs. Richard Davidson and Nathan Fox, reported in the *New York Times*, 22 November 1988, p. C1, by Daniel Goleman, shows that infants watching a smiling, laughing face on television have different brain wave patterns compared to infants watching a neutral or sad face. There is also evidence that cognitive style "reflects a constellation of genetic, endocrinological, and neurological features." See Deborah Waber, "Biological Substrates of Field Independence," *Psychological Bulletin* 84 (1977): 1,076ff. I know of no evidence to support Adam Smith's concept of a universal "propensity to truck, barter, and exchange."

[62] See M. E. P. Seligman and J. L. Hager, eds., *Biological Boundaries of Learning* (New York: Appleton-Century-Crofts, 1972).

[63] See Albert Bandura, *Social Learning Theory* (Englewood Cliffs, NJ: Prentice-Hall, 1977), 73. Whether particular cognitive styles have biological substrates is still uncertain. Waber argues that the established relationship between sex and stage of maturation, on the one hand, and Witkin's "field-independence," on the other, suggest such biological roots. Waber, "Biological Substrates of Field Independence," 1,076.

not called upon to resolve the dispute. We turn to two other features of market behavior: (1) acquisitiveness or the tendency to claim possessions as private property, and (2) the desire to "earn" rewards as evidence of one's control over one's personal environment. If these reflect the workings of innate drives or biologically given motives, we would expect them to be more important sources of happiness.

Acquisitiveness. Over fifty years ago Beaglehole sought to discover whether there were grounds for believing in an acquisitive instinct, such as Tawney suggested in reporting that "acquisition of riches [is] . . . one of the most powerful human instincts."[64] From his inquiry into animal behavior Beaglehole concluded that for the most part acquisitiveness among animals was limited to storing food, a prudential measure, although there were nest-building and adornment purposes served as well. Since acquisitions were instrumental for other purposes, he concluded that there was no acquisitive instinct, per se.[65]

Becker, a property lawyer, reviewed the literature on *territoriality* as a possible source of some instinctual basis for arguments supporting property rights. It failed the test. One reason is that "the territorial imperative" is often collective, implying, if anything, a drive not for private but for collective ownership. In any event, the evidence suggested that although there are clearly preferences for controlling one's own immediate space, they may be satisfied in a variety of ways without owning that space. "If a fixed term, inalienable untransmissable lease on an apartment will satisfy it [the territorial or property acquisition motive] as well as full ownership of a house . . . then the territorial imperative gives virtually no commands to a property theorist."[66]

Cross-cultural studies of children's behavior provides some evidence of biological or instinctual acquisitive instincts. Lita Furby reviewed the material in the Human Area Files and concluded: "The large majority of references stated or implied that children are naturally possessive and acquisitive and that society must inculcate something different if so desired." Since the material was gathered by anthropologists for purposes other than discovering instinctual bases, "most of the material was too general and fragmented for any solid conclusions. . . . They are deserving of further systematic study."[67] On the other hand, White's experimental studies mentioned previously, found that for young children "a disproportionately high amount of time spent procuring objects is negatively related with good development." The object procurement of these children is quite different from the useful exploratory behavior of the healthy child, partly because it is solipsistic and prevents the child from engaging in a "rich social life."[68] The normal, nonacquisitive children seem more likely to represent nature's preferred pattern.

[64] R. H. Tawney, *The Acquisitive Society* (1920; reprint New York: Harcourt, Brace, 1964).
[65] Earnest Beaglehole, *Property: A Study in Social Psychology* (London: George Allen & Unwin, 1931).
[66] Lawrence D. Becker, "The Moral Basis of Property Rights," in J. R. Pennock and J. W. Chapman, eds., *Property*, NOMOS 22 (New York: New York University Press, 1980), 201. The conclusion may be correct, but Becker's inference is weak. It does not follow that because a motive can be satisfied in other ways, a given way of satisfying it draws no support from the biological endowment expressed by that motive. Ownership might be a sufficient condition for satisfying the need for space (or personal control) but not a necessary one.
[67] Furby, "Possessions."
[68] White, "Exploring the Origins of Competence," 40–5.

The evidence available regarding innate acquisitive instincts is very slight; I conclude, with Beaglehole and Becker, as reinforced by White's observations, that there is no support for an "acquisitive instinct." But there is an indirect route, via the concept of personal control, that tends to reinforce acquisitive behavior.

Personal control. As pointed out in our discussion of "internality" in Chapter 9, there is evidence for an innate desire to control one's own environment, to be effective, and to see the world respond when one acts upon it. The desire is reflected in two economic behaviors: earning and owning. Seligman believes that mood, joy and sorrow, are evolutionary devices for reinforcing active control over the environment. He first asks about the utility of emotion and answers that it is to guide efforts at control:

What selective pressure produced feeling and affect? It may be that the hedonic system evolved to goad and fuel instrumental action. I suggest that joy accompanies and motivates effective responding; and that in the absence of effective responding, an aversive state arises, which organisms seek to avoid. It is called depression. *It is highly significant that when rats and pigeons are given a choice between getting free food and getting the same food for making responses, they choose to work.* Infants smile at a mobile whose movements are contingent on their responses, but not at a noncontingent mobile. . . . These activities, because they entail effective instrumental responding, produce joy.[69]

(Observe how Seligman reverses the telic order: Nature, he says, uses happiness as a means to promote what might broadly be called the economic order; mankind, however, holds that the economic order exists only to promote the happiness or well-being of the species.)

The evidence on the desire to control one's own environment challenges the finding that the drive for acquisition is unsupported by biologically given motives, because acquisitions, or possessions, extend a person's ability to control the environment. The source of the satisfactions derived from earning, the sense of control, operates in making possessions, the fruit of earning, a source of satisfaction as well. As mentioned in Chapter 17, Furby's research on the way possessions give people satisfaction shows that: "The central feature of possession – its principle defining characteristic – is causal efficacy or control over aspects of one's environment."[70]

Payment contingent on effort, that is, pleasure from *earned rewards* (as contrasted to public goods) is supported by appropriate biological substrates. That very important feature of the market system is at least compatible with and very likely supported by biologically given tendencies.[71] The desire to be a cause, thought to be innate[72] and illustrated by the persistent *illusion of control*[73] (our tendencies to convert chance situations to skill situations over which we have more influence), is gratified by earning as well as owning. As B. F. Skinner has said, we pay too much

[69] Martin E. P. Seligman, *Helplessness* (San Francisco: Freeman, 1975), 98; emphasis added.
[70] Furby, "Possessions," 322.
[71] To what extent this apparent biological support for rewards contingent on effort implies a biogram favoring the justice of deserts is quite uncertain. The fact that people have two, often incompatible, justice preferences, one for rewarding individuals and one for the shape of the distribution of these rewards, would certainly cloud any inferences to be drawn on this matter.
[72] Robert W. White, "Motivation Reconsidered: The Concept of Competence," *Psychological Review* 66 (1959): 297–333.
[73] See Ellen J. Langer, *The Psychology of Control* (Beverly Hills, CA: Sage, 1983).

attention to wealth and not enough to the process of earning wealth. This view is supported as well by research on "process benefits," suggesting, and to some extent proving, that the pleasures of *doing* and *making* are among the main rewards of economic activity.[74]

Resonance with quality-of-life studies. In the quality-of-life studies there is evidence that the sense of control over one's environment, indicated by reward for effort, is indeed a major contribution to happiness; in that sense, the theory that those motives informed by biological substrates are more likely than others to make people happy is supported. In the most extensive of Andrews and Withey's analyses of contributions to satisfaction with life-as-a-whole, an "efficacy index" ranks first, making by far the largest contribution (beta = .26) to overall life satisfaction.[75]

We know from cross-cultural studies that modes and norms of happiness vary across cultures;[76] we know from experience that individual moods vary from time to time; and we know that within a culture what makes one member of our species happy does not make others happy at all. None of this is incompatible with the two hypotheses sketched so briefly and inadequately here: (1) A "talent for happiness" may depend in part on the endocrinal endowment of an individual, and (2) whatever the cultural specificity of expressive outlets, pursuits of happiness in harmony with a biologically reinforced motive for feelings of control over one's immediate environment are more likely to find their targets than pursuits of happiness that violate this drive. The market reinforces and therefore teaches the sense of internal control (Chapter 9).

Moods and market performance

We have been examining how biologically influenced moods influence the way the market satisfies human wants, but it is also important to look at the way these physiological factors might influence market performance. We may speculate on the nature of their influence on the market itself.

In some ways biologically influenced moods will influence demand. Although marginal utility curves may assume roughly the same shapes for those whom nature has made happy or unhappy, they will start at different origins and slope by differ-

---

[74] F. Thomas Juster, "Preferences for Work and Leisure," in Juster and Frank P. Stafford, eds., *Time, Goods, and Well-Being* (Ann Arbor, MI: Institute for Social Research, 1985). Juster observes that this source of utilities is nearly totally ignored by economists.

[75] Andrews and Withey, *Social Indicators of Well-Being*, 124. Beta = .27; the second-ranking contribution had a beta of .19. The items in this index were: "How do you feel about . . . "The way you handle the problems that come up in your life?" "What you are accomplishing in your life?" "Yourself?" The reason for calling a combination of these items "efficacy" is their relation to the underlying concepts in Robert White's theory of competence and effectance. See White, "Motivation Reconsidered." A further indication of the enhanced contribution of biologically reinforced motives is suggested, but only that, by the second most important contribution to overall satisfaction with life: satisfaction with family life. The biological substrate here is not so much sexual motivation as the bonding instinct that Edward Wilson finds universal among primates. Edward Wilson, *Sociobiology: The New Synthesis* (Cambridge: Harvard University Press, 1975).

[76] Klaus R. Scherer, Herald G. Walbott, and Angela B. Summerfield, eds., *Experiencing Emotion: A Cross-Cultural Study* (Cambridge, UK: Cambridge University Press, 1986). On the reported sources of joy and happiness, see pp. 52–4,

ent decrements or increments. Similarly, the urgency of wants will be less for those with a "talent for happiness" than for those with no such talent, though this may be masked by the fact that happy people are more outgoing and active.

But the more important influence is on productivity. Happiness releases energy for productive activity. One might think that happy people are likely to be less eager to exert themselves, but it is not happiness but depression that leads to passivity;[77] as mentioned in Chapter 4, the happy person has initiative and imagination: "Good feelings seem capable of bringing out . . . our creativity in thinking and problem solving" and people with these feelings are more imaginative and experimental.[78] In this sense, they seem to advance economic enterprise. And they facilitate teamwork, for a predisposition to happiness makes people more cooperative, easing economic conflict.[79]

There are other ways in which positive affect, good mood, or at least transient happiness helps people to be more efficient in their lives as in their work. Although a happy person will certainly have worries, these worries are likely to be about things deemed soluble, perhaps unrealistically so because of the tendency of good feelings to exaggerate the probability of favorable events (it is the depressed who are more accurate in their estimates of future events).[80] Finally, although transiently happy people tend to be risk averse (they fear that they will lose their precious happiness),[81] those endowed with a biologically programmed happiness need have no such fear of loss; their optimism may indeed lead them to take unfavorably loaded risks that a more prudent, or depressed person, would not take. Happy people should consult depressives on risky enterprises.

In these several ways, the unconscious force of physiology not only affects how the market may alter moods but, conversely, also influences how biologically given moods influence market performances.

Biological imperatives give loose instructions on property arrangements. If acquisitiveness and possessiveness have no biological foundation, but attempting to control one's environment does, economic systems that seek to maximize satisfaction have considerable freedom in the incentives, practices, and structures they select. They do not need to rely on private property and they may use tokens of achievement that lack some of the specific qualities of money (such as store of value) for their purposes. How private property and money may best serve human purposes is a practical question, subject to experimental validation; argu-

---

[77] Norma D. Feshbach and Seymour Feshbach, "Affective Processes and Academic Achievement," *Child Development: Special Issue on Schools and Development* 58 (1987): 1,335–47.

[78] Alice M. Isen, "Positive Affect, Cognitive Processes, and Social Behavior," in L. Berkowitz, ed., *Advances in Experimental Social Psychology,* vol. 20 (New York: Academic Press, 1987). The quotations are from a report on Isen's work: "Feeling Happy, Thinking Clearly," *APA Monitor,* April 1988, pp 6–7.

[79] Isen, "Feeling Happy," 6.

[80] Lauren B. Alloy, Lyn Y. Abramson, and Donald Viscusi, "Induced Mood and the Illusion of Control," *Journal of Personality and Social Psychology* 41 (1981): 1,129–40; Alloy and Anthony H. Ahrens, "Depression and Pessimism for the Future: Biased Use of Statistically Relevant Information in Predictions for Self and Others," *Journal of Personality and Social Psychology* 52 (1987): 366–78.

[81] Alice M. Isen and Robert Patrick, "The Effect of Positive Feelings on Risk Taking: When the Chips are Down," *Organizational Behavior & Human Performance* 31 (1983): 194–202.

ments from a supposed "state of nature" or "human nature" are, it seems, spe-
cious. With great suffering, the twentieth century has provided a variety of economic experiments whose answer, at the end of the century, is reasonably clear:
Market economies do better. But this is not because nature says so, nor is this the
end of history.

*Endowed happiness reduces some sources of misinterpretation of the grounds
of happiness.* A predisposition to happiness counteracts some of the sources of
misinterpretation mentioned: ego-alienation, compensatory strivings, misreading
arousal. (1) For a happy person, there is little that is ego-alien. Ego presents a face
and not a mask to a world that prefers faces, and being well-received, there is less
to be unhappy about. By definition, the happy person is less internally conflicted
and can therefore choose ego-syntonic goals that genuinely increase a sense of well-
being. (2) The potential for feelings of frustration is given in situations; happiness
cannot prevent frustration. But when frustrated, the person with a happy mood turns
to *alternatives,* rather than to compensatory goals, for such a person can choose
without the resentment and mourning that prompt and follow compensatory choices.
(3) Emotions are likely to be as labile among the happy as among the unhappy, but
when aroused, the happy search for favorable explanations compatible with their
positive affects: Difficulties are soluble and temporary; if the person cannot solve
them, it is because of a local deficiency of skill, not a global deficiency; where the
unhappy seek explanations in their own defects, the happy turn to solutions relying
on their own capacities.

The misinterpretation of income

For my purposes in explicating the misinterpretation of the sources of a person's
happiness, the crucial question is whether these processes of misinterpretation apply
to income and wealth. On this point Campbell says:

It has repeatedly been shown that when people are asked how the quality of their lives might
be improved, they tend to answer in terms of more money. . . . People appear to overestimate the beneficial effects that additional income will have on their lives, . . . but its ability
to enhance these feelings [of well-being] appears to be restricted to those material domains
of life which relate to the need for having, which in turn has only a limited relationship to a
person's general sense of well-being.[82]

This is a confirmation of and support for the other data presented in Chapter 26 on
buying happiness. Money is immediate, personal, and, at least in its symbolization
and effects, vivid. Because of well-known laws of cognition,[83] it will not be easy
to accept the pallid background statistics that support what we all know but lightly
pass over: People with more income than we have do not seem to be happier, at
least not for that reason.

Summary

Accurate insight into the sources of one's own happiness is obviously more important in the satisfaction of human wants than those features of rationality that form

[82] Angus Campbell, *The Sense of Well-Being in America* (New York: McGraw-Hill, 1981), 66.
[83] Daniel Kahneman, P. Slovic, and Amos Tversky, eds., *Judgment Under Uncertainty: Heuristics and
Biases* (New York: Cambridge University Press, 1982).

the staples of market analysis. In order to explain the problems of such an accurate insight, I have reviewed four theories of why people misinterpret the nature and causes of their own moods: (1) the separation of thought and feeling exhibited in ego-alienation and inauthenticity; (2) selection of compensatory goals because, for some reason, the original goal is denied; (3) interpretation of one's own feelings of arousal based on false attributions derived from conventional social theories and behavior; and (4) the influence of biologically given moods and of biological programs favoring market activities. These processes of misidentification, misattribution, and biological fixity are closely relevant both to market behavior and to the justification of the market as a device designed to satisfy human wants.

The use of inauthentic or ego-alien personae leads people to adopt life-styles that mislead them about what is truly satisfying. In seeking to find a satisfying personality–economy fit, the ego-alien person finds the wrong niche in the economy. At the level of choices among domains, they invest in domains that cannot provide for them what they genuinely want.

People seek money and material things as compensatory goods that cannot satisfy their needs or wants as well as the original goods would have done. On the other hand, research evidence seems to show that it is possible to "compensate" for lack of social support by high levels of personal control, the belief that a person controls the events that affect his or her life.

Often people who are emotionally aroused are uncertain of the causes for the arousal; they must then infer from the context why they are aroused and in doing so use the theories of arousal in similar situations offered by their culture or by their own more intimate groups. In this respect they are like outside observers of their own behavior and therefore unable to choose goals uniquely able to satisfy their own wants.

The market is an arousal mechanism. Its contingency rules require alertness of threats and opportunities; its frequent presentation of novelty, its competition as both rivalry and as alternatives, all tend to increase arousal levels during an ordinary day and over the life span. Having aroused participants, markets help them to construe their arousal: (1) The market's emphasis on self-reliance leads to constructions of personal responsibility; (2) the market's focus on price and exchange tends to focus on economic causes; and (3) post-hoc inference tends to justify what has been chosen, making the market's feedback mechanism less informative.

There are probably biological and inherited causes of positive and negative moods that narrow the capacity of market events to change levels of satisfaction. For those with a given "talent for happiness" marginal utility curves start higher and slope more gradually than for others and insecurity is less troublesome. Happy people are more energetic and adventurous; transiently happy people are more risk averse than others but those with a "talent for happiness" need not fear the loss of their happiness.

Of two of the market's thematic activities, we have tentatively concluded that there is no biological substrate for one – acquisitiveness – thus loosening the relationship of the market to private property, but that there is for the other – personal control – expressed in earning and owning, which seems to be resonant with biologically given traits and needs (restoring some of the lost basis for property).

The market has stakes in the happiness of its participants, for hedonic moods influence demand and productivity. They do this by influencing the nature and urgency of demand and the energy, creativity, cooperativeness, and risk aversion of workers. Happy people are simply more productive.

We are dealing here with choices far more important than cereals and cars: choices between domains of life, choices of life plans. Believing that it is my religious faith that yields genuine satisfaction, I invest more and more time in religion with no greater happiness on this earth. And, believing that it is income that gives me happiness, I spend more and more time earning money that brings me a little joy but no relief from sorrow. The rational life plan suffers as much as the pantry and garage from my inability to discern what makes me happy.

28 Summing utilities and happiness

Why is it that summing utilities does not produce a total that is equivalent to happiness? Indeed, given their diversity, is it possible to sum utilities at all? And if they may be summed, can we avoid mixing the sources of utility, like income and commodities, with the consumption process that yields the final pleasure, that is, utility? In concluding Part VII on happiness, I cannot avoid these questions. In seeking to answer them, I am also adding to earlier discussions on how we may best understand the idea of happiness (Chapter 22), on the nature of wants and their satisfaction (Chapter 23), on the relation between pleasure and pain (Chapter 24), and especially on the various structures of happiness (Chapter 25). Indeed, the problem of summing utilities is a facet of the structure of happiness neglected by economists, but fortunately treated by utilitarian philosophers, some of whom, however, confound the idea of a happy life with the idea of a valuable life. In this chapter we seek to find reasonable answers to the questions raised by those discussions.

Summing market utilities

The summing of utilities is an analytic device, not a description of a cognitive process. People may "count their blessings," but they do not count their utilities or their satisfactions. They do have two mental states that serve as substitutes, however: (1) summary views of their happiness or overall satisfactions with their lives that provide a strategic criterion of how a life plan is progressing, and (2) preferences that people treat in ordinal fashion to provide tactical criteria on smaller matters.These local satisfactions refer to the familiar "schedule of preferences" – implicit, rarely articulated, mostly unconscious, but operative. These two elements, a strategic evaluation of a life and a tactical evaluation of the fulfillment of local preferences, offer the empirical basis for the analytical device of summed utilities. (I use the term "utility" here to make connection with the literature; it may be read as "satisfaction," or "positive affect.")

Most treatments of the summing of utilities ignore the properties of what, inelegantly, may be called the *summator*, the person doing the summing.[1] Yet, as the previous chapter on misinterpretation of one's own feelings and inferences about their causes clearly shows, individual processing of cognitions and emotions are certain to affect outcomes.

[1] For example, see James Griffin, *Well-Being: Its Meaning, Measurement, and Moral Importance* (Oxford, UK: Clarendon Press, 1986); Robert E. Goodin, *Political Theory and Public Policy* (Chicago: University of Chicago Press,1982).

Choosing high hedonic activities

The development of skills in choosing high hedonic yield activities might be learned in the market. But is the market a good teacher? (1) The market fails to teach "leisure competence"[2] but there is some weak evidence that it is a better teacher of *hedonic competence,* the ability to select those activities that make the largest contribution to overall life satisfaction and happiness. There is a positive association between age and "process well-being," the enjoyment of activities in which one engages. As Juster and Courant point out, "we could be observing a learning process in which preferences change as consumers [and producers] are exposed to [new] activities."[3] Similarly, (2) the market concept of human capital,[4] that is, skills contributing to productivity, is valued by the market, but skill in making hedonically satisfying choices is not. This kind of Epicurean human capital is sometimes expressed as a capacity for enjoyment, often associated with "life's little pleasures." People learn to adapt, of course, but possibly also to select activities in a hedonically more satisfying way.

(3) For people to learn hedonic competence from the market, the market would need to offer a *corrective feedback system* superior to the one it now offers, which is too narrowly confined to its own products and commodities, and does nothing to correct for ego-alien, compensatory choices. The feedback in the family is probably better, but the feedback from government and other sources of collective goods is almost certainly worse

(4) The market's emphasis on extrinsic rewards tends to usurp the *proper role of self-rewards* – of conscience, standards of excellence, the call of duty (no longer "prowling about our lives like the ghost of dead religious beliefs"). As we saw in the studies of the hidden cost of rewards (Chapter 18), without intrinsic rewards, people do not learn how to do work but rather how to make money. They lose the powers of *self*-regulation. "People respond self-critically to inadequate performances for which they hold themselves responsible but not to those which they perceive are due to irregular circumstances."[5] To exaggerate, they are not so much taught as conditioned when they believe that they work only for pay.

The market does not teach hedonic competence effectively.

The satisfaction standard: ranking and summing

In considering the problem of summing utilities, three methodological problems must be disposed of: (1) the relation of money to utility (again), (2) the relation of

[2] Robert E. Lane, "The Regulation of Experience: Leisure in a Market Society," *Social Science Information* 17 (1978): 147–84.

[3] F. Thomas Juster and Paul N. Courant, "Integrating Stocks and Flows in Quality of Life Research," in Frank M. Andrews, ed., *Research on the Quality of Life* (Ann Arbor, MI: Institute for Social Research, 1986), 167.

[4] See Theodore W. Schultz, *Investment in Human Capital: The Role of Education and Research* (New York: Free Press, 1971); and Idem, *Investing in People: The Economics of Population Quality* (Berkeley: University of California Press, 1981).

[5] Albert Bandura, *Social Learning Theory* (Englewood Cliffs, NJ: Prentice-Hall, 1977), 132–3, 134.

ordinal ranking to cardinal summing, and (3) problems of varying intensities, durations, and differences between pain and pleasure.

Why money is a poor measuring rod. The inadequacy of money as a measure of utility may be summarized as follows: (1) Because of the intrinsic value of work, money earned does not reflect the utility or disutility of work; (2) because of consumer rent and various process benefits and costs, money spent is not equivalent to consumer utilities; (3) because of the discrepancies in times of appraisal and possibly because of "savers rent" (which might be negative), money saved is similarly unreflective of the hedonic value of savings. And (4) because they do not include self-rewards, money rewards cannot measure satisfaction. Summed, these money items do not add up to the hedonic economic values of the individuals who earn, spend, and save these funds.

Commensurability: ranking and summing. To be ranked, a series must be composed of comparable items but it might be that an individual's values and preferences, and the satisfactions or utilities derived from their fulfillments, are of such different kinds that they cannot be ranked on any single dimension. Two kinds of circumstances previously mentioned suggest this incompatibility: (1) Something of infinite worth or inestimable value, such as Kant's "dignity," is part of the series; (2) something that is a condition for the ranking process itself, such as Rawls's lexicographically preferred "liberty," must be considered. Yet to achieve these privileged statuses, these goods must *have been* compared with others. For the individual, if not for the moral philosopher, there are no incomparable values that cannot, for that reason, be entered into a summation process. "Incomparability . . . is too strong." says Griffin. In his canvas, he says: "We do not find values that are strictly incomparable," with the modification that a person may take the position that "enough of A outranks any amount of B"[6] – which still leaves values comparable. If values can be compared, so can utilities, and they can also be ranked.

But for summing, cardinal ordering is necessary.[7] As mentioned, the market's solution is to use as a measure the amount of money a person is willing to give up to attain some good. Money, of course, offers cardinality, but given the weak relation between money on the one hand, and utilities, life satisfaction, or happiness on the other, the sum achieved would not be meaningful.[8] It is not preferable to the contribution-to-life-satisfaction standard. But satisfactions tend to be ordinal; how can they be summed?

Contributions to overall life satisfaction as the standard. The quality-of-life studies do not sum satisfactions directly but rather they sum contributions of

[6] Griffin, *Well-Being,* 82 and 89. Griffin explicitly rejects both Dworkin's idea of rights as trumps and Rawls's lexicographic ordering of liberty. (p. 91)

[7] Ian Little comments that summing utilities "sounds like nonsense because addition is a precise mathematical operation, which requires the possibility of counting." I. M. D. Little, *A Critique of Welfare Economics,* 2d ed. (London: Oxford University Press, 1957), 53.

[8] Griffin's proposal to employ hours of leisure given up as the standard runs into the obstacle that leisure activities may be less valuable than what is chosen in its place. *Well-Being,* 101–2.

local satisfactions to overall life satisfaction (beta weights). The flaw is that the weights are for collectivities and may not be strictly appropriate to any individual, but Andrews and Withey's finding that their measures apply without distortion to all groups in the population[9] is some reassurance that their measures of contributions to subjective well-being are roughly applicable to most individuals. And beta weights, of course, permit summing in cardinal fashion within any single schedule of satisfactions. Given the vagaries of money as an expression of satisfaction, the contribution-to-life-satisfaction standard seems preferable to a money standard for summing utilities.

The quality-of-life studies also offer an answer to the question of the commensurability of pain and pleasure. For example, Griffin's concern (Chapter 24) that pains are more hurtful than pleasures are enjoyable[10] suggests some process of weighing intensity beyond simple addition and subtraction of pains and pleasures. Andrews and Withey's scoring system assessing contributions to overall life satisfaction embraces intensity of feeling without difficulty: A close association of a concern with assessments of overall quality of life is a measure of intensity; if some concern is both painful and closely associated with feelings about life-as-a-whole, the pained individual will achieve a net summary score of "unhappy" or "terrible," a meaningful, if infelicitous, outcome.

Griffin also feared that the pains have longer duration than pleasure. If that were generally the case, one would accumulate sorrows while the joys tended to disappear and, therefore, one would find that the present tended to be worse than the past.[11] Indeed, it is the case that negative feelings tend to last longer than positive feelings, but that difference does not seem to mean that as the pains persist and the pleasures evaporate people have an increasingly painful view of life. As roughly indicated by answers to questions asking people whether they regard their quality of life in the present better or worse than the past (and the probable future) this cumulation of pains does not occur: Young adults in their thirties saw the most improvement over the past five years, but all but the elderly (over age 64) saw their futures as likely to be a little better than their present.[12] Moreover, life satisfaction increases with age.[13] Again, the contribution-to-happiness standard takes such differences into account and permits a summing unweighted by such considerations.

[9] Groups that "might be assumed to have somewhat different values show remarkable similarity in the way they seem to combine evaluations of live concerns when evaluating life as a whole. . . . This is not incompatible with the groups having different values . . . that generate affective evaluations that we observe and analyze. *Homogeneity* between groups in the way affective evaluations are manipulated is compatible with *heterogeneity* in the generation of affective evaluations." Frank M. Andrews and Stephen B. Withey, *Social Indicators of Well-Being: Americans' Perceptions of Life Quality* (New York: Plenum Press, 1976), 17–18.

[10] Ibid, 84.

[11] Darlene E. Goodhart, "Some Psychological Effects Associated with Positive and Negative Thinking about Stressful Outcomes: Was Pollyanna Right?" *Journal of Personality and Social Psychology* 48 (1985): 216–32.

[12] Andrews and Withey, *Social Indicators of Well-Being*, 326.

[13] Ronald Inglehart and Jacques-Rene Rabier, "Aspirations Adapt to Situations–But Why Are the Belgians So Much Happier than the French? A Cross-Cultural Analysis of the Subjective Quality of Life," in Andrews, *Research on the Quality of Life*, 13.

Hedonic assets and hedonic income

Counting utilities as both the item that produced the satisfaction, like income, and the satisfaction from consuming this product is a form of double counting that is common in summing utilities; it can be corrected by borrowing from financial accounting the concepts of balance sheets (or capital accounts) and income statements, as Juster and Courant have suggested.[14] Mixing objective and subjective categories is the most common cause of confusion: A person is rich and enjoys economic security. But wealth is a hedonic *asset;* it yields *psychological income* in the form of enjoyment of security (and other sources of satisfaction). Economics deals exclusively with the capital accounts of income and wealth, purchases and savings, work and economic productivity. The assets are confounded with their "income," the pleasure they produce. The true income accounts are thus abandoned to other disciplines willing to analyze the contents of the categories of utility and disutility and their allied concepts of enjoyment and/or satisfaction.[15]

The income account, which alone is of interest in "summing utilities," includes all forms of *enjoyment.* Part V on work was an exploration of the nature and consequences of enjoying work activities but, of course, enjoyment of leisure activities and of the consumption of commodities are also parts of the income account. Where economics stops at the purchase of a commodity providing the purchaser with an asset, the income account must include both the act of purchasing (often hedonically negative)[16] and the subsequent act of consumption. The assumption that an individual derives satisfaction commensurate with the sacrifice in money required by the purchase has no empirical foundation, although repeated purchases of the same item makes the assumption more plausible. The assumption that the process of satiation follows repeated purchases, the concept underlying the belief in declining marginal utility, is equally suspect.[17]

The capital account is by no means limited to the economic assets possessed by or available to an individual, for, as discussed in Chapter 27, the biologically or culturally given "talent for happiness" may be equally important. Many dispositions other than moods, then, must be entered into the capital account, for example, the positivity and negativity biases and such attributional dispositions as to credit the self for success and to blame circumstances for failure. The unity of personality and the hedonic skills mentioned are assets, too, and given the low relationship between money income and satisfaction with life-as-a-whole or with happiness, they are probably more important than any conceivable economic assets.

This conceptualization invites very broad extensions. Anything that might con-

---

[14] I have greatly modified the concepts presented in Juster and Courant, "Integrating Stocks and Flows in Quality of Life Research."

[15] Compare Juster and Courant's idea that economics deal with "flows" and social psychology with "stocks" or states of being. Ibid., 149.

[16] F. Thomas Juster, "Preferences for Work and Leisure," in Juster and Frank P. Stafford, eds., *Time, Goods, and Well-Being* (Ann Arbor, MI: Institute for Social Research, 1985).

[17] Albert O. Hirschman, *Shifting Involvements: Private Interest and Public Action* (Princeton: Princeton University Press, 1982).

tribute to subjective well-being can be thought of as an asset. Juster and Courant include "available time," and define "wealth . . . to include not only conventional capital assets like factories, houses, and cars, but also human capital skills, environmental assets, stocks of associations between individuals, the social and political infrastructure, and so forth."[18] One might add a congenial spouse, successful and loving children, loyal friends, and circumstances that are just sufficiently challenging. Economists distinguish between primary and intermediate capital (or fixed and variable capital). What is primary and what is intermediate depends on one's analytical purposes. Focusing on individuals, one might claim that the biological endowments of individuals, including their temperaments, is their primary capital and their hedonic competences represent their intermediate capital. Focusing on the environment, one might think of, say, the roster of jobs in a community as primary and an individual's current job as intermediate. A crucial environmental asset is a job that offers opportunities for self-direction; a crucial internal asset is a sense that life has meaning and an absence of cynicism.[19] Thus, possessing a belief in the meaning of life is an asset and happiness is its income; the two should not be confounded – and yet income can be quickly converted into capital.

This distinction between happiness and the meaning of life is useful because it helps to sort out different processes of acquisition: learning and inheritance in the case of personal capital, and exploitable opportunities in the case of environmental capital. For most people the market (like marriage) is an environmental asset, relatively fixed, ready to yield the intermediate assets, at different stages of production, first of income and then of goods and services, which, when consumed or enjoyed in themselves, yield "income" or utilities.

One other advantage of distinguishing between personal capital and environmental capital is that personal capital alone provides the resources for what Scitovsky calls "self-stimulation," Bandura calls "self-rewards," and what I have treated as intrinsic pleasures (Chapter 18). When personal capital is used in conjunction with environmental capital one sees, through the translucent metaphor, the familiar problem of environmental stimuli, mediated by personality, leading to a response, in this case a hedonic response.

These capital goods have various efficiencies, some yielding utilities at less hedonic cost than others. The summing of utilities, then, is a consequence of ascertaining the hedonic yields of these intermediate capital goods in a fashion reminiscent of Bentham's accounting process. And the prudent manager of the enterprise – a person and his or her life – reinvests in the most efficient agents of production.[20]

People enlarge their hedonic capital by investing some portion of their income.

[18] Juster and Courant, "Integrating Stocks and Flows in Quality of Life Research," 149.

[19] "The only attitude that is important for adult happiness is the certainty that life has meaning and direction, a religious principle in only the broadest sense." Philip Shaver and Jonathan Freedman, "Your Pursuit of Happiness," *Psychology Today* 10 (August 1976): 27–32, 75 at 75. The philosophical origins of the market have been indicted for their ignorance of this aspect of the foundations of a good life: "There has been a long tradition of complaint against utilitarianism that it puts *happiness* where *the meaning of life* belongs." Griffin, *Well-Being*, 13, n. 14.

[20] Like Gary Becker and Theodore Schultz, Juster and Courant make time the original and ultimate scarce resource. Thus the way time is invested becomes the determinant of efficient hedonic yield. Juster and Courant, "Integrating Stocks and Flows in Quality of Life Research."

Here the feedback cycle mentioned in Chapter 25 helps to explicate the model. Starting with a given capital asset of a *disposition* for happiness, the top-down theory says that daily experiences will then be more satisfying, that is, the yield from this capital asset will result in a flow of daily satisfactions. And the bottom-up theory says that these satisfying experiences will be returned as an investment in the capital state of being. Alternatively, a learning model explains how we learn over a lifetime what experiences are satisfying so that hedonic selective skills become part of hedonic capital. With hedonic competence the learning processes discussed in relation to cognitive development, money, work, and rewards may be applied to the development of what might be called *Epicurean capital*.

As "the most saleable of all commodities," money has a special status among assets, for to some extent it may be exchanged for higher yielding assets, such as free time (leisure), and certain kinds of (psychological) income-producing goods, such as entertainment and various forms of purchases with their consumption potentials. But the capital market is not made exclusively of freely exchangeable goods, composed as it is of biological endowments, skills, money, benign government, and other hedonic assets. Some of these, indeed, are particularistic goods, like biological endowments, which cannot be exchanged at all; others, like good government, are banned from sale, and still others, like certain hedonic skills, might be taught but cannot be exchanged. As with intrinsic enjoyments, the lack of exchangeability in a market does nothing to diminish the chain of hedonic causation and therefore the values of the capital assets in the hedonic balance sheet.

Summing current utilities versus summing lifetime utilities

A person's current happiness can be an asset or a debit in the capital account, an asset because it helps to build, in a bottom-up fashion, the dispositional happiness that can later yield hedonic income (in top-down fashion), and a debit for at least two reasons. The first reason follows from the opponent process theory developed in Chapter 24 that says that every great pleasure is followed by a counterbalancing pain: as the "highs" of addiction create dependence with potentially unhappy withdrawal symptoms when the source of pleasure is extinguished.[21] And the second reason follows from Parducci's notion of the benefits of negative skewness in the distribution of highly pleasurable experiences on the grounds that as people compare any current event with past events in their lives, they will find more pleasure in the current event if they do not find the contrast with previous events unfavorable.[22] In this conflict of hedonic processes, one would guess that the first, building up a happy disposition, is the more important, providing the current experience is not more than usually addictive.

The reverse process, where some hedonically negative experience is a means to achieve future hedonic gains, is more common. Learning skills are the most familiar

---

[21] Richard L. Solomon, "The Opponent-Process Theory of Motivation: The Costs of Pleasure and the Benefits of Pain," *American Psychologist* 35 (1980): 691–712.
[22] Ed Diener, "Subjective Well-Being," *Psychological Bulletin* 95 (1984): 542–75 at 568, citing Parducci (1968).

example, the possible pain of learning serving as a condition for the pleasure of using the skills once they are learned.[23] Delayed gratification, as in saving, also falls in this category, as does any form of abstinence for reasons of health, such as stopping smoking. Whether in these three kinds of cases the glow of virtuous self-denial or self-satisfaction from duties performed is sufficient recompense to put the current account in a state of credit is always uncertain. For example, it seems that during the early and middle stages of adult life, savers are less happy than spenders.[24] In any event, when one is storing up happiness for the future, the current account is not a sufficient indication of happiness or life satisfaction over the life cycle.

Spreading gratifications over a life to maximize the summed utilities of experiences over a lifetime requires institutional cooperation. The market fails to do this in two respects: (1) It does not match needs and opportunities to serve those needs; that is, anxieties of early adulthood are exacerbated by the insecurities and uncertainties of market performance, opportunities for training and opportunities are not matched to the availability of jobs, mobility of industry is out of phase with population expansion and contraction, and rapid occupational obsolescence is not matched with adaptive skills. And (2) the postponement of gratification in the three kinds of acts mentioned – undergoing training now for skills later, saving for the future, and abstinence from health-damaging indulgences in food and drink – is more difficult in a market society where advertising encourages indulgence in the present without consideration for the future. Advertising serves as the normal, everyday equivalent of "pushers" in the related problems of drug abuse.

These problems are formed by the relationship of individuals to their institutions, but there is an additional set of problems posed by the relationship among the various kinds of desires and the goods sought by individuals to satisfy their desires. We turn to these next.

Structures: the relationships among the goods

Griffin poses the problem:

> To understand aggregation [the summing of utilities], we have to understand how desires are given structure. . . . To some degree, estimating the values of these various [desired] ends is like determining the value of ingredients in cooking. . . . With our different ends, too, the important estimate of how valuable they are . . . [depends on] their contribution to a whole life. . . . In any case once we talk about *amount* of utility we have to see these items as part of a life. So the amount of value cannot be decided by attaching a value separately and then adding.[25]

Many of Griffin's (and others') difficulties come from confusing a happy or satisfying life with a *valuable life,* a confusion stemming from a long line of thinking identifying happiness with virtue, as illustrated by Aristotle's treatment of happi-

---

[23] Education is perhaps wrongly justified in this fashion – wrongly because the justification seems to sanction painful learning when, with some exceptions, learning can be made a pleasure in itself.

[24] Carin Rubenstein, "Money and Self-Esteem, Relationships, Secrecy, Envy, Satisfaction," *Psychology Today* 15 (1981): 29–44.

[25] Griffin, *Well-Being,* 35–6, emphasis added.

ness or Spinoza's view that happiness must necessarily be in accord with the will of God (Chapter 22). We turn to this later in the chapter. But the empirical point about structure remains and is not resolved by the fact that the quality-of-life studies do sum satisfactions and find that these sums relate well to a measure of overall life satisfaction. Consider the following difficulties in summing utilities in the absence of a sophisticated theory of hedonics:

Confounding objective characteristics with satisfactions. The first difficulty is the confusion between assets and income compounded by its materialistic emphasis. The market has so closely identified wealth with happiness that a person counts his or her blessings in market terms: ''I have a big house, an expensive car, an expensive education, and a large bank account. I should be happy.'' But he or she was looking at the capital account and was counting low-yield assets, rather than examining a statement of operating income or utilities.

Redundant information. When a person has a strong positivity (or negativity) bias, summing utilities beyond a few crucial items tells us nothing of the person's happiness because those few items already tell us what any further summing might say. This is because the strong positive disposition imposes colinearity among the functions describing contributions to overall subjective well-being. In fact, this is the way it works out in the quality-of-life studies. For example, Andrews and Withey find that in their lists of from twenty-three to thirty concerns contributing most to life satisfaction, the cumulative additions of concerns beyond twelve is minimal.[26]

The sum of utilities is significant only in the light of a life plan. The same data suggest an alternative hypothesis: Sums of most utilities are irrelevant unless they reflect what a person considers central to his or her life – the ''psychological centrality''[27] mentioned as a condition of self-esteem in Chapter 10 and in the discussion in Chapter 25 of dominant and recessive influences on happiness. For the family man, lowered utilities in the market are not very important if his satisfactions from the family are preserved; for the market achiever, the feeling of having met and conquered economic obstacles will capture the important variance, and contributions from family matters will not alter life satisfaction very much.[28] In this sense Griffin is right. The simple aggregation of utilities is not informative until one understands what is important to an individual: ''If desires are fairly well informed, the structures are plans of life,'' although ''not necessarily highly planned.'' Desires must be seen in fairly long-range terms ''as ways of living, which exclude

[26] Ibid., 128, 130–1.
[27] See Morris Rosenberg, *Society and the Adolescent Self-Image,* (Princeton, NJ: Princeton University Press, 1965).
[28] This is implied by the importance of the way contributions to life satisfaction are entered in the list; the low scores of the later entries are low because most important items for the entire sample were entered first; for an individual with different priorities, later items in the sample list might explain more of the variance.

other ways of living, all of which have – in these terms – to be ranked.''[29] If they are ranked in such a way as to reflect the priority of the individual's central concerns, the point made previously regarding "redundant information" applies: Later items in the rank list will not add much to total utility or to satisfaction with life-as-a-whole.

The market's tendency to increase aspirations far beyond a person's capacity to satisfy them seems to some critics to guarantee unhappiness, but in fact the consumer aspirations the market creates would be weighted rather modestly in this summing process (because satisfaction with goods and services and actual income have so slight a relationship to life-satisfaction) and so would not diminish felicity as much as has been alleged.

Utilities depend for their value upon context. The summing of utilities that is under consideration runs into further difficulties because of the dependence of the value of any given good on its context. Three examples illustrate this point:

1. The first example of the context effect simply illustrates again the effect of *expectations* in changing the value of money. Let us say that the protective work clothing that has always been provided by a firm is now chargeable to employees. In other circumstances, the payment involved might have represented something close to an equivalence to the satisfaction received, but in this new circumstance the payment buys no satisfaction whatsoever.

2. The second example also illustrates a point made earlier (Chapter 25). The preference for *like-for-like exchanges* revealed by Foa's research[30] suggests that the utilities derived from exchanges are minimal unless repayment is made in the coin of the original offer, gift, or payment by the other party. In any event, the market's emphasis on exchange is inappropriate for particularistic, person-specific goods.

3. The problem of *labeling* activities mentioned earlier (Chapter 4) illustrates the contextual effect very well. If the same task is called a game it has positive utilities; if a chore, the utilities are negative.[31]

Ambivalent and intransitive preferences: self-rewards. Summing particular satisfactions to yield life-satisfaction scores, or, in certain cases, happiness scores, is complicated by the instability and intransitivity of preferences, such as those indicated in the discussion of ambivalence, approach–avoidance, and feasibility gradients in Chapter 23. For intransitive preferences, there will be at least two sums at any one time, each of which is as valid as the other. For unstable preferences, there will be fluid sums, changing as the elements of the addition change. The point

---

[29] Griffin, *Well-Being,* 34. There is much in common between this formulation and William James's concept of happiness as the ratio between achievements and aspirations. See William James, *Psychology: The Briefer Course,* ed. G. Allport (1892; reprint New York: Harper Torchbook, 1961), 54. James adds a characteristic human touch: "How pleasant is the day when we give up striving to be young – or slender."

[30] Uriel Foa, "Interpersonal and Economic Resources," *Science* 171 (2 January 1971): 345–51.

[31] Status goods, whose value depends on their uniqueness, create an "adding up problem." But the problem is one of adding up utilities for a collectivity, not for an individual. Fred Hirsch, *Social Limits to Growth* (Cambridge: Harvard University Press, 1976), 4.

returns us to the discussion in the previous chapter and the opening of this one: The most important aspect of assessing and summing utilities has very little to do with the market and much to do with the unity and integrity of the personality of the assessor and summator.

The list of difficulties in summing utilities in the absence of a sophisticated theory of hedonics continues, taking into consideration interaction effects:

Mutually inhibiting sources of satisfaction. The interactions among pleasures make simple summing difficult (but permits net measures). The most prominent example of this is the reduction of the pleasure of intrinsic work enjoyment by pay that under other circumstances is also a pleasure. But the problem is more general: The enjoyment of anything intrinsic, like friendship, may be spoiled by extrinsic intrusions.

Complementarity among utilities: the recipe metaphor. Griffin's comparison of the elements of a happy life to "the value of ingredients in cooking" suggests a particularly exacting interaction effect: enough baking powder for the cake to rise, enough shortening to give it texture, enough sugar to sweeten the chocolate, and enough chocolate to satisfy the taste. This is an Aristotelian model of a good life, the formula for *eudaemonia*. Compared to the accounting metaphor, it is a constraining formula suggesting that there is a limited number of ways of combining the elements of a good life just as there is in making a cake.[32] The answer is implied in the metaphor: People bake cakes to suit their tastes; each is free to mix the elements to suit his or her taste.

The market's selective facilitation of some kinds of choices is crucial. Its bakery favors commodity-rich tarts and leaves barren shelves for community-rich pancakes.

Conditional relationships. Summing utilities runs into other difficulties when one good is conditional on another. Consider the following four examples:

1. LEXICOGRAPHIC AND SECOND-ORDER PRIORITIES. The lexicographic conditional relationship mentioned in connection with the priority that Rawls gives to freedom is an answer to the apparently impossible task of summing finite and infinite values. Or, to put the matter in the context of the cybernetic model used in Chapter 25, second-order systems that make possible the operation of the first-order system cannot be included in the same systemic account. As mentioned, the values of the elements of the two orders are comparable, but are not easily summed – as the values of Epicurean capital and its yield in happiness cannot be summed.

2. FECUNDITY OR CONSEQUENTIAL IMPLICATIONS. Bentham suggests that assessments of net utility take into account the "fecundity" of each pain or pleasure, that is, its tendency to generate further pains or pleasures, it's immanent consequences. Adding up pleasures pregnant with future pain gives us tentative current

---

[32] Griffin, *Well-Being,* 36. The metaphor borders on treating external ingredients of a life (assets) as though they were themselves utilities; it deals with baking and not the physiology of taste.

sums, but they are spurious[33] because future regret will detract from any momentary happiness in a ledger, which turns out to be a "loan" rather than a true "credit" in the happiness account. The opponent process theory, represented by the problems of addiction, illustrates the problem of summing utilities premised on future pain, as, conversely, so do the problems of deferred gratifications previously mentioned.

3. FEEDBACK LOOPS AND THEIR CONSEQUENTIAL IMPLICATIONS. What Lasswell and Kaplan call "agglutinative values" and what Merton refers to as "The Matthew Principle" ("For unto every one that hath shall be given, and he shall have abundance . . .") may also be conceived as a benign feedback loop. The person with an endowed disposition (asset) yielding a sense of well-being has, by the top-down principle, more satisfying experiences, which, according to the bottom-up principle, increases the sense of overall well-being. The reverse is a malign feedback loop, illustrated by feelings of low personal control that interpret every failure as due to global and permanent personal deficiencies and every success as due to luck or, if accounted for by internal attribution, to accidental and unrepeatable personal qualities.[34] The market is an instrument for these self-fulfilling feedback loops: Success, with its trophies of economic gain available for reinvestment, breeds success, whereas failure, with its load of debt and impaired credit, breeds failure. To sum the *assets* at any time might give a picture of the bright or dim futures of an individual, but to sum the psychological *income* or utilities gives no hint of what is to come.

4. CONDITIONAL INTERACTION WHEN ONE GOOD IS ENHANCED BY ANOTHER. The pleasure of a sense of personal control offers genuine utilities; personal control is also a condition for favorable interpretation of the feasibility of various experiences.[35] For example, middle-class worries and working-class worries are about equal in frequency, but middle-class worries tend to deal with at least partially controllable events, like taking out mortgages or, more frequently, achieving better relations with one's children. Working-class worries tend to be about things that are more difficult to control, like death and poor health.[36] Middle classes benefit from the double pleasure of a sense of control and the reduced pain from anxieties that, they believe, may be resolved by their own acts. For the working classes, the

---

[33] "'Utility,' we might try saying, is the fulfillment of desires that persons would have if they appreciated the true nature of their objects." But since people might not want the necessary "daunting improvements," if this meant doing something they don't want to do, Griffin settles for: "Utility must, it seems, be tied to desires that are actual when satisfied." Ibid., 11.

[34] Carol I. Diener and Carol S. Dweck, "An Analysis of Learned Helplessness: Continuous Changes in Performance, Strategy, and Achievement Cognitions Following Failures," *Journal of Personality and Social Psychology* 36 (1978): 451–62; and Idem, "An Analysis of Learned Helplessness: II. The Processing of Success," *Journal of Personality and Social Psychology* 39 (1980): 940–52.

[35] B. Weiner, "A Cognitive (Attribution)-Emotion-Action Model of Motivated Behavior: An Analysis of Judgment of Help-Giving," *Journal of Personality and Social Psychology* 39 (1980): 186–200; Idem, "The Emotional Consequences of Causal Attribution," in M. S. Clarke and T. Fiske, eds., *Affect and Cognition: The 17th Annual Carnegie Symposium on Cognition* (Hillsdale, NJ: Erlbaum, 1982); Susan T. Fiske and Shelley E. Taylor, *Social Cognition* (New York: Random House, 1984), 322–4. On economic implications, see E. R. Smith and J. R. Kleugel, "Cognitive and Social Bases of Emotional Experience: Outcome, Attribution, and Affect in Data from a National Survey," *Journal of Personality and Social Psychology* 43 (1982): 248–59.

[36] Gerald Gurin, Joseph Veroff, and Sheila Feld, *Americans View Their Mental Health* (New York: Basic Books, 1960).

depression associated with their feelings of helplessness[37] makes every pain that much more painful, because relief, if there is to be any, is in the hands of unpredictable external forces.

Interaction effects themselves yield net satisfactions, correlative to Marshall's net manifested motivational force. Interaction effects are present when hidden cost psychologists consider the "net incentive" remaining after the effects on intrinsic satisfaction of extrinsic rewards have been accounted for.[38] The theoretical problem of these interactions is probably minor compared to practical difficulties in overtaxing people's capacities for taking them into account when calculating "expected utility," or overall life satisfaction. As we saw in the previous chapter, people are not very good at assessing their own moods of satisfaction and especially of assessing the causes of these moods. What the interaction does is to overload an already heavily taxed faculty.

Moral goods and hedonic goods

Happiness and virtue

The root of Griffin's difficulty in treating a happy life as though it were commensurate with a *valuable life* is the unwillingness to conceive of an immoral or trivial life as happy, an unwillingness grounded in the idea that virtue and happiness must somehow go together.[39] Empirically, they *do* go together: People's moods improve after an altruistic act and people who are in a happy mood are more likely to help other people.[40] Kant noted one-half of this relationship: "To secure one's own happiness is a duty, at least indirectly; for discontent with one's condition, under a pressure of many anxieties and amidst unsatisfied wants, might easily become a great temptation to transgression of duty."[41]

But the relationship between moral behavior and mood is looser than that between *beliefs* about one's behavior and mood. Beliefs that they are in some sense deficient in virtue, make people feel guilty and therefore unhappy. Freud's argument to this effect is supported by Freedman's finding that one of the clearest early symptoms predicting unhappiness in adulthood is a hypertrophic conscience in

[37] Martin E. P. Seligman, *Helplessness: On Depression, Development, and Death* (San Francisco: Freeman, 1973), 98.

[38] Alfred Marshall, *Principles of Economics*, 8th ed. (London: Macmillan, 1938), 15–16; Mark R. Lepper and David Greene, "Overjustification Research and Beyond: Toward a Means–Ends Analysis of Intrinsic and Extrinsic Motivation," in Lepper and Greene, eds., *The Hidden Costs of Rewards: New Perspectives on The Psychology of Motivation* (Hillsdale, NJ: Wiley/Erlbaum, 1978), 125.

[39] Because of his special more-than-ethical view of virtue, Aristotle belongs only partly to this tradition. Spinoza represents it better. Some portion of this identification of virtue and happiness is based on a form of empathy, which, in turn, is evidence of knowledge of God (Chapter 22). Baruch Spinoza, *Ethics Demonstration in Geometrical Order*, in Monroe C. Beardsley, ed., *The European Philosophers: From Descartes to Nietzsche* (New York: Random House Modern Library, 1960), 197, 209. (Original work published 1677.) Such critics of utilitarianism as Ross and Rescher do not say a person *cannot* be happy if he or she is evil, but they insist that he or she *should* not be happy – a very different matter.

[40] See Leonard Berkowitz, "Mood, Self-Awareness, and Willingness to Help," *Journal of Personality and Social Psychology* 52 (1987): 721–9; Weiner, "A Cognitive (Attribution)-Emotion-Action Model of Motivated Behavior."

[41] Immanuel Kant, *Theory of Ethics*, trans. T. K. Abbott, in Theodore M. Greene, ed., *Kant: Selections* (New York: Scribner's Sons, 1920), 277, emphasis in original.

childhood: "Those who often feel guilty as children are less optimistic as adults, less happy and more likely to experience fears, anxiety, insomnia, loneliness and feelings of worthlessness."[42] Similarly, feelings of positive virtue, altruism, measured by the question, "How do you feel about how much you are contributing to other people's lives?" does influence overall feelings of life satisfaction; in one list they rank ninth out of twenty-three concerns, just below financial security and above feelings of acceptance by others.[43] Feelings of virtue contribute to happiness and life satisfaction; feelings of deficient virtue (guilt) detract from them. Like other qualities that people like to have, such as skill and intelligence, the belief that one has sufficient virtue (an asset) yields psychic income.

One does not normally think of the market as a moral agent, but indirectly it is one: When it satisfies human wants it increases altruistic behavior quite outside its own sphere of operations, and its failures contribute to delinquency.

Ethical and commercial utilities in the same utility function

Like so many others, Robert Goodin has assumed that combining ethical and commercial goods in the same account will result in "moral pollution," ethics for sale, a price on human dignity. And like Durkheim's sacred–secular division, Goodin's division holds that moral utilities or satisfactions cannot be combined with economic ones in a single utility function.[44] This violates Griffin's belief that all values are commensurable; it also impugns the combination of moral utilities (satisfaction with one's contribution to others) and economic utilities (satisfaction with one's standard of living) in a single summed analysis of variance given by the quality-of-life studies.

The survey instrument is crude for interpreting Goodin's problem, but it reveals no evidence that people's *assessments* of their own altruistic records were polluted by their assessments of their commercial concerns. Their satisfaction with their altruistic records was at an average level, which means that, like the other items, it was influenced by a positivity bias: A full 73 percent were at least "mostly satisfied" with their "contribution to other people's lives," whereas only 8 percent were at least "mostly dissatisfied."[45] Many more are dissatisfied with their economic performances; apparently the high standards of performance required in the economy have not generalized to the rather more self-indulgent areas of moral performance.

The contextual effects mentioned have specific relevance to the partitioning of

---

[42] Jonathan Freedman, *Happy People* (New York: Harcourt Brace Jovanovich, 1978). The quotation is from a report on Freedman's study by Jane Brody, "Studies Asking: Who's Happy?" *New York Times*, 16 January 1979, p. C1.

[43] Andrews and Withey, *Social Indicators of Well-Being*, 135, 263.

[44] Robert E. Goodin, *Political Theory and Public Policy* (Chicago: University of Chicago Press, 1982), chap. 6. Goodin's solution is to establish an ethical framework within which commerce takes place rather than attempt to regulate immoral behavior. This framework is to be reinforced by a "polite fiction." See Chapter 2 in this book.

[45] Andrews and Withey, *Social Indicators of Well-Being*, 272–3. Feelings of satisfaction and guilt in this area of concern were almost identical with those revealed in a separate question on "helping people or groups in the community."

life into domains. The fact that an individual's moral performances vary from do-main to domain has two significant implications. (1) It reminds us of one of the oldest findings in behavioral science: A person is not "honest" or "dishonest;" he or she is honest in school but less so in tax matters, honest in business but not on the golf course.[46] In the usual trait × situation explanatory model, situation ex-plains at least as much of the variance in behavior as does a moral trait. Thus the additivity of moral utilities across domains already obscures one important feature: Moral traits are domain specific. (2) There exists a strong possibility of concealed interaction of moral satisfactions with other satisfactions according to domain set-tings: altruism in the home is *additive* to other family satisfactions (and its absence is more keenly felt because of high expectations), whereas altruism in business is *interactive* because it produces tension, potentially detracting from both the plea-sures of altruism and the pleasures of making money. We can add utilities derived from moral acts, but moral utilities are especially vulnerable to the various settings (domains) where a moral question arises.

If the market is an uncertainly reliable moral agent, at least it does not seem to discourage satisfactions derived from moral acts and (at least a few) guilty feelings of moral deficiency. Survey evidence reveals much guilt in the middle classes over failure to meet family obligations,[47] and depth interviews reveal some anxiety over meeting civic obligations,[48] but I know of no substantial evidence of guilt from engaging in market activities, though there is much shame for failing to be success-ful in the market.[49]

Without going deeper into the problem of moral teachings and deficiencies in the market,[50] we find that on the single issue of summing utilities there is little evidence or reason to believe that summing moral satisfactions and market satisfactions in a single function pollutes either moral principles or market efficiency principles, both of which are valuable to society.

Summary

The summing of utilities is as crucial to the market's capacity to satisfy human wants as it is to the analysis of happiness, but it is a much more complex problem than market analysts have assumed. Summing utilities is an analytical device with-out actual expression in normal human behavior; the practical equivalence is com-posed of summary views of life satisfaction (or happiness) and a schedule of pref-erences on local satisfactions. Although people do seem to learn a form of hedonic

[46] Hugh Hartshorne and Mark May, *Studies in Deceit* (New York: Macmillan, 1928).
[47] Gurin, et al., *Americans View Their Mental Health*, 130–6.
[48] Robert E. Lane, "The Tense Citizen and the Casual Patriot: Role Confusion in American Politics," *Journal of Politics* 27 (1965): 735–60.
[49] At least when people are asked about how they feel about money, it is less likely to be guilt than "shameful failure" that marks their answers. Paul F. Wernimont and Susan Fitzpatrick, "The Meaning of Money," *Journal of Applied Psychology* 50 (1972): 218–26.
[50] See Allen Buchanan, *Ethics, Efficiency, and the Market* (Totowa, NJ: Rowman and Allenheld, 1985); Gerald Dworkin, Gordon Bermant, and Peter G. Brown, eds., *Markets and Morals* (Washington, DC: Hemisphere/Wiley/Halsted, 1977).

competence over the years, the market's informational feedback system is inadequate to teach hedonic competence effectively.

Referring choices to a contribution-to-life satisfaction standard avoids the misleading measuring rod of money, permits cardinal orders necessary for summing, makes comparable various intensities of pleasure and the differences between pain and pleasure, and thereby permits summing of "utilities."

The concepts of financial accounting can be usefully applied to hedonic accounting. The capital account is composed of all assets that yield psychic income, including such economic assets as income and wealth, biological assets including health and an endowed disposition toward happiness, learned skills that are a pleasure to use, and so forth. The income account comprises utilities and other psychic income. Economists deal only with the capital account; psychologists and some philosophers treat the income account. By distinguishing between environmental and personal hedonic assets, we can also distinguish the different modes of acquisition and, within the personal account, explain intrinsic satisfactions. Psychic income may be reinvested in hedonic capital to increase a more or less enduring disposition toward happiness, thus creating a benign cycle. Given their heterogeneity and person-specificity (as in biological endowments and skills), assets have no capital market, but the lack of a market is not a significant influence on the value of the assets.

The sum of utilities can represent a current sum or a lifetime sum, but if the latter, only periodic inventories will yield the appropriate figure. Such periodic inventories will uncover more- and less-favored cohorts, the outcome often depending on the performance of the market during the cohort's formative years. The market is especially responsible for the insecurities that depress the life satisfactions of young adults, the marginal and the poor, as well as the difficulties people have in postponing gratifications.

The relationships among utilities and their sources influence the process of summing in the following ways: confounding assets and income, accounting for colinearity and redundancy, acknowledging relevance to life plans, responding to prior expectations, including Bentham's fecundity, and discounting for ambivalence.

Summing must also take into account such interaction effects among the goods that yield utilities as: mutual inhibition, combinatorial effects, contingent relations among utilities, and feedback cycles.

The market lacks corrective influences for benign and malign cycles, favors present over future utilities, has no handle on second-order market protective devices, and mixes trivial and important utilities in a disorderly cafeteria of choice.

Positive feelings increase altruistic behavior and altruistic behavior increases feelings of well-being; thus the market's success in satisfying human wants, and thereby increasing feelings of satisfaction, contributes to moral behavior or moral delinquency. Moral pollution by the market is diminished by two processes: (1) People weigh separately the contributions to their happiness of moral acts and economic acts, and (2) people apply different codes appropriately to different domains. Based on relatively weak evidence of the influence of the market on moral standards, I conclude that, aside from the interaction problems among domains mentioned, there are no serious difficulties in adding moral and commercial utilities in the same accounting system.

As Griffin said: "We can never reach final assessment of ways of life by totting up lots of small, short-term utilities."[51]

[51] Griffin, *Well-Being*, 34.

PART VIII

Conclusion

29 Can the wheel of history turn again?

As I approach the end of my long exposition I address the promise of reforming economic institutions along the lines suggested in this book. What are the elements of culture and society that promote and retard these economic reforms? Selectively, I turn to underlying economic and ethical ideas, to values, practices, resources, and to the inherent features of the market that may favor the producer economy (Part V) and, beyond that, the broader goals of well-being and human development.

Ultimately (or penultimately, for materialists) it is ideas expressed in institutions that shape the market experience. Like many other institutions, the market can perform only as well as the intellectual disciplines that guide and criticize it. When medical practice followed the "doctrine of signatures," ringworm was treated with fowl feces because the patterns of these feces resembled the pattern of the ringworm. Later, when medicine identified ringworm as a viral infection, the treatment changed accordingly. Similarly, without an adequate economic theory of market behavior, market institutions cannot cure their illnesses. And without adequate guiding theories, market institutions currently fail to achieve their own ends, facilitating utility maximization. (Human development is not acknowledged as an appropriate end by most market economists.) In Chapter 27 we found some fundamental causes accounting for people's misinterpretation of the sources of their own happiness; in like fashion we seek here some underlying causes accounting for the misinterpretation of the market experience by the disciplines that interpret and criticize it.

The first topic in this final chapter, therefore, deals with certain features of the parent disciplines, disciplines that might be called the deep structure of our knowledge system. I will point out flaws in the way the humanist critique[1] conceives of human development and embraces the hidden causal explanations in ethics, a philosophical discipline quite devoid of any causal theory. For the reasons given throughout the discussion in this book, the microeconomic defense of the market is also considered deeply flawed, especially its theories of human behavior. Both ethics and microeconomics rely upon interpretations of behavior without reference to any scientific theory of that behavior.

The second topic in this chapter deals with a proposed rotation of the axis about which the major politicoeconomic debate of this century revolved. An *axis* of this kind has two central properties: First, it offers to whole societies a central theme

[1] The roster of humanist critiques is extensive. Illustratively, for the eighteenth century I might cite Montesquieu as a critical proponent and Ferguson as a major Scottish Enlightenment critic; in the nineteenth century Thomas Carlyle and William Morris represent competing lines of criticism; in the twentieth century the Frankfurt School authors, Horkheimer and Adorno, precede the important work of the Frankfurt School diaspora, Erich Fromm, Herbert Marcuse, and Leo Lowenthal; Lewis Mumford represents an aesthetic–social critic and Hannah Arendt a more purely philosophical one. Recent British critics include Robert Goodin and Bernard Williams; and French critics include Jean-Paul Sartre and Alain Touraine. There are many more. I have not included the Marxist critics, who often agree with the humanists but have an underlying materialist (as well as economistic) critique.

giving purpose and direction to their striving while it gives meaning to themes ancillary to the central ones. As we shall see, the principal politicoeconomic axis in the twentieth century turned on the question of jurisdiction over the economy by market or state. This axial question then enlisted and gave meaning to arguments about the "natural" human propensities thought to favor or oppose laissez-faire economics. Second, an axial theme creates major partisan camps whose shifting alignments produce the dominant patterns of political life. The idea of a *rotated* axis signifies a change in the *agenda* of debate, as contrasted to new arguments supporting the positions taken along the old axis. One may think of a rotated axis as a shift in Kuhnian paradigms but without the implied need for a change in cohorts.

In order for market institutions to "triumph," a change from religious and communal axes to an economic axis was necessary.[2] After the triumph, as mentioned, the major politicoeconomic axial problem turned on the scope of the triumphant market – "socialism" and "capitalism" are the blunt terms sometimes used for this much more complex set of problems. A third axial change is proposed here, a change from an economistic axis to one that focuses not on local "utilities" but on satisfaction with life-as-a-whole, and not on physical capital but on a kind of "human capital" quite foreign to most economists. Schumpeter is an exception: "One may care less for the efficiency of the capitalist process in producing economic and cultural values than for the kind of human beings that it turns out and then leaves to their own devices, free to make a mess of their lives."[3]

The proposed new axis needs a name. Because of the consumer bias of the economistic axis, I have called the economy designed to replace that consumer economy the "producer economy." But that term refers to a proposed kind of economy instead of an axis of argument and rationalization of performance. It does not characterize an axis. For want of a better name, I call the proposed new axis, the *well-being–developmental* axis, thus embracing the two ends I have claimed to be final goods.

Axial rotations occur when some exogenous force (such as technology) finds or develops supporting ideas, practices, and resources. The rotation needs supporting values and concepts of human nature sufficiently weighty to make a rotation possible. Rotations also require the new skills and practices that institutions quietly, almost secretly, develop to implement the proposed rotation. And a rotation needs sufficient resources to feed its needs. In a third section we will examine the sources of support and resistance, the practices and behavioral patterns that might facilitate or hinder the proposed axial rotation.

Even when many of their members know something is seriously wrong, societies cannot easily change their ways. Anthropology and history are teachers of the many devices societies employ to maintain patterns yielding to the majority of their populations only inferior solutions to their problems – and sometimes yielding misery,

[2] Albert O. Hirschman, *The Passions and the Interests: Political Arguments for Capitalism Before Its Triumph* (Princeton: Princeton University Press, 1977).
[3] Joseph A. Schumpeter, *Capitalism, Socialism, and Democracy,* 3d ed. (London: Allen & Unwin, 1950): 129.

alienation, dumb endurance, and poverty. In conclusion, I turn to three paradigms of change and "pattern maintenance" (Parsons), locating the sources of resistance to economic change. This is the fourth main topic.

Misinterpretation of the market experience

A critique of humanist criticism

In the brief compass of this conclusion we will examine two features of the humanist critique of the market experience, a theory of human development and a related theory of ethical behavior. These two aspects of the humanist critique offer major weaknesses in the deep structure of the humanist analysis.

Human development. The dominant humanist ideology (or, by some accounts, the liberal ideology) from Locke to Smith to J. S. Mill to Rawls has been altered from time to time, most notably to accommodate Manchester liberalism and then to modify this view and accommodate the welfare state. But persistent through the changes has been the ideal of individuals developing themselves to their fullest capacities. The unreconstructed laissez-faire supporters of this ideal have employed too hopeful a view of what they regard as an autotelic motivation to develop, and the "reconstructed" or welfare branch has been overpoliticized. This second group has failed to understand the positive contribution made to human development by the market experience.

The laissez-faire theories of spontaneous human drives for self-development, well expressed earlier by Enlightenment theorists and later by social Darwinists, holds that people are motivated to develop themselves. Thus the chief social Darwinist, Herbert Spencer, argued that mankind's striving nature, if permitted to run its course, would create a superior person as well as a superior civilization.[4] In recent thought Fromm also expressed this view: "Man," he said, has certain "inherent . . . tendencies to grow, to develop and realize potentialities which man has developed over the course of history – as, for instance, the faculty of creative and critical thinking and of having differentiated emotional and sensuous experiences."[5] If that were the case, our common task would be one of removing obstacles to these inherent tendencies. Unfortunately, we have found no evidence of any strong indigenous motive for cognitive or moral development similar to those hypothesized by hopeful liberal thinkers from Condorcet and Holbach to Fromm and Maslow. Wanting to be "a better person" is quite general, of course, but that particular human want is not self-activating; to be realized, it needs both social support and institutionalized means, and possibly extrinsic rewards. What is missing in laissez-faire economics is an account of how economic life provides these supports, means, and rewards.

[4] Herbert Spencer, *Social Statics: Or The Conditions of Human Happiness* (1850; reprint New York: D.Appleton, 1878), 483. In the latter part of the nineteenth century in the United States, but much less so in Great Britain, this Spencerian doctrine was the orthodoxy of the committed supporters of the market. See Thomas C. Cochran and William Miller, *The Age of Enterprise* (New York: Harper & Row, 1961).
[5] Erich Fromm, *Escape From Freedom* (New York: Rinehart, 1941), 288.

Ethical preferences for self-help do not settle the question of under what circumstances people *can* help themselves.

Whereas liberals of the Manchester school were content to let individuals find their own way to develop themselves or to "make a mess out of their lives," liberals who opposed the human injuries of the unreconstructed market turned to the state for help. Their theories were overpoliticized in the sense that they relied too much on governments and not enough on markets to foster development. One can understand why Aristotle should have held that the state, rather than commerce, was responsible for developing the virtue and excellence of individuals, but much later, after the market had prospered, John Stuart Mill still relied on government to "promote the virtue and intelligence of the people themselves,"[6] and Durkheim, perhaps because of his concern with the raging appetites encouraged by markets, still held that in modern society the development of individual personalities and their liberation from the families and villages that "absorbed" them was primarily a state function. A strong state, he said, is not a danger to human development but a condition for it.[7] T. H. Green and Rawls follow in this path. It is as though an institution capable of conscious direction is somehow more consequential to human development than one, like the market, that is autocephalic and self-regulating. The state may be more amenable to direction, but there is no reason to believe that it is more consequential.

The reconstructed liberals' and other humanists' antipathy to the market has blinded them to its capacity to educate and teach developmental skills. One source of this antipathy lies in the humanist preference for the intrinsic, the self-motivated, the unconditioned response. Governments may foster situations, but at work or elsewhere, where intrinsic satisfactions are encouraged, markets, which rely on exchange and contingent reinforcement, cannot. The intrinsic cannot be exchanged. Humanist critics, therefore, adopted a morbid antipathy to exchange and were thereby blinded to the ways exchange itself teaches self-attribution and personal control by means of these contractually contingent responses (Chapter 9).

But the main reason why the humanist critique of market influences on human development falters is that the ethics on which humanists rely is, as a discipline, devoid of any causal theory of how people learn. All causal inferences are the province of science; when philosophy trespasses on this province, as it does whenever it seeks to assess the consequences of, say, a moral rule, it does so at the risk of violating the standards of its philosophical neighbor, the philosophy of science. We turn next to this problem of ethical theory.

Ethical theories of behavior. In addition to a misinterpretation of the social sources of human development, the humanist critique is flawed by its reliance on ethical theories that are often unhelpful. These theories may be broadly divided among deontologists, intentionalists (who may also be deontologists), and conse-

---

[6] John Stuart Mill, "Considerations on Representative Government," in R. B. McCallum, ed., *On Liberty and Considerations on Representative Government* (Oxford, UK: Blackwell, 1946), 127.
[7] See Steven Lukes, *Emile Durkheim: His Life and Work* (London: Allen Lane/The Penguin Press, 1973), 326.

quentialists. *Deontology* is a nonconsequentialist ethics that focuses on the right without regard to the good. This pattern of thinking is a disaster when applied to any *system* where acts affecting one element of a system will inevitably affect other elements, for any change in these other elements reverberates back on the original ethical purpose (Chapter 2). For example, moral codes that substantially reduce productivity, like the Christian economics of the medieval period, reduce the *affluence effect* that we found to be a fruitful condition for ethical behavior.

Intentionalists rule out consequences on the grounds that only intentions qualify as moral, for one cannot say that a man who intends good but mistakenly, even after prudent inquiry, achieves only harmful consequences is ethically to blame. Only benevolence or, as Kant would say, good will, is ethically good. But it will be recalled that Adam Smith pointed out that we do not expect our dinner from the benevolence of the butcher, the baker, and the brewer. Rather, it is their self-interest (selfishness) to which we appeal. Ethical condemnation is not relieved by the benign outcome of the hidden hand, which is a mainstay of the market analyst's consequentialist argument.

Consequentialist ethics suffers from what is fatal to any analysis of consequences: neither ethics nor philosophy in any form has within its own arsenal of skills a capacity to analyze cause and effect nor to ascertain facts. Two examples will illustrate the point about its ad hoc causal theories: Rawls's theory of the effects of civil rights on self-esteem is, by the evidence analyzed in Chapter 10, quite wrong, whereas Kant's idea that unhappy people are likely to be less moral is, by other evidence on the influence of "positive affect," correct. In Chapter 4 we found in this Kantian understanding a reason for attributing to the market a benign, if derivative, influence on ethical behavior.

If causal theory is one of the weaknesses of ethical reasoning, attitudes toward "facts" is another. The two are related; since "facts" are observations in the light of a theory, relevant "facts" will not be acknowledged without a relevant theory. Furthermore, since interesting facts (especially facts dealing with relations) rarely lie on the surface of things, they require an investigatory apparatus to ferret them out. Without that, one must not only rely on the observations of others but also be able independently to assess their worth. It is for this problem of assessing the evidence that ethics is unprepared.

More seriously, ethical theorists sometimes claim that factual observations do not affect the standards of ethical behavior; to say otherwise, they say, is to commit (one version of) the naturalistic fallacy, going from is to ought. Ethics, however, is loaded with factual assumptions where ought depends on is. For example, like economists, many humanists believe that well-being is roughly measured by level of income, and they therefore draw the inference that to achieve significant equality of well-being society must equalize incomes. The findings reported in Chapter 26 that well-being is, above a decent minimum, relatively unaffected by level of income reveal how a corrected understanding of facts can lead to a fairly radical change in ethical priorities. More generally, it is a rule in ethics that one cannot impose a moral obligation beyond human capacities, that is, "ought" implies "can." Thus, recent findings on the limits of cognitive abilities also limit moral obligation.

Ethicists demand of people a kind of moral accountability that is beyond their capacities.[8]

Together these (and other) errors in interpreting the right and the good constitute the *ethical fallacy* that makes the humanist criticism of the market prone to error. The failure to take account of research on well-being as well as on economic motives, thinking, and behavior produces an ethically attractive, compassionate, often elegant version of utopian thinking that all will admire and none implement. But the failure of ethics to mount a credible critique is not ethically neutral, for it leaves intact a market economy that not only fails to advance the ends of well-being and human development, but also the high ethical ends of the ethicists.

Yet humanists sometimes have a wisdom that both economists and behavioral scientists lack. The multidisciplinary analysis of society transcends the limits of the social sciences.

A critique of microeconomics

This is not a book on economics, certainly not on macroeconomics with its sophisticated analyses of, for example, the money supply, the effects of interest rates on production, international trade, money and banking systems, and determinants of factor prices. It is a criticism of microeconomics, already under siege from many sources, including economists.[9] My criticism focuses on those features of microeconomics dealing with the determinants of economic behavior. As noted in Chapter 1, there is a difference between the discipline of microeconomics and the market phenomena it analyzes. In this discussion of concepts and theories underlying market failures, we turn first to the discipline and deal later and more briefly with the inherent defects of the market that it interprets.

It is, of course, in the discipline and not the market that methodological problems are located. Of the discipline, Schumpeter said that economics derived from interpretation of our "common experience," but this was not, he thought, an experience held in common with other disciplines. He said that economic theory, or at least important parts of it, is a system of logic, not of psychology.[10] It is in the spirit of

---

[8] Also, few ethical theories give an accounting of either the rule to follow when obligations are in conflict or, more generally, the limits of obligation. See James S. Fishkin, *The Limits of Obligation* (New Haven: Yale University Press, 1982). The conflict between market and bureaucratic ethical prescriptions are illustrated by the experiment reported in Chapter 11, showing that whereas the children of civil servants, with their rule-governed ethic, without consideration of exchange tended to help others asking for help, the children of entrepreneurs tended to give help only if the help could be reciprocated. See Leonard Berkowitz, "A Laboratory Investigation of Social Class and National Differences in Helping Behavior," *International Journal of Psychology* 1 (1966): 231–42.

The entrepreneurial children's concept of self-reliance is congruent with recent work in ethics suggesting that donors have an obligation to consider the effects of help on the donee, perhaps as a guard against developing dependency in another. The conflict between two concepts of justice, with their implied moralities, is further illustrated by the conflicting accounts given by Rawls and Nozick. John Rawls, *A Theory of Justice* (Cambridge: Harvard University Press, 1971); Robert Nozick, *Anarchy, State, and Utopia* (New York: Basic Books, 1974).

[9] "A number of our fellow economists do share with us a sense of general malaise afflicting contemporary microeconomic theory." Richard R. Nelson and Sidney G. Winter, *An Evolutionary Theory of Economic Change* (Cambridge: Harvard University Press, 1982), 4.

[10] Joseph A. Schumpeter, *History of Economic Analysis*, ed. from manuscript by Elizabeth Boody Schumpeter (New York: Oxford University Press, 1954), 28, 1,058.

the latter observation that economists rely on deductions from a few simple axioms in their efforts to account for economic behavior. But because two of the principal axioms regarding human behavior, that is, people may be characterized by their rationality and greed, are thoroughly misleading, economists fail to account for much of the complexity of economic behavior. Nor have the laws of large numbers saved economic analysis of individual behavior from the perils of this axiomatic treatment, although economists' success in accounting for the behavior of *firms* is substantial and should be a lesson to psychologists on the limits of their individualistic discipline. And the elegance of economists' systemic analyses where each element relates to other elements in predictable ways can teach all of us a great deal that is valuable.

Of course, Friedman is right when he says that for any discipline it is not the accuracy of its assumptions but their fruitfulness that determines whether or not they should be accepted.[11] But throughout this work we have found that the fruit of many of the economists' assumptions were, in fact, not nourishing. Fruitfulness, like efficiency, is relative to the goals pursued, and if the goal of economics is to account for human behavior to the end that utility may be maximized, Friedman must be disappointed. In an ongoing discipline the use of the accepted principles of science would seem to imply a constant effort to correct its assumptions so as to improve each successive observation.

It would be tedious to recapitulate the many criticisms of microeconomics reported in this book, but in this critique of the way that discipline monitors the market experience, we may recall some of the main criticism: Economics cannot understand economic behavior without a general theory of behavior;[12] it cannot understand the actual working of the economic *system* without understanding the social system of which it is a part.[13] Economics cannot understand a money economy without understanding how people think about money and its symbols (Chapters 5 and 6); it should not assume that people employ a particular form of cognition, rationality, when the evidence shows that they do not (Chapter 3). It is wrong to think of work as the sacrifice made by workers to acquire commodities and leisure when work has intrinsic value for many workers (Chapters 18 and 19); a discipline that does not have independent measures of its dependent variable, for example, utility, risks its standing as a scientific discipline (Chapters 23 and 27); a discipline cannot deal sensibly with the "satisfaction of human wants" without inquiring into the nature of satisfaction and of wanting (Chapters 22 and 23); and where processes are the sources of both satisfaction and the development of human capital (Chapter 13), evaluating the system exclusively on the basis of its outcomes must be regarded as a form of tunnel vision.

In many ways our problems with the discipline of economics refer to its claim to be a science dealing with how to satisfy human wants. Adam Smith and John Stuart Mill saw economics as the science of wealth, but Edgeworth, Jevons, Marshall,

---

[11] Milton Friedman, *Essays in Positive Economics* (Chicago: University of Chicago Press, 1953), 14.
[12] See Stephen E. G. Lea, Roger M. Tarpy, and Paul Webley, *The Individual in the Economy* (Cambridge, UK: Cambridge University Press, 1987).
[13] C. West Churchman, *Challenge to Reason* (New York: McGraw-Hill, 1968).

Mises, and now, as Stigler points out, the entire discipline, have all accepted the idea that economics is the science of satisfying human wants, or at least of relieving dissatisfaction. The change is unfortunate because it identifies wealth with satisfaction and, by extension, with happiness, a claim that is quite unjustified. The identification of wealth with happiness and with satisfaction focused on life-as-a-whole is the *economistic fallacy*.

The behavioral sciences. The sciences of behavior do not solve the problems either of the humanists' critique or of the economists' defense, or, of course, the defects inherent in markets (see following). What they do is to offer to both approaches a body of theory and research findings that should inform the work of each approach. The arguments among psychologists over the relative explanatory strength of situations, for example, market institutions, and of persons, for example, workers and consumers, is fruitful[14] and, suitably focused, might give us a picture of persons responding to market situations. I have, however, found no psychology of the market (although consumer psychology and industrial psychology offer partial pictures) and have had, in tentative fashion, to create my own. In the process I have found many instances where the laws and findings of economics would be useful to behavioral scientists were they but recognized.[15]

Only by a convocation of these several disciplines in invisible colleges will a proper interpretation of the market experience be possible. In the meantime let us examine how the change in focus from *economic* welfare to more promising pursuits of happiness and human development alters the current lines of politicoeconomic argument.

Changing the axis of the century-old debate in political economy

Schumpeter once said: "Though we proceed slowly because of our ideologies, we might not proceed at all without them."[16] Most of our ideologies were framed by the familiar issues of the twentieth-century politicoeconomic axial debate over the role of the state in the production and distribution of wealth. The implications of this book simply do not fit the framework of an ideology thus framed. This section explains how the ideologies of our time fail to fit the social science evidence presented in earlier chapters and explains why we "proceed so slowly" and why we may not "proceed at all" without new ideologies. Claims in the 1950s and 1960s about "the end of ideology" represented an early intimation of this needed ideological change.

The axis of the familiar debate between Left and Right has been largely economic on the correct assumption that economic welfare was the foundation of life and the incorrect assumption that quality of life or happiness was (above a decent minimum)

[14] See, e.g., Walter Mischel, *Personality Assessment* (New York: Wiley, 1968).
[15] For an exception, see Lea et al., *The Individual in the Economy*. What psychology needs above all else is the kind of systems theory exemplified by economics, a theory that would integrate the many particular findings of a fragmented discipline or, really, set of disciplines.
[16] Joseph A. Schumpeter, "Science and Ideology," *American Economic Review* 39 (1949), 359.

directly related to levels of income and wealth. With new information on the relation between wealth and happiness, information that reflective introspection tends to confirm, we can now see that it is time to change the axis of that debate so as to focus on happiness and human development. This does not ignore economic issues but rather reformulates them so that they serve these widely accepted ends. Let us examine the effects of the proposed change in axis on the conventional ideological partisans, the Left and the Right.

The Left–Right dimension

In a period when Left in command economies seeking to break out of their unhappy molds refers to capitalists and the Right to communists, the Left–Right dimension becomes totally relativistic and can refer only to support or opposition to some status quo, whatever it may happen to be. Prior to this semantic catastrophe, Left has meant greater egalitarianism than that favored by the Right, a greater disposition to favor collective (public) goods than the Right, and less faith in the market processes than the Right. Both Left and Right commit the *economistic fallacy* and both place their faith in rationality, the Left preferring to call it Reason.[17] These dimensions of the Left–Right debate do not properly address the promotion of happiness and human development.

One reason for this deflection is that both Left and Right follow in the footsteps of economics and commit the same errors: They allow consumer interests to dominate producer interests. In their quarrel over income distribution both groups fail to see that it is not individual wealth but, though individually owned, the collective wealth of a society that most influences well-being. Their particular quarrel over title of ownership of the means of production is mistaken because ownership does not make much difference to workers if the processes of production remain the same. More generally, the Left–Right quarrel turns on outcomes, whereas (as mentioned) it is the *processes* of producing these outcomes that embrace the important experiences affecting happiness and human development.

Both Left and Right must, in the process of framing their world-views, formulate a version of human nature. But we are no longer free to do this in a folk medicine fashion and without understanding the characteristic strengths and weaknesses of human thinking processes, the nature of motivation, the processes of interpersonal attraction, the way people characteristically think of justice, and the bases of altruistic and selfish behavior; in short, if not human nature at least human behavior.

Each of the poles of the Left–Right dimension has its own characteristic failings.

The political Left. The emphasis of the Left on *economic* equality is mistaken not only because after a decent minimum, income does not affect the quality of life very much, but also because subjective well-being is already much more equally distributed than is income; to change the distribution of income above that decent minimal level will not affect the current pattern of subjective well-being.

---

[17] For a sensitive analysis of the role of reason in Left and Right, see Silvan Tomkins, "Left and Right: A Basic Dimension of Ideology and Personality," in Robert W. White, ed., *The Study of Lives* (New York: Atherton, 1963), 388–411.

The emphasis on economic *equality* is also mistaken because what gives people a sense of dignity is the opportunity to achieve and control their own environments and to develop along the unique paths (ladders) that life confronts them with or that they have chosen. Providing that these paths offer genuinely open opportunities for movement, it does not matter for either happiness or human development whether or not the paths start from the same level plateau. Furthermore, equality is undemocratic in that it does not reflect popular wants – almost no one wants it.[18] Moreover, emphasis on equality of outcome increases invidious social comparisons for it makes salient each person's position with respect to others (Chapter 12). On the other hand, genuine equality of opportunity, the Right's form of equality (though espoused more in the abstract than in practice), not only fails to increase invidiousness, but also positively increases cognitive flexibility, self-esteem, democratic orientations, and the value to the individual of self-direction. Finally, because the Left employs ethical criteria without regard to the consequences that a behavioral theory might suggest, it commits the *ethical fallacy*.

Between Left and Right. Both the Left and the Right have branches that are essentially communitarian, and communitarianism is one position that transcends the old ideological boundaries. Where the *economistic fallacies* of both Left and Right hold that economic rewards are closely identified with happiness, the doctrines of communitarianism imply that economic productivity is subordinate to the happiness and well-being of community life. It is inattentive to the economic consequences of the supremacy of community ideals, ideals that are generally dysfunctional to productivity and threaten to deprive society of what I have called *the affluence effect,* the effect of increases in social income that improve people's well-being and the features of human development treated in the text (Chapter 26). The substitution of affiliative motives for productive motives risks a level of poverty that has the damaging influence on cognition pointed out in Chapter 7. To understand these economic effects, communitarians must become systems analysts who take pains to understand both the economic importance of lack of mobility, lumpy factors of production, and markets failing to respond to changes in demand on the one hand, and the behavioral consequences of a return to gemeinschaft on the other.

The political Right. The unreconstructed, "Manchester" Right is, of course, an apostle of economic laissez-faire and the more or less unbridled market. For the reasons we have so laboriously examined in this book this position is untenable. Its underlying defects are the same as those I identified as defects of the theories of microeconomics – and of the market itself, as we shall see.

Psychic income from work or consumption: dilemmas for Left and Right. The shift from the money axis to the work axis jumbles the Left–Right argument in other ways. For example, the shift to the work axis should please the Right, recently

---

[18] Robert E. Lane, "The Fear of Equality," *American Political Science Review* 53 (1959): 35–51; Lee Rainwater, *What Money Buys: Inequality and the Social Meaning of Income* (New York: Basic Books, 1974).

so critical of the decline of the work ethic, attitudes of dependency among welfare recipients, and the alleged hedonism of the time. And it should alarm the Left because it deemphasizes the treasured doctrine of income equality. But, ironically, because the purpose of this shift is neither the fulfillment of duty nor increased productivity, but rather work enjoyment and learning at work, it should offend the Right and please the Left. This combination of offensiveness and gratification is a sure sign that we are working on a different axis.

The shift from (psychic) income derived from consumption to (psychic) income derived from working upsets the usual partisan alignment in another way. The Left favors redistribution of income by the state, but the change in axis has a strange consequence for the capacity of the state to redistribute sources of gratification from the haves to the have-nots. One can distribute self-direction at work widely or narrowly depending only minimally on technology and somewhat more on the available distribution of the skills on which self-direction relies. But *redistribution* is different. Although one can *redistribute authority* so as fruitfully to help one person at the expense of another, one cannot take *self-direction* or pride of achievement and personal control from one to give to another. Thus, the Left's preference for state redistribution of goods is frustrated by the change in axis while the Right's preference for laissez-faire is well served.

Self-direction and work satisfaction are distributed along the lines of the privileged-class hierarchy, the hierarchy of those who derive their (psychic) income from work (Chapter 15). This puts urban professors at the top of the ladder. Whereas the top of the *income* hierarchy is vulnerable to a *re*distribution of its particular resources, the top of the hierarchy based on psychic *income from work,* especially professors, scientists, professionals, artisans, and artists, is secure from depredations of this kind. They are thus doubly privileged.

In short, the strange effects of making work a positive utility discussed in Chapter 21 includes a radical change in the partisan debates between what has historically been a recognizable Left and Right.

We now turn from the partisan effects of a change along the well-being–developmental axis to a different question: What cultural and institutional features of society favor or impede the proposed axial rotation? Along the way we seek to learn something from the mostly eighteenth-century rotation where the precepts of the market were themselves the elements of the then newly proposed economistic axis.[19]

The challenge of axial rotation

Predisposing changes in beliefs, values, and motives
Major institutional changes are usually prompted by changes in objective circumstances, such as technology, trade routes, and economic or military dominance. But the sparks thus kindled must have tinder to make a blaze. Changed objective circumstance must find supporting themes in culture, especially in social *values* stipulating what is worth striving for and in *beliefs* about what causes what. Among

[19] See Hirschman, *The Passions and the Interests;* Milton L. Myers, *The Soul of Modern Economic Man: Ideas of Self-Interest, Thomas Hobbes to Adam Smith* (Chicago: University of Chicago Press, 1983).

these themes, attributional beliefs are crucial: Is it fate, or "the authorities," or economic "laws" beyond individual control that determine outcomes, or is it individual effort and skill? And if individual effort causes relevant changes, whose efforts count? Changes in *motives* follow from these changed beliefs and values, for, with some exceptions, people will be motivated to support or pursue or worship objects embodying the new values only if they can in some manner influence or attain them.[20] However, those features of a culture that indiscriminately support the themes of both the old axis and the new one are not helpful to an axial rotation; to be helpful they must be discriminating, selectively promoting the themes of the new axis. In this section we seek to identify the elements of culture that prepare us for a rotation embodying the themes of the *well-being–developmental* axis.

What we will find is an integrated culture whose values, beliefs, and motives are bound together by the tenets of the economistic fallacy, the belief that an individual's sense of well-being is primarily a function of income and wealth. This causal belief is supported by ethical values, namely that to pursue happiness through material gain is ethically acceptable. To penetrate this well-armored belief, some chinks in the armor, some contrary beliefs, values, and motives must be found or created.

Changes in predisposing beliefs. Since most people's beliefs that higher income will increase their long-term sense of well-being are largely false, the problem of changing from an economistic axis to a well-being axis seems to be *only* a matter of persuasion. It is a cognitive matter first and only after that a matter of motivation or evaluation. But given the evidence that people often do not know what makes them happy and must rely on prevalent social theories of the general sources of happiness (Chapter 27), these popular theories must first be corrected. We are returned again to what seems to be the current fountainhead of materialist theories of utility, microeconomics (and, strangely, also to its socialist and humanist – but economistic – critics). Is microeconomics, then, the central source of human unhappiness and the frustration of wants? Probably not.[21]

There are at least two reasons for believing that microeconomics plays only a minor role in perpetuating the economistic fallacy. First, everyone has *experiential* evidence that a sense of well-being is increased by an increase in income and decreased by a decrease in income. But these changes in hedonic states are only temporary (Chapter 26). Adaptation rapidly erodes these feelings and the new *level* of income is no more likely to increase a sense of well-being than did the previous level. But people do not normally differentiate temporary increases in well-being because of a *change* in income from the enduring sense of well-being that might be associated with any particular *level* of income.

[20] John W. Atkinson, "Motivation for Achievement," in Thomas Blass, ed., *Personality Variables in Social Behavior* (New York: Halsted/Wiley, 1977); Milton Rokeach, *The Nature of Human Values* (New York: Free Press, 1973), 14–16.

[21] Without help from microeconomics, the Enlightenment contained a strong materialistic theme. For example, the French philosopher, Mercier de la Riviere, argued in 1767 that "humanly speaking, the greatest possible happiness for us consists in the greatest possible abundance of objects suitable to our enjoyment and the greatest possible liberty to profit by them." Mercier de la Riviere, *l'ordre naturel et essential des societé politiques* (1767) reported in John Bury, *The Idea of Progress* (1920; reprint New York: Macmillan, 1932), 173.

Second, there are broad historicocultural reasons for the economistic fallacy. If helped by religion, or, better still, by secularism, *scarcity* will always generate materialistic theories of happiness. The cultural themes offering resistance to these theories can only emerge in an era of relative affluence – hence the crucial importance of the affluence effect. But given the long tradition of reasoning about scarcity, persuading even the members of the middle class that their sense of well-being does not stem from their incomes and their possessions will be uphill work. As Karl Polanyi points out, those who doubt the verity of this belief that they work primarily for money are in trouble: "He who would have refused to imagine that he was acting for gain alone was . . . considered not only immoral, but also mad."[22]

Nevertheless, the evidence in the quality-of-life studies showing a decline among the better off in the correlation between wealth and self-reported happiness suggests why prosperous people may now begin to doubt that it is income that makes them happy.[23]

Changes in predisposing values. The predominantly eighteenth-century axial change from reliance on religious piety and communitarian values to material and individualistic values was preceded by helpful religious changes making good works, rather than faith alone, a source of salvation (Luther) and then by other changes making the prospects of salvation evident to a person by his material prosperity (Calvin).[24] In Northern Europe, especially in Britain, this largely eighteenth-century change in values was also favored by early manifestations of acquisitiveness. In addition, readiness for the market's anticommunitarian individualism facilitated acceptance of the new economistic axis, as revealed by Alan MacFarlane's study of the development of individualism prior to the market.[25] There are many more such claims giving credit to a variety of predisposing cultural changes,[26] including the

[22] Karl Polanyi, "Our Obsolete Market Mentality," in his *Primitive, Archaic, and Modern Economics,* ed. G. Dalton (Boston: Beacon, 1971), 70.
[23] Angus Campbell, Philip E. Converse, and Willard L. Rodgers, *The Quality of American Life* (New York: Russell Sage, 1976), 28.
[24] Max Weber, *The Protestant Ethic and the Spirit of Capitalism,* trans. T. Parsons (New York: Scribner's, 1958). The British version seems more clearly "capitalist" than the American. Baxter says: "If you . . . choose the less gainful way, you cross one of the ends of your calling, and refuse to be God's steward, and to accept His gifts and use of them for Him when he requireth it." But in Cotton Mather's version, there were cautions against "overcharging" and "uncharitable . . . preying upon the weakness of another." Even though a market economy provided a field for testing one's salvation, the American version of the Protestant ethic was less enterprise oriented, for, says Mather, a man should "not launch out beyond his estate" in his business life. Richard Baxter, *Christian Directory,* quoted in Weber, *The Protestant Ethic and Spirit of Capitalism,* 162; Cotton Mather, "A Christian at His Calling," in Moses Rischin, ed., *The American Gospel of Success* (Chicago: Quadrangle Books, 1965). See also Kenneth Silverman, *The Life and Times of Cotton Mather* (New York: Harper & Row, 1984). Similarly, McClelland finds the origins of the achievement motive in religious orientations. See David C. McClelland, *Motivational Trends in Society* (Morristown, NJ: General Learning Press, 1971).
[25] Alan Macfarlane, *The Origins of English Individualism: The Family, Property, and Social Transition* (New York: Cambridge University Press, 1978).
[26] Hagen suggests another cultural basis: the creative force of ambition of a minority group with its own high standards, as among the Jews, Scots, and Ibos. Everett E. Hagen, *On the Theory of Social Change: How Economic Growth Begins* (Homewood, IL: Dorsey, 1962); Landes, an authority on technological change, reports that rationalism is a condition of modernization and, at least by implication, acceptance of the market. David Landes, *The Unbound Prometheus* (London: Cambridge University Press, 1969).

idea that the market corresponds to the pattern variables that Parsons and Shils say characterize modernity.[27] That earlier axial rotation was, indeed, favored by many predisposing changes in values.

Are there such cultural preparations available for the new axial rotation proposed? Consider the availability of support for elements in the well-being–developmental axis. The value of *happiness* is almost universal; relatively few today would agree with St. Augustine and the Puritans that happiness is not to be found in this world (Chapter 22). If the false beliefs of the economistic axis can be corrected, that universal value is a major source of support for the well-being portion of the well-being–developmental axis. The value of *self-esteem* is now also generally accepted (Chapter 10) and seems, like happiness, to be universal in the sense that everyone wants to think well of the self. If it can be shown that more people will believe in their self-worth when the axis of practice and debate have rotated off the economistic axis, another powerful value comes into play to support the new axial rotation. The value of *personal control* is less certainly universal, for, as Seligman and others have pointed out, it must be exercised to be learned.[28] If it is not learned it may not seem relevant to an individual. Yet, in some guise, the desire for personal control is said to be a cross-cultural and even cross-species value, or at least animals behave as though they valued highly some control over their own environments.[29] Under the name of *freedom* this value has been appropriated by market theorists for their economistic axis. But as *self-attribution* and especially as *personal control* the value seems more likely to fit the specifications of the well-being–developmental axis, for these terms focus on the values and skills that must be learned in order for a person to use environmental freedom.

But the value of cognitive complexity seems to have no internal correlative, no native drive to give it universal value. Support must come from external sources. In an affluent society those sources are available in the tendency for work to become more complex and therefore more demanding of complex cognition. This is true, at least, for those who do not fall out of the working labor force entirely or who are not displaced from complex industrial jobs to routine service sector jobs.

These mutations of common values prosper only if the dominant economistic, materialist values wane. Two accounts of a decline in materialistic values seem to suggest some preparation for a society less dependent on economistic values: Inglehart's findings on the postwar rise of a postmaterialist culture in Europe and the United States[30] and Veroff, Douvan, and Kulka's reports on a shift by an American

As we saw in Chapter 7, the greater capacity for cognitive differentiation among hunters and gatherers, compared to agriculturalists, may also rank as a kind of favorable predisposition for both the eighteenth-century and the proposed twenty-first-century rotations.

[27] Talcott Parsons and Edward A. Shils, "Values, Motives, and Systems of Action," in Parsons and Shils, eds., *Toward a General Theory of Action: Theoretical Foundations for the Social Sciences* (1951; reprint New York: Harper Torchbook, 1962), 80–4.

[28] Martin E. P. Seligman, *Helplessness: On Depression, Development, and Death* (San Francisco: Freeman, 1973).

[29] Ibid.; Robert W. White, "Motivation Reconsidered: The Concept of Competence," *Psychological Review* 66 (1959): 297–333; Herbert M. Lefcourt, *Locus of Control: Current Trends in Theory and Research* (Hillsdale, NJ: Erlbaum/Wiley, 1976).

[30] Ronald Inglehart, *The Silent Revolution* (Princeton: Princeton University Press, 1972).

population toward internal, nonmaterial standards of self-worth.[31] It is a slender hope, but it may be that the predispositions we seek are slowly becoming available for the proposed turn of the wheel of history.

Consumer values versus producer values. The wheel will not turn if consumer values remain dominant over producer values. As mentioned, economists' belief that work is a disutility to be endured only for the purpose of earning the utilities yielded by commodities and leisure (Chapter 21) is a brake on the rotation of history's ever-turning wheel. But there are reasons to believe that this particular conflict between consumer and producer values is different from other forms of value conflict. In this case each of the parties to the conflict has, so to speak, a minority interest in the victory of the other. Where each contestant is both a consumer and a worker, the conflict is not only over who will get what, but also over which of a person's plural values and roles will get more and which will get less. The axial rotation, then, relies on converting what is for some a purely subordinate interest into a dominant interest. That internalization of the conflict should ease the burden of change. Moreover, the group with a dominant interest in work values (because they derive their psychic income from work satisfaction more than from pay) is already powerful. Following my analysis in Chapter 15, this privileged class, as I have called it, may be increasing along with the decline in unskilled labor.

Changes in predisposing motives. Motives follow from two *beliefs:* the belief that one can actually attain some object and the belief that the object is valuable. It is the combination of these two beliefs that makes efforts to attain the object seem worthwhile. In our discussion of the pay maximization hypothesis (Chapter 17) we found reason to believe that most people do not, if they have alternatives, seek to maximize their pay. In spite of research showing that both blue- and white-collar workers often *do* work primarily for pay, later research shows that this is primarily by default: When jobs that are challenging and relatively unsupervised are available, almost *all* workers prefer these kinds of intrinsically satisfying jobs and will usually give these job characteristics priority.[32] There is a substantial literature showing a new priority for work with intrinsic, challenging characteristics.[33]

The proposed axial rotation, then, presents us with the task of giving intellectual grounds for practices that have no justification in the rationales of the economistic axis. Where the conflict between consumer values and producer values was characterized in part as an internal conflict between values present in the minds of most

[31] Joseph Veroff, Elizabeth Douvan, and Richard A. Kulka, *The Inner Americans: A Self-Portrait from 1957 to 1976* (New York: Basic Books, 1981).

[32] Edward E. Lawler, III, "Strategies for Improving the Quality of Work Life," *American Psychologist* 37 (1982): 486–93; Frederick Herzberg, *Work and the Nature of Man* (1966; reprint New York: Mentor/New American Library, 1973); Melvin L. Kohn and Carmi Schooler, *Work and Personality: An Inquiry into the Impact of Social Stratification* (Norwood, NJ: Ablex, 1983).

[33] See, for example, Christopher Jencks, Lauri Perman, and Lee Rainwater, "What Is a Good Job? A New Measure of Labor-Market Success," *American Journal of Sociology* 93 (1988): 1,322–57; Daniel Yankelovich and John Immerwahr, *Putting the Work Ethic to Work* (New York: Public Agenda Foundation, 1983).

working people, here we find a conflict between official doctrine and unofficial practice. (In some modest way, this book seeks to provide a theoretical basis for what people actually *do* and as such seeks to give a rationale to these untutored practices.) But that theory will not be accepted until the prevailing economistic fallacy is laid to rest.

In the next section we leave the sphere of culture and turn to the patterns of conflict proposed by the new axial rotation, comparing it with conflict along the economistic axis once instituted in part because of its promise of peaceful and mutually beneficial conflict.

Patterns of conflict in the economistic and well-being–developmental axis

What is so striking about the economistic argument is its promise of harmony. One route to this happy state is via the proposition that each person gains from an exchange where each is, in a sense, pitted *against* a partner. This apparent mutuality of interest is not only said to be true of individual relations, but through the manipulations of the hidden hand, it is also true socially. The hidden hand makes universal selfishness beneficial to all. Even more beneficently, as the economy grows *all* may profit. Together these three features of markets may seem to offer a variable sum game in which, as in Pareto optimality, individual gains are not at the cost of *anyone's* losses. The eighteenth-century axial rotation was defended on these principles, prior to Adam Smith on the grounds of a providential harmony that ensured peaceful relations and then, and apparently conclusively, on the basis of the hidden hand.[34]

But the actual market experience did not turn out to be so free of conflict. The competitive feature of market economics means that one person's gain may well be at the cost of another's loss. Also, although it may be true that over the long run, collective money income is not a fixed sum, in the short run it is: the condition for a zero sum game. These latter two features increase the intensity of the conflict.

The well-being–developmental axis may not be favored by support from divine Providence or a hidden hand, but it has other assets that mitigate the intensity of conflict. In only a few cases is it true that the happiness of one implies the unhappiness of another, such as where positive affect is derived from "downward comparisons,"[35] but in many other cases the happiness of one *increases* the happiness of others, as in work situations where the enjoyment of work by others increases one's own enjoyment.[36] Few think of the pursuit of happiness as a zero sum game for few believe in a limited "happiness fund" where one person's withdrawal leaves

---

[34] Myers, *The Soul of Modern Economic Man*, chap. 4. A variation on this view is the belief that "Providence favors trade between peoples as a means of promoting the universal brotherhood of man." See Jacob Viner, *The Role of Providence in the Social Order* (Princeton: Princeton University Press, 1972), 32. Finding this unpersuasive, still others employed the emerging concepts of physics: As in the heavens, some sort of human gravity must harmonize interests. Myers, *The Soul of Modern Economic Man*, chap. 6.

[35] Thomas Ashby Wills, "Downward Comparison Principles in Social Psychology," *Journal of Personality and Social Psychology* 90 (1981): 245–71.

[36] See Jencks et al., "What Is a Good Job?"

less for others. In this respect the pursuit of happiness is less conflictful than the piecemeal pursuit of utility.

Nor is human development a genuinely zero sum game (in spite of Hirsch's belief that the education of others limits the benefits an individual may derive from his or her own education).[37] Both Left and Right seem to agree on the possibility of reciprocal gain from personal development. Spencer says: "The ultimate man will be one . . . who, in spontaneously fulfilling his own nature, incidentally performs the functions of a social unity; and yet is only enabled so to fulfill his own nature by all others doing the like."[38] Marx and Engels conclude Part II of the *Communist Manifesto* with the following: "In place of the old bourgeois society, with its classes and class antagonisms, we shall have an association, in which the free development of each is the condition for the free development of all." The underlying argument is very like that of the market's ideas of the advantages of mutually satisfactory contracts, the beneficence of the hidden hand, and the social product of economic growth: Each person may gain without jeopardizing another's gains. But what is missing along the well-being–developmental axis is the kind of *guaranteed* mutual gain offered by market arguments.

Institutions, however, are not infinitely malleable. Just as one cannot adapt a dictatorship to a participatory system nor a church to the practices and ethos of a business firm without changing the institution beyond recognition, so it may be that one cannot adapt a consumer-driven market economy to an economy where producer benefits are given priority. The inner logic of institutions is such that certain demands made upon them are simply beyond their capacities. Can the market itself adapt to the changes demanded by the well-being–developmental axial rotation? We turn to that question now.

Adaptability of market institutions

None of the cultural and ideational predispositions mentioned could make possible the proposed axial rotation if the central institution, the market, is so designed as to frustrate the necessary changes. Thus, we must assess what features of the market are inherently, by the very constitution and purpose of the institution, resistant to these proposed changes. These resistances are not trivial. It is inherent in the market that it give consumer welfare priority over worker welfare because consumers are the sources of profits and workers are costs. Inasmuch as exchange is central to the market network of transactions, giving price signals for the self-regulating system, it is inherent in the market that intrinsic satisfactions, none of which can be exchanged, should lack consideration. For the same reason it is inherent in the market that outcomes should be the focus of concern, as opposed to the *processes* that contribute so much to life satisfaction. Competition, a necessary feature of the market, inherently creates a degree of insecurity detracting from the enjoyments of market outcomes and processes. And it is inherent in the market that price should be the measure of value, for there is no register for our preferred metric, "contribution to satisfaction with life-as-a-whole" (Chapter 25). It is not inherent that the

---

[37] Fred Hirsch, *Social Limits to Growth* (Cambridge: Harvard University Press, 1976).
[38] Spencer, *Social Statics*, 483.

measures of the value of production, GNP and its kin, should be employed by analysts to measure welfare, for there are substitutes such as Measure of Economic Welfare (Chapter 22), but it is inherent in the market economy that it use the "measuring rod of money" to register value and imputed value.

Would the proposed axial rotation toward a well-being–developmental axis be able to employ an institution so recalcitrant to its values? It will take an act of social invention to find the way, but perhaps within the nascent discipline of socioeconomics there are people with ideas who can contribute to the creative acts required for such a social invention.

In the meantime the market contributes in its way to both happiness and human development, principally through the *affluence effect* providing the material resources on which education, leisure, and moral development depend. By relieving poverty, the market takes a large step forward both in contributing to cognitive development and in making salient a variety of nonmaterial, or as Inglehart says, "post-material," values. By encouraging technology the market makes possible (but does not require) an increase in the kinds of work that are hedonically more satisfying and developmentally more stimulating. Along the way, the market encourages self-attribution and the sense of personal control, removes people from "the idiocy of rural life," and provides a stimulating environment that enriches cognition up to the point of overload. These benefits in well-being now flowing from a system based on an economistic axis serve as resistances to an axial rotation that may put the benefits at risk. The benefits of a less adequate solution are enemies of a better one.

Among the circumstances that favor axial rotations the level of available resources is a crucial element. We might even believe that if only the *affluence effect* could triumph over the market's *exchange effect* (Chapter 7), all would be well. Keynes seems to be saying something like this.

Will affluence promote an axial rotation favoring well-being and development?

As mentioned in the introductory chapters, in 1930 Keynes wrote an essay to his grandchildren advising them that the "permanent problem of mankind" would confront them squarely: How to live well. He proposes that when people are rich enough, there should be an axial rotation in practice and debate from problems of productive efficiency to problems of living an ethical, civilized, and prosperous life. He believed that when the miracles of compound interest and growth had made society rich enough,

all kinds of social customs and economic practices affecting the distribution of wealth and of economic rewards, which we now maintain at all costs however distasteful and unjust they may be in themselves, because they are tremendously useful in promoting the accumulation of capital, we shall then be free, at last, to discard. . . . We shall be able to afford to dare to assess the money-motive at its true value.[39]

[39] John Maynard Keynes, "Economic Possibilities for our Grandchildren," in his *Essays in Persuasion* (London: Macmillan, 1931), 63.

There are two points here: the consequence of affluence and the need to postpone the benign fruits of this affluence until the moment of sufficient social wealth has arrived. On the first of these, the character of "the permanent problem of mankind," I disagree with Keynes. In Keynes's treatment there is no indication that human development is a goal, whereas it is one of the two goals I have claimed to be paramount; where Keynes depreciates the *processes* of production, I find in them the key to happiness and development; the grounds on which Keynes depreciates the money-motive seem to be mainly ethical grounds (we are to call the motive by its right name, "avarice") but I depreciate the money-motive on hedonic grounds, for I find it to be a motive that misleads people in their pursuit of happiness. Keynes believes that the wealth that permits people to live well can be at least maintained, if not increased, without the conventions and motives that sustain the market in the period of accumulation, but we have found that it is not possible to promote the worker values contributing most to happiness in a market system that inherently makes it necessary to give priority to consumer values, that is, to the material aspects of Keynes's idea of "living well." Yet for all of that, as I pointed out in Chapter 1 and in the previous section, economic growth improves the quality of life as well as the level of living, and demonstrably increases people's sense of well-being (Chapter 26). Affluence makes it possible to address "the permanent problem of mankind" even if it does not tell us the solution to that problem.

In the meantime, are we condemned to "distasteful and unjust" practices that promote affluence? Our discussion of the affluence effect and the exchange effect partially supports this belief. In a line of argument parallel to Keynes's we would have to say that until the well-being–developmental axial rotation takes place, society must endure most of the "distasteful" features of the exchange effect.

Social diagnosis and social change

At the conclusion of this book I will classify the maintenance systems that preserve intact the kinds of ills that beset humankind and will seek to locate in this classification the social ills that we have been discussing in this book. Like physical illnesses, the relief of social illnesses depends upon their diagnosis, for, as mentioned earlier, no axial rotation is possible without understanding what sustains the axis that must be replaced. Diagnosis comes before remedy.

What might lead a society to devise and retain institutions that fail to foster as well as they might the happiness and personality development of its members? One answer depends upon whether the values of the society lend themselves to the tests of experience. If the central values are religious, as they were for a thousand years of Western history, they do not, and without possible confirmation or disconfirmation the society may persist in its misery-making, stultifying policies for a very long time. Deontological ethical values would suffer the same fate were it not for the fact that their expositors are secret consequentialists concerned with observable outcomes. Another answer is based on simple social lag; the learning curves of societies often have a low gradient, though they seem to be accelerating: Communism is a bundle of this-wordly, empirically testable propositions and, favored by the empirical nature of its predictions, history took only seventy years to show that the initially plausible tenets of communism are misleading. That is a relatively short historical time.

Three other patterns of explanations seem more relevant to the case at hand.

Type I: ignorance of the causes of social misery. One explanation follows from the thesis that people do not know what makes them happy (Chapter 27). Then imitation of more successful societies and trial-and-error are the only ways to learn. If one thinks of the various human societies as social experiments such that each can learn from the experience of others, isolation from other societies with more felicitous institutions would permit the patterns of misery-making institutions to continue without any ready means of correction. Or, in their isolation, if the evolutionary method of *accidental* experiments fails to reveal the benefits of mutant forms, societies will not learn from their own experience. Among the natives of Dobu, an island in the Western Pacific, belief in sorcery created such mutual suspicion that those friendly relations were missing that in other societies make people happier and life more rewarding.[40] Among the Manus, each newly wedded couple was so burdened by debt that they were required to spend the rest of their lives suffering from the obligations thus imposed. The leading elders of the society had experienced these burdens and passed them on to the relatively powerless young.[41] There seem to be few immanent forces in these societies to change their dysfunctional patterns; in these matters, at least, there is no dialectic. Under these circumstances one need not attribute social misery to defects of individuals or exploitation, but rather to the inadequacy of information and knowledge of the causes of well-being. We will call these kinds of endogenous dysfunctions based on local ignorance of the causes of their malaise, Type I.

The very idea that the social order could itself be a cause of unhappiness is said to be a product of "the modern age."[42] The modern age may have its own variants of Type I, however, where success limits progress. Pleased with second-best performances, converting an empirical hypothesis to a quasi-religious, heavily symbolized faith, employing deductive thinking "proving" that, in spite of evidence to the contrary, the given arrangement *must* be the best, even scholars could easily persist in their adoption of an unsatisfactory model. (Newton's success must have seemed to him good reason to reject Kepler's theory.)

Type II: exploitation. In other societies dysfunctional cultural patterns may be seen to benefit a leading group at the expense of others; those patterns can then be explained on the basis of elite interests in maintaining the pattern and thus serve as examples of exploitation and domination. Marx saw history as a succession of such social patterns, and because there are groups with more or less conscious

[40] R. F. Fortune, *Sorcerers of Dobu*, rev. ed. (London: Routledge & Kegan Paul, 1963).
[41] Margaret Mead, *New Lives for Old* (New York: Morrow, 1956).
[42] Albert O. Hirschman, "Rival Interpretations of Market Society: Civilizing, Destructive, or Feeble?" *Journal of Economic Literature* 20 (December 1982): 1,463–84 at 1,464–5.

interests in opposition to those of the elite, a dialectical diagnosis is at least possible. This category is Type II, a type to which the market economy has been assigned by socialists for well over a century. But, reinforced by the evidence already cited to the effect that people do not know what makes them happy, we should consider the possibility that the market pattern shares some features of the endogenous dysfunctionality of Type I as well.

   Type III: value conflict. As Ruth Benedict pointed out, every society must choose only a few of the many possible values that are available for human expression. A society that chooses piety will likely forego wealth; one that chooses honor in war will suffer the losses of war. The current conflict over the benefits of market societies falls mainly into this Type III category. Recognizing that for every chosen value there are opportunity costs, which values shall we emphasize? Okun's *Equality and Efficiency: The Big Tradeoff* represents one such choice between values in market societies;[43] the quality-of-life studies suggest other tradeoffs for national wealth: insecurity, possibly erosion of family life, a deprived underclass. I am suggesting a third tradeoff: between consumer values and producer values, or more drastically, between the pleasures of consumer wealth and producer happiness.

   The conflict over who gets what share of the money rewards is a Type III problem, but a conflict over what rewards shall be emphasized, a dispute over the *kinds* of tradeoffs to be made available, falls in Type III. But the selection of values is often framed in ignorance and governed by tradition – a Type I pattern. Support for the market, therefore, represents some combination of support for the interests of the better off (Type II), conscious preference for wealth over other values (Type III), and ignorance about alternatives available in a producer economy combined with the simple persistence of tradition (Type I).

   The remedy depends upon the illness. For the ills of Type I, ignorance of better alternatives, the remedy is to *teach* the members of the ill society about the alternatives. For the ills of Type II, exploitation of the weak by the strong, the remedy is to *mobilize forces* strong enough to relieve that exploitation. For the ills of Type III, the selection of values that one thinks unsatisfactory for some reason, the remedy is to *persuade* the misguided of their errors. To teach, persuade, and mobilize; there is no other way.

   But first we must *discover* how to make the market a better agent for promoting happiness and human development. I take my leave with that task only just begun.

[43] Arthur Okun, *Equality and Efficiency: The Big Tradeoff* (Washington, DC: Brookings Institution, 1975).

Author index

615

Subject index

abstraction, 253–4

acculturation, and cognitive complexity, 145–6

achievement, 471–2; socialization for in primitive economies, 119; and self-esteem, 186; motivation for, 367–8, 389–90, 488; and intrinsic satisfaction, 408; and happiness, 510–11

achievement–aspiration ratio, 446–7

acquisitiveness, lack of biological support for, 566

active life, hedonic value of, 488

actors and observers, effect of on attribution, 560

adaptation, 534; theory of, 73, 447; to economic change, 120; to environmental complexity, 147; and regression, 149–52; and dissatisfaction, 463; to unsatisfied wants, 464–5; and pain of withdrawal, 499; and homeostasis, 511; to higher incomes, 524; to income changes, 537, 604–5; and long-term income change, 538; and individual vs. collective income changes, 539–41; and materialist treadmill, 545

advertising, 466

affect balance, 479–80, 492–3; effect of income on, 499; see also felicific calculus; utilities, summation of

affect, negative, 67; see also depression, emotion

affiliation, 151; and work, 252–3; and pay, 357

affluence effect, 24, 27–8, 230, 540, 602; dependence of on extrinsic rewards, 419; as redeeming virtue of market, 422; and materialist treadmill, 545; effect of axial rotation, 610; see also economic growth

agricultural employment, 310–11

algorithms, 559–60

alienation, 256, 276–7, 459; and influence on work, 249

altruism, 98–9; effect of extrinsic rewards on, 373; and happiness, 585

ambivalence, 54–5, 107, 112, 343, 457, 582

American character, 214; humility in, 201; and "greed," 541–3

anomie, 97–8, 194, 463

antiintellectualism, 22, 133

anxiety, 29, 75, 300, 483; and money, 103

approach/avoidance, 342–3, 457–8

approval, social, as information, 212

arousal: by market, 60, 560–3; relation of to potential achievement, 97; and stress, 140; curvilinear theory of, 140–1; of aspirations, 188–9, 446–7, 458–9; and self-esteem, 186, 193–5; and indifference to money, 102–3; and ratio to achievements, 193–4; and internal locus of control, 464; hedonic effects of, 536; interpretation of, 556–63; labeling of, 557; see also emotion

assets, hedonic, and hedonic income, 577–9

attributions to self, 11, 157–79, 357, 562; as basis for interpreting success, 64; measure of, 160; and failure of work role, 163; and income, 169; and benign cycles of reinforcement, 171–2; in less marketized societies, 172–3; Japanese variant of, 172–3; and cognitive complexity, 173–4; and incidental learning, 174; and resistance to authority, 174–5; and stress, 175; and social stratification, 175–6; as socially useful fiction, 176; and Protestant ethic, 178; undermined by equality, 178–9; and self-esteem, 89; and happiness, 490; and income increases, 540; see also personal control

attributions: external, in success and failure, 64; internal, relation of to income, 64–5; and guilt, 65; and money, 80–1; to dispositions or circumstances, 157–8; fundamental error of, 158; and disposition–situation interaction, 158; as trait or state, 159; theory of, 159; and contingent responses, 159–60; and conservative ideology, 176; and intrinsic satisfaction, 176–7; as dogma, 177; veridical distortion of, 177; and loss of ethical perspective, 177–8; effect of modern work on, 245; and work, 255; by dispositions or circumstances, 343; and intrinsic motivation, 404; see also attributions to self

authoritarianism, 145, 551–2

automation, 276; in command economies, 282; in Britain and France, 283; see also technology

autonomy, see self-determination

avarice, 28, 541–3

axis of debate, 3, 593–613; definition of, 593; rotation of, 594; proposed change of, 600–11; and predisposing values, 603–8; change of in eighteenth century, 605–7; and challenge to economistic axis, 607–8; see also well-being–developmental axis

basic economic sequence (BES), 26–7

behavioral sciences, 600

Belgium, effect on happiness of income changes in, 535–6

biological substrates, and happiness, 563–70

blood, sale of, 210

bookkeeping, double-entry, 479–80

boredom, 140, 256–7

bottom-up theories of happiness, 509; see also happiness

bureaucracy, 241, 250, 275, 304–6

bureaucrats, and entrepreneurs, socialization practices of, 152–3

business ideology, 359; see also ideology, market doctrine

buying, and selling, 266; as intermediate goal, 365–6; see also exchange, consumer behavior

cash nexus, 207

challenges, meeting, 459

change, economic, and cognitive overload, 142

child labor, 274

children, as consumer goods, 21

choice, in market society, 264; effects of, 329; benefits of, 474, 562

coercion, 210

cognition: limits of, 27, 79–80; and economic growth, 31; market feedback, 52; and emotion, 62–3, 71–2; in philosophy, 71; and affect, 150; and intelligence, 116; and happiness, 448, 569; see also learning, rationality

cognitive complexity: defined, 10, 116; elements of, 43; and rationality, 43–54, 75–6; and happiness, 75–6; and money, 79–95; low popular value of, 133; and authoritarianism, 145; limited desire for, 606

cognitive development, 115–35; and wage labor, 119; relation to economic needs, 120–1; in socialist economies, 121–2; in kibbutzim, 122–3; and poverty, 123–6; and health, 124; and industrialization, 125–6; decline of in recessions, 125–6; and economic